Seshat History of the Axial Age

Edited by Daniel Hoyer and Jenny Reddish

Seshat Histories Vol I

Beresta Books

 Seshat

Seshat: Global History Databank

Beresta Books
Published by BERESTA BOOKS LLC
Chaplin, Connecticut, U.S.A.

**SESHAT HISTORY OF THE AXIAL AGE / edited by Daniel Hoyer
and Jenny Reddish**

Cover design by Marta Dec
Layout and typesetting by Grzegorz Laszczyk
Cover illustration: artistic interpretation of details from Achaemenid royal tombs at
Naqsh-e Rustam, Iran. © 2019 Kinsey Hotchkiss

Financial assistance for the research and writing of this book was provided by grants from
the John Templeton Foundation, the Tricoastal Foundation, the Economic and Social Research Council, and the European Union Horizon 2020 Programme for Research and Innovation. The editors were supported in their work by the Evolution Institute, the University
of Oxford, and the Complexity Science Hub, Vienna.

ISBN: 978-0-9961395-6-4

Library of Congress Cataloging-in-Publication Data
Seshat History of the Axial Age / edited by Daniel Hoyer and Jenny Reddish
p. cm.
Includes bibliographical references and index
1. World history. 2. History, ancient. 3. Religion and politics. 4. Kings and rulers – religious
aspects. 5. Social evolution. I. Title.

Acknowledgments

Seshat gratefully acknowledges the support of our sponsors, without whom this book could not have been written. Hoyer and Reddish were supported in their work on this volume by the Evolution Institute, the University of Oxford, and the Complexity Science Hub, Vienna. Research funding provided by a John Templeton Foundation grant ("Axial-Age Religions and the Z-Curve of Human Egalitarianism"), a Tricoastal Foundation grant ("The Deep Roots of the Modern World: The Cultural Evolution of Economic Growth and Political Stability"), an ESRC Large Grant ("Ritual, Community, and Conflict": REF RES-060-25-0085), a grant from the European Union Horizon 2020 research and innovation programme ("Aligned": 644055), and the program "Complexity Science," which is supported by the Austrian Research Promotion Agency FFG under grant #873927.

A 2017 workshop on "Testing the Axial Age" was held at the University of Oxford, while the Complexity Science Hub, Vienna hosted Seshat team members during the writing-up period. We would like to thank all of the participants at those meetings. We would also like to thank our research assistants as well as the many historians, archaeologists and anthropologists who have contributed to the project by sharing their expertise with us. A full list of expert contributors can be viewed at http://seshatdatabank.info/seshat-about-us/contributor-database/.

Finally, we would like to acknowledge the generous support given over the years to Seshat: Global History Databank by Bernard Winograd and James Bennett.

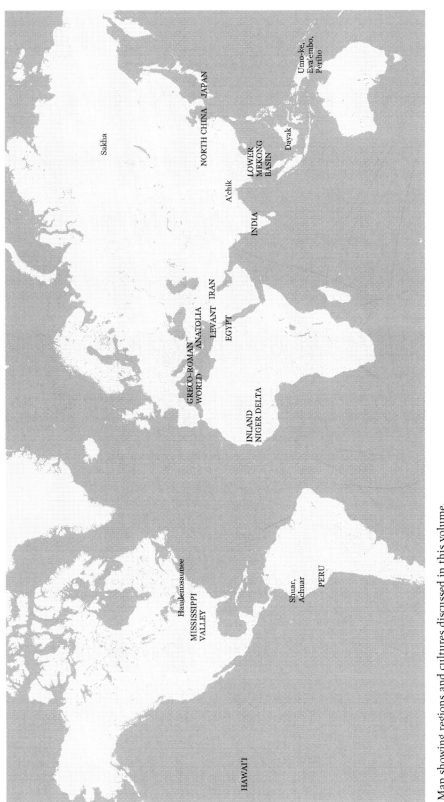

Map showing regions and cultures discussed in this volume.

Contents

FOREWORD

For What It's Worth: Evidence and Models in the History of the Axial Age
Ian Morris

Articles of faith

> There's something happening here.
> What it is ain't exactly clear.
> Buffalo Springfield, "For What it's Worth" (1967)

"For What it's Worth" could almost be the theme song of Axial Age scholarship. Something, something big, was happening in multiple places along the axis running from China to the Mediterranean in the first millennium BCE—and yet, despite nearly 150 years of study, what it was still ain't exactly clear. But that is changing, thanks to the unparalleled exercise in data collection that has led to the Seshat History of the Axial Age.

No one, I suspect, contributed more to making the Axial Age unclear than Karl Jaspers. Despairing for Europe in the aftermath of the Second World War, Jaspers looked into the past to find a secure basis for rebuilding the continent's moral order. He found it in the years between 800 and 200 BCE, when, he said, five societies—China, India, Iran, Israel, and Greece—had experienced moral breakthroughs, leading them to embrace ideals of equality, freedom, universalism, peace, enlightenment, and the individual's ability to chart his or her own course toward happiness and salvation. Men of letters had been talking about such a mid-first-millennium BCE "moral revolution" since the 1870s, but their work had been largely forgotten by the 1940s (Halton 2019), and Jaspers' book *The Origin and Goal of History* has been the starting point for most modern analysis. Jaspers called the upheaval the Axial Age (*Achsenzeit*), because, as he saw it, it formed the axis around which the moral history of the world turned. "The middle of the last millennium BCE," he concluded, was a time "for which everything which preceded it would appear to have been a preparation, and to which everything subsequent actually, and often in clear consciousness, relates back" (Jaspers 1953: 262).

Although nearly all discussions of the Axial Age begin from Jaspers' *Origin and Goal*, most historically minded social scientists appear to find it impenetrable. Jaspers had begun his career as a psychologist before turning to existential philosophy, and only small parts of his book—just 31 out of 267 pages—focus specifically on what happened 2,500 years ago. This, he explained, was because he was interested in the past not for its own sake, but "to light up the consciousness of the present epoch and [show] us where we stand" (1953: 81). Rather than testing a hypothesis or even making inductions from a mass of facts, his book "is based on an *article of faith*: that mankind has one single origin and one goal" (xv). The origin is the axial societies of the first millennium BCEE, when "Man, as we know him today, came into being" (1); the goal, "the faith of the future [which] will continue to move within the fundamental positions and categories of the Axial period" (225).

Origin and Goal was a tract for the times, not a piece of historical sociology, and its studied vagueness is at least partly to blame for why no two scholars seem to agree on what it was that happened in the first millennium BCE, when and where it happened, what to call it, or how to study it—let alone on why it happened or what it meant. Not until the 1970s, when the American Academy of Arts of Sciences invited a distinguished group of ancient historians to discuss the concept in the pages of its journal *Daedalus* (Schwartz 1975), did the Axial Age receive much professional attention; and only in the 1980s, when the sociologist Shmuel Eisenstadt injected some order into the conceptual morass (Eisenstadt 1982, 1986d), did the Axial Age scholarship really acquire much rigor. Even in the 2010s, reading the literature often feels like wrestling with jello. This is the problem that *Seshat History of the Axial Age* tries to solve.

The shape of the elephant
One of the most valuable things that Eisenstadt did was to concentrate scholarly interest on empirical questions (the whats, whens, wheres, and whys) of the first-millennium BCE Axial Age, as necessary preludes to the normative questions that had attracted Jaspers. Scholars of all stripes—anthropologists, biologists, historians, philologists, philosophers, political scientists, psychologists, sociologists—then picked up the gauntlet that Eisenstadt threw down. Despite this disciplinary diversity, though, research has broadly followed a single set of methods. We might call this the traditional humanistic approach, in which a lone researcher or a small team of scholars reads as much as possible, thinks hard about it, and then offers an interpretation. They regularly offer these interpretations at conferences, which are then published as edited multiauthor books; but even the best of this work offers us bundles of competing voices rather than genuinely collaborative projects.

There is an obvious problem with this way of working. Wildly different cultural traditions flourished across Eurasia between 800 and 200 BCE, recorded in multiple difficult dead languages and idiosyncratic literary genres. Most of the materials that once existed have been lost to selection processes that we rarely understand, and what has survived to our own times is usually subject to thorny analytical problems. Despite the formidable learning of many of the academics who have addressed the Axial Age, none has had the skills or time to tackle first-hand more than a sliver of the daunting dataset. Small wonder that the outcome is like the Indian story of the blind men and the elephant, in which one sage grabs the pachyderm's trunk and thinks he is holding a snake, while a second, holding a tusk, thinks he has seized a spear, and a third, clutching a leg, thinks it is a tree (and so on).

Social and natural scientists often approach similarly messy evidence very differently. Rather than competing to produce the best virtuoso reading, researchers get together. They work out common definitions, questions, and methods, pooling their resources to produce a systematic, large-N database, against which interpretations can be tested. Increasingly, they make their databases available online, so that rival interpreters can engage in transparent debates over coding, scores, and ambiguities, avoiding the pitfalls of cherry-picked data. (Such debates are, in fact, already raging over Seshat's classification of the data for early religions: Beheim et al. 2019; Savage et al. forthcoming; Slingerland et al. 2019; Whitehouse et al. 2019.) Such open and explicit datasets, which have survived the trial by fire of rigorous reanalysis by rivals, could potentially make it possible not only to clarify the similarities and differences among Jaspers' five axial societies, but also to see whether axial thought already existed before 800 BCE or only kicked in after 200 BCE and to know whether axiality really was limited to Jaspers' five cases or can in fact be found outside the China–Mediterranean band. Finally, having established an agreed-upon foundation of facts, scholars can consider causes and consequences.

Anthropologists have been generating cross-cultural catalogues of customs and behavior for more than a century (beginning, I believe, with Steinmetz 1898/99), and in many ways, Seshat is continuing just this tradition (Turchin et al. 2015). However, scholars will search in vain for information on attitudes, values, and ideals in most of these datasets. Categories of thought are difficult to reduce to forms (especially numerical forms) that can easily be compared between cultural contexts, and so cataloguers have tended to skip over them—as I did myself in my one venture into index-making (Morris 2013).

Yet difficult is not the same thing as impossible, and some sociologists have found ways to use cleverly designed opinion polls to quantify values and ideas. Drawing on over 400,000 interviews in 100 countries, the World Values Survey has produced sophisticated statistical analyses of changing attitudes (Inglehart and Welzel 2005; Inglehart 2018). However, its data-gathering only began in 1981, and it is not obvious how anything similar could be done for earlier centuries. For instance, we learn from Jill Levine and Miriam Stark that Jayavarman VII, who ruled the Angkor Empire between 1181 and 1218 CE, put up inscriptions that sound distinctly more axial than those of earlier Angkor emperors, let alone the poorly known, semi-divinized kings of the seventh- and eighth-century Chenla state. But how much more axial? That would be hard to quantify; and, given the limits of the epigraphic record, even if we could rank Angkor and Chenla monarchs on some sort of axiality scale, it might not tell us much about their societies as wholes.

Making matters even more difficult, the words ancient writers used to discuss the core concepts of axiality—fairness, justice, respect, and so on—constantly shifted meaning. In the millennium separating the epic poet Homer from the Stoic philosopher Epictetus, for example, Greek authors wrote an enormous amount about *nomos* (law, order) and *dike* (justice), but just what they thought orderly and just societies should look like varied enormously. Worse still, from Greece to China, the axial founding fathers all agreed that their fundamental concepts were indefinable. Nirvana—literally "blowing out," a state of mind in which the passions of this world are snuffed out like a candle—cannot be described, said the Buddha; even trying is inappropriate. For Confucius, *ren*—often translated as "humaneness"—was similarly beyond language. "The more I look up to it, the higher it is; the more I penetrate it, the harder it becomes: I see it ahead of me and suddenly it is behind ... in speaking about it can one avoid being hesitant?" (*Analects* 9.11, 12.3 [Dawson 1993: 32, 44]). Likewise, when pressed to define *to kalon*, "the good," Socrates threw up his hands: "It's beyond me, and if I try I'll only make a fool of myself" (Plato, *Republic* 506e).

Least definable of all was *dao*, the "Way" that Daoists follow:

The Way that can be spoken of is not the true Way;
The name that can be named is not the true name ...
Both may be called mysterious,
Mysterious and still more mysterious,
The gateway of all subtleties!
(Laozi, Daodejing 1 [de Bary and Bloom 1999: 79–80])

Confronted by so many mysteries wrapped inside subtleties, historians regularly conclude that social scientists' efforts to reduce values and ideas to cross-culturally comparable scores are doomed from the outset (Fogel and Elton 1983 remains a classic discussion of the pros and cons of quantification). If they are right, then the traditional humanistic method of approaching the Axial Age, ineffective as it has proved, nevertheless remains the only game in town. Yet there are signs that this negative conclusion might be an overreaction to life's messiness. In the case of ancient Greece, for instance, the classicist Josiah Ober has shown how one large-scale, collaborative database, the Inventory of Archaic and Classical Poleis (Hansen and Nielsen 2004), can be used to quantify and compare the literary and artistic accomplishments of different Greek city-states (Ober 2008: 39–79, 287–88; 2015: 34–37). However, Ober's study also shows just how deep into the details scholars need to go to reach reliable results. It may well be that the kind of large-*N* comparisons beloved of social scientists studying the modern world, often based on easily accessible, government-issued data, are simply out of the question for the first millennium BCE.

But large-N number crunching and the connoisseurship of the detailed historical case study are not the only options. Social scientists often identify a third way to approach problems, which they call "analytic narratives" (Bates et al. 1998). These are linked sets of case studies, numerous enough to allow cross-cultural comparisons but few enough to allow a serious plunge into the data, teasing out subtleties and idiosyncrasies as well as broad patterns. This, I would say, is where *Seshat History of the Axial Age* comes in. For the first time, a large team of researchers has systematically worked through the scholarly literature, using the same definitions, asking the same questions, and deploying the same methods. Burrowing into the details of evidence and interpretation, they have worked their results up into more than a dozen analytic narratives, which look back beyond 800 BCE, forward after 200 BCE, and beyond Jaspers' five core axial cases to take in most of the continents. They have, in fact, solved the blind-men-and-elephant problem, creating a treasure trove of data that might be the most important contribution yet made to understanding the Axial Age.

As clear as mud

So, what is in the treasure trove? First of all, there are some things that would not have greatly surprised Jaspers. While each of the chapters on Greece, the Levant, India, and Iran insists that its particular region is not a perfect fit with any general axial model, they also confirm that each place becomes more axial (in one way or another) in the period 800–200 BCE. By contrast, Jill Levine and Barend ter Haar's North China chapter concludes that "while there was a rise in diverse intellectual thought in the latter first millennium BCE, in line with Jaspers' Axial Age timeline, the ideologies that developed in this period expressed very few, if any, typically axial features."

If regional specialists accept this characterization, it will be a serious dilution of most theories of a first-millennium BCE Axial Age; but this is only the first of several dilutions to come out of Seshat's data. Jaspers left Egypt, Anatolia, and Mesopotamia off his list of axial societies, even though they are geographically sandwiched between axial Greece, Israel, and Iran; but the Seshat data suggest that Egypt, Anatolia, and Mesopotamia not only experienced axial developments but also experienced them before 800 BCE, the supposed start date for the Axial Age (understandably, Jenny Reddish and Julye Bidmead sidestep the contentious issue of dating Zarathustra in their chapter on Iran).

Looking beyond the China–Mediterranean region, Dennis Spencer, Alan Covey, and Agathe Dupeyron's chapter portrays Inca society much as Jaspers might have expected, with few signs of axial attitudes before the arrival of Christianity in the sixteenth century. The Mekong Basin was apparently even more immune to the charms of axial ideas, with its rulers taking several centuries to embrace them even after the arrival of Mahayana Buddhism; but Hawai'i, which was still further isolated from the Eurasian axial world than Peru or Southeast Asia, had already generated some distinctly axial-sounding ideas by the time Captain Cook arrived in 1778 CE.

It would have been very valuable if the *Seshat History of the Axial Age* could have been expanded to add more case studies from premodern societies outside the China–Mediterranean zone, but there are major empirical limits to what can be done. The chapters on the Mississippi Valley (Cahokia) and the Inland Niger Delta (Jenné-jeno)—extremely illuminating contributions, since these regions are hardly ever included in discussions of the Axial Age—illustrate the problems. In each case, we can only reconstruct the society's intellectual and moral life by retrojecting recent ethnohistorical accounts back across centuries or even millennia. The bind this puts us in has long been known: dismissing such speculative accounts as "conjectural history," the anthropologist A. R. Radcliffe-Brown explained that the objection "is not that it is historical, but that it is conjectural ... To establish any probability for such conjectures we should need to have a knowledge of laws of social development which we certainly do not possess and which I do not think we shall ever attain" (Radcliffe-Brown 1952: 50). We are no closer to such knowledge now than in his day, and we should probably concede that we will never know the extent to which axial values prevailed at Cahokia or Jenné-jeno—or, for that matter, at Teotihuacan, or Çatalhöyük, or any other specific prehistoric town.

The approach that Eva Brandl takes in her "Survey of Late Complexity Socie- ties," presenting accounts collected by early ethnographers in Oceania, Asia, and the Americas, is perhaps sounder. "Intriguingly," she notes, "some proposed axial traits are present in these cultures, albeit ambiguously." While she observes that the "wide geographic spread [of certain ideas] and commonality with many hunter-gatherers suggest that egalitarianism has deep roots in human history," when it comes to trying to reconstruct the past of any specific group, she follows Radcliffe-Brown's maxim. "We make no attempt to trace the historical depth of these traditions," she says, "and we do not treat them as pristine remnants of archaic cultures ... They pro- vide a glimpse into ritual practices and belief systems as they were encountered by anthropologists in the nineteenth and early twentieth centuries."

At this point, I suspect that Jaspers would have thrown his hands up in exasper- ation. Seshat's empirical "clarification" of the Axial Age has dissolved his claims for the uniqueness of the five first-millennium BCE societies, and left matters as clear as mud. It seems at least possible that axial-type ideas were widely found around the world in prehistoric foraging bands; probable that they were anticipated well before 800 BCE in Elam and Egypt; probable too that they were not very influential at all in China before 200 BCE; and almost certain that they had at least some parallels in eighteenth-century Hawaii. The *Seshat History of the Axial Age* shows, beyond reasonable doubt, that the pattern we need to explain is much messier than Jaspers' model of a moral and intellectual revolution in first-millennium BCE Eurasia.

Better questions

One of the biggest lessons I learned as a graduate student was that historical theories are rarely simply right or wrong. More often, what happens is that the further we go with analysis, the more the conceptual, methodological, and empirical challenges pile up, until, at a certain point, any reasonable scholar feels compelled to go back to the drawing board. That, I would say, is what the Seshat data have done to Jaspers' first-millennium miracle. It still looks like there was something happening here; it's just that what it was now seems even less clear.

Conceptually, the Seshat data break down Jaspers' stark before-and-after contrast between pre–800 and post–200 BCE worlds. Axiality starts to look less like a state of being, unknown until a few intellectual and moral giants discovered it around 500 BCE, and more like what the sociologist (and early theorist of the Axial Age) Max Weber called an "ideal type." An ideal type, he explained, is an analytical tool achieved by the one-sided accentuation of one or more points of view and by the synthesis of many diffuse, discrete, more or less present and occasionally absent individual phenomena, which are arranged according to those one-sidedly emphasized viewpoints into a unified mental construct. In its conceptual purity, this mental construct can never be found empirically in reality. It is a *utopia* (Weber 1949: 90).

There is no such thing (and never has been) as a purely axial society or person, let alone a distinct Axial Age. Rather, axiality is an analytical construct, distilled from real-world properties because it makes it easier for scholars to think about the infinitely varied messiness of the world we actually live in. Axiality, like love, is all around us: real individuals and societies can be rated as more axial or less axial, but not completely axial or completely un-axial. Within every individual mind and larger community, axiality is always debated and contested, and it is constantly changing. We will be able to think about axiality and the Axial Age a lot better if stop asking how and why four or five Eurasian societies became axial in the first millennium BCE and start asking why, in certain places, axial-type ideas appealed more after 800 BCE than they had done before.

Second, we need to broaden our questions chronologically, because even setting the first millennium BCE into the context of the whole period from the Agricultural to the Industrial Revolution still only shows us part of the elephant. When we ask questions about axiality, we are talking about human values. We therefore need to take the whole of human history as our subject. We certainly need to go back as far as the origin of *Homo sapiens* (perhaps 300,000 years ago) and arguably as far as the origin of the genus *Homo* (some 2.4 million years ago), and also to come all the way forward to our own time.

Despite my discomfort with conjectural histories of Cahokian or Jenné-jeno values, I suspect (for reasons I explain at length in Morris 2015: 25–43) that Eva Brandl is quite right to assume that at least some axial-type values were widespread in the foraging world before 10,000 BCE. If we want to explain what made these values regain their attractiveness in at least some places after 800 BCE, we must first explain both why they had been attractive to prehistoric hunter-gatherers in the first place and why they had become *less* attractive once agriculture began. After that, we will need to know what made them reach a peak of attractiveness since the Industrial Revolution. I suspect that most academic analysts will end up disagreeing with Jaspers' claim that the real history of humanity began in China, India, Iran, Israel, and Greece in the first millennium BCE and is now approaching its goal, but there is no denying that the axial values of equality, freedom, universalism, peace, enlightenment, and the individual's ability to chart his or her own course toward happiness and salvation have been more widely embraced in recent times than ever before.

There is nothing very remarkable about these proposals. They are, in fact, perfectly consistent with Seshat's own agenda of trying to shift discussion of the past away from historical and philosophical models toward ones based in cultural evolution. Several cultural evolutionists have already written books treating the Axial Age along roughly these lines (e.g. Bellah 2011, forthcoming; Norenzayan 2013; Turchin 2016).

Nor should anyone really object to treating the history of values as an evolutionary issue. The biologist E. O. Wilson was already arguing in the 1970s that "the time has come for ethics to be removed temporarily from the hands of philosophers and biologicized" (Wilson 1975: 562), and in the last 15 years, evolutionary psychologists have made a strong case that values are biologically evolved adaptations. We humans are not the only species with senses of fairness and justice. Values, including human values, differentially affect the likelihood of individual animals passing their genes on to the next generation, and are subject to natural and sexual selection (Brosnan 2013; Brosnan and de Waal 2014; McAuliffe and Santos 2018).

Human values are also, though, subject to cultural selection, and it is this that makes humans different from all other animals. With only trivial exceptions (discussed in Whiten 2011), we are the only animals that have evolved biologically to have brains capable of evolving culturally too, adapting a cumulative body of shared information that we have acquired from other people through teaching, imitation, and other kinds of transmission. In some times and places, people have responded to the selective pressures exercised by their environment by adapting this cumulative body of information in ways that moved it closer toward the axial ideal type; in other times and places, adaptations moved it further from the axial ideal type. Seshat's data make it difficult to go on looking at the first-millennium BCE Axial Age as the discrete phenomenon that Jaspers imagined. Driven back to the drawing board, we should perhaps reframe the question as one about how and why selective pressures changed, in some first-millennium societies, in ways that encouraged people to adopt and adapt axial-type values.

Better answers?

I would not be taking the time to write this essay if I did not have thoughts of my own about the answer to this question, so I will close with a few. I can be brief about them, since they fill a large part of my book *Foragers, Farmers, and Fossil Fuels: How Human Values Evolve* (Morris 2015). In a nutshell, I believe that the whole story is one of cultural adaptations to changing energy inputs.

Before 10,000 BCE, when there is some reason to think that axial ideas were quite widespread, everyone on earth was a hunter-gatherer, living by hunting wild animals and gathering wild plants. These foods normally provided only small amounts of energy per unit of land or water, with the result that population densities were extremely low (among recent foragers, densities of less than one person per square kilometer have been normal), group size was tiny (in modern times, again, typically less than twenty people in a residential band), and people moved around constantly as plants ripened and animals migrated. In recent societies operating under these constraints, hierarchy of any sort was usually difficult to create and maintain, and sharing, humility, and restraint were often core values. Upstarts (especially successful young male hunters) certainly did challenge these ideals, but most bands developed methods—ranging from mockery to murder—to keep them in line.

In her chapter in this book, Eva Brandl stresses the variety of modern small-scale societies, and that variety was probably even greater in prehistory, since foragers then had access to every kind of ecological niche on the planet. Some sites, most famously Sungir in Russia (c. 26,000 BCE), have produced extraordinary concentrations of Stone Age riches in burials. Others, such as Star Carr in England (c. 8000 BCE), have proved to be much larger than any modern hunter-gatherer camp. A tiny handful, like Göbekli Tepe in Turkey (c. 9500 BCE), have even yielded grand stone monuments, long believed to have been beyond the organizational capacities of hunter-gatherers. All in all, there was probably greater economic, political, social, and cultural diversity among prehistoric foragers than among those of recent times; but, having said that, the archaeological evidence does suggest that most prehistoric bands were indeed tiny, thinly spread, mobile, poor, and egalitarian, like most modern ones. This is the basis for thinking that before the invention of agriculture, selective pressures favored (but did not require) the success of ideas somewhat like axial values.

This all changed after the last ice age ended, around 9600 BCE, and global warming made possible the domestication of plants and animals. This process got underway in West Asia around 9500 BCE, the Andes around 8000, Mesoamerica and South and East Asia around 7500, New Guinea around 7000, and the Sahel area of Africa around 3500. Farming and herding released a flood of energy per unit of land, which fed an astonishing population boom. In 10,000 BCE, there had been about 5 million foragers and no farmers on earth; in 1 BCE, there were about 250 million peasants, who had driven most of the few hundred thousand surviving hunter-gatherers back into marginal lands that farmers did not want.

Population densities climbed above 10 people per square kilometer and sometimes even over 100, and by 1 BCE, the city of Rome probably had a million residents. All this required organization, and the chances are that just about any system we can imagine was tried by some farmers at some point. Overwhelmingly, though, competitive pressures pushed people toward the organizing principles of hierarchy, patriarchy, and extreme inequality. Forced labor—slavery, serfdom, debt bondage—became almost universal in farming societies, because although premodern agriculture regularly required collective action above the household level, it was rarely profitable enough to pay wages that would tempt many workers into the labor market. Violence effectively lowered the unit cost of labor; without systematic brutality, ancient and medieval societies would not have worked. As in the age of foragers, there was enormous variation, but it is hard to identify many (perhaps any) egalitarian farming societies.

Members of industrial societies have sometimes romanticized agrarian villages as happy, organic communities, but people who have spent time in them rarely feel that way. Maxim Gorky, for instance, moved to a village in the 1890s, hoping to discover an egalitarian model for a new Russia. Instead, he found that "The [village] was governed by an assembly of peasant elders which, alongside the land commune (*obshchina*), regulated virtually every aspect of village life ... Some dog-like desire to please the strong ones in the village took possession of [the poor], and then it disgusted me to look at them" (Gorky, *My Universities* [1923], cited from Figes 1996: 86). Similar tales of inequality, oppression, and just plain mean-spiritedness can be told about villages everywhere from fourteenth-century Montaillou in France (Le Roy Ladurie 1978) to Kerkeosiris in first-century BCE Egypt (Crawford 1971).

People responded to these economic imperatives with a remarkable piece of cultural evolution, reinterpreting what fairness meant. Whereas recent foragers often seemed to feel that the most important thing about humans is that we're all basically the same, with the result that fairness meant treating everyone in basically the same ways, farmers inclined toward saying that the big fact is that we're all different, and that fairness therefore demands treating everyone differently. After all, if one of us is so rich and powerful that he genuinely seems like a god on earth, would it be fair to treat him the same as everyone else?

It is this background that makes the axial thought of the first millennium BCE so surprising. To be sure, very few individuals and no entire societies became radically axial, renouncing hierarchy, wealth, violence, and exploitation. In Classical Athens, often called the birthplace of democracy, no women had any political rights whatsoever and one-third of the population was enslaved. In early Christian Rome, despite Jesus' famous line that "It is easier for a camel to go through the eye of a needle than for a rich man to enter the kingdom of God" (Matthew 19:24), the thoroughness with which a super-rich elite colonized the upper ranks of the Church leads the historian Peter Brown to joke that "I am tempted to call this period the Age of the Camel" (Brown 2012: xxiv). But even so, as Chapters 2–6 in this book show, something did happen. Athens did give all its male citizens—roughly one-third of the adult population—an equal vote on all major decisions, regardless of wealth, ancestry, or education; and Rome did gradually commit to a religion that was open to all and gave everyone access to the same afterlife.

So, just what was it about the environment of the first millennium BCE in certain places between China and the Mediterranean that exerted selective pressures encouraging people to reverse so many (but by no means all) of the trends of the agrarian age? In an earlier book, I suggested that axial ideas were initially a response by marginal groups, mostly on the lower rungs of the elite and in societies around the edges of the great empires, to rising social development and the invention of new ways of managing states (Morris 2010: 245–63). The earliest axial ideas, offered by Confucius, Mozi, the Buddha, the Mahavira, the Hebrew prophets, and Socrates, were often quite countercultural, smacking of rebellion and alternative lifestyles. Everywhere from Rome to China, rulers found these threatening; but everywhere from Rome to China, rulers also learned that it was easier to co-opt axial leaders than to persecute them. In the last few centuries BCE and first few CE, Confucians, Buddhists, Zoroastrians, Yahwists, and Stoics all bent their knees in the service of the state, and were often handsomely rewarded for it.

Axiality is a steadily evolving set of adaptations, not a stable state of being achieved between 800 and 200 BCE. Further transformations therefore followed in the mid-first millennium CE as the great ancient empires disintegrated. In a world where centralized authority was weakening, new, simpler versions of axial ideas—Christianity, Islam, and Mahayana Buddhism, which I like to lump together under the heading of Second-Wave Axial Thought (Morris 2010: 320–29)—proved more attractive than the old, complicated ones. We might also speak of a Third Wave of Axial Thought in the twelfth and thirteenth centuries, as theorists such as Thomas Aquinas, al-Ghazali, and Zhu Xi systematized Christianity, Islam, and Confucianism to fit new environments; and even a Fourth Wave in the sixteenth.

This interpretation of the Axial Age, like most of interpretations offered since the 1870s, rests on traditional, humanistic methods, and whether my account or any of the other theories can survive rigorous testing against Seshat's data remains to be seen. We are surely on safer ground, though, in recognizing that the past 200 years have seen the most spectacular axial expansion of all. Our ability to extract energy from our environment has increased by orders of magnitude, as has our population size and density, our wealth, and our stock of knowledge. Institutions of exploitation and oppression that had thrived for thousands of years—slavery, serfdom, the patriarchal family, the rule of godlike kings—crumbled across the course of a few decades. Hoary barriers of sex, race, and class dissolved. "All fixed, fast-frozen relations, with their train of ancient and venerable prejudices, are swept away, all new-formed ones become antiquated before they can ossify," Marx and Engels observed, even though the process was still in its infancy in their lifetimes. "All that is solid melts into air" (Marx and Engels [1848] 1977: 244).

Jaspers claimed that history had an origin and a goal, but if a cultural evolutionary framework is the right way to think about axiality, he was wrong. Evolution is directionless. No one is in charge; as the environment changes, whatever adaptations prove advantageous will drive disadvantageous ones into extinction. However, as Marx and Engels understood better than most, older adaptations do not go gentle into that good night. When farmers began valuing hierarchy above equality in Early Neolithic societies, old-fashioned egalitarians probably fought back; when radicals reversed this valuation in first-millennium BCE China, India, Iran, Israel, and Greece, powerholders certainly pushed back. In the nineteenth century, aristocracies fought back hard enough to defeat the revolutions of 1848, and in the twentieth, the Nazi and Communist fightback was so violent that Jaspers feared that the entire course of history had been derailed. In the 2010s, it is tempting to see the rising tide of nationalism and xenophobia as parts of a new fightback, and many analysts (myself included) suspect that the twenty-first century is bringing a new round in the endless struggle over axial values, between a liberal, Western version and an authoritarian, Chinese one.

In a way, this brings us full circle back to Jaspers' *Origin and Goal of History*. Seshat's data muddied Jaspers' empirical claims about the uniqueness of the first millennium BCE to the point that they became untenable. The solution to that problem, I believe, is to make axiality part of a 300,000-year evolutionary story about human values. Inevitably, this will bring us back from facts to the normative questions that so exercised Jaspers—but now in a new form, asking whether axiality really is the origin and goal of history, or one set of cultural adaptations to humanity's changing environment. And when we put things that way, it seems that Jaspers, and Buffalo Springfield, both had a point. There's something happening here, even if what it is ain't exactly clear. But thanks to Seshat, how we got here, at least, is now clearer than it was—and that's worth a lot.

Acknowledgments
I would like to thank Dan Hoyer and Jenny Reddish for inviting me to contribute to this volume, and for their extraordinary patience in bearing with me through one delay after another; and Veronica Shi for discussing Karl Jaspers' work with me, allowing me to read her unpublished paper on his historical thought (Shi 2016), and making valuable comments on an earlier draft of this essay.

INTRODUCTION
Daniel Hoyer and Jenny Reddish

The Axial Age

The term "Axial Age" refers to a historical period in the mid-first millennium BCE during which a cluster of changes in cultural traditions are said to have occurred in some of the complex social formations across Eurasia. Notably, many thinkers contend that this period saw the rise of moralizing, universalizing and egalitarian ideals expressed through novel religious and philosophical systems—Buddhism, Confucianism, Hinduism, Judaism, Greek philosophy and Zoroastrianism—which developed independently, but nearly synchronically, in a handful of areas across Afro-Eurasia. The period is seen as axial not only for the changes experienced in these few ancient societies, but because this is often pointed to as one of the key turning points for humanity as a whole; proponents hold that these new cultural traditions, along with the novel forms of social and political organization that they helped spawn, formed the basis of what is sometimes called "modernity." Put simply, Axial Age theories hold that the spread of the major world religions practiced around the globe today; the fundamental principles held in many parts of the world about the importance of equal rights and opportunity, the benefits of representative forms of governance and the sanctity of the rule of law; and the institutions put in place in many modern nations to limit the arbitrary, excessive, tyrannical use of power all claim common descent from the novel ideologies awakened during this single, great epoch. At least, that's the way the argument goes.

The claim that there was a pivotal period in the mid-first millennium BCE that launched the (Western) world towards modernity is almost 150 years old, but the concept has enjoyed a surge in popularity in recent years, both among scholars from various disciplines and religious leaders, political reformers and the media (e.g. Armstrong 2006; and popular articles in the *Guardian, Wall Street Journal, Huffington Post* and *New Statesman*).[1] These recent reworkings typically present the Axial Age as a period of intense, transcultural religious and philosophical development worthy of emulation by contemporary policy makers, political and religious leaders, business

---

1   Andrew Anthony. 2014. "Interview: Rebecca Newberger Goldstein: 'Science Is Our Best Answer, but It Takes a Philosophical Argument to Prove That.'" The Guardian, October 19.
Peter Thonemann. 2016. "A Radical Retelling of Ancient History." *The Wall Street Journal*, December 9.
Nathan Gardels. 2016. "How Science Is Resurrecting the Religious Imagination." *HuffPost*, June 3.
Craig Calhoun. 2016. "Are We Really Living in the Age of the Second Renaissance?" *New Statesman*, June 12.

managers and the public. Indeed, some say we are in the midst of a second axial epoch, in which telecommunications, increased mobility, the rise of failed states and the continued scourge of sectarian violence have been leading people to question traditional religious and political realities. In their place, they seek a new "axiality," new ideas leading to more inclusive, more socially and environmentally conscious ways to engage in worship, to interact with others and to build communities. But are we really living in a second Axial Age? And, for that matter, what exactly *was* the Axial Age to begin with?

The developments of the Axial Age idea

The first glimmerings of the concept of an "Axial Age" can be traced to the eighteenth century, when the French scholar Abraham-Hyacinthe Anquetil-Duperron observed parallels between the ancient Iranian religion of Zoroastrianism and spiritual and intellectual developments in China, Greece, India and the Levant during the mid-first millennium BCE (Anquetil-Duperron 1771; discussed in Assmann 2012: 369).[2] Related ideas resurfaced in the nineteenth century in the work of Scottish barrister and part-time historian John Stuart-Glennie (1873): he proposed a "moral revolution" occurring around 600 BCE in roughly the same regions. The idea became a key preoccupation in some of the influential works of brothers Max (2013) and Alfred (1935) Weber in the period before the Second World War. But its most prominent and enduring articulation comes from philosopher and sociologist Karl Jaspers (1948; 1953). Writing amid the chaos of mid-twentieth-century Europe, Jaspers sought through historical investigation to find a universal, binding principle that could heal the wounds of a divided world. What he found was, as he called it, *die Achsenzeit* (literally "the axis-time")—his observation that broadly similar changes in moral fiber, philosophical dispositions and political institutions had occurred in five separate regions all within a period of about 600 years; 800–200 BCE. For Jaspers, these five centers of axiality were (what is today) Greece, Israel-Palestine, Iran, India and China. The critical and perhaps most surprising realization for Jaspers was that these transformations were not only very similar and occurred nearly simultaneously, but that each was entirely independent from the others, at least in his reading of history. Indeed, he stressed that each of his five axial regions were philosophically autochthonous—each being completely "independent," "isolated," and experiencing only "interrupted contact" with the others while these changes were occurring (1953: 10–11, 23).

The thrust of Jaspers' analysis, though, lay not in understanding these axial societies by illuminating the broader sociopolitical contexts in which these changes

---

2   Though see the chapter on Iran in this volume for an overview of debates over when the prophet Zarathustra lived.

occurred, but rather on the men he deemed to be the great thinkers of the day, sages who conjured the revolutionary ideas on which the axis of history turned: for Greece, this meant the ancient philosophers, especially Plato; for the Levant, the Hebrew prophets and scholars who helped shape early Jewish thought; in Iran, it was the elusive figure known as Zarathustra, whose eponymous Zoroastrianism had a deep impact on subsequent thought throughout Central Eurasia; in India, it meant Siddhartha Gautama, better known as the Buddha; and for China, Jaspers selected out of many possible sages the political philosopher Confucius. From these great minds, according to Jaspers, new ideologies and profound sociopolitical transformations took root, spread and eventually morphed into what we (at least in the West, and at least for the most part) take for granted as simply the way that modern society works. In this respect, Jaspers' original idea of the Axial Age was both sharply delimited—it refers explicitly to only a handful of thinkers, movements and regions within a roughly 600-year period—but was at the same time a truly global theory, as it sought to explain the gulf between the period of "primitive" and "archaic" human history before the Axial Age and what we know today as the modern world.

Over the years, the epoch has been described in various terms: Jaspers' *Achsenzeit* or Axial Age is most common, but it has been known also as the "Moral Revolution," the "Moral Axial Age," the "Prophetic Age," the "Ecumenic Age," the "Age of Transcendence," an "Age of Criticism," and, most recently, as the "Great Transformation" (Armstrong 2006; Habermas 2010; Momigliano 1975; Schwartz 1975; Torpey 2017; Voegelin 1974). Most proponents of the idea since the 1950s have followed Jaspers' original articulation, at least in broad outline. Indeed, several prominent recent studies have sought to revitalize the idea, focusing on different features, but each supporting the basic notion that some critical bundle of changes occurred in some select societies that then had tremendous influence on subsequent developments throughout the world. Eisenstadt, for example, has written several influential works that focus largely on the institutional reforms and the ways that the "tyrannical" authority of rulers began to be systematically curtailed with the adoption of axial ideologies (Eisenstadt 1986b, 2005). Bellah, perhaps the most well-known proponent of the idea after Jaspers, has written extensively on the psychological and intellectual underpinnings of the other transformations, particularly the way novel, axial ideologies encouraged and formalized critiques of prevailing social structures (Bellah 2005, 2011; Bellah and Joas 2012).

Even more recently, scholars have begun to explore some of the *causes* of these axial transformations, along with their lingering *effects*. Baumard and colleagues, notably, have argued that a dramatic rise in the general affluence of the core axial societies generated the prosperity and freedom required for thinkers to begin engaging in the sort of social critiques that Bellah points to, thus setting themselves on the path towards a dramatic, axial-type overhaul of their societies (Baumard et al. 2015a,

2015b). Others argue that one of the most important, lingering impacts of the Axial Age was not any immediate societal change in ideologies or institutions, but that the period laid the foundations for a radically new, powerful way of enforcing societal norms; namely, modern, moralizing religions like Buddhism, Christianity and Islam, which quickly spread from humble origins to become the most prominent religious and ritual systems practiced around the world today (Baumard and Boyer 2013; Norenzayan 2013; Purzycki et al. 2018).

One reason that these arguments have had such a lasting hold on generations of scholars is that the Axial Age idea seems really to have something in it that appeals to everyone. The notion has been championed by scholars from a variety of disciplines and specializations—history, anthropology, sociology, religious studies, philosophy, evolutionary psychology—each of whom has brought a unique perspective and a different approach to the topic, and added their own nuances and interpretations to the still-growing body of Axial Age theory (or theories). In fact, the one constant in work on the Axial Age is its sheer variety; scholars have differed on just about every single aspect of the concept, from the temporal bounds of the "age"[3] to its geographical extent (for instance, several scholars add Egypt to Jaspers' original five core regions). There are further debates about what exactly is the set of cultural transformations that should be seen as diagnostically "axial" and disagreements over the precise role and importance of the supposed great axial sages, while others argue over whether this really was a single epoch or should rather be understood as a continuous process involving "secondary" breakthroughs, such as those associated with the rise and spread of Christianity and Islam in the first millennium CE.

Core elements of the Axial Age idea

With all of this diversity, then, we are still left wondering: what exactly *was* the Axial Age, and does it have relevance today? With this question in mind, some colleagues (Mullins et al. 2018) sought to investigate the Axial Age idea using a powerful tool for conducting such large-scale, historical research: Seshat: Global History Databank.[4] We started by outlining the core elements that are common to the most prominent and influential of the Axial Age theories (though not all). We identified five central, step-wise assertions:

1. The Axial Age is defined by a specific temporal boundary (roughly 800–200 BCE, though this varies).
2. The Axial Age is defined by a specific geographic boundary (typically this includes the five regions initially identified by Jaspers, though this too varies).

---

3   For a full discussion of the wide range of "ages" that have been associated with the Axial Age over the years, see Mullins et al. 2018.
4   http://seshatdatabank.info/.

3. That during the specified period, these specified regions experienced critical transformations in their prevailing cultural, ideological and religious systems, including in particular: the rise of explicitly moralizing ideologies; the promotion of egalitarian thought; the onset of (or rise in prevalence of the use of) second-order thinking and widespread critical re-examinations of inherited traditions; the development of more formal, institutionalized legal systems; and limits to the absolute, often divinely sanctioned authority of rulers.

4. By implication from assertions #1 and #2, these transformations should not have occurred before the defined Axial Age temporal boundary; nor should they have developed in any other region until after the defined Axial Age and then mainly by diffusion from or contact with one of the "original" axial cultures.

5. These transformations were founded upon the novel ideas of a specific group of identifiable "sages," which then took root and spread throughout the major, largely imperial polities of Eurasia, leading (eventually, and after a series of fits and starts) to what many would now call modernity.

It is easy to see why this theory has enjoyed such long-lived popularity. It is an elegant, fairly simple notion about cross-cultural similarity that nevertheless seeks to illuminate a host of complex, interconnected dynamics in many key aspects of human society: religion and normative philosophy, moral and ethical precepts, legal and political structures. Further, it is at once localized, able to highlight interesting and compelling evidence from some of the most well-known and interesting ancient societies, and also expansive, generalizable and global, seeking to connect some of the more humanitarian and honorable cornerstones of modern societies through a single, common origin.

On the other hand, as noted, there is a great deal of variation and disagreement between the different scholars who have written on this topic. More significantly, all of the work done on the Axial Age to date has accepted, more or less, Jaspers' original premise; scholars have argued about some of the particulars, extended or contracted the temporal boundaries, and argued over where exactly qualified as a "core" axial region, which developments were primary or most significant, and who should be counted among the "great sages" of the time. But few ask the bigger questions[5]: is it useful to talk about an Axial Age at all? Were the supposed axial developments really independent from each other? Is it really true that none of these key developments had taken place prior to the axial period, and, once introduced, were they more or less stable thereafter? What exactly was happening in the non-axial regions? Were these typically "archaic" societies just waiting to be "enlightened" through exposure to axial thought, or do they exhibit similar complex cultural, ideological and

---

5   With some important exceptions, e.g. Assmann 2012; Baumard et al. 2015a; Shults et al. 2018.

political dynamics of their own? Much of the information contained in this volume was collected and analyzed in an attempt to examine these crucial questions systematically and holistically.

Exploring the limits of the Axial Age

As noted, our earlier work exploring the five core assertions of Axial Age theory (Mullins et al. 2018) utilized empirical data collected through the Seshat Databank,[6] which offers an immense volume of structured historical material on a host of topics, including the key topics of axiality. In order to take a broader, more holistic look at the topic, we explored the periods both before and after the mid-first millennium BCE, looking to identify when each of the different axial transformations occurred (if at all). This allowed us to assess whether the appearance of each trait during the supposed Axial Age was indeed a novel development of the period rather than a heritage from earlier traditions. Further, we chose a more comprehensive geographical sample than is normally offered, adding to the five core axial regions typically highlighted (Greece, the Levant, Iran, India and China) another five regions throughout Afro-Eurasia (modern-day Italy, Turkey, Egypt, Cambodia and Japan) to test claims that the five core regions were in fact the first to experience these profound cultural transformations and that the other regions experienced similar developments only by diffusion from or contact with the "original" axial societies.

In brief, we found some very interesting, but somewhat conflicting patterns. First, it became immediately clear from our broad historical investigation that the traditional temporal and geographic bounds of the Axial Age are problematic at best. The evidence is clear that the five core regions normally highlighted as the original centers of axiality were not alone in experiencing the transformations during this period—places like Egypt, Anatolia and Mesopotamia had each started to develop certain "axial"-type ideologies before the developments in the core regions in the mid-first millennium, in some cases centuries earlier. Moreover, even in the core regions, the so-called axial transformations were not as stable as they are often described; rather, not every region experienced similar transformations in each aspect of religious, philosophical and political life, as is typically suggested. This belies the notion of a single, coherent concept of axiality. Likewise, the transformations that are evidenced in both the core and other regions do not appear to have arisen entirely independently from each other, for recent historical and archaeological work[7] has illuminated how interconnected all of these regions and societies were during the axial period (and before), with significant transcultural exchange of goods, people and ideas.

---

6   See below for details on Seshat's approach and methods.
7   E.g. Beckwith 2009; Frankopan 2015; Hansen 2012; Heldaas Seland 2011.

On the other hand, we found that many of the key traits traditionally associated with axiality *did* develop together in nearly all of the societies we looked at—not always when and where they are said to have, but the transformations themselves do look fairly "axial." After all, Stuart-Glennie, Weber and Jaspers did not create their ideas out of thin air; there does appear to be some common causal force, or mutually reinforcing dynamic, between the spread of moralizing, equality-promoting, authority-limiting (or, better, regularizing) ideologies, at least as evidenced in our initial cross-cultural sample. These developments were not confined to Jaspers' five core regions, nor to his (or any other scholar's) single time period. Still, these axial traits emerged largely together in one way or another in nearly every Eurasian society we examined. In other words, even though the concept of the Axial Age as a single, sharply delimited temporal and geographic "movement" of similar yet independent developments does not stand to up to historical scrutiny, there is nevertheless some *there* there.

Does the Axial Age still have relevance?

Historical schemas of the Axial Age and the spread of axial ideas, following Jaspers' original conceptualization, have generally argued (or assumed) that most societies and cultures in the world were typified by "archaic" forms of governance and religious ideas until the arrival of transformative axial ideologies. Even if the idea of an Axial Age as typically presented is problematic, the topics that the theory explores are of the utmost relevance and importance for modern societies around the world. Surely, understanding the complex dynamics and interconnections between religious and ideological systems; moralizing and egalitarian principles; regulations limiting the arbitrary, authoritarian use of power; and institutions promoting social mobility, supporting public goods, and generating equitable access to resources and opportunities is a critical task: a necessary precondition for reforming social norms and improving the well-being of people throughout the world. This volume argues that a full, comprehensive exploration of where we come from—where we *all* come from, in every corner of the globe—offers the best means to understand how we got to where we are today, which in turn will allow us to correct course (where needed) in the quest to improve our collective future. Axial Age theories, then, which attempt to illuminate these long-term, large-scale, interconnected dynamics, still have tremendous relevance.

While neither Jaspers nor most subsequent proponents of the Axial Age idea directly discuss the relevance of the concept to areas outside of Afro-Eurasia[8]—such

---

8   Apart from Jaspers' (1953: 22) dismissive remark that "the vast territories of Northern Asia, Africa and America ... were inhabited by men but saw the birth of nothing of importance to the history of the spirit." For a recent account of Jaspers' pessimistic outlook on non-axial regions, see Halton 2014.

as sub-Saharan Africa, Polynesia or the Americas—the theory is described as being global in scope. The implication, then, is that areas outside of Afro-Eurasia ought to have experienced an "axial" turn only with the introduction of one of the core axial ideologies or their offshoots. Our earlier work identified interesting axial-like trans-formations in areas outside of the original five core regions, both before and after the traditional age in the mid-first millennium BCE. But this work was still limited to Afro-Eurasia. What is needed is a more comprehensive exploration of developments in these key traits in every corner of the globe; this is the goal and inspiration for the current volume.

The Seshat History of the Axial Age

Scope and purpose

Having ascertained that the temporal and geographic bounds of traditional notions of the Axial Age do not hold up to systematic empirical scrutiny, yet that there was something worthwhile in the idea that key cultural transformations tend to arise together, the pressing questions then became: how far can we push this? Do the patterns we find in Eurasia hold true *everywhere*? Are there "indigenous" axial-type developments in places like Polynesia, Africa and the Americas that mirror those in Eurasia, or, as is often implied, did axiality reach these shores only with Euro-pean colonization and (in the African case) trans-Saharan trade with the Islamic Mediterranean? Would a truly global history of the Axial Age—or, better, axiality in general—reveal a common ancestry to modern society, as Jaspers and others have so passionately argued, or would we find that all societies developed along their own, unique paths?

The identification of the key regions and ideologies associated with axiality are also problematic. Jaspers and most subsequent proponents of the Axial Age describe the regions where these axial developments arose using modern country names—a practice we follow in this introduction only to facilitate comparison with and evalu-ation of previous scholarship on the topic. It is important to point out, however, that modern geopolitical entities like "Greece" or "India" have little to do with the politi-cal, social or cultural boundaries in antiquity. When Jaspers and others talk about "Greece" experiencing an axial breakthrough, then, do they mean all of what is today Greece, do they mean only mainland Greece or perhaps just Attica (the home of Ath-ens, site of the major philosophical schools considered to have spawned axial ideas), or do they mean the wider Greek *koine* (common cultural area) of antiquity, which covered not only the territory of the modern country but also what is today Cyprus, western Turkey, Albania, Macedonia and Bulgaria and (at times) northern Egypt?

Likewise, the simple identification of an axial "sage" with a particular religious system or philosophical school that is then associated with a specific region presents many complications. Often, several different religious and ritual practices coexisted within a particular region, and it is not always clear that the system being high-lighted as "axial" was the dominant practice. Similarly, the ideologies that, arguably, spawned key cultural, political and institutional changes are said to be attributable to a set of axial sages as identified by Jaspers and others, but often the ideologies reached maturity only centuries after the sages' lifespan—the ideas of Confucius come to mind—begging the question: is it the period when the sage *lived* that is axial, or only the period when their ideas became formalized as a specific school of thought and gained widespread practice?

Lastly, as noted above, a central insight of the original concept of the Axial Age, going back at least to Alfred Weber, is that each example of an axial transformation was similar in form and function to the others, yet was at the same time entirely independent and unique. Recent research has questioned such notions of cultural separation, highlighting instead the connections and interdependencies of societies across Afro-Eurasia throughout the last few millennia BCE. This leads one to won-der if the supposedly axial transformations were, in fact, a response to an extended, cross-cultural interchange of peoples, goods and ideas. These are some of the burn-ing questions that past work on the Axial Age has largely left unanswered.

Structure of this volume

The Seshat History of the Axial Age offers a suite of regional studies sampling a wide swath of the globe. The historical information presented in each chapter is taken primarily from the Seshat Databank, supplemented with additional research and the expertise of the chapters' authors. Together, the chapters here provide a larger, more representative and thorough investigation of a selection of historical material than any previous work on the Axial Age; both through the lengthy time frame and the global scope, including, notably, regions generally ignored in works on the Axial Age, such as Southeast Asia, Polynesia, West Africa and North and South America.

To accomplish this ambitious task, we brought together a formidable team of scholars. We paired early-career researchers with more established experts to pen a series of chapters, each exploring the same themes and developments in a broad, accessible historical overview. The idea behind the volume is a fairly simple one: if we want to figure out the applicability and utility of the Axial Age as a concept, we need to take a deep dive into the history of a large number of regions from across the globe, tracing the dynamics of the key markers of axiality in a large time frame.

Each chapter focusses on one specific part of the world, sketching out that re-gion's experience in relation to the purportedly axial traits through a broad historical trajectory, encompassing essentially the last two millennia BCE through the first millennium CE, though the timescale differs depending on relevance and availa-bility of evidence. We employ an analytic narrative to offer detailed information, yet without getting bogged down in immersive exegesis on primary material. We offer reference to the most current scholarship on the areas in question, providing quantitative and qualitative summaries of key information and sources, trying to remain accessible to non-specialists. The narratives focus on the key themes of the Axial Age, using information taken from the Seshat: Global History Databank, and supplemented with additional research into relevant primary and secondary material as needed.

All authors were asked to focus on the same topics and to follow a similar structure of presentation to increase readability and to facilitate an overall, global comparison. With some variations, each chapter contains the following:

— **Introduction** situating readers in the region and historical periods to be discussed
— **Historical background** providing background information essential for understanding the region's historical trajectory, explaining major transitions and outlining the different political entities that controlled, or fought over, the area during the period covered
— **Religious-ideological overview** introduces readers to the major religious and ideological systems practiced in these societies, noting differences between popular practices and "official" or elite practice where important
— **Universalizing morality and egalitarian ethics** explores what may be considered *the* key marker of axiality: the rise of explicitly moralizing ideologies and ethical formulations stressing equality and making claims to universal participation
— **Rulership and institutions of authority** explores the supposed legal and political corollaries of axial ideologies, namely the idea that "archaic" forms of rulership, centered on the absolute, often divinely sanctioned authority of rulers and the arbitrary application of law gave way to more institutionalized, formalized political practices that limited rulers' authority, set out explicit rules and procedures in law and largely denied any claims to a divine right to rule
— **Egalitarianism, social mobility and prosociality in practice** explores differences between the prevailing ideologies concerning morality and equal distributions of resources and access to power. This section also discusses the actual manifestation of these principles, focusing on the limits of social mobility in practice along with prosocial activity such as charity, the production of public goods and other signs of "moral" practice. Further, there is an eye to the limits of egalitarianism in each region, especially the application of supposedly universal, egalitarian ideals in many of the axial ideologies to women and other marginalized populations, another underexplored aspect of Axial Age history
— An **Interaction** section rounds out many of the offerings, exploring the ways that the key traits explored throughout the chapter arose not autochthonously or independently of other developments, but through a cross-cultural transfer of

people and ideas, which stands in sharp contrast to Jaspers' and others' formulations about each distinct axial transformation
- **Short conclusion** summarizing the key arguments and dynamics, helping to lead from one chapter to the next

Not every chapter will have this exact division, as not every region provides enough information on each and every topic; these gaps in our knowledge, however, are just as important as the evidence we do possess, so such limitations are noted when they occur. We also sought to be flexible enough in our organization to conform to the diverse historical realities of each region. Some chapters, for instance, combine information on moralizing and egalitarian norms exhibited by the dominant religious ideology into a single section, while others separate these out, perhaps combining a discussion of egalitarianism with discussion of the development of institutional reform. Still, we wanted to ensure that each chapter would feature discussion of the same critical features and developments, even if the structure was somewhat pliable, to facilitate comparisons between each region. While each chapter is written as a stand-alone offering, we hope that this volume is read cover-to-cover, offering a consistent and engaging story in each chapter, along with an overall unity in structure and tone that is often missing from large, edited volumes such as this.

Importantly, all authors were asked to remain agnostic about the existence—or non-existence—of an "Axial Age." We are interested rather in offering a series of chapters outlining how the critical traits developed and changed over time in the different regions. Granted, the choice of these traits is directly and explicitly inspired by Axial Age theory, and most chapters make direct mention of the idea at some point. Still, each chapter is meant to stand on its own merits as a broad but detailed historical overview of these themes—key elements in human society, past and present.

Chapter breakdown

INTRODUCTORY MATTER: The selection of chapters was dictated by our primary aim for the volume—to test, explore and think through the various aspects of the Axial Age idea in as broad a scope as possible. The volume begins with this Introductoy chapter, then an **Overview of "Axial" Religions** chapter, which provides general background summaries of several important ideologies that appear in multiple chapters—Hinduism, Zoroastrianism, Buddhism, Confucianism, Christianity and Islam—for readers who may not be familiar with the traditions. These overviews also set the stage for understanding for how these ideologies express the key axial tenets, which frees up the regional chapters in which they reappear to focus on the peculiarities and the effects of the actual practice of these faiths on the societies being explored.

AXIAL CORE. This section offers a chapter on each of the five regions initially selected by Jaspers as centers of axial transformation: the **Mediterranean Basin (Greco-Roman World), the Levant, Iran, India,** and **North China.**[9] As readers will learn, the detailed discussion of these region's histories from the second millennium BCE to the first millennium CE reveals a mixed picture; some developments adhere quite well to the claims made by previous work on the Axial Age, while other aspects contradict the idea.

One common thread that emerges from the chapters on these five "axial" cases is the limited nature of the egalitarianism promoted by the new ideologies. While gulfs between rich and poor or ruler and ruled received a level of critical attention that does appear to be fairly novel in the historical record, the positions of slaves, foreigners and especially women were often overlooked. We learn in Jenny Reddish and Oren Litwin's chapter on the **Levant,** for instance, that the Hebrew prophets of the mid-first millennium criticized their kings for disobeying YHWH, railed against the exploitation of the poor by the rich and lamented the oppression of their people by the Neo-Assyrian and Neo-Babylonian Empires. Their attitudes to gender roles, on the other hand, were decidedly patriarchal, reminding us that modern Western notions of "human rights" cannot be projected backwards onto societies separated from our time by two and a half millennia. Likewise, the chapter on the **Mediterranean Basin** written by Jenny Reddish and Franco De Angelis highlights the exclusion of women, slaves and foreign residents from participation in the much-vaunted Athenian democracy: this was an experiment in political equality, but one that was both strictly circumscribed and relatively short-lived. Moreover, many of the thinkers whose names crop up again and again in the literature on axiality in Greece—notably Socrates, Plato and Aristotle—were mostly hostile to democratic modes of governance.

The chapter on **North China** (Jill Levine and Barend ter Haar) notes that there were elements within the "Hundred Schools of Thought"—a later Chinese term for the febrile intellectual activity of the first millennium BCE—that promoted such values as fairness, impartiality in application of the law, meritocracy and the personal cultivation of virtue. However, these were counterbalanced by expressions of support (for instance among thinkers later classed as belonging to the *fajia* school) for existing hierarchies and hereditary privileges in the name of preserving social

---

9   It is important to note that Jaspers, and many scholars following him, use only the modern country names to describe the regions (China, India, Israel-Palestine, etc). We include some of these as well for continuity and comparability with this earlier work, but also note the larger region in which they are situated (East Asia, West Asia, etc.). The chapters themselves concentrate on the area encompassed by the modern countries, but are concerned also with developments at different scales—sometimes smaller regions within the countries (e.g. the Susiana region of Iran), at others larger (e.g. the Mississippi River Valley beyond the site of Cahokia).

order. In **India** (Enrico Cioni, with contributions from Vesna Wallace), the concept of karma first emerged in the mid-first millennium BCE. It shaped thinking within a wide range of philosophical and religious traditions, including Buddhism, Jainism and the Brāhmaṇic thought associated with the Upanishads. But although karma imbued all human activity with moral dimensions and repercussions, supporting the idea of a florescence of universalizing morality in Axial Age India, it could also serve to justify inequality and suffering in the world by explaining it as a result of the individual's actions in a previous life.

The ancient history of **Iran** (Jenny Reddish and Julye Bidmead) presents a challenge to the idea of simultaneous and independent axial breakthroughs. Many scholars now believe that Zarathustra, the prophet whose religious reforms led Jaspers to include Iran among his Axial cases, in fact lived many centuries before "sages" such as Gautama Buddha, Confucius or Plato. In addition, by the mid-first millennium BCE, a network of interactions had developed between south-western Iran and Afro-Eurasian regions to the west and east, mediated through the Achaemenid Empire (whose rulers worshiped Ahura Mazda, the Zoroastrian supreme deity) but stretching beyond its borders. These issues aside, Zoroastrianism shows a complex mixture of universalizing and equity-promoting features (a stress on common spiritual purpose and ethical imperatives for all people) with doctrines and practices whose claim to axial status is less clear (such as purity rituals that applied most stringently to women). This chapter also makes the case for greater consideration of the contributions of the Elamite civilization, present in the region as early as the mid-third millennium BCE, to later Iranian religious and political history.

OTHER AFRO-EURASIAN REGIONS. For a more complete reassessment of the proposed geographical boundaries of axial developments, the next section offers four chapters on regions that are within Afro-Eurasia but have been absent from most accounts of the Axial Age: **Anatolia**, **Egypt**, the **Lower Mekong Basin**, and **Japan**.

The chapters on **Egypt** (Jenny Reddish and J. G. Manning) and **Anatolia** (Jenny Reddish, Sharon Steadman and Gregory McMahon) highlight the evidence for (proto-)axial features in societies often deemed not to have undergone such transformations. Written evidence from the Hittite Empire of Anatolia (c. 1650–1200 BCE), displays a deep concern with divinely bestowed morality and the workings of the gods in human history that foreshadows Judaic thought in the following millennium.[10] Egyptian civilization too, as Egyptologist Jan Assmann has argued in several publications (e.g. 1989, 2005, 2012), displays many precedents of axiality, beginning

---

10 Similar features can be identified in Mesopotamian religious systems, which—though this volume does not include a chapter dedicated exclusively to the Mesopotamian case—crops up in the chapters on Iran, the Levant and Anatolia. See Michalowski (2005).

as early as the Old Kingdom. As in the "axial core," impulses towards social mobility, an emphasis on personal ethical responsibility, and universalizing forms of religion coexisted alongside entrenched social hierarchy and the near-absolute power of the ruler.

In other regions, too, the introduction of axial traditions or their offshoots did not result in institutional transformations aimed at constraining the power of rulers: in fact, they frequently had the opposite effect. Despite their critical attitudes towards unconstrained temporal power, these ideologies were regularly co-opted by the ruling elite of the societies that encountered them in order to legitimize their status and right to rule. In **Japan** (Thomas Cressy with contributions from Gina Barnes and Eugene N. Anderson), Buddhism (from India via Korea and China) and Chinese Confucian-influenced statecraft were valuable tools for the incipient palace elite from the first millennium CE onwards. In the **Mekong Basin** (Jill Levine and Miriam Stark), Sanskrit literacy allowed the rulers of Funan, Chenla and Angkor to exert increasingly effective administrative control over village communities, while Brāhmaṇic and Buddhist rites and symbols enhanced their special status, particularly through the association of individual kings with Śiva or Viṣṇu. Indeed, one has only to recall the elevated status of Hellenistic divine kings as well as Roman emperors both before and after Christianization, or Hindu concepts of the *cakravartin* ("world monarch"), to see that the societies of the "axial core" demonstrate similar dynamics in ruling ideology, as well as comparable gaps between ideology and institutionalized practice regarding inequality and constraints on executive power.

REGIONS OUTSIDE AFRO-EURASIA. In the final section of the volume, we expand our scope still further, leaving behind Eurasia and North Africa to investigate whether the bundle of developments associated with axial-type transformations was experienced in societies with no relation to the European and Asian ones traditionally singled out; at least, before colonizers arrived on their shores. To this end, we have six chapters focusing on areas that have been almost completely ignored in prior work on the Axial Age: the **Inland Niger Delta**, **Highland Peru**, the **Mississippi Valley**, **Hawai'i** and a survey chapter on **Late Complexity Societies**, which addresses the question of whether and which "axial" traits can be identified among small-scale societies from a handful of regions in Oceania, the Indian subcontinent, Southeast Asia, South America, North America and northern Asia.

The **Inland Niger Delta** in modern Mali (Jenny Reddish with contributions from Susan McIntosh) presents an illuminating case study of a complex and populous civilization that appears to have lacked centralized or despotic power structures for much of its history. Archaeological work in the region over the past half-century or so has revealed an alternate societal response to the problem of the distribution of resources and power, based on economic specialization and interdependence: "heterarchy" rather than hierarchy (McIntosh 1999). Towards the end of the first millennium CE, however, more coercive political formations began to emerge, culminating in vast empires that stretched across West Africa. The introduction of Islam around the same time—often portrayed in Axial Age literature as a late-flowering product of the Judaic axial turn—did little to mitigate against this. Despite the religion's doctrinal stress on the equality of all people before Allāh and its strict monotheism, in practice local rulers benefitted from a syncretic mixture of indigenous and Islamic sources of legitimacy.

The chapters on **Hawai'i** (Dennis Spencer and Tim Earle), the **Mississippi Valley** (Jill Levine and Peter Peregrine) and **Highland Peru** (Dennis Spencer and Alan Covey) present case studies of regions that had no contact with the Afro-Eurasian landmass until just a few centuries ago. Would anything akin to an axial transformation be discernible here?

In the Hawaiian archipelago, Polynesian social complexity reached its peak, and when British explorer Captain Cook arrived in the late eighteenth century, he and his crew encountered a state-level society stratified into classes of elites (*ali'i*) and commoners, presided over by a divine king (*ali'i nui*). The concept of *mana* (a kind of vital energy force that flowed from the realm of the gods) and the *kapu* system, which stipulated a range of taboos and restrictions, together served to reinforce the status of the *ali'i* and create social distance between them and the rest of society. We cannot know whether this primary state would have undergone an "axial"-type transformation if left to its own devices, however, because its development was truncated by the arrival of Europeans from Cook onwards. The introduction of Christianity—heir to the Judaic and Greek axial traditions—may have contributed to the Hawaiians' abandonment of the *kapu* system. However, these processes cannot be disentangled from the other changes brought about by the colonial encounter: a series of epidemics, drastic population decline and the replacement of customary land tenure with private land ownership in a process that dispossessed much of the native population.

Levine and Peregrine's chapter on the **Mississippi Valley** charts the rise of a complex, populous society, now known as Cahokia, between the tenth and thirteenth centuries CE. Scholars disagree on whether this was a chiefdom, a small state or another type of polity not encompassed by these terms. What is clear is that Cahokia was unlike most early states in Eurasia: though burial evidence and human sacrifice indicate the presence of elites, the society lacked a literate bureaucracy and has produced no evidence of a king or a royal palace. It was succeeded by more egalitarian social formations in which villages were politically autonomous, but the belief systems and norms that accompanied the waxing and waning of centralized power in the American Bottom are sadly all but lost to us today. The introduction of Christianity in the course of European incursions was accompanied by demographic collapse due to Old World pathogens, along with an increase in slaving practices among the Illinois and other peoples.

In **Highland Peru**, a deep history of state formation and disintegration culminated in the vast Inca Empire, which—despite lacking written records—featured a complex administrative hierarchy, a class of hereditary nobles and a divine king with few formal constraints on his power. On the other hand, indigenous cosmology and religion placed a high value on reciprocity as a structuring force of the social as well as natural world, as well as encouraging prosocial behavior by rulers and ruled alike. As Spencer and Covey note, Inca royals sometimes styled themselves as "friend of the poor." In an echo of the history of Hawai'i and the Mississippi Valley, the introduction of Catholic Christianity through the Spanish Conquest was accompanied by epidemics and population decline, and was thoroughly integrated into a system of colonial rule that privileged those of European ancestry over all other subjects of the empire.

In her chapter (with contributions from Harvey Whitehouse), Eva Brandl explores what **small-scale societies**, typically roundly ignored or dismissed in the Axial Age literature, can teach us about the prevalence of egalitarian ideologies, universalizing ethics and constraints on the power of rulers across different social formations. She notes a widespread focus on egalitarianism within the group, along with a range of formal and informal mechanisms intended to maintain equable distributions of wealth and power. Contrary to unspoken assumptions in much writing on the Axial Age, small-scale societies are not inherently egalitarian and therefore in no need of mechanisms for curbing the centralization of power; rather, they appear to have developed their own responses to the problem of inequality.

Admittedly, there is a risk here of projecting ethnographic detail observed within the last few centuries back into the past, and we do not claim that modern-day small-scale societies existing within the orbit of powerful states are representative of ancient pastoralists or hunter-gatherers. The paucity of written evidence from these societies makes it extremely difficult to reach any solid conclusions about the development of ideologies and institutions through time. Still, it is important that these areas are not simply cast aside, for they too have something important to add to any truly global exploration or cross-cultural comparison.

CONCLUDING MATTER: Finally, a **Conclusion** (Harvey Whitehouse, Pieter François, Enrico Cioni, Jill Levine, Daniel Hoyer, Jenny Reddish) rounds up the volume, highlighting both similarities and differences in the developmental trajectories experienced by the regions discussed in the other chapters, pointing out also areas where we need further research to discover even more. The chapter ends by offering some thoughts about the broader ramifications for our understanding of the Axial Age idea, what the historical surveys presented in this volume can teach us about the shape of modern society—and about where we might be headed.

A brief explanation of the Seshat approach

Goals and methods of Seshat

No investigation of the idea of the Axial Age has been attempted before with the scope offered in this volume; indeed, the sheer amount of historical information needed to accomplish the feat is generally prohibitive. Luckily, this volume has the advantage of being able to call on the work done by Seshat: Global History Databank, a large international collaboration that brings together the collective intelligence of scores of researchers, collecting a tremendous amount of information about past societies from all over the globe—precisely the sort of detailed, fine-grained yet expansive data needed for a truly systematic exploration of these ideas. Below, we offer a brief overview of the Seshat project, noting how exactly we collected the information on which the chapters in this volume are based.[11]

Seshat collects information about our shared past culled from primary and secondary sources. As far as possible, we seek advice from academic historians, archaeologists, anthropologists and other scholars to make sure we are interrogating the cutting-edge information. We gather data on a variety of topics, exploring and testing different theories about the world in consultation with our collaborators. The overall goal of Seshat is to enable researchers to conduct comparative analyses of human societies and rigorously test different hypotheses about the social and cultural evolution of societies across the globe, spanning long periods of human history.

Seshat has a global scope, as we seek to gather evidence for societies from every corner of the globe. Still, we cannot do everything at once and there are gaps in our databank as we work toward filling them in, one at a time. As a first step, we focused on a sample of different areas—what we term "Natural Geographic Area" (NGA)—making sure to grab NGAs in every world region. NGAs, though, are simply a sampling scheme, a way to ensure that we are not over-sampling one particular type of society (for instance, those across Afro-Eurasia that developed large-scale and complex social systems relatively early, like Greece, Iran and Egypt). NGAs really just act as "anchors" on the map; our real unit of analysis is the various social formations that occupied all or part of each NGA over time. We call these *polities*, which we define as an independent political unit that ranges in scale from villages (local communities) through simple and complex chiefdoms to states and empires.[12]

With our NGAs as anchor points, we then populate a list of every polity that occupied the NGA over time, starting typically with the Industrial Revolution or the

---

11   For more detail on Seshat's methods and approach, see http://seshatdatabank.info/methods/. Also see François et al. 2016; Manning et al. 2017; Mullins et al. 2018; Turchin et al. 2015; and Turchin 2018.

12   We also capture information on *quasipolities*: areas without clear political unity, but with some degree of cultural homogeneity distinct from surrounding areas: roughly speaking, an "ethnological 'culture'" (Murdock and White 1969) or an archaeological subtradition (Peregrine 2003).

point of colonial contact for regions outside of Afro-Eurasia (ca. 1800 or 1900 CE, depending on the location) and working back in time to the Neolithic Revolution or equivalent period (subject to the limitations of data). Currently, there are over 450 such polities in Seshat. It is important to point out that our use of polities and quasipolities is simply a way for us to explore the vast literature on past human societies and should not be thought of as any static or essential framework being imposed on these societies.

The next step is to systematically gather information about each of these polities and quasipolities. We gather information on a host of topics, from basic political structures to war-making capacity, technology, informational complexity, economic instruments and measures of output, as well as the various features of the polity's different cultural, religious and ideological systems. For every one of these topics, we generate a series of variables—the specific information we would need to test the various theories that have been proposed about the topic. These variables are listed in the Seshat Codebook.[13] The databank, then, consists of the information gathered on each of these variables (including cases where none is available) for each of the polities generated through our NGA sampling scheme.

Data collection

The "data" itself is actually quite complex. Every "Seshat record" consists of three essential components:

1. **The value** assigned to each variable for the polity in question
2. **A descriptive text** explaining the reason the assigned value was given
3. **Citations** to the relevant scholarship used to determine the value

The data values can take several forms; typically, they consist either of a numerical value or a "binary" value indicating whether a particular trait or technology is thought to have been present or absent in the polity in question. For numerical values, this can be either a single number or (more frequently) a range approximating the 90 percent confidence interval. Binary values include: present, absent, inferred present, inferred absent and unknown (numerical variables can also be coded as unknown). The inferred present and absent values indicate uncertainty, either due to inconsistencies or gaps in the historical record. For example, if iron smelting has been attested both for the period preceding the one that is coded and for the subsequent period, we code it as "inferred present" even if there is no direct evidence for it (assuming there are no indications that this technology was lost and then regained). We also preserve scholarly disagreements in the data itself, rather than trying to make (what would be arbitrary or ill-informed) decisions about which side to take.

---

13   http://seshatdatabank.info/methods/codebook/

Where two or more scholars offer different ideas about a variable, we simply code both, tagging it as "disputed," and explain the arguments in the descriptive text. We also try to capture temporal uncertainty. If, for instance, iron smelting appeared in a polity at some point between 300 and 600 CE, we code this variable as absent for the time before 300 CE, present for the period following 600 CE, and for the period between 300 and 600 CE we code as "either absent or present," which is different from a simple "unknown" code (as that would indicate the value is unknown, rather than the date range).

Overall, then, our approach to transforming the rich historical record into a single coded "value" seeks to avoid forcing information about a past society into an arbitrary scale (e.g. "rate the social complexity of this society on a scale from 0 to 10"), a problem that has plagued previous attempts to construct large stores of cross-cultural historical and archaeological information (for a critical review, see François et al. 2016). Instead, we break down complex, multidimensional categories like "social complexity" or "morality" into a suite of distinct variables in order to better capture the complexity and nuance of human society.

The descriptive text and citations are just as critical as the coded value. These elements link the data in Seshat to the rich scholarly record, citing both primary and secondary literature and summarizing the opinions of various domain experts. The descriptive text is important too for providing qualitative nuance to the quantitative data presented in the coded value. Not every "present" or "absent" in each polity or in different variables is the same, so the descriptive text provides critical details on why the coded value is deserved and how exactly experts in the area think about that particular variable.

With all of these elements of each Seshat record, we can construct robust time series, tracking the dynamics in a particular theme or topic in each NGA over the very long term and comparing different regions, polities and cultures. We can perform complex statistical analyses with the quantitative values, or offer thick, descriptive narratives from the descriptive text, engaging with the most current and relevant scholarship on the issue. Or, better yet, we can combine the two approaches, drawing on the best features of traditional humanistic and scientific approaches to investigating the past.

The actual process of gathering all of this information is equally complex, an iterative and labor-intensive exercise involving dozens of collaborators working together:

— First, members of the Seshat project define a topic of interest—like the Axial Age—and we then define the variables we need to explore it. Experts in these topics and areas of interest are invited to workshops, where a comprehensive research plan is formulated.

- Then a group of Research Assistants (RAs), supervised by senior members of the Seshat team (a mixture of postdoctoral researchers and more well-established scholars) scour existing scholarship, searching through published articles, books, and archival material on a particular polity in order to find information about each variable. These RAs generate the first draft of each Seshat record.
- Next, we reach out to expert collaborators, scholars specializing in history, archaeology, anthropology and a host of other fields. These collaborators check our data, offer corrections or alternative interpretations, provide advice to the RAs on sources that may have been overlooked, and point out debates or controversies in the scholarship that were missed. Sometimes we hold additional workshops; sometimes we correspond digitally. Importantly, such experts are also the only ones who can indicate that a variable deserves a code of "unknown" (RAs code these as "suspected unknown," pending expert feedback).
- Each RA and expert collaborator who worked on a polity is "tagged" as having contributed to the databank, which allows us to both track the work and maintain control of version history, but also to give the appropriate acknowledgement[14] to the dozens of people whose hard work and indispensable knowledge goes in to each and every Seshat record.

Most of the information provided in the following pages is, at least in the first instance, based on Seshat records. The authors of these chapters are current or former Seshat RAs and expert collaborators. This volume, then, represents one way of expressing and distilling the collective knowledge gathered in the Seshat Databank.

Some caveats

Each chapter in this volume focuses on the key tenets of the Axial Age idea, as described above. This is intended to facilitate comparison between the different regions noted here and to emphasize the way different parts of the world do, or do not, conform to the expectations of a seminal, mid-first millennium BCE, Afro-Eurasian "Axial Age." Not every chapter, though, is the same. Some are longer than others, due largely to differences in the historical record—length here is in no way indicative of importance. We know a lot more about developments in the Susiana region of modern-day Iran, stretching back in time to the Neolithic transition, for instance, than we do about the Yakut people who occupied the Lena River Valley in modern Russia, who only show up on the historian's radar in the thirteenth century CE. Moreover, we do not always have the same depth or detail about each of the key axial tenets for every period of every region. While each author was instructed to focus

---

14 See http://seshatdatabank.info/seshat-about-us/ for a list of everyone who has helped build the databank so far.

on the same subjects, they did not always have the same type of source material available. Consequently, discussions of, say, moralizing ideology in some regions are much more circumscribed than in others. Further, the exact presentation of the material varies, as each author was given leeway to decide how best to present the very complex and deep historical record for each region, though, again, always centered around the same essential topics.

These topics also deserve some further explanation, if not an apology. The cornerstone of nearly all arguments about the Axial Age is a transformation in ideology and in ways of thinking, or viewing the world. This takes us into somewhat fraught territory, as ideology by this meaning is often equated with religion. And rightly so, as in most societies the dominant source of normative thought and behavior was what we generally call "religion." Here, what we really mean is *normative ideology*, which we define as any thought system concerned with the correct behavior of people, governments/leaders and other groups (and particularly the relationships between these groups). Mainly, this will be a religious or ritual system—Buddhism, Zoroastrianism, etc. But they include other thought systems as well, such as philosophical systems or anything that prescribes a particular pattern of behavior—Platonic philosophy, for instance, or Confucianism (see the "Overview of 'Axial' Religions" chapter for discussion of how Confucianism has been classified as religion and/or political philosophy). Again, the authors in this volume were given the freedom to decide how exactly to define normative ideology for their regions. Generally, they chose to focus on religious systems, especially those tied to the "official cult," namely the set of collective religious practices that are most closely associated with legitimation of the power structure (including elites, if any). But many of the chapters also discuss differences between official religion, philosophical ideals and what may be termed "popular" religion, pointing out how each system expressed the different "axial" traits. Most chapters also highlight differences between expressions of axial traits in ideology—in sacred texts, or proclamations by religious officials—and the actual practices, as demonstrated by legal regulations or particular historical events. For instance, there is a sharp distinction between the egalitarianism espoused in Buddhist scriptures and the strict hierarchies observed in many societies where Buddhism was an official religion, including acceptance and even justifications of slavery. The chapters, thus, look not only at ideology, but also institutions and the behavior of rulers to discern how far supposedly "axial" ideas had penetrated different societies at different times.

To learn more about these important and, hopefully, interesting differences in where, when and how different parts of the world adopted moralizing, universalizing, equality-promoting, tyranny-limiting ideals—in other words, began to act in "axial" ways—we refer readers to the many illuminating chapters in this volume.

Overview of "Axial" Religions

Enrico Cioni*

Introduction

This chapter introduces some of the major religious and ideological systems treated in several different chapters throughout this volume: Hinduism, Zoroastrianism, Confucianism, Buddhism, Christianity, and Islam. Many of the societies discussed in the regional chapters throughout this volume shared ritual practices as well as normative ideologies. Indeed, the very notion of an "Axial Age" implies that particular ideological systems have come to dominate religious practice throughout the world today in the form of "world religions." The area-focused chapters concentrate on developments that are distinctive to the areas under discussion. Providing some general background information here will hopefully aid readers who may be unfamiliar with these traditions.

Zoroastrianism is included despite the fact that it is usually neglected in Axial Age scholarship as well as histories of world religions more broadly. The reason for its inclusion is that it was not only an early adopter of the moralizing, universalizing precepts associated with later ideologies, but it also exerted an important influence on later developments throughout western Eurasia. Similarly, Confucianism, while not often considered to be a religion at all (more on this below), also provided a critical foundation for moralizing ideology and especially the institutional structures and ideas of rulership that later developed throughout East Asia. Indeed, an underappreciated aspect of the Buddhist notions and practices that emerged in the region during the first millennium CE was their adoption and mixing of earlier Chinese traditions, including Confucianism. The description of Confucian thought provided here should therefore also provide helpful context for the discussions of Buddhist practice in China, Japan, and the Lower Mekong Basin (modern Cambodia) elsewhere in this volume.

Lastly, it is worth noting that two of the other key axial ideologies frequently discussed by scholars—Rabbinic Judaism and Platonic philosophy—are not treated in this overview chapter. The reason for this is simple: whereas the other ideologies discussed here provide a useful background to several area-focused chapters in this volume, the origins and nature of Judaic and Platonic thought and their relationship with ideas of axiality are sufficiently explained in the Levant and Greco-Roman chapters, respectively.

---

*   Harvey Whitehouse also contributed to this chapter by reading and providing feedback on previous drafts.

Below, we treat each ideology in turn (organized *roughly* chronologically by origin): Hinduism, Zoroastrianism, Confucianism, Buddhism, Christianity, and Islam. We offer first a brief description of their *origin and spread*, then turn to a discussion of how each expressed the *core traits associated with axiality*, namely strong moralizing norms, egalitarian ideals, universal inclusion, and support for institutions limiting the authority of rulers and organizing society.

Hinduism

Origins and spread

According to some recent scholarship, there was no such thing as "Hinduism" in precolonial South Asia. Instead, prior to European colonization, several different religious systems coexisted in the subcontinent. According to this view, it was only during the nineteenth century that these were assembled into a single, unitary religion, arbitrarily labelled "Hinduism" by Western scholars (Frykenberg 1989). There is no consensus on this matter, however, and some have argued that the idea that Hinduism is a recent Western construct stems from a reluctance of modern-day Western scholars to regard Hinduism as a religion, because it is so different from its Abrahamic counterparts, which itself suggests a distorting bias on their part (Asad 1993).

Unlike every other religion considered in this chapter, Hinduism lacks a traditional founding figure, which makes it difficult to pinpoint its exact origins. Did it originate outside of South Asia, or was it an indigenous development? If it came from outside, where did it come from? Did it emerge as far back as the Indus Valley Civilization (c. 2500–1500 BCE), or was it more recent? Or was it older? How much did it borrow from preceding traditions, and did it borrow from certain traditions more than others? None of these questions have clear answers, and indeed the subject of the religion's origins is rather controversial, as different theories have been used by different political groups to bolster their agendas. Even if we were to say that Hinduism began with the date of composition of the earliest Hindu (orally transmitted) scriptures, the Vedas—which mostly focus on the theory and practice of early Hindu ritual—these have also been difficult to date, with estimates ranging from 1500 to 600 BCE (Whaling 2009: 14–16).

However, we do know that Hinduism formed the dominant ritual-religious system in parts of what is today northern South Asia by the seventh century BCE. Moreover, the Upaniṣads were composed some time between 600 and 300 BCE: these are sacred texts that codified many essential aspects of Hindu thought and practice, most notably the karma system, that is, the idea that one's actions result in more or less favorable rebirths after death. The Upaniṣads also focused less on the external trappings of religion—group or public rituals, symbolic dress, etc.[1]—and more on worshipers' interior experience of their faith (Whaling 2009: 17–19). Around the same time, however, Jainism and Buddhism also emerged, and they both eventually eclipsed Hinduism in importance, starting with Mauryan rule (322–187 BCE). Nevertheless, even this time of relative obscurity saw the composition of further Hindu sacred texts: specifically, the epic poems known as the *Rāmāyaṇa* and the *Mahābhārata*, both of which weave popular traditions and Hindu philosophy into the framework of a single extended narrative, and the *Bhagavad-gītā*, a philosophical dialogue meant to teach how to reconcile the religion's apparent contradictions and how to incorporate religious practices into one's daily life. In the fourth century CE, with the rise of the Gupta Empire, whose influence extended to the subcontinent's far south, Hinduism re-emerged as the predominant ideology in South Asia. By the end of the Gupta period, around 540 CE, another set of sacred texts had been composed, this one known as the Purāṇas, though additions were made up to at least 1000 CE. The Purāṇas provide instruction on correct moral behavior and modes of worship, and they each also focus on a single deity as the being responsible for the creation of the world and maintenance of cosmic order. Three gods, in particular, began to attract increasingly large followings: Viṣṇu, Śiva, and the goddess Devi. The cult of Viṣṇu is known as Vaiṣṇavism, that of Śiva Śaivism, and that of Devi Śāktism (Shattuck 1999: 38–51). The shifting focus of Hindu ideology between a large polytheistic pantheon of equally powerful—and important—deities, and the more henotheistic flavor of the Purāṇas, which at times even verges toward monotheism, is one of the reasons that Hinduism has been so difficult for modern Western scholars to classify.

From the Gupta period up until the arrival of Islam into the region in the thirteenth century, Hinduism—particularly Śaivism (Sanderson 2009)—benefited from the financial support of virtually all dynasties that rose and fell in South Asia. State sponsorship led to the blossoming of religious scholarship, art, and architecture. Hinduism's dominance mostly came at the expense of Buddhism, whose presence waned in the subcontinent (Whaling 2009: 25)—precisely as its influence was on the rise in East and Southeast Asia—while Jainism continued to attract followers and some government funding and support (Dundas 2002).

Between the twelfth and thirteenth centuries, powerful Islamic polities, most notably the Delhi Sultanate and the Mughal Empire, established themselves throughout the northern subcontinent. As a result, tensions between the Muslim establishment and the Hindu majority occasionally resulted in violent conflict. However, Islam's message of equality and straightforward monotheism also attracted many

---

1   Compare this with the other axial religions discussed below, which combined an importance placed on highly visible ritual activity with a focus on the internal expression of faith.

converts, especially among the lower castes. Moreover, practitioners of the more mystical branches of Islam adopted some of the more esoteric elements of Hinduism in their worship and, in the sixteenth century, Guru Nanak combined aspects of Islam and Hinduism into the movement that became Sikhism. In the south, the Vijayanagara Empire and its immediate predecessors and successors each maintained Hinduism as the dominant ideology; the most notable religious development in this region at this time was the rise of devotional traditions (Whaling 2009: 26–28). Devotional Hinduism was spread by wandering poet-saints who garnered large followings through their songs, in which they emphasized the personal relationship between worshiper and deity. Much of the appeal of devotional Hinduism came from its simpler, more open, and more egalitarian nature, evident in part from the fact that both men and women could become poet-saints and that their songs were usually written in the vernacular. Such practices set this devotional worship apart from the more hierarchical and inaccessible dominant Hindu practice (Shattuck 1999: 58–63).

Core traits associated with axiality

Morality, universalism, and egalitarianism

According to the karma system, which Hindus and Buddhists share, one's actions in this life have consequences after death. On the one hand, the more good actions one performs in life, the more merit one accumulates, and the more likely one is to be reborn as a more elevated being and/or in a more "heavenly" realm. On the other hand, a preponderance of bad actions leads to one's rebirth as a lower being and/or in a more hellish realm (Shattuck 1999: 29). Bad actions are ones motivated by hatred, dishonesty, deceit, jealousy, and avarice, while good actions are motivated by benevolence, restraint, and dutiful conduct. Through many iterations of life, death, and rebirth, people seek to break free from the cycle (achieving *mokṣa*) and unite with Brahman—a Sanskrit term denoting the Hindu notion of the ultimate, eternal, and divine unity of existence. While Hindu deities do not judge human actions or punish moral transgressions, at least compared to the "moralizing" deity of the Abrahamic faiths (discussed below), the karma system and the conception of Brahman as eternal, unchanging, and perfectly ordered does lend some moralizing weight to Hindu thought and practice.

Hindu society has long been organized by caste, that is, it is constituted by segments whose members observe various restrictions, for instance with regard to what they can eat and whom they can marry. There are four major castes, or *varṇas*: *brāhmaṇas* (priests and scholars), *kṣatriyas* (warriors and rulers), *vaiśyas* (farmers and traders), and *śūdras* (servants). The scriptural basis for this classification is *Ṛg Veda* X.90.11–12, which draws parallels between human anatomy and the correct division of society: *Brāhmaṇas* correspond to the mouth, *kṣatriyas* to the arms, *vaiśyas* to the legs, and *śūdras* to the feet. All four *varṇas* fulfill an essential role, but they are also ordered hierarchically, with *brāhmaṇas* at the top and *śūdras* at the bottom. Each *varṇa* is also subdivided into thousands of sub-castes, or *jātis*, which are usually associated with distinct professions (Whaling 2009: 73–75). The more esoteric professions are considered superior and the professions more closely associated with death and decay are considered inferior (Quigley 2003). Indeed, according to Louis Dumont's classic anthropological treatise *Homo Hierarchicus* (1980), the caste system is based entirely on notions of purity and pollution. However, many have since argued that Dumont's theory is overly simplistic. Throughout history, several *jātis* have succeeded in "elevating" themselves, for example through economic advancement, migration, religious conversion, propaganda, and disputing their own status (Whaling 2009: 74–75). It is also worth noting that there is a dissenting minority, within Hindu scholarship, that argues that Hinduism and the caste system are not, in fact, as closely linked as may be supposed (Brockington 1981; Quigley 2003).

Within traditional Hindu society, women are also normally attributed lower status than men, largely because menstruation is regarded as polluting (Whaling 2009: 81). Although records show that female sages took part in debates around the Upaniṣads in Hinduism's early centuries, by the first century CE they were not allowed to study the scriptures. Indeed, by this time, interpretation of these texts cast the relegation of women to the domestic sphere as crucial for the maintenance of the universal order; women were instructed to focus on running a house, raising children, and serving their husbands, and any education they may receive was meant entirely as preparatory for these activities (Shattuck 1999: 33). Once a woman's husband died, remarriage was considered an impossibility. Some have also observed that the arrival of Islam in northern South Asia in the twelfth and thirteenth centuries resulted in a conservative turn within northern Hinduism, perhaps in response to the "threat" of Islamic conversion, and a more progressive turn in southern Hinduism (Whaling 2009). With regards to women, this led to more rigid gender norms in the north, including the rise of *sati*, that is, the practice of burning women to death following their husbands' demise. Around the same time, the devotional movements of the south allowed women to reach some degree of equality with men in the religious sphere, if not in everyday life (Whaling 2009: 81).

Institutions of authority and social organization

In Hindu thought, punishment or reward for certain behaviors is believed to occur mainly through the karma system, not through the action of other humans. "Hindu law" does exist, and, though it likely originated as a branch of sacerdotal studies, it soon became its own independent field of study, generating norms of behavior that do not necessarily reflect the tenets of Hindu scripture. Indeed, the *Arthaśāstra*, an influential treatise on statecraft that was probably written between the second century BCE and the third century CE, recognized that politics and administration lie outside the boundaries of the sacred (Mathur 2007: 1–2). Nevertheless, as noted, many South Asian polities actively promoted and endorsed Hindu belief and practice and, while their laws and institutions may have been nominally "secular" as a modern commentator would understand it, many practices were nevertheless influenced, if not directly inspired by, Hindu thought. For instance, during many periods, the caste system described above was codified in secular law, and included, in many cases, prohibitions from intermarriage.

It is also worth noting that, for millennia, Hindu thought fostered the notion that rulers are in some way divine. This notion first emerged in South Asia during the Vedic period, between 1500 and 500 BCE. According to the earliest known written myth regarding the origins of kingship as an institution, which may be found in the *Aitareya Brāhmaṇa* (c. eighth or seventh century BCE), the gods were only able to gain the upper hand and win their war against an army of demons by appointing someone to lead them into battle: thus, the very first king was a god, Indra (Basham 1967: 82–83). Vedic texts also contain descriptions of a number of rituals meant to imbue the king with divine power, including the *rājasūya* or Royal Consecration, which consisted of a year's worth of sacrifices and ceremonies through which the new king was identified first as Indra himself, then as the god Prajapati, then as Viṣṇu. The notion that kingship was in some way divine or at least divinely sanctioned persisted throughout South Asian history: Gupta monarchs claimed an association with Viṣṇu in inscriptions and coins (McKnight 1977); later, the Rāṣṭrakūṭas assumed the title *pṛthvī-vallabha*, that is, they claimed that they were Lords of the Earth and an emanation of Viṣṇu himself (Keay 2013: 191); later still, rulers of the Chola Dynasty were worshiped as gods in temples (Basham 1967: 86). Divine kingship became such an integral aspect of Hindu ideology that, as the latter spread beyond the borders of the subcontinent, notions of divine kingship went alongside it (Legendre de Koninck 2004: 149). However, the South Asian king's divine associations were by no means exceptional (Basham 1967: 88); the entire caste of *brāhmaṇas* was also in some ways seen as divine, as were particularly saintly ascetics, and even commoners who sponsored and financed a sacrificial ceremony were raised to divinity for the ceremony's duration. It is also worth observing that divine kingship did not equate to absolute rule (Basham 1967: 89). In the eyes of his subjects, the king's priority was to promote and maintain the Dharma, the fundamental principle of cosmos, which largely depended on humankind's adherence to moral righteousness. Therefore, sacred texts and other religious literature authorized rebellion against any king who behaved immorally. Indeed, the king depended for his legitimation on *brāhmaṇas*, who were the only caste authorized to perform rituals (including the above-mentioned rituals of kingship), as well as the caste tasked with preserving and transmitting knowledge of the Dharma (Roy 1994: 75; Smith 1994: 142).

Zoroastrianism

Origins and spread

Of all the religions considered in this chapter, Zoroastrianism is in many ways the least well understood. The surviving sources simply do not provide a clear sense of its founder's life; nor do they illuminate the process by which it spread after his death (Nigosian 1993: 10, 25).

Zoroastrianism owes its name to its founder, Zarathustra, known in Greek as Zoroaster. According to tradition, Zarathustra was born between the seventh and sixth centuries BCE, in a land that would fall within the borders of modern-day Azerbaijan. Both his date and place of birth have been the subject of debate: some scholars favor the traditional date, while others place him centuries earlier, in the second half of the second millennium BCE (see the Iran chapter in this volume for a discussion). Nigosian (1993: 11–17) favors the traditional date, arguing that no persuasive alternatives have yet been advanced. This was a time of turmoil across central Eurasia, as once-dominant powers (like the Assyrian Empire) fell and new ones emerged (Media, Chaldea, and eventually the Achaemenid Persian Empire) (3–10). Again according to tradition, Zarathustra began his training to become a priest at an early age, most likely in one of the local Mesopotamian traditions prominent at the time. Around the age of 20, however, he rebelled and left home to pursue the "true" or "good" religion, which he found 10 years later, following a mystical revelation (11–12). Based on a comparison between Zoroastrian and early Hindu scriptures, Boyce (1979: 3–16) infers that the dominant religion at the time across South and Central Asia was essentially a polytheistic system centering on the worship of fire and water and preoccupied with the notion of purity. If this was indeed the case, then Zoroaster's "true" religion shared many similarities with its predecessor, but sources say that the prophet struggled for a long time to spread his teachings: after 10 years of preaching, he succeeded in making only one convert. Tradition says that the turning point came with the conversion of King Vishtaspa of the Kingdom of Bactria in the seventh century BCE, though, again, this has been difficult to confirm (Nigosian 1993: 13).

Indeed, as already mentioned, it is far from clear how Zoroastrianism first spread across the region. By the end of the sixth century BCE, the Achaemenids had firmly established themselves as the dominant power in West Asia, with an empire that stretched from northern South Asia to the eastern Mediterranean. According to some scholars, the empire's rulers were Zoroastrian (Herzfeld 1936: 20), while others believe that they still followed pre-Zoroastrian beliefs (Benveniste 1929; Duchesne-Guillemin 1953). Others still argue that, under Darius (552–486 BCE), the official state religion was "Zarathustrianism," that is, the prophet's original teachings, while from Artaxerxes I (465–24 BCE) onwards it became "Zoroastrianism," that is, a mixture of the prophet's teachings and pre-Zoroastrian beliefs (Gershevitz 1959:

8–22). Each of these views has some merit, and each flaws. Only two things are clear: first, that under Achaemenid rule, Zoroastrianism coexisted with pre-Zoroastrian belief systems; and second, that the end of Achaemenid rule and the period of foreign domination throughout Persia—first by Alexander the Great and then by his successors, particularly the Seleucids—threatened the religion's very survival. Alexander, in particular, a zealous follower of Greek philosophy and theology, ordered the execution of large numbers of Zoroastrian priests and destroyed the two archetype copies of the Zoroastrian scriptures held in Persepolis and Samarkand—again, at least according to tradition (Nigosian 1993: 30–31, 47).

However, Zoroastrian practice managed to survive this period of persecution under the Seleucids and, indeed, flourished under the Parthians (247 BCE–226 CE) and their successors, the Sasanians (224–651 CE). As with the Achaemenids, our knowledge of the religious situation in Parthian lands is incomplete, but it seems that Zoroastrianism coexisted peacefully with other religions (Nigosian 1993: 31–32). This seems to have changed under the Sasanians. The first two Sasanian rulers, Ardashir I (224–240 CE) and Shapur I (240–272 CE), are considered the founders of a form of Zoroastrian orthodoxy known as Mazdayasna, which focused particularly on worship of the high Zoroastrian deity, Ahura Mazda. Although the key Mazdayasnian tenets are far from clear, it is likely that the elimination of rival religions was required. A high priest by the name of Kartir or Karter, for example, left an inscription in which he boasted of the attacks he directed at other religions, including Judaism, Christianity, Mazdakism, Manichaeism, Hinduism, and Buddhism, and several sources suggest that Manichaeans and Christians, in particular, were frequent targets of persecution (32–42). This demonstrates not only the Sasanians' harsh attitudes to pluralistic practice, but also reveals that these religious communities had comprised significant populations under the previous ruling dynasty. It is not entirely clear why the Sasanians deviated from the Parthian policy of religious acceptance, though it has been suggested that Sasanian administration was relatively weak, leaving room for the Mazdayasnian priestly class to assume administrative, judicial, and fiscal responsibilities, particularly in the provinces (Daryaee 2009: 2012). By this reading, Mazdayasnian priests may have sought to consolidate their power by eliminating rival ideologies in the empire, leading to these persecutions. Unfortunately, however, our sources are not able to provide more conclusive details.

Zoroastrianism was dealt two heavy blows in quick succession between the seventh and the eighth centuries: first, the death of the last Sasanian ruler, Yazdgird III, in 651, and then, not long after, the arrival of Islam. Islam's replacement of Zoroastrianism as the dominant ideology in the region was slow and complex, but Malandra (2005) provides the following list of key factors. First, compared to Mazdayasna, Islam was a religion with a simpler message and simpler rituals, which did not require the mediation of a priestly class. Second, Islam and Zoroastrianism shared several common elements, in part because Islam ended up absorbing many elements of the older religion as it spread eastward into modern-day Iran and northern India: notably, a shared focus on duality (i.e. good vs. evil) and eschatology (i.e. the final destiny and judgment of humankind).[2] Third, several centuries of social and religious oppression under the Sasanians likely made Islam's message of equality, and the relative tolerance of the Islamic sovereigns toward their non-Muslim populations, appealing, particularly to the minority groups that had suffered oppression under the Sasanians.

Zoroastrian still survives today, albeit with a greatly reduced following, mostly in Iran, on the west coast of India, and in diasporic communities in many major Western cities (Nigosian 1993: 45).

Core traits associated with axiality

Morality, universalism, and egalitarianism

Much of what is known about the Zoroastrian faith as it was practiced in ancient times derives from the religion's scriptures, known as the Avesta. Unfortunately, only a small portion of the latter survived Alexander the Great's invasion in the fourth century BCE, and much of what was reconstructed through the later efforts of Parthian and Sasanian rulers and priests was lost again with the Arab conquest of Persia in the seventh century CE (Nigosian 1993: 46–47). This makes it particularly difficult to understand how the religion evolved through time. The following summary, then, applies most solidly to the most recent and best-documented period of Zoroastrian dominance in Iran, the time of Sasanian rule, and can only be cautiously applied to Parthian and Achaemenid rule. Moreover, many matters are still far from clear.

For example, scholars still debate whether Zoroastrianism was monotheistic, polytheistic, or dualistic. Zarathustra replaced the traditional polytheistic pantheons of ancient Iran with a system in which the god Ahura Mazda reigns supreme as "self-created, omniscient, omnipresent, holy, invisible, and beyond human conceptualization" (Nigosian 1993: 71), but which also includes a group of abstract entities known as the *Amesha Spentas*. Indeed, that this system was somewhat unintuitive may partly explain why a straightforwardly monotheistic religion such as Islam eventually came to replace Zoroastrianism as the dominant religion on the Iranian Plateau (Malandra 2005).

Ahura Mazda was also in charge of punishing those who transgressed moral norms and rewarding those who obeyed them. Though the most detailed account

---

2 Elements shared also by the other Abrahamic faiths, Judaism and Christianity; all these traditions co-developed seemingly in conversation with each other in the last two millennia BCE (Stepaniants 2002).

of the Zoroastrian hell, the *Arda Viraz Namag* (*"The Book of the Righteous Viraz"*) is "impossible to date with any amount of accuracy" (Stausberg 2000: 238), it does shine a light on the kinds of behaviors that Ahura Mazda was thought to punish. These included: stealing, homicide, "neglecting crying and hungry children," "denying hospitality to travelers," "violation of contracts," "selling items with false measures and weights," "making false promises," "disrespect of husband,"[3] "disrespect for one's parents," "sodomy," "sexual intercourse during menstruation," "polluting water and fire through excrement and carrion" and "performing worship while thinking that the gods do not exist" (241). By contrast, gratefulness, generosity, and righteousness were all virtues that Ahura Mazda rewarded (231–32).

The Zoroastrian approach to social equality was seemingly rather ambivalent. On the one hand, Zoroastrian eschatology holds that the potential for resurrection and salvation is universal, in contrast with more ancient Iranian traditions, which held that neither women and slaves could hope to access heaven, but were consigned to "the kingdom of shadows beneath the earth" (Boyce 1975: 132). On the other hand, the religion was also thought to provide cosmological justification for social hierarchies:

> The omniscient Mazdean religion is likened to a mighty tree with one trunk (the mean [or moderation]), two main boughs (action and abstention), three branches (good thoughts, good words, and good deeds), four small branches (the estates of the priests, warriors, husbandmen, and artisans), five roots (the lord of the house, the village headman, the tribal chieftain, the ruler, and the highest religious authority, the representative of Zoroaster on earth ...), and above them all the head of all heads ... the king of kings, the ruler of the whole world (Shaki 1994: 279–81).

Moreover, with regards to gender, Choksy (2002) points to a number of malign images of women and femininity from a variety of Zoroastrian texts and argues that these symbolic structures would have had direct implications for women's daily lives. In the fifth century CE, a new sect known as Mazdakism advocated the equal sharing of wealth and property, but it included women in the latter category (Rose 2015: 131), which again demonstrates that notions of gender equality were still far from accepted.

Institutions of authority and social organization

With regards to the way that Zoroastrianism affected rulership and the law in polities where it was the dominant ideology, sources are, once again, rather patchy. Some texts specifically dealing with legal matters have survived from Achaemenid

---

3   Note that, as with Hinduism, this marital morality applied only to women; there is no indication of a similar exhortation against the "disrespect of wife."

times, but only from the empire's peripheries (Magdalene 2009); next to nothing is known with regards to the Parthians (Shaki 2009); and no legal texts have survived from Sasanian times, but much can be reconstructed by looking at other types of documents (Macuch 2009). Overall, it is clear that Zoroastrianism was closely intertwined with rulership and the administration of justice, at least for the Achaemenids and the Sasanians. Both dynasties promoted the notion that Ahura Mazda bestowed "divine fortune" or "glory" (*xwarrah*) upon the monarch, legitimating his rule (Rose 2014: 105; Schmitt 1983). Moreover, all forms of punishment meted out by the Achaemenid ruler were seen as carrying out the will of Ahura Mazda; indeed, under the Achaemenids, the Zoroastrian equivalent of sin, "the lie," came to encompass resistance to Achaemenid power (Stausberg 2000; Wiesehöfer 2013: 48–49). Similarly, the Sasanian legal system was explicitly based on Zoroastrian ideals, with crimes categorized as either moral transgressions against religious teachings or offenses against other members of the Zoroastrian community (Macuch 2009). There is not enough evidence to say whether or not Zoroastrian clergy punished moral wrongdoing, though the distinction itself is misleading; under Sasanian rule, Zoroastrian priests often acted as judges. Indeed, the highest legal official was also the head of the Zoroastrian Church (Macuch 1981: 188–208).

Confucianism

What is "Confucianism"?

First, there is the question of whether or not Confucianism can be considered a "religion." Many people today do not consider it a religion, and indeed even the Chinese government excludes it from its official list of the five major religions (Daoism, Buddhism, Islam, Catholicism, and Protestantism) (Sun 2017: 1). Confucianism has no official clergy, no institutions equivalent to churches or mosques, and no conversion rites. The Chinese term for Confucianism, *rujiao*, is more accurately translated as "Confucian thought" than "Confucian religion" (though it is also worth noting that the notion of religion in a Western sense is just over a century old in China) (3–4, 21). The very name "Confucianism" was used for the first time in Western publications in the 1860s and only in the following decade did Western scholars classify it as a "world religion" alongside Christianity, Islam, and so on (20–21).

Second, Confucianism is often misleadingly confused with Chinese culture as a whole (Goldin 2014: 3–4). This is largely due to the writings of Matteo Ricci (1552–1610 CE), a Jesuit missionary who argued that, just as he viewed European society to be founded on the teachings of Christ, Chinese society was founded on those of Confucius. In fact, Ricci was also the one who first used "Confucius" as a translation for the sage's Chinese name, Kong Qiu. Many scholars believe that the term has been misused so much that it should no longer be used, one of the suggested alternatives being "classicism" (e.g. Nylan 2001: 2).

The primary consideration that motivates the inclusion of Confucianism in this chapter, however, is that it was an important, moralizing ideology, sociopolitical philosophy, and series of ritual behaviors that developed in the first millennium BCE and eventually came to exert a major influence over powerful premodern states throughout East and Southeast Asia. Further, it was identified by Jaspers (1953) as a key axial ideology, with Confucius himself designated an "axial sage," a designation followed by most subsequent proponents of the Axial Age idea. Whatever it is called, then, it certainly belongs alongside Buddhism, Zoroastrianism, and the other ideologies presented here.

Origin and spread

Confucius himself lived between the sixth and fifth centuries BCE, at a time when the territory of what is today the People's Republic of China was splintered into small, independent states that were often at war with each other and were ruled by lords who maintained their authority mostly through the use of force, as opposed to the moral example they set or a genuine concern for their subjects' welfare (Gardner 2014: 2). This, at least, was Confucius's own evaluation of the country's circumstances, which he believed to be dire compared to those it had enjoyed under Zhou rule several centuries before. After a disappointing experience as the minister of crime for his native state of Lu, Confucius spent much of his life wandering from one state to the next, seeking a ruler he could mold into his own ideal notion of what a perfect ruler should be (Sun 2017: 16). However, here too he was disappointed, as none of the rulers he approached found his message appealing (Gardner 2014: 3). Confucius therefore shifted his focus to teaching his disciples (72 [Gardner 2014: 3] or 3,000 [Sun 2017: 16], depending on the tradition), so that they could carry on his ideas and pass them down to future generations. Indeed, his disciples and their own followers demonstrated such devotion to their master that, several centuries after his death, a collection of his thoughts, the *Analects*, appeared in written form. These would form the founding canon of Confucianism, alongside the "Five Classics": the *Book of Changes*, the *Book of Odes*, the *Book of History*, the *Book of Rites*, and the *Spring and Autumn Annals*. Traditionally, these have all been in some way attributed to Confucius (either as author, compiler, or editor), but the attribution has not withstood critical scrutiny, especially as some of these texts were likely written long before Confucius was even born, and others long after his death (Gardner 2014: 3-4). Among Confucius's early followers, two stand out for the long-lasting influence of their own interpretation of the sage's teachings: Mencius and Xunzi (see below).

Although Confucius is seen as the great sage of his eponymous school of thought, it took a long time for Confucianism to emerge as a dominant ideology, centuries after his death; indeed, though within the traditional bounds of the Axial Age in its origin, the effects of Confucian thought only really started to manifest well into the first millennium CE. At first, it was simply one of several competing ideologies, alongside Daoism, Legalism, Yin-Yang cosmology, the teachings of Mozi, and the theories of the Military Strategists, Diplomatists, Agriculturalists, Logicians, and so on. Though they each had their own unique vision, all these schools of thought were interested in exploring matters such as what makes a good ruler, what makes a good society, and what place the individual has within a family, within society, and within the cosmos (Gardner 2014: 4–5). Only during the Han Dynasty (202 BCE–222 CE) did Confucians manage to assert their dominance, at least at the level of government. Specifically, they persuaded Emperor Wu (141–87 BCE) to banish all non-Confucian officials and create a panel of advisors, known as the "Erudites of the Five Classics," who were experts in the Confucian canon (6). From this moment until 1912 CE, Confucianism functioned as an essential ideological prop for the legitimation of government in mainland China. Indeed, over the centuries, an elaborate system took shape which made it essential for the Chinese bureaucratic class to know the Confucian classics to perfection (Gardner 2014: 6–7). Still, it is worth noting that the influence of Confucianism periodically waned, particularly when that of Buddhism waxed, for example during the Sui and Tang dynasties. Moreover, the imperial cult also provided essential support to rulership and its associated institutions (see below).

From China, Confucianism spread to what is today Vietnam, Korea, and Japan (Gardner 2014: 8–9). With the exception of some brief periods of independence, the region now occupied by Vietnam was subject to Chinese dynasties for over a millennium, from 111 BCE to 939 CE, and even afterwards, local polities retained the Chinese tradition of selecting bureaucratic officials based on their expertise of the Confucian classics. A similar system also emerged in the Korean Peninsula, where Confucianism was first introduced around 370 CE, and where it dominated over all other systems of thought during the Chosŏn Dynasty (1362–1910 CE). By contrast, Japan never developed a bureaucratic system comparable to those that emerged on the East Asian mainland, and that may explain why, even when Confucianism was championed by the Tokugawa Dynasty (1603–1868 CE), it never became an exclusive orthodoxy in the archipelago, blending instead with Buddhism and Shintō.

Core traits associated with axiality
Morality, universalism, and egalitarianism
Goldin (2014: 5) offers the following useful summary of the key tenets that Confucians share:

> (i) human beings are born with the capacity to develop morally; (ii) moral development begins with moral self-cultivation, that is, reflection on one's own behaviour and concerted improvement where it is found lacking; (iii) by perfecting oneself in this manner, one also contributes to the project of perfecting the

world; (iv) there were people in the past who perfected themselves, and then presided over an unsurpassably harmonious society—these people are called "sages."

Not all Confucians agree on what exactly "moral self-cultivation" entails; indeed, two of Confucius's most influential early followers had diametrically opposed ideas on the matter, with Mencius arguing that one must develop one's own innate good-ness in the face of external corruption, and Xunzi arguing that human nature is in-herently evil and may be corrected only by looking at one's culture and environment (Gardner 2014: 50–51).

Overall, however, most Confucians agree on the benefit of cultivating a number of key virtues, either by finding and developing them within oneself or by looking to the outside world for examples. These are: filial piety, intended mainly as revering one's parents, both in life and, through ritual activities, after their death (Goldin 2014: 34; Puett 2002); dutifulness, intended as putting the interests of one's supe-rior, whether father or ruler, before one's own (Rainey 2010: 30); and honesty and sincerity, intended as living up to one's word and moral ideals (30). As implied in Goldin's summary, a person who dedicates themselves to moral self-cultivation does so in order to perfect the world (intended mainly as human society), not with the aim of achieving some kind of reward in the afterlife. Though contemporary Chinese culture includes elaborate notions of merit, punishment, and reward in the afterlife, these largely derive from the Buddhist traditions that were most influential in the region throughout the medieval and early modern periods (Thompson 1989: 35). Indeed, though Confucius believed in the existence of gods and ancestral spirits, and though he believed that these beings could all intervene in human affairs, including by providing moral guidance, he also believed that it was the human realm that required urgent intervention, and that it was therefore his duty, and his followers' duty, to direct people toward earthly matters rather than heavenly ones (Gardner 2014: 13–14; Sun 2017: 16).

According to traditional Chinese ideology, dating back to the Han Dynasty, men who were well versed in the classics (i.e. scholars and state officials) were superior to other social groups—specifically farmers, artisans, and merchants. However, it is worth noting that it was possible for farmers, artisans, and merchants to become literate, and join the ranks of their social superiors. Indeed, according to Confu-cianism, the path to social betterment is open to anyone who has the willpower and persistence necessary to study the classics and cultivate the fundamental vir-tues—regardless of status, family background, or natural talent. Those who applied themselves with particular diligence to moral self-cultivation and the study of the classics could even take the exams for becoming a civil official, and, if they passed, they could join the vast bureaucratic machine that was meant to amplify the ruler's own unparalleled wisdom and morality (see below) by putting his ideas into practice throughout the polity's territory (Frederickson 2002).

The only insurmountable obstacle in one's path to moral cultivation and social betterment was gender: there is no indication that any of Confucius's teachings or those of his followers were meant for women, and indeed the *Analects* include the pronouncement that "Women and petty men are especially hard to handle" (17.23) (Gardner 2014: 104–05). In families, only sons could continue the family line and ensure the fulfillment of ancestral obligations, while daughters were expected to marry out, and therefore fill the ranks of other families (Ebrey 1993: 7–8). In public life, women were excluded from serving as civil officials (Gardner 2014: 105).

Institutions of authority and social organization

According to Confucian thought, a prosperous and orderly society is the direct result of good rulership. A good ruler is an exemplar of virtue for his people to imitate. At the same time, a good ruler must protect and promote his people's well-being, so that they may prosper, and so that they may willingly and gladly accept his rule. Moreover, a good ruler possesses the willpower and persistence necessary to constantly cultivate the virtues expected of a person in a position of power (including, for example, benevolence, wisdom, and humility), especially as he cannot rely on institutions to improve his rule or benefit society without his guidance. According to Confucian thought, institutions simply provide rigid rules and norms, but only a good ruler can wield these in the way that best suits the times in which he lives, while a bad one could easily manipulate them to his own advantage (Chan 2014). Indeed, when Chinese emperors did not embrace Confucian morals, there was no legal system of checks and balances to constrain their actions, so that they could abuse their power or neglect their responsibilities and suffer no consequences. One might expect, perhaps, that state officials might speak out against bad rulership, especially as many would have been well versed in the Confucian canon, but in practice they could only do so at great personal risk (Gardner 2014: 99–100), though the freedom granted to administrators to censure or critique rulers varied widely from dynasty to dynasty and ruler to ruler. This autarchic power provided to, and frequently taken up by, rulers of Chinese dynasties derived from that other dominant Chinese ideology, the imperial cult, according to which rulers were divine figures (Puett 2014: 243) and had a direct—and unquestionable—mandate from the gods to govern the people (Gardner 2014: 46).

Buddhism

Origin and spread

Siddhārtha Gautama, later Buddha, the founder of Buddhism, was born somewhere on the Nepalese side of the modern-day border between India and Nepal, in either the sixth or fifth century BCE (Keown 2013: 17).

It is likely that many different beliefs mingled in that region at that time, but, of these, the only one that has left texts behind is the early Hindu practice of Brāhmaṇism (Gombrich 1988: 25). According to Brāhmaṇic thought, the cosmos was created through the creator god's self-sacrifice by fire, and regular fire sacrifices were essential for maintaining the proper functioning of the universe, though the fire sacrifices that humans were required to perform did not involve self-immolation. Fire sacrifices, then, were significant acts whose consequences appeared to be invisible, but were in fact vastly important. Such significant acts were referred to with the Sanskrit word karma, and the proper functioning of the universe that these acts maintained was known by the Sanskrit word Dharma. At death, if an individual had performed acts of karma in the correct manner, and had achieved a clear understanding of Dharma, his or her soul would be reabsorbed into the creator god, who had not died as a result of his immolation, but rather had become a vast cosmic soul. Otherwise, one would spend millennia cycling between "our" world and several layers of afterlives, through a complex system of rebirths and reincarnations (Bechert and Gombrich 1984: 11–12).

Because Brāhmaṇism held that there was a single proper way for the cosmos to function, Brāhmaṇic society also followed strict rules. Most notably, people were born into hereditary, hierarchically organized castes, and, with very few exceptions, intermarriage between castes was not allowed. The most powerful caste was that of the *brāhmaṇas*; they were the only ones allowed to perform rituals, and they were therefore seen as responsible for the upkeep of the universe (Hamilton 2013: 24).

However, as already mentioned, just as it is likely that several other religions existed alongside Brāhmaṇism, so were there people who lived outside of the Brāhmaṇic caste system. These outsiders were usually celibate wanderers with no ties to family and no economic or ritual role within the communities they passed through (Hamilton 2013: 34). Gautama was one of these outsiders. Legend holds that he was born to a wealthy, perhaps royal family that followed the Brāhmaṇic tradition. Raised in luxury and shielded from trouble, he one day came upon people who were sick, disabled, and poor, coming to realize the sufferings of the "real" world that he had been spared to that point. He left his home (and, by some accounts, his wife and child) to learn how to best help end people's suffering. After first studying under a Hindu guru (a spiritual teacher, guide, and mentor), he eventually achieved enlightenment on his own while meditating under a bodhi tree. Once enlightened, Gautama became known as the Buddha, or "enlightened one." His path was exemplified by what came to be known as the "Middle Way," a rejection of both the extreme ascetic self-mortification of the Brāhmaṇic wandering sages he had once sought to emulate as well as the life of excess led by wealthy, powerful families like the one he was born to: according to the Buddha, a person should live a simple, humble life, but also one devoid of discomfort (Hamilton 2013: 49–50). He further rejected the authority of the *brāhmaṇas* and their scriptures (Bechert and Gombrich 1984: 12), did not believe in the existence of a permanent "soul" or "self" (Sanskrit *ātman*), and did not believe that the gods were concerned with human affairs (Keown 2013: 37), though he never argued against their existence.

Other than that, however, the Buddha maintained many of the other key aspects of Brāhmaṇic thought, though in a few cases he reinterpreted them. For example, he shared the Brāhmaṇic understanding of karma, the belief that one's actions had consequences for one's afterlife, but he believed that it was the intention behind these actions that made them good or bad and therefore determined their exact consequences (Keown 2013: 43). And, like adherents of Brāhmaṇism, he believed that the universe was governed by a law called the Dharma, and that this law was also the "Truth" underlying all things, as well as a doctrine for his students to follow (Bechert and Gombrich 1984: 12–13). He did not believe the caste system should be abolished, but he did say that caste would become irrelevant to anyone who joined his *saṅgha*—that is, his community of monks, nuns, laymen, and laywomen.

Buddha acquired hundreds of followers in his lifetime and, shortly after his death, five hundred senior monks and nuns gathered to codify his teachings. These monks and nuns mostly lived in monasteries in what is today the Indian state of Bihar, but, over the following centuries, both they and their founder's teachings spread gradually throughout the northern subcontinent (Bechert and Gombrich 1984: 60). Around a century after the Buddha's death, the religion experienced its first schism, most likely over the questions of how to honor/worship the Buddha himself and whether or not Buddhism should mingle with other religious and cultural traditions as its geographic range expanded. Eventually, the two opposing factions—the Universal Assembly and the Elders—fragmented into several sub-schools. Of these sub-schools, the only one to survive today is Theravāda, whose name ("the Way of the Elder" in Pāli) refers to the senior monks who preserve its tradition, hinting also toward Theravāda's relative conservatism. Other schools paved the way for the emergence of the Mahāyāna tradition between the first century BCE and the first century CE. Mahāyāna Buddhism introduced two main innovations. First, it emphasized the figure of the *bodhisattva*, that is, a person who, motivated by selfless love, works tirelessly to ensure the well-being and bring about the enlightenment of his or her neighbors. Second, it transformed the Buddha into a benevolent god-like being. Indeed, in general, while Theravādins see salvation as an individual responsibility, Mahāyānists seek the aid and intercession of an elaborate hierarchy of *bodhisattvas* and supernatural beings. Today, most Buddhists think of themselves as Mahāyānists or Theravādins in the same way that most Christians think of themselves as either Catholics or Protestants (Keown 2013: 61–66).

In the third century BCE, Buddhism experienced its first great expansion throughout the whole Indian subcontinent and Central Asia, as a result of the conversion of Aśoka, ruler of the Mauryan Empire. However, in South Asia, the religion lost much support by the middle of the first millennium CE: first it was supplanted in popularity by a renewed interest in Hinduism and Jainism, and then it was nearly obliterated by the Muslim invasions of the thirteenth century onwards. In Central Asia, Buddhism had been supplanted by Islam a few centuries earlier. Similarly, in China, Buddhism spread among the elites in the fourth century CE, experienced its heyday under the Sui and Tang dynasties between 589 and 960 CE—a number of Chinese sects arose, more scriptures were translated, and monasteries accrued significant wealth through official state support and patronage—then never fully recovered from state suppression in the late tenth century, surviving today mostly in the form of popular devotionalism. Buddhism was more successful in Tibet, Śrī Laṅkā, and Southeast Asia, particularly in what is now Myanmar, Cambodia, and Thailand, where it remains the dominant religion today, and in Japan, where it was introduced from Korea in the sixth century CE, eventually spawning countless native sects, and incorporating traditional Shintō beliefs (Bechert and Gombrich 1984: 60, 116, 172).

Theravāda became the main form of Buddhism in Śrī Laṅkā and much of Southeast Asia, while Mahāyāna Buddhism prevails everywhere else. In each of its regions, Mahāyāna Buddhism mingled with other belief systems, resulting in the emergence of several distinctive variants. In Japan, for example, early sects transformed Buddhism in a highly elaborate system of esoteric beliefs that at one point became virtually indistinguishable from ancient shamanistic and animistic beliefs and practices, and which were used to provide supernatural protection for the state; from the thirteenth century onwards, Amidism, Zen, and Nichiren Buddhism promoted a simpler, more straightforward interpretation of Buddhism, which held greater appeal for the general population (Gombrich 1984: 172). In China, many accepted Confucian scriptures as the most authoritative guide to the world of the living, but turned to Buddhism for guidance about the afterlife, a topic on which Confucianism is largely silent (Keown 2013: 85). In Tibet, esoteric forms of Mahāyāna Buddhism, known as Tantra or Vajrayāna, flourished. Like Esoteric Buddist practices in Japan, these made use of shamanistic formulas and utterances, secret languages, and mystical diagrams; to many modern audiences, Tibetan Tantra distinguishes itself by the emphasis it places on sex no longer as an obstacle to personal development, but as a potent force that actually speeds up personal development if harnessed correctly (Keown 2013: 94). Tibetan Buddhism spread into Mongolia from the thirteenth century CE, and there it blended with local variants of shamanism and folk beliefs and practices (Wallace 2015).

Core traits associated with axiality

Morality, universalism, and egalitarianism

We have already seen that, according to Buddhism, though many gods exist, they are remote beings who do not involve themselves in human affairs; moreover, like humans, they are subject to karma and participate in the cycle of rebirth (Keown 2013: 37). In other words, unlike in the Abrahamic faiths, Buddhist gods are uninterested in morality, they do not punish or reward humans for their behavior, and indeed they themselves may suffer from the consequences of their own actions if they contradict the Dharma. Strictly speaking, to talk about "reward" and "punishment" is incorrect, reflecting Judeo-Christian and Islamic preoccupations rather than Buddhist thought. It is easier to understand the way one's actions in Buddhism have consequences in one's afterlives by comparing this process to a natural law, like gravity, with good deeds resulting in upward movement toward reincarnation into more elevated beings and life in more serene planes of existence, and bad deeds resulting in downward movement toward reincarnation into more lowly beings and lives of greater turmoil (Keown 2013: 43). The more good deeds one performs, the more good karma, or "merit" (*puṇya* in Sanskrit) one accrues.

For lay followers, a key way of accruing merit is to support the order of monks, for example by placing food in the bowls of monks as they pass on their daily alms round, providing them with robes, and donating funds for the upkeep of monasteries and temples (Keown 2013: 44). Moreover, lay followers must obey the following five precepts: (1) avoid harming living beings, (2) avoid stealing, (3) avoid sexual transgressions, (4) refrain from false speech, and (5) avoid intoxicants that cause reckless behavior (Gethin 1998: 118–19). Conversely, bad deeds include killing, stealing, sexual misconduct, lying, fomenting division or causing offense through one's words, frivolous speech, and covetousness. Each of these bad deeds is seen as motivated by one or more of the following three negative states: greed, hatred, and delusion or ignorance. Deeds motivated by greed are thought to lead to reincarnation as a "hungry ghost," that is, a permanently unsatisfied being; deeds motivated by hatred lead to one's rebirth in one of many possible hell realms, where one suffers terrible pain; and deeds motivated by delusion or ignorance lead to one's rebirth as a dumb animal (Gethin 1998: 136).

Buddhist ideology is fundamentally egalitarian, as every human being is thought to have the potential to achieve what the Buddha achieved, regardless of class or ethnicity. Indeed, at least theoretically, even rulers are generally seen as mere lay followers, though usually they are also seen as lay followers who are slightly wiser and more virtuous than their subjects, and who only act for the welfare of others

(Schmidt-Leukel 2006: 86). However, as has already been mentioned, Gautama Buddha himself did not attempt to overturn the caste system in South Asia and Buddhist doctrine does not challenge the existence of slavery; indeed, Buddhist scriptures lay out the proper conduct that masters should follow with regards to their servants, and vice versa (Schmidt-Leukel 2006: 65), runaway slaves were not allowed to become ordained, and throughout history and in virtually all regions where the religion spread Buddhist temples routinely kept (lay) slaves (Gombrich 1988: 30).

As for the question of gender equality, most Buddhist scholars, today as in the past, accept a fundamental ideological equality between the sexes, believing that one's gender does not affect one's capacity for personal development. Indeed, Buddhism was one of the first religions to give rise to a female religious order, though the Buddha himself opposed it at first and nuns no longer exist in the Theravāda tradition. However, in line with its acceptance of slavery and the South Asian caste system, Buddhist practice has done little, historically, to challenge gender inequality in the cultures and societies that adopted it, and in many cases it absorbed misogynistic notions, leading for example to the commonplace idea, still extant in some traditions, that to be reborn as a female is less fortunate than being born as a male (Keown 2013: 140–42).

Institutions of authority and social organization

Though Buddhists believe that moral transgressions are ultimately punished—and that meritorious actions are ultimately rewarded—through karma, Buddhist scriptures exhort rulers to punish transgressors and reward the virtuous in their lifetime. Specifically, the *Golden Light Sūtra* says that, in doing so, a ruler demonstrates the basic principle of karma, i.e. that good deeds lead to good outcomes and bad deeds to bad outcomes. Moreover, the *Golden Light Sūtra* points out that if a ruler that does not punish moral transgression, the polity might descend into lawlessness, leading to an increase in violent, impious behavior. Indeed, even though Buddhism generally promotes non-violence, in the case of rulers, texts like the *Golden Light Sūtra* argue that a non-violent ruler—and specifically a ruler who does not use violent means to punish evil-doers and deter potential evil-doers from committing transgressions—may indirectly lead to greater violence overall within a society. However, a ruler's use of violence must be selfless and lawful and based on impartial judgment, and his punishments must fit the crime (Emmerick 1970: 57– 73).

Christianity

Origins and spread

Like Confucius, Jesus did not leave writings of his own. Also as in Confucius's case, none of Jesus' contemporaries recorded his words and actions as he pronounced or performed them. Instead, the definitive accounts of his life and teachings, the

Gospels, were written some time after his death, between the first and second centuries CE. The Gospels present many similarities, but also several differences, and many of the teachings they preserve are riddle-like and ambiguous. As in Zarathustra's case, then, it is challenging to assemble a historically solid reconstruction of Jesus' life and teachings (Woodhead 2004: 3–5).

According to the gospels, Jesus was born in Galilee (which falls between modern-day Israel, Palestine, and Lebanon) at a time when the region was part of the Roman Empire. The Gospels leave much unsaid about his childhood, other than noting that, from even before his birth, it was clear that he was an exceptional individual, uniquely favored by God. Much of the Gospels' narrative is concerned with Jesus' public ministry in Galilee, as a man in his late twenties or early thirties, wandering the region, spreading his teachings, performing miracles, and attracting followers. The latter were mostly part of the large Jewish population who had been living in the Levant since the beginning of the first millennium BCE, and whose God—creator of the universe, omniscient and omnipotent—and scriptures—the Hebrew Bible—Jesus acknowledged, but whose priestly class he criticized, favoring instead the poor and the socially despised (Woodhead 2004: 7).

At the time, Judaism was hardly a monolith, with different groups (e.g. the priesthood, the Pharisees, and the Essenes, known to us from the so-called Dead Sea Scrolls) each aiming for the attainment of "purity" amongst Jews in the region; that is, the creation and/or preservation of communities that were free of "corruption." None of these groups agreed on what either purity or corruption entailed, but each believed their own interpretation to coincide most closely with that of their forefathers, and they excluded and used vituperative language against those who disagreed (Young 2006: 24–25). One could argue that Jesus was a natural fit in this milieu: he, too, wished to build a community based on his own specific interpretation of Judaism, and one that excluded those he deemed "corrupt" but included those he deemed "pure." Because Jesus placed the powerful and wealthy in the former category, and because he favored the poor and downtrodden, his preachings alarmed both Jewish and Roman authorities as he traveled southward to Jerusalem. The Romans, who had long promoted religious plurality and accepted numerous faiths within their borders, were particularly concerned about the proselytizing aspect of this new religious movement, something the other Judaic groups had not pursued. Early Christians sought not only to attract other Jews, but also to convert Roman pagans away from the official state cults and the rituals that, to the Roman authorities, kept the empire in the gods' favor. Jesus was therefore arrested and executed by crucifixion. The Gospels then say that, mere days after his death, his followers visited the grave where he had been buried, and found it empty. Three of the Gospels say that Jesus then appeared miraculously to some of his followers, claiming to have been resurrected by God. The Gospels' message is clear: those who follow Jesus and his teachings will be rewarded with eternal (after)life (Woodhead 2004: 7–8).

It is difficult to say how many followers Jesus managed to attract in his lifetime, how many were left after his death, and indeed how large Christian communities tended to be as the religion spread across the Roman Empire. The problem, again, is with the sources (Fox 1986: 269–70). Though Christian writers suggest that Christianity spread rapidly, very few non-Christian sources mention the religion or its practitioners, including some of the more comprehensive histories, which suggests that, for a long time, Christians were a negligible minority. However, the letters of St. Paul to different Christian communities—foundational texts for Christians, especially as the letters' main aim was to regulate practices and beliefs at a particularly formative developmental stage for the religion—do show that their geographic spread, at least, was significant (271). Most likely, by the third century CE, there were Christian communities in towns and cities of all sizes throughout the Roman Empire,[4] while Christians were much fewer and farther between in rural areas. There is also evidence that the Christian teachings were preached in most major languages spoken across the empire (notably Latin and Greek), but not in the minor dialects (293).

Many of the early converts likely came from the "middle" classes, that is, they were neither very poor nor very wealthy. Woodhead (2004: 40) specifically mentions "fairly prosperous traders, merchants, and craftsmen, who moved freely across the Roman Empire," while Fox (1986: 311) argues that "the humbler free classes" (educated, but not highly, and with modest property) would have found Christian ideas particularly appealing. Jesus' anti-establishment message also appealed to many wealthy Romans who engaged in trade but were barred from translating their economic success into political or social privilege due to the fact that these positions remained dominated by Rome's noble lineages. Many women, including high-status women, also swelled the ranks of the early converts. Most likely, most converts were attracted by the Christian notion of spiritual equality regardless of class or gender, as well as by the strong sense of solidarity and the mutual support that characterized Christian communities. Christians also attempted to appeal to elites by claiming that they believed in spiritual, not social equality, creating the potential for conflicting interpretations of the message about the corrupting power of wealth (Fox 1986: 325; not unlike early Buddhists in South Asia, who did not substantially challenge the caste system). Conversely, Christians did little to evangelize slaves, who, according to St. Paul, must simply "submit" to their masters (Fox 1986: 297); a further complication of the "core" Christian message of equality of all under God, accepting the legal and social hierarchies of Rome's status quo.

---

4   Covering at the time some 4 million km^2 around the wider Mediterranean Basin.

Because Christianity did not seem to pose a great threat to fundamental Roman institutions such as slavery, Christians were only persecuted sporadically between the first and fourth centuries, mostly because they refused to participate in some of the most important rituals of (Eastern) Roman pagan practice, notably the imperial cult (Woodhead 2004: 41–42). These persecutions increased over time as Christians became more vocal and visible members of Roman society, culminating in Emperor Diocletian's Great Persecution between 303 and 312 CE (Brown 1996: 26). Because it came right after this final period of persecution, Emperor Constantine's conversion to Christianity in 312 CE was experienced by many as an unexpected event (Fox 1986: 609). Indeed, at the time, Rome's large Christian community had been bishop-less (that is, leaderless) for several years due to internal disputes, and breakaway groups had begun to form in North Africa and the eastern Mediterranean based on new and unorthodox interpretations of the scriptures (Fox 1986: 609–10). Constantine's conversion, and the fact that his successors largely kept to the Christian faith, resulted in renewed prestige for the Church, greater wealth due to official state support, and a definitive end to persecutions; moreover, Constantine's successors gradually banned fundamental pagan rituals such as public sacrifices, closed (and occasionally looted) pagan temples, and even colluded in violent attacks against pagan cult sites (Brown 1996: 42–43). At this time, Christianity was particularly successful in the eastern Mediterranean and North Africa—and, not coincidentally, the Roman Empire's center of power shifted eastward following Constantine's move of the capital to Byzantium, renamed Constantinople (modern-day Istanbul) (Woodhead 2004: 56). Christianity's expansion to the east was checked, at the empire's border, by the popularity of Manichaeism (Brown 1996: 42–43), an Iranian religion based on the dualistic notion of the struggle between good and evil, which was enjoying a final resurgence under the Sasanians in Persia and throughout West Asia. In western Europe, Christianity spread more slowly, mostly as a top-down process, that is, through the conversion of Germanic tribal leaders (Woodhead 2004: 56).

Two very different Churches eventually developed, each with its own rituals and interpretations: an Eastern Church, still under the control of the emperor in Byzantium, and a Western Church, headed by the bishop of Rome—later known as the pope (*papa* in Latin, or "father" of the Church)—and which gained increasing power following the fragmentation of the western half of the Empire into many smaller polities beginning in the mid-fifth century CE (Woodhead 2004: 58). The two Churches split permanently around 1054 CE, over differences in ritual (for example, the use of unleavened versus leavened bread in ceremonies) and disagreements over the authority that should be accorded to the pope versus the authority that should be accorded to the ecumenical council that grouped representatives from the major Christian cities (Kolbaba 2008: 223).

The Eastern Church struggled to spread farther east into Asia and south into Africa due to the advent and rapid spread of Islam, whose promise of comprehensive social reform held great appeal for local populations. However, Eastern Christianity did secure a lasting presence and influence in eastern Europe and Russia, both through the spread of monasteries into the region and through the conversion of ruling families. Indeed, when the Byzantine Empire was engulfed by the Ottoman Empire in 1453 CE, Russia became the largest and most powerful Christian empire. By contrast, the Western Church had established a firm hold over western Europe, where political fragmentation allowed the pope to claim leadership of the whole of Western Christian society. However, secular authorities did not always meekly accept the Church's dominance; indeed, the struggle for power between popes on one side and kings and emperors on the other was a recurring theme for much of medieval and early modern European history, and was one of the key factors in the fragmentation of the Western Church into Catholic and Protestant branches following the Reformation in the sixteenth century (Woodhead 2004: 46–50, 65).

Core traits associated with axiality

Morality, universalism, and egalitarianism

Like Judaism and Islam, Christianity is a monotheistic religion in the Abrahamic tradition, whose god punishes moral transgressions and rewards virtuous behavior. Broadly speaking, the Christian God is thought to reward acts born out of love for one's neighbor with an afterlife of eternal peace and harmony, and acts that harm one's neighbor with one of eternal suffering. Virtuous acts include forgiving one's enemies, providing financial support to those in need, and honoring one's parents, while sinful acts include stealing, killing, bearing false witness, committing adultery, and even simply desiring one's neighbor's property. Acts born out of love of God are also rewarded (for example, fasting and persevering in one's faith in the face of persecution [Sullivan 2003: 155]), while sacrilegious ones are punished (for example, misusing God's name and worshipping other gods [Lachowski 2003: 144]).

As already mentioned, many commentators argue that much of Christianity's appeal derived from its call for spiritual egalitarianism: all, regardless of class or gender, could be rewarded with eternal life after death, provided they acted righteously on earth. This did not equate to social egalitarianism: most early Christians did not wish to upend the institution of slavery, for example; nor did they criticize the elite's riches and status, regardless of what Jesus may have said on the matter. Indeed, by medieval times, Christian scholars had developed an elaborate theological cosmology according to which all of God's creation was ordered hierarchically, including human society (Evans 2007: 65).

Spiritual egalitarianism also did not coincide with gender egalitarianism. Even in the third century CE, when women were a likely majority in the Christian community, Church leaders usually dismissed them as weak creatures whose irra-tional natures made them likely to spread heretical views (Fox 1986: 310–11). Indeed, St. Paul's letters clearly state that women should not teach the Christian doctrine. Part of this prejudice derives from the Old Testament (for example, Eve's culpability in leading Adam astray in the Book of Genesis), but these attitudes were likely in-fluenced by the broader misogynistic cultural and philosophical attitudes prominent throughout the Mediterranean Basin in antiquity, according to which women were imperfect beings, and wives should be subordinate to their husbands and confined to the domestic sphere. Nevertheless, Christian women enjoyed greater opportuni-ties for welfare support than their pagan counterparts, and they could more easily attain positions of influence and even leadership. Indeed, the very fact that St. Paul forbade them from teachings suggests that some did teach (Woodhead 2004: 39–40).

Institutions of authority and social organization

As has already been mentioned, following the fall of the Roman Empire, Rome's bishops came to be known as popes and claimed leadership of the Christian world: over its kings, emperors, and other secular rulers. Indeed, elaborate ceremonies and protocols soon emerged through which the pope legitimized secular rulers and, when the latter did not meet the pope's approval, the pope could excommunicate them. In other words, he could cast them out of the Church, withholding the promise of eternal salvation and encouraging their subjects to rebel against them (Woodhead 2004: 48–49). Not all secular rulers accepted this state of affairs, but, all the same, legitimating authority by claiming to uphold Christian values, signified at the ex-treme by the pope's approval, became a de facto requirement for European rulers during the Middle Ages. By the eleventh century CE, a rich genre of literature had emerged describing the attributes of the good Christian ruler—mostly written by clerics, but in some notable cases written by rulers themselves, for example Stephen of Hungary. In essence, a good Christian king was expected to support the Church and its representatives, act as an exemplar of the rightful Christian way of life for his subjects to imitate, and defeat the enemies of the Church, including heretics and other moral transgressors in their own land and followers of rival religions (above all, Islam) in foreign ones.

In the Byzantine Empire, as in the West, the emperor was also expected to uphold Christian teachings, but the power balance was reversed: the emperor's power over the Church was unlimited, at least officially, and he (and his spouse) could unilater-ally intervene in doctrinal issues that would normally be reserved to Church author-ities (Hunt 2007: 77–80).

In practice, in both Eastern and Western Christendom, local Church figures would have been responsible for enforcing Christian morals in day-to-day life. From the eighth century onwards, Western clerics could rely on instruction manuals known as "penitentials" when establishing how best to punish acts such as homicide, perjury, sacrilege, drunkenness, various types of sexual transgressions (including adultery, incest, sodomy, and bestiality), sorcery, disrespect toward one's parents, and theft (McNeill and Gamer 1990). In the East, from at least the fourth century CE onwards, it was common for clerics to punish mild transgressions with equally mild penalties known as *epitimia*—usually consisting of prayer, fasting, prostrations, charity, the reading of scriptures, and, sometimes, temporary exclusion from certain aspects of Church life (Papadakis 1991: 723–24).

Islam

Origin and spread

On the eve of the rise of Islam, West Asia was largely divided, both directly and indirectly, between the Byzantine Empire to the west and the Sasanian Empire to the east. The dominant ideology in the former was Christianity, and in the latter it was Zoroastrianism, but both polities included multiple different religious communities. The Arabian Peninsula was distant from both Byzantine and Sasanian centers of power, but, because it occupied a strategic position with regards to Indian Ocean trade, both Byzantium and the Sasanians established footholds in the region, mostly through protectorates and alliances. Partly as a result of this, religions that had developed outside the peninsula also began to establish themselves there, particularly Christianity, Judaism, and, to a lesser extent, Zoroastrianism. The influence and popularity of the local animistic and polytheistic cults that had existed long before the advent of these scriptural religions began to wane, though strongholds remained in towns such as Ṭāʾif and Mecca. Worshipers of these cults attributed divine qualities to natural objects such as the sun, the moon, and certain sacred rocks and trees, and one of these sacred rocks, the Kaʿba, was held in a sanctuary in Mecca, where it was regularly visited by pilgrims. Because of the Kaʿba, fighting was forbidden in Mecca, which made the town an important center for both trade and other social interactions (Donner 2010).

It was in Mecca that the Prophet Muḥammad was born, in 570 CE. In 610 CE, Muḥammad began to receive revelations from the Archangel Jabrāʾīl (Gabriel), which he shared among friends, family, and eventually other inhabitants of Mecca. These revelations persuaded him and others of the spiritual importance of fasting and charity, as well as the existence of only one God. In 622 CE, the hostility of Mecca's polytheistic majority forced Muḥammad and his supporters to flee the city. This event, known as the *hjira*, has been taken as the beginning of the Islamic calendar. These first Muslims settled in Medina, whose significant Jewish population saw similarities between Muḥammad's revelations and their own beliefs and practices. For the next 10 years, Muḥammad received more revelations and built a community (*umma*) of followers and fellow believers, with whose help he was able to return to and establish control over Mecca, in 630 CE. Seeing his success as a sign of divine favor, tribes throughout Arabia also converted to Islam and joined the *umma* (Silverstein 2007: 9–10).

Muḥammad's first successor, or "caliph," was Abū Bakr (r. 632–34 CE), whose tenure as head of the *umma* was mostly consumed by the so-called "wars of apostasy" (*ridda*). Specifically, Abū Bakr fought to bring back into the fold those Arabian tribes who believed that with Muḥammad's death they were free to abandon their new religion and/or withhold their taxes and allegiance from the *umma*. Once the majority of the Arabian tribes were again Muslim and unified under the rule of the second caliph, 'Umar (r. 634–44 CE), they began spreading their religious message (and extending their political hegemony) into both North Africa and Persian territory, including what is today Tunisia, Egypt, Syria, Iraq, and Iran. In this, they met little opposition from the great empires of the time, who had been weakened and fractured by war, or from the people of the newly conquered lands, who had accrued a number of political and religious grievances toward their rulers, and who included significant populations of monotheists quite receptive to Islamic ideas. By the mid-eighth century, the Islamic world extended from the Iberian Peninsula to the Punjab, mostly as a result of the military campaigns of the Umayyad caliphs (r. 661–750 CE) (Armstong 2002: 35–43).

However, to many Muslims at the time, the rule of the Umayyads was illegitimate, as they were not related to Muḥammad's family. The 'Abbāsid family, whose leader was a descendant of Muḥammad's uncle al-'Abbās ibn 'Abd al-Muṭṭalib, managed to seize control of the Islamic Empire in 750 CE, which they ruled until their decline in the thirteenth century. However, the 'Abbāsids were also seen as illegitimate by a vocal minority who believed that only the descendants of Muḥammad's son-in-law 'Alī—a figure of great charisma and piety, who was assassinated by rival Islamic sects in Kufa—should be allowed to rule. This faction called itself the party (*shī'a*) of 'Alī (Armstrong 2002: 31) and they are now commonly known as Shī'a. The majority of Muslims, both in the past and today, are known as Sunnī. Historically, Shī'a Muslims have often suffered persecution at the hands of Sunnī governments, due to the fact that they did not accept the latter as legitimate and there have been several Shī'a rebellions throughout the centuries all across the Islamic world (e.g. Armstrong 2002: 52–56). Though Sunnīs and Shī'as share a core set of beliefs and practices, over time Shī'as developed distinctive approaches to some key aspects of Islam. Most notably, they developed their own set of rituals centering on the figures of 'Alī, his wife Fāṭima, and their son Ḥusayn, commemorating their struggle and 'Alī and Ḥusayn's martyrdoms under the Umayyads (Hussain 2005). Ṣūfīs are sometimes misunderstood to be the third major branch of Islam besides Sunnīs and Shī'as, but they are in fact Sunnīs with a more esoteric, mystical approach to the religion; still, it is worth noting that this approach has sometimes manifested itself in the promotion of beliefs and the performance of rituals that have led to conflict with the establishment due to their apparent heterodoxy (Armstrong 2002: 62–65).

After a long "golden age" of expansion, Islamic world experienced a phase of political fragmentation between the eleventh and fourteenth centuries. After the late eleventh century, Muslim lands suffered repeated invasions on the part of European armies, motivated by the belief that it was their duty as Christians to wage war against Muslims. These invasions are known as the Crusades. Moreover, in the fourteenth century, the Black Death epidemic swept the Mediterranean. Beginning in the early thirteenth century, the Islamic world also suffered from the expansion of the Mongol Empire, which invaded and established its rule over large portions of West Asia, seizing control of vital trade routes, and even burning the ʿAbbāsid capital, Baghdad, in 1258 CE. More than anything else, the Mongol invasions marked a decisive end to Islamic political unity, and though the ʿAbbāsids survived for a few centuries longer, ruling from Cairo, they were leaders of the entire *umma* in name only (Sonn 2010: 79–112). However, the Islamic world eventually experienced a second golden age under the rule of the three so-called "gunpowder empires":[5] the Ottomans in the Mediterranean (1299–1922 CE), the Safavids in Iran (1501–1736 CE), and the Mughals in northern South Asia (1526–1857 CE). Notably, the Safavids were a Shīʿa dynasty (Sonn 2010: 95–98), and Shīʿa Islam remains the dominant ideology in Iran today.

Core traits associated with axiality

Morality, universalism, and egalitarianism

In many ways, Islam is not very different from Christianity. For one thing, it is monotheistic—though, unlike the Christian God, Allah has no direct children and no parents (Yaran 2007: 23). Moreover, the Islamic God is also omnipresent and omniscient: "To Allah belongs the East and the West. Whichever way you turn, there is the face of Allah. Allah is All-Embracing, and All-Knowing" (Qurʾān 2:115, quoted in Yaran 2007: 24). He is also described as omnipotent (Yaran 2007: 23–24): he created and governs the cosmos, and he actively directs the moral evolution of men and women, sending prophets to teach them proper conduct and, on the Islamic equivalent of the Christian day of resurrection (known as the Last Day, or *Qiyāmah* in Arabic), rewarding those who followed these teachings by welcoming them into paradise (*Janna*) and punishing those who knowingly disobeyed them by sending them to hell (*Jahannam*).

---

5 This term was coined and popularized by Hodgson (1974) and McNeill (1993) in reference to the military technology that, according to the two scholars, allowed these polities to establish and maintain their power for several centuries.

The types of moral behavior proscribed by the Islamic God are also overall similar to those punished by the Christian and Judaic ones, including harming the weak, cheating on one's spouse, killing other people (unless for a just cause), cheating in trade, believing falsities, and being prideful:

Do not slay your offspring for fear of want. It is We who provide for them, and for you. Indeed their killing is a great sin. Do not approach adultery, for it is an indecent thing and an evil way. Do not take the life which Allah has rendered sacrosanct, except for a just cause ... Do not approach the property of an orphan except in the way that is best (responsible investment) until he attains majority. Keep your covenants, for one is responsible for one's covenant. Give full measure when you measure, and weigh with even scales (when you weigh). This is better, and will be the best in the end. Do not go after that of which you have no knowledge, for (man's) eyes, ears and heart, each of these (senses) shall be closely questioned. Do not walk proudly on the earth (Qur'ān 17:31- 7, quoted in Yaran 2007: 43–44).

As for positive moralizing commands, there are seven main ones: to acknowledge the existence of only the one God, to show respect to one's parents, to be righteous (which includes avoiding the above-mentioned sinful behaviors and carrying out the ones mentioned in this current list), to give to the poor, to spend with moderation, to speak kindly, and to be generous (Yaran 2007: 43). Moreover, chastity and modesty is praised both in men and in women ("Behold; [...] men who guard their modesty and women who guard (their modesty), [...] Allah has prepared for them forgiveness and a vast reward" [Qur'ān 33:35, quoted in Yaran 2007: 45]). As in Christianity, however, the question of gender equality within Islam is a fraught one (see below). In general, the Islamic God rewards "[k]indness and equity, compassion and mercy, generosity, self-restraint, sincerity, the moral fellowship of the believers, honesty, truthfulness, the keeping of commitments, fair-dealing, humility, patience, endurance, courage, thankfulness, dignity, purity, modesty and chastity, helpfulness, cooperation, charitableness, hospitality, brotherliness, warmth and lovingness, striving and hard work" (Yaran 2007: 43).

All men are considered equal in Islamic thought, and indeed even the Prophet Muḥammad is described by early sources as a fallible, ordinary mortal, who, in the Qur'ān, is even occasionally rebuked by God—though later sources do denote him as infallible (Silverstein 2010: 10). Muslim rulers are not usually sanctified, except, to some extent, in cases where Islamic traditions mix with pre-Islamic ones (most notably, in Persian and Persian-influenced cultures, such as Safavid Iran [Matthee 2010: 245–48]). Indeed, because of this belief in the equality of all men, Islam forbids the enslavement of foundlings and orphans—not to mention the fact that it does not allow debt slavery, or the enslavement of both Muslims in general and non-Muslims who live in Muslim polities (*dhimmīs*). However, Islamic law does allow the enslavement of enemies captured in a legitimate war, as well as of the children of slaves.

Moreover, there is considerable controversy over the Islamic stance on equality between the sexes. On the one hand, the Qur'ān explicitly states that men and women have equal religious responsibility before God and that men and women will be rewarded equally on the Last Day (33:35; 40:8); on the other hand, it differentiates between their roles and rights, in some cases assigning lesser roles to women compared to men, and depriving them of rights that men enjoy (though also giving them rights that men lack) (Young and Müge Göçek 2013). Some scholars argue that the gender imbalance common in Islamic societies derives from pre-Islamic cultural traditions, rather than Islam itself. For example, Ahmed (1992) points to the rise of the ʿAbbāsid Dynasty and its adoption of patriarchal customs from Persia and Byzantium.

Institutions of authority and social organization

Traditionally, regardless of the exact form of government, the law in Islamic polities is meant to be based on Islamic principles and doctrine. In his *The Ordinances of Government*, eleventh-century scholar al-Māwardī specifically writes that a ruler's greatest responsibility is to ensure that the religion's established principles are safeguarded, and that legal judgments and penalties are enforced accordingly. In practice, however, Islamic governments have had little to do with the direct enforcement of Islamic law, which has normally been articulated and administered by a class of scholars who are trained, supported, and operate autonomously from the state, particularly within majority Sunnī contexts. The discussion of the exact contents of Islamic law led, from the eighth century CE onwards, to the emergence of several schools of legal thought, many of which still exist today, and are prevalent in particular geographic regions: the Mālikī in North and West Africa, Ḥanafī in India and areas that used to be part of the Ottoman empire, Shāfiʿī in Southeast Asia, Ḥanafī in the Arabian Peninsula, and Jaʿfarī in predominantly Shīʿa regions such as Iran. These schools do not differ significantly and are mutually acceptable. They all agree that some actions are required of all good Muslims, some recommended but not essential, some neutral, some discouraged, and some forbidden. Only forbidden actions and the willful refusal to perform required actions must be punished. Islamic law is particularly concerned with criminal matters, economic transactions, familial matters, and matters of inheritance (Sonn 2010: 41–51).

Conclusion

It should be clear why the six ideologies discussed above so captivated Karl Jaspers and most other Axial Age proponents who followed: they each display a strong penchant for moralizing norms, articulating a series of strict, immutable dos and don'ts for adherents to follow—crucial for adherents seeking eternal salvation in order to enter the kingdom of heaven, or to escape the turmoil of endless cyclicality. The thrust of morality is also notably similar across these traditions, as honesty, caring for kin and neighbors, and fidelity (to parents and other authorities as well as to the ideology itself) are generally rewarded, whereas transgressions such as lying, cheating, failing to help those in need, disrespecting authority, and various types of "impure" acts (such as certain sexual behaviors, intoxication, improper worship, etc.) are to be punished, in this life or the next (or both). While the specific formulation of the norms differs, the basic concern for similar norms promoting ingroup coop-eration, cohesion, and stability is often seen as a hallmark of modern human social life, a point emphasized in nearly all articulations of the Axial Age idea. Whether these similarities are confined to the so-called "axial" religions, however, has been the source of some controversy, as many scholars insist that the moral concerns ex-pressed in the ideologies described here are, in fact, universal, rather than a heritage of developments from the mid-first millennium BCE (see e.g. Haidt 2007; Curry et al. 2019).[6]

We likewise see a close relationship between ideology and institutions in all of these formulations—specifically in the way that political authorities and social organization more broadly were inexorably tied up with the ideas—and ideals—ex-pressed in scripture; another key argument made in much Axial Age work. Rulers of societies where these ideologies took hold tended to embrace their traditions, concepts, and rituals, often going so far as to explicitly legitimate their authority on religious or ideological grounds: as caretakers of the faith, defenders of the righteous, and punishers of transgressors. Legal systems developed and became increasingly formalized, with laws and procedures often grounded directly in religious and philo-sophical notions of right and wrong. Broadly speaking, the societies that functioned as homes to these traditions came to be defined and organized in large part around their ideals, norms, and practices.

However, this chapter should have also made clear that these ideologies do not conform to all expectations of fully formed, properly "axial" traditions. While they all include claims to universality—specifically, the notion that all people, regardless of race, ethnicity, nationality, and so on have the same access to spiritual fulfillment and salvation—along with several explicit appeals to notions of egalitarianism and equal rights, in practice these lofty ideals were heavily circumscribed. In attested historical practice in all of the traditions discussed above, women were frequently denied the opportunity to attain positions of power—secular or otherwise—or to en-gage as equals in key rituals, seemingly relegated to inferior positions in the afterlife

---

6   See the Introduction chapter in this volume for further discussion.

as in the mortal realm. Slavery was not only tolerated in many of the societies where these religions prevailed, but often the ideologies themselves were (re)interpreted to justify and sanction the practice. Even the institutionalization of the supposedly axial principles that stemmed from these ideologies—setting formal limits on the arbitrary use of power by rulers, abandoning the idea of rulers as divine beings, supporting just and equitable treatment of different groups within society—never really took hold. Instead, we see time and again, from western Europe to West Asia to South and East Asia, that rulers who expressed and supported these traditions continued to claim nearly unlimited powers, often even claiming divine status or at least basing their authority on their "special" commitment to religious or philosophical practice. Laws were put in place and society regulated, but in such a way as to support, if not advance, strict hierarchies and iniquities in various spheres of life: religious, political, economic, and cultural.

How, then, do the ideologies discussed here fit into the wider picture of an "Axial Age"? Do they deserve to be grouped together as similar developments, part of this supposedly critical and singular moment in human history, along with Classical Greek philosophy and Rabbinical Judaic interpretation? Are there differences in the ways that different societies at different places and times have articulated their norms? Are the so-called axial ideologies really so different from other religious and customs, those that arose before and after the "age" or that existed outside of the Afro-Eurasian core? The rest of this volume presents various regional chapters that explore precisely these ideas.

CHAPTER 3

MEDITERRANEAN BASIN | The Greco-Roman World

Jenny Reddish & Franco De Angelis

Period	Polity	Approx. dates
Bronze Age	*E. Mediterranean*	
	Minoan (Prepalatial, Palatial)	3000–1400 BCE
	Mycenaean (Palatial, Postpalatial)	1600–1100
	W. Mediterranean	
	Central Italian Bronze Age (Proto-Villanovan)	1800–1000
Iron Age	*E. Mediterranean*	
	Dark Ages (Protogeometric, Geometric)	1100–750
	W. Mediterranean	
	Central Italian Iron Age (Southern Villanovan)	
Archaic	*E. Mediterranean*	
	Archaic Aegean (Orientalizing)	750–500
	W. Mediterranean	
	Roman Kingdom (Etruscan)	716–509
Classical	*E. Mediterranean*	
	Classical Greek *poleis*	500–323
	W. Mediterranean	
	Early Roman Republic	509–264
Hellenistic	*E. Mediterranean*	
	Hellenistic kingdoms	323–31
	W. Mediterranean	
	Middle Roman Republic	264–133
Roman Imperial	Late Roman Republic	133–27
	Principate	31 BCE–284 CE
	Dominate	284–394
Late Antique	*E. Mediterranean*	
	Eastern Roman / Byzantine	395–607
	W. Mediterranean	
	Western Empire	395–454
	Dominion of Italy (Kingdom of Odoacer)	454–493
	Ostrogothic Italy	489–554

Table 1. Polities and periods mentioned in text that were based in or that occupied the Mediterranean Basin

Introduction

This chapter turns the spotlight on the "Classical" civilizations of Greece and Rome, along with the regions they drew into their cultural or political orbit. While other chapters in this volume have reviewed evidence of universalizing thought and egalitarianism in the regions bordering the easternmost Mediterranean (Egypt, Anatolia, the Levant), this focus allows us to extend our analysis to the western and northern shores of what the Romans called *mare nostrum* ("our sea"), including the Iberian, Italian, and Balkan peninsulas.

Greece—at least parts of what is today Aegean Greece—forms one of the proposed "axial cores." It was singled out by Karl Jaspers and subsequent Axial Age theorists (e.g. Bellah 2011: 324–98; Eisenstadt 1986a; Raaflaub 2005) as the site of key intellectual transformations in the mid-first millennium BCE. In this literature, we find repeated references to the new philosophical and artistic traditions of the Archaic and Classical Greek city-states, mainly Athens, to reflexive critique of existing patterns of government, and to the development of new forms of political organization—most notably, "radical" Athenian democracy. While insisting on the commonalities between Greece and the other societies that underwent axial transformation, Jaspers (1953: 62–63) nevertheless stressed the distinctiveness of Greek "political liberty" and "rationality" as ideas divorced from religious ideology. As discussed in other chapters in this volume, this divide was largely absent in the other "core" axial traditions (areas in what are today northern China, Iran, India, and Israel-Palestine).

In this chapter, we are less concerned with the more purely theoretical aspects of the "axial breakthrough" as it has been described for mid-first-millennium BCE Greece, such as scientific enquiry or tensions between the transcendental and mundane orders (Jaspers 1953: 62–63; Eisenstadt 1986a: 29). Our emphasis is instead on the presence or absence of universalizing and egalitarian ideologies and the degree to which these were put into practice in the Greco-Roman world, along with how these ideologies supported different and evolving concepts of rulership. We also examine the period before and after the eventful few centuries of the mid-first millennium BCE: can precedents in this region be identified for the so-called "Greek miracle"? How was the heritage of Classical Greece received, transformed, and institutionalized through cultural Hellenization and through Rome's territorial expansion? Lastly, we address the doctrines and concrete sociopolitical consequences of Christianity, an explicitly universalizing and moralizing religion that combined elements of the Jewish and Greek "axial transformations" of several centuries before.

Historical background: From the Bronze Age to Late Antiquity

The eastern Mediterranean during the second half of the second millennium BCE, when we begin our analysis, was home to a range of complex societies, including New Kingdom Egypt, the Hittite Empire in Anatolia, and—most importantly for this chapter—the Aegean's Minoan and Mycenaean cultures. Minoan civilization on the island of Crete flourished somewhat earlier than the Mycenaean, arguably reaching its peak of political complexity and artistic exuberance between around 1700 and 1400 BCE (Adams 2004; Castleden 1990: 4). Intricately chambered monumental "palaces," apparently serving as administrative and ritual centers, emerged from 2000 BCE onwards (Rehak and Younger 1998; Schoep 2006). Palaces with quite different architectural forms were also built from c. 1600 BCE onwards at Mycenae, Tiryns, Athens, and other Greek mainland sites; the regions they controlled and administered are collectively known as the Mycenaean city-states (Shelmerdine and Bennet 2008).

With the exception of Knossos, the majority of the Minoan palaces were violently destroyed and burnt around 1450 BCE (Rehak and Younger 1998: 148). Cretan material culture and burial practices after this date show clear Mycenaean influences, but earlier assertions of a wholesale conquest of the island by more warlike northerners are not well supported by the evidence (Nafplioti 2008). What we can say with more certainty is that the final centuries of the Bronze Age saw a greater degree of cultural integration and exchange across the Aegean: between Crete, the mainland, the smaller Aegean islands, and the west coast of Anatolia (MacSweeney 2008; Wallace 2018). The distribution of trade goods, for instance the finds of Mycenaean pottery in Cyprus, Italy, Sardinia, and Sicily, reveals wide links across the Mediterranean (Alcock and Cherry 2013: 12–13). But like its West Asian neighbors, this interconnected world succumbed to a wave of societal collapse shortly after 1200 BCE: the so-called "Late Bronze Age Crisis." Palatial administration and written record-keeping ceased both in Crete and on the mainland, marking the beginning of what has traditionally been known as a "Dark Age" in Greece (Lemos 2010; Papadopoulos 1996; Snodgrass [1971] 2000).

In the wake of the disintegration of the palatial systems, migrations took place within the Aegean, especially from west to east, and new Greek settlements sprang up on the Anatolian coast and nearby islands (Pomeroy et al. 2004: 36–37; Vanschoonwinkel 2006). Less centralized patterns of political organization now held sway, and it was within this Early Iron Age context that the distinctive Greek form of the city-state, the *polis*, began to take shape (Papadopoulos 1996). Recent reappraisals have questioned how "dark" the period after c. 1150 CE really was for Greece, with Papadopoulos (1996: 254–55) asserting simply that "too much was happening in Early Iron Age Greece for it to warrant the term 'dark age.'" However, it is true that a lack of written records affects our ability to understand ideological changes and how the inhabitants of the region viewed their societies at this time.

Citing evidence for renewed trade links, literacy, and technological and artistic innovation after a gap of several centuries, some scholars have written of a Greek "renaissance" in the late eighth century BCE (Hägg 1983; critiqued in Morris 1988).

The historical framework adhered to by most scholars of ancient Greece thus designates the time span between around 750 and 480 BCE as a new period, the Archaic. Another significant development of this time was that both Greek and Phoenician cities (the latter clustered along the coasts of modern Syria, Lebanon, and Israel, and covered in more detail in the chapter on the Levant in this volume) began to send out groups of colonists and traders, who founded new settlements around the Mediterranean and Black Sea (Tsetskhladze 2006; van Dommelen 2005). Italy, Sicily, Sardinia, and other Mediterranean islands now hosted communities of both Aegean and Levantine origin, while Phoenician expansion also produced the city of Carthage on the North African coast and reached as far west as the Atlantic coast of Iberia (Niemeyer 2006).

The late sixth and early fifth centuries BCE brought momentous political changes to the small Greek city-states that lay beyond the western edge of the Achaemenid Persian Empire—especially (perhaps) Athens. By the mid-fifth century, this city was possessed of an institutional framework for the exercise of direct democracy by all free male citizens. It also used its superior naval power to exert control over other Greek cities as the head of the Delian League, a de facto Athenian empire (Rawlings 2008). Overall, the Classical period, 480–323 BCE, was an age of great experimentation in art, politics and philosophy in Greece.

In the mid-fourth century, however, the formerly peripheral Kingdom of Macedonia rose under Philip II to become the dominant power in the region, subjecting several formerly prominent city-states (*poleis*) to what Thonemann (2016: 20) has called "unequal and humiliating alliances." His son and successor Alexander III ("the Great") expanded his father's conquests eastwards as far as Afghanistan and northern India. The Hellenistic kingdoms, sprawling across a vast region of south-eastern Europe, Egypt, and western Asia, were Alexander's legacy, as after the conqueror's death in 323 BCE his great empire was divided among various generals. The Greek cities, respected as they were for their cultural achievements by Alexander and his Macedonian successors, occupied an anomalous position within these Hellenistic kingdoms, slipping in and out of direct control. Even during the periods when Macedonian monarchs had a strong hold over the peninsula, they often made ideological gestures towards recognizing the "freedom" of the Greeks and the autonomy of the poleis (see e.g. Wallace 2014).

Meanwhile, the western Mediterranean in the second half of the first millennium BCE was the arena for struggles between Carthage in modern-day Tunisia—originally a Phoenician colony and now an expansionist state in its own right—the western Greek settlements in Sicily, and the burgeoning Roman Republic (Bagnall 2003; Scullard 1989). The monarchy of Rome had been overthrown in an internal revolt during the late sixth century BCE (Cornell 1995: 218). In its stead, new political institutions emerged over time, including what we now recognize as prototypically representative democratic (if still aristocratic) governance featuring elected consuls, a Senate, and citizens' assemblies with legislative powers. The armies of the republic finally captured and destroyed Carthage in 146 BCE (Bagnall 2003) and, over the succeeding centuries, Rome annexed territory throughout the Mediterranean, encroaching on the Hellenistic kingdoms in the east. The Battle of Actium of 31 BCE, in which Octavian defeated Cleopatra VII (last ruler of the Ptolemaic Dynasty in Egypt) and her Roman ally Mark Antony, was only one particularly decisive moment in an ongoing process of shifting power relations in the Mediterranean. Octavian made Egypt a Roman province and attained such an unassailable political position that the nature of government in the state was changed permanently. More commonly known as Augustus, the title bestowed on him by the Senate in 27 BCE, he is now viewed as the first emperor of Rome (Ando 2011).

As an empire or "principate" (after the emperor as head—*princeps*—of state), Rome proceeded to conquer more and more territory in Europe, North Africa, and West Asia, introducing new administrative structures and a Greek-inspired model of urban life. However, the third century CE brought conflicts over the imperial succession, economic decline, and military difficulties in retaining control over the vast region administered from Rome, particularly the volatile western European provinces (de Blois 2002; Hoyer 2018; Liebeschuetz 2007). It was in this context that the Emperor Diocletian split the empire administratively into Western and Eastern halves in 293 CE (Corcoran 2000: 1–2). Diocletian's accession in 284 is considered to mark the transition from the Roman Principate to the Dominate, a term that conveys the less constrained nature of the power henceforth exercised by emperors.

Though the effects of many of Diocletian's reforms were long-lasting, the new divided administration was not the guarantor of stability he had envisaged. In the early fourth century, the empire's capital was moved from Rome to Constantinople (named after Emperor Constantine I), a more strategic location on the site of modern Istanbul. The East and West slowly became more isolated from each other, however, and in 395 CE the empire was split again, for the last time (Barnwell 1992: 6). The West also began to lose territory to Germanic peoples such as the Visigoths, Franks, Vandals, and Burgundians, who established their own kingdoms. One particular turning point, the deposition of the last Western emperor by the military leader Odoacer in 476 CE, has traditionally been taken as the date of the fall of the Western Roman Empire (Humphries 2009: 107).

The East, on the other hand, survived until the fifteenth century and referred to itself as the "Roman Empire" until the very end (Papaioannou 2009), though it is now more commonly known as the Byzantine Empire (Byzantium was the ancient Greek name for the city later refounded as Constantinople). In the seventh century, it acquired a powerful new rival in the Islamic Umayyad Caliphate, which expanded outwards from Arabia in a remarkable series of conquests. We end our analysis at the close of the first millennium CE. At this point, the Eastern Roman Empire had developed the distinctive administrative system, religious institutions, and culture now referred to as "Byzantine"; Muslim states dominated North Africa, the Levant, and southern Iberia; and Christian kingdoms and principalities occupied much of western and central Europe.

Universalizing morality and egalitarian ethics

In this section, we review the evidence for expressions of "axial"-style moralizing, egalitarian, and universalizing thought in this region from the mid-second millennium BCE to the late first millennium CE.

Because the script used by the Minoans, Linear A, remains undeciphered (Perono Cacciafoco 2017), the religious beliefs and practices of Bronze Age Crete can be reconstructed only through the analysis of architecture, iconography, and other forms of material culture. It is unsurprising, then, that a wide range of opinions have been expressed on the subject since the first excavations of the Palace of Knossos in the late nineteenth century. To Arthur Evans, the British archaeologist who excavated at Knossos from 1900 onwards, the Late Bronze Age Cretans were peaceful, nature-loving, and adhered to kind of matriarchal quasi-monotheism: he believed they worshiped a great mother goddess (Eller 2012; Hamilakis 2006).

This has since been heavily criticized. In fact, it is likely that Cretan religion in both the Middle and Late Minoan periods involved the worship of a range of both gods and goddesses, some of whom would have been familiar to the polytheists of the Classical period (Budin 2004: 233; Marinatos 2004: 205–06). Evidence of fortifications and weaponry dating to the second millennium BCE also makes it difficult to maintain a view of Minoan society as pacifist (Manning 1986; Starr 1984). Nevertheless, the prominence of representations of both human and divine women in frescoes, seals, and other media is striking and hints at a strong role in public life and ritual for Minoan women (Olsen 1998; Younger and Rehak 2008). Cretan Bronze Age society may therefore have been relatively egalitarian in outlook when it came to gender—perhaps more so than later societies in the same region and elsewhere.[1] As Armstrong (2006: xvi) notes, a concern with gender equality is only weakly expressed in the mid-first-millennium BCE religious and philosophical movements typically identified as "axial."

On Crete, Linear B documents have been unearthed from Postpalatial contexts at Knossos and provide clear testimony of social and economic hierarchy (Tartaron 2007: 96). While earlier theories of a wholesale "Mycenaean conquest" have been criticized (e.g. Catling 1989; Nafplioti 2008), the arrival in Crete after c. 1450 BCE of

---

1   Indeed, the rarity of evidence for such structural gender equality will strike readers in the chapters throughout this volume.

administrative structures, burial practices, and modes of elite display that show striking affinities to mainland Greek cultural patterns cannot be denied. MacSweeney (2008) has written of an emerging "pan-Aegean elite identity," expressed through rich *tholos* burials, fine ceramics, and iconography depicting warriors in distinctive dress, including boar's-tusk helmets. Though the Linear B archives from the mainland palaces as well as from Knossos on Crete are concerned almost exclusively with administrative matters and shed little light on contemporary attitudes to social (in) equality (Shelmerdine 2008), the archaeological evidence from the final centuries of the Aegean Bronze Age thus gives a strong impression of consolidating elite power and status and the development of an aristocratic warrior ethos. Mycenaean religion incorporated several Minoan features and involved communal feasting and making offerings to an array of gods and goddesses—including deities like Zeus, Hermes, and Poseidon, who were still being venerated many centuries later across the Greek and Roman world (Marinatos 2004).

Overall, then, the surviving evidence gives few indications of universalizing and egalitarian ideologies among the societies of the Late Bronze Age Aegean. Some scholars (e.g. Driessen 2002; Schoep 2002) have argued that Neopalatial Minoan society was less centralized and hierarchical than was initially assumed by early excavators on Crete and that the presence of kings ("priest-kings," as Arthur Evans thought) is not supported by the archaeological record. However, alternative models often posit the existence of competing elite factions, using material culture and performance to shore up their own status (e.g. Logue 2004; Soar 2009); a far cry from the radically universalizing ideologies considered to characterize axial transformations, instead fitting fairly comfortably with models of pre-axial or "archaic" societies (Baumard and Boyer 2013; Bellah 2011). Likewise, what we know of Mycenaean beliefs and ritual practice suggests that the religion provided sacred legitimacy to existing political hierarchies rather than challenging them (Elkana 1986: 44–45; Marinatos 2004: 208–09). Still, the possibility of heterodox, more universalizing ideologies in the societies of Late Bronze Age Crete and Greece—perhaps historically invisible because they did not produce a corpus of texts—cannot be excluded.

The centuries between the collapse of the Mycenaean administration and the emergence of an alphabetic Greek script (adapted from Phoenician models) in the eighth century BCE present obvious challenges for the reconstruction of religious and political ideologies. On the one hand, there are some signs of cultural continuity from the earlier literate period to the later, for instance in the names of some gods and goddesses. Burkert (1992: 3–4) takes this as indicating the survival of a "living cult," but notes the widespread archaeological evidence for a break or transformation in cultic practice in mainland Greece. Whatever precise forms the beliefs, rites, and festivities of the post-Mycenaean Aegean took, it is evident that religious practice served different ideological ends: it no longer centered on the palaces or the sanctified person of the *wanax* (king).

The relationship between expressions of egalitarianism in the late Archaic and Classical Greek *poleis* and the religious beliefs and practices of their populations is complex and not easily summarized here. The Greeks conceived of the world as ordered in accordance with the gods' interests and honored them through celebrations and offerings, especially sacrificed animals (Pomeroy et al. 2004: 30). In return, worshipers hoped to be favored with worldly success and prosperity. In ritual life, clearly defined roles for men and women and restrictions on the participation of foreigners in civic cults reinforced gender and ethnic hierarchies (Jennifer Larson, pers. comm. 2016). However, the gods themselves were almost proverbially capricious and amoral, while power relations between them "temporary and fragile" (Osborne 2013: 277; Pomeroy et al. 2004: 30). Osborne (2013) has suggested that the lack of absolute sovereign power and moral good in the world of the Olympian deities—even Zeus must ensure the support of other gods in order to act effectively—offered a model of negotiated power and pluralistic values that chimed well with the democratic life of the polis. Though in a broad sense the gods were thought to punish injustice and hubris, the absence of universal moral imperatives from the Greek religious system arguably left ethical questions open to debate within human communities.

Egalitarian and democratic ideologies are certainly in evidence in Classical Greece, especially as expressed by some of the region's prominent philosophical schools. Critically, however, they were both limited and counterbalanced by alternative strains of thought. Even in Classical Athens at the height of its experiment with radical democracy, the widespread practice of slavery and the exclusion of women, children, slaves, and metics (foreign residents) from the city's democratic institutions received ideological support from theories of the inherent inferiority of these groups. Aristotle's doctrine of natural slavery posited that certain categories of people, particularly non-Greek "barbarians," were intrinsically suited to enslavement, being incapable of fully rational thought and action (Garnsey 1996: 77; Heath 2008). And, with the exception of some of Plato's writings, Classical Greek thought held that women were less capable physically and mentally and more emotional than men: their duty was to preside over the home and bear children, not to participate in public life (Murray 1986: 207–10). Nor should we assume that contemporary political philosophers approved of the forms of collective governance they saw being exercised around them. As Arnason et al. (2013: 2) have written, "[i]t is easier to find critics of democracy than supporters" in this period. Socrates, Plato, and Aristotle all expressed deep skepticism about the advantages of rule by the *demos*, the people of Athens.

Perhaps more influential among the broader Mediterranean population than these somewhat rarified philosophies were the religious societies dedicated to particular deities (including the initiatory religions dubbed "mystery cults"), which became especially popular during the Hellenistic period and continued to flourish under Roman rule (Martin 2018: 51–58). Many of these were more universalizing and egalitarian in outlook than either the public "*polis* religions" of the Greek world or the traditional cults supported by the Roman state. For instance, women, slaves, and foreigners could all be initiated into the secret rites of the goddesses Demeter and Persephone at Eleusis in Attica (Jennifer Larson, pers. comm. 2016). Religious communities called *thiasoi* and *eranoi* thrived in the cosmopolitan port cities of the Hellenistic world, promulgating a "spirit of brotherhood and equality" among their diverse members (Martin 2018: 21). Another newly prominent feature of religion in the post-Classical Mediterranean was a concern with the afterlife and the salvation of the individual "soul." The Eleusinian Mysteries as well as the cults of Dionysus, Isis, and the Phrygian mother goddess Cybele all used ecstatic ritual practices to bring about a personal experience of the divine and promised adherents a blessed life after death (Tripolitis 2002: 15–36).

There also grew in this period a strand of philosophical argument embracing universalizing and egalitarian values; indeed, it is these arguments which proponents of the Axial Age theory tend to point to in support of Classical Greece as exemplary of the axial transition. While the evidence for such claims is clear in the writings of Plato and Aristotle and the Hellenistic schools their ideas spawned, these social critics nevertheless stopped short of calling for the redistribution of wealth or the abolition of slavery, for example. The early Stoics of Greece, including Zeno of Citium and Cleanthes of Assos, held that women and men were equally capable of cultivating virtue, but this did not spur them to advocate radical change in gender roles; nor did Roman Stoics agitate for the removal of gender discrimination enshrined in Roman law (Engel 2003). We should also bear in mind that far from representing the dominant ideologies in contemporary societies, these schools of thought were largely confined to elite circles within the Hellenistic kingdoms and the Roman Republic.

A similar dichotomy between the philosophical and religious ideologies subscribed to mainly by elites and the ritual practices traditional to different parts of the Mediterranean littoral persisted through the Roman Imperial period (after 27 BCE). Hellenistic philosophical traditions, with their focus on egalitarian and universalizing principles, continued and found a foothold among the upper echelons of Roman society (Colish 1990). For example, the first-century CE Stoic philosopher Musonius Rufus advocated gender equality in matters of education. Nevertheless, the Stoics' excoriation of luxurious lifestyles was perfectly compatible with their idealization of the aristocratic Roman man, exercising complete control over his passions as well as his family and slaves (Grimm 2006: 355–56). In this sense, philosophy served to legitimize existing hierarchical relationships. Initiatory religions were also an important part of the Roman cultural milieu, however, and in some cases provided a space where social status in everyday life was temporarily set aside in favor of graded hierarchies internal to the cult. Older religious associations persisted alongside newcomers such as Mithraism, which (though it excluded women) was popular among soldiers, slaves, and low-status men.

Of course, the territories incorporated into the Roman Empire were home to innumerable local religious traditions as well, which Roman officialdom generally tolerated as long as their practitioners made the required gestures of deference towards the imperial state. Some of these traditions are discussed in other chapters in this volume, for instance Judaism and Egyptian religion in the Levant and Egypt chapters, respectively. However, the impact of Christianity on Roman civilization— from its origins in the province of Judea to its position of dominance in Byzantium and the Christian West at the close of the first millennium CE—is worth considering here. The religion spread in the decades after Christ's crucifixion beyond its initial Jewish, Levantine context, becoming one among many cults in this cosmopolitan empire (Heid 2007). In Axial Age discussions, Christianity often appears as a synthesis of the axial transformations of first-millennium BCE Greece and the Levant: Jaspers (1953: 58) stressed its continuity with the Jewish prophetic tradition, but also the influence of Greek and Hellenistic philosophy on its theology. In its early forms, it was quite radically egalitarian and universalizing, aiming to transcend ethnic and (in some contexts) gender divisions (Beavis 2007; Buell 2002). Emphasis was placed on the equality of all people before God and the universal potential for salvation through faith.

The overall impression the sources provide of the intellectual climate of the late first-millennium BCE Hellenistic-Roman Mediterranean, then, is of a complex and ever-changing mixture of ideas: one in many ways more culturally open and fluid than what had come before. Egalitarian and universalizing currents of thought were certainly present, for instance playing a role in new religions and philosophical schools, but were counterbalanced by anti-democratic arguments and the legitimizing role religion and philosophy could play for still-pervasive social hierarchies.

In Late Antique society in both the West (both before and after the collapse of the Western half of the empire) and the East, concepts of a divinely decreed "great chain of being" made the entrenched inequalities of the time seem natural and inevitable (Evans 2007: 65). This held true throughout the period under review here, up to the end of the first millennium CE. For example, from the cathedral school at Laon in what is now France, late eleventh- to early twelfth-century texts have survived that discuss the ethical implications of servitude and conclude that it could serve as a worldly punishment for one's sins, or else be willed by God in order to test believers (65). In Byzantium, too, Christian writers used Biblical verses and the teachings of the early Church Fathers to argue for the inferiority of women and slaves (James 2008). While the fundamental spiritual equality of all people according to Jesus' teachings occasionally found expression in Late Antiquity and the early Middle Ages, this was tempered by a resignation to the inequities and injustices of the temporal world (James 2008; Papio 2004: 1049–52).

Rulership, institutions of authority, and social hierarchy

Minoan attitudes towards the proper relationships between the ruler, elites, and the general population before c. 1450 BCE (that is, before the destruction of most of the palaces and the arrival of "Mycenaean" cultural patterns) are difficult to discern. More concrete evidence of social stratification has come from Neopalatial Crete than from the preceding Protopalatial periods. In terms of ideology, we are again restricted by our inability to read Linear A, but the evidence of iconography and architecture suggests that religion and ritual came to play a greater legitimizing role for elite status in the Neopalatial period (Peatfield 2016; Tartaron 2007: 95). Nevertheless, the precise role and composition of elite Minoan groups at this time, and their relationships to the palatial administrations, are not well understood. It is likewise unclear whether the society was headed by a hereditary monarch, and unambiguous representations of kings or queens are absent (Rehak and Younger 1998; Tartaron 2007).

After the mid-fifteenth century BCE, with the creation of a Mycenaean cultural *koine* (a set of shared symbols and practices) across the Aegean world, including Crete (MacSweeney 2008), the image swims into focus somewhat. In mainland Greece, Linear B tablets from this period testify to the existence of centralized and hierarchical polities, each headed by a king called a *wanax* (Shelmerdine and Bennet 2008: 292). Like contemporary rulers in North Africa and West Asia, including New Kingdom Egyptian pharaohs and Hittite kings, the legitimacy of the *wanax*'s power was bolstered by rites and religious symbols and he appears to have served as the chief priest (Palaima 1995: 131–34). This close relationship between institutionalized religion and political power is one of the features considered decidedly "archaic" or "pre-axial" in the Axial Age literature. However, though the *wanax* received offerings of fragrant oil, a gift suitable for the gods, we have no indication that he was believed to be a living god (Shelmerdine and Bennet 2008: 293; Thomas 1976: 111).

The disappearance of written sources from the Aegean after the Late Bronze Age collapse of the palatial system creates difficulties in reconstructing the nature of rule and the organization of political authority during the so-called Dark Age in Greece. For the Phoenician context of the Levantine coast, however, there are some hints in various sources of deliberative assemblies of citizens in Late Bronze and Early Iron Age cities, exercising power independently of monarchs. One historian (Stockwell 2010, 2012) has portrayed these developments (addressed more fully in our chapter on the Levant) as a form of proto-democracy. Unfortunately, expressions of the ideological bases of early experiments in communal governance in Tyre and other cities are lost to us; very few texts written within the Phoenician city-states themselves or their colonies and "workshops" in the west have survived (Lipiński 1995: 1321–22). The possibility remains that anti-monarchical, egalitarian values were exported around the Mediterranean by Phoenician and Punic traders and colonizers (Stockwell 2012). As a group notably open to interaction with foreigners, their political and religious ideas would certainly have contributed to the overall intellectual climate of the Early Iron Age Mediterranean (Niemeyer 2006: 158–59; Quinn 2018: 83). In the context of this chapter, it is worth bearing in mind that contacts with the Phoenicians and other West Asian cultures had a considerable influence on Greek cultural development in the early first millennium BCE, so much so that the span of time between the late eighth and mid-seventh centuries BCE is often referred to (though mostly in older scholarship) as the "Orientalizing period" of Greek history (Burkert 1992).

The *Iliad* and the *Odyssey*, great epic poems likely composed in the eighth or seventh centuries BCE, are considered to incorporate and rework older traditions and have therefore been used to shed light on the cultural contexts of the later "Dark Age" (Graham 1995). The world of these poems is populated by heroic warrior-aristocrats who command respect but—unlike the rulers of the Late Bronze Age—seem to have little institutionalized authority (Finley 2002b). They often exchange precious gifts with their peers, forging alliances and enhancing their status through deeds rather than relying on inherited prerogatives. Both the Homeric literature and the material record (discussed in the following section) point to a social context in which power was less centralized than in the Bronze Age and bureaucracy completely absent.

It is also likely, as Donlan (1973) has argued for the Archaic period (eighth to sixth centuries BCE), that the Homeric valorization of the aristocratic ideal—lauding individual honor, bravery, and glory—represents only one aspect of the wider set of beliefs and ethical norms that structured contemporary Aegean societies. For Elkana (1986: 45), the roots of later, egalitarian political thought are likewise to be found in this "heroic" age. It is in the Archaic period too that signs of a florescence of anti-aristocratic and, by the fifth century, properly "democratic" ideologies become abundant. Some of the earliest surviving Greek verse, including that of the great poets Hesiod, Archilochus, and Tyrtaeus, takes a less than deferential attitude to the existing social order and the supposedly natural superiority of the *aristoi* (Balot 2013: 183; Donlan 1973). The early sixth-century Athenian statesman Solon, whose legal reforms we discuss in the following section, wrote poetry that criticized wealthy elites for their excessive greed and injustice and instead stressed the common good of the *polis* (Donlan 1973: 147).

The Archaic period also led to the birth of the *polis* and the foundation of new Greek communities in the west, especially in Sicily and southern Italy. In their search for self-definition, Greeks (especially Athenians) of the Classical period often looked back to these centuries as a time of tyranny and injustice with which their enlightened democracy could be contrasted. Certainly, Archaic Greek society was riven with social divisions compared to the "Dark Age": new wealth from trade and manufacture was unequally distributed and chattel slavery was practiced on an unprecedented scale (Austin and Vidal-Nacquet 1977: 53–56). However, these developments, along with the perceived preoccupation of the elite class with *symposia* (drinking parties) and luxury goods from West Asia, provoked a reaction from contemporary writers. As we saw above, Greek literature of this period already displays a critical attitude towards inherited wealth and status and pays attention to problems of social justice. In the context of legal frameworks and political institutions, too, measures were taken to increase access to the judicial system and impose constraints on the exercise of executive power. As far as we know, laws began to be codified in the seventh century BCE. Some of the oldest come from the city-states of Gortyn, Axos, and Dreros on Crete (Perlman 2004). Though the early legal codes in many ways served to reinforce inequality by, for instance, setting out harsher penalties for offenses against free people than against slaves (Gagarin and Perlman 2016: 81–84), they also represent the increasing importance of the "rule of law" in Greek societies and the tenet that no one, not even the ruler, was above it. Most early Greek laws show a clear concern with controlling and regularizing elite power. For instance, the Dreros law set term limits, enforced by penalties, for the powerful office of *kosmos* (Wallace 2016: 1–2). In Athens in the 590s, still well before the emergence of direct democracy, the statesman-poet Solon made a number of reforms aimed at broadening access to the law courts and preventing enslavement for debt (Balot 2013: 182; Harris 2002: 415). In urban planning, too, there are signs of egalitarian ideals being put into practice. Aristotle credited a fifth-century city planner, Hippodamus of Miletus, with the gridded design of equal plots that reified the ideal of *isonomia* (equality before the law) in the physical structures of the city. In fact, this type of plan has also been found in Archaic cities, for instance the Greek colony of Megara Hyblaea in Sicily (Fitzjohn 2007: 217–19), but in this case the town plan could simply be a reflection of equality among elite clan members (De Angelis 2016: 136–41).

Though city-states had existed for millennia, the Greek *polis*, which emerged in the Archaic period and reached maturity in the Classical, was an entirely new form of political organization: made up of citizens, not subjects. Its institutions of collective governance were informed by notions of the basic equality of all its free, male, adult members, irrespective of wealth or aristocratic lineage (Raaflaub 2013: 324–29). Classical Athenian thinkers extolled the virtues of *isonomia* as well as *isēgoria* (freedom of speech for all), thought to be necessary for democratic governance to function (Raaflaub 1996). The Archaic and Classical periods also saw the emergence of what has been termed "second-order thinking" about the ideal forms of human society and the nature of knowledge (Elkana 1986).

In the wake of Alexander's conquests in the late fourth century BCE, Greek culture and religion spread far beyond their original home, becoming transformed in the process. Successive *poleis* now became part of kingdoms spanning the eastern Mediterranean and western Asia. At the level of ruling ideology, Alexander's successors in the eastern Mediterranean managed to carve out a position for themselves as divine kings, complete with religious honors such as incense offerings, animal sacrifices, and cult images (Eckstein 2009: 252). In mainland Greece itself, where strong federated political units such as the Achaean and Aetolian Leagues (Hahm 2009: 191) prevented total domination by these new monarchs, concessions were sometimes made to old ideals of "freedom" and democratic rule. However, Greek opposition to monarchy in principle quickly fell by the wayside, as illustrated by the Athenians' treatment of the Hellenistic kings Antigonus "the One-Eyed" and his son Demetrius as "Savior-Gods" after they wrested control of the city from their rival Cassander in 307 BCE (Eckstein 2009: 252). More generally, shifting power relations after 323 allowed anti-democratic elements within Greek communities to gain influence, and there are indications of a decreasing emphasis on the basic equality of all adult male citizens within the *polis* (Davies 2006: 87; Green 1990: 36–38). This may also have been linked to changes in military organization and land tenure, discussed in the following section (Davies 2006: 87).

Meanwhile in the western Mediterranean, Republican Rome, especially from the second century BCE onwards, defined itself in opposition what it saw as the decadent tyrants of the east and their subjugated populations (Connolly 2007; Erskine 1991). A deep mistrust of absolute power, a commitment to the freedom (*libertas*) of the Roman people, and the valorization of this group as a sovereign body were key political values of the republic (though how these ideas played out in practice is a matter for the next section of this chapter) (Connolly 2007: 160–1; Mouritsen 2004: 1–17). As in Classical Greece, however, these ideals applied primarily to the freeborn, adult, male citizen. Women, children, and slaves were generally perceived as inferior and, as we shall see below, this inequality was enshrined in law.

The attitudes of Greek and Roman philosophers in the late first millennium BCE to social inequality and different forms of government varied greatly. The Platonic-Socratic and Aristotelian traditions, founded in the Classical period, lived on under the Hellenistic kings as well as finding some purchase within the expanding Roman Republic and were joined by new schools such as Stoicism and Epicureanism in the late fourth and early third centuries BCE (Martin 2018: 13–14). Several thinkers either evinced support for traditional aristocratic values and authoritarian forms of rule, or recommended quietistic withdrawal from politics (Brown 2009; Connolly 2007: 131; Green 1990: 38).

The Roman Senate's decision to award Octavian the title "Augustus" in 27 BCE should be seen in the context of longer-term developments, namely the increasing concentration of political power in the hands of individual statesmen over the preceding century. Interestingly, though, the early emperors continued to pay lip service to republican values, at least in their interactions with Roman audiences. Augustus continued to refer to the will of the Senate and the Roman people in his speeches and, until the late third century CE, emperors maintained in certain contexts that they were merely the *princeps*: first among equals (G. Rowe 2006: 114–16). However, at the same time, there was a rapid development and spread of an imperial cult, in which offerings were made to the gods on behalf of semi-divine emperors and their families (Galinsky 2007: 80–82). These cult activities gained a particularly strong foothold in the eastern reaches of the empire, where Hellenistic ruler cults provided a precedent (81). It is noteworthy that Rome, the cultural inheritor of the Greek "axial breakthrough" of the mid-first millennium BCE, developed (perhaps *re*-developed?) what was essentially a form of sacral kingship—cast as a defining trait of "archaic" societies in the Axial Age literature—as its power and territory grew.

Above, we noted the strong tendency within early Christianity towards universalizing morality and support for radical social reform. Several centuries after its birth, however, Christian symbols and institutions were working to cement social hierarchy, constituting a potent source of legitimacy for those in power and playing a similar role to the earlier, pagan imperial cult. The Church was growing in political influence and, in the early fourth century CE, the emperor Constantine I adopted Christianity—a persecuted minority faith under his predecessors—and gave official sanction and protection to Christian practice within the empire (Leppin 2007: 104–07). This in no way entailed the abandonment of the rites, dress, and other symbols that marked out the emperor as a sacred persona (McCormick 1990, 1991). The ruler's status from the late third century onwards was in fact elevated and he became hedged about with rituals designed to set him apart from ordinary mortals. In the Eastern Roman Empire, he was "God's representative on earth" (McCormick 1991).

Egalitarianism, social mobility, and prosociality in practice

In this section, we consider how the religious and ideological traditions and the exercise of political authority discussed above relate to more concrete realities, including economic inequality, legal rights, and prosocial activity throughout the Greco-Roman world.

Our understanding of the degree and type of inequalities existent in the Minoan context is complicated by the presence of multiple competing models of the sociopolitical structure of the state or states. As we noted above, it is uncertain whether Minoan societies were ruled by kings and, hence, whether "palace" is an accurate term for the labyrinthine architectural complexes of the Cretan Late Bronze Age (Tartaron 2007: 93–94). However, archaeological excavation in residential contexts has furnished evidence of wealth and status differentials: Younger and Rehak (2008:

179) contrast the densely built houses at Gournia with the "more elegant" living quarters at Nirou Chani, and note how dress functions as a marker of status in Minoan artwork. Overall, the Neopalatial period seems to have involved the construction of even more elaborate elite architecture than the Protopalatial period (Younger and Rehak 2008). While law codes from contemporary West Asian societies demonstrate the differing values placed on the lives and legal testimonies of men and women, free people and slaves, no comparable texts survive that could shed light on legal rights in Minoan Crete.

The "pyramidal" hierarchies that structured Mycenaean societies towards the end of the Bronze Age are somewhat clearer, in large part due to the presence of administrative archives written in the deciphered script Linear B (Tartaron 2007: 93–94). In each polity, the palace, seat of the *wanax*, appears to have constituted the core of a centralized economy, drawing taxes in kind from its hinterland and disbursing rations to dependent workers (Dickinson 1994: 81–86). This structure is reminiscent to some of the contemporary redistributive and corvée systems in place in nearby Egypt, Anatolia, and Iran (see those regional chapters in this volume for further discussion). However, representations of Mycenaean palace societies as rigidly hierarchical have been challenged in recent years (Tartaron 2007: 93–94). Focusing on the polity at Pylos, Nakassis (2013: 24–27) argues that its social structure was much more flexible than has been hitherto recognized and that relationships between the palace and surrounding communities (known as *damoi*) were often mutually beneficial rather than founded on coercive power. Local elites and overseers within the *damoi* may have had considerable scope for autonomous political action (Cavanagh 2008: 334; Lupack 2011: 212–15). Overall, though, strong evidence for communal governance is lacking before the early Archaic period (Raaflaub and Wallace 2007: 24).

After the collapse of the palatial systems in the early twelfth century BCE, archaeological indications of centralized power and wealthy elites become much scarcer in Greece and the Aegean. By many accounts, population levels fell during this period, building in stone declined, and the surplus agricultural production needed to support a wealthy elite and a bureaucratic hierarchy was no longer available (Snodgrass [1971] 2000; though see also Lemos 2010 for a less pessimistic view). Against this background, the archaeological record does provide some hints that these societies were not completely egalitarian. As we noted above, the Homeric epics likely reflect the presence of an aristocratic warrior ethos in the Iron Age. Material support for processes of elite self-aggrandizement and competition is provided by the large, "chiefly" houses excavated at various settlements and by finds of valuable metal objects and exotic prestige goods in a restricted number of graves (Donlan 1993; Lemos 2010; Morris 1986). Beneath a tenth-century monumental structure at Lefkandi on Euboea, for instance, a woman adorned with gold jewelry, the cremated remains of a man with iron weapons, and four (probably sacrificed) horses were interred (Lemos

2010: 89–90). The site has been interpreted as evidence of continuing social stratifi-cation after the Mycenaean collapse (Alcock and Cherry 2013: 486–87). Nevertheless, the considerable diversity in material culture across the Greek mainland and Aegean makes it difficult to make valid generalizations about political organization in the Iron Age.

The picture comes into focus only in the Archaic period. It is clear that this was a time of far-reaching social and economic changes throughout the Aegean and that deep inequalities coexisted with the evolution of political and legal institutions premised on the theoretical equality of freeborn males within each *polis* (Morris 1996). This process reached its peak during the Classical period and, in this sense, arguments for Greece as a site of axial transformation during the mid-first millen-nium BCE are supported by the evidence. However, we should not lose sight of the fact that democratic and egalitarian elements of Greek life were limited both in principle (as we saw in the preceding section) and considerably more so in practice. While the egalitarian political ideals of certain *poleis* were expressed in the allotment of voting powers to all native-born, free male citizens regardless of wealth or lineage, in practice richer citizens could exert a greater influence over decision-making pro-cesses (Black 2008: 28). With very few exceptions, running for public office across the Classical Greek world required candidates to own a certain amount of property (Foxhall 2002: 218).

Beyond the formally defined citizenry of the poleis, evidence of egalitarian in-stitutions and practices is scarcer still. A substantial portion of Athens' wealth de-rived from the silver mines of Laurium in Attica, which were worked with gangs of slaves (Murray 1986: 261). Likewise, it has been argued (Cartledge 1975) that it was the labor of the helots, the subjugated population of Laconia and Messenia, that made the economic and political equality of free Spartan citizens possible. As some scholars note (Jennifer Larson, pers. comm.), Archaic and Classical Greek ideals of "freedom" are only fully intelligible in contrast to the conditions of the less fortu-nate inhabitants of the *polis* territories. On the other hand, when it came to gender relations, social realities may have in fact been more equable than the political and philosophical literature suggests. Women may have played a greater public and legal role in Classical *poleis* than the (overwhelmingly male) authors of the time thought was ideal. Though they could not legally own or dispose of property in Athens, they had stronger rights in other *poleis*, such as Sparta (Osborne 1997: 20).

During the Hellenistic period, economic growth across the Mediterranean and West Asia was coupled with a trend towards more unequal distribution of wealth, as the gap between the general population and the "very tip of the social and political pyramid" widened (Green 1990: 385–86). Changes in military organization may have exacerbated this process. The dominant form of warfare in the Archaic and Classical Greek world had been waged by heavily armed infantrymen known as hoplites, who were citizens fighting for their *polis* rather than professional soldiers. While hoplite warfare arguably fed into an egalitarian ethos by stressing cooperation on the battlefield and requiring states to maintain a robust force of free, male citizens with enough wealth to provide their own armor and weapons, the rise of professional armies after the mid-fourth century lifted this restriction (Davies 2006: 87; Raaflaub and Wallace 2007: 27). In step with these developments, elites monopolized more and more of the available land and movable wealth during this period as well. They also made large donations to help the poor and fund public works—a practice known as euergetism—but the importance of this type of gift-giving arguably demonstrates the greater degree of economic inequality in the Hellenistic world compared to earlier periods (Cecchet 2014: 171–76). Euergetism served in many ways to bolster the special status of elites and their generosity was recognized through monuments and inscriptions (171–76).

Turning our attention now to the Italian Peninsula, we can identify concrete institutional correlates of the republican ideals of the Romans of the mid-first millennium BCE (Connolly 2007). Checks and balances were instituted from the late sixth century BCE onwards to prevent the monopolization of executive power by individuals, including the powers of the Senate and popular assemblies, which could vote on legislation and elect officials, and restrictions on terms of office (Adkins and Adkins 1998: 38–41; Beck et al. 2011: 10). However, as in Classical Greece, the Roman ideal of the free citizen was limited in scope, in both theory and practice. In line with discriminatory attitudes to women, the lower classes, and foreigners (Connolly 2010; Finley 2002a; Gruen 2010; Uhalde 2012), full political rights—at least before c. 300 BCE—were reserved to Roman men of the elite "patrician" class (Crawford 1986: 26). As the republic grew, slavery also expanded to a scale not seen in the Archaic and Classical Greek periods, so that—according to one estimate—30–35 percent of the population of Roman Italy were slaves by the late first century BCE (Scheidel 2005).

From the late first century BCE onwards, long-term trends towards the concentration of power in the hands of one man intensified, ushering in the Imperial period of Rome's history (Connolly 2007). This resulted in the emergence of contradictions between Roman republican values, such as cultural antipathy towards hereditary kingship and the political reality of the emperor's role. While checks and balances were nominally still in place, they were increasingly ineffective in practice. For instance, the Senate could technically override the emperor's decisions and even remove him from power, but the former power was practiced very rarely and the latter never (Harris 2010). Augustus also introduced strict new marriage laws (which disadvantaged women in particular, and barred unmarried people from inheriting their parents' wealth) and placed restrictions on the numbers of slaves who could be freed (Dunstan 2011: 243–44). In all, the legal and economic structures of the empire allowed the upper classes to enjoy their privileged lifestyles in relative peace, benefiting from the labor of their slaves and less wealthy inhabitants of the provinces. The exhortations of Stoic philosophers, very popular in Roman imperial elite circles, to live austerely and refrain from unnecessary entanglements in public life (Brown 2009), were not always followed even by the thinkers themselves. Seneca is a good example of a Stoic philosopher who failed to apply his own ideals to his personal life: he was very wealthy, owned many slaves, and was active in politics at the highest level.

On the other hand, certain aspects of life under Roman imperial rule may be seen as truer to "axial"-style universalizing ideals than even the mid-first-millennium BCE Greek world was. Most importantly, Roman citizenship was much more open than that of the Classical Greek *poleis*. After Augustus, birthplace and ethnic background were no bar to becoming a Roman citizen, with all the legal and social benefits that conferred (Mathisen 2006). Even freed slaves could become citizens and did so in great numbers: a practice "potentially shocking" to Greeks and not found anywhere else in the ancient world (Dench 2003: 295). The intense legal and bureaucratic apparatus built up to support the massive empire (Eich 2015; Hoyer 2018) likewise followed more closely than most classical Greek *poleis* the institutionalization and regularization of political authority highlighted by several prominent Axial Age proponents (notably Eisenstadt 2011). Further, Greek and Hellenistic practices of civic benefaction by wealthy elite patrons—the euergetism discussed above—not only continued in the Republican and Imperial periods, but in many ways served as the backbone of Rome's economic and urban expansion throughout the wider Mediterranean world (Fischer-Bovet 2014; Hoyer 2018). The emperor himself is often said to have based his authority less on formal, institutionalized powers than on his prosocial activities: gifts of "bread and circuses" to the Roman populace (Lomas and Cornell 2003).

As the Western and Eastern halves of the empire gradually split from one another, further transformations in both political ideology and socioeconomic realities took place. In the preceding section, we highlighted the increasingly elevated and sacred role played by the Roman emperor from the late third century CE onwards, somewhat ironically coinciding with the adoption as state cult of a religion (Christianity) that made a stark conceptual division between God and humankind. This ideological shift was complemented by moves towards the removal of yet more constraints on executive power (McCormick 1991), so that the government of the Eastern Roman Empire has been described as a "bureaucratic absolute monarchy" (Loewenstein 1973: 238). Social mobility also fell in Late Antiquity: under Diocletian, peasants became legally bound to their land and certain professions were made "essentially hereditary" (Lim 2010: 551). Economic patterns reveal the growing concentration of wealth in the hands of a few from the mid-fifth century CE, when large estates proliferated (Baker 2011: 245–46).

In this context, the egalitarianism of early Christian thought became de-emphasized, particularly as widespread expectations of Christ's imminent return and the establishment of a perfect, divine kingdom on earth were disappointed. The Church became a powerful and wealthy landowner in its own right (Madigan 2015: 20) and, as we discussed above, provided ideological justification for a range of social divisions and inequities. However, charitable activities provided a way in which Christian universalism and attention to the plight of the least fortunate could be put into practice. State-funded philanthropic institutions that distributed alms, provided medical care, and supported orphans and the elderly were established from the fourth century CE onwards (Miller 2003: 4, 2008). Indeed, parallels can be drawn between philanthropic institutions under the Byzantines, the tradition of euergetism in the Hellenistic world, and public donations by the Roman elite in the Republican and early Imperial periods. All three practices, stressing the responsibilities of the rich to help the poor, may perhaps owe something to traditions of thought dating back to mid-first-millennium BCE Greece and Israel (see the chapter on the Levant in this volume) (Black 2008: 33). However, as this review chapter has made clear, the egalitarian and universalizing thought of the Axial Age Mediterranean was both tempered by rival arguments (such as anti-democratic political rhetoric in Greece) and—to take a longer-term view—failed to prevent the concentration of wealth and power at the top of the social pyramid.

Conclusions

Our review of the evidence for universalizing and egalitarian ideologies in theory and practice in the Greco-Roman world provides some degree of support for Axial Age schemas that localize these developments to the Greek mainland in the mid-first millennium BCE. Overall, the Mycenaean societies of the Late Bronze Age appear to have been largely hierarchical, centralized, and equipped with religious systems that bolstered the position of the ruling classes. Minoan sociopolitical structure is less well understood and may have had strong heterarchical tendencies; nor should we dismiss the possibility that Mycenaean polities were more fluid and less coercive than was initially assumed after the decipherment of Linear B in the 1950s (Nakassis 2013). Even with these caveats in mind, though, it remains difficult to point to any signs of flourishing egalitarianism in the architecture, material culture, or written record of this period.

Phoenician commercial expansion in the late second and early first millennium BCE introduced beliefs, rituals, and cultural norms from the Levant into the western Mediterranean. There are some indications that political structures in the mother cities included proto-democratic forms of communal governance, but the near-complete absence of written records from Phoenician contexts, including the great city of Carthage and the smaller "workshop" settlements in the west, means that the ideologies that may have accompanied such experiments are inaccessible to us. For similar reasons, it is difficult to give an account of religious and political thought in the Aegean world during the early Iron Age. However, research in settlement and landscape archaeology suggests that more decentralized political patterns characterized Greek life in the period, and while elites may have indulged in self-aggrandizing activities, they lacked the authority of the Mycenaean *wanax*.

Some of the very first written records in the Greek alphabetic script to appear, in the eighth and seventh centuries BCE, already show a concern with justice and fairness and engage in reflexive critique of the established order. The poet Hesiod is perhaps the most well-known and clearest example of this in the Archaic Greek world. We can find precedents for later Classical ideals of equality among the archaeological as well as written evidence for the Archaic period. It was nevertheless in the Classical period (480–323 BCE) that ideologies of egalitarianism reached their fullest expression and had an impact on legal and political structures. As we note above, Greek ideals of freedom and equality were limited and to a lesser or greater extent excluded women, slaves, and non-Greeks. A similar mismatch between the universalizing claims of some prominent ideologies and the actual scope of egalitarian precepts, along with stark contrasts between ideology and practice in socioeconomic inequalities and the legitimation of authority, characterizes the Roman period.

What we are presented with, then, is a conflicting picture of Classical Greece's position as a core axial region. On the one hand, we see egalitarian claims and moralizing thought arise in the eloquent works of Athenian philosophers and ideals of civic responsibility and the exercise of popular self-government gain a foothold in several *polis* constitutions of the Classical period. This looks like an "axial turn" away from the sharply hierarchical societies and absolute rule of tyrants and kings that typified the Dark Age and Archaic periods. On the other hand, however, this ostensibly axial florescence was not only limited in scope—equality and political representation were confined largely to adult male citizens—but also short-lived; the subsequent Hellenistic age witnessed the reappearance of the god-king with his unchecked authority, a form of rule put aside for a time by Republican Rome only to reemerge once more under the empire. In short, we see precisely the opposite pattern to that predicted by theories of an Axial Age. It is perhaps worth reflecting here on the risk of historical distortion posed by the idealized image of Greece that emerged during European Romanticism and remains influential to this day. With the portrayal of Classical Athens in particular as the intellectual and political ancestor of latter-day Europe, other expressions of Hellenism—such as that of the cities of Sicily and southern Italy or the Hellenistic empires of the late fourth to first centuries BCE—are often marginalized, treated as pale reflections of developments in the Aegean core region (De Angelis 2016: 5–9).

In the context of ancient Rome, it is also important to point out that the "axial"-type features that do appear in the early Roman Republic, such as constraints on centralized power and institutions for collective decision-making, were not imported from Greece, but homegrown and suited to the Roman social context. Nor was Rome the only republic to emerge in the western Mediterranean. In the later first millennium BCE, Carthage was ruled by elected judges in conjunction with a senate and people's assembly (Markoe 2005: 103–04; Stockwell 2010) and, as we discussed above, these forms of political organization appear to have precedents in the Phoenician city-states of the late second and early first millennia BCE (see also the Levant chapter in this volume). These facts beg the question: do Axial Age proponents disproportionately credit Greece for the emergence of axial features in the Mediterranean world?

Further complicating the picture is the fact that Rome was likewise full of contradictions, at least as far as axiality is concerned. For one, it maintained the complex mixture inherited from the Greek world of ideologies promoting moral, egalitarian behavior along with realities of sharp structural inequalities. In some ways, Republican Rome represents the culmination of Classical Greece's axial turn, particularly in the explicit, formalized, institutionalized body of laws and procedures regulating the activity of both citizens and rulers alike. Further, the prominence and importance of civic euergetism not only helped support Rome's great expansion in the later first millennium BCE, but this prosocial spending by elite benefactors helped to distribute material and other resources to a relatively large segment of the population. On the other hand, the extensive use of slave labor, the exclusion of women from positions of authority, and the lack of any widespread explicitly moralizing ideology clearly indicate an absence of axial values. Interestingly, even the adoption of Christianity, a religious system built on decidedly axial foundations, as the official state cult did not usher in a wave of moralizing, egalitarian ideals and practices, but rather was accompanied by an increase in authoritarian, hierarchical institutions and realities, even if official dogma made strong claims to the contrary.

The last point that deserves space here is that none of the ideological, social, and institutional developments presented in this chapter came from nowhere. From the early Bronze Age onwards, the Mediterranean was a multicultural world, which developed under the influence of and in interaction with large and powerful states in Egypt, Anatolia, the Levant, and Mesopotamia. We did not spend a great deal of time here describing these "outside" influences, as their home-grown developments, institutions, and ideologies are treated more fully in their respective regional chapters in this volume. Our survey here of the Greco-Roman world, from the Bronze Age to Late Antiquity, reveals a muddied picture, one of contrasting traits, complex dynamics, and a host of influences, upheavals, and countermovements throughout this long period. The only real conclusions that can be offered are 1) yes, the Greek world saw the rise in the mid-first millennium BCE of novel ideals of egalitarianism, political participation, and the institutionalization of popular authority; traditions which were inherited and expanded under the Romans; but 2) no, there was no systematic "turn" during the Classical period that saw any meaningful or lasting implementation of truly universal morality, structures facilitating an equitable access to power and resources, nor even effective limitations of authoritarian, divinely sanctioned rule. This world remained both "axial" and "archaic" at once.

WEST ASIA | The Levant
Jenny Reddish & Oren Litwin

Period	Polity	Approx. dates
Bronze Age	Early Canaanite city-states	2000–1350 BCE
Iron Age	Later Canaanite city-states	1350–1500
	New Kingdom Egypt	1500–1180
	Phoenician city-states	1180–1030
	Northern Kingdom of Israel, Kingdom of Judah	1030–721
Archaic	Neo-Assyrian Empire	721–608
	Twenty-sixth (Saite) Dynasty of Egypt	608–604
	Neo-Babylonian Empire	604–538
Classical	Achaemenid Persian Empire	538–331
Hellenistic	Macedonian Empire	331–300
	Hellenistic period	300–62
	Ptolemaic Kingdom	300–200
	Seleucid Kingdom	200–103
	Hasmonean Dynasty of Judea	103–62
Roman Imperial	Late Roman Republic	62–31
	Roman Principate	31 BCE–284 CE
	Roman Dominate	284–394
Late Antique	Byzantine Empire	394–614
	Sasanian Empire	614–628
	Byzantine reconquest	628–638
Early Medieval	Early Islamic Caliphate ("Rāshidūn")	638–663
	Umayyad Caliphate	663–750
	ʿAbbāsid Caliphate	750–946
	Ṭūlūnid, Ikhshīdid Dynasties	868–969

Table 2. Periods and dates of polities mentioned in text that were based in or that occupied the Levant

Introduction

The cradle of monotheism and fulcrum of empires, the territory encompassing biblical Israel and its northern neighbors is typically called the southern Levant by archaeologists. The fractious city-states that occupied the region in the Late Bronze Age until about 1200 BCE are now known as "Canaanite" and saw themselves as part of a shared culture. Caught between powerful empires—Egypt to the south, Hittites to the north-west, and various Mesopotamian empires (notably the Assyrians) to the north-east—the Canaanite cities were typically vassals of whichever empire was most formidable at the time (usually Egypt). The sudden weakening of Egyptian power c. 1200 BCE and the contemporaneous collapse of Canaanite civilization is poorly understood; but the resulting power vacuum allowed the emergence of two rather small, but historically prominent societies: the Israelites and the Phoenicians. During this period, Judaism first took shape, while Phoenician sailors developed an advanced culture with writing, ceremonial sports, and (very probably) constitutional government, all of which they would spread to the Greeks. Yet again, however, a succession of expansive empires would soon dominate the area. Assyria conquered first the Phoenician city-states and then, c. 722 BCE, the Northern Kingdom of Israel; and the Southern Kingdom of Judah would fall to the Neo-Babylonians c. 587 BCE. The region would then be successively ruled by Achaemenid Persia, Alexander the Great's Macedonian Empire, the Ptolemaic Dynasty in Egypt, and by the Seleucid kings from their capital of Antioch in the northern Levant. A faction known as the Maccabees briefly won independence from Seleucid control for the Jewish residents of the Levant c. 140 BCE, before elite infighting and the eastward expansion of the juggernaut of Rome once again put the region under "foreign" control. During the following period of ideological and social foment, as new religious sects sprang up to address the theological problem of enduring imperial domination, Christianity would be born and would eventually remake the Roman Empire in its own image.

Israel, and Judaism in particular, have been an important part of Axial Age theory all the way back to Karl Jaspers (1953), who included the Levant as one of his axial regions. However, the historical dynamics in the Levant of so-called axial cultural features such as universal egalitarian ethics are not straightforward—nor are the dynamics of factors thought to facilitate or impede the development of "axiality," such as cosmopolitanism or sociopolitical complexity. As this chapter will discuss, there is some evidence that egalitarian ideas existed on the margins of urban Canaanite society in the Late Bronze Age, if not earlier, and that those ideas periodically were the driver for uprisings and revolution—potentially leaving their mark on the development of Judaism. Additionally, the gradual curtailing of the power of Phoenician kings and the rise of ruling city councils likely had less to do with ideology and more to do with material factors such as the power of the merchant class; though, due to the scarcity of reliable written sources from this period, the reasoning and intentions of these political struggles remain difficult to reconstruct.

This chapter will first briefly outline the history of the Levant, focusing on the south of the region, from c. 2000 BCE to c. 1000 CE. It will explore the polities intersecting the region through time, focusing on key variables relevant to Axial Age theory and concentrating on the earlier periods (Bronze and Iron Ages), as many of the later developments were strongly influenced by polities originating outside of the Levant and covered more fully in other chapters of this volume. This will include the differing religions of the region and what each had to say about the ideal structure of society and social relations between classes; the political and institutional position of the ruler and the regime; and the presence or absence and the development over time of universalizing morality and egalitarianism in the Levant. Finally, the chapter will discuss the degree to which ideas about universalism, moral norms, or egalitarian principles were carried out in practice.

Historical background

An identifiably Canaanite culture had emerged at least by the Middle Bronze Age, if not earlier; it is thought to have developed from the prehistoric Ghassulian culture, which practiced agriculture and long-distance trade. Though the southern Levant lagged behind neighboring regions such as Egypt and Syria in its development of cities, at some point in the Early Bronze Age (beginning c. 3500 BCE), major urban centers had emerged, such as Jericho, Ebla, Hazor, and Jerusalem. However, for reasons that are poorly understood, the so-called proto-Canaanite culture suffered a collapse at the end of the Early Bronze Age and cities were abandoned as their populaces returned to farming villages and pastoralism.

By the Middle Bronze Age (c. 2000 BCE), cities had reconstituted, and the material culture shows strong influences from Mesopotamian Amorite society. In the southern Levant, these Amorite populations developed into a differentiated culture that was called "Ka-na-na" or "Ki-na-a" by surrounding cultures such as Egypt—hence Canaanite (Cline 2004: 13). It featured dozens of small city-states, some strong enough to lead regional confederations against each other or against outside invaders. These city-states appear to have been significantly institutionalized, featuring standing armies, proto-bureaucracies and public works, and official cults. The social structure was highly unequal; most of the land was concentrated in the hands of the small ruling class, while the vast majority of inhabitants were serfs, slaves, or landless vagabonds or nomads. Many Canaanite cities boasted imposing fortifications, which required massive investments of labor and wealth. These perhaps indicate that—as in surrounding societies—the populace was heavily taxed, both in goods and in corvée labor. The economy depended heavily on trade, with intensive cultivation of staples such as wine and oil meant for export in exchange for prestige goods such as imported pottery and tin for making bronze.

During the Middle Bronze Age, Canaanite polities were wealthy and powerful enough to extend their influence into the Nile Delta (via the so-called "Hyksos" invaders). However, the end of the Middle Bronze Age (c. 1550 BCE) is marked by the military campaigns of the pharaoh Thutmose I, who expelled the Hyksos and then campaigned into Canaan proper, imposing Egyptian overlordship over many of the Canaanite cities. As the Bronze Age progressed, Canaanite cities were marked by increasing social turmoil, wracked by repeated uprisings against Egyptian officials or against local elites, and facing periodic invasions from the sea or pressure from the Hittite Empire.

For our purposes, the popular uprisings of the Habiru or ʿApiru deserve comment. The name had been used since about 1800 BCE in various Sumerian, Egyptian, Hittite, and other sources to refer to an amorphous group of landless outcasts, present throughout the Fertile Crescent. At times, they are described as mere migrant laborers; other times they are feared as mercenaries, bandits, and outlaws (e.g. Rainey 2008). Where the ʿApiru appear in the Amarna Letters, a collection of Egyptian diplomatic correspondence dating from the fourteenth century BCE, they are considered a serious military threat to the city-states of Canaan. City mayors repeatedly warned the Egyptian pharaoh that ʿApiru forces were threatening several cities and had actually captured some of them; additionally, rebellious nobles were making common cause with the ʿApiru in order to overthrow Egyptian rulers. In particular, Rib-Adda, the ruler of Byblos, wrote in a panic that ʿApiru leaders had appealed to the people of Ammiya to kill their ruler and join them: "And they have been won over in accordance with his [wo]rds and they are like the *apîru* troops ... Thus they have made an alliance among themselves and thus I am very much afraid because there is no man who can deliver me [fr]om their hand" (Amarna Letter 74 in Rainey 2015).

Some scholars identify the ʿApiru with the biblical Hebrews, but the evidence for this identification is insubstantial (Rainey 2008). More relevant for this discussion is the tantalizing possibility that the ʿApiru represented a revolutionary opposition to the existing, starkly hierarchical Egyptian regime. Even if the ʿApiru did not have an explicit ideological commitment to egalitarianism, the practical effect of such uprisings would likely be to challenge the legitimacy of highly unequal regimes and provide the possibility for "exit" (cf. Hirschman 1970), that is, for the peasantry to defect away from their rulers. Such a challenge may well have had lingering effects on the intellectual development of the region.

Finally, the Bronze Age Canaanite civilization fell victim to the wave of calamities that swept the eastern Mediterranean and West Asia in the early twelfth century BCE. In the southern Levant as elsewhere, famine and drought struck, population fell, and urban sites were destroyed (Langgut et al. 2013). Egypt, facing internal instability and invasions from the sea and surrounding desert, lost its grip on Canaan around 1150 BCE (Matthews 2013: 463). The role played by mobile populations in these upheavals remains uncertain. Groups now collectively known as "Sea Peoples" appear in Egyptian and other sources as violent raiders and pirates, but most scholars today no longer attribute the Late Bronze Age collapse solely to the disruption caused by their activities. They may have been groups displaced by the region-wide aridification of the climate around this time and its detrimental effects on agriculture.

In the vacuum left by the collapse of the great powers, new polities and ethnic groupings appeared in the Levant. Changes in ceramic styles and architecture at the Late Bronze/Early Iron Age transition testify to the presence of newcomers to the region, many of them culturally linked to the Aegean world (Dothan 1989). One group of Sea Peoples, the Philistines, likely migrated from Greece and western Anatolia to settle the south-western coastal plain and coalesced around the sites of Gaza, Gath, and Ashkelon (Miller 2014: 187–89; Stone 2014: 136–37). To their north, freed from the yoke of both Hittite and Egyptian hegemony, the Phoenician city-states—autonomous units that nevertheless shared a distinctive material culture and political structure—developed from the hitherto relatively homogenous Canaanite society (Dixon 2013: 13). However, the outcome of the migrations and political disintegration of the late second millennium BCE with the most direct relevance for this chapter is the appearance in Canaan of a community identifying itself as "Israel" and cohering around the worship of a single god, YHWH (Stone 2014: 127–30).

Understanding the early history of the Israelite polity is fraught with controversy. For the present purpose, we must set aside the origins of the Israelites, the Exodus narrative in the Bible, and the conquest of Canaan that is depicted there. While some scholars associate the 'Apiru with the Israelites, or point to other possibilities for the Israelites' emergence, there is not enough evidence to say for certain. What we can say is that their first likely appearance in the archaeological record is in small agricultural settlements in previously uninhabited areas of the Judean highlands. Over time their settlements became more developed and Israelite control extended through more of the former Canaan, until an elaborated Israelite state emerged during this Iron Age period.

How this happened is disputed. The Bible depicts a stateless tribal confederation that lasted some centuries before the people decided on a king (Saul, then David and Solomon), who ruled over the entire Israelite people. Within a few generations, the northern tribes rebelled and split off to form the Northern Kingdom of Israel, while the Davidic dynasty was left with the truncated Kingdom of Judah. This broad sequence is accepted by archaeologists such as Amihai Mazar (e.g. 2010); however, Israel Finkelstein and his supporters argue that the Northern and Southern kingdoms in fact arose independently of each other, with the Northern Kingdom emerging first (e.g. Finkelstein 2013; for an overview of the debate see Thomas 2016).

Either way, Israel and Judah had deep interrelations throughout their history; usually, Israel was the dominant actor. At its height, Israel imposed tribute on many of the surrounding kingdoms, not only Judah but Moab, Edom, and perhaps others as well. The Israelite population primarily lived in cities and towns in the hills, with fortified cities protecting the frontiers on the plains and dominating major trade routes through the region. Trade linked Israel with its northern neighbor Phoenicia, particularly through the port of Dor. At the height of its power, Israel was also a significant military force, contributing the largest contingent to the regional coalition that turned back Assyria's first attempt to conquer the Levant (the Battle of Qarqar, c. 853 BCE) (Finkelstein 2013: 133). Israel possessed a standing army that included a strong chariot corps with weapons of iron and bronze. Fortifications were many and imposing, and the Palace of Omri was one of the grandest in ancient West Asia.

However, starting with the assassination of the Omrid king Jehoram by Jehu (c. 841 BCE), Israel's fortunes waned; and it spent the rest of its existence as the tributary of either Aram or Assyria, depending on which of the two neighboring states was ascendant. Even when the economy of Israel flourished during certain periods of the next century (as attested by the greater incidence of luxury goods in archaeological finds), Israel was still subject to the authority of powers outside the Levant, being invaded several times. Ultimately, following an ill-fated rebellion against Assyria, the polity of Israel was dissolved (c. 722 BCE), its people exiled, and the land turned into an Assyrian province.

The Phoenician city-states, too, were organized into a province of this great Mesopotamian empire in the late eighth century (Oded 1974). Nevertheless, due to their importance as trade centers, the Phoenicians kept much of their traditional forms of government; and with Assyria blocking territorial expansion to the east, the Phoenician cities instead established colonies across the Mediterranean—and particularly the Tyrian colony of Carthage (Niemeyer 2006; Tsetskhladze 2006; van Dommelen 2005). These colonies would have a tremendous impact on the development of ancient Greek culture.

The smaller kingdom of Judah fared better than its northern neighbors, retaining a degree of independence under the Davidic line of kings as a vassal state of Assyria. However, with the exception of a brief period in the second and first centuries BCE, it would remain subject to one or another large empire for the remainder of its history (Soggin 1999: 248–49, 259); a characteristic condition of most Levantine statelets in antiquity. In 587/6 BCE, Jerusalem was sacked, and Judah annexed to the Neo-Babylonian Empire. This state had been founded in 626 by Nabopolassar and had rapidly risen—at the expense of Assyria—to become the paramount power of West Asia (Van de Mieroop 2007: 270–71). Though Babylonian imperial policies in the Levant were arguably less oppressive than those of the Neo-Assyrian kings, they did include the exile of King Zedekiah and many of the Judahite elite to Babylon, an event of great significance for the development of Judaic thought and religious practice (Lipschits 2005: xi–xiv). The Twenty-fifth and Twenty-sixth Dynasties of Egypt also periodically intervened in Sinai and the Levant between the eighth and sixth centuries BCE, sometimes fomenting local rebellions against Mesopotamian powers (Soggin 1999: 5, 248).

Just as Assyrian hegemony had weakened and collapsed less than a century earlier, the Babylonian Empire fell apart in the mid-sixth century in the face of the military campaigns of Cyrus "the Great," founder of the Achaemenid (or first Persian) Empire. Cyrus occupies an unusual position in the Jewish historiographic tradition. According to various written sources from across West Asia (as well as the Greek histories), the Persian conqueror-king was received in Babylon and its territories as a liberator (Vanderhooft 2006: 351–52). The Book of Isaiah goes so far as to name Cyrus as YHWH's "anointed" (45:1) and his "shepherd" (44:28), a position linked to the Persian policy of allowing the various peoples exiled to Babylon to return home. Nevertheless, Judah was controlled and administered by Persian-appointed officials, initially as part of the large satrapy of Babylonia and Across the River, and after 482 BCE as Across the River, comprising the regions of Phoenicia, Palestine, and Syria west of the Euphrates (Dandamayev 2006: 376; Lipschits 2006: 25–26).

In 332/1 BCE, the Levantine territories of the Achaemenid Empire fell, from north to south and in quick succession, to the armies of Alexander III of Macedon (Betlyon 2005), marking the beginning of the Hellenistic period in the region. The independent power of the Phoenician polities was permanently broken, with Tyre being destroyed by Alexander (allowing its colony Carthage to become independent). The southern Levant was incorporated into the Ptolemaic Empire in 301 BCE and was ruled from Alexandria until the Seleucid king Antiochus III conquered it in 200 BCE (Smith 1990: 123). The Seleucid Dynasty's control waxed and waned, however, and at times certain areas of the Levant were able to assert their political autonomy. In Judea, the local Hasmonean Dynasty ruled a mostly independent Jewish state from the mid-second century BCE until 63 BCE, when it was annexed to an increasingly powerful Roman Republic (Gafni 1984: 17; Regev 2013: 17).

In 6 CE, the regions of Judea, Samaria (to its north), and Idumea (to its south) became the Province of Judea within the Roman Empire (Schäfer 2003: 105). The southern Levant would remain under some form of Roman rule—though not without considerable, if perhaps periodic, resistance, notably the Bar Kochba revolt of 132–135 CE—until the early seventh century, when the Sasanian (Persian) Empire wrested Jerusalem from Byzantine control (Eshel 2006; Sivan 2008). The Persian occupation was brief, however, and by 640 the entire Levantine coast had been conquered by Muslim armies and incorporated into the expanding Islamic Empire (Schick 1998: 75–76). For the remainder of the first millennium CE, the region was ruled by various Islamic governments, including the ʿAbbāsid caliphs and their rivals in Egypt, the Ṭūlūnid and Ikhshīdid Dynasties (76–78).

Universalizing morality and egalitarian ideologies
Bronze and Iron Age Canaan

Unfortunately, the Canaanites left few writings behind and none at all on religious matters; some scholars have even speculated that there was an active taboo against creating religious writings (Shai and Uziel 2010). Similarly, the Phoenicians (heirs to the Canaanites) left almost no writings behind on any subject, despite their legendary literature; in a bitter irony, their adoption of papyrus meant that their heritage crumbled into dust while older societies' stone and clay writings survived (Lipiński 1995: 1321–22). A common practice among scholars is to make inferences about Canaanite religion from the discovered writings of Ugarit, which was just outside of Canaan proper yet shared cultural elements with it, and has similarities with the descriptions of Canaanite religion found in the Hebrew Bible (Noll 2007).

There were four ranks of gods in the Ugaritic literature. A "high god," El, and his consort Asherah ruled the others; in the second rank were the "cosmic" gods, each of which ruled over some aspect of the natural world. In the third rank were gods of everyday activity such as gods of craftsmanship, gods of child-bearing, and deified ancestors. Lowest were the messenger gods. It is believed by modern scholars that these four ranks corresponded to the four classes of Canaanite society: royal, noble, peasant, and slave (Noll 2007). And it would follow that these religious beliefs were used to legitimate the power of the ruling class, given the precarious, manifestly unequal social structure. However, unlike the surrounding cultures, Canaanite cities have left almost no iconography glorifying city rulers (Yasur-Landau et al. 2015); any discussion of the political uses of Canaanite religion is hence speculative.

In Canaan itself, archaeologists have discovered cultic temples called *migdals*: large, thick-walled rectilinear structures housing an altar or niche opposite a single entrance (Nakhai 2003: 337). The rituals that took place there are unknown, though they are believed to have featured animal sacrifice and communal feasting. In the Middle Bronze Age, such temples seem to have been the focus of popular ritual activity; in the Late Bronze Age, on the other hand, cultic figurines were often found in people's homes, leading some to posit increasing religious plurality from the Middle to the Late Bronze Age (Shai and Uziel 2010).

Canaanite afterlife beliefs, as with all other facets of their religion, are obscure. Some scholars argue that Canaanite beliefs held that only kings, prominent householders, and great heroes were reborn into a divine afterlife, while most commoners could expect none (Noll 2007). Others note that many of the burials that have been found included grave goods and infer that an afterlife of some sort was common to all (even if only kings and the like became actual gods) (Shai and Uziel 2010). No one, however, suggests any sort of divine judgment for moral behavior or its lack.

As noted, the four-tier structure of the divine pantheon is thought to have corresponded to the actual social structure of kings, nobles, peasants, and slaves; it would therefore have served an ideological purpose, justifying the class structure. Kings were hereditary and had the endorsement of patron deities. Any sort of social-egalitarian philosophy seems absent. Similarly, men were seen as inherently superior to women; in the writings we have, such as the Amarna Letters, almost no women are spoken of even when the authors are describing their families (Kennedy 2013: 67). There is no evidence for or against discrimination against foreigners, however; and given the extensive trading links between Canaanites and their Amorite cousins in Mesopotamia, it is possible that Canaanites did not believe in their own inherent superiority—but again, no evidence exists.

From the evidence we have, the Canaanite ideology was very much not axial (or, perhaps better, pre-axial), in the sense of valuing egalitarianism or of positing a judging god concerned with human morality.

Moving forward in time from this obscure formative period, the picture, unfortunately, fails to lend much clarity. The religion of the Israelites during the later Bronze and Iron Age is likewise the subject of much argument. Some scholars contend that the greater part of the Hebrew Bible was written after the fall of the Northern Kingdom, with a few arguing that it was written centuries later during the Babylonian exile. The dating of the biblical law and whether it was ever put into practice is particularly disputed, which is unfortunate for our purposes—for the laws of the Bible depict the first overtly "axial" religion in the Levant. According to the Bible, all people are created in the image of God; kings are fellow humans and not quasi-divine beings, and are bound by the same laws as the people; debts are periodically canceled, and land repatriated to its ancestral families.

As noted by Axial Age scholars, Judaism was also unusual in that it posited a deity concerned with all aspects of human morality. However, contra these scholars, divine judgment did not necessarily take place in an afterlife; while post-biblical Jewish writings were replete with descriptions of God's judgment in the "world to come," the Bible itself has almost no explicit references to an afterlife. The patriarch Jacob worries about descending to "Sheol," and some of the Psalms claim that there is no praise of God in Sheol, making it seem more like a Greek-style realm of pale spirits (Johnston 2002); there are no descriptions of judgment in Sheol.

According to biblical ideology, the Israelite people (understood in the broad cultural sense here, covering the Iron Age peoples living in Judah and the Northern Kingdom) were vassals of the Jewish God—YHWH—who was considered the one true king. However, that shared vassalage also meant that no individual had standing to oppress another, a perspective which underwrote a religious claim to something akin to egalitarianism (though a patriarchal one, to be sure) (Finer 1999; Walzer et al. 2000). Some assert that such egalitarian streaks in biblical Judaism in fact derive from earlier periods, perhaps under the influence of 'Apiru-led rebellions discussed above. These scholars contend that the pre-monarchic ideology of the Israelite people was already broadly egalitarian, deriving from the time of the early Bronze Age tribal confederations (Finer 1999); and that enough of that tradition survived to give bite to the prophecies of figures such as Amos, who castigated the Israelite elites in the mid-eighth century BCE for oppressing the poor:

> Therefore, because you trample on the poor
> and take from them levies of grain,
> you have built houses of hewn stone,
> but you shall not live in them;
> you have planted pleasant vineyards,
> but you shall not drink their wine.
> For I know how many are your transgressions,
> and how great are your sins—
> you who afflict the righteous, who take a bribe
> and push aside the needy in the gate (Amos 5: 11–12).

While this ideological commitment to egalitarian ideals may have been exerted in the cultural and spiritual sense, it was countered by explanations, if not justifications, of difference. The Hebrew Bible indicates that divine reward takes the form of material blessings in this world. Repeatedly, the great wealth of the patriarchs and other notable Israelites in the Bible is taken as a mark of divine favor. One might imagine that such a theology would be used to legitimize inequality. Again, a paucity of direct evidence leaves this view speculative, though the actual existence of fairly stark class and wealth inequalities is well evidenced (see below for the discussion of morality and egalitarianism in practice).

There is a similar tension in the universalism expressed in Judaic thought, a cornerstone of many Axial Age theories and a significant reason for the inclusion of Judaism and the Levant as typically axial instances. God is portrayed as responsible for and holding authority over all creation, a clear and unambiguous universalizing appeal. For instance, Psalm 117 reads: "Praise the Lord, all you nations! / Extol him, all you peoples! / For great is his steadfast love towards us..." Yet the notion of YHWH-worshipers and Israelites in particular as a "chosen" or "favored" people among others just as clearly belies such claims (Gürkan 2008).

There is also a notable patriarchal streak in early Judaic ideology (Noll 2007). Priestly legislation, based on interpretations of biblical passages and further elaborated in the Persian and Hellenistic periods, clearly regarded women as "unclean" in ways not affecting men—primarily due to menstruation and childbirth—and this view led to stark restrictions on their activities and opportunities. Biblical literature itself provides a clear picture of this sort of attitude. In 2 Samuel 11–12, for instance, King David is said to covet another man's wife. He sleeps with her and, after she becomes pregnant, engineers the death of her husband in battle. YHWH is angered at this, but not because David has had sex with a married woman and sent her husband to his death; rather, YHWH expresses displeasure that David has taken the wrong man's wife; had he slept with the wives of other men, there would have been no offense. Further, as punishment for David's sin, it is declared that the child shall die and another man shall rape several of David's other wives. Noll (2007: 71) summarizes the moral lesson from this story well, noting that "the values of Canaanite culture are clearly on display in this tale: the divine patron punishes a man by killing a child and orchestrating the rape of other women, protecting the property of males by violating or destroying the property of other males."

Intermixing of ideologies: From Assyrians to caliphates

One of the recurring themes in the history of the Levant in this period is its position on the edge of empire. This peripheral, provincial status is perhaps more pronounced than for any other region reviewed in this volume. Many of the powers that dominated the Levant—including New Kingdom Egypt, the Achaemenid Empire, the Ptolemaic and Seleucid Kingdoms, and Rome—are addressed more fully in other chapters, and we will not rehearse discussions of their "axial" features here. Instead, we review the impact of foreign hegemony on the presence or absence of universalizing morality and egalitarian thought in the Levant from the Assyrian to the Islamic period. In the following sections, we ask how these ideological currents related to levels of social, political, and economic equality and to "prosocial" activity; and how rulership in the region was affected both in theory and practice by this turbulent political history.

Assyrian, Babylonian, and Persian domination further engendered an intellectual tradition of anti-imperialism in the southern Levant, which can be seen running through much of Judaic ideology from its formative period. Some commentators have gone as far as to suggest that "Israel was the first nation in world history to raise its voice against imperialism" (Weinfeld 1986: 172), although, as can be seen from this and other contributions to this volume, such claims are somewhat hyperbolic. Still, this focus on "freedom" from oppressing powers is a recurrent theme in biblical literature and commentary and seems to bolster Judaic notions of universal rights and the importance of the freedom of all people (or at least all devotees of YHWH) to worship and pursue moral fulfillment. On the other hand, one prominent strand in Jewish thought held that their subjection to foreign powers was a punishment willed by their God for their disobedience—it followed that political submission rather than rebellion was required of them (Goldstein 1990: 292). These conflicting attitudes were present alongside each other, leading to an ideology that both developed many syncretic elements, or at least incorporated influences from other normative systems, yet remained committed to keeping "traditional" beliefs and practices intact.

The exposure of a segment of the Judaic elite to a wide range of influences while resident in Babylon—which had been an intellectual and religious center of West Asia for over a millennium—did much to shape the development of Jewish thought over the following centuries. Narratives of "exile and return"— from Babylon to Zion, from Egypt to Canaan in earlier periods, from across Europe back to the Levant in modern times—remain an important strand in Judaic thought, emphasizing the resilience of Jewish practice in the face of hardship. Nonetheless, changes to Jewish thought and practice from the earlier Bronze and Iron Ages were inevitable. Post-exilic Judaism, notably, had to come to terms with the destruction of YHWH's temple in Jerusalem (the First Temple, destroyed during the Babylonian conquest in the mid-sixth century BCE). Judaic ideology from the outset had been deeply localized; YHWH resided in a particular place (the Temple), surrounded by the territory considered to be ancestrally sacred, divinely protected, and promised to his worshipers. With the Temple's destruction, YHWH was no longer localized in this way. Conceptions of YHWH's divine nature instead began to emphasize his transcendence (Burkes 2003: 14–17). The universalizing claims of Jewish thought also may have developed around this time, a response to the literal scattering of practitioners away from the Levant during the exilic period. At the same time, this strand of Jewish thought may have as much, if not more, to do with intermingling with Zoroastrian universalism, a prominent ideology throughout western Asia during this time (see the Iran chapter in this volume for more details).

It was this post-exilic period—also known as the "Second Temple" period in reference to the rebuilding of YHWH's temple in Jerusalem after the return from exile in Babylon—that saw the rise of the Rabbinic tradition; elders looking to interpret, reinterpret, and come to terms with changes undergone during the Temple's destruction and the exile in Babylon. Biblical exegesis later flourished during the Hellenistic period, when the Levant was surrounded by great powers on all sides (Ptolemaic Egypt, the Seleucid Empire, and Anatolian states such as the kingdoms of Pergamon, Pontus, and Cappadocia). This led to a fairly intense period of development in Jewish thought and, indeed, many of the traits often pointed to in support of Judaism as an axial tradition developed during this time, not before.[1] The "Golden Rule," for example, a paradigmatic universalizing moral norm, is not attested from before this time, and indeed the expression of the rule in Jewish thought can be attributed to the wider influence of Hellenistic moral philosophy (Graeber 2011).

---

1   Note that the Hellenistic period belongs at the very tail end of the period 800–200 BCE, the conventional span of time denoted by the term Axial Age.

As noted above—and discussed further below—it is nearly impossible to distinguish those universalizing, equity-promoting moral norms that developed "natively" among Jewish practitioners and Rabbinic interpreters from those deriving from "external" influence, notably the similar traits expressed in Zoroastrianism, Classical Greek philosophy, and Pharaonic Egyptian ideology. Nevertheless, Jewish ideology and the relatively small group of practitioners living in Jerusalem and other growing cities throughout the southern Levant maintained some autonomy in their practices during the Hellenistic period and through the Roman hegemony. These practices and ideals survived also the final destruction of the (Second) Temple in Jerusalem by the Romans in 70 CE. This was a somewhat typical Roman response to the rebellion by the Province of Judea against Roman authority, which centered on issues of taxation and self-rule.[2] The empire's Jewish populations maintained an uneasy communion thereafter, at times engendering a fairly seamless integration of Jewish and non-Jewish communities in economic, political, and social relations, while at others leading to hostility, anger, and open revolt. Roman social historian Seth Schwartz (2011: 562) summarizes well the contradictory experience of Jews living in the Levant in the first two centuries CE, noting that:

> The Jews as discrete national group were unintegrable in the Roman world, a fundamental fact that explains the devastating consequences of the three revolts against the Roman state. Concurrently, some Jews gradually developed a social institution, the local religious community, which fostered limited acculturation but also enabled moderate separatism. Even this did not completely defuse the tensions in some respects inherent in the relations between Judaism and Rome's relative interventionism. Nevertheless, the local community did sometimes work, especially in the later empire, since Christian emperors were inclined to treat the Jews as members of a separate, inferior but legitimate, religious community/ church. It was in this decentralized form that the Jews were subsequently incorporated into the kingdoms of Rome's Christian and Muslim successor states.

Even as Rome Christianized in the later third and through the fourth centuries CE, traditional Jewish practices continued, and many Late Antique Jewish communities in the Levant seem to have actually flourished, their autonomy sanctioned by the Eastern Empire's Christian rulers (Schwartz 2004). This is not to suggest that relations between Christian and Jewish Romans were always amicable, and there is evidence for increasing hostility against Jewish authority and privileges fomented

---

2   It was not, as is sometimes contended, a defense against Roman attempts to eliminate Jewish practice within the empire. See e.g. Horsley 1999 for an argument for "oppressive" Roman treatment of its Jewish population and (e.g.) Goodman 1987 for the view that the Jewish populations of Judea were not dissimilar to other Roman provincials.

by certain Christian bishops in the fourth and fifth centuries. These hostilities, in fact, led to another period of diaspora in which Jews migrated west through Europe as well as east to Sasanian Persia (Hezser 2004; Schwartz 2004). The point is that through the first millennium CE and beyond, Jewish communities in the Levant largely maintained that uneasy balance between assimilation and cultural mixing with steadfast adherence to the "old ways."

The diaspora communities have been an important feature of the Jewish experience and ideology, from the First Temple destruction right to the present day. Diaspora communities both acted as loci for the continuation of traditional practice and also fostered an intermixing of ideology with local, non-Jewish populations. To the east of the Levant, parts of West Asia, particularly Babylon, continued to host large Jewish populations even after the exilic period, numbers that swelled during the first few centuries CE when Roman-Jewish hostilities flared up (Schwartz 2004). This resulted in the Babylonian Talmud,[3] a compendium of traditional religious writings and Rabbinic interpretations that comprises the primary source of orthodoxy and orthopraxy utilized by Jews since its compilation around the mid-first millennium CE (Hezser 2004). These same Jewish populations were able to maintain their social, legal, and religious practices under the Islamic caliphates, which were generally encouraging of cultural and religious pluralism as long as Islamic authority remained paramount, similar in style to imperial Roman rulership. Indeed, many Jewish communities in West Asia joined with the Arabs in their conquest of former Persian and Roman territory, perhaps looking to supplant the increasingly hostile Christian authorities in Constantinople with a new, more lenient hegemon (Schwartz 2004).

Universalizing morality and egalitarian ideologies in practice

What little we know (or can infer) of Canaanite social structure in practice points to a deeply unequal and stratified society. The proportion of slaves in the general population has been estimated at between 20 and 50 percent, at least in the Late Bronze Age (Kennedy 2013: 70). Slaves would have been captured in wars, seized for non-payment of debt, or sold by their parents. Most of the populace were so-called *hupsu* farmers, who were essentially enserfed to the powerful landowners who made up a tiny portion of the population. Women were generally excluded from power, and even from most official correspondence; authors of the Amarna Letters only rarely name their wives or their daughters, unless discussing marriage arrangements (Kennedy 2013: 67).

---

3   There is a parallel Talmudic tradition known as the Palestinian Talmud, compiled in Jerusalem slightly earlier than the Babylonian Talmud.

The Amarna Letters do record a single cryptic instance of a woman who ruled an unidentified Canaanite city, bearing the name (or title) "Lady of the Lions" or "Mistress of the Lionesses." Two of her letters to the Egyptian pharaoh survive in which she describes herself as "Queen Mother" and warns of cities being lost to the 'Apiru. Nothing else is known of her. A 2009 find at Tel Beit-Shemesh of a ceramic plaque of a ruler or deity in female dress has led some archaeologists to speculate that the Mistress of the Lionesses ruled there (AFTAU 2009), but there is no other evidence to support this. How she became ruler, the basis of her power, and her eventual fate are all unknown.

Little evidence exists for social mobility. The only direct evidence we have for people advancing beyond their initial station are cases in which Egyptian overlords replaced the "mayor" of a city (see below). However, it was the occasional practice in Egypt for rulers to make land grants, for example to soldiers who had exhibited heroism in battle. Probably, something similar would have occurred in Canaan.

The various empires that occupied the Levant over the millennia had different strategic aims and needs, but for all of them extracting tribute was a central focus. Neo-Assyrian and Neo-Babylonian rule have been noted as relatively harsh for conquest populations, especially in economic terms, in that heavy burdens were placed on peripheral peoples to finance military and administrative costs, building programs, and other major outlays in the imperial centers (Perdue 2008). The Persians are often seen as much more laissez-faire, though this picture derives largely from post-exilic Jewish historiography that expressly sought to depict the rule of Cyrus and his descendants in a more positive light than the preceding period of Neo-Babylonian domination. Recent archaeological work, however, has shown that both the exile itself and the return were relatively insignificant in demographic terms, involving only a very small segment of the Jewish population (Lipschits 2005: 271).

What does all of this, though, say about the levels of social or economic inequality in the Levant through the first millennium BCE? Unfortunately, very little. There are hints of periods in which poverty and indebtedness were widespread among the peoples of the Levant (Berquist 1995; Cohen 2014; Lipschits 2005). Whether this is an exaggerated claim intended to vilify the external powers occupying the region, or whether, if true, it reflects any change in the egalitarian ideals espoused in Jewish thought (or indicates the foisting of Assyrian, Babylonian, or Persian ideologies with justification for inegalitarian treatment of subject peoples into the region)—our evidence simply does not provide simple answers to such questions.

What is clear, however, is that at various times these external powers effectively "tightened the screw of dues and taxes" (Hengel 1990: 44) levied on the Levantine Jewish populations. These fiscal burdens tended to become heavier during times of interstate conflict, as the ruling authorities needed to cover military costs; this is particularly noticeable during the repeated bouts of armed conflict between Hellenistic rulers in Egypt, Anatolia, Mesopotamia, and Syria fighting for hegemony in the Levant and elsewhere (Eckstein 2008; Monson 2015). The growing inequality between Jewish and non-Jewish populations, then, is understandable in large part as a result of prevailing political and economic realities rather than as an expression of ideologies promoting either egalitarianism or social hierarchy.

The fiscal policies of Persian, Hellenistic, and later Roman powers drew wealth and agricultural products away from the Levant (and elsewhere) for consumption in the major imperial centers like Sardis, Persepolis, Ephesus, Antioch, and Rome itself. This certainly would have placed a burden on the poorer, largely agrarian Jewish commoner. At the same time, the imperial administrations and their needs also created a host of lucrative roles for the Jewish elite as administrators and tax collectors facilitating these transfers (Schwartz 2004). The flourishing of the Levantine economy is indicated by clear archaeological evidence showing a revival of urbanism in the southern Levant during and after the Persian period. The rebuilding of the Temple in Jerusalem accompanied a demographic expansion, along with the rise of "Greek-style" civic architecture (e.g. judicial and administrative buildings and theaters), growing populations, and a proliferation of consumer goods, identifiable archaeologically (Aperghis 2011). The Jewish religious-administrative elite, thus, acted as nodes connecting the Jewish populations in the Levant to the robust Mediterranean-to-West Asian trade networks supported by the *Pax Romana*.

However, increasing wealth in the region was not distributed equitably and Jerusalem's revival coincided with the emergence of a privileged urban elite of Greek-speaking immigrants and "Hellenized" Jews. According to the Jewish written tradition, it was the inequities of this period and the attempts of Seleucid rulers to suppress local religious practices that lay behind the revolt of Judas Maccabeus, which was successful in establishing the (mostly) independent Hasmonean Dynasty and enhancing the temporal powers of the High Priest (Gruen 1998: 1–2).[4]

Rulership and institutions of authority

We now look at how these cultural systems and ideas about universality, moralizing norms, and egalitarian ideals were expressed in the forms authority took in different periods. The role of Canaanite rulers in society is uncertain. Few writings shed explicit light on governmental institutions; however, the evidence we have suggests that city kings (and later, under Egyptian domination, "mayors") were hereditary. Interestingly, the wealthy landowners upon which the regimes depended were also very likely hereditary; on the evidence of the Amarna Letters, Egypt would on rare

---

4   Similar issues were at least a contributing factor to the so-called "Great Revolt" of the late 60s CE and the second-century Bar Kokhba uprising against Roman authorities (Aperghis 2011; Bazzana 2010: 91; Marfoe 1979; Pfoh 2016).

occasions replace a Canaanite city mayor for disloyalty, and would most likely draw his replacement from the landowner class. These local authorities would command the city's army, which would typically number some several hundred armed men out of a city population of between around 5,000 and 50,000 people.

Rulers would also oversee a city "bureaucracy," though its structure and composition is uncertain and likely varied from city to city. While elaborated royal administrations can be reasonably inferred at pre-eminent cities such as Hazor, most cities show little evidence of a redistributive economy. Royal palaces in cities such as Megiddo, Kabri, and Lachish lack large-scale storerooms or workshops, as were common in Mesopotamia or Egypt. Further, no evidence has been found of any structured, literate administrative apparatus for the larger Canaanite economy. Some scholars infer from this that most Canaanite regimes were more similar to an Aegean-style household *oikos* economy than the larger, centralized redistributive states known elsewhere (Yasur-Landau et al. 2015).

The only solid evidence we have of Canaanite law codes comes from two fragments of a tablet found at Hazor (designated Hazor 18), which follows a similar format to the Code of Hammurabi. By implication, law codes were set directly by the king, rather than the king being subject to an independent body of law (Horowitz et al. 2012).

Another tablet found at Hazor (Hazor 5) contains a fragmentary account of a lawsuit, which was judged by the king personally. Whether all cases were judged by the king, or only those involving important officials, is impossible to know given the current body of evidence. Later biblical parallels such as the judgments of Solomon suggest that the king might have been expected, in principle, to judge all of the people; but that may have been due to the relative universalism and egalitarianism of Israelite society, so may not reflect the practice of earlier Canaanite regimes.

The formal and informal constraints under which Canaanite rulers operated are likewise nearly unknown due to the lack of data. We have no evidence of a formal process of protest, censure, or impeachment, or of their absence; nor have signs emerged of any kind of popular assembly, elite council, or even a ranked military hierarchy. On the other hand, we know of several cases from the Amarna Letters in which rulers were violently overthrown, by disaffected nobles or by peasant or 'Apiru uprisings. There are likewise some tantalizing hints in biblical passages concerning the later Iron Age Israelite kingdoms. Internal critique of both individual kings (e.g. the identification of "bad" Davidic kings) as well as the institution of kingship itself (e.g. Psalm 99, "The Lord is king; let the peoples tremble!" and Psalm 118, "It is better to take refuge in the Lord / than to put confidence in princes") are attested, suggesting at least informal, ideologically based constraints.

The evidentiary basis for uncovering the formal institutional powers of Israelite kings is also quite sparse beyond what is written in the Bible. Still, notwithstanding the interpretive difficulties of basing historical narratives on biblical traditions—discussed above—there is much that can be inferred from those traditions. In particular, the story of the vineyard of Naboth (I Kings 21) offers a glimpse into what was expected or perhaps demanded of Israelite rulers. In this episode, King Ahab desires a plot of land belonging to Naboth, and offers to buy it from him. Naboth refuses because it is his ancestral heritage. Ahab retreats sullenly; then, his Phoenician wife Jezebel arranges for Naboth to be brought up on trumped-up charges of blasphemy before a local court of elders. Upon his execution, Jezebel tells Ahab to take ownership of the dead man's field—where he encounters the prophet Elijah and learns of his divine punishment.

Assuming that this story reflected some historical realities, we can infer much about the limits of Israelite kingly authority. First, Ahab could not simply seize the land, or execute Naboth, by fiat. Second, the courts of elders were nominally independent of the king (though certainly biddable in this case). Third, ill-defined "nobles" (I Kings 21:8, 11) played an important role in the king's support coalition.

This picture is consistent with the Mosaic picture of a king who is constrained by the law, rather than the absolute ruler of society. Ahab is stymied by societal norms concerning the inviolability of ancestral property and apparently cannot indiscriminately murder without justification. On the other hand, for practical purposes the king is still able to get his way, by hook or by crook. Thus did the pre-eminent power of the king exist uneasily alongside the notional—perhaps formalized—restraints on his authority.

In the military realm, Israelite kings were paramount. Often, they commanded their armies in the field, as did Ahab and others, at least if the biblical stories are to be taken as accurate. Sometimes, kings were overthrown and replaced by military commanders. The king's military role was indeed the main justification for having one in the first place, according to the narrative in I Samuel 8.

Israelite kings were certainly not considered to be divine beings. However, they did all that was in their power to give their regimes the legitimacy of divine endorsement. We can see this illustrated in the United Monarchy in the many Psalms in which David is portrayed as claiming special favor from God as his anointed king; and the Bible attests (I Kings 12: 25–33) that with the formation of the Northern Kingdom of Israel, its kings established royal cult centers as a way of severing the connection of the people to the cultic center in Jerusalem. Ahab in particular is subjected to biblical excoriation for importing Phoenician deities and supporting their worship. Whether or not this is literal history, it surely reflects the practice of the day, as the kings of the Canaanites and their neighbors frequently claimed to act on behalf of their patron deities (Noll 2007).

From what little we can tell, it does not appear that either the Northern or Southern monarchies became more egalitarian over time. If anything, the reverse is true; the monarchies were established in a context of limited authority and a broad sort of proto-egalitarianism, and over time consolidated their power and elevated themselves and their wealthy supporters over the majority. Often, kings borrowed institutions or ideologies from surrounding civilizations such as the Assyrians in order to buttress their own positions. Pfoh (2016: 154) has argued recently, for instance, that the position and authority of Bronze and especially Iron Age kings in the Levant were solidified largely through patrimony, with the king as chief patron presiding over a network of patron-client relationships among various elites, a strategy mirrored throughout West Asia: "patronage constituted not only a main socio-political practice but also the matrix which crafted the ancient perception of reality which we read about in our extant texts from the ancient Near East."[5] This process seemingly continued until the very end of the Northern, and later Southern, kingdoms.

On the other hand, the reverse seems to have happened in the Phoenician cities. While the early Phoenician kings were absolute rulers and commanded their militaries directly, their power was radically reshaped by Assyrian overlordship (Glassman 2017: 499). Though their land-based military adventures were heavily curtailed, the kings were still admirals over their navies and correspondingly shifted their activity seaward. Yet naval campaigns would take the kings away from their cities for months at a time and, in their absence, broader assemblies emerged, likely made up of the powerful merchant class. The travelogue of Egyptian priest Wen-Amun discusses an "assembly" at Byblos that governed alongside the king and discussed affairs of state, over which the king presided. A similar assembly was recorded in the fourteenth-century BCE Amarna Letters, where it was called the Council of Elders. In the seventh-century BCE treaty between Tyre and Assyria, the members of the council are called the "elders" of the city. There was also a larger body called the People's Assembly, which apparently "was made up of the 'enfranchised' population of the city, i.e. its free male citizenry" (Markoe 2000: 88).

These assemblies gradually cemented their power, partly displacing that of the king. The first-century CE historian Josephus noted that during the invasion of Nebuchadnezzar II in the sixth century BCE, Tyre lacked a king for seven years, during which time the council of Tyre ruled; and magistrates were popularly elected for short periods. Stockwell (2010, 2012) argues that by the time of Alexander's siege of Tyre, the power of the council had essentially eclipsed that of the king; and, furthermore, that the "proto-republican" form of Phoenician government would powerfully influence the development of republicanism in Classical Greece.

---

5   See also Dutcher-Walls (2002) on the ways Israelite kings limited their authority in the face of Assyrian, Babylonian, Egyptian, and Persian hegemony.

The development of such institutions need not have been *caused* by any sort of "axial" philosophical tendency, however. Ruling a mercantile society with powerful seafaring merchants, the regime would have needed some way to encourage cooperation with royal power, and especially with its tax demands, since brute coercion would be unlikely to work well. Thus, there would be strong pressures to grant rights or powers to the wealthy merchant class to some extent, and perhaps extending further to the enfranchised population. One can draw a parallel with the governmental structures in the Dutch Republic, a similarly wealthy mercantile empire that featured both oligarchic rule by its merchant class and a high degree of political inclusion for the time (cf. Tilly 1992). Unfortunately, owing to the previously noted lack of Phoenician writings (Lipiński 1995: 1321–22), an accurate picture of their institutions remains inaccessible to us.

Institutions of rulership became at once more complicated and also somewhat clearer with the end of Assyrian dominion in the area. Throughout the Classical and Hellenistic periods, the region of Palestine was subject to quasi-divine kings: Assyrian and Neo-Babylonian rulers, both firmly within the Mesopotamian tradition of sacral kingship, as well as the various Hellenistic kings with their ruler cults. However, Jewish monotheism (especially after Cyrus' conquests) maintained that both local and foreign kings were as human and fallible as their subjects, though their rule may have been approved by YHWH. Judaic thought, then, presented a consistent alternate view of kingship to the "official" positions of the rulers themselves, resulting in a very complex and, at times, fraught interplay between obedience to or assimilation with the ruling society and the maintenance of Jewish notions and practices (Schwartz 2011).

This persisted through the period of Roman control and well into Late Antiquity and the arrival of the Islamic caliphates, beyond the period discussed in this chapter. The realities of rulership and authority during the first millennium BCE and beyond, then, present no clear answer to the question of whether the Levant exhibits the traits and developments that Axial Age scholars have often pointed to (e.g. Bellah 2012: 452). The above discussions do, however, show quite plainly that the region was much more complicated, subject to various interleaved traditions and entangled developments, than is often acknowledged; a topic we turn to now.

Interaction and cross-cultural influence in the Levant

An important feature of the initial articulations of the Axial Age idea by scholars such as John Stuart-Glennie, Alfred Weber, Max Weber, and later Karl Jaspers (see the introduction to this volume) was the supposed autochthony of the transformations being highlighted; the period was "axial" to these thinkers precisely because of the incredible coincidence that such similar developments could have occurred in several different spots throughout Eurasia with no meaningful connections between them.[6] Several chapters in this volume complicate this picture, illustrating how deeply intertwined many of the religious, cultural, and political developments in the various polities throughout Europe, North Africa, and West, South, and East Asia really were. The Levant is certainly one of these areas, where we can see clearly how interaction and cross-cultural influences undergirded the region's historical dynamics, rather than exemplifying an "independent," "isolated" culture experiencing only "interrupted contact" with other societies and ideologies, as Jaspers contended (1953: 10–11).

Jaspers' reasons for nominating the Jews as one of his five "axial peoples" are somewhat unclear. He argued that the Judaic prophetic tradition produced a "*conscious inwardness of personal selfhood*" that "achieved ... a perennially decisive absoluteness," mirroring the ethical and political philosophy of Greek and Roman tradition (1953: 63, emphasis in original). Elsewhere, he notes that "the prophetic religion of the Jews set the minds of men free from magic and the transcendence of objects with a radicality such as had not occurred anywhere else on earth; although it did so only for an historically limited moment and for a small number of men, it left its message in the Book for all who came after and who were capable of hearing it" (1953: 75). Here he foreshadows the identification of Christianity and Islam as key secondary breakthroughs, following up and expanding this "radicality" beyond the "limited moment" and "small number of men" involved in the proposed Jewish axial breakthrough itself.

Interestingly, Jaspers' insistence on the autonomous nature of the five axial breakthroughs is tempered by his recognition that "the prophetic religion of the Jews came into being while they stood powerless between two warring empires and were delivered over to powers against which all struggle was vain, when politically their world was in ruins" (1953: 64). As discussed above, however, this rather apocalyptic view of Jewish devastation at the hands of imperial conquerors is often overstated.[7] More germane to our purposes here, such views overlook the influences that ideologies and practices from elsewhere had on the origins and continued development of Jewish thought—from Assyria, Mesopotamia, Egypt, Persia, and the Greco-Roman Mediterranean. We discussed above how some of the paradigmatically "axial" features of Jewish thought that coalesced especially in the Second Temple and Hellenistic periods have strong parallels in some of the universalizing, moralizing, and equity-promoting threads in Zoroastrian, Pharaonic Egyptian, and Greek philosophical ideologies. The "Golden Rule," for example, is more Hellenistic in character than specifically Jewish, and even practices such as charity and utopian ideals of

---

6   Though see Mullins et al. (2018) for a critical review of this argument.
7   Schwartz (2004) offers a useful, critical overview of arguments about "destruction" narratives in Jewish scholarship.

egalitarian cooperation are at least mirrored by other communities around the Mediterranean from ancient times right through to Late Antiquity. On the other hand, there is evidence that the egalitarian, almost anti-authoritarian strands in later Jewish thought were inherited from earlier Bronze Age Canaanite ideals, rather than borrowed from other cultures. Further, the universalizing strand in Jewish thought, insisting on the mortality of rulers and forcefully pursuing social and economic (if not gender or class) equality appear precociously early compared to other nearby traditions, suggesting that Jewish ideology does stand out as formative, perhaps axial. While it is impossible to determine conclusively which tradition was primary and which "derivative" in terms of the origin of any of these supposedly axial traits, or whether they all matured in conservation with each other, the central point to take away from this discussion is that neither Jewish, nor Persian, nor Egyptian, nor Greco-Roman developments can be fully understood without contemplating the effects of interaction and intermixing between them all.

This is especially significant when investigating the Jewish tradition, as there is something of a contradiction in the Jewish experience with other cultures; as Schwartz (2011) and various other commentators have noted, "the Torah prescribed for the Jews a life lived in the profoundest possible state of separation from their neighbors. Jews were not to worship their neighbors' gods, eat their food, or marry their sons or daughters." Yet, it is clear that this commitment to isolationism and self-imposed segregation did not prevent assimilation with prevailing norms nor interaction with other thought systems, at least to some degree and at certain periods. This led to, as Schwartz (2011) goes on to argue, "problems of integration, both external and internal" faced by Jewish communities struggling to maintain autonomy, yet coexist with the various imperial powers who claimed rule over the Levant.

We can see these "problems of integration" playing out through the centuries, as Jewish communities in the Levant benefited at times from inclusion in wide-ranging political and economic relations with societies throughout Europe, North Africa, and West Asia; while at other times, these same communities struggled under the fiscal demands of what were often viewed as "occupying" forces. Similarly, the Jewish thought that emerged after the Babylonian exile and especially within the cosmopolitan world of the Hellenistic kingdoms—the Jewish thought that is highlighted for its supposed "axial" expressions—clearly developed in conversation, if not coevolution, with ideologies from across Afro-Eurasia; conversely, notions of monotheistic absolutism and strands of egalitarianism became tightly guarded hallmarks of Jewish communities, to be kept separate from the customs of imperial settlers.

Conclusions

The Levant, like many of the regions examined in this volume, presents a generally murky picture in terms of Axial Age notions. There were without doubt some important "axial"-type developments in the Levant in the mid-first millennium BCE. Bronze and Iron Age Canaanite, Phoenician, and Israelite communities exhibit strong evidence of moves to curtail the absolute power of rulers and establish constraints on executive power (e.g. King Ahab cannot simply order the execution of the man whose land he covets). As in Classical Greece, the idea of a "rule of law" to which all people are subject, including the most powerful, emerges fairly early on in the Levant. There is also a strong egalitarian tradition within Jewish thought, evidenced by traditions about prophets' diatribes against both imperial domination by external powers and the oppression of the poor by the rich within their own society. It is easy to see, then, why Jaspers and others have singled Jewish thought out as typifying the sort of axial transformation they wish to advance.

Not all evidence confirms traditional Axial Age arguments, however. For instance, in contrast to the Greek tradition concerning limits to rulers' authority, the "rule of law" for the Israelites was conceived of as God's law and was thus crucially different from the Greek *nomos*, a complex body of customary practices and statues that drew their authority from long usage and shared social norms (Ostwald 1986: 89–93). The extent of such institutional reforms as well as notions of egalitarianism, universalism, and social cooperation were, thus, highly circumscribed, meant to apply *only* to the relatively small group of YHWH-worshipers in the southern Levant, persisting as a separate, never fully integrated group within wider imperial contexts. Further, much of what we now consider characteristic of Judaism was a product of the Hellenistic and Roman—i.e. post-axial—periods.

"Traditional" Jewish thought and practice was in large part maintained throughout the periods of occupation after the Babylonian exile, though the ideology nevertheless experienced important changes in response to the sociopolitical realities of the time. This includes the importance of influence from neighboring powers with their own thought systems and practices, including several of the other so-called axial traditions as noted above. All of these ideologies, practices, cultures, and subcultures mixed and merged within the cosmopolitan context of first the Hellenistic Levant and later the Roman province of Judea to coalesce as the Jewish tradition we know today.

While this all makes it difficult to assess whether Judaism fits within traditional notions of the Axial Age or not, it certainly makes the Levant a key piece of the puzzle when looking at the intersection of the various belief systems and political philosophies that emerged and coevolved together through Afro-Eurasia in the last millennium BCE and the first millennium CE.

WEST ASIA | Iran

Jenny Reddish & Julye Bidmead

Period	Dynasty / Polity	Approx. dates
Bronze Age	Proto-Elamite Susa	3100–2675 BCE
	Early Awan Dynasty	2675–2250
	Akkadian Empire	2675–2250
	Third Dynasty of Ur	2112–2004
	Old Elamite (Shimashki, Sukkalmah Dynasties)	2004–1500
Late Bronze / Iron Age	Middle Elamite (Kidinuid, Igihalkid, Shutrukid Dynasties)	1500–1100
	Neo-Elamite	1100–647
Archaic	Neo-Assyrian Empire	646–612
	Neo-Elamite revival	612–539
	Achaemenid Empire	539–331
Hellenistic	Greco-Macedonian Empire	330–312
	Seleucid Empire	312–63
	Parthian Empire	147 BCE–244 CE
Late Antique	Sasanian Empire	224–642
Early Medieval	Rāshidūn Caliphate	643–663
	Umayyad Caliphate	663–750
	ʿAbbāsid Caliphate	750–946
	Būyid Dynasty	947–1056
	Seljuq Empire	1037–1194

Table 3. Periods and dates of polities mentioned in text that were based in or that occupied the south-western Iranian Plateau

Introduction

In south-western Iran lies the historically important region of Susiana, the fertile alluvial plain created by three main rivers—the Karkheh, Karun, and Dez—in the modern-day Iranian province of Khuzestan (Diakonoff 1985: 1; Petrie 2005). Situated to the west of the mountainous Iranian Plateau and on the eastern periphery of Mesopotamia, the area has witnessed a long and complex sequence of cultural development and been incorporated into empires stretching to both west and east. Indeed, its namesake, the city of Susa, was founded in the late fifth millennium BCE and still occupied by the time of the Mongol invasion in the thirteenth century CE, making it one of the oldest and longest-lasting cities in world history (Gropp

2005; Harper et al. 1992b: xiv; Hole 1987: 41; Potts 2004: 46). This chapter covers the period from the very end of the third millennium BCE to the beginning of the second millennium CE. During this time, Susiana saw the rise and fall of the Elamite, Achaemenid, Seleucid, Parthian, and Sasanian states and, from the seventh century CE onwards, formed part of a series of imperial Islamic states.

Iran[1] featured in Karl Jaspers' (1953) Axial Age theory as one of the five sites across Eurasia where an axial transformation, including the emergence of reflexive critique of the political order and a rise in egalitarianism, moralism, and universalizing ideologies, took place more or less independently between 800 and 200 BCE. His inclusion of Iran was motivated by the prophet Zarathustra's teachings that the universe was structured by a "struggle between good and evil" (Jaspers 1953: 2), though Jaspers notably did not develop his thoughts on Iran beyond a nominal inclusion among the other axial regions.[2]

As discussed in more detail below, it is not at all certain that Zarathustra was alive during the mid-first millennium BCE and he may predate Jaspers' Axial Age by almost a thousand years. Our sources for Zoroastrianism, the religion that developed from Zarathustra's teachings, and early Iranian history in general are rather poor, at least compared to more richly documented areas like Egypt, so it is difficult to reconstruct a clear timeline of ideological development in this region. Indeed, in his recent well-known account of the Axial Age, Bellah (2011) excluded Iran from consideration as an axial region precisely due to the incomplete historical record. It is nevertheless clear that Iran has had an interesting and dynamic past in terms of its political, social, and religious history. The region also sits on the crossroads between western and eastern Eurasia and has played a critical role in the history of nearby regions, including the decidedly axial areas in Greece and India as well as Egypt, Anatolia, and Central Asia. Iran, thus, certainly deserves exploration as a potential axial region, as does its probable role in the axial-type transformations of other areas.

Historical background: From the Old Elamite period to the Seljuq Empire
South-western Iran is one of the world's earliest centers of civilization—societies there were among the first to develop complex urban sites, formalized writing, bureaucratic governance, and other markers of social complexity. Although we begin this chapter shortly before the second millennium BCE, it should be noted that by this time, complex societies based on settled agriculture and structured by hereditary

---

1   In the absence of a concise term for the region encompassing the Susiana Plain and the Iranian Plateau (and one that would apply equally to all historical periods), we generally use "Iran" as shorthand in this chapter.
2   Jaspers has been criticized for this by other proponents of the Axial Age, e.g. Arnason (2012: 342).

inequality were already several thousand years old in the region (Abdi 2012: 17–23). "Elam," the name given to this region by Mesopotamian scribes, is a geographically imprecise term that refers to slightly different areas at different points in time (Potts 2004: 1–4). Generally, however, it refers to the region governed by the Elamite state, which emerged in the early third millennium BCE and straddled the lowlands of Susiana and the highlands of modern-day Luristan and Fars (Potts 2012: 38). The rulers and much of the population of this kingdom spoke Elamite, a language isolate unrelated to either the Semitic tongues spoken to the west, the Sumerian language (another language isolate), or the Indo-European languages that were introduced to the region later in its history (Liverani 2014: 25; Potts 2012: 37–38).

The earliest known ruling dynasty of Elam originated in Awan, an area that has yet to be located by archaeologists (Liverani 2014: 142). Around 2350, Sargon, founder of the famed Akkadian Empire centered around the city of Akkad close to the Tigris river, began to expand his territory outwards from southern Mesopotamia in a series of military conquests unprecedented in scale at the time (Potts 2004: 85). By Sargon's death, the area from the Persian Gulf to Tuttul on the Middle Euphrates was under direct Akkadian control, with commercial networks stretching further north-west to the Mediterranean and east to the Indus Valley (Liverani 2014: 133–35). Elam, for many centuries a political rival of states to the west, was not spared by the conquering Akkadians (Abdi 2012: 29; Liverani 2014: 135). Akkadian governors were appointed in Susa and a treaty between an Elamite king and Naram-Sin, Sargon's grandson, obliged the former to defend Akkadian interests in Elam (Potts 2012: 41). After the empire fell to the nomadic Gutian people in the twenty-second century BCE, Elam also suffered a decline, notwithstanding a brief period of military strength under Puzur-Inshushinak, the first Elamite king whose name is attested in the documentary evidence (Liverani 2014: 142; Potts 2012: 41).

A subsequent period of domination of Susiana by a Mesopotamian power began in the late twenty-second century BCE when the area was ruled by the powerful Third Dynasty of Ur, centered in Sumeria to the west of Elam. After this, the Awan, Shimashki, and Sukkalmah Dynasties held dominion over Elam in succession; these dynasties together make up the Old Elamite period (c. 2000–1500 BCE) (Amiet et al. 1992; Harper et al. 1992a; Potts 2012). The political structure of the Elamite state in this period is unfortunately not well understood, except that the Elamite cities were under the control of regional governors or vassals from more powerful states to the north and west. (Liverani 2014; Potts 2012). The Susiana lowlands had become a more significant center of Elamite power towards the middle of the second millennium (Potts 2004: 187). This trend continued during the Middle Elamite period (c. 1500–1100 BCE), as the dynastic rulers who controlled Elam carried out building projects in the ancient city of Susa and also founded new sacred sites such as the famed ziggurat (terraced ritual compound) at Chogha Zanbil in the highlands

(Liverani 2014: 460; Potts 2004: 188). The Middle Elamite period is considered to end with the Babylonian king Nebuchadnezzar's invasion of Susiana around 1100 BCE (Amiet et al. 1992; Potts 2004).

An almost complete lack of historical evidence for events in south-western Iran characterizes the period following the Babylonian invasion. Scholars disagree about the extent to which this represents the disintegration of the Elamite Kingdom; some argue that it split into multiple autonomous chiefdoms in the early first millennium BCE, while others believe it maintained its political unity (Hansman 1985: 30; Wouter Henkelman, pers. comm. 2016; Potts 2004: 249; Waters 2000: 10). In comparison, the written record from the mid-eighth century onwards is much more complete and we know the names of most of Elam's kings from this time until the sack of Susa by the Neo-Assyrian king Aššurbanipal in 647/6 BCE (Amiet et al. 1992: 13; Diakonoff 1985: 23; Liverani 2014: 526).

The sixth century BCE was another period of relative obscurity in Susiana and the adjacent highlands, though the sources we have make clear that the region was host to a diverse mixture of languages and ethnic groups (Henkelman 2008; Potts 2012: 46–47). Many scholars now believe that the destruction wrought by Aššurbanipal's forces, once thought to have put an end to Elam as an independent state, may not have been as complete as the Neo-Assyrian king claimed (Carter and Stolper 1984: 182; Wouter Henkelman, pers. comm. 2016; Potts 2004: 288). Still, it was within a context of political decentralization throughout the plateau that the ancestors of Cyrus "the Great," founder of the Persian Achaemenid Empire, were able to carve out a foothold in the ancient Elamite region of Anshan (Potts 2012: 47). Cyrus' childhood, defeat of the Median king Astyages, and conquests across West and Central Asia attained an almost mythical status over the succeeding centuries, and he is lauded in sources including the Old Testament and Greco-Roman biographies and histories (Cizek 1975; Frye 1984: 82–83; Shahbazi 2012: 124). Cyrus and his successors built the largest empire the region had yet seen, stretching from Macedonia and the North African littoral in the west to north-western India in the east (Daryaee 2012a: 3; Kuhrt 2001: 93). Conquered regions, including Elam, became provinces (satrapies), compelled to pay tribute to their new Persian rulers, though retaining a great deal of independence (Briant 2002: 448; Kuhrt 2001: 114–15; Wenke 1981: 306). Susa, with its long tradition of Elamite literacy and bureaucracy, served as one of the most important centers for the administration of the new empire (Briant 2002).

After some two centuries of Achaemenid rule, the combination of an attempted coup and the arrival of Alexander the Great brought an end to the first Persian Empire. In 330 BCE, the last Achaemenid king, Darius III, was assassinated by two high-ranking Persians, one of whom, Bessos, declared himself king in eastern Iran and Bactria (Kuhrt 2001: 95). However, through a combination of diplomacy and military prowess, the invading Alexander was able to achieve recognition as the new rightful ruler of the Achaemenid territories, adopting the title "Lord of Asia" (Green 2013: 297; Wiesehöfer 2009: 92). His death in Babylon in 323 BCE precipitated civil war among his followers, the so-called *diadochoi* ("successors") (Hölbl 2001: 12–14; Lindsay Adams 2006: 28). This conflict resulted in the break-up of Alexander's vast empire, with different regions ruled by his former generals and advisors. The territory of Asia Minor, Syria, and Iran fell to Seleucus (Lindsay Adams 2006: 43), who created a polity now known as the Seleucid Empire. Cities built on a Greek-style plan—complete with gymnasiums, theaters, and stadiums—sprang up across Seleucid territory and immigrants from Greece and Macedonia arrived in great numbers (Lindsay Adams 2006: 45).

In the third century BCE, however, while the Seleucid kings were preoccupied with the western half of their empire and their wars with the Ptolemaic Dynasty of Egypt, separatist revolts and external invasions began to cause trouble in the neglected east (Dąbrowa 2012: 168; Schippmann 1987). As the Greek satraps of Bactria and Parthia mounted rebellions, declaring themselves rulers of independent kingdoms, a nomadic Eastern Iranian people known as the Parni were gathering strength on their frontiers (Dąbrowa 2012: 168; Lerner 1999: 11). In 247 BCE, according to later sources, a Parni leader called Arsaces was crowned king, inaugurating the "Arsacid era" (Schippmann 1987). His descendants conquered Greco-Bactrian and Seleucid territories across Asia, founding the Parthian or Arsacid Empire. Remnants of the once-vast Seleucid Empire persisted for some time in Anatolia and Syria (Yarshater 1983: xviii), but the Parthian kings now became rulers of one of the most powerful states in Eurasia, flanked on the west by Rome and on the east by the Chinese Han Dynasty (Schippman 1987). Due to a lack of sources, much is still unknown about the political and sociocultural history of the empire, but it is likely that existing administrative institutions were retained in many of the conquered provinces (Dąbrowa 2012: 164–68). For instance, the Greek cities were allowed to remain more or less autonomous, with their own governing councils (Koshelenko and Pilipko 1994: 141).

Parthian rulers claimed to be restoring Achaemenid Persian heritage and aimed to retake lands that they saw as rightfully theirs to rule (Dąbrowa 2012: 170–71; Yarshater 1983: xxxii). It is somewhat ironic, then, that the old Achaemenid heartland of south-western Iran was a particularly rebellious and troublesome province from its conquest (c. 140 BCE) onwards (Wenke 1981: 306). From the early first century CE to around 215, the Parthian satrapy of Elymais (including Susa) was effectively an independent state (Rezakhani 2013: 771; Wenke 1981: 306). The Arsacids were also weakened by perennial conflict with Rome, whose rulers pursued aggressive policies against Persia from Republican times onwards, and by dynastic struggles within the royal family (Cornell 1993: 143–45; Daryaee 2012b: 187). This allowed a Zoroastrian priest, Pabag, and his son Ardashir to mount a rebellion against local rulers in the the province of Fars (Daryaee 2012b: 187). Ardashir proceeded to conquer much of the Iranian Plateau and eastern Arabia, and in 226 CE was crowned "king of kings" at the Parthian capital of Ctesiphon in modern Iraq (Daryaee 2012b: 187). This state is known to us as the Sasanian Empire, after Ardashir's grandfather, Sasan (Wiesehöfer 1986).

A more centralized and elaborate bureaucracy developed within the Sasanian Empire, and by the fifth century CE the power of the administrative elite and hereditary Zoroastrian priesthood rivaled that of the Great Kings they served (Daryaee 2012b: 191–96). However, this was to be the last pre-Islamic Iranian empire. In an echo of the events that had brought their own dynasty to power, the Sasanian kings' succession conflicts and wars with the Eastern Roman Empire made Persia ripe for conquest by the armies of Islam in the seventh century (Al-Husain Zarrinkub 1975: 4; Morony 2012: 208). Beginning with raids across the empire's western frontiers after the death of the Prophet Muḥammad in 632 CE, the invading Arabs won victory after victory against Sasanian forces (Al-Husain Zarrinkub 1975: 4–6; Morony 2012). In 651 CE, the last Sasanian king, Yazdgird, was assassinated, leaving no heir (Al-Husain Zarrinkub 1975: 4–6, 25). Though local resistance was fierce even after Yazdgird's death (26), the Iranian Plateau and Susiana were now inexorably absorbed into the Islamic world both politically and culturally. By the same token, the Persian inheritance profoundly influenced patterns of Islamic rule, arts, and literature both within Iran and beyond its borders (Katouzian 2009: 66–67; Nasr 1975: 419).

Until 661 CE, Iran formed part of the Rāshidūn Caliphate, named after the "rightly guided" early successors of Muḥammad (Bosworth 1996: 1–2).[3] After the assassination of Caliph ʿAlī in that year by a member of a dissident sect (the Khārijites), Muʿāwiya, the governor of Syria, founded the Umayyad Caliphate, a powerful imperial state stretching at its height from southern Spain through North Africa and Egypt to western Asia as far as north-western Pakistan, making it one of the largest empires in history (Bosworth 1996: 2–3; Lapidus 2012: 80–90). The last Umayyad caliph was defeated in 750 CE in a revolt led by the House of ʿAbbās, descendants of Muḥammad's uncle, with the aid of many Persian fighters (Katouzian 2009: 73). During both the Umayyad and the early ʿAbbāsid periods, Persia was ruled by Arab families with their seats of power to the west of the Iranian Plateau and Susiana (72–73). Their control of the region, particularly its eastern reaches, was often only

---

3   The term *rāshidūn* is not accepted by Shīʿa Muslims as an epithet for the first three caliphs, because they believe that Muḥammad's cousin and son-in-law ʿAlī ibn Abī Ṭālib—rather than his father-in-law Abū Bakr—was the prophet's chosen successor (Sowerwine 2011: 5). Having been passed over, ʿAlī was eventually elected fourth caliph in 656 CE and is considered in Shīʿa Islam to be the first *imām*, an infallible ruler whose accession was divinely preordained (Katouzian 2009: 67–68).

nominal, however, as several semi-autonomous Persian dynasties arose from the early ninth century onwards (Daryaee 2012a: 6; Katouzian 2009: 81–89).

One of these dynasties, the Shīʿa Būyids (or Buwayhids) from northern Iran, seized control of Baghdad in 945 CE, turning the ʿAbbāsid caliph into a mere figurehead (Katouzian 2009: 86; Lapidus 2002: 108). The Būyid amirs exercised control over Mesopotamia, Susiana, and a large portion of the Iranian Plateau, but were defeated by a rival dynasty, the Seljuqs, in the mid-eleventh century (Donohue 2003: 2–11; Katouzian 2009: 90–91). The Oghuz, a Turkic people originating in the Altai Mountains of Central Asia, had converted to Islam shortly before the turn of the millennium. In the eleventh century, under Oghuz chiefs belonging to the Seljuq family, they swept through Persia, first conquering regions of the eastern plateau held by the Ghaznavid Dynasty (also Turkic-speaking) and eventually seizing Baghdad in 1055 CE (Katouzian 2009: 90–91; Lapidus 2002: 117). They reconstructed an empire out of the former parts of the ʿAbbāsid Caliphate and extended their domination from the Mediterranean to Khorasan on the eastern Iranian Plateau (Lapidus 2002: 117). We end our period of analysis with the death of the Sultan Sanjar in 1157 CE, which ushered in the final disintegration of the Seljuq state (Katouzian 2009: 97).

Religion and rulership in the history of Susiana
From the earliest periods, leaders in Iran and throughout Mesopotamia based their rule on divine authority; the well-being of the people and the proper functioning of the land, indicated by plentiful harvests, were considered signs of the gods' favor, implying their approval of the current ruler (Darling 2013: 15–17). The Akkadian King Naram-Sin (r. 2254–2218 BCE) went so far as to actively proclaim himself a living god, though this was unusual in Bronze and Iron Age Iran (Van De Mieroop 2007: 68). Most Akkadian and Elamite rulers in Iran associated themselves with the gods and presented their rule as divinely legitimated, but do not seem to have claimed to be living gods; this represents an interesting contrast with contemporary rulers in Egypt (Vallat 1998).

During the Ur III period, south-western Iran was under the control of *ensi*, provincial governors appointed by the *lugal* (king) in Ur. The area formed one part of the wider Mesopotamian sphere of Ur's authority, though appears to have been fully integrated on both a political and administrative level. Interestingly, the rest of Elam remained independent, interacting with the territory under Ur control through peace treaties and diplomacy (Liverani 2014). Iran in the later third millennium BCE thus stood at the intersection of a powerful Mesopotamian polity and smaller, though formidable, political formations centered on urban sites as well as more mobile tribal confederations such as the Amorites (Hamblin 2006). This perhaps led to the confederate structure of political authority that held sway during the Middle Elamite period. The various *sukkal* (governors) of the period each retained autonomous control of different regions, paying only nominal allegiance to the *suk-kal-mah*, ruler of the wider Elamite confederation (Henkelman 2011). Moreover, the "Elders of Elam," attested from the Middle and Neo-Elamite periods, placed an additional layer of constraint on Elamite rulers (Henkelman 2008). This loose political centralization is notably misaligned with the typical characterization in the scholarship of pre-axial, "archaic" states as ruled by autarchic, unchallenged god-kings (this is discussed throughout this volume).

Conceptions of divine protection and approval of rule, known as *kitin* (Elamite for god-given royal power) or *farnah* (Old Persian for "glory" given by gods to the rightful ruler) extended from the Elamite periods into the Achaemenid Empire, and may have influenced Zoroastrian ideas concerning the role of religion in political life (more on this below) (Daryaee 2012b; Henkelman 2011). The popular perception of the Achaemenid ruler, the "king of kings," is as the epitome of the absolute, all-powerful, divine monarch (Daryaee 2012a: 4). This picture comes to us largely through the descriptions of Persian kings by contemporary Greek writers, notably Herodotus. It is important to stress, however, that all of the evidence from Persia itself suggests that Achaemenid kings did not claim to be living gods in the way that, for instance, Egyptian pharaohs did (Kuhrt 2001). Further, the legitimization of Achaemenid authority on religious grounds seems to have placed informal constraints on the king's autarchy, for the king was considered legitimate only insofar as his actions were supported by the gods, indicated by the overall well-being of the people and interpreted by the Zoroastrian priestly elite.

On the other hand, some scholars challenge the view that the priests during this period had any real power to critique or challenge the kings' authority (e.g. Llewellyn-Jones 2003: 7). Moreover, there were few formal limits to the king's authority, even if adherence to Zoroastrian principles carried certain informal constraints. The Achaemenids did not develop a systematically formulated legal code that applied across the full range of their territory (Katouzian 2009; Shahbazi 2012), a hallmark of axiality according to many proponents of the Axial Age (Bellah 2011: 264; Eisenstadt 1986b: 8). The king, in any case, was the dispenser of justice, not its subject. It is interesting that the areas of the empire that enjoyed relatively formalized, codified legal systems were in the west, not the regions in which the potentially "axial" Zoroastrian ideals held most sway. The Persians incorporated law codes from conquered peoples, notably from Babylonian, Egyptian, and Judaic law, while much of the population was governed with reference to Zoroastrian principles and precedent based on royal decree and local tradition. Achaemenid kings were responsible for preventing and punishing injustice, though this was interpreted largely based on loosely defined religious—Zoroastrian—principles, rather than as an institutionalized duty to uphold a written law code (Skjærvø 2014; Wiesehöfer 2013).

The conquests of Alexander triggered many important changes in Persia, though many elements of Achaemenid rule were retained under the Seleucids. To their Greco-Macedonian audience, the Seleucids presented themselves as soldier-kings, upholders of Alexander's legacy, and presided over a complex, urban-based administrative empire backed by formal, institutionalized rules. For Persian audiences, they adopted many of the symbols and conventions of Achaemenid rule, seeking to appease the conquered populations and instill a sense of continuity (more on the ideological consequences of this double identity below) (Tuplin 2008; Wiesehöfer 2009). What is interesting about this period is that Seleucid emperors, like other Hellenistic monarchs, did make some claims to divinity, which their Achaemenid predecessors had not done, encouraging the development of a ruler cult and identifying themselves at various points with Zeus or Apollo (Strootman 2015). The Seleucids also brought more formalized and institutionalized rule than had existed under the Achaemenids, installing Greek law and legal principles throughout the empire, though they still allowed traditional and customary judicial practices to function alongside the new systems (Bickerman 1983). They retained many of the old administrative forms including the satrapal divisions, but also created a more centralized bureaucratic apparatus, especially in terms of fiscal matters, seeking to increase the transfer of resources from the various satrapies to the central state coffers (Monson 2015). Large portions of this revenue were used to fund the Seleucids' frequent and costly campaigns against the other Hellenistic states, notably Ptolemaic Egypt (Monson 2015; Yarshater 1983).

Under the Parthians, once they took over from the Seleucids, Iran entered another phase of more decentralized rule, in which various satraps and vassal kings enjoyed great autonomy in regional administration and finance (Katouzian 2009). This is not to suggest that Parthians were constrained by any formal institutional or legal limits on their power (Katouzian 2009: 47). Rather, their authority over empire-wide matters was theoretically absolute, but in practice heavily circumscribed by the autonomy they were forced to concede to regional leaders (Kaizer 2009). Like the Achaemenid Persian royals, they worshiped Ahura Mazda and maintained Zoroastrian rites and practice within courtly contexts, providing an example to be emulated by elites across the empire (de Jong 2015: 94–96). The religious aspects of Parthian rulership, however, have not often been emphasized in the scholarship: partly because the Parthian kings did not attempt to impose their religion on governed populations, and partly because Sasanian propaganda presented the older dynasty as bad stewards of the Zoroastrian faith (94–96). Indeed, some argue that the apparent "eclipse" of Zoroastrianism during the Hellenistic and especially Parthian periods, along with the Hellenization of the Parthians, was overstated by the Sasanians in an effort to present themselves as the true keepers of the ancient Persian heritage (Stepaniants 2002: 160). However, it is generally accepted that the association between rule and religion became institutionalized to a much greater extent under the Sasanian kings, who sought to promote Zoroastrian worship more than any previous dynasty (Daryaee 2012b). In addition, they managed to create a greater degree of administrative centralization than their predecessors (Canepa 2009; Daryaee 2010), at least in the west, though some historians maintain that this was very limited in extent (e.g. Pourshariati 2009). This period also saw a formalization and codification of the legal system to bring it into line with Zoroastrian principles (Macuch 2009).

During both the Parthian and Sasanian periods, diverse political and legal practices survived throughout the territories governed by Iranian kings, allowing different regions to maintain traditional forms of administration and justice. This not only created disparities in the formalization of rule between different satrapies and vassal states, but also helped to facilitate a great deal of interaction and cultural mixing, especially in the west, where Persian, Greek, Egyptian, Judaic, and Anatolian traditions coexisted. We discuss further the importance of this intermingling in Persian cultural and ideological history at the end of the chapter. Although they generally presented their rule as returning Persia to its original (namely, pre-Seleucid) glory, both Parthian and Sasanian rulers occasionally made claims to divine descent, a practice more in line with Hellenistic ruler cults than with Achaemenid royal ideology (Kuhrt 2001; Shayegan 2013; Yarshater 1983). From Shapur II (r. 309–379 CE) onwards, however, Sasanian royal propaganda dropped these pretensions and returned to the older emphasis on divinely bestowed "glory" as the source of the reigning king's legitimacy (Daryaee 2012b; Gnoli 1999). Furthermore, perhaps inadvertently, Sasanian state support for Zoroastrian institutions provided the priesthood with tremendous influence, creating an increasingly powerful counterweight to royal power (Daryaee 2012b). These are important dynamics, not only for understanding the history of rule in Iran, but also because they provide meager support for Axial Age arguments that rulers became decreasingly tied to divine legitimation after the acceptance of "axial ideologies" like Hellenic philosophy or Zoroastrianism.

In the seventh century CE, the Islamic conquest brought fairly drastic changes to the region, though there were also many continuities. The earliest successors of the Prophet Muḥammad, followed by the Umayyads, 'Abbāsids, and several local Islamic dynasties in Iran after the disintegration of the 'Abbāsid Caliphate, continued to draw legitimacy from religious sources, holding authority by virtue of their support of Islam (Lapidus 2002: 122). Justice was conceived of in religious terms, as it had been since the Mazda-worshiping Achaemenids, although law under the caliphs was significantly more formalized and uniformly applied than in any earlier period (Lapidus 2012; Weiss 1998). At the same time, the Christian, Jewish, and Zoroastrian populations of the Iranian Plateau and Mesopotamia were generally permitted to continue traditional religious and judicial practices, especially in rural areas (Abulafia 1999; Floor 2009; Khanbaghi 2006). It has also been argued that many medieval Islamic ideas of good governance or "righteous rule" owe their articulation to the Iranian cultural context in which they developed, and especially to Zoroastrian ideals (Yavari 2012, 231): a chain of influence consistent with Axial Age arguments and the idea of "secondary" axial breakthroughs.

Universalizing morality, egalitarianism, and social mobility

Religious ideology in early Iran

In this section, we examine the evidence for three key trends viewed as characteristic of Axial Age societies—universalizing morality, egalitarian ideology, and social mobility—in south-western Iran during the roughly three thousand years between the Akkadian occupation of Elam and the rise of the Seljuq Empire. If Axial Age proponents are correct, the history of Iran should reveal the initial emergence of universalizing morality and egalitarian thought, coupled with increasing social mobility, between 800–200 BCE rather than earlier or later.

At the beginning of this period, we find Susiana and, to a lesser extent, the adjacent highlands under the influence of powerful Mesopotamian polities from the west: first the Akkadian Empire, then the Neo-Sumerian Empire under the Third Dynasty of Ur (Álvarez-Mon 2012: 745; Liverani 2014). The cultural as well as political impact of these occupations is evident in material culture and the use of Akkadian and Sumerian in administrative documents (Amiet et al. 1992: 7; Vallat 1998; Van De Mieroop 2007: 67). However, Elamite culture was not destroyed and it appears that local rulers and officials maintained some degree of autonomy, especially during the reign of Elamite King Puzur-Inshushinak at the end of the third millennium BCE (Van De Mieroop 2007: 67–68). The names of both Mesopotamian and Elamite deities are attested at Susa in the late third millennium BCE (Vallat 1998). Over the following centuries, during the Middle and Neo-Elamite periods, the prominence of Mesopotamian gods in Elam waxed and waned (Vallat 1998).

Religious ideology in Elam is not well understood for either the periods of strong Mesopotamian influence or the "elamizing" periods under the Kidinuid, Shutrukid, and Neo-Elamite kings (Henkelman 2008: 61; Vallat 1998). However, certain general observations can be made. Libations and offerings of sacrificed animals to the various gods were widespread and frequent from earliest times and depictions of what are probably rites of purification appear in the iconography (Henkelman 2008: 299–303; Hinz 1972: 50; Potts 2004: 239–40). This much is entirely in keeping with characterizations of pre-axial or "archaic" religion as centered on rites of sacrifice (e.g. Armstrong 2006: xiii; Bellah 2011; Casanova 2012: 196). Indeed, the arrival of Zoroastrian (or at least Mazda-worshipping) Iranian-speakers in Elam was interpreted in the older scholarly literature as bringing an "enlightened faith" to the region, tolling the death knell for the "primitive and fearful" Elamite religion (Henkelman 2008: 58–63).

The historian Wouter Henkelman (2008) has recently challenged this view, arguing that the influence of Elamite religious beliefs and practices on later Iranian history has been significantly underestimated. For instance, texts from Susa dating to the mid-third millennium BCE, at the end of the Old Elamite period, reveal that the Elamites had a concept of a divine tribunal after death, in which the deceased would be judged by Inshushinak, "weigher of souls," and his assistants Ishmekarab and Lagamal (Carter 2011: 46; Potts 2004: 172–73; Vallat 1998). Possible echoes of this belief may be found in the "Netherworld triad" of later Zoroastrianism: Mithra, Sraosha, and Rashnu (Henkelman 2008: 62; Potts 2012: 48); arguments that the concept of individual judgment after death originated with the Prophet Zarathustra (e.g. Boyce 1979: 29) may therefore have to be modified. In the absence of any contemporary religious literature,[4] it is unclear which criteria were employed to judge the Elamite dead. Whether the tribunal of the underworld was believed to be universal—an inevitable feature of the journey between this life and the next for all people—is also unknown. Nevertheless, the available evidence does imply that Inshushinak was concerned with the morality of human behavior and that one's conduct in life would bring either reward or punishment in the afterlife.

Divinely sanctioned moral principles that appear in the Mesopotamian literary corpus may also have featured in Elamite religion and ethical norms, considering the clear mutual influence of the two cultural traditions. For instance, the Akkadian *Šurpu*, a compilation of prayers and spells dating to the late second millennium BCE but incorporating older material, includes pleas to three Elamite gods to forgive the sinful deeds of an afflicted person and "release" them (Bottéro and Finet 2001; Tavernier 2013: 482). However, the motifs of the divine tribunal and the weighing of the soul do not feature in contemporary Mesopotamian iconography or literature and can be considered an indigenous Elamite development (Henkelman 2008: 61–62).

The fragmentary historical and archaeological record thus provides tantalizing hints of a moralizing ideology in pre-Achaemenid south-western Iran, but it is not currently possible to say whether this found expression in universal ethical imperatives. It is also difficult to discern whether egalitarian currents—another commonly cited feature of the Axial Age—were present in Elamite religion. No texts have survived that make doctrinal statements on the position of men and women, different

---

4   By comparison, such literary evidence is available from Pharaonic Egypt. The *Book of Going Forth by Day*, for example, provides declarations of innocence to be made by the deceased before the council of gods (Ockinga 2005; Quirke 2005). Egyptologist Jan Assmann (2005: 136–39) has interpreted the Egyptian belief in the universal judgment of the dead, for which there is evidence from at least the late third millennium BCE, as one of the "antecedents of axiality," entailing the transference of sociopolitical concepts into a transcendent otherworldly realm.

ethnic groups, or elites and the general population. There are some suggestions from the material culture: rock reliefs at Kul-e Farah, an open-air sanctuary founded in the Middle Elamite period but in use into the Neo-Elamite period, depict an "intricate social pyramid" in which higher status is conveyed through dress and hairstyle as well as proximity to the king (Henkelman 2011: 128–32). As in ancient societies the world over (both pre-axial and axial), Elamite iconography thus served to reinforce social hierarchy, but neither the written nor the visual sources shed much light on whether elites were believed to be fundamentally different sorts of being from the general population. Likewise, the position of Elamite religious ideology on the status of non-Elamite ethnic groups is not well understood, but the evidence we have suggests that Susa was a cosmopolitan and multilingual city from earliest times (Stolper and André-Salvini 1992: 257).

Often noted in discussions of the Elamite civilization is the apparent high esteem in which women were held. Elamite woman enjoyed considerable legal rights, for instance in matters of inheritance, and played an active role in public life (Brosius 2016; Nashat 2003: 14–15). Higher-ranking women used seals that indicate their control over economic resources (Brosius 2016; Carter et al. 1992: 211). Though men still dominated the most important political offices, it appears that gender inequality was less pronounced in Elam than in neighboring Mesopotamia, a fact reflected in the importance of goddesses in the Elamite pantheon (Nashat 2003: 14; Vallat 1998). Interestingly, some scholars have suggested that the politics of gender in Elam were an important influence on those of the Achaemenid Empire (Brosius 2010; Nashat 2003). For example, it is possible that the power and prominence of women at the Persian court owed more to Elamite precedent than to Zoroastrian teachings about gender equality (Brosius 2010; Rose 2015: 273).

In sum, aside from the hints of a moralizing ideology in the concept of the divine tribunal and the relatively high status of women, the evidence currently available does not provide a clear sense of the extent to which universalizing morality and egalitarian ethics were present in Elamite society. The majority of Axial Age discussions simply do not mention Elam even as an example of a pre-axial society (Michalowski 2005: 158). Rather, it was the next phase of Susiana's history that has been the focus of scholars from Jaspers onwards and prompted the inclusion of Iran among other sites of supposed axial transformation; the period in which the first Persian Empire emerged and came to dominate a vast swathe of western Asia as well as peripheral regions of Europe and Africa. In order to contextualize these historical developments, a brief outline of current thinking on Iranian religion and its origins is necessary.

Religious ideology under the Achaemenids: Zoroastrianism as an axial tradition

The Achaemenids who founded an empire in south-western Iran in the sixth century BCE were inheritors of an Iranian religion that most likely originated among cattle-keeping pastoralists on the steppes of Central Asia in the second millennium BCE (Boyce 1987; Grenet 2015: 22; Malandra 2005; Skjærvø 2012: 57). Closely related to the religious tradition from which the Sanskrit Vedas emerged, it featured a pantheon of gods, a three-tiered cosmology including a heavenly realm and a land of darkness, and a priesthood responsible for conducting rites of sacrifice (Bryant 2001: 130; Malandra 2005). Several peoples, including the Persians and Medes, appear to have migrated from this north-eastern homeland over the Iranian Plateau, bringing new gods, rituals, and religious ideologies (Boyce 1987; Malandra 2005). However, Iranian religion was not transmitted unchanged: at some point between the mid-second and the mid-first millennium BCE, a prophet known as Zarathustra emerged and began making a number of religious reforms.

Zarathustra did not introduce new gods, but insisted on the supremacy of one deity—Ahura Mazda, the creator god, lord of truth and cosmic order—above all others (Malandra 2005). He claimed to have received visions from Ahura Mazda and taught that two fundamental moral forces structured the universe: *asha* (goodness, order, and truth) and *druj* ("the lie") (Malandra 2005; Armstrong 2006: 8–9). This dualism had not been absent from the ancient Iranian substrate, but it was Zarathustra who turned the opposition between *asha* and *druj* into an all-encompassing cosmic principle (Stausberg and Sohrab-Dinshaw Vevaina 2015: 9). Zoroastrian theology included a belief in divine judgment after death for all people; the dead would have to account for their good and evil deeds before they could cross the bridge from this world to the next (Malandra 2005). Those deemed virtuous and true would enjoy eternal life in heaven, while all others would go to the "abyss" (Boyce 1979: 29; Malandra 2005). The prospect of an imminent apocalypse also loomed large in Zarathustra's teachings, influencing later concepts of the Last Judgment within Judaism, Christianity, and Islam (Starnes 2009). According to Zarathustra, the arrival of a future savior figure, the Saoshyant, on Earth would herald a final reckoning and the triumph of Ahura Mazda in battle against Angra Mainyu, the embodiment of evil (Boyce 1979: 29; Malandra 2005; Starnes 2009: 30).

Several aspects of Zoroastrianism have led Axial Age proponents to consider it a quintessential axial faith and consequently to include mid-first-millennium BCE Iran among the axial civilizations (Jaspers 1953; Wittrock 2012). For instance, Zarathustra's eschatology was more universalizing than what had come before. Zoroastrianism has been described as the first Indo-Iranian religious tradition structured according to "worldview and belief" instead of ethnic identity (Kreyenbroek 2006). Zoroastrian ideals sought to transcend ethnic boundaries with a shared, universal set of moral and ethical precepts (precursors of the teachings of later prophets like

Jesus or Muḥammad). Similarly, while in more ancient Indo-Iranian belief women and servants could not hope to enter paradise after death but were consigned to a subterranean "kingdom of shadows," the new religion held that all human beings had the potential for salvation (Armstrong 2006: 11; Goldman 2012; Gould 1994: 143–45). Eternal life was obtained by cleaving to *asha*, worshiping Ahura Mazda, and rejecting the forces of *druj*, that is, Angra Mainyu and the lesser evil deities (*daivas*) (Skjærvø 2014: 177–78). Humanity was thus divided according to individual conscience rather than along the lines of tribal affiliation, sex and gender, or social status (Kreyenbroek 2006; Skjærvø 2014: 178). Some scholars have argued that the emphasis on free will and the prospect of divine judgment would have encouraged a greater degree of moral introspection and self-examination among worshipers (Boyce 1968: 270; Stepaniants 2002: 167). Zarathustra's approach has even been called "ethical individualism" (Erickson 1999), chiming with representations of the Axial Age as the era in which personal moral responsibility and the "inner man" came to the fore (Assmann 2005: 140; Jaspers 1953). Not all scholars have accepted the inclusion of Zoroastrianism among the truly axial religions, however. For Karen Armstrong (2006: 11), the "deeply agonistic" character of Zarathustra's religious vision—its transformation of the violence encountered on earth into a primordial cosmic principle—is a decidedly pre-axial, archaic feature.

In addition to disputes about whether Zarathustra's worldview belongs among the axial religions and philosophies, there are significant historiographical issues that influence what can be said about Achaemenid Iran as a potential site of axial transformation. Our understanding of early Zoroastrianism comes overwhelmingly from sacred texts set down after the Islamic conquest, incorporating ancient oral traditions (Skjærvø 2012: 57–60, 2014: 175). These scriptures (the Avesta) and commentaries (Zand) were first codified and written down in the Sasanian period by Zoroastrian priests. Those manuscripts have been lost, however, and the earliest extant sources (with the exception of a limited corpus of royal inscriptions) date to the thirteenth and fourteenth centuries CE (Malandra 2005; Skjærvø 2012: 58–60). The gap between the forms of Mazda-worship practiced during the Achaemenid period and the date of the oldest surviving Zoroastrian texts means that any attempt to reconstruct religious ideology during the sixth to fourth centuries BCE, as well as during the Seleucid, Parthian, and Sasanian periods, will always involve some degree of speculation.

Several other problems arise from the scarcity of early sources on Zoroastrianism. For instance, the dating of Zarathustra's lifetime and the identification of his homeland remain open questions. According to the traditional Zoroastrian, Greek, Hebrew, and Islamic interpretations, he was alive just before the Persian Empire was founded in the mid-sixth century BCE, placing him comfortably in the middle of the Axial Age along with other figures like the Buddha, Confucius, and Plato. However, most contemporary researchers now believe that he was a much earlier historical figure. Archaeologist Frantz Grenet (2015: 22), reviewing recent contributions to the debate, concluded that he probably lived among pastoralist speakers of an Iranian language (Old Avestan) on the northern steppes of Central Asia between 1500 and 1200 BCE. His teachings likely spread from here—or from the eastern Iranian Plateau, according to another interpretation—and gradually transformed older Iranian beliefs and forms of worship rather than replacing them wholesale (Malandra 2005; Parpola 1999: 196).

To complicate matters further, even the prophet's historical existence is in doubt. As early as the nineteenth century, the French Iranist James Darmester was arguing that Zarathustra was a "mythical priestly hero" rather than the author of the Avestan hymns known as the Gathas (Sohrab-Dinshaw Vevaina 2015: 228; Stausberg and Sohrab-Dinshaw Vevaina 2015: 9). Writing recently, Prods Oktor Skjærvø (2014: 181) noted the lack of concrete evidence for Zarathustra's historicity and several historians working on the origins of Zoroastrianism view him as a "literary creation that lent credibility to an evolving belief system" (Waters 2014: 152). In one sense, whether Zarathustra was a real person or a convenient name for a collection of religious trends and emerging beliefs is not a question that should substantially affect our analysis, but it does undercut the "great man" theory of history that inflects many accounts of the Axial Age (e.g. Armstrong 2006; Runciman 2012; discussed critically in Boy and Torpey 2013: 252–54).

It is these uncertainties and gaps in the historical record that have led a number of Axial Age proponents (e.g. Armstrong 2006; Bellah 2005, 2011) to refrain from any prolonged discussion of Iran in their work. Karen Armstrong (2006: xvii, 10–11) also cites the shift in the dating of Zarathustra's lifetime and her conviction that the morality espoused by Zoroastrian teachings merely foreshadowed the emergence of fully axial ideologies based on compassion and self-transcendence. Keeping these caveats in mind, it is nevertheless possible to make some general observations about religion in mid-first-millennium BCE Iran. The rulers of the first Persian Empire from Darius the Great (r. 522–486 BCE) onwards were certainly worshipers of Ahura Mazda, the "all-knowing lord" of Zoroastrian belief (Skjærvø 2014: 177–78). Zarathustra himself is not mentioned, leading earlier scholars to question whether the Achaemenid kings were "orthodox" Zoroastrians (Skjærvø 2014: 181). However, the notion of orthodoxy may be anachronistic in the religious context of first-millennium BCE Iran and it is in any case clear that the Achaemenid inscriptions share the dualistic morality and cosmology of the Avestan texts (Skjærvø 2014: 181). Zoroastrian or "Mazdaist" beliefs and practices were likely also found among non-royal Persians and members of other Iranian-speaking groups; according to the Achaemenid King

Darius I's famed Behistun Inscription, Ahura Mazda was the "god of the Aryans," not just the Persians (Frye 2002: 81; Gnoli 1993).[5]

The worship of Ahura Mazda and other Iranian gods was only one mode of religiosity—albeit the mode favored by the ruling elite (Gnoli 1993)—among many within the empire. Even in western Iran, the center of Persian culture and religion in the Achaemenid period, the worship of Elamite deities remained very much alive. The archive of Achaemenid administrative documents known as the Persepolis Fortification Texts reveals that ancient Elamite gods including Humban and Napirisha received sacrificial offerings funded by the Persian state (Henkelman 2011: 96–97); indeed, Henkelman believes it is futile to attempt to separate "Elamite" and "Iranian" beliefs and practices in this context. Summing up the religious landscape of Achaemenid Iran, historian Richard Frye (2002: 79) identified the dominant form of worship as "henotheism or monolatry," in which different groups of people venerated particular gods without denying the existence of others or seeking to eradicate rival faiths (Baldick 1990: 24).

Perhaps unsurprisingly given the central position of Iran on the Eurasian landmass, we are thus dealing with an extremely complex situation with regard to religion. Some of the forms of religion and philosophy present in the various Achaemenid satrapies—for instance, the cults of Mesopotamian, Elamite, and Egyptian deities[6]—are considered typically "archaic" in theories of the Axial Age. Others, namely Zoroastrianism, Judaism, and the schools of philosophy that emerged in the Greek cultural sphere in the mid-first millennium BCE, comprise three of the five "core" axial traditions identified by Karl Jaspers as well as by those contemporary Axial Age proponents who do not exclude Iran (e.g. Wittrock 2005, 2012). Because the axial traditions originating in the Levant and Greece are treated more thoroughly elsewhere in this volume, in this chapter the emphasis is on Mazda-worship and Zoroastrian ethics. However, it should be borne in mind that both "pre-axial" and "axial" ideological developments coexisted, coevolved, and exerted considerable influence over one another in the first Persian Empire.

---

5   Surviving today in the name of the nation-state of Iran, the term ārya (Old Persian ariya-, Avestan airiia-) was used by speakers of Indo-Iranian languages from pre-Avestan times through to the Sasanian period to refer to their own ethnolinguistic group and had a broader meaning than names for individual "tribes" like the Persians and Medes (Bailey 1987; Schmitt 1987). Its meaning in the ancient Iranian context (and its use here) is to be clearly distinguished from its pseudoscientific use in twentieth-century National Socialist racial ideology.

6   Egypt was absorbed into the empire in 525 BCE, although the Persian kings periodically lost control of the territory due to local resistance and frequent separatist revolts over the following centuries (Ruzicka 2012).

Religious ideology in later Iranian history

The Achaemenid Empire fell in 330 BCE to Alexander the Great and his conquering Macedonian armies. The Hellenistic[7] period that began after this conquest witnessed a great mixing of cultures, as Greek and Macedonian settlers came in large numbers to the former Achaemenid territory (Daryaee 2012a). This change would have been felt especially at the top of the social hierarchy, as the ruling elite of the Hellenistic Seleucid Kingdom were Greek-speaking Macedonians, followers of traditional Greek pagan ritual, supplanting the Persian Zoroastrians who had ruled the Achaemenid Empire. The arrival of Alexander in Persia along with the throngs of Greek-speaking migrants who followed in his wake certainly increased the influence of religious and philosophical currents from the Greek world on Iran (Kreyenbroek 2006), though it is important to stress that these ideals had not been absent in Iran during previous periods. Persia had always been a diverse, multicultural empire, and this diversity was only increased after Alexander's victory. In eastern Iran, syncretic traditions began to emerge that incorporated elements from Zoroastrianism, Hellenic religion, Hinduism, and other South Asian ideologies such as the developing Buddhist ideas (Kreyenbroek 2006; Venetis 2012: 158). In the west, in Anatolia as well as modern-day Israel, Palestine, Syria, and Lebanon, Greek ideas of governance and urban development mingled with established Jewish and Zoroastrian Persian populations (Sherwin-White and Kuhrt 1993). The Greek-style *polis* (urban center), governed by popular assemblies and organized around a standard set of public infrastructure, became a widespread form of settlement throughout Persia as far east as modern Afghanistan (Katouzian 2009: 40).

The religious life of much of the population remained largely unchanged under the Seleucids, as did many Achaemenid state institutions; like their predecessors, Seleucid rulers chose to leave most traditions intact, allowing different populations to keep their traditional faiths and maintaining older administrative structures, for instance the satrapy system. Moreover, like the Ptolemies in Hellenistic Egypt and as the Achaemenid kings had done in Mesopotamia, the Seleucids were careful to cultivate multiple images of themselves as rulers. To their Greco-Macedonian subjects, especially in the western part of the empire, they appeared as conquerors, rulers of the land by "right of the spear" as direct successors of Alexander himself (Bickerman 1983: 7); for the benefit of Persian audiences, they adopted the trappings of Achaemenid rule, preserving and patronizing Zoroastrian temples and legitimating their rule, in part, by claiming to be favored by the gods, in this case a syncretized amalgam of the Greek and Iranian pantheons. It is, however, a controversial topic

---

7   "Hellene" is an ancient term for the wider Greek-speaking peoples. The Hellenistic period refers to the time after Alexander the Great's conquests when much of the eastern Mediterranean and West Asia was ruled by his successors and scores of Macedonians and Greeks settled in Persia, Anatolia, and Egypt.

among Iranists whether Seleucids directly worshiped any Zoroastrian deities or claimed to rule by the favor and in the service of Ahura Mazda as the Achaemenids did (Colpe 1983: 825; Strootman 2015). This disagreement may stem from the fact that Seleucid rulers seem to have very deliberately displayed themselves in different ways to different audiences, so perhaps both sides are correct. Further complicating the issue is the status of the Seleucid period as something of a "dark age" from an Iranian perspective; the available documentary evidence is overwhelmingly in Greek or Latin, representing a history written by the victors (Venetis 2012: 142). In any case, it is clear that diversity of religious and cultural practice typified Seleucid as it had Achaemenid Persia.

The Parthian Empire embraced a similarly complex mixture of influences, customs, and religious practices to that under the Seleucids. Parthian rulers presented themselves as "philhellenes"—lovers of Greek culture—in order to curry favor with the substantial Greco-Macedonian population and the Iranian nobility, who had become Hellenized during the Seleucid period (Katouzian 2009: 45). However, they also supported Zoroastrian temples and ritual practices, showing particular reverence for three old Iranian deities: Ahura Mazda, Mithra, and Anahita (45). At the same time, the substantial populations who practiced Greek ritual as well as the Jewish communities in the west also maintained their temples and traditional forms of worship.

Interestingly, Zoroastrianism became the official state religion only under the Sasanians. The founders of the Sasanian Dynasty came from a family of Zoroastrian priests (Daryaee 2012b: 188–89) and under their rule the beliefs and practices of the now-ancient religion became codified and set down in writing, receiving the support of the ruling elite. Zoroastrians not only made up the majority of the ruling class and priestly elite during this period, but Christians, Buddhists, Jews, and followers of other religions throughout Persia were actively persecuted at times under Sasanian rule (191). The religious and cultural plurality that had typified Iran in the preceding centuries came under attack as Zoroastrian ideals became institutionalized and entrenched in Sasanian law and practice, accompanied by a decreasing religious tolerance (Shaki 1981: 117–19; Skjærvø 2012). Unfortunately, as with earlier expressions of Mazda-worship, our understanding of the institutionalization and practice of Zoroastrianism under the Sasanians is hobbled by the poor state of preservation of the literature produced in the period (Katouzian 2009: 48). We know that there was a genre called *andarz*, consisting of tracts on "manners and morals," as well as texts written to advise those in power on principles of good rulership, but, frustratingly, this body of work survives only in the form of echoes in Islamic-period manuscripts (48).

In spite of the favorable treatment shown to Zoroastrian worshipers and clergy by the Sasanian elite, other religions continued to be practiced throughout Persia.

The region was also affected by two new "axial"-type religions promoting moralizing and universalizing ideals that arose in the early first millennium CE: Manichaeism and Christianity (Kreyenbroek 2006). The Prophet Mani, who lived in Persian-controlled Mesopotamia in the early third century CE, famously posited a cosmological opposition between the forces of good and evil (Daryaee 2012b: 190; Fowden 1999: 95). Drawing on a wide array of influences including early Christianity, Gnostic philosophy, Buddhism, and Zoroastrianism, it was a "religion of the book" but a remarkably universalizing and dynamic one (Fowden 1999; Laine 2014: 86; Sundermann 2009). Manichaeans promoted the idea that every people had their own messenger from god and that the various religions were different paths to the same end: the liberation of the "world soul" or "living self" from its prison of demonic matter (Sundermann 2009). Mani thus presented himself as the successor to Zarathustra, Gautama Buddha, and Jesus Christ: as the "seal of the prophets" whose message was intended for the whole world (Laine 2014: 86; Sundermann 2009). Like the "axial sages" before him, as well as later prophets like Muḥammad, Mani became a voice of reform in a Zoroastrian context during the third century CE, stressing universal ideals and the importance of ethical conduct. His activities were tolerated and even sometimes supported by the Sasanian kings Shapur I and Hormizd I, but Hormizd's successor, Bahram II, had the prophet imprisoned and then executed in 276 CE (Daryaee 2012b: 190–91). It is noteworthy that Mani is almost never included in the company of the other "axial sages," in spite of the commonalities between his message and the other axial traditions as well as the striking similarity of his life to that of other "axial" prophets.

Alongside the growing influence of Manichaeism in Persia, Christian practice gained a foothold in the region during the mid-first millennium CE. Notably, Susiana became a "hotbed of Christian activity" in the fourth century (Daryaee 2012b: 193), along with the urban centers in Mesopotamia and the more Hellenized western satrapies where Zoroastrian had never fully penetrated (Laine 2014: 86). Christian practice became so cemented in the city of Susa that the Sasanian king Shapur II (r. 309–379 CE) reportedly sent 300 war elephants to crush Christian resistance there (Gropp 2005). Later kings, such as Yazdgird I and Bahram V, were more tolerant of minority faiths and in this period Christian and Jewish communities became more firmly established within the Persian Empire, paying taxes to the Sasanian kings in return for relative autonomy (Daryaee 2012b: 194–95).

By the end of the seventh century, a new political landscape had emerged; the entire territory of Persia had been taken over by conquering armies from the fledgling Islamic Caliphate centered in the Arabian Peninsula. As the philosopher of religion Marietta Stepaniants (2002: 159) has commented, the meeting between the Zoroastrian and Islamic faiths (and, by extension, between the Persian and Arab cultural worlds) was "one of the most dramatic" of all historically known cultural encounters. Inhabitants of rural areas and the more strongly Zoroastrian Fars held onto their old religions for some time (Katouzian 2009: 66), but it is clear that by the mid-ninth century CE, the vast majority of the population living on the Iranian Plateau, as well as in most of Mesopotamia and the wider West Asian region, had converted to Islam (Daryaee 2012a: 6).

As could be expected, the early Islamic period in Persia did not differ drastically from the experience of other regions within the caliphate throughout the Mediterranean and West Asia. Because this period is discussed extensively throughout this volume, we will not devote much space here to the topic. A few notable facets of Islamic Persian history do require comment, however. First, it is worth stressing that so much of what we know about the literature of the Sasanian period in Iran, along with Classical Mediterranean philosophy, is owing to the diligence and erudition of scholars in medieval Islamic Mesopotamia and Iran, who produced many translations and commentaries on pre-Islamic Persian texts and the philosophers and thinkers of the Classical world, running the gamut from Zoroastrian scripture to Aristotle and Plato (Daryaee 2012a: 4). The arrival in Persia of a new and dominant faith, then, did not mean the eclipse of older "axial" traditions in the region; scholars instead preserved this intellectual heritage and debated its merits.

A second point is that Islamic rule in Persia largely restored the religious and cultural pluralism enjoyed in the region prior to the Sasanian period. In response to the need to govern religiously and ethnically diverse conquered peoples, successive Islamic ruling dynasties institutionalized protection for the *dhimmīs*, certain non-Muslim inhabitants of the caliphate, including Jews, Christians, and, in the former Persian territories, Zoroastrians (Kumaraswamy 2007; Lapidus 2002: 36). The ʿAbbāsids in particular adopted a relaxed attitude towards minority groups as they sought to appeal to their various constituent communities, including Greek and Persian populations, Aramaic-speaking Christians and Jews, Syriac speakers, a significant Turkic population, and other groups (Yavari 2012: 229).

Another important characteristic of Islamic rule in Persia was the early and influential presence of Shīʿa Islam. One form of Shīʿa gained a foothold in eastern Iran in the early tenth century and formed a locus of resistance to Sunnī ʿAbbāsid power (Lapidus 2002: 107). The ethnically Iranian Būyid Dynasty, who all but overthrew the ʿAbbāsid caliphs in the mid-tenth century and wielded military and political authority across modern Iraq and western Iran, were also Shīʿa Muslims (Yavari 2012: 230). However, it was only in the sixteenth century CE under the Safavid Dynasty that Shīʿa became the official Iranian state religion (Katouzian 2009: 68). Medieval Shīʿa political theory typically emphasized the religious role of the ideal ruler of the Muslim community, the divinely inspired *imām*, whereas Sunnīs more readily accepted the political compromises made by caliphs (Esposito 1984: 13–14; Lapidus 2002: 47). The relationship between religion and temporal power in the Persian territories remained a point of contention throughout the Islamic periods, though Iranian political and cultural heritage helped to bolster the emergence of Islamic ideas of the ruler as a "protector of religion" (Yavari 2012: 236–37). In the 'Abbāsid period especially, his authority was also enhanced through his interventions into scholarly and religious debate and his patronage of institutions of learning.

Cultural and religious pluralism under Islamic rule was not entirely free from problems, moreover. The legal protection bestowed on the *dhimmī* populace was accompanied by a set of discriminatory regulations (Emon 2012: 1–4; Esposito 1984: 11) and, as discussed below, non-Arab converts to Islam sometimes found that the promise of equal treatment for all believers was not fulfilled. Several novel religious systems, often incorporating both Muslim and Zoroastrian elements, emerged in reaction to the growing disparities in power and privilege between Muslims and non-Muslims, or between Arab and non-Arab Muslims, under the 'Abbāsids (discussed more in the following section) (Morony 2012: 224). In particular, a radically egalitarian sect known as the Khārijites, who had split from the Muslim community during the time of the first four caliphs, found followers in early Islamic Persia. Rejecting the principle of dynastic succession, they argued that each caliph should be elected by the wider Muslim community (the *umma*) and that, if he sinned while in office, he should be deposed (Lapidus 2002: 47). A Khārijite revolt in the late ninth century resulted in the massacre of tax collectors in eastern Iran before being suppressed (Morony 2012: 225).

Egalitarianism, social mobility, and prosociality in practice
Egalitarianism, social mobility, and structural inequalities
Given the difficulty of reconstructing early Zoroastrian ideology, is it possible to discern concrete social and economic correlates of the supposedly axial (and, specifically, universalizing and egalitarian) features of Zoroastrianism? Due to the nature of the available written sources, the links between religious ideology, state institutions, and social structure in the Achaemenid period remain largely opaque. What we can do is compare Zoroastrian teachings—as expressed in the royal inscriptions and the Avestan oral traditions and commentaries set down in medieval Iran—on the role of men and women, different ethnic groups, and elites and commoners with what is known of levels of inequality and strategies of rule in the empire. This section focuses on the Achaemenid Empire, the polity occupying Iran and much of western Asia during the height of the so-called Axial Age, but will also ask the same questions of later Iranian history.

Popular representations of Achaemenid Iran—both in our own time and among the empire's own subject peoples and neighbors—have tended to cluster into two opposing extremes. On the one hand, we have the image filtered through the Classical (and later) Greek texts of the autarchic, debaucherous Persian god-kings. Threatened

by the vast and militarily powerful state to their east, Greek writers generally projected an image of "Oriental despotism" onto Achaemenid society, contrasting their own
supposed liberty with Persian servitude (Briant 2002: 268; Cartledge 1993: 40–41, 48,
1997: 29–30; Miller 2002). In this view, the inhabitants of the empire were subject
to the whims of a cruel and all-powerful king whose judgment was corrupted by the
constant scheming of palace women and eunuchs (Briant 2002: 268–70). An exception was nevertheless sometimes made for Cyrus the Great, lauded in the Greek
historian Xenophon's semi-historical *Cyropaedia* as a virtuous and strong ruler (Cartledge 1993: 104–05; Sage 1995: 164). His conquests were also positively portrayed in
the Jewish scriptural tradition (Daryaee 2012a: 3; Kuhrt 1983: 83–84). A passage in
the Hebrew Bible, Isaiah 45, a controversial chapter among scholars of Judaism,
presents Cyrus as YHWH's "anointed" one, chosen to defeat rival kings and restore
the temple in Jerusalem (Fried 2002, 2004: 180).[8]

There is also a prominent strand of thought among scholars holding that the
expansion of Achaemenid power across West Asia heralded a new era of benevolent and humane rule (discussed critically in Dusinberre 2003: xiii; Kuhrt 1983: 84;
Wittrock 2005: 77, 120). For instance, grand claims are often made about the religious and cultural "tolerance" of the Achaemenid rulers (Kuhrt 2001: 120; Wittrock
2005: 77). This can sometimes stray into anachronism, as in 1971 when the clay cylinder recording the decree given by Cyrus the Great after conquering Babylon (the
Cyrus Cylinder) was described by Iran's last Shah as the world's "first declaration of
Human Rights" (Kuhrt 1983: 84). Nevertheless, there is a kernel of truth in such
representations. Local cults survived and even thrived under the Persian kings, and
royal iconography and inscriptions emphasize the religious and cultural diversity of
the empire's many subject peoples (Haerinck 1997: 28; Shahbazi 2012: 120; Wittrock
2005: 77). After capturing Babylon, Cyrus proclaimed himself a "beloved servant" of
the ancient god of the city, Marduk, and restored the deity's temple (Boyce 1983a;
Schwartz 1985: 684). Adopting a similarly favorable attitude towards other religions,
Darius I is said to have provided funds for the restoration of the Jewish temple in
Jerusalem (Boyce 1982: 127–28).

In older scholarship in particular, this clemency is sometimes linked to the Zoroastrian faith of the Persian kings and their quasi-monotheistic focus on one god—
Ahura Mazda—above all others (Kuhrt 1983: 84). However, it is unclear how this can
be reconciled with Cyrus' willingness to present himself as the servant of Marduk, or
with the references to the old gods of Egypt in Persian royal propaganda intended
for consumption within Egypt (for example, Darius I's Tall al-Mashūṭa stele; see

---

8   The return of Jews living in Babylon to Jerusalem and the building of the Second Temple may
    in fact have taken place after Cyrus' death (van der Spek 2014: 236). On the basis of archaeolog-
    ical evidence from Jerusalem, Oded Lipschits (2006: 32) argues that this "return" was a gradual
    process rather than a sudden mass movement of people in the wake of the Persian conquest.

Lloyd 2007: 101–04). In many ways, Cyrus' recognition of local gods and proclamations of "freedom" followed long-established precedent for conquerors of cities in Mesopotamia. For instance, some 1800 years earlier, the victorious Sargon of Akkad had paid homage to the Babylonian gods and reinstated old privileges for the cities of the region (van der Spek 2014: 245). There is even evidence that several Assyrian kings, whose heavy-handed imperial policies have often been held up as typical of archaic rule and the antithesis of the more tolerant, possibly axial mode of rule under the Achaemenids, allowed peoples living in forced exile to return to their homelands after successful Assyrian conquests (van der Spek 2014: 246).

Statements (generally confined to non-academic texts) that Cyrus abolished slavery[9] are also misleading, and the passage from the Cyrus Cylinder in which the king claims to have relieved the servitude of the inhabitants of Babylon (see Kuhrt 2007: 71) should be seen in its proper historical context. Such rhetoric belonged to a pre-existing set of conventions observed by conquerors in ancient West Asia (Kuhrt 2007: 74) and did not signal that "slavery" in the modern sense would henceforth be banned. Individuals could be bought and sold and various forms of unfree labor certainly continued to be utilized within the Achaemenid Empire (Dandamaev and Lukonin 1989: 153; Frye 1984: 129; Llewellyn-Jones 2013: 50). If there was any kind of doctrinal prohibition on slave-owning, it was evidently not observed by the Persian elite (Dandamayev 1988); nor did it appear to pose an ethical dilemma under the Zoroastrian Sasanian kings (Macuch 2015: 292). Nevertheless, it should be noted that the contribution of bound labor to the overall Achaemenid economy was relatively minor in comparison with other complex societies of the Axial Age, notably the Classical Greek *poleis* (Dandamayev 1988; Lewis 2011: 91; Llewellyn-Jones 2013: 50).

Achaemenid tolerance of non-Zoroastrian practice also had its limits: the Persian kings sometimes used the exalted position of their god, Ahura Mazda, to justify their suppression of the worship of other gods, portrayed as evil *daivas* (Lincoln 2007; Skjærvø 2014: 180). Tolerance likewise did not imply equality of peoples and religions; it is clear that Iranians occupied a privileged position within the empire, legitimized at least in part by their religion (Wittrock 2005: 77). Amélie Kuhrt (2001: 103) summarizes this ideological position: "the great god Ahuramazda had set [the Persian king] over the varied lands and peoples of the earth and given Persia supremacy over them." Marriage between Iranians and non-Iranians was likewise discouraged in Zoroastrian scripture (the Avesta) (Nashat 2003: 16), expressing a form of ethnoreligious hierarchy that existed alongside widespread policies of tolerance for diverse traditional religious and cultural practices. It seems that the Persian elite

9   For example, Kimberly Halkett. 2013. "The Story behind the Cyrus Cylinder." *Al Jazeera: Reporter's Notebook*. http://www.aljazeera.com/blogs/americas/2013/03/65976.html (accessed September 24, 2019).

also maintained the ancient Iranian concept (found in the Avesta) of the division of society into three "classes": priests, warriors, and farmers (Briant 1992). There is no indication that these classes were formally institutionalized in the Achaemenid Empire, but certainly the empire was deeply structured by inequalities in wealth, power, and access to land (Briant 1992). Finding themselves atop a religious and ethnic hierarchy, the Persian nobility considered the social order to be god-given and saw it as their duty to preserve it (Wiesehöfer 2013: 45). Social stratification remained in place throughout the Hellenistic, Parthian, and Sasanian periods, although its specific manifestations and the groups it benefited changed over time (Dąbrowa 2012: 182–83; Daryaee 2012b: 189; Sherwin-White and Kuhrt 1993: 124). As with other aspects of administration, the Sasanians formalized these traditional Avestan social divisions, establishing Zoroastrian temples for the use of different classes and thereby conferring highly visible forms of religious legitimation on social divisions within Persian society.

As we have seen, certain aspects of Sasanian rule also represented a departure from the traditionally relaxed attitude towards religious plurality shown by Persia's rulers, as the promotion of Zoroastrian worship was accompanied by the persecution of other religious communities. However, this antagonism may be slightly exaggerated in our sources and in practice it is indisputable that a diverse set of religious and other cultural practices coexisted throughout the Sasanian Empire. The absorption of Iran into the Islamic Caliphate then brought a state religion that held that—in theory—all men were equal, regardless of ethnic or cultural origin (Yaran 2007: 12). For instance, though the Umayyads were criticized for favoring members of the Arab tribal aristocracy, they in fact adopted several Sasanian administrative and royal practices and employed Persian-speaking Muslims as officials in the conquered regions to the east (Lewis 1993: 72–73; Morony 2012: 217).

Nevertheless, in practice, substantial inequalities existed not only between religious groups, but also within the Islamic population. Arab Muslims and non-Arab converts to Islam (*mawālī*) were treated differently. Non-Muslims were subject to higher taxes on their land and property (Katouzian 2009: 48; Yavari 2012: 228). A special poll tax, known as the *jizya*, was applied only to non-Muslims (Katouzian 2009: 48). That the position of non-Arab Muslim converts was considered a problem is shown by the revolt of al-Ḥārith ibn Surayj of Tamīm against the Umayyad rulers in the mid-eighth century. Though an Arab himself, Ḥārith agitated for the equality of Iranian and Arab Muslims (Morony 2012: 222). The discontent of Iranian *mawālī* likely also played a role in bringing the ʿAbbāsid dynasty to power in 749/50 CE; the Arab ʿAbbāsid family justified their revolt against the Umayyad caliphs by appealing to the suffering and inequitable treatment of non-Arab farmers (Lapidus 2002; Morony 2012: 222–23).

Gender equality in practice

With regard to the question of gender inequality in Iranian history, women occupied an ambiguous position within Zoroastrianism. As mentioned above, it has often been argued that the reformed teachings of Zarathustra represented a more "gender-inclusive philosophy" than the more ancient Indo-Iranian religious traditions, particularly in terms of eschatology (Boyce 1975: 308; de Jong 1995; Goldman 2012; Gould 1994: 145). However, these egalitarian impulses have been counterbalanced over the long history of Zoroastrian worship by representations of women as a polluting and corrupting influence. For instance, Drug, the incarnation of evil and deceit, was portrayed as female (Nashat 2013: 16). In a 2002 book, the Iranist Jamsheed Choksy pulled together various malign images of women and femininity from a variety of Zoroastrian texts and argued that these symbolic structures would have had direct implications for women's daily lives; menstruation and childbirth, both involving the production of "dead matter," rendered women ritually impure and justified restrictions on their behavior and their exclusion from important ritual spaces (Choksy 2002: 91; Rose 2015). In one sense, then, the lives of women in Persia may have improved under Islamic rule, at least for Muslim women and converts, as Islam imposed fewer restrictions based on ideas of feminine ritual impurity.

At the same time, such representations did not prevent royal or noble women within the Achaemenid Empire from exercising considerable economic and political power. The iconography of Achaemenid-period administrative seals and funerary monuments reveals that they were entitled to hold formal audiences[10] like their male counterparts, and there is evidence from administrative texts that some women owned and managed large estates (Brosius 2010; Llewellyn-Jones 2013: 112; Kuhrt 2001: 116). The prominent female presence at royal and satrapal courts was likely the source of a favorite trope of Greek writers: the decadent and cruel Persian noblewoman, a corrupting influence (along with the ubiquitous scheming eunuchs) on the Great King (Briant 2002: 268, 285; Sancisi-Weerdenburg 2013). The lives of nonelite women under Achaemenid rule are less well understood, but when compared to older Anatolian and Mesopotamian judicial systems, their legal status appears to have improved (Magdalene 2009). Levels of gender inequality varied widely between different satrapies—for example, Egyptian women always enjoyed a particularly favorable legal status—but in Achaemenid-period Elam and Babylonia as well as Egypt, women could own property and dispose of it independently (Allam 1990: 33; Dandamaev and Lukonin 1989: 124). Linking these realities with Zoroastrian religious ideology is a daunting task and is complicated by the myriad other cultural

---

10   The formal audience offered a venue for subjects of the empire to meet with Persian administrators, including the king himself, to make requests or complaints.

patterns that shaped gender relations in the first Persian Empire, especially the influence of the Elamite heritage on the court and bureaucracy.

In sum, many aspects of Zoroastrianism during the Achaemenid period as well as the more ancient Iranian religion, which was not completely abandoned, served to reinforce inequality and provide it with sacred justifications. Expressions of egalitarian ethics were clearly present in Zoroastrian thought, but they were counterbalanced by other teachings—including concepts from the older Indo-Iranian religion—that stressed the polluting nature of women and the special status of privileged ethnic and religious groups. The division of humanity into followers of good and evil was also easily manipulated to justify violence against outgroups. In one notable example, when Darius I ascended to the throne, he conducted a systematic campaign against rivals throughout the empire, presenting his conquests as divinely justified wars against "liar kings," a clear allusion to the Zoroastrian (or "Mazdaist") dichotomy of truth and falsehood (Wiesehöfer 2013). Later Persian rulers likewise justified their military campaigns against the Roman Empire by claiming that Roman leaders were liars (Daryaee 2012b: 189). After reviewing the evidence, it is clear that we can draw no simple connections between the development of Zoroastrianism (and its favorable position within the Achaemenid, Parthian, and Sasanian Empires) and the emergence of new, more equable, and less oppressive sociopolitical structures in Iran.

Prosociality in practice

Historian of ancient Iran Alberto Cantera (2015: 331) has noted that Zoroastrianism, from its earliest beginnings, imposed an "ethical imperative of assistance to the needy members of the community." Achaemenid kings portrayed themselves as protectors of the weak, continuing a motif that in fact recurs throughout Iranian history from the Elamite through to the Islamic periods. For instance, an inscription in the tomb of the Achaemenid king Darius I proclaims:

> (It is) not my desire that the weak should be treated wrongly for the strong one's sake, (and) that (is) not my desire that the strong one might be treated wrongly for the weak one's sake (Wiesehöfer 2013: 41).

This encapsulates two related duties of the Persian king: to guarantee the just and fair treatment of his subjects, and to bestow peace and prosperity on his empire (Wiesehöfer 2013: 47). Although the principle of the king's duty to ensure justice had precedent in earlier Iranian traditions, it was not until Darius I that Achaemenid modes of administering justice became institutionalized and codified in a formal legal system (Shahbazi 2012). The empire, however, incorporated legal practice from Babylonian, Jewish, and Egyptian traditions, consistent with the rulers' habit of allowing cultural diversity and permitting different satrapies to maintain traditional practices (Dandamaev and Lukonin 1989).

The second element of the king's role is also notable, highlighting an apparent contradiction in Zoroastrian thought. On the one hand, Zoroastrian ideology emphasized self-reliance and personal salvation (Boyce 1968: 270), ideals echoed in later, post-axial religions including Christianity and Islam. Zoroastrians considered themselves responsible for their own conduct and expected ultimately to receive judgment for it in the afterlife, as explained above. On the other hand, a component of "good conduct" was to carry out good deeds that benefited others, especially in terms of material comforts. This included charitable giving as well as the creation and maintenance of irrigation works, a critical need in the more arid areas encompassed by the empire in northern and eastern Iran, parts of Anatolia, and Egypt (Balali et al. 2009: 98). The *qanat* system, an innovative method of transporting water across great distances in underground channels leading down from mountainous areas, was developed during this period, though the technology may be somewhat older (Wilson 2008: 291–92). *Qanats* were exported along with Persian dominion throughout Mesopotamia, the Levant, and North Africa, built and maintained by the state using corvée labor (English 2009). Zoroastrian ideals of good deeds, along with Achaemenid kings' sense of their royal duties, thus supported prosocial activity; a trend consistent with the notion that the Achaemenid period represents a typical moment of axial transformation.

As noted above, there were significant continuities in political ideals and institutions from the Achaemenid period until the arrival of the Islamic conquerors, although Zoroastrian principles became more formalized and integrated into administrative institutions under the Sasanians. The rulers of the Seleucid, Parthian, and Sasanian Empires continued to look after the well-being of their diverse population, supporting the temples and rites of a variety of faiths. Festivals were held, *qanats* were maintained and new ones built, and goods were collected in state storehouses for alimentary support (Aperghis 2004; Boyce 1983b; Mahmoudian and Mahmoudian 2012; Raschke 1976). A new office entitled "protector of the poor and judge" was instituted in the sixth century by the Sasanians, influenced by prosocial tendencies within Christianity and Zoroastrianism (Daryaee 2012b: 197). The office was meant to ensure the well-being of the people, supporting Zoroastrian temples and distributing alms to the poor and aid to the sick and infirm (Ragab 2015). Islam likewise is noted for its strong incentives towards prosocial practice, from rulers, elites, and the general population alike; medieval Islamic Iran was certainly no exception (Daryaee 2012a; Katouzian 2009; Yaran 2007).

Interaction and cross-cultural influence in Iran

We have touched above in several places on the role of Persia as an intermediary power, situated amid important connections and conflicts stretching from the Mediterranean littoral in the west to China in the east. Developments on the Iranian Plateau both influenced and were influenced by developments in societies across Afro-Eurasia, including the other typically "axial" regions according to Jaspers and followers: the Levant, Greece, India, and China. Even Egypt, perhaps more self-contained than these other regions for much of its early history, saw a period of Achaemenid occupation in the late first millennium BCE and, before that, interacted with Persian territory in the Levant—both "friendly" interaction in the form of trade and diplomacy and "hostile" interaction in the form of warfare (Briant 2002; Horky 2009).

The Iranian Plateau has thus long been a crossroads for the movement of people, goods, and ideas across Afro-Eurasia. As we describe above, influences from northern South Asia, Mesopotamia, Anatolia, and the Levant played no small role in the development of Persian cultural and political forms, including Zoroastrianism. Iran, in turn, played a key role in later supposedly axial developments in Egypt, Greece, and South Asia (Bellah 2011; Horky 2009). Influences from east and west only intensified with the development of Silk Road trade, encouraged by the Parthian kings, in the late first millennium BCE (Beckwith 2009; Daryaee 2012a; Frankopan 2015; Hansen 2012). The movement of goods and people between Persia and the Mediterranean world in the early first millennium CE remained significant, despite continual hostilities between the Roman Empire and the Parthians and Sasanians. This cultural exchange led to the widespread adoption of a Persian ideology—Mithraism, a cult that grew out of Zoroastrian thought—throughout the Roman world until Christianity became the dominant religion in the empire starting in the fifth century CE (Daryaee 2012a: 5).

Conclusions

During the height of the proposed Axial Age in the mid-first millennium BCE, Egyptian religious ideology, early Judaic thought, and Zoroastrianism as well as a variety of local Anatolian and Mesopotamian religious systems all coexisted in what is today the Sinai Peninsula, Israel-Palestine, Lebanon, Syria, southern Turkey, Iraq, and Iran. It is extremely likely, though difficult to demonstrate unequivocably from the material evidence, that these traditions coevolved in this context of high contact and interaction. In any case, it is clear that the areas and traditions traditionally associated with axiality cannot be considered isolated cases.

Iran, and its native Zoroastrianism, are often neglected in accounts of the Axial Age, relegated to a mention without much explanation or investigation, due largely to problems with sources. Yet, as the above discussions make clear, we are able to uncover much about this important, central region over the course of its long history from the third millennium BCE all the way to the Islamic caliphates and minor dynasties of the early medieval period. Indeed, there is a growing appreciation among regional specialists of the extent to which Persia was the "heir of Elam," inheriting a complex bureaucracy already thousands of years old in south-western Iran (Álvarez-Mon et al. 2011: 8–9; Henkelman 2011: 91). Not only is Achaemenid-era Persia often undervalued, but the vital early innovations of the Elamite states receive very little attention in the scholarship (Michalowski 2005: 158).

This chapter attempts to put Iran back in its rightful place among the important regions throughout Afro-Eurasia that witnessed key cultural, ideological, and political transformations at an early date. Whether it ought to be considered an "axial" region or not is debatable. Certainly, many of the elements associated with axiality—strong moralizing ideologies, claims to egalitarianism, and universal applicability of norms and cosmic justice, along with inducements to prosociality—seem to have been key features of Zoroastrian thought from its conception. Yet these features were also clearly present in the ideologies of Iran, Mesopotamia, and Anatolia from much earlier times, a millennium or two before the traditional Axial Age of 800–200 BCE (see other chapters in this volume for more on these ideologies). Further, the egalitarianism of Zoroastrianism was circumscribed, and the formalization and institutionalization of law often said to characterize the "modernizing" changes brought by axial ideals were absent at least until the Sasanian period. Moreover, Persian ideologies were both influenced by and had a large impact on developments in the other key regions of Afro-Eurasia, belying the idea of autochthonous or independent development that has been a hallmark of work on the Axial Age since Jaspers. In conclusion, then, we assert that Iran played a central role in many of the important innovations that occurred throughout Afro-Eurasia over the course of the first millennium BCE to the first millennium CE and that, whether it is axial or not, it ought to retain a prominent position in any global, cultural history that touches on this period.

CHAPTER 6

SOUTH ASIA | India
Enrico Cioni and Vesna Wallace

Period	Polity	Approx. dates
North-west India		
Neolithic	Aceramic Neolithic	7500–5500 BCE
	Ceramic Neolithic	5500–4000
	Chalcolithic	4000–3200
	Pre-Urban Period	3200–2600
Bronze Age	Indus Valley Civilization	2600–1900
Iron Age	Post-Urban / Proto-Historic Period	1900–550
Archaic	Achaemenid Empire	550–329
	Macedonian Empire	325–303
Classical	Mauryan Empire	303–194
	Greco-Bactrian Kingdom	194–179
	Indo-Greek Kingdom	179–160
	Greco-Bactrian Kingdom	160–145
	Indo-Greek Kingdom	145–95
	Parthian Empire	95 BCE–21 CE
	Indo-Parthian Kingdom	21–81
	Kushans	81–251
	Sasanian Empire	251–496
	Hephthalites	496–532
	Sasanian Empire	532–642
Islamic	Umayyad Caliphate	670–750
	'Abbāsid Caliphate	750–862
	Sind	862–1193
	Ghūrid Sultanate	1166–1207
Medieval	Delhi Sultanate	1207–1340
	Mughal Empire	1523–1740
Southern India: Deccan Plateau		
Neolithic	Neolithic Deccan	3000–1200 BCE
Iron Age	Iron Age Deccan	1200–301
Classical	Mauryan Empire	300–206
	Sātavāhana Empire	100 BCE–203 CE
	Vākāṭaka Empire	286–335
	Early Pallava Empire	335–350

Period	Polity	Approx. dates
Late Antique	Kadamba Empire	451–540
	Cālukya Empire	541–642
	Late Pallava Empire	643–675
	Cālukya Empire	675–752
	Rāṣṭrakūṭa Empire	753–973
	Cālukya Empire	974–1155
	Kalacurī Empire	1155–1185
	Cālukya Empire	1185–1190
Medieval	Hoysala Empire	1192–1280
	Seuna Empire	1254–1270
	Kampili Kingdom	1280–1327
	Delhi Sultanate	1327–1336
	Vijayanagara Empire	1337–1646
	Mughal Empire	1687–1720
North-eastern India: Ganges Plain		
Neolithic	Neolithic Ganges	7000–3000 BCE
	Chalcolithic Ganges	3000–600
Iron Age	Mahājanapada Era	600–300
Classical	Mauryan Empire	300–200
	Śuṅga Empire	200–100
	Ayodhya Kingdoms	100 BCE–100 CE
	Kushans	100–200
	Ayodhya Kingdoms	200–319
	Gupta Kingdom	320–514
	Hephthalites	515–550
Late Antique	Magadha	550–606
	Empire of Harṣa	606–550
	Kanauj	650–547
	Rāṣṭrakūṭa Empire	780–810
	Gurjar	810–1030
	Chandela Empire	1030–1090
	Gahadavala	1090–1202
Medieval	Delhi Sultanate	1203–1526
	Jaunpur Sultanate	1394–1478
	Mughal Empire	1526–1803

Table 4. Periods and dates of polities that were based in or that occupied South Asia

Introduction

Jaspers (1953) included "India" as one of the five core regions that saw the more or less independent emergence of ideologies that could be described as moralistic, egalitarian, universalizing and critical of existing power structures. In other words, Jaspers argued that India contributed as much to the Axial Age as did Greece, the Levant, Iran and China (Jaspers 1953: 2). The aim of this chapter is to examine India's place within Axial Age theory.

As with other chapters in this volume, we start with a general summary of the region's history from about the middle of the third millennium BCE to the beginning of the second millennium CE: that is, from the emergence of the Harappan Civilization in the Indus Valley to the arrival of Islam. Unlike other chapters (e.g. the Iran chapter, centered on the Susiana region), we have not opted to anchor ourselves to a circumscribed region of the subcontinent, as, due to its sheer size, it would have been reductive to do so. Indeed, as we will show, at different moments in time, complex societies arose in different regions (most notably, the Indus Valley to the north-west, the Gangetic Plain to the north and the Deccan to the south). Privileging one over the others would result in a skewed reconstruction of South Asian history, especially as only a small number of polities were able to rule over a majority of the subcontinent in the period under consideration. As a consequence of this choice, however, we have also been unable to provide as much detail on many of these polities as they deserve: faced with the need to summarize more than three millennia of history spread across more than 3 million square kilometers, it seemed most economical to focus on the rise of the main indigenous religions of South Asia and of the largest and most powerful polities, hinting at developments that occurred outside of the Brāhmaṇic and śramaṇic traditions, such as Jainism and Buddhism, only when necessary.

The historical summary is followed by a section discussing shifting ideological perceptions of rule: we start by reviewing scholarly theories about the nature of power among the Harappans, then move on to the emergence of divine or divinely sanctioned kingship and attempts to critique or curb the ruler's power from within Hinduism, Jainism, Buddhism and in Kautilya's seminal treatise, the *Arthaśāstra* (which was most likely composed sometime during the Mauryan period[1]). We will then look at the development of moralistic, egalitarian and universalizing thought, showing that the way this took place in South Asia does broadly correspond to the basic predictions of the Axial Age theory, some important nuances notwithstanding. Finally, we will provide a broad outline of cross-cultural interactions and influences between India and other parts of the Old World (Europe, Africa, and the rest of Asia) in the period under consideration, with the aim of illuminating the connections

---

1   Patrick Ollivele (2013: 29), however, argues that as a recension of different earlier treatises, the Arthaśāstra was composed sometime between 50 and 125 CE.

between the subcontinent and the other Axial Age regions, but also in order to provide a glimpse of the ripple effects of ideological developments in India with regards to the rest of the world, and vice versa.

Historical background

Around 2600 BCE, the Indus Valley, in the north-western corner of South Asia, on the modern-day border between India and Pakistan, witnessed the emergence of one of the world's earliest complex societies, popularly known as Indus Valley Civilization. This society, also known as the Harappan Civilization, emerged later than comparably complex societies in Mesopotamia, the Nile Valley of Egypt and the Middle Yellow River Valley in northern China, and it did not last as long; it came to an end around 1900 BCE, long before the rise of Hammurabi of Babylon in Mesopotamia (1792–50 BCE), the establishment of the Shang Dynasty in China (1650–1045 BCE) and the splendors of the Egyptian New Kingdom (1570–1069 BCE; see other chapters in this volume). However, the Indus Valley Civilization also covered a much wider area, at over a million square kilometers. This included 544,000 km2 of cultivable terrain, against about half that number in Mesopotamia and 33,657 km2 in Egypt (Maisels 1999: 253). Moreover, Harappan Civilization left behind evidence for many of the same markers of social complexity as its predecessors and contemporaries in the rest of the Old World: most notably, cities (the largest, Mohenjo-daro, likely exceeded 250 hectares, with a population of around 100,000 inhabitants), a well-developed bureaucracy (as suggested by inscribed material such as seals, copper tablets and stone bangles) and writing (which remains undeciphered). Overall, however, the Indus Valley Civilization remains relatively enigmatic, partly because it was only rediscovered in the 1920s (McIntosh 2008).

In particular, it is worth dwelling on the fact that, despite the aforementioned evidence for bureaucratic administration, the overall political organization of the Indus Valley Civilization is still unknown. It is possible that the valley never merged into a single, unified political unit. It is also far from clear how individual sites were governed, as they do not feature anything that can be recognized as typical evidence for the existence of a ruling elite; there are no clearly identifiable palaces, wealthy burials, luxury artefacts, monumental inscriptions or any form of iconographic propaganda. This is perhaps the most remarkable difference between the Harappan Civilization and comparable societies in Mesopotamia, Egypt and China, and indeed the only other highly complex society that is yet to yield any clear and explicit evidence for the existence of a ruling elite is the Niger Inland Delta Civilization, which flourished in the latter half of the first millennium CE in modern-day Mali (McIntosh 2005; see the chapter on the Inland Niger Delta in this volume). Possehl (2002: 57) posits that the Harappans felt a "marked distrust in [...] strong, centralized government," which leads him to speculate that the Indus peoples were governed by a heterarchy of councils, that is, councils that were not ranked, but had overlapping and/or equally important duties and responsibilities. Alternatively, McIntosh (2008: 392–93) suggests that they were governed by a theocracy of priests, citing, among other things, the fact that sites like Mohenjo-daro include monumental structures that have been interpeted as fulfilling a religious function.

It also remains unclear why the Indus Valley Civilization collapsed around 1900 BCE. No strong evidence has yet been found of warfare at any point in its long history. Most likely, the decline of the Indus Valley Civilization was due to several different environmental factors, combined with the population's overall worsening health, possibly due to cholera outbreaks and/or endemic malaria (McIntosh 2008: 392–400). Eventually, major sites were abandoned, and the disappearance of weights, writing and standardized architecture points to the disappearance of bureaucratic administration as well. Most recently, Green and Petrie (2018) have demonstrated that, following 1900 BCE, the density of settlements across the alluvial plain of north-western India increased, suggesting that the people who left the Harappan cities subsequently established new, small-scale settlements in this region, or even, in some cases, reoccupied sites that had been abandoned around the time of the Harappan cities' rise. This demographic shift likely both contributed to and resulted from the process of de-urbanization that has been interpreted as the key symptom of Harappan collapse. Petrie et al. (2017) suggest that changes in the monsoon cycle led to the increased reliability of rainfall in this north-western region and decreased reliability of rainfall in the Harappan heartland.

Meanwhile, farther south, the subcontinent was transitioning from the Neolithic period (2700–1200 BCE) to the Iron Age (1200–300 BCE). Neolithic communities appear to have been small, egalitarian (as suggested by only minor variations in house size, design and content, as well as in mortuary practices) and reliant on pastoralism (mostly cattle), agriculture (mostly millet and pulses) and hunting and gathering. The prevalence of cattle motifs in rock art, as well as the number of ashmounds (large mounds of burned cattle dung) dotting the landscape, points to the symbolic importance of cattle in south Indian Neolithic ideology as a whole (Johansen 2014: 62–65). Iron Age residents in the south also largely relied on agriculture and pastoralism, but ashmounds ceased to be the most prominent expression of the dominant ideology, and were replaced by megalithic structures (which, as Johansen [2014] has observed, were nevertheless often built near ashmounds, suggesting some continuity in people's relationship to the landscape). These structures have been found all across the modern-day Indian states of Maharashtra, Karnataka, Andhra Pradesh, Kerala and Tamil Nadu (Brubaker 2000–2001). Differences in the scale, design and materials of mortuary megalithic structures and associated grave goods point to the growing hierarchization of south Indian societies at this time (Johansen 2014: 65). However, there was some variation in terms of the sociopolitical organization of individual communities; for example, it is likely that some chiefs with limited decision-making powers ruled over single settlements; that more powerful leaders based in large centers exerted some control over surrounding settlements; and that some polities were made up of several settlements ruled by a hierarchy of leaders who answered to a single paramount chief. The first type of polity probably prevailed at the beginning of the Iron Age, while the second and third type likely became more common towards its end (Brubaker 2001–2002: 287–91).

Back in the north, as we have seen, the Indus Valley ceased to be the center of complex development in South Asia. From the sixth century BCE onward, and with only one notable exception (the Mauryan Empire), north-west India largely fell within the orbit of Central Asian empires, whose rulers were based well outside the subcontinent. Indigenous Indian societies whose complexity was comparable to the Harappan cities next emerged in the Ganges Valley. Indeed, in the nineteenth and early twentieth centuries, when the Harappan Civilization was even more nebulously understood than it is today, most scholars believed that it was along the Ganges that complexity first emerged in India, following invasion by the "Āryan" people, to whom the introduction of the Vedas (a body of religious texts, originally transmitted orally) and Vedic ritual tradition into the subcontinent is mostly ascribed. "Āryan," of course, has become a rather fraught term, with very specific associations that have very little to do with South Asian history and culture. Moreover, beginning in the latter half of the twentieth century, much doubt has been cast on the Āryans' true identity and origins, and on whether they were even a distinct, non-Indian people (Thapar 1971).

Indeed, though the adjective *ārya* appears throughout the Brāhmaṇic literature, it is never clearly and explicitly meant as an ethnic label. Even allowing for the fact that the original meaning of the word *ārya* is hard to pin down, most likely it simply meant something like "pure," "moral," "respectable," "noble," or "wealthy" (Keay 2013: 20). The idea of an Āryan "race" derived from European scholars of linguistics—for example, English polymath Sir William Jones—who noticed commonalities between Sanskrit, Persian and several European languages. This observation led other scholars, for example the Oxford professor of Sanskrit Friedrich Max Müller (1867), to hypothesize that there once was a nomadic race who brought their language to India, Europe and Persia through invasion. European scholars called this race "Āryan" from the Persian word *ārya*, which, unlike the Sanskrit term, was indeed an ethnic label (and the origin of the name Iran). The idea soon emerged that Āryan culture had obliterated preceding indigenous cultures due to its superiority; in some reconstructions, the Āryans were tall, fair and refined, while the indigenous peoples they subdued were short, dark and primitive. British colonialists began to see parallels between their own endeavors in India and the Āryan invasions; to them, both were comparably laudable attempts at bringing higher civilization to a benighted land.

However, in the 1930s, it became clear that the Harappan Civilization, and therefore the emergence of social complexity in the subcontinent, had preceded any Āryan invasion. Moreover, Nazi appropriation of "Āryan heritage" on the one side and the reclamations of Indian nationalists on the other have cast further shade on the theory (Keay 2013: 22). Sir Mortimer Wheeler (1947), who at the time was one of the world's pre-eminent experts in prehistoric India, proposed that the agricultural Harappan Civilization had collapsed precisely *because* of the Āryan invasions, but the evidence he adduced to bolster this theory (including skeletal remains he interpreted as bearing traces of warfare-related trauma) has since been shown to be inconclusive (Dales 1964). Nowadays, many (though not all) scholars agree that traditional theories surrounding the Āryans were based on tenuous assumptions and racist, imperialistic ideologies (Keay 2013: 19, 22).

The overall consensus now is that social complexity emerged gradually along the Ganges, developing from a combination of indigenous and foreign influences. It is likely that, in the first half of the second millennium BCE, Sanskrit-speaking, cattle-herding peoples from Central Asia settled the Punjab region, and from there spread throughout northern India, probably through multiple waves of migration that took place across several centuries. Between 1500 and 500 BCE, these migrating peoples both introduced new technologies and domesticates, including the horse and the war chariot, and adopted agricultural techniques via interaction with indigenous populations. They also founded polities, enforced their borders, built cities, established trade relations and waged war against their neighbors. We know about all these developments from the aforementioned sacred texts, but, unfortunately, these texts do not clarify the exact processes through which these developments came about. Nor do they shed much light on the emergence of two of the more influential aspects of these Sanskrit-speaking, cattle-herding cultures: a strict social hierarchy in which different groups are divided into hereditary "castes" with little possibility for intermarriage, and the dominance of the priestly caste, known as *brāhmaṇas* (Keay 2013: 28–29).

By the seventh century BCE, northern India—more specifically, the regions in and to the east of the Middle Ganges Basin—was divided into sixteen polities, known today as the Mahājanapadas. These were characterized by fortified urban settlements, the use of indigenous coins, Brāhmī writing and a distinctive pottery type known as Northern Black Polished Ware. The balance of power shifted frequently from one Mahājanapada to the next; Kosala and Magadha often vied for absolute dominance over the region. Of the lesser Mahājanapadas, Vajji is notable for its republican form of government, with annual general assemblies in which representatives of the polity's major clans elected political officials, who would form a small council headed by a chief. The other Mahājanapadas were monarchies (Chakrabarti 2000). In the fifth century BCE, Magadha finally established itself as the largest and most powerful polity in the region and, under the leadership of Mahāpadma Nanda, it extended its rule across the whole of the Ganges Delta, reaching into the Kaliṅga Kingdom on the subcontinent's north-east coast (Stein 1998: 75). However, the Nanda Dynasty survived only a few decades, due partly to external pressures resulting from Alexander the Great's incursions into northern India between 326 and 324 BCE, and partly, though less clearly, to the rise of Candragupta Maurya, founder of the Mauryan Empire (see below).

Our main sources of information about the Mahājanapadas are Buddhist and Jain writings produced between 600 and 200 BCE. Buddhism and Jainism developed alongside other "śramaṇic" traditions—a term derived from the Sanskrit śramaṇa, meaning "who exerts himself" or wandering ascetic—which rejected the authority of the Vedas, denied the efficacy of sacrificial ritual practices and criticized the Brāhmaṇic caste system that conferred prestige and power on the caste of brāhmaṇas. Around the sixth and fifth centuries BCE, both traditions spread relatively rapidly across the Mahājanapadas, especially in the region of Magadha (now Bihar) and Bengal. Notably, the prevalence in this period of śramaṇa or beggars (bhikkhu) who subsisted on laypeople's alms was only possible in a society with enough surplus wealth to distribute as alms. This prosperity was grounded in the rise of a merchant class and increasing class differentiation based on economic prosperity and property ownership. Personal liberation through asceticism (which involved cutting the roots of attachment through renunciation of possessions and mundane concerns); the notions of reincarnation and karma, implying personal responsibility for one's experiences in this and future lives; the emphasis on the eradication of ignorance; and the use of vernacular languages to spread teachings challenged the belief in the efficacy of sacrificial ritual; the exclusive ritual authority of brāhmaṇas; and the view that the lower castes were inherently polluted and spiritually inept while the higher castes were inherently pure and attuned to spiritual matters.

However, it was only with the emergence of the Mauryan Empire, founded in 320 BCE by the Nanda general Candragupta Maurya, that Buddhism spread throughout South Asia and to some parts of Central Asia. Mauryan emperor Aśoka (268–32 BCE), a patron of Buddhism, sent both dhamma-mahāmātras ("ministers of Dharma") to spread Buddhist teachings (Dharma) across his own lands and Buddhist missionaries (his son included) to Śrī Laṅkā in the south and the Macedonian Empire's successor states to the north-west. Most famously, Aśoka commissioned the erection of large pillars along the major trade routes his empire encompassed, encouraging his subjects to follow Buddhist ethical principles. If we were to calculate the extent of the Mauryan Empire based on the location of the outermost of Aśoka's pillars, then it covered over 4.5 million square kilometers, from eastern Afghanistan to the Deccan Plateau, from the Arabian Sea to the Bay of Bengal. However, the empire was more likely made up of five core regions (the eastern Gangetic Plain, the Hindu

Kush foothills, the Malwa plateau, the north-east coast of India and the western portion of the Deccan Plateau) separated by large, autonomous territories. Each core region may have been governed by a relative or vassal of the emperor. However, it should be also said that, overall, the Mauryan system of governance remains poorly understood. Until relatively recently, it was thought that the treatise of statecraft known as the *Arthaśāstra*, which was composed by one of Candragupta Maurya's advisors, provided a detailed description of Mauryan administration (which, it seemed, relied on an elaborate hierarchy of ministers and a vast network of spies and secret agents), but many now believe that the text more accurately describes the succeeding Magadha-Nanda administrative system.

The Mauryan Empire went into rapid decline after Aśoka's death in 232 BCE, eventually shrinking back to its core northern region. The last of its rulers, Bṛhadratha, was assassinated in 187 BCE by his military commander, Puṣyamitra, who went on to found a new dynasty, the Śuṅgas. The Śuṅgas briefly ruled over what remained of the Mauryas' territory. Relatively little is known about them or indeed any of the polities that emerged shortly after the fragmentation of the Mauryan Empire.

As previously mentioned, the north-west had been invaded by Alexander the Great around the same time as the Mauryan Empire was founded in the northeast, and for much of the second century BCE it was home to a succession of small polities ruled by an ethnic Greek minority. Of these, the so-called "Indo-Greek" kingdoms are known almost exclusively from their coinage and therefore rather poorly understood, but, farther to the west, the remains of the city Ai Khanoum, of the Greco-Bactrian kingdom (in modern-day Afghanistan), suggest a certain degree of continuity with their culture of origin (particularly through the presence of a theatre, a gymnasium and Greek-style statuary). At the same time, however, cultural intermingling likely also occurred, and there is no indication that indigenous beliefs were obliterated (Docherty 2008; Mairs 2015).

The next extensive empire to appear in South Asia arose around 100 BCE. Unlike the Mauryas, the Sātavāhanas were based in the south, specifically in the Deccan Plateau. Although they covered a smaller area, they ruled over a significant portion of both the southern and northern subcontinent and touched both eastern and western coasts. According to the most widely accepted hypothesis, based on numismatic, archaeological and textual evidence, this polity lasted until the end of the second century CE, though many scholars are reluctant to assign absolute dates to specific kings. It also seems likely that the empire experienced a period of increased regionalization and decreased centralization—maybe even temporary collapse—in its middle century (Sinopoli 2001: 166). Notable Sātavāhana rulers include Gautamiputra Śatakarani, Vasiṣṭhiputra Pulumavi and Yajñaśrī; under their governance, South Asian commerce with Southeast Asia intensified (Stein 1998: 92) and there was a florescence of the arts, particularly in the field of Buddhist iconography (Murthy and Ramakrishnan 1978: 25–26).

Meanwhile, to the north, the subcontinent experienced successive invasions of several different Central Asian peoples, culminating with the Kushans. Between 115 and 140 CE, the Kushans' best-known ruler, Kaniṣka, conquered and governed an area that rivaled the size of Aśoka's empire, stretching from eastern Afghanistan to the eastern Gangetic Plain, and reaching as far south as the Saurāṣṭra Peninsula in the Gujarat region. The Kushan Empire benefited from its strategic position between the South Asian and Mediterranean worlds, which allowed it to profit from levies on land and sea trade routes that ran through its domains. In the matter of religion, though the Kushans funded the construction and maintenance of many Buddhist monasteries, and though Buddhist lore places Kaniṣka alongside Aśoka as one of the religion's first great benefactors, Kushan coins included depictions and dedications of Greek, "Hindu," and Persian deities (Stein 1998: 91). Some time between the third and fourth centuries CE, the Kushans would eventually succumb to the Sasanian rulers of Persia, who would therefore also take control of a small portion of the Kushans' domains in north-west India.

Farther south, the fall of the Sātavāhanas (which remains poorly understood) was followed by the rise of two new empires. The polity ruled by the Vākāṭaka Dynasty lasted from about 250 to 550 CE and mostly covered the central South Asian region of Vidarbha, while that ruled by the Guptas, which eventually came to cover most of the subcontinent's northern portion, emerged around 320 CE and lasted two centuries, until about 515 CE. The two dynasties never went to war against each other; instead, they contracted a marriage alliance late in the fourth century CE. The period of Vākāṭaka-Gupta rule is considered a "golden age" of Indian history. Following the two empires' initial phase of expansion, the subcontinent entered a period of relative peace and stability, the only wars mostly taking place on the north-west borders with the Kushans. The Chinese monk Faxian, who visited the Gupta Empire around 400 CE, remarked that there appeared to be no crime or violence and that no groups appeared to be oppressed, with the one exception of the outcastes (caṇḍālas), who were universally shunned because they were responsible for disposing of the dead. Trade flourished, both within and beyond South Asia. In the arts, painting reached great heights (most notably with the Ajanta frescoes, which depict opulent courtly scenes); a style of sculpture emerged that would be as influential on South Asian art in the following centuries as Hellenistic sculpture was in Europe; and one of the great Sanskrit playwrights and poets, Kalidāsa, was most likely also active at this time. In the sciences, the length of the solar year was calculated with a precision that was as yet unprecedented in the ancient world, the value of pi was correctly calculated to four decimal places and a number of medical and astronomical treaties were produced (Keay 2013: 145–54).

In terms of religion, the Vākāṭaka-Gupta period saw the beginning of Buddhism's decline and the rise of Hinduism (understood as a revival and adaptation of earlier Brāhmaṇic ideology). Both religions received royal patronage under both dynasties, although the Vākāṭakas were officially devotees of the Hindu god Śiva (Śaivas) and the Guptas of Viṣṇu (Vaiṣṇavas). Moreover, the Gupta period was marked by the establishment of great Buddhist monastic and educational centers, one of which— Nālandā—became an internationally renowned monastic university and a city in its own right. However, Faxian noted that both the Buddha's birthplace and Aśoka's palace were neglected, the former looking "like a great desert" and the latter in ruins. He also noted that Buddhist monasteries were commonly located outside cities, while Brāhmaṇic educational establishments could be usually found within them, and close to the court (Keay 2013: 146).

Indeed, it is also worth noting that, of the two religions, it was Hinduism that witnessed the more important shift in its evolution in this period, with the composition of some of the Purāṇas, a set of eighteen scriptures that discuss the creation, history and dissolution of the world of South Asia and its dynasties, as well as instructions regarding the proper way of living one's life and performing rituals. While each Purāṇa is dedicated to a different Hindu deity, they collectively expressed the idea that all deities are ultimately manifestations of the supreme deity Brahman. Purāṇic teachings had been transmitted orally for generations prior to being written down and codified (Shattuck 2002: 41–44).

The fact that, under the Guptas, many Jains migrated from the city of Mathura and its environs to Vallabhi on the Saurāṣṭra Peninsula, which at the time was part of the kingdom of the Maitraka Dynasty, might perhaps be seen as indicating that they suffered some form of persecution or discrimination. Indeed, the Purāṇas describe the archetypal heretic as an amalgam of the Buddhist monk and the Jain ascetic. However, according to Dundas (2002: 115), the migrating Jains were simply responding to the external and internal political pressures on the Gupta state that would eventually lead to its collapse.

Both the Gupta and the Vākāṭaka dynasties disintegrated in the sixth century CE. Both were weakened by tensions over succession, and the Guptas also faced repeated invasions by the Hephthalites, a nomadic group belonging to a wider tribal confederation known as the "White Huns." Indeed, for a few decades following the fall of the Guptas, the Hephthalites nominally ruled over much of what had previously been Gupta territory (Bauer 2010: 182). By contrast, the Vākāṭakas, possibly after a few decades of regionalization, were succeeded by another Indian dynasty, the Cālukyas or Western Cālukyas.

The Cālukyas started out as vassals of the Vākāṭakas' southern neighbours, the Kadambas, but they rebelled in the early sixth century CE, taking over much of the Kadambas' territory and founding a new capital at Badami (modern-day Vātāpi) in

543 CE. Eventually, their empire grew to encompass much of central and southern South Asia, much of it conquered under Pulakeśin II in the first half of the seventh century CE. Though Vātāpi is a small town today, it may have reached a population of as many as 70,000 in its heyday. The Cālukyas' only true rivals were the Pallavas, who ruled the south-east, and whose influence ranged far from the subcontinent itself, as they established trade connections with China, intervened in dynastic disputes in Śrī Laṅkā and may have played an important role in the spread of Hinduism and South Asian culture generally across Southeast Asia, from the Mekong Basin to Java (Keay 2013: 176–77).

Under Pulakeśin II, the Cālukyas also managed to drive back the great empire ruled by Harṣavardhana (also called Harṣa, r. 606–47 CE), which covered most of north India. Harṣa's empire is particularly well documented thanks to the writings of his court poet Bāṇabhaṭṭa and a Buddhist pilgrim from China, Xuanzang, who stayed at Harṣa's court and travelled across his lands for 15 years in the seventh century. Although the influence of Buddhism had been waning in India, it experienced a revival of sorts under Harṣa, who later became a great patron of the religion. Most notably, he convened a grand assembly at Kanauj to propagate the teachings of Mahāyāna forms of Buddhism. Several monarchs from neighboring states and thousands of priests from a number of different Buddhist sects attended. However, the assembly ended in disaster: a huge monument to the Buddha that Harṣa had commissioned for the occasion was set on fire and both Xuanzang and Harṣa were almost assassinated. In response, Harṣa ordered the arrest and exile (and in a few cases, the execution) of 500 *brāhmaṇas* (Sharma 2007: 262–63). The fact that Harṣa failed to turn around the fortunes of Buddhism in his lands suggests that the decline of the religion in the region could not be reversed. According to Schmidt (2015: 28), it appears that Harṣa's charisma and authority was the only thing keeping his empire together, since it fell apart almost immediately after his death. It is notable that he was the last indigenous ruler to build a large empire in north-west India; all subsequent large empires in the region were founded by foreign dynasties from Central Asia or Europe (28).

Back in the south, the Cālukyas held on to power for over a century after their conflict with Harṣa in 633. When they finally lost their empire in the mid-eighth century CE, it was to their own feudal subordinates, the Rāṣṭrakūṭas, who would go on to rule almost until the end of the tenth century CE. The Rāṣṭrakūṭas rapidly became the undisputed rulers of the Deccan Plateau, and organized several successful expeditions in northern India. Though these expeditions resulted in important territorial gains, these never lasted more than a few years. Indeed, it seems that their main aim was not to extend Raṣṭrakūṭa rule, but to advertise its might (Basavaraja 1984: 62–83). Under the long and peaceful reign of Amoghavarṣa I (814–78 CE), also known as Nṛpatuṅga, literature and the arts flourished, and the capital of Malkhed was built (Madan 1990: 120–22). Malkhed may have had a population of as many as 100,000 (Chase-Dunn 2001, pers. comm.), but accurate estimates are made difficult by the fact that much of it was destroyed by Chola armies in the tenth century CE, and what was left was subsequently destroyed by the armies of the Delhi Sultanate and the Mughals. Today, the Rāṣṭrakūṭa capital is little more than a village. Moreover, what little information exists about the city's heyday appears to be strongly influenced by Jain tradition, which may be biased, as Malkhed used to be a major centre for the religion (Mishra 1992: 208). The Rāṣṭrakūṭa Empire collapsed around 973 CE when, weakened by a Pallava raid and an ineffectual king, it was unable to quash the rebellion of one of its feudatories, Tailapa II Cālukya, who happened to be a descendant of the Rāṣṭrakūṭas' former overlords, and who took Malkhed (Basavaraja 1984: 82–83). Subsequently, a number of other feudatories declared independence from Rastrakūṭa rule, but the newly re-established Cālukya Dynasty managed to bring them under control.

Meanwhile, in 750, the Pāla Dynasty of Bengal, whose kings followed Mahāyāna and Vajrayāna Buddhism, established the other large South Asian Buddhist empire of the "Classical" era, which eventually came to encompass most of the subcontinent's north-east (including modern Bangladesh, Nepal and part of Pakistan). The founder of the Pāla Dynasty, Gopala, was the first ruler to come to power through democratic election since the time of the Mahājanapadas. Pāla kings, who were great supporters of Buddhism and Buddhist art, built large monasteries and temples and financed large Buddhist monastic universities such as Nālandā and Vikramaśīla. In the eighth century, Dharmapāla built Somapura Mahāvihāra, the largest Buddhist temple in the subcontinent at that time. The Pālas were skilled diplomats and military strategists who developed trade with West Asia. After the empire's power considerably weakened in the eleventh century, they were replaced by the Sena Dynasty, who supported Hinduism.

To the south, the Cālukyas, now ruling from the city of Kalyani in what is now West Bengal, held power over much of the subcontinent. The new Cālukya Empire covered a similarly large area to the Rāṣṭrakūṭa polity and the previous Cālukya Empire; it probably reached its peak during the reign of Vikramāditya VI (1076–1126 CE), during which its borders expanded, its capital grew (possibly reaching a population of 125,000), and its scholarship flourished. Most notably, the jurist Vijñāneśvara wrote the *Mitākṣara*, a commentary on the Hindu text titled the *Yājñavalkyasmṛti*, which became an influential legal treatise in the development of Hindu law. Toward the end of the twelfth century CE, the throne was seized by Bijjala II Kalacurī, and he and his few successors managed to rule their former overlords' empire for about twenty years. Under the Kalacuris' brief reign, India witnessed the emergence of Vīraśaivism, a Śiva-worshiping branch of Hinduism that rejected all hierarchy and promoted the idea that one did not need *brāhmaṇa* priests to mediate one's relationship with Śiva, but that one should cultivate a personal, direct relationship with him. This would have significant consequences in the history of Hinduism (Schouten 1995: 2–5). It may also mark the beginning of the (admittedly slow) decline of Jainism's fortunes in southern South Asia, specifically the Karṇaṭaka region, as hagiographies of the founder of Vīraśaivism, Basava (1106–67), portray Jains as tricksters and sorcerers whose attempts at leading Śiva worshipers from a righteous path were punished through bloody massacres (Dundas 2002: 128–29).

When the Cālukyas managed to retake the throne, they were unable to hold on to it for long, as, only a few years later, they were once again usurped, this time definitively, by the Hoysalas. At around a similar time as the Hoysalas' rise to power in southern South Asia, the Delhi Sultanate established itself in the north of the subcontinent. Muḥammad Quṭb-al-Dīn, who ruled over the city of Delhi and its environs on behalf of the Ghūrid Dynasty (itself based in modern-day Afghanistan), rebelled and declared his independence from his overlords in 1206 (Wolpert 1997: 110, 212). His son and successor managed to obtain official recognition of his polity's sovereignty by a representative of the ʿAbbāsid Caliphate of Baghdad (Kulke 1990: 157). The Delhi Sultanate lasted over 300 years and was ruled by five consecutive Turko-Afghan dynasties: the Mamluks, the Khaljis, the Tughlaqs, the Sayyids and the Lodis. Most notably, by directly ruling such an important centre as Delhi over several centuries, the sultanate firmly established both Islam and the use of Persian as the language of administration in the northern subcontintent (Habib 2004: 37–44).

The Delhi Sultanate rapidly expanded between the thirteenth and fourteenth centuries, reaching far into the south of the subcontinent by c. 1300 CE. The Hoysalas and lesser southern rulers (including the Kampilis and the Seunas) were unable to resist the sultanate's advance. However, though the Delhi Sultanate was able to easily conquer new territory thanks to its large, well-managed standing army, it lacked a strong, centralized administrative system: only Delhi and its environs were directly governed by the sultan, while the rest of the empire was largely left in the hands of local (Hindu) rulers and landowners (Habib 2004: 37–44). Asher and Talbot (2002: 33) observe that conventional maps showing the extent of the sultanate's dominions are deceptive; they depict solid blocks of land, which suggest that the sultan uniformly held sway throughout his territories, when in fact most of the sultanate's power outside of Delhi's environs was concentrated in fortified garrison towns that did not necessarily manage to successfully assert dominance over the surrounding countryside. Indeed, it proved too challenging for the sultanate to maintain control over the south of the subcontinent, and within only a few years a new dominant power emerged in the south and repelled the invaders from Delhi: the kingdom of Vijayanagara, the last large, long-lasting Hindu-ruled polity to appear in India before the advent of the Mughal Empire.

Religion and rulership

As already noted, very little is known about rulership among the Harappans. Indeed, archaeologists are yet to unearth clear evidence for the very existence of any kind of elite, be it secular, religious or both. Scholars have therefore advanced a broad range of hypotheses regarding Harappan political organization. One of these hypotheses is that the dominant ideology at the time was founded on egalitarian principles (e.g. Maisels 1999); indeed, one scholar has suggested that Harappa may have been the first democracy (Naqvi 1993). However, it is also possible that elites, and by extension rulers, did exist, but expressed their power in different ways from what one would expect based on how power was expressed in similarly complex societies. For example, McIntosh (2008: 269–71) speculates that the populations of cities like Mohenjo-daro were organized into an early version of the caste system and governed by a priestly caste that drew its authority precisely from the fact that it kept itself strictly segregated from the rest of the population. Noting that, in addition to all this, transgressors may have also been threatened with divine punishment, McIntosh (269–71) suggests that this may have been a strong enough organizing principle that law and order could be maintained without explicit demonstrations of power on the part of this ruling caste. Alternatively, Possehl (2002: 57, 153) points out that it is also plausible that Harappan cities were ruled by "councils" or gatherings of leaders; based on his sense that Harappans had a "marked distrust in government, per se, especially strong, centralized government," Possehl suggests that there may have been a council for each individual settlement, one for each region, and perhaps an overall supreme council. As already noted, however, all this remains speculative. Generally speaking, the fact that none of the conventional hallmarks of ancient rulership appear in any of the Indus Valley sites does suggest that they were most likely not ruled by the self-aggrandizing, authoritarian god-kings that are traditionally associated with "archaic" forms of rule (as discussed throughout this volume).

There can be no doubt, however, that divinely sanctioned kingship first emerged in India during the Vedic period (c. 1500–500 BCE). The god Indra, depicted as the king of heavens (*svarga*) and gods (*deva*), was extolled in the Ṛg Veda (the first of the four Vedas) for his might and courage, displayed in killing the demon Vṛtra and saving all living things on the earth. A similar story regarding the origins of kingship as an institution is told in the *Aitareya Brāhmaṇa* (a Vedic ritual treatise from the eighth or seventh century BCE), according to which the gods were able to gain the upper hand and win their war against an army of demons only by appointing someone to lead them into battle, namely Indra. In a later variant of this myth, the gods do not appoint a king themselves, but perform a sacrifice to the high god Prajāpati, who sends his son Indra to lead them. Indeed, it soon became traditional to ascribe some degree of divinity to kings, and Brāhmaṇic texts describe a number of rituals meant to imbue the king with divine power. Most notably, the *rājasūya*, or royal consecration, consisted of a year's worth of sacrifices and ceremonies through which the new king was identified first as Indra himself, then as Prajāpati, then as the god Viṣṇu; at the ceremony's conclusion, the chief priest addressed the gods thus: "Of mighty power is he who has been consecrated; now he has become one of yours; you must protect him." Throughout a king's reign, his divine power was routinely restored through lesser rituals, such as the *vajapeya* (a rejuvenation ceremony), the *aśvamedha* (a horse sacrifice) and the *puruṣamedha* (a human sacrifice, though it is up for debate whether this was real or symbolic[2]). The notion that kingship was in some way divine or at least divinely sanctioned persisted throughout Indian history. In the fourth and fifth centuries CE, Gupta monarchs claimed an association with Viṣṇu in inscriptions and coins, indicating that their authority to rule over their domain came directly from the god himself (McKnight 1977). In the eighth and ninth centuries, the Rāṣṭrakūṭas assumed the title *pṛthvī-vallabha*, where *vallabha* meant "husband," and *pṛthvī* referred to both "the earth" and to the earth goddess who was one of Viṣṇu's consorts. In other words, the Rāṣṭrakūṭas claimed that they were lords of the earth and an emanation of Viṣṇu himself (Keay 2013: 191). In the eleventh century, rulers of the Chola Dynasty were worshiped as gods in temples (Basham 1967: 86). Divine kingship (including the notion of the *cakravartin*, or "universal emperor") became an integral part of Hindu, Jain and Buddhist world views, which spread beyond the borders of the Indian subcontinent to Southeast Asia, China, Tibet and Mongolia (see other contributions to this volume). For example, in the Mekong Basin, Jayavarman II, founder of the Khmer Empire, declared himself "universal emperor" in 802 CE (Legendre de Koninck 2004: 149), while on Java, Airlangga, who ruled in the eleventh century, was the first Javanese monarch to be given the title *ratu cakravartin* in epigraphic references (Hall 1993: 211). In Buddhist Mahāyāna scriptures, for example, the *Golden Light Sūtra* (*Suvarṇaprabhāsottama Mahāyāna Sūtra*), the god Brahmā speaks of kings in this way:

Under the blessing of the divine kings, he will enter the womb of his mother. Having first been blessed by the gods, he afterwards enters her womb. Although as king he is born and dies in the world of man, yet since he comes from the gods, he is called a divine son. The thirty-three divine kings have given a portion to

---

2   Many scholars, particularly in the nineteenth and early twentieth centuries, believed these acts to have been intended as merely symbolic (e.g. Colebrooke 1805; Winternitz 1887: 37; Gait 1913: 849). Some have suggested that these texts were meant to present human sacrifice as a horrific act that should ultimately *not* be performed (Keith 1914; Roth 1850: 457-64). However, more recent scholarship suggests that human sacrifice probably was part of the ritual repertoire of ancient South Asians. For example, Houben (1999) argues that such rituals are described in too much detail for it not to have been at least an accepted practice.

the king (saying): "You (are our) son, a lord of man magically created by all the gods" (Emmerick 2004: 61).

However, divine kingship did not equate to absolute rule. According to the principle of the king's duty (*rājadharma*), found in all major Indic traditions, the king was charged with promoting and maintaining the Dharma, encouraging his subjects to perform virtuous actions, supressing lawlessness and supporting religious groups and ascetics. Therefore, the Dharmaśāstras (texts setting out proper ethical conduct) authorized rebellion against any king who behaved immorally. For example, the *Mahābhārata* epic explicitly sanctions revolt against an immoral king, who "should be killed like a mad dog." The legend of King Vena depicts him as being so impious that he was murdered by divine sages armed with blades of grass that miraculously transformed into spears. In the Hindu context, the king depended on *brāhmaṇas* for his legitimation, who were authorized to perform rituals (including the above-mentioned rituals of kingship) and who fulfilled prominent roles in his council, most notably that of *purohita* ("chief priest"). Likewise, the king's duty to uphold the Dharma also included upholding the caste system, and by extension the *brāhmaṇas'* position of privilege and power.

All the same, formal mechanisms designed to check the king's power appear not to have existed. Certainly, no such mechanisms are described in Kauṭilya's *Arthaśāstra*. However, the very existence of the *Arthaśāstra* testifies to its author's conviction that a king must be guided in his thoughts and actions by wise advisors. According to Kauṭilya, a king should begin receiving guidance even before he is a king, from tutors tasked with teaching him the virtue of self-control; if a prince cannot dominate his natural human tendencies toward vices such as gambling, drinking and sex, Kauṭilya believed his tutors should construct elaborate scenarios that would transform the prince's passion for these things into revulsion (for example drugging his liquor). If even these scenarios fail to work, then the tutors should report this to the current king, and the king should arrange for the prince to be killed, so he may never attain the throne (Boesche 2002: 38–40). A newly crowned king, then, should already be able to demonstrate considerable self-control, but he must still surround himself with able advisors or *mantrins* (including the aforementioned *purohita*), whom he is expected to consult before initiating any task (Olivelle 2013: 41). It is not clear to what extent Kauṭilya's recommendations informed the governing strategies of contemporary rulers such as Candragupta Maurya or any of the rulers who followed him throughout South Asian history. In some cases, even the composition of kings' councils is in doubt. For example, the only *mantrin* explicitly mentioned in Cālukya inscriptions is the *saṃdhivigrāhika,* the minister of war and peace (Dikshit 1980: 210–14). However, most sources agree that South Asian kings were normally aided by a number of skilled *mantrins*, who, besides the *purohita* and *saṃdhivigrāhika*, also included the *mahāsenapati* (commander of the army), a figure in charge of revenue and/or treasury, a superintendent of stores and a minister of justice.[3] Overall, the persistence, throughout South Asian history, of both the king's council as an institution and Kautilya's *Arthaśāstra* as an influential treatise reflects the enduring legacy of Kautilya's notion that a king can never govern by himself, but should always receive guidance.

According to Kautilya, a king's primary duty should be to maintain peace and order among his people. Specifically, he advocates a kind of "royal paternalism" that involves taking care of the sick, the elderly, the poor, women, children and other vulnerable individuals, even when these do not actively seek his aid. Kautilya also recommends that the king regularly hear his subjects' grievances at a specially designated assembly hall. Kautilya justified this advice by arguing that subjects who believe that their king cares for them are less likely to rebel. Candragupta Maurya appears to have taken these ideas to heart. According to the Greek geographer Strabo, he even listened to his subjects' complaints while being massaged. Both Candragupta and Aśoka had an assembly hall built, and Aśoka also established a comprehensive social welfare system that included medical centers for both humans and animals (the ideal king, according to Aśoka, also took care of horses whose old age, illness or injuries made them incapable of working [Boesche 2002: 541]), wells for the supply of drinking water and the planting of trees along roads to provide shade for tired travellers. He also frequently toured the countryside to keep in touch with his poorer subjects (Thapar 1997: 70, 152, 158, 160–61, 180). Aśoka's ideals inspired later Buddhist conceptions of an ideal "Dharma king" (*dharmarāja*) both within the borders of South Asia and far beyond.

It is worth briefly dwelling on the Jain approach to rulership as well, particularly as Jainism was relatively influential in the region of Karṇataka, where some of the southern subcontinent's more important dynasties were based. According to early Jain scriptures, it is unethical for ascetics, who adhered to the principle of nonviolence, to accept alms from kings, because it was inconceivable at the time for a king not to frequently wage war on his neighbors in order to gain riches and territory. Nevertheless, in Karṇataka, Jain ascetics frequently developed close ties to rulers, who were likely attracted, first, by the way the religion's Digambara "sect" celebrated the ideals of heroic individualism and self-perfection through the use of bellicose imagery, and second by their northern origins and the prestige that this entailed. The clearest expression of the Jain approach to rulership may be found in the *Ādipurāṇa*, composed in the ninth century CE by Jinasena, and likely intended to be read at the court of Jinasena's patron, Amoghavarṣa Rāṣṭrakūṭa. According

---

3   See Kamath (1980: 25, 38, 137) for the Sātavāhanas, Kadambas and Hoysalas, respectively, and Altekar (1958: 358) for the Rāṣṭrakūṭas.

to the *Ādipurāṇa*, a king must govern by following Jain doctrine and surrounding himself with Jain advisors. He must protect not only himself and his subjects, but also the Jain tradition and its followers, ensuring that his land is free from heretics and their teachings. The *Ādipurāṇa* also notes that a king will achieve true mastery of the world by becoming an ascetic. Although even rulers with very close ties to the Jain world might not have had a full committment to the Jain doctrine, the last Rāṣṭrakūṭa emperor is said to have embraced asceticism later in life, eventually committing the supreme ascetic act of fasting to death (Dundas 2002: 118–20).

Buddhist political theory formulated the ideal of the *dharmarāja*, a just and moral king who, unlike other monarchs, rules his kingdom according to Buddhist ethical norms. In the Kūṭadanta Sutta (written in the Pāli language), the Buddha speaks of a wealthy king who wishes to gain lasting happiness for himself only by means of great sacrifices. However, his kingdom is beset by thieves, the countryside is filled with bandits, and towns and villages are being destroyed. The Buddha then points out that the problem of crime cannot be solved through executions, imprisonments, confiscations, threats and banishment, but only through economic justice, which can be achieved by distributing grain and fodder to farmers and cattle herders, providing capital to merchants and traders and giving proper living wages to those in government service. Greedy, cruel or violent kings are often included in standard Buddhist lists of the causes of catastrophes that may befall people and their land. In another early Buddhist *sutta*, the *Cakkavattisīhanāda Sutta* ("The Lion's Roar on the Turning of the Wheel"), the Buddha lists the duties of and characteristics of the universal monarch, including the following:

1. He acknowledges the Dharma and acts in accordance with it.
2. He protects his household, towns, countries, troops and ascetics, as well as birds and other animals, without resorting to violence.
3. He prevents crimes by giving to those in need.
4. He is willing to receive spiritual advice.
5. Once he brings the entire world under his dominion by peaceful means, he must ensure that his people live in comfort and in freedom from poverty. He is to his people like a father to his children. His people trust him and they are loyal to him.

In the same *sutta*, the Buddha also describes how social, moral and physical degradation takes place. He says that not giving to the needy leads to killing, lying, envy, harsh speech, greed, hatred and incest. These, in turn, would lead to the reduction of people's lifespan to ten years. People would end up seeing each other as beasts and kill each other, ultimately causing the collapse of society. Buddhist texts therefore encourage rulers to be forces for good and offer instructions and advice on how to rule justly and compassionately. Above all, Buddhist scriptures assert that a good ruler should live and act as a pious Buddhist layman, providing his subjects with a model of good conduct. He should regularly seek the advice of Buddhist monastics, protect all the people and animals dwelling in his country, show no tolerance for wrongdoing and help the poor. A *dharmarāja* conquers only by means of righteousness, without resorting to violence. Although he may have an army, he establishes his power without using it.

In a number of early Buddhist texts, we are presented with situations in which the Buddha acts as a mediator and prevents war by demonstrating its futility through logical reasoning. A king should try to avoid violence, using it only as a last resort, and only if his motivation is righteous. In the *Golden Light Sūtra* specifically, we read that a king must encourage his subjects to perform virtuous actions so that they may reach the abode of the gods. Gods have blessed the king so that he may demonstrate the results of good and bad actions to his subjects. He must not neglect lawlessness nor leave the evildoers unpunished. If he ignores the evil in his land, the chief gods in Indra's heaven will become angered; his territory will be overcome by wickedness and destroyed by foreign armies, natural disasters, famine and plague; his ministers will die; and he himself will become separated from his loved ones and his wealth. Therefore, he should impose restraint on evildoers in accordance with their crimes and should never take sides, but remain impartial even at the cost of his life (Emmerick 2004: 61–65).

The *Sūtra of the Ten Wheels of Kṣitigarbha* (*Daśacakrakṣitigarbha Mahāyāna Sūtra*) prescribes a proper time for electing a ruler and the types of individuals qualified for selecting a king—namely, those who are wise, impartial, educated and of mature age, characterized by diligence, impartiality, compassion, education, wisdom and physical fitness. The text also provides detailed policy advice, including the idea of eliminating unemployment and fostering prosperity by assigning those of lesser education, intelligence or knowledge to work that is suitable for their abilities and needs. The king should also bring people who follow different religious traditions into harmony to prevent strife. He must protect his cities, towns and villages, as well as visitors and his subjects by means of strong walls and a strong army. The king himself must be always mindful of his position and background and must guard himself from evil temptations or from being blinded by power (Rinpoche 1972). According to the same *sūtra*, the king must always try to prevent war by finding a compromise with his adversary; if war is truly unavoidable, then the king and his people must face it with skill and bravery. They must be ready to sacrifice themselves for the greater good and they should try to minimize the loss of lives on both sides. Another Mahāyāna *sūtra* (*Bodhisattvacaryāgocaropāya-viṣayavirkurvaṇa Sūtra*), says much the same.

Early Pāli canonical and post-canonical sources as well as several Mahāyāna *sūtras*[4] include unequal distribution of wealth as a major cause of crime in the country. These texts therefore argue that the best way for the king to prevent crime is to improve the economy through such acts as providing loans to merchants and fodder to farmers and saving failing businesses. When punishing a wrongdoer, the king should impose a bearable and purposeful punishment that would improve the actions of the wrongdoer. Capital punishment must be avoided (Rinpoche 1972).

Finally, let us briefly turn to Islamic notions of rulership, which were first introduced to India by the Delhi Sultanate, the first polity to establish direct Muslim rule in the subcontinent.[5] In Islamic tradition, the ideal ruler is one who acts in accordance with the Prophet Muḥammad's teachings, recognizes the authority of the ʿAbbāsid caliphs (who claimed descent from one of the Prophet's uncles) and promotes Islamic law in his own land. Indeed, the narratives produced by historians at the court of the Delhi sultans address the latter with titles such as "sultans who protect the faith" and "path-followers of the predecessors"; they point to parallels between the deeds of the sultans and those of the Prophet; and they praise the good sultans who diligently enforce Islamic law as opposed to making their own. Moreover, the Delhi sultans often sought investiture from the ʿAbbāsid caliphs and even had caliphs' names and titles inscribed on their own coinage (Auer 2012: 10–16). More relevant here is the expectation that the Islamic ruler invest in his subjects' welfare; specifically, the virtuous ruler was expected to make pious endowments, called *awqāf* (singular *waqf*), resulting in the creation of mosques, schools, hospitals, fountains and other structures and institutions meant to fulfill his subjects' basic spiritual, cultural and medical needs. It is well documented that the Delhi sultans established a number of structures (tanks, dams, artificial lakes, reservoirs and other infrastructure) meant to ensure a reliable water supply across their land, including in the more arid regions (Siddiqui 1986). They also established several hospitals, where medicine, the patients' meals and the physicians' salaries were all paid for by the state. The hospital founded by Sultan Fīrūz Shāh (r. 1351–88) in his capital of Firuzabad is notable for including a wing dedicated to veterinary medicine (Siddiqui 2012: 16–18).

Overall, the patterns we have described above fit somewhat, but not entirely, with what proponents of Axial Age theories predict. For example, Black (2008: 33)

---

4   E.g. the *Cakkavattisīhanāda Sutta, Agañña Sutta, Milindapañña,* and *Bodhisattvacaryāgoca-ropāya-viṣayavirkurvaṇa Mahāyāna Sūtra,* among others.

5   This is the only section of this chapter where we look at Islam's contribution to the development of a specific aspect of ideology in South Asia, simply because Brāhmaṇism/Hinduism, Jainism and Buddhism were on the whole more influential in the time period considered. However, since this section deals specifically with rulership and because the historical summary we provided above includes a few words on the Delhi Sultanate, it seems important to briefly summarize the ideological approach to governance of the subcontinent's earliest Muslim rulers.

notes that the axial "breakthrough" resulted, in many regions, in the emergence of the ideas that power should be based on merit instead of birth, that rulers and administrators should be virtuous and wise, and that the wealthy and powerful should respect and demonstrate generosity toward the poor and disenfranchised. As we have seen, Jain and Buddhist scriptures as well as the *Arthaśāstra* all attempted to mould rulers into virtuous, wise figures who dedicated time and attention to even their poorest subjects. Rulers from the Maurya Dynasty, starting with Aśoka, seem to have followed some of these instructions, and there is certainly a tradition of Indian monarchs investing in their subjects' welfare—for example, the custom of kings founding "pilgrims' feeding houses" beginning in the tenth century CE (Mack 2002: 99–100) and the Vijayanagara Empire's widespread construction of water tanks and irrigation canals to cope with water shortages (Prasad 1998: 93). And, of course, Islam has its own tradition of rulers investing in their subjects' well-being, as seen, for example, in the public projects carried out by the Delhi sultans.

We have also seen that early Hindu texts, such as the epic *Mahābhārata*, contain the notion that a ruler's subjects should rebel if a ruler demonstrates disreputable behavior, implying that a king should ideally behave in a wise and ethical manner. Of course, many such texts were composed by *brāhmaṇas*, who benefited from propagating the notion that a ruler's behavior was to be kept in check—after all, who could better guide the ruler than a *brāhmaṇa* caste that was responsible for preserving and transmitting the highest forms of knowledge? Moreover, as we will explore in more depth below (and as scholars such as Black [2008] note), South Asian ideological approaches to power relations were moderated by the idea that one's social status derived from the merit one acquired in past lives, which led to the notion that a person in a position of power must have been virtuous and wise almost by default, for otherwise they would not have attained power. This is not quite the same as the moralizing, institutionalized constraints on rulers traditionally posited in arguments about axial transformations.

Universalizing morality, egalitarianism and social mobility

If proponents of the Axial Age hypothesis are correct, universalizing morality and egalitarianism (and a consequent rise in social mobility) should have first emerged in South Asia between 800 and 200 BCE, not earlier or later. However, as already noted, there is a distinct possibility that the social ideology of the Indus Valley Civilization was already founded on egalitarian principles. This conjecture is mostly based on the facts that Harappan sites lack clearly identifiable evidence for class, gender or race inequality, and that archaeological evidence for Harappan daily life and mortuary practices suggests a high degree of standardization (Lowe 2004: 182–85). For example, all Harappans appear to have lived in two-story burnt-brick houses placed over mud-brick platforms, with no significant differences in house layout, architectural design or even brick size. Burials tend to include only a few modest grave goods. Precious metals demonstrate proportionally equal distribution across rural and urban sites, which also suggests no great wealth differentials; similarly, objects with inscriptions have been found both in the largest urban sites and in the smallest rural ones, which suggests equal access to literacy.

Then again, as mentioned above, scholars such as McIntosh (2008) interpret certain aspects of the Harappan archaeological record to be indicative of the existence of an early version of the South Asian caste system. The apparent importance of fire and water to Harappan ritual and the presence in most Harappan houses, of both sophisticated plumbing systems and female figurines that were used to burn fire or incense suggest a preoccupation with notions of purity and pollution: concepts that would later be used to underwrite caste distinctions. Furthermore, Harappan spaces show a clear demarcation between public and private, which could indicate segregationist practices. However, as Lowe (2004) observes, there is no clear evidence that Harappan society was organized by caste or that elites were considered "purer" than others. This theory of social segregation is highly speculative and can be easily disputed. For example, the Great Bath, the Harappan structure interpreted by some as the location for large-scale water-based rituals, may have simply been a public bath; similarly, Harappan plumbing may have been constructed to meet basic hygienic needs. Lowe also critiques Kenoyer's (1989) and Maisels's (1990) studies suggesting structural gender inequality among the Harappans. Kenoyer's study revealed that female skeletons show a higher proportion of dental caries (cavities) than male ones, while Maisels demonstrated that female skeletons show greater signs of stress; however, neither a higher proportion of caries nor greater physical stress necessarily correlate to lower social status. There is also no clear evidence for a moralizing aspect to Harappan ideology, though here again McIntosh (2008: 393) speculates that law and order may have been maintained in Harappan settlements through the threat of divine punishment.

Regardless of whether the Indus Valley Civilization constitutes an exception to the Axial Age theory, Brāhmaṇic tradition largely conforms to conventional models of pre-axial ideology. First, Brāhmaṇic ritual focussed predominantly on the act of sacrifice and its efficacy in maintaining the cosmic order (*rta*). According to the Vedic *Hymn to the Primordial Man* (*Puruṣasūkta*), the cosmos was created through the primordial man's (Puruṣa's) self-sacrifice; and regular fire sacrifices of animals, animal products, and later only plants were essential for maintaining cosmic order and balance. As the prominent Axial Age proponent Bellah (2005: 70) argues, sacrifice was a key aspect of ritual in pre-axial, "archaic" religions, as it provided a spectacular display of elites' power over life and death.

Second, Brāhmaṇism promoted a strict social hierarchy based in part on the Puruṣasūkta, according to which, after the first man's sacrifice, different parts of his body gave rise to different social classes (*varṇa*), one of a number of terms that is sometimes translated as "caste": from Puruṣa's mouth arose the class of *brāhmaṇas* (Vedic priests and scholars); his arms gave rise to *kṣatriyas* (rulers and warriors), his legs to *vaiśyas* (farmers and traders) and his feet to *śūdras* (providers of services and labor). *Brāhmaṇas* held the most exalted status due their superior knowledge of the cosmos, Vedic hymns and the exact ways of performing Vedic rituals. As already mentioned, many of these rituals were aimed at maintaining the proper functioning of the cosmos, but some were also meant to confer legitimacy on the *kṣatriyas'* rule; and in return, *kṣatriyas* conferred fees and gifts on the *brāhmaṇas*. Although both *vaiśyas* and *śūdras* were tasked with providing sustenance to the two upper social classes, *vaiśyas* were deemed inherently superior to *śūdras*. Those who did not fall into any of the four mentioned categories, the *caṇḍālas*, were associated with highly "polluting" occupations—such as leather working, disposing of dead bodies, and disposing of sacred cattle after their death. One could not become a member of a social class in which one had not been born, and marriage was largely restricted to within a single social class. Mobility between classes was therefore limited, though to some degree intermarriage was permitted between members of different *jātis* (occupation-based castes) *within* these broader classes.

The Vedic approach to gender relations is complex. Some Vedic hymns make references to both male and female seers (*ṛṣi*); women are at times presented as equal or superior to men in their commitment to asceticism; texts written in dialogue form include both male and female speakers; and there are clues that women were allowed to speak and walk freely in public, choose their own husbands, inherit property and remarry after the death of their consorts. Then again, Vedic texts also include numerous contradictory references to the supposedly evil nature of women, and promoted the notion that a woman's main purpose in marriage was to produce sons who would honor their ancestors through sacrifices and other rituals.

Brāhmaṇism was not an entirely moralizing ritual tradition. It included moralizing elements, but it was not founded on moralistic principles in the same way as Axial Age religions. At death, the soul of a Brāhmaṇic priest travelled by the path of the sun to heaven, a place of eternal rest, light and joy, where the dead feasted on milk, honey, ghee and *soma* juice (extracted from the *soma* plant and believed by some to be a type of a hallucinogenic drink), sang and played music, and were able to experience the delights of love. The souls of others followed the path of smoke, which led to the land of ancestors. Although the gods Yama and Varuṇa are portrayed in the Vedas as ethically concerned deities, they ultimately grant unconditional pardon to the higher castes. There are, however, exceptions, who are confined to the world of hell (*narakaloka*). In later Vedic texts, the category of those who may expect to be condemned to eternal punishment included those guilty of ritual transgressions, such as breaking taboos and/or failing to correctly perform rituals.

In the *Jaiminīya* and *Śatapatha Brāhmaṇas*, hell is said to be reserved for those who cut wood or eat animals (Obeyesekere 1980: 156–58). One's fate in the afterlife, then, had very little to do with one's behavior toward other people and very much to do with one's relationship with the gods—and with the *brāhmaṇa* priests, whose nature partook of the divine.

Karma

As predicted by standard Axial Age theories, we see a qualitative shift in South Asian thought between the seventh and the fifth centuries BCE, with the emergence of the notion of karma as the moral quality and repercussions of one's actions, fundamental to Buddhism and Jainism, and later to the Hindu tradition as well. Buddhism and Jainism were also radical in their promotion of relatively egalitarian ideals, as seen, most notably, in the fact that their ideas were initially spread not through Sanskrit, the language of the learned classes, but through Prakrit, a language that was accessible to a broader range of people (though, as we will see, neither Buddhism nor Jainism pushed egalitarianism as far as is implied by some proponents of Axial Age ideas). Moreover, both religions championed non-violence (*ahiṃsā*). Both were influential in South Asia for a relatively limited number of centuries, and only ever prominent in certain regions.

In all three main South Asian religious traditions, the theory of karma centers on the notion that individuals are responsible for the results of their own actions in this and future lives. The word karma ("action") makes its earliest known appearance in Vedic texts, where it primarily denotes a ritual action. In the *Bṛhadāraṇyaka Upaniṣad*, which dates to between the seventh and sixth centuries BCE, we find the idea that "one becomes good by good actions, and one becomes bad by bad actions." However, this and other early Brāhmaṇic and Upaniṣadic texts did not offer a comprehensive system of recommended ethical conduct; instead, they reserved punishments for specific crimes that involved injury to a *brāhmaṇa*. There is evidence that the ascetic sect known as the Ājīvikas also had similar ideas. Some scholars have argued that the notion of karma emerged far from the Brāhmaṇic heartland. For example, Obeyesekere (1980) points to Gangetic "tribal" religions as originators of the notion of karma. However, as Doniger O'Flaherty (1980: xiii) observes, "it might be argued that 'tribal' is simply a scholarly way of saying 'we do not know who they were.'"

In the Buddhist context, all sentient beings (not only humans) are interconnected through karma; all desire happiness and seek to avoid suffering. Also, all composite phenomena (physical and mental, individual and social, as well as historical) are impermanent and devoid of inherent existence, as they arise and cease due to the confluence of causes and conditions. Nothing has autonomous existence or occurs independently. Along with the role of the person's effort, this idea of the interdependence and causality of all phenomena has implications for Buddhist ethics, which focus on the removal of one's own and others' suffering. Specifically, according to Buddhism, one's actions can be ethically virtuous, non-virtuous or neutral. An action's moral quality is determined by the motivation or intention behind it. However, good intentions do not always lead to positive results, so it is only when an action does not harm oneself or others that it is a morally positive action. While a person has a certain degree of freedom to choose his actions, he is also constrained to a degree by the habitual propensities carried over from previous lives and this life. The cycle of rebirths and accompanying suffering stems from negative karma, with derives from mental afflictions such as delusion, attachment, aversion, greed and the like, which, in turn, derive from ignorance of impermanence, personal and phenomenal lack of identity and so on. In order to attain freedom (*nirvāṇa*) from the perpetual cycle of rebirth and suffering, one must perform wholesome bodily, verbal and mental actions, cultivate loving-kindness, compassion, empathetic joy and equanimity toward all beings, and study and meditate until one is able to penetrate the nature of reality. Indeed, the Noble Eightfold Path consists of right view, right aspiration, right speech, right action, right livelihood, right effort, right mindfulness and right meditation, that is, the state of profound meditative concentration (*samādhi*) that results in unwavering mental peace and profound insight into the nature of reality. The purpose of the five main Buddhist vows that must be followed by lay Buddhists—abstinence from killing, lying, stealing, sexual misconduct and intoxicants—are meant to prevent both the accumulation of negative karma and the infliction of harm on others.

Long after the Buddha's lifetime, Buddhist doctrine and practices continued to evolve throughout Asia, and giving rise to several schools and movements, all of which endorsed personal responsibility. The Mahāyāna tradition introduced the figure of the *bodhisattva*, a person who cultivates the altruistic motivation (*bodhicitta*) to achieve enlightenment in order to lead others to freedom from rebirth and suffering.

In Jain cosmolology, the world (*loka*) is also subdivided into a set of hierarchically organized planes of existence similar to those in Buddhism. In this tradition, too, the combination of good and bad actions that one has accumulated in past and present lifetimes determines the nature of one's rebirth and experiences. However, in the Jain tradition, karma is not a mere consequence of one's actions, it is also a physical substance that attaches itself to the soul (*jīva*), just like dust sticks to a sweaty body. The karmic substance that attaches itself to the soul forms a "subtle body" that clings to it in the cycle of transmigration and hinders it from ascending to the the realm beyond the world (*aloka*), where it can abide in a perpetual bliss of liberation (*mokṣa*). The main goal of Jain practices, then, is to liberate the *jīva* from the bonds of karmic matter by avoiding both morally negative and positive karma through ascetic practices that entail stopping the influx of new karma and shedding the already accumulated karma. The four fundamental causes of karma are attachment to sensual pleasures; the mental impurities of anger, deceit, greed and pride; activities of the body, speech and mind; and false view. To prevent the influx of new karma one must cultivate right view, right knowledge and right conduct. As in Buddhism, right view refers to the removal of one's own preconceptions of the way things are. Right knowledge is the knowledge of the structure of the world. Right conduct includes the development of the five virtues—namely, non-violence, truthfulness, abstinence from stealing, chastity and non-attachment to mundane things—as well as mindfulness and self-restraint. Right conduct is cultivated through the Great Vows (*mahāvrata*) taken by ascetics and the less stringent Lesser Vows (*anuvrata*) designed for lay practitioners. The Great Vows involve abstinence from killing any living being, from lying, from taking what is not given, from sexual intercourse, from attachment to food and the like, and from eating after dark. The Jain prohibition against eating eggs, root vegetables, honey and various other substances is based on the idea that one must avoid harming living beings, including those found in these types of food. Similarly, the Lesser Vows oblige lay practitioners to limit harm to other living beings, avoid swindling customers or business partners, avoid stealing, enjoy sex in moderation and practice generosity. Lay practitioners also have the choice of following three Subsidiary Vows (which limit travel, the enjoyment of basic pleasures such as food and clothes, and idleness) and four more Vows of Instruction (which compel one to further limit travel, perform specific rituals, observe fasting days and engage in charitable activity) (Dundas 2002: 157–59, 189–92).

Ultimately, the principle of non-violence lies at the root of all the vows mentioned above. According to the Jain tradition, all forms of life have equal dignity, and harming another being is tantamount to harming oneself. It is clear how killing, lying and stealing may harm others. Sexual immoderation, attachment and the excessive enjoyment of other mundane pleasures are deemed causes of the mental defilements of envy, jealousy and greed, which may lead one to acts of violence. Some of the vows may seem at first sight not to have anything to do with non-violence. But they can be explained by the Jain view that even the smallest fraction of space is inhabited by some form of life. The *Ācārāṅga Sūtra*, one of the earliest surviving Jain texts, states: "All beings are fond of life; they like pleasure and hate pain, shun destruction and like to live life, they long to live. To all, life is dear" (AS 1.1.3). Hence, vows that limit travel are meant to reduce the likelihood of accidentally trampling another living being. Indeed, the first Great Vow can be expanded to include an injunction to avoid wandering during the monsoon season, when the general burgeoning of new plant life makes it particularly likely that a traveler will step on a living being. Similarly, the sixth Great Vow, which compels ascetics not to eat after dark, derives from the fact that someone who wanders looking for food after dark is likely to accidentally trample over living beings he or she cannot see (Dundas 1995: 158–60). As already indicated, Buddhism also champions non-violence, which extends to all sentient beings, not just humans. It is worth noting that, in these two traditions, non-violence extends to mental or psychological as well as to physical harm.

Unlike Jainism and Buddhism, the Brāhmaṇic tradition was relatively slow to embrace the notion of karma. One of the key obstacles to this was the fact that karma came from outside this tradition, so its adoption would suggest that *brāhmaṇas* were not the guardians of all sacred knowledge. However, in the course of time, the Brāhmaṇic tradition incorporated and adapted elements from śrāmaṇic and Upaniṣadic traditions into its own system of thought.

Social (in)equality

In the Upaniṣads, we encounter a passage that connects a person's karma from their previous life with their social status in the present one: "people [...] whose behavior is pleasant can expect to enter a pleasant womb, like that of a woman of the Brahmin, the Kshatriya, or the Vaishya class" (Bronkhorst 2011: 48). Passages like this one are relatively rare and contradict the notion of Brāhmaṇic exceptionalism, grounded on the inherent superiority of a *brāhmaṇa* who knows the Vedas and Vedic rituals, by implying that anyone can become a *brāhmaṇa* in the next life purely through morally positive actions, and that a *brāhmaṇa* whose conduct is "unpleasant" can be conceived in the womb of a lower-caste woman in the next life. However, later Hindu texts, such as the *Laws of Manu* (*Manusmṛti*, (c. 200 BCE–third century CE) and other Dharmaśāstric texts, take the position that due to his inherently pure nature, a *brāhmaṇa* cannot act immorally; it is inconceivable that he would be reborn in the next life as a member of a lower social class or as an outcaste (*Manusmṛti* 1.28–30). The *Manusmṛti* is of particular importance for our discussion due to its clear explication of caste relations and the rules or duties of the four castes, including a section (the longest in the text) on the fourfold Dharma of a *brāhmaṇa*. The text recommends the practice of virtues such as not harming any living being, truthfulness, abstention from stealing, chastity, vegetarianism and so on, for all four social classes. However, *śūdras* and *caṇḍālas* were not allowed to listen to the recitation of the Vedas. Moreover, *caṇḍālas*—whom Manu refers to as "dog-cookers"—could not own property and were forced to live outside villages and perform the lowliest tasks, including sweeping and removing excrement. If a *caṇḍāla* touched someone from a superior social group, that person required ritual purification (Knott 2000: 82).

As for Buddhism, though at first the religion may appear to be fundamentally egalitarian, its approach to class and gender inequality is in fact nuanced and varied. Buddhist texts may certainly be interpreted as refuting notions of Brāhmaṇic exceptionalism and throwing doubt on the foundations of the caste system. After all, the path to enlightenment was open to all regardless of birth, social status or gender. In the Vāssettha Sutta of the Suttanipāta, one of the earliest Buddhist canonical texts, the Buddha asserts that one cannot classify human beings into different species in the way animal and plants are differentiated. Diverse social classes exist by mere designation or social convention and in accordance with their occupation. The moral superiority of individuals is not related to their *varṇa* or *jāti*, or the clan or family into which they were born, but in their freedom from mental afflictions (*kilesa*) and their ethical conduct (*sīla*). In the same text, the Buddha states:

> I do not call a man a brahmin because of his mother or because of his breeding. Just because a man is entitled to be called "Sir," it does not mean that he is free from habit and attachment. He who is free from attachment, he who is free from grasping is the person I call a brahmin.
>
> When all the chains are shattered, where there is no more agitation, and a man has freed himself and thrown off his shackles—that is a person I call a brahmin.
>
> He who has cut off the strap [of ignorance] and harness [of false views], who has removed obstacles and is enlightened, is one I call a brahmin.
>
> He who, without getting annoyed, endures insults and violence, whose strength and army is endurance, is one I call a brahmin (Saddhatissa 1994: 72–73).

However, Buddhism did little to overturn the caste system, even at the height of its influence. In the scripture known as the *Aṅguttaranikāya* (III: 363), the Buddha provides ethical instructions for the three higher social classes only, which may lead some to think that he did not care for the lowest social class and the *caṇḍālas*. Moreover, though caste distinctions ceased to be important among those who joined the Buddhist monastic community (*saṅgha*), the Buddha did not admit slaves into his *saṅgha*, as they were seen as someone else's property, though it is worth noting that he also did not admit soldiers who "belonged" to a king or debtors who were yet to discharge their debts. In the "Mahāvagga" section of the Pāli Vinaya scripture, we read that at one time when Bimbisāra, the king of Magadha, was engaged in a war with a bordering kingdom, some of his soldiers, believing that fighting was a non-virtuous act, left the army and joined the Buddha's monastic community. This angered the king's army commanders, who reported the incident to him. Bimbisāra's legal advisors suggested capital punishment for a person who ordained soldiers in royal service. The king, who was a great patron of the *saṅgha*, reported this to the Buddha and asked him not to ordain his soldiers, and the Buddha, not wishing to disturb the military administration, complied by barring soldiers from the monastic community.

With regards to unfree labor, it is also worth mentioning that, instead of questioning the institution, there are Buddhist texts that describe the proper conduct servants should have toward their masters and vice versa: for example, in the Pāli *sutta* titled *Sigalovāda Sutta*, the Buddha instructs the layman Sigala not to over-burden his workers with labor but to give them work they were able to carry out, proper wages and vacation, and to take care of them when they are sick. Further, throughout history and in virtually all regions where Buddhism spread, large Buddhist monasteries had their own slaves, though some experts would argue that the word "serf" is more accurate.

Similarly to Buddhism, though Jain texts assert that all souls are inherently the same, that one's rank should depend on one's ethical conduct rather than one's birth, and that purity is something that may be achieved through rigorous practice rather than inherited from one's parents, one cannot say that Jainism promotes completely egalitarian principles. Over time, the Jain tradition has developed its own hierarchy of social groups, which usually originate from the patronage relationship between one or more families and a single Jain teacher. One shares one's caste with other descendants of those original families, and the caste usually takes its name from the families' original geographic location (Dundas 1995: 47–49).

Gender equality

Early in the Vedic period, women seemed to enjoy considerable freedom; later, how-ever, they were faced with significant constraints. For example, only young men were allowed to study the Vedas and rituals, and only the sons in a family were allowed to perform ancestral rites and funeral rites for their father. Later still, the *Manusmṛti* clearly argues that women are inferior to men: women were prohibited from hearing the recitation of the Vedas or from taking part in sacrificial rituals in the absence of their husbands; they had no access to religious institutions; and they were the de-nied the possibility of achieving *mokṣa* through asceticism. According to the *Manusmṛti*, women should be controlled by their husbands, must serve them and bear them many children even if their husbands mistreat them. Even though a husband should endeavor to treat his wife with respect, a woman should never leave a bad husband and should not remarry after his death (Knott 2000: 83). Women were regarded as unfit to be independent; hence, while living in her father's house, a girl was subjected to him; when married, she was subjected to her husband; and when widowed, she was subjected to her son. In accordance with this role, her religious duty (Dharma) was to serve first her father, then her husband and finally her adult son. Similarly, women were seen as overly sexual, which made them less trustworthy, so their sex-uality was to be controlled as well.

In the Upaniṣads and in the texts of the śrāmaṇic, ascetic traditions (which abandoned the need for sacrificial rituals and therefore also the need for sons to perform them) we find references to women who were allowed to study, debate, be ordained as nuns and engage in religious practices. In the early Buddhist Pāli texts, the Buddha is said to have taught his Dharma not only to monks and laymen but also to nuns and laywomen. Likewise, the early texts show that women were accepted into the *sangha* and could achieve arhatship (that is, insight into the true nature of existence); at the same time, a fully ordained, senior nun still held a lower status than a young male novice. Some Mahāyāna *sutras* such as the *Ugraparipṛcchā* ("*Questions of Urga*") include explicitly derogatory statements about women. It is not until the rise of Esoteric Buddhism (c. seventh century CE) that we see women as Buddhist Tantric practitioners and teachers equal to men. One of the vows of Tantric Buddhism is to respect women. In the doctrines of both Mahāyāna and Tantric Buddhism, one is not intrinsically female or male; gender is not ultimately real, it is provisional. In the cycle of *saṃsāra*, every person has been born as a male and as a female at different times in previous lifetimes. Moreover, in Tantric Buddhism, a woman is an equal partner in Tantric sexual practice and she can achieve enlightenment within a single lifetime.

Jain attitudes to gender relations are likewise complex. Or, rather, the two main Jain sects demonstrate very different approaches, the Śvetāmbara approach being more nuanced and the Digambara one being more clear-cut. The difference that is most relevant to our discussion is that Śvetāmbaras ("dressed in white clothing") believe that women can achieve liberation, while Digambaras ("dressed in space," that is, naked) hold that only a *jīva* that is housed within the body of a man can achieve liberation.

There is evidence that, at its origins, Jainism unambiguously promoted the notion that men and women were spiritual equals. The Kalpasūtra clearly states that, by the time of the death of Mahāvīra (an important Jain figure of the sixth century BCE), the number of Jain nuns and laywomen exceeded the number of monks and laymen, respectively, as did the number of women who attained liberation compared to the number of men who did the same. Indeed, according to the Śvetāmbaras, the very first person to achieve liberation was a woman, Marudevī. There are many other spiritually heroic women in Jain legends, including Malli, who, like Mahāvīra, is considered a *tīrthaṅkara* ("fordmaker"), that is, she was a pioneer in the attainment of liberation, making a path for others to follow. Similarly, the nun Rājimatī dissuaded her monastically ordained brother from seducing her, and compelled him to return to his vows. In early Digambara texts, too, dating to the third and/or fourth centuries CE, nuns are said to be able to attain liberation.

The contemporary Digambara stance on women's spiritual inferiority emerged in the fifth century CE, although the most comprehensive argument defending this position, authored by the Jain ascetic Prabhācandra, dates to the eleventh century. The cornerstone of Prabhācandra's argument is that, since nakedness is essential for the attainment of liberation, and women are not allowed to wander naked because of the risk of rape, their souls can become liberated from the cycle of rebirths only when dwelling in a male body. Prabhācandra also argued that women are incapable of following the Jain teachings with the necessary dedication, due to an innate tendency towards delusion and immorality, and that birth as a woman suggests some moral failing in a previous life.

Although a number of Śvetāmbara texts criticize Prabhācandra's arguments, this does not mean that Śvetāmbara' beliefs and practices are completely devoid of misogyny and patriarchal attitudes. The above-mentioned examples of Jain "spiritual heroines" are few and far between compared to the many cautionary tales in which devious and lustful women attempt to lure men away from the path of righteousness. As in the early Buddhist Vinaya, according to Śvetāmbara monastic law, even a nun of great seniority must pay homage to a newly initiated monk (Dundas 1995: 55–59).

Interaction and cross-cultural influence in South Asia

Evidence for interaction between South Asia and far-flung lands dates to as early as the Aceramic Neolithic (7500–5500 BCE). Mehrgarh, the earliest farming settlement in the Indo-Iranian borderland region, has yielded craft items made from exotic materials, specifically turquoise and lapis from Turkmenistan and Afghanistan and shell from the Arabian Sea. It is even possible (though far from certain) that domestic plants and animals reached north-west India from West Asia. Trade networks may therefore have stretched across the entire Iranian plateau, reaching all the way to East Asia, though most likely goods moved from one region to another through sequences of short-distance exchanges rather than planned, deliberate long-distance commerce (McIntosh 2008: 59–60).

These trade networks gradually expanded throughout the region's prehistory, culminating in a major shift shortly after the emergence of the Harappan Civilization: the invention of seagoing vessels. These allowed Indus traders to sail to what are now Oman and Bahrain on the Arabian Peninsula, as well as the cities of southern Mesopotamia (McIntosh 2008: 86). Mesopotamian texts, which refer to the Indus Valley as Meluhha (McIntosh 2008: 46), show that Harappan imports to the lands between the Tigris and the Euphrates included timber, copper, red pigments for cloth dyeing, gold, ivory, pearls and precious stones; in return, the Harappans likely received grain, animal products and tin (Stein 1998: 49–50). Ideas moved from region to region alongside goods, as attested, among other things, by shared iconography, such as the widespread image of a sacred mountain and a tree, or that of a hero or god wrestling ferocious beasts—lions or tigers, bulls or water buffaloes, depending on the region (McIntosh 2008: 290). The collapse of the Harappan Civilization did not interrupt the flow of goods and ideas between South Asia and the rest of the world; the key trading node simply shifted from the Indus Valley farther to the south, to

Gujarat, which retained its intermediary role until at least 1600 BCE (McIntosh 2008: 399).

We have already seen how, between the second and first millennia BCE, the migration of Central Asian Sanskrit-speaking, cattle-herding migrants into the northern subcontinent, and their interaction with indigenous populations, resulted in lasting changes to South Asian culture: most notably, the ideological justification of social stratification and of the power and privilege enjoyed by the priestly caste. We have also already nodded at the presence of Greek-ruled polities in the subcontinent's northern regions, but here it is worth noting that Greek culture, too, engendered a not insignificant ripple effect across the arts and sciences of northern South Asia: for example, the adoption of Hellenistic-style Gandharan stone sculpture and an enrichment of astronomical knowledge (Stein 1998: 76). As noted above, the so-called "Indo-Greeks," and indeed most other peoples who occupied all or part of north India in the succeeding centuries, were in turn influenced by South Asian culture—most obviously as attested by numismatic and some textual evidence concerning the development of South Asian religion, particularly Buddhism and Hinduism.

Readers may turn to the religion overview chapter to learn about Buddhism's expansion from India to the rest of Asia in the second half of the first millennium CE. At around this time, the Pallavas, the first great power to emerge in what is now the Indian state of Tamil Nadu, established extensive diplomatic and commercial ties across both Mainland and Island Southeast Asia, which also led to the spread of Hinduism and Sanskritic culture generally (Stein 1998: 127). Fifth- and sixth-century rulers in modern-day Thailand, Cambodia and Vietnam adopted Sanskritic names and, in particular, the Khmer kings of the Mekong Basin bore names ending in -varman, like the Pallava kings; an eighth-century inscription found in Java uses the Pallava script, and the region's earliest Hindu temples show clear similarities with the architecture of the main Pallava port of Mamallapuram (Keay 2013: 177). Texts similarly record the participation of Southeast Asian religious scholars at seminaries in India, where they learned of the most up-to-date scriptural interpretations and were able to observe new forms of worship, as well as aspects of South Asian politics and society. Some aspects of South Asian culture were reinterpreted and forged into something altogether new once they reached Southeast Asia. A prominent example is the notion of divine kingship, which, though present in the *Naradasmṛti*, a Dharmaśāstra dealing with legal matters, never truly took hold in South Asia, while in Southeast Asia it became a key aspect of elite ideology (Stein 1998: 127–28).

As for cross-cultural interaction with the Mediterranean world, there are many Greek references to trade with South Asia, and we have already seen how the Kushans played an important role in commercial exchange between the subcontinent and the Roman Empire. The Romans, in particular, benefited from an improved understanding of monsoon cycles compared to previous trade partners with the sub-continent, which enabled them to navigate there directly across the Arabian Sea, significantly shortening travel times and allowing them to avoid pirate-infested coasts (Stein 1998: 103). On the subject of cultural influences between South Asia and the Classical world, it is particularly worth noting that the figure of the South Asian ascetic, first encountered by Alexander the Great's followers in the third century BCE, and known to Classical authors as the gymnosophist or "naked philosopher," recurred in the writings of thinkers such as Lucian and Cicero and, later, Ambrose of Milan (Keay 2013: 77).

By the eighth century CE, the Indian Ocean had become the main setting for trade between China and West Asia. Shortly thereafter, as Islam expanded from the Arabian Peninsula to the Fertile Crescent and then Central Asia, it turned its commercial interests towards the east and south. By 1000 CE, cosmopolitan trade emporia managed by Arabs, Jews and Armenians, among others, were established along South Asia's western coasts, and once again the subcontinent found itself at the centre of a vast exchange network, due to both its geographical position and its valuable products, particularly textiles and spices (Stein 1998: 147).

As we have seen, the expansion of Islam did not stop in Central Asia, but continued onto the subcontinent. No Muslim ruler ever attempted mass conversion of his subjects, and much of pre-Islamic Indian culture remained untouched; indeed, southern polities such as the Vijayanagara Empire experienced a resurgence of strict Hindu orthodoxy, perhaps as a reaction to the perceived threat of an Islamic takeover. Nevertheless, cross-cultural influence inevitably occurred, in architecture (where styles mingled), gender relations (where the more patriarchal elements of Islamic and pre-Islamic Indian culture combined to result in an overall diminishment of women's status) and religious scholarship (which saw the emergence of the Chisthī Ṣūfī tradition, which, unlike other Ṣūfī traditions, looks to South Asia, as opposed to Central or West Asia, as its spiritual home) (Stein 1998: 144–50).

Overall, then, there is an abundance of evidence for cross-cultural interaction between South Asia and the rest of Eurasia. However, its inclusion as a "core" Axial Age region was based on supposedly entirely autochthonous phenomena. Indeed, as we have seen, the evidence does suggest that South Asian developments in ideology and forms of rule were largely indigenous. In fact, these developments had a significant impact on political trajectories throughout the rest of Asia and into Mediterranean southern Europe, perhaps more so than South Asian ideology was itself impacted by external forces.

Conclusion

This chapter has shown that, broadly speaking, ideological developments in India partially correspond to the predictions of the Axial Age theory. Most notably, between the fifth and fourth centuries BCE, the Gangetic Plain witnessed the emergence of Buddhism and Jainism, two strongly moralistic religions founded on egalitarian, universalistic principles; shortly thereafter, Brāhmaṇism adopted a number of axial notions from both as it transformed into Hinduism, particularly the principles of karma and non-violence. Moreover, it is likely no coincidence that a seminal treaty regarding proper governance, Kauṭilya's *Arthaśāstra*, was composed around the same time, circa 300 BCE. Interestingly, the South Asian case also appears to adhere to Jaspers' original Axial Age theory in that the emergence of karma, Buddhism and Jainism were all indigenous phenomena, even though, from the earliest times, key regions of the subcontinent were enmeshed in a network of contacts that stretched across the length of Eurasia.

Nevertheless, we have also shown that, as far back as 2600 BCE, egalitarian principles may have already constituted an important part of Harappan ideology, though this is speculative, and any connection between this hypothetical Harappan egalitarianism and later axial developments would be difficut to prove. Finally, it should be clear that, at the height of the Axial Age, neither Buddhism, nor Jainism, nor Brāhmaṇism/Hinduism pursued egalitarianism and universalism to their logical conclusions; the caste system remained firmly in place and ended up even being legitimized by Buddhism and Jainism. All three ideologies also promoted misogynistic notions of men's superiority to women, though they also encompassed more positive attitudes to women, according them at least spiritual equality to men. All told, developments in South Asian ideology in the time period under consideration demonstrates a complex interplay between the key traits encompassed by notions of axiality, not unlike what we see in many regions across the world, as attested by other chapters in this volume.

EAST ASIA | North China

Jill Levine & Barend ter Haar

Period	Dynasty	Approx. dates
Bronze Age	Shang	c. 1550–1045 BCE
	Western Zhou	1045–771
Iron Age	Spring/Autumn	771–476
	Warring States	475–221
Early Imperial	Qin Empire	221–202
	Former Han	202 BCE–9 CE
	Wang Mang Interregnum	9–24
	Later Han	25–220
Six Dynasties	Three Kingdoms	220–265
	Western Jin	265–420
	Northern Wei	386–554
	Northern and Southern dynasties Period	420–581
Early Medieval	Sui	581–618
	Tang	618–907
	Five Dynasties	907–960
	Northern Song	960–1127

Table 5. Periods and dates of polities mentioned in text that were based in or that occupied northern China

Introduction

The Middle Yellow River Valley has been home to complex societies since the fourth millennium BCE. The rulers of the Bronze Age[1] societies in northern China (roughly 2000 to 700 BCE) controlled ritual capitals and carried out predatory expeditions in surrounding territories. After a long period of interstate warfare during the Iron Age (roughly 700 to 200 BCE), the numerous independent states of the region were unified under the Qin Empire and first emperor of China, Qin Shi Huangdi ("the First August Emperor of the Qin"). China was recurrently unified under successive imperial dynasties, with only short-lived disruptions, until the overthrow of the Qing in 1911 CE. The emperors of imperial China at times expanded their territory into Central Asia, Champa (modern Vietnam), and the Korean Peninsula, and also

---

1   It is important to note, however, that these designations reflect a largely Western preoccupation with discrete periods; bronze and, later, iron both remained critical metals for much technological and economic activity well after the supposed end dates of these periods. We employ the terms here simply to aid readers in making comparisons across other regions in this volume.

exerted control over Tibet. Key developments during imperial rule include the creation and expansion of central and provincial bureaucracies along with the implementation of civil service exams.

This chapter begins with a brief outline of Chinese history and religion from the Late Shang period (1250 BCE) to the fall of the Northern Song Dynasty (1127 CE). China was singled out by Karl Jaspers as one of the regions that underwent an "axial" transformation in the mid-first millennium BCE (Mullins et al. 2018: 42). The Axial Age as it has been interpreted by Jaspers and followers, c. 800–200 BCE, begins at the end of the Bronze Age in northern China and ends in the first century of the Western Han Dynasty. Axial Age proponents point to Confucianism as a strong moralizing force in Chinese political and intellectual life. While Confucius did live during this period, Confucianism as a cohesive philosophy was not institutionalized as a state ideology until the Han period at the very end of this time span (Mullins et al. 2018: 39). How much of an impact did Confucian teachings have on first-millennium BCE rulers? Were there any earlier axial moralizing forces in Chinese history? We will examine the concepts of morality, equity, and prosociality that define the Axial Age thesis in order to determine its relevance in north China.

Historical and religious background
At the end of the second millennium BCE, the late Shang Dynasty ruled over a hierarchical society centered around modern Anyang. Thousands of bronze, jade, and ceramic artifacts have been uncovered from the ruins of the late Shang settlement of Yin—evidence of a highly complex society (San 2014: 18). The Shang were eventually overthrown by the Western Zhou and their allies, whose rulers asserted that the Shang regime had fallen into degenerate and immoral behavior, making their rule illegitimate. The first king of the Western Zhou Dynasty in fact claimed a "Mandate of Heaven"—a right to rule given by divine powers. In the late Shang and Western Zhou periods, kings ruled central capitals, while local elites controlled surrounding territory in a "proto-feudal" political system (29). The Shang were in constant conflict with neighboring settlements, and conquered polities presented tribute to the kings in Anyang to recognize their authority (Keightley 1999: 236). The Western Zhou held several capitals including one at present-day Luoyang in conquered Shang territory. In the early Western Zhou period, lesser royals and their allies controlled surrounding polities, consolidating Zhou control over a large section of north China (von Falkenhausen 2006: 4). This network of allied polities was centered around Zhou royal power (4).

Early Chinese religion was characterized by the connection between the living and spirit worlds. Ritual practices meant to appease and interpret signs included sacrifices and divination based on plants, dreams, the environment, and natural events (Lewis 2007: 182–3). The primary state cult of the Shang and Western Zhou centered on ancestor worship (185). These ideas laid the foundation for the indigenous Chinese religion that continued to evolve throughout the next millennia. The Western Zhou adopted many of the traditions and rituals of the previous Shang Dynasty, and specific Zhou rituals were not invented until around 850 BCE (von Falkenhausen 2006: 2). The Western Zhou's Mandate of Heaven pitched the ruler as a Son of Heaven who received his right to rule from the gods. According to this concept, the Son of Heaven was the only legitimate ruler of China.

The collapse of Western Zhou rule in north China ushered in the Spring and Autumn period. The name of the era comes from the early annalistic work traditionally ascribed to Confucius, *Chunqiu* ("Spring and Autumn Annals"), which chronicles the events from the mid-eighth to the late fifth century BCE as seen from the ducal court of Lu. In a period of political turmoil and rebellion, the Western Zhou had fled eastward in 771 BCE and founded the Eastern Zhou after their capital was sacked by invaders from the north-west (Hsu 1999: 545; von Falkenhausen 2006: 4). The weakened Zhou court became symbolic rulers, while regional nobles gained political power and influence (von Falkenhausen 2006: 4). The Spring and Autumn period was marked by intense conflict between these regional powers.

In the early fifth century BCE, the vassals of the Eastern Zhou were replaced by independent military rulers, marking the beginning of the Warring States period (Lewis 1999a: 587). As can be deduced by the name of the era, there was constant interstate warfare. The central governments of individual states were run by military officials, and ruling strategies were characterized by increasing control over the people and state bureaucracy (Lewis 1999b: 356). The rulers of the Warring States concentrated on expanding military capacity, extracting resources (including labor) from the peasantry, and consolidating authority in their own states in order to prevail in conflict with neighbors.

Archaeological evidence suggests that the traditional ancestral worship rituals and aristocratic ranking systems of the Shang and Western Zhou were transformed due to the changing social and geopolitical realities of the Spring and Autumn and Warring States periods (von Falkenhausen 2006: 397). The state cult of Eastern Zhou continued traditional ancestor worship rituals and sacrifices, while rulers of individual states reinterpreted the same rituals through the worship of nature and outdoor sacrifice. Rulers and elites in these independent states started to use their own objects for rituals, distinct from those traditionally used by the Eastern Zhou court (397). The shift might have been an attempt to weaken the power of the Eastern Zhou court, as the king (*wang*) was an important figure in traditional ancestor worship (Lewis 2007: 185). It is unclear how these changes impacted the balance of power between the Zhou and the independent regional rulers, but von Falkenhausen (2006: 397) writes that the restructuring of traditional ritual practices in this period should be seen merely as "a refreshed version of the old system." The material evidence suggests regional rulers had more flexibility in ritual practices, but ultimately did not stray far from tradition.

This period is traditionally classified as the era of the Hundred Schools of Thought. It also coincides with the Axial Age as understood by Jaspers and subsequent writers, c. 800-200 BCE. This was the time of thinkers like Confucius (551-479 BCE) and Mozi (468-391 BCE)—an era characterized by a "plethora of writing and ideas" (Kirkland 2002: 177). While we know a number of scholars compiled texts and worked with students, it is difficult to determine how formally distinct their teachings were. Scholars might not have had much tangible influence on state policy. Confucius, for example, was unable to find a ruler who would put his ideologies into practice in his lifetime (Van Norden 2011: 20), and the five Confucian classics were not formally compiled and edited until the first century CE (Nylan 2001: 175). The concept of discrete philosophical schools of thought like Confucianism and Mohism certainly did not exist in this period. In fact, modern scholars generally dismiss the notion of cohesive philosophical schools in China in any period.

Before Qin became the region's first major empire, it was a relatively small state on the western border of the modern country of China. One by one, Qin conquered all of the other independent Warring States in the course of the third century BCE, as well as overthrowing the Eastern Zhou court. This was an important ideological move in 256 BCE, after which other states followed suit in cutting ties with the Zhou court. Qin Shi Huangdi claimed the Mandate of Heaven and unified for the first time nearly all of modern-day China under a single managerial system, ushering in China's imperial era, which lasted until the overthrow of the Qing Dynasty in 1911 CE. Qin's unification was not only political and military, but included the introduction of a common written script to be used throughout the newly-formed empire along with standardized weights and measurements (which applied even to the length of a wagon axis). This era saw also major expansion of public works throughout northern China. Qin Shi Huangdi used massive corvée labor forces to construct great projects including the Qin Great Wall and his grandiose tomb complex; the home of the famed terracotta warriors. By the end of Qin's brief rule, the central government faced conflict with nomadic northern tribes. The Qin were overthrown after 14 years by peasant rebellions and revolts from conquered states.

Succeeding the Qin was the Han Dynasty, founded by Liu Bang, the leader of one of the largest rebellions against the Qin. Han rule is divided into the earlier Western Han and the later Eastern Han periods, separated by the coup of an official named Wang Mang, who seized the throne and founded the short-lived Xin Dynasty (9-24 CE). In its early years, the Western Han had a strong central government ruling over a combination of centrally controlled and semi-autonomous provinces (San 2014: 73). The rise of great landlord families weakened the central government, paving the way for Wang Mang's official coup (Lewis 2007: 22). This coup, however, was felt only at the court level–Wang Mang already held great influence at court before 9 CE because of his family's connections to the empress dowager. After the Han restoration, the Eastern Han eventually faced major rebellions from regional religious groups, including the Yellow Turbans and Five Pecks of Rice / Way of Celestial Masters dissident groups. The weakness of the central government in the face of violence and disorder led to the rise of powerful regional warlords, who became de facto rulers of the many Han provinces.

The first emperor of Qin and his advisors believed the dynasty needed to provide ideological traditions supported by the central government (Lewis 2007: 208). An older view (e.g. Seidel [1978] 2008: 134) contends that that philosophical texts like the *Mengzi* (traditionally attributed to the philosopher Mengzi, also known as Mencius) and the Confucian *Analects* had already been codified in the fourth and fifth century BCE, but lacked official titles or authors. The Han attributed authors to the works retroactively, using the names of ancient sages and personalities. Recent consensus holds that these texts were not codified at these early dates, nor were there really distinct "philosophical schools"; there were, rather, retroactive designations by followers of already-mature traditions.

In the Western Han, the concept of ideological schools was in its infancy. Sima Tan (165–110 BCE), grand historian to the first Western Han emperor, further categorized writings from the Spring and Autumn and Warring States period into "the six houses of thought," or *jia*. The most influential were the *mo, ru, fajia,* and *daojia* teachings (Goldin 2011: 88). These four *jia* were precursors to some of the "-isms" that evolved in later centuries: Mohism, Confucianism, Legalism, and Daoism, respectively (Kidder 2003: 130), though again it is important to note that these terms are (largely Western) inventions from the nineteenth and twentieth centuries and would not have been familiar to practitioners of the time. Texts later classified as "Mohist" emphasize the need for impartiality and common standards of evaluation (Van Norden 2007: 144). *Fajia* is traditionally translated as "Legalism," but modern scholars take issue with the term. Goldin (2011: 94), for instance, writes that "the concept of *fajia* is itself partisan and anachronistic; it was invented retrospectively by Sima Tan for his own discursive purposes." Daoists only began to distinguish their practices and beliefs from those of Confucians and Buddhists in the early medieval period (Kirkland 2002: 177).

The ideology that evolved into Confucianism emphasized the importance of traditional rites and ceremonies, social hierarchies, and filial piety. In Confucian texts, Confucius and his followers promote a return to past ideals and traditions, and the path of virtue—the "Way"–in response to the chaos and militarism of the Spring and Autumn and Warring States periods (Van Norden 2007: 67). However, in an analysis of archaeological evidence from the Zhou period, von Falkenhausen (2006: 2) suggests a more complicated narrative: "Confucius and his contemporaries, far from either reverting to the past or being radically innovative in their own time, reflected on, and gave philosophical expression to, currents of comprehensive change that had been ongoing for about a century, and which broadly manifested themselves in the ritual practices of the epoch."

In the Western Han, the imperial academy became increasingly important in the promotion of court officials. Future imperial scholars mainly studied Confucian classics at the academy, which led to the rise of Confucian classicism in court (Lewis 2007: 67–69). Wang Mang's short-lived equal field policy, an attempt at an equitable distribution of land, was inspired by Confucian texts (23). Mohism faded into obscurity during the Western Han and was not reintroduced into the Chinese intellectual sphere until the Ming period (Fraser 2016: x). While classic texts influenced imperial scholars, popular religion based on ancestor worship and polytheism was still an essential part of court and common life. Buddhism arrived in China in the Western Han and soon became an important component of state ideology.

The development of religious Daoism has a complex history. Religious Daoist movements starting in the second century CE were inspired by values and ideas in ancient texts. Daoist leaders often lived among their communities and had close ties with local communities. They were therefore able to incite rebellions and uprisings against perceived immoral behavior from leaders (Barrett 1996: 16-7). Daoist movements in this period include the Tianshi Dao in Sichuan (also known as the Five Pecks of Rice movement) and the Taiping Rebellion in eastern China (also known as the Yellow Turbans), the latter often credited as a direct cause of the fall of the Eastern Han (Raz 2012: 2). Some Daoists attempted to create a more cohesive religion in the fifth and sixth centuries. This included the compilation of Daoist canon from a diverse set of classical texts. The authors of these texts would not have identified as part of the same school or religion (Kirkland 2002: 177).

After the fall of the Han in 220 CE, China was divided into the states of Wei, Shu, and Wu, the so-called Three Kingdoms period. Buddhism gradually came to dominate north-central China during the Six Dynasties period (the Three Kingdoms, Western Jin, and Northern and Southern periods) (Xiong 2009: 68).

Mahāyāna Buddhism had first entered China in the first century CE, either due to contact with South and Central Asian merchants through the Silk Route, or along the maritime trade route in the south. There was little interest in Buddhism among the Han Chinese until the Three Kingdoms period. Buddhism became more widespread in the Western Jin period (Knechtges 2010: 183), and was supported by medieval Chinese rulers. Mahāyāna Buddhists believe in powerful *bodhisattvas*—those who have almost reached enlightenment but choose to stay on earth and help others reach *nirvāṇa*. This concept was integrated into traditional indigenous religion, inspiring popular millenarian sects that anticipated the breakdown of social order before the arrival of messianic figures such as the *bodhisattva* Prince Moonlight

(Ownby 1999: 1525–28). Buddhists were actively suppressed and persecuted three times in medieval China, twice in the Northern and Southern period (in 446 CE and 575–77 CE), and once in the Late Tang in 845 CE.

The Western Jin reunified China briefly in the third century CE, but their rule was marked by political turmoil and rebellion. Western Jin rulers fled the capital during a large-scale uprising of northern nomadic tribes and founded the Eastern Jin Dynasty, with a capital near modern Nanjing. The fall of the Western Jin ushered in the Northern and Southern period in which the Tuoba tribe of the northern steppe federation (modern Mongolia) ruled north China as the Northern Wei Dynasty. Buddhism was the state religion during most of Northern Wei rule, and Tuoba emperors are famous for constructing Buddhist caves in Longmen and Yungang. Daoist reformer Kou Qianzhi promoted Daoism to the Northern Wei court (Xiong 2009: 11). Han Confucian rituals and ceremonies along with traditional ancestor worship rituals were still incorporated by the court (Chen 2010: 53); Emperor Xiaowen and Empress Dowager Feng ordered the construction of temples for Confucius in the late fifth century CE (Holcombe 2011: 66–67).

China was once more unified by the Sui after the Northern and Southern period. The first Sui emperor, Emperor Yang Jian, claimed Northern Zhou territory after a palace coup forced out the ruling family then conquered Southern Chen, reuniting much of mainland China, and reestablished Confucian rituals at court. The second Sui emperor, Emperor Yangdi, used corvée labor for large construction projects including the Grand Canal and a new capital at Jiangdu and spent massive funds in attempting to conquer the Korean Peninsula. Yangdi and the Sui fell to large-scale peasant rebellions.

Following the collapse of the Sui, the Tang Dynasty rose to power. This dynasty was also marked by the rise in eunuch power—in the Late Tang the royal department controlled by eunuchs became the most powerful government institution (Dalby 1979: 571–72). The An Lushan Rebellion (755–63 CE) ushered in an era of powerful regional warlords (Lewis 2009: 58). The weakened Tang Dynasty collapsed in the ninth century CE after a series of agrarian revolts. After a century of political turmoil, the Northern Song reunited China ushering in an era of economic advancement and growth. Northern Song society was extremely complex and sophisticated. The central government was staffed by scholar-officials, rather than aristocrats (Hartman 2015: 20), and civil service exams became a more important factor in the official selection process (Ebrey 1996: 136).

Medieval China was influenced by Daoism, Buddhism, Confucianism, and traditional popular religion. Daoist leaders often served as advisors to the emperor (Kirkland 2004: 145), and Tang emperors generally favored religious Daoism. However, Buddhism received state support in the seventh century CE under Tang empress Wu Zetian. The Northern Song saw the rise of Neo-Confucianism, a more secular and rationalistic version of Confucianism. While the state examinations only included Confucian classics under the Northern Song, scholars set up large private academies for Neo-Confucian studies (Zhao 2015: 337). Neo-Confucianism continued to influence the court in the succeeding Ming period. These Neo-Confucian elites, however, still held Daoist and Buddhist beliefs.

Religion and the chief executive

Kings and emperors in China were never seen as gods themselves, but were thought to be "chosen" representatives. The actions of the chief executive had implications for the forces that connected the worlds of the spirits and the living (San 2014: 16). In the early Bronze Age, kings and diviners are thought to have performed oracle-bone readings and ancestor worship rituals (Keightley 1978: 2). The idea of a divine right to rule or Mandate of Heaven was introduced in the Western Zhou. The Mandate of Heaven said that rulers were chosen by the gods and that there could only be one legitimate king. Ritual specialists interpreted natural signs, and it was believed that a disaster or good harvest could be influenced by the behavior of the chief executive. Therefore, chief executives likely faced informal constraints from nobles and ritual specialists who interpreted and formulated cosmological theories (Peter Bol, North China Workshop 2016). However, we know of no significant formal, institutionally backed constraints on rulers in "pre-axial" north China.

Early Iron Age China was characterized by a weak central administration. The Eastern Zhou court and king performed the traditional rituals and ceremonies, but real power lay in the hands of regional rulers. These rulers were legitimized by their military strength rather than divine authority (Loewe 1999: 989). The rulers of independent states had the power over their own legal systems, tax collection, and military forces (Van Norden 2007: 65). While the first legal code in China dates to the Tang Dynasty, there is evidence for the creation of penal laws in the states of Zheng and Jin in the late Spring and Autumn period (cf. Barbieri-Low and Yates 2015; Hulsewé 1955; Lau and Staack 2016). The creation of these early legal codes might have slightly constrained the power of regional rulers, but it is unclear to what extent; largely, these rules were focused on the general population. In all, there seem to be few if any constraints on rulers of vassals and independent states in this period.

The following imperial dynasties made a great show of returning to "traditional Western Zhou" ideology in which the chief executive was both a religious authority (claiming the Mandate of Heaven) and claimed certain political authority, though in practice these later rulers held much more real centralized authority than Zhou kings ever had. The authority of emperors largely followed Legalist principles, positioning them as true heads of state. The first Qin emperor created the title of *huangdi* ("august thearch"), which classified the emperor as a "supreme divine being" (Lewis 1999b: 167). Emperors were immortalized and deified through rituals (Lewis

2007: 52) and became powerful "royal ancestor spirits" after death (Puett 2014: 243). Ideologies from the previous era continued to influence court politics. There are numerous examples of religious agents and officials offering advice or criticizing the emperor on the basis on their political or religious philosophy (Lewis 2007: 64). The Censorate—a class of censors in charge of monitoring and criticizing the behavior of the emperor—was present throughout the imperial period (Benn 2002: 2). However, while emperors were expected to behave in accordance with the dominant court ideology and with popular traditions, there is no evidence of formal constraints on their authority. In addition, while officials could make recommendations to the emperor—and it seems many in fact did—it was up to him whether or not to take the advice, or which advisor to follow.

Universalizing morality and egalitarianism in North China
Morality
Indigenous Chinese religion encouraged moral behavior during the late Bronze and early Iron Ages in the form of the Mandate of Heaven. In the Western Zhou, rulers might have been concerned with moral activities in order to placate Di (the concept of the earth) and ancestor spirits (Keightley 1999: 72). With the adoption of the Mandate of Heaven, there was also the concept that Tian (heaven) would punish rulers who promoted certain immoral behaviors. In the following example from a 998 BCE bronze inscription, King Kang speaks to his high minister Yu about the relationship between correct behavior and the Mandate of Heaven:

> Yu! Brilliant King Wen received the great Mandate from Tian. When King Wu succeeded King Wen, he created a state, opening hidden lands, possessing all the four quarters, and setting right their peoples. In ceremonial affairs involving wine, oh! he permitted no excess; at sacrificial rites, he permitted no drunkenness. Hence Heaven in its greatness watched closely over its sons and protected the former Kings in their possession of the four quarters. I have heard that the Yin (Shang) lost the Mandate because the greater and lesser lords and the many officials assisting the Yin sank into drunkenness and so were bereft of their capital ... (Eno 2009: 100–101).

In the passage, King Kang notes that heaven punished a king for allowing improper behavior and allowed another king to retain power for banning the same behaviors.

The period Jaspers classifies as China's Axial Age is marked by the emergence of competing ideologies. Spring and Autumn and Warring States writings give diverse views on morality. Notably, morality receives in-depth discussion in the Zuo Zhuan (Commentary of Zuo). The Zuo Zhuan was likely composed in the Warring States period, but includes material from earlier periods (Goldin 2001: 93). According to

Pines (2002: 85), "Whereas some of the Zuo protagonists hoped that sacrifices would suffice to ensure extrahuman protection, others believed that deities would bestow favors only on the moral person; still others considered morality as important in itself and denied the immoral person even the right to communicate with the deities." From this text, it seems the concept of a divinely audited morality was growing, but not universally accepted in China by the Warring States period. An increased emphasis on morality might be explained by the shift away from ancestor worship in the Eastern Zhou. Support from the spirits, in this case, would come from proper behavior rather than sacrifices. In the late Spring and Autumn period, an emphasis on morality became important for proper conduct among the elite and a way to maintain social order (Pines 2002: 84).

Other examples further demonstrate the diversity of opinions present in this period. The writings of Han Feizi (279–233 BCE) and Shen Dao (350–275 BCE) were later classified as *fajia* thought. Han Feizi did not believe the promotion of morality could greatly influence the behavior of rulers or the general population (Pines 2009: 97). Shen Dao believed political power was more important than morality, writing: "worthiness does not suffice to subdue unworthiness, but power and position suffice to bend the worthies" (quoted in Pines 2009: 47). In contrast, Warring States philosophers Mengzi (372–289 BCE) and Xunzi (310–217 BCE) both believed that moral behavior was important for rulers (Pines 2009: 35, 96). It is difficult to assess the extent that the ideologies introduced in the Spring and Autumn and Warring States periods influenced the rulers of vassals and independent states.

Jaspers marks the teachings and ideas of Confucius as a moralizing turn in north China. The Confucianism manifested by the Western Han period—notably at the very end of the widely accepted Axial Age end point of roughly 200 BCE—does fit traditional "axial" arguments on a superficial level. Confucian definitions of morality, however, are complex and nuanced. As Yao Xinzhong (2000: 33) points out, "What is meant by 'morality' in Confucianism is in fact quite different from that defined in Western ethics." Western morality is often concerned with heaven and hell and ethical behavior. Confucian morality encompasses more than just metaphysical or ethical issues—for Confucius, morality was linked to both religion and politics (34). Confucius believed that morality was best achieved through behavior including performing traditional rites and ceremonies. Maintaining harmonious family relationships is another important factor in Confucian morality. This applied to the common people and to rulers alike (33). In addition, the widespread adoption of explicitly moralizing normative ideologies like Buddhism did not occur until the early medieval period—centuries after the traditional bounds of the Axial Age.

Like Confucianism, Buddhism promotes a shared, universal moral code that can be followed by all social classes. The five precepts of Buddhism are an example of a moral code promoted by the ideology: "not to kill, steal, lie, engage in illicit sexual activity, and imbibe intoxicants" (Gregory and Ebrey 1993: 13). The core tenets of medieval Chinese Daoism are difficult to untangle, but Daoist teachings focused on rituals to placate spirits, and were less concerned with moralizing behavior (Barrett 1996: 16).

Egalitarianism

There is also no evidence of the promotion of egalitarianism in the religious traditions of the Bronze Age. Bronze Age China maintained strict social hierarchies, supported and sometimes endorsed by the prevailing ideology. Elite status was hereditary, and elites held separate privileges from the common people.

In the late fourth century BCE, the authors of the *Mengzi* wrote about the well-field system (also called the equal-field system), which they attributed to the Western Zhou. The equal-field system is also discussed in the *Rites of Zhou*, a text from the Warring States period later labeled a "Confucian text" (Schrecker 2004: 26). Such land arrangement regimes can be interpreted as legal and economic manifestations of growing ideological commitment to egalitarianism in the later first millennium BCE. On the other hand, in spite of some egalitarian elements, there are reasons not to read too much idealized or "socialist" intent behind their implementation in the Chinese context. In addition, the concept of egalitarianism in historical Chinese context often refers to the concept of fairness rather than the more Westernized idea of sameness. According to the *Mengzi*, a plot of land was organized into nine equal squares. Individual families owned eight of the plots, and a feudal lord owned the last plot, which was farmed communally as tax to the lord. It is not clear whether this was a new idea in this period. This kind of equal grid system had already been put into practice, for example, by reformer Shang Yang (390–338 BCE) of Qin (Lewis 2006: 249). These land systems could be considered egalitarian as households all have the same landholdings. In theory, the well-field system described by the *Mengzi* would ensure that each household was self-sufficient (von Glahn 2016: 75). However, it is important to note that equal-field systems are also a form of social control. In addition, Mengzi (the philosopher) is recorded as mocking the ideology of Xu Xing, who promoted egalitarianism and utopian communalism in the Warring States period (Schrecker 2004: 27). No writings of Xu Xing survive (in fact, it is unlikely he had any in the first place) and it is unknown if he had any influence over rulers in this period—his ideas have only been preserved through Mengzi's discussion with his disciple.

The equal-field system was put in place by the Qin, but was replaced in the Han period (Holcombe 2001: 136). Inspired by the *Rites of Zhou*, Wang Mang attempted to implement an equal-field system during his short rule (Lewis 2007: 23). The system was not successfully installed, though, until around 485 CE during the Northern Wei (386–534 CE). The land allocated to farmers was a mix of heritable (and taxable) and non-heritable land given to the male head of a family for as long as he was able to work on it (Leeming 1980: 164). In the Northern Wei equal-field system, land was given to households based on their amount of labor power rather than their needs; smaller plots were also to given to women and children, and sometimes even slaves—it was more about practicality (raising more total grain and revenues) than egalitarianism (von Glahn 2016: 175). The system remained in place until after the An Lushan rebellion (755–63 CE) during the Tang Dynasty. As the Tang declined, powerful families and Buddhist monasteries were able to obtain large plots of land.

In the Western Han, Sima Tan (quoted in Goldin 2011: 89) complimented *fajia* thought for its emphasis on rigid social hierarchies, noting that *fajia* rulers "are strict and have little kindness ... But as for honoring rulers and derogating subjects, and clarifying social divisions and offices so that no one is able to overstep them— none of the Hundred Schools could improve upon these." *Fajia* texts were mostly written in the Warring States period. Confucians in the Warring States era did not promote equality (Schrecker 2004: 26). Most major philosophical texts—including the so-called Confucian texts that were heavily promoted in the Western Han and later periods—emphasize maintaining, if not reinforcing, clear political and social hierarchies. The concept of filial piety, or respecting one's elders, is important to Confucianism. In a family hierarchy, children must obey their parents, and younger brothers must obey their older brothers. Outside of the hierarchies of the family, however, there is no indication, in Confucian literature, that social elites are in- herently superior to commoners.[2] It was, thus, possible for lower-class citizens to become educated and join the ranks of Confucian scholars. Still, it is important to note that Confucian literature does not explicitly promote egalitarianism or this sort of social mobility.

Confucius' bias against women impacted Chinese society for thousands of years past his lifetime. Confucius valued sons, because women could not continue a fam- ily line to fulfill their obligations to the ancestors (Despeux and Kohn 2003: 1–2). Female children were considered a burden who would eventually move into their in-laws' home and be unable to care for their parents in old age. Confucius did not promote education for women apart from for household chores (1–2), though it is important to note that education was not widespread in these periods among males either.

Egalitarian ideologies found in Daoism and Buddhism were not used to fur- ther the position of Chinese women in society. Universal egalitarianism is a core philosophical tenet of Buddhism, but historically did not include equality between women and men (cf. Keown 2013; Schmidt-Leukel 2006). While Daoists believe that

---

2   With some exceptions in certain periods: for instance, the Fallen People, Music Households, Tanka/Boat People and others were viewed as low status in the Ming and Republican periods.

women are expressions of yin and are necessary to maintain balance in the universe, Daoist ideology was used to deter women from participating in the public sphere. Patricia Ebrey (1993: 7–8) notes that "Daoism throughout its history has lived and breathed the social version of mainstream Confucian society, which was patriarchal, patrilineal, and patrilocal, and saw women as inferior to men." Throughout Chinese history, women generally did not serve in government positions and had no significant role outside the home.

The *Mozi*, a work traditionally ascribed to the philosopher Mozi (also known as Mo Di), discusses egalitarianism in terms of government appointments through the doctrine of "promoting the worthy" (likely referring exclusively to men), which states that government officials should be appointed on merit rather than social status (Fraser 2016: 96). China's civil service examination system was created to open access to bureaucratic positions for non-elites, breaking the monopoly of power in the hands of a few leading families. Starting in the Han Dynasty, scholars and state officials were educated in the Confucian classics. Lower-level professionals like farmers and merchants could, in theory, study the classics as well to become scholars. However, in reality, the meritocratic system was weak (Peter Bol, North China Workshop 2016). In the periods before the Northern Song, men mainly entered the political system through official recommendation or on the basis of their family's nobility (Elman 2000: 5). The Sui and Tang promoted appointment on the basis of merit, but it is difficult to establish that this extended much beyond the gentry—education had to be funded by candidates or their families, meaning that it was mainly only elites who could afford to demonstrate "merit." In any case, these limited egalitarian reforms to China's system of government selection and promotion were implemented centuries after the axial period.

Prosociality

Mohists promoted the doctrine of "inclusive care," arguing that people should care about the lives of others as much as they care for their own and that they should try to help others (Fraser 2016: 158). Fraser (ix) writes, "the Mohist ideal of inclusive care appears ultimately to have been absorbed into Ruism [Confucianism] itself." This might be an example of how ancient texts were cobbled together to form invented "schools" of philosophy. Confucianism as realized in the Han Dynasty does promote the idea of caring for and respecting others (Laliberté et al. 2011). While Confucians believed that it was primarily important to care for one's immediate family, the concept of *ren* (benevolence or humanity) was also important in Confucian thought. There is no explicit mention of charity in Confucian texts, but emperors would perform charitable acts in the name of the Mandate of Heaven, supported by Confucian exhortations towards magnanimous rule. Families followed Confucian beliefs by caring for the old and sick within their family (Simon 2013: 65). Widespread

Confucian charity, however, was not realized until later periods. In the Ming and Qing Dynasties, there were charities and benevolent halls based on moralizing Confucian ideology, though clearly influenced by Buddhist ideology as well (Weller et al. 2018: 25-6).

Prosociality in Buddhism is well documented, as compassion is an important element in Buddhist teachings (Laliberté et al. 2011). The Buddhist drive to lessen human suffering led to great works of charity in medieval China, including the construction of hospitals and orphanages. Charity for the masses was not common in China until the rise of Buddhism in the medieval period. In earlier periods, charity was practiced, but was more limited in scale. Private "charity" (perhaps better: "personal magnanimity") has been recorded in the Han period (Lewis 2007: 123). Emperors presented private gifts to select individuals and performed other acts of charity in line with Confucian ideology (Lewis 2007: 124-5; Loewe 1986: 746). There is evidence suggesting that the first "mutual aid societies" date to the Han period; however, these societies generally operated within a single community (Simon 2013: 62). Before the rise of Buddhist monasteries in the medieval period, charity in China was mainly confined to elite private giving within one's lineage (60).

Works of mass, public charity like constructing wells and other infrastructure and helping the homeless are encouraged by Buddhist ideology (Weller at al. 2018: 96). In China, Buddhists gave alms to monasteries and donated private goods including land (Benn 2004: 29). In turn, monasteries supported the construction of public works. The first Buddhist hospitals were constructed in the Northern and Southern dynasties period. By the Tang period, Buddhist monasteries and societies ran hospitals, kitchens and orphanages for the poor, and provided housing for the elderly. Buddhist organizations also constructed large public works including roads and bridges (Simon 2013: 63). However, after monasteries were persecuted by the state in the late Tang, state-run institutions began to provide charity and relief in the Northern Song (65). Daoists promoted charitable works in medieval China (Kleeman 1998: 61), and Daoist masters provided free medicine and care to the poor (Laliberté et al. 2011). The work of Buddhist charitable halls continued into the late Ming period. Thus, the golden age for religious prosocial action in China began centuries after Jaspers' Axial Age.

Conclusion

Along with Egypt, Mesopotamia, northern India, and Anatolia, northern China has been home to some of the world's earliest complex societies, beginning in the 4th millennium BCE. Over its very long history, the region experienced periods of growth and unification as well as intermittent periods of strife, conflict, and dissolution. Traditional ritual practices and concepts of divinities and spirits arose early in the Bronze Age and evolved over the millennia. The ideologies that developed amid the chaos and turmoil of the later Iron Age experienced numerous rises and falls in popularity and influence over the years, often becoming intermingled with each other. Buddhist thought was introduced into China early on, but only became popular during the early medieval period. Once it did, however, it began to exert a tremendous influence on the political, social, and even economic life of China.

These different ideologies all promoted something like a universalizing conception of the world and of the things that bind all humans together. Apart from the somewhat less mainstream schools like Daoism or the much later principles of Mahāyāna Buddhism, the major ideologies of China during the Iron Age and early imperial periods really do not look like typical "axial" religions. Although China, and specifically early Chinese Confucianism, was singled out by Jaspers as one of the prototypical instances of an Axial Age religion, a designation followed by nearly all Axial Age scholars, there is very little evidence to support these notions. Morality was only a minor concern of Confucianism and most other Chinese ideologies of the period, and the morality that was expressed was very different from the way the concept is formulated by most proponents of the Axial Age idea. While texts from the traditional "axial" period of the mid-first millennium BCE espouse egalitarianism through the promotion of the equal-field system and merit promotion for government positions, variations on these concepts were not implemented on a large scale until centuries later. Even then, the equal-field system emphasized stable revenue and social order over egalitarianism, and the civil service exam system favored the gentry. Typically, axial ideals of institutional/formal limits on ruler's authority, as well as promotion of charity and other forms of prosociality were, moreover, almost entirely absent, at least until the heyday of state-sponsored Buddhism in the eighth to ninth centuries CE—a millennium after the traditional Axial Age.

Thus, while there was a rise in diverse intellectual thought in the latter first millennium BCE, in line with a traditional Axial Age timeline, the ideologies that developed in this period expressed very few, if any, typically axial features. Moreover, these schools of thought did not exert influence over China as a unified nation until later periods, belying the traditional timeline of axial transformation. Even when Buddhism, Confucianism, and Daoism became influential state ideologies in China, there was little impact on the typically axial traits—there was no clear rise of moralizing thought or calls for increased egalitarianism in early medieval China, despite the messages of compassion and respect in state ideologies and religion.[3] Rulers

---

3   The history of popular religious and philosophical movements and uprising in China is long and complex. Daoist movements like the Yellow Turbans (184–205 CE) and Five Pecks of Rice or Way of Celestial Masters (founded 142 CE) did missionary work to spread their teachings and attract followers (Kohn 2000: 140), which could be argued to be "axial" in nature. While the Way of Celestial Masters held great influence over the state of Wei, these movements did not seem to directly inspire institutionalized "axial" changes in the central state.

from the early Shang kings all the way to the powerful emperors of the imperial dynasties were only informally constrained by these ideas, while in reality both the institutional structure and political ideology of states from the time of the Zhou kings allowed for nearly unimpeded autocratic rule. The rise of charity in China from Buddhist organizations would be an example of axial intellectual and social changes, but did not happen until after Jaspers' Axial period.

In all, China saw many fundamental ideological and political developments over its history, changes that have had tremendous impact on the modern world. However, its historical trajectory provides little support for the idea of an Axial Age in the last millennium BCE.

WEST ASIA | Anatolia
Jenny Reddish, Gregory McMahon, and Sharon R. Steadman

Period	Polity	Approx. dates
Late Bronze Age	Hittite Middle Kingdom	1500–1400 BCE
	Mitanni	1500–1300
	Arzawa	1400–1200
	Hittite New Kingdom	1400–1180
Iron Age	Neo-Hittite	1180–900
	Tabal Kingdoms	900–730
	Urartu Kingdom	860–590
	Phrygian Kingdom	836–695
	Cimmerian Period	714–626
Archaic	Lydian Kingdom, Mermnad Dynasty	670–546
Classical	Achaemenid Empire	559–330
Hellenistic	Greco-Macedonian Empire	359–294
	Kingdom of Lysimachus	323–281
	Seleucid Kingdom	312–63
	Kingdom of Pergamon	282–133
	Later Cappadocian Kingdom	323–93
	Kingdom of Galatia	275–75
	Kingdom of Pontus	302–64
Roman Imperial	Later Roman Republic	133–27
	Roman Principate	27 BCE–283 CE
	Roman Dominate	284–394
Late Antique	Early Byzantine / Eastern Roman Empire	395–607
Early Medieval	Sasanian Empire	224–642
	Middle Byzantine Empire	608–866

Table 6. Periods and dates of polities mentioned in text that were based in or that occupied Anatolia

Introduction

Anatolia is the landmass bordered by the Black Sea to the north, the Aegean to the west, the Mediterranean to the south, and, less precisely, by the Lesser Caucasian highlands to the east and the plains of Mesopotamia to the south and south-east (Palumbi 2011: 205). It corresponds roughly to the Asian portion of modern Turkey, but in some definitions also includes parts of the modern countries of Georgia, Armenia, Iraq, and Syria (McMahon and Steadman 2011). A high plateau occupies much of central Anatolia, separated from the coastal regions by the Pontic and

Taurus mountain ranges to the north and south, respectively. The Zagros mountain range, which forms an arc through present-day south-eastern Turkey, Iran, and Iraq, has produced some of the earliest evidence for cereal cultivation anywhere in the world, while some communities of both the Zagros and the central Anatolian plateau were practicing livestock management over 9,000 years ago (Arbuckle 2014; Arbuckle et al. 2014; Stiner et al. 2014; Zeder 2011). The region consequently occupies a position of great significance in the history of the earliest settled agricultural societies. In later periods, it witnessed the rise and fall of myriad kingdoms and empires (including the Hittite, Phrygian, Lydian, and Cappadocian states) and was at various points under the domination of other Eurasian powers (such as the Achaemenid Empire and the Roman Principate).

In Axial Age discussions, Anatolia sometimes features as a peripheral region to the "core" West Asian and Mediterranean sites of axial transformation in the last millennium BCE: Greece, the Levant, and Iran. Some recent publications depart from Karl Jaspers' (1953) essentialist formulation of axial innovations as an achievement of certain ethnic groups—the "axial peoples"—by addressing the eastern Mediterranean world between around 800 and 200 BCE as a whole, stressing mutual influence and interaction (e.g. Halpern and Sacks 2017). For the most part, however, Anatolian societies' specific contributions to cultural, intellectual, and political innovation during the last two millennia BCE have been underplayed, if not completely overlooked. Yet, as this chapter demonstrates, the region witnessed precocious development of "axial" ideas like formalized, universally applied laws well before other supposedly axial powers did, as well as serving as a conduit for the transmission and interchange of people, technologies, and ideas, linking more traditionally heralded societies in the Mediterranean, Levant, and wider West Asia (discussed throughout this volume). Anatolia was, at the very least, an important node in the axial transformations observed elsewhere, if not an essential driver of such developments. The inclusion of a chapter devoted to Anatolian history here, then, seeks to give the region its proper due in discussions of the Axial Age along with global, comparative histories more generally.

This chapter examines the evidence for universalizing morality, egalitarian ethics, and reflexive critique of the existing political order (all identified as key features of the Axial Age in the relevant literature) in Anatolia from the mid-second millennium BCE to the early Byzantine period, ending in the ninth century CE. While our main focus is on the highlands of central Anatolia, important developments in the west and east will also feature in the following discussion.

Historical background, c. 1400 BCE–866 CE

The start date we have chosen for this historical review, 1400 BCE, marks the beginning of the imperial period or "Hittite New Kingdom" (Van de Mieroop 2007: 156).

However, because the more ancient political and religious history of Anatolia sheds light on this Late Bronze Age history, it is worth giving a brief introduction to the key events of the early second millennium BCE here. Anatolia in this period, the Middle Bronze Age, was populated by an array of communities of differing scales of political integration, including several small kingdoms and city-states, and with diverse ethnic and linguistic affiliations (Michel 2011). Between the early twentieth and late eighteenth centuries BCE, merchants from the city of Aššur on the river Tigris set up substantial trading settlements (kārums) close to urban sites on the Anatolian Plateau, bringing Mesopotamian cultural traditions and cuneiform writing (Barjamovic, Hertel, and Larsen 2012; Larsen 2015). The Old Assyrian trade network was centered at Kültepe-Kaneš, but Ḫattuša (modern Boğazköy)—later to become the Hittite capital—was also home to a substantial merchant community (Matthews 2013: 453–55). This commercial system collapsed sometime before 1700 BCE, possibly due to violent conflict between rival Anatolian kingdoms.

The early second millennium in Anatolia was thus a time of state-building, growing urbanism in certain locations, and increasing commercial contacts with Mesopotamia, as well as with western Iran and the Caucasus (Laneri and Schwartz 2011; Michel 2011). After a hiatus in written records following the burning and destruction of key sites and the departure of the Assyrian traders, a new royal dynasty at Ḫattuša is attested in the early seventeenth century (Bryce 2002: 8; Hawkins 1986). These kings soon began to extend their domination through military conquest. The term "Hittite," which in older scholarship was thought to be an obscure "tribe" mentioned in the Hebrew Bible, is now applied to the large Bronze Age state that emerged through this process, rediscovered in the late nineteenth and early twentieth centuries through excavations at Ḫattuša (Genz and Mielke 2011: 2–3; van Seters 1972). It also refers to the ethnolinguistic group from which the governing elite of the polity were drawn: speakers of an Indo-European language, who are thought to have entered Anatolia around 2000 BCE (Klengel 2011: 31–32). However, though the main languages used for administrative documents and public monuments were indeed Indo-European (Hittite, also known as Nešite, and the related Luwian), the nascent kingdom also incorporated many of the traditions of the central Anatolian Hattic-speaking people (Bryce 2002; van den Hout 2011: 48–49). It is from this group that the name of the Hittite heartland on the Kızılırmak river—Ḫatti—derives.

The period between c. 1500 and 1400 BCE, sometimes called the "Middle Kingdom," is characterized by the comparative scarcity of sources for reconstructing Hittite political history, though whether this necessarily implies instability or decline has been a matter of much debate over the past century or so (Archi 2003). Records from the "New Kingdom," c. 1400 to the early twelfth century BCE, are much more numerous and reveal the transformation of the Hittite state into a full-blown empire, one of the most powerful polities of Late Bronze Age West Asia (Bryce 2002: 9).

Local kingdoms across Anatolia, Upper Mesopotamia, and the northern Levant were brought into relationships of vassalage with the Great King at Ḫattuša, who also engaged on equal terms in diplomatic correspondence with New Kingdom Egypt and the Middle Babylonian Empire (Beckman 1995; Bryce 2003: 8–37).

Though Hittite rule at its greatest extent stretched from the eastern reaches of the Anatolian Plateau as far west as the Aegean coast (Seeher 2011: 378–79), it was far from the only political force in Late Bronze Age Anatolia. For instance, Mitanni, a large state ruled by an ethnically Indo-European dynasty but inhabited chiefly by people known as Hurrians, occupied northern Mesopotamia and parts of south-eastern Anatolia until it was conquered by the Hittite king Šuppiluliuma I in the late fourteenth century (Van De Mieroop 2007: 123–34, 143). To the west of the Land of Ḫatti, the large Kingdom of Arzawa slipped in and out of Hittite control (Bryce 2011; Matthews 2013). Moreover, in common with contemporaneous and later West Asian rulers, the Hittites were tolerant of religious and cultural diversity within their territory, leaving local traditions largely intact. In particular, the importance of Luwian-speaking people, who probably made up a large proportion of the indigenous/pre-Hittite population of central and western Anatolia, has only recently begun to be appreciated (Mouton et al. 2013; Yakubovich 2011).

Archaeological evidence reveals that the Hittite Empire, along with several other powerful states of the Near East and Aegean, disintegrated rapidly after 1200 BCE (Kaniewski et al. 2013). Ḫattuša was largely abandoned by about 1180 BCE, at least by the ruling elite, and other central Anatolian sites (such as Maşat and Kuşaklı) were destroyed by fire (Hawkins 2009: 164; Seeher 2011). The Late Bronze Age crisis ushered in a period of political fragmentation across the region. In south-eastern Anatolia and northern Syria, it appears that branches of the Hittite ruling dynasty did survive, drawing on the illustrious heritage of the empire and still using old royal titles, rites, and iconography (Bryce 2012; Sams 2011). These kingdoms are known as "Neo-Hittite" or "Syro-Hittite." As Assyria expanded under a series of conquest-oriented kings from the ninth to the seventh centuries BCE, the small Neo-Hittite kingdoms south of the old Hittite heartland, collectively known as Tabal, became vassal states of this resurgent Mesopotamian power (Bryce 2012: 43).

In the rest of the landmass, new polities arose during the early Iron Age (c. 1200–700 BCE), notably Urartu in the east around Lake Van and Phrygia on the western plateau (Voigt and Henrickson 2000; Zimansky 1995). The precise origin of the Phrygian people, who spoke an Indo-European language related to Greek, is not known, but one popular hypothesis holds that they migrated from south-eastern Europe in the wake of the political upheavals (Muscarella 1995; disputed by Drews 1993). Further Greek immigration to the Aegean coast and nearby islands also took place; these eastern Greeks, collectively known as Aeolians, Ionians, and Dorians, would make a considerable contribution to the flowering of Hellenic philosophy, art, and literature in the late first millennium BCE (Bryce 2012: 35). From the eighth century, Greek efforts at colonization also led to the foundation of settlements around the Black Sea and along the southern Anatolian seaboard (Harl 2011: 753–54).

Just as the Hittite Empire had struggled to impose control over the semi-sedentary Kaška of the north-central plateau and Black Sea coast (Glatz and Matthews 2005), incursions by the nomadic Cimmerian people weakened the Tabal kingdoms, Urartu, Phrygia, and other early Iron Age Anatolian states (Bryce 2012: 44; Yakubovich 2011). Cimmerian attacks were likely one cause of the eclipse of Phrygia by the Lydian Kingdom, with its capital at Sardis, from the early seventh century onwards (Bryce 2012: 44; Greenewalt Jr. 2011). The Lydian kings of the Mermnad Dynasty extended their hegemony both westwards, attacking Greek states, and eastwards towards the Kızılırmak River (the Halys in the Classical sources), where they clashed with the Indo-Iranian Median people (Dusinberre 2013: 1; Roosevelt 2012).

The mid-first millennium BCE heralded the arrival of a new imperial power in Anatolia: the Achaemenid Persians. After 550 BCE, beginning with the conquests of Cyrus II, vast swaths of West Asia were unified under a Persian "king of kings" (Kuhrt 2001). Accounts of Cyrus' victory over the Lydian king Croesus were preserved and no doubt embellished by Greek writers such as Herodotus and Ctesias (Kuhrt 2007: 48). Croesus' territories, as well as those of eastern Anatolia, now became satrapies (provinces) of the Achaemenid Empire (Jacobs 2006). Several centuries of Persian rule were brought to an abrupt end in the late fourth century BCE by the arrival of the Macedonian conqueror Alexander the Great.

After Alexander's death in 323 BCE, the future of the vast territories he had conquered was uncertain, and civil war ensued between several Macedonian generals who had been part of his entourage. After decades of conflict, a comparatively stable settlement was reached: by the 270s CE, the Antigonid and Seleucid dynasties were installed in Macedonia and Alexander's Asian territories, respectively, while the descendants of Ptolemy had been firmly in control of Egypt for some time (Braund 2003; Lindsay Adams 2006). Within Anatolia, frontiers between the warring *diadochoi* ("successors" of Alexander) shifted frequently. For a brief time, Lysimachus, another of Alexander's companions, controlled most of Anatolia from his capital in Thrace, but he was defeated and killed in battle against ruler of the Persian territories, Seleucus, in 281 BCE (Lund 1992: 1, 184). Lysimachus' Anatolian possessions passed to the Seleucids, only for yet more new dynasties, notably the Attalids of Pergamon and the Hellenized Anatolian monarchs of Bithynia, Pontus, and Cappadocia, to emerge and assert their independence (Lindsay Adams 2006; Thonemann 2016: 40–41).

Regardless of which dynasty was in power, religion and politics among Anatolian communities became increasingly Greek in character in the aftermath of Alexander's invasion. New administrative structures were established, immigrants from the west arrived, and cities built on Hellenic-style grid plans were founded across the region. At the same time (from the 270s BCE onwards), a group of Celtic-speaking peoples known as Galatians arrived and settled central Anatolia (Mitchell 2003; Thonemann 2016: 40). The Romans, growing in territory and influence across the Mediterranean, increasingly interfered in this fragmented political landscape—with mixed success—from the early second century BCE onwards (Sherwin-White 1977). In the following century, Rome annexed parts of Anatolia to its empire, for instance creating the province of Bithynia-Pontus in the north, and installed tributary kings in others (Rawson 1986: 52–53).

Roman rule of some form would survive in Anatolia for some 1600 years, until the Ottoman conquest of Constantinople. In the third century CE, the empire's center of gravity shifted eastwards from its traditional home in Italy and the "eternal city" itself, Rome, in particular with the accession of Emperor Diocletian in 284 CE. He instituted the first of several divisions of the empire into a Western and an Eastern half, each ruled by a senior and junior emperor (Augustus and Caesar) and presided over the East as Augustus from the city of Nicomedia in western Anatolia (Chadwick 1986; Rees 2004). This arrangement, known as the Tetrarchy, lasted only until 306 CE (Corcoran 2000: 1), but the split between West and East was more enduring. In 324 CE, Emperor Constantine moved the Eastern capital to a strategic location on the Bosphorus. It was from this city, now renamed Constantinople (*née* the Hellenic city of Byzantion), that what we now know as the Eastern Roman Empire—or, especially for later periods, the Byzantine Empire—was governed.

The period covered by this chapter ends in the mid-ninth century CE, with the replacement of the Amorian Dynasty of Byzantine emperors by the Macedonian Dynasty, named after the birthplace of its founder, Basil I (Treadgold 1997: 455). By this date, the frontier between Byzantium and the 'Abbāsid Caliphate, the product of rapid Islamic expansion over the preceding two centuries, ran through eastern Anatolia and northern Mesopotamia (Haldon and Kennedy 1980).

Universalizing morality, egalitarianism, and ideologies of rule
Bronze and Iron Age Anatolia, 1400–546 BCE

In this section, we review the evidence from Anatolia for three key ideological currents identified in the Axial Age literature as characteristic of the mid-first millennium BCE in the five core regions of China, India, Iran, the Levant, and Greece: egalitarian ethics; expressions of universal moral responsibility for all people; and critical, questioning attitudes towards existing political structures. The following section will ask how these shifting beliefs over the course of Anatolian history manifested in practice, for instance through economic (in)equality or differential legal rights for men and women or those of different social status.

The various communities of Late Bronze Age Anatolia practiced forms of religion that had much in common with those of wider West Asia; in the west, there was also some interface with Hellenic cultures across the Aegean. Indeed, it is reasonable to suggest that the people living under Hittite rule in the second millennium BCE participated in a common West Asian culture, drawing on a shared inheritance of religious symbols, rituals, and ideologies spreading from the eastern Mediterranean all the way through Iran and northern Afghanistan. Written and iconographic sources reveal that the religion promoted by the Hittite state during the New Kingdom period entailed the worship of an array of anthropomorphic gods and goddesses (Taracha 2009). As the empire expanded across Anatolia and into modern Iraq and Syria, deities of many different origins—Hattian, Luwian, Hurrian, Palaic, Syro-Mesopotamian—were welcomed into the pantheon, and some of their images were erected in Ḫattuša (Karasu 2003; Taracha 2009). Not for nothing did the Hittites know their capital as the "city of a thousand gods" (Seeher 1995).

The gods of Ḫatti not only demanded but were believed to be dependent on offerings of slaughtered animals, food, and drink as well as festivities in their honor (Collins 2007: 165). They were neither all-knowing nor omnipresent, and under certain circumstances could even be tricked (Bryce 2002: 134; Collins 2007: 174). Linked to their fickle and fallible nature was the lack of a clear boundary between the divine and the human (Beckman 1995: 100). One New Kingdom-period Hittite text (in Bryce 2002: 139) reads:

Are the desires of gods and men different? In no way! Do their natures differ? In no way!

As in other "pre-axial" societies including Shang China, Babylonia, and Assyria, the Hittite king stood between the realms of the gods and of humankind. On the one hand, he was the gods' chosen ruler and earthly representative, and on the other he led rituals on behalf of his people to assure the continuance of divine favor (Bryce 2002; Yakubovich 2005). In Beckman's (1995: 101) memorable phrase, he was the "linchpin of the universe." And, in framing both the relationships between the king and the people and between the gods and the king as master/servant relationships, Hittite religion lent an air of inevitability to social hierarchy as the natural order of the cosmos (Beckman 2013).

The precise nature of the king's own divinity in imperial ideology is the subject of debate among scholars. Harry Hoffner (2006: 144–45) notes that the expression "the king became a god," commonly used to indicate that the monarch had died, has been taken by some historians as an indication that he attained godhood only after death. After reviewing the textual evidence, however, Hoffner (145) concludes that the king "even during his lifetime ... was more like a god than a man." Royal ideology also shifted over time; there was a trend towards greater sacralization of kingship in the late New Kingdom as Tudḫaliya IV (r. c. 1237–1209 BCE) and Šuppiluliuma II (r. c. 1207–1180 BCE), both facing internal challenges to their rule, presented themselves as living gods (Beckman 2002; Collins 2013: 96).

These features of Hittite state-sanctioned ideology—sacred kingship, divine legitimation of the human political order, and the existence of many gods demanding worship through sacrificial rites—align well with models of "archaic" religion found in the Axial Age literature. In all, there are few signs of universalizing or egalitarian currents in the surviving sources, and little evidence of critique of existing sociopolitical structures. Nevertheless, we can point to certain hints of moralizing thought and, arguably, incipient axial transformations in Late Bronze Age Anatolia. First, the Hittite concept of *arā*, meaning appropriate or virtuous behavior, drew its force from ideas of divinely bestowed morality (Collins 2013). Its opposite, *natta arā*, may be glossed as "sin" and has several parallels in Mesopotamian and Egyptian religious thought.[4] In Anatolia during the Hittite New Kingdom, sins such as theft and murder could invoke divine anger and risk punishment through earthly misfortune (Collins 2007: 91). In such cases, the gods had to be placated through rituals, offerings, and the confession of wrongdoing to priests (91). Intriguingly, the Hittite rites of expiation have much in common with first-millennium Levantine practices, and Feder (2011) posits a common origin, perhaps in Bronze Age Syria, for certain Hittite and later Jewish beliefs about the power of blood to atone for sin and impurity.

The existence of behavioral norms enforced by morally concerned gods in Anatolia and wider West Asia several centuries before the proposed Axial Age is a challenge for attempts to enshrine the mid-first millennium BCE as the period in which moralizing religions emerged. For instance, Baumard and Boyer (2013: 272) claim that such faiths first appeared in the Yellow and Yangtze River valleys, northern India, and the eastern Mediterranean between 500 and 200 BCE. However, it is not entirely true to say that the gods of large, complex societies (e.g. in Mesopotamia) before this date "did not care whether people followed moral codes" (272). Though the various deities of Late Bronze Age Anatolia were hardly embodiments of pure goodness, they could not be described as entirely amoral, and they were increasingly perceived as taking an active interest in human conduct as the Hittite state developed. As Collins (2013: 106) writes, by the time of the New Kingdom, the gods were "manifest in history." Muršili II (r. c. 1321–1295 CE), interpreting a devastating plague as a sign of the gods' displeasure, sought possible explanations in the conduct of his

---

4   For instance, the Assyro-Babylonian incantatory text known as *Šurpu*, dating in its most well-known form to the period of Kassite rule in Babylonia (1400–1100 BCE); and the confessions of guilt on stelae dedicated to the gods in New Kingdom Egypt (Assmann 2004; Cranz 2017: 33–35).

father Šuppiluliuma I, who had broken a peace treaty with Egypt guaranteed by the Storm God of Ḫatti (Bryce 2002: 140; Singer 2002: 9–10).

In Muršili's prayers, as well as other late Hittite royal texts such as the Deeds of Šuppiluliuma, we see a level of historical detail unprecedented in the West Asian written record (Assmann 1990: 10–13). An analogous, though more fully developed, concern with the workings of the Israelite God (the God of Abraham) through human history (and with adherence to divine covenants) is a recurring motif in discussions of mid-first-millennium BCE Israel as a site of axial transformation (e.g. Liverani 2005: chap. 10; Uffenheimer 1986). Indeed, Assmann (1990) draws parallels between what he calls the "theologization of history" in both Late Bronze Age Ḫatti and the Iron Age Levant. However, key differences between the two contexts remain. These Hittite sources, composed by kings or those under their direct control, do not mount a critique of the political institutions of the Hittite state, but rather identify specific actions by previous rulers as the possible sources of present misfortunes. In contrast to Israel during the time of the prophets (Blenkinsopp 1995; Eisenstadt 1982), there are no signs of a heterodox intellectual elite in Hittite Anatolia who provided a dissenting voice from dominant religious and political ideologies (Collins 2013: 107).

One further development within Hittite imperial-period state religion that should be considered here is the episode in which King Muwatalli II (r. c. 1295–1272 BCE) left Ḫattuša and founded a new capital, Tarḫuntašša (d'Alfonso 2014; Singer 2006). This king promoted the worship of a new or formerly obscure deity, the Storm God of Lightning, over the more traditional guarantors of royal authority, the Sun Goddess of Arinna and Storm God of Ḫatti (Bryce 2002: 146; Tatišvili 2010). Itamar Singer (2006) has noted the suggestive parallels to the religious reforms of the fourteenth-century Egyptian pharaoh Akhenaten, who also moved the capital. It is true that the Storm God of Lightning held a special position in Muwatalli's prayers, but both iconographic and written evidence shows that this was no radical revolution in theology. Muwatalli did not deny the existence of the other gods, instead addressing them through the Storm God as his personal intercessor (Singer 2002: 91–92). The case for a proto-axial transformation seems weaker in this context than for Akhenaten's more purely monotheistic and universalizing "Amarna revolution" (see e.g. Assmann 1992; discussed further in the Egypt chapter in this volume). Moreover, both these reforms in fact served to bolster the ideological position of the reigning ruler and his proximity to the divine realm, distinguishing them from later egalitarian religious movements.

This highlights a broader issue for the study of religion in Hittite Anatolia: texts from this period tell us very little about the beliefs and religious practice of the majority, non-elite populace (Collins 2013: 96, 104). The written record on such matters is skewed towards royal and elite practice to a much greater degree than in

New Kingdom and Late Period Egypt, where scholars have argued for a florescence of "personal piety" among the general population (Szpakowska 2010). The apparent contrast between the religious contexts of Late Bronze Age Egypt and Anatolia may thus stem from differences in the nature of the surviving written evidence. Another, related problem for historians of Anatolian religions is the scarcity of information about doctrinal attitudes to gender, social status, and other axes of inequality. Iconography and written sources both suggest that female ritual specialists played a prominent role in Hittite worship. Likewise, both gods and goddesses were revered and occupy symmetrical and equal positions on the rock carvings of Yazılıkaya near Ḫattuša (Beckman 2000; Collins 2013). However, as we discuss in the following section, there is ample evidence for concrete forms of sexual discrimination and, more generally, economic inequality and social stratification in the Late Bronze Age Hittite state. As a rule, beyond marking out a special, exalted status for the king, the religious texts we have do not provide clear statements either lending legitimacy to these divisions (for instance through separate origin myths for elites and commoners) or challenging them by insisting on human equality.

After the disintegration of the Hittite state, our sources for reconstructing religion and ideology in Anatolia are even fewer and further between. The small states that occupied the south and south-east of the peninsula during the early to mid-Iron Age are known as "Neo-Hittite" because they preserved certain aspects of older Hittite culture, especially the iconography and rhetoric of kingship, but the degree of religious continuity after 1200 BCE remains unclear in many cases. Hittite cuneiform script (and possibly also the Nešite language) disappeared completely, but bureaucratic institutions did not, especially at sites like Carchemish on the southern fringes of Anatolia (Bryce 2012: 16, 54). As in the Bronze Age, a hieroglyphic script was used to write Luwian inscriptions on stone monuments (Thuesen 2002: 43). In light of the strong evidence for a Luwian cultural orientation for the Neo-Hittite states, it is probable that Luwian religious practices—already identifiable in the archives at Ḫattuša before 1200 BCE—now came to the fore. These included bird augury and certain types of rituals and festivals (Hutter 2003; Mouton and Rutherford 2013). As implied by the alternative name for the south-eastern Anatolian Iron Age kingdoms, the "Syro-Hittite" states, this was also a period in which the various Anatolian traditions underwent further mixing with northern Syrian and Levantine practices, forming the widely shared religious culture from which a distinctive Jewish theology would emerge over the course of the last millennium BCE. However, within the specific contexts of the Neo-Hittite kingdoms from c. 1200 to their incorporation into the Neo-Assyrian Empire in the mid-eighth century BCE, clear evidence has yet to emerge of universalizing morality, egalitarian strains of thought, or other developments that could be considered "axial" or "proto-axial."

Elsewhere in Iron Age Anatolia, the two new states of Urartu (in the east) and Phrygia (on the western plateau) emerged and expanded. What we know of Urartian religion suggests that the king occupied a divinely legitimated position like the monarchs of both Ḫatti and Mesopotamia (Kravitz 2003: 90–92; Zimansky 1995: 1144). Also, in line with other known religious traditions within the centralized states of Bronze and Iron Age West Asia, the many gods of Urartu had diverse origins in the various cultural milieu brought under the control of the Urartian kings (Taffet and Yakar 1998). Both the supreme god Haldi, a warlike deity who supported the king's conquests, and the lesser gods required regular animal sacrifices and festivities in their honor (Taffet and Yakar 1998; Zimansky 1995). Overall, the impression conveyed by Urartian iconography and epigraphy is of a religion that served to bolster royal legitimacy rather than promote egalitarian or universalizing ideals (Smith 2000). However, as in the Hittite case, it should be kept in mind that the surviving sources are heavily biased towards royal and elite ideologies.

Phrygian religion is still less well understood due to the very small corpus of extant textual evidence. It has been suggested, though not universally accepted, that the cultural make-up of the kingdom was a product of the mixing of imported Phrygian traditions from south-eastern Europe and those of the Muški. The latter appear as a "fierce, aggressive, tribal people" in Assyrian records and may have been related to the Kaška who resisted Hittite control in the Bronze Age (Bryce 2012: 40; Mellink 1992). Stone-built architecture at Gordion, the center of the nascent Phrygian state, has been interpreted as residential quarters for the elite, and rich burials in tumuli represent considerable mobilization of labor, likely for the aggrandizement of a few powerful members of society (Roller 2011: 562). Though archaeological dating methods have shown that the so-called "Midas Mound" predates the late eighth-century Phrygian king Midas, it is the most impressive of these burial tumuli, and its occupant was evidently a powerful ruler (Sams 2005: 20). Written inscriptions and carved images at sacred sites associated with the polity have led scholars to suggest that Phrygian religion was polytheistic but with a focus on Matar, a "mother goddess" (Roller 2011: 570–72). Indeed, it is widely accepted that the cult of the goddess Kybele (Greek) or Cybele (Latin) in the Greco-Roman world derived from earlier Phrygian practices (Alvar 2008; Roller 1999). The name of one Midas, possibly the aforementioned historically attested king, is inscribed at one of Matar's sanctuaries, hinting that—whatever the disruptive potential of later ecstatic Greek and Roman rites in her honor—in Phrygia she had close ties to the state and to royal power (Joukowsky 1996: 374–78; Roller 1999: 69–70).

The limited evidence we have tells a similar story for the Lydian kingdom, which was socially stratified and ruled by an "absolute" monarch with the aid of a wealthy elite (Joukowsky 1996: 409). Lydian material culture testifies to strong links with the Aegean world (Greenewalt Jr. 1995: 2011), and religious life at Sardis involved the worship of Greek as well as local Anatolian gods (Roosevelt 2009: 80–84). King Gyges appears in the written record both dedicating lavish gifts to the sanctuary of Apollo at Delphi and humbly requesting military aid from the Assyrian king Aššurbanipal (Cogan and Tadmor 1977; Kaplan 2006: 130–31). It seems likely that such external connections served to bolster Lydian royal power—especially as the polity expanded and exacted tribute from a range of Anatolian and eastern Greek populations—by providing impressive symbols of the kings' wealth and proximity to various deities. Though our impressions of Lydia are colored by Greek authors' stereotypes of Eastern decadence and tyranny, it must be admitted that indications of egalitarian or universalizing ideologies in the kingdom are lacking.

Imperial rule of Anatolia, 546 BCE to 866 CE

Anatolia came under the Achaemenid yoke in the mid-sixth century BCE in the course of Cyrus' conquests. Claims for the "axiality" of the Achaemenid Empire are addressed in the chapter on Iran in this volume, but here it is sufficient to note that the transformation of Anatolian kingdoms and other independent polities into Persian satrapies had starkly different effects in different regions. As we discuss in the following section, Thonemann (2013: 8–14) has argued that in Phrygia, the Achaemenid occupation had a "flattening" effect on local hierarchies. If his interpretations are correct, it is possible that egalitarian and universalizing ideologies accompanied and promoted processes of "state evasion" in Phrygia. However, because the collapse of older, hierarchical political institutions went hand in hand with the abandonment of writing here, evidence of such ideologies is lacking.

Elsewhere in Anatolia, the Persian conquest shaped the practices and beliefs of local elites in the image of the imperial center, and these elites prospered from their associations with distant royal power (Dusinberre 2013: 69–71). Importantly for our purposes, the Achaemenid period brought the rites and institutions of Zoroastrianism, which survived into the Hellenistic period and beyond. Zoroastrian practices in Anatolia are attested in the reports of Greek and Roman historians as well as in archaeological remains, such as the presence of a fire altar at a sanctuary in Hellespontine Phrygia (Hjerrild 1990; Roller 2011: 564–65). Lydia shows particularly clear cultural and religious "Iranization," including the arrival of Persian nobles (Sekunda 1985).

It was the character of the Prophet Zarathustra's teachings that prompted Karl Jaspers to include the Persians among his five "axial peoples" (Jaspers 1953: 2). According to his theories, the transfer of Persian religious ideas and motifs to Anatolia should have effected a profound ethical transformation in local modes of thought. However, at least by the Hellenistic period (to which most of our evidence for Zoroastrian worship in Anatolia dates), it appears that the radically egalitarian aspects of earlier manifestations of the religion had given way to more rigid and prescriptive forms, dominated by the priesthood (Hjerrild 1990: 144–46). As we discuss in the chapter on Iran, Jaspers' concept of simultaneous axial breakthroughs in the mid-first millennium BCE falters when it comes to the Persian case because current scholarly consensus dates Zarathustra to the second millennium BCE. There are few indications of a florescence of universalizing and equity-promoting beliefs associated with Mazda-worship as it was practiced under the Achaemenid kings.

Alexander's conquest in the late fourth century BCE and the emergence of Hellenistic kingdoms did not result in a wholesale replacement of Anatolian and wider West Asian ideologies in the region, but it did add new, Greco-Macedonian elements to its complex cultural mixture. Again, we see the importation of the traditions of one of the "axial peoples"—the Greeks—but neither egalitarian ethics nor universalizing morality, nor indeed reflexive critique of the existing social order, gained ascendancy in the process. Instead, sacred legitimization for the institution of monarchy was provided by a well-developed ruler cult, in which incense offerings were made and monuments dedicated to the Seleucid (and later Pergamene-Attalid) kings (Lindsay Adams 2006: 46). The new rulers could also use invasions of Celtic Galatians in the third century BCE as a valuable propaganda tool, presenting themselves as "saviors" of Greek civilization from the "barbarian" hordes (Mitchell 2003: 284).

Concessions were occasionally made in this period to Greek ideals of "freedom," but, as elsewhere in the Hellenistic world, this now most often took the form of a defense of the political autonomy of the culturally Greek cities (Dimitrov 2011; Lund 1992). Hellenistic schools of philosophy such as Stoicism, Epicureanism, and Cynicism, many of which made decidedly "axial" ethical recommendations (see the Mediterranean Basin chapter), also featured in the intellectual life of fourth- to first-century BCE Anatolia. However, it appears that they did not penetrate far beyond the Hellenized urban elite of the (mainly coastal) cities, and the majority of the population likely continued older cultic practices without much regard for the thought of Epicurus, Diogenes the Cynic, or Zeno of Citium.

As Anatolia gradually came under Roman hegemony and then direct rule from the mid-second to the first centuries BCE, cultural exchanges took place in both directions. While Greco-Roman deities such as Jupiter, Juno/Hera, and Aphrodite/Venus received worship at new temples across Anatolia, eunuch priests conducted rituals in Rome itself in honor of the Phrygian mother goddess Cybele (Fear 1996: 43; MacMullen 1981: 7, 43; Rubin 2008: 65–68). We can also point to significant continuities in religious practice, as the Eastern portion of the Roman Empire retained a substantially Hellenic cultural character. The Roman imperial cult—institutionalized in Anatolia from the reign of Augustus onwards (Rubin 2008)—merely replaced Seleucid, Attalid, and other local ruler cults with another version of sacral kingship. Within the varied religious landscape of Hellenistic and Roman Anatolia, certain universalizing and egalitarian elements can be identified. Notably, some of the "mystery religions" that gained popularity in this period were open to people excluded from participation in traditional, state-sanctioned cults.[5]

The interconnected and cosmopolitan nature of the post-axial Mediterranean enabled the rapid spread of Christian beliefs and practices, and Anatolia saw the formation of some of the earliest Christian communities beyond the Levant. By the mid-third century CE, "powerful Jewish and Christian communities" were present even in the mountainous interior (Mitchell 1993: 10). The religion was explicitly universalizing and—at least in spiritual terms—egalitarian, particularly in its early incarnations across the empire. However, early Christian groups' millenarian expectation of the imminent arrival of the kingdom of God, in which all human distinctions would be dissolved or reversed, soon gave way to an acceptance of earthly hierarchies as the Church grew in power (Beavis 2007: 46–49). This process was intensified after Constantine's legalization of Christianity within the Roman Empire and the eastward shift of the seat of imperial power. As we note in the Mediterranean Basin chapter, the Church served to legitimize a range of increasingly rigid social divisions in the Eastern Roman or Byzantine Empire. Anatolia, now at the very heart of empire, was no exception.

Universalizing morality and egalitarian ethics in practice: From the Hittite Empire to the early Byzantine period

In this section, we ask how the ideological developments reviewed above related to more concrete aspects of equity and modes of governance in Anatolia between the Bronze Age and the Byzantine period.

Given the exalted position held by the kings of the Hittite New Kingdom, it comes as no surprise to learn that royal power was almost completely unconstrained. As well as chief priest and military leader, the king headed the judiciary as the most important judge in the empire, and challenging his judgments was punishable by death (Bryce 2002: 29; Collins 2013: 107). While in the Old Kingdom an assembly of officials, known as the *panku*, may have acted as a moderating influence on the kings' activities, after c. 1400 BCE references to the *panku* disappear (Trevor Bryce, pers. comm. 2016).

We noted above how the available texts on Hittite religion do not provide a clear picture of attitudes to economic and gender inequality or to the practice of slavery. Legal texts, however, lent institutional backing to class distinctions and the inferiority of women and slaves, which must have shaped the everyday lives of the Hittite Empire's subjects significantly (Beckman 2000; Bryce 2002: 38–40, 52). Slave owners were permitted to punish, mutilate, and even execute their slaves (Bryce 2002: 52).

---

5   For a brief discussion of mystery religions and their relationship to axial-style ethical thinking, see the Mediterranean Basin chapter in this volume.

The *Hittite Laws*, a compendium of case law preserved in several different versions dating between 1650 and 1200 BCE, set out harsher penalties for causing harm to a man than a woman and valued a slave's life at around half that of a free person (36–40). In this respect, Hittite legal practices were similar to those of wider Bronze Age West Asia (Wells 2005: 190–92). The socioeconomic position of women in general also appears to have been less favorable than the prominent role enjoyed by female ritual specialists in religious life might suggest. Beckman (2000: 22), though noting the lack of clear expressions of religious ideology, ventures the opinion that religion "was an aspect of Hittite life resistant to the patriarchal hegemony of the culture."

Moderating this rather gloomy picture of life under Hittite rule is the apparent absence of discrimination based on ethnicity or birthplace. Late Bronze Age Anatolia was culturally diverse and mixed; in the archives of Ḫattuša, for example, at least eight different languages were in use (Bryce 2002: 6, 251–52). Patterns of enslavement appear to be unconnected to ethnic or linguistic identity, and the *Hittite Laws* do not specify differential rights along these lines, though the evidence for this is somewhat sparse. In general, the mid- to late second millennium BCE in West Asia was an age of large-scale interregional trade accompanied by extensive cultural interchange (Matthews 2013: 454; Van De Mieroop 2007: 129–48), supporting a multicultural and (in some ways) open, though hierarchical and patriarchal, social environment.

We should also acknowledge that certain features of Hittite legal texts were evidently intended, at least in theory, to guarantee fairness and equality before the law for all people (Bryce 2002: 38–40). As Bryce notes, the *Laws* insist that justice be administered fairly and impartially, without bias or favoring the interests of the elite over others. At the same time, it is clear that, in spite of such universalizing ideals, certain social and class distinctions were nevertheless reinforced legally, as noted above.

Several Axial Age proponents (e.g. Bellah 2011; Eisenstadt 1986b) have described a respect for the "rule of law," and in particular salvoes made to its universal application, as a characteristic of societies undergoing axial transformation, such as Classical Athens. This underscores how complex the situation in Bronze and Iron Age Anatolia was regarding any sort of axial transition; in many ways, the strong authoritarianism and clear class and gender differences fit well within traditional models of archaic (i.e. pre-axial) society, but in other respects, such as the strong institutionalization of widely applied legal rights, societies like the Hittites appear rather as precocious, almost proto-axial.

It is interesting, if not entirely surprising, that the Iron Age in Anatolia seems to have resulted in a greater centralization and entrenchment of social, economic, and political hierarchies in the smaller, wealthy kingdoms that emerged in the wake of Hittite collapse. The Kingdoms of Phrygia, Urartu, and Lydia display clear signs of hierarchy, for instance in the citadel uncovered in the Phrygian capital of Gordion. Gordion's architecture reflects a "privileged society prepared for war and siege," one that stockpiled provisions and wealth and likely cemented social hierarchies by imposing restrictions on movement within the citadel (Mellink 1992: 629). Lydia presents us with a similar story, evident from the power and privilege of the military and economic elites in the capital, Sardis (Joukowsky 1996: 409). It is less clear, however, whether the smaller, outlying towns in Anatolia enjoyed a more equitable, "heterarchical" social organization, as some evidence suggests. For instance, Phrygian Kerkenes lacked a citadel and clear markers of status difference (Liverani 2016: 204). Still, royal authority in the heart of the Anatolian kingdoms was near absolute in this period, with well-established and legally enforced differences in class, rank, and gender.

With the Persian conquest of Lydia in the mid-sixth century, a layer of Achaemenid imperial bureaucracy was overlain onto indigenous Anatolian institutions. We noted above how the historical trajectories of different regions of central Anatolia diverged from each other during this process. According to Thonemann (2013: 8), there was a process of "de-statification" in Phrygia between 550 and 330 BCE and, for centuries afterwards, society here remained mostly rural, "post-literate" and "largely non-stratified." In his view, the disappearance of rich burials and monumental architecture after the mid-sixth century marks not a generalized collapse of society, or even of urban life, but an "internal process of radical simplification" (12–13). The patterns observable in Achaemenid-period Phrygia are very different from those of Lydia, where luxury goods and administrative documents show a prosperous elite tied into the Persian state bureaucracy (14). Thonemann raises the possibility that the dramatic decrease in social hierarchy in Phrygia in this period was a (perhaps intentional) "rational adaptation" to demands for tribute from the region's conquerors (14). This view, however, should not necessarily be taken as a sign of an axial transition for Anatolia as a whole, as the "flattening" of social hierarchy in Phrygia was balanced by the numerous layers of military and bureaucratic hierarchy elsewhere, creating a large group of privileged elite at the level of cities, satrapies, and the royal courts and bureaucratic centers in Mesopotamia and on the Iranian Plateau. In short, Achaemenid rule in Anatolia brought the same complexities and contradictions as it did further south:[6] on the one hand, prominent, politically supported ideals of universalizing morality and social and cultural egalitarianism, arguably linked to the Zoroastrian inheritance of the Persian elite; yet on the other, strict administrative hierarchies and a privileged elite class led by an autocratic, semi-divine Great King.

---

6   See the discussion of morality and egalitarianism in practice under the Achaemenids in the Iran chapter in this volume.

Similar contradictions were present in Hellenistic Anatolia. Like the other successor states that carved out pieces of Alexander's great empire, the Anatolian kingdoms mixed existing (in this case Achaemenid) institutions and practices with Greek ideals, adapting each to the chaotic political and military realities of the eastern Mediterranean of the period. In spite of the popularity of certain strands of Greek philosophy espousing the rule of law, opposition to tyranny, and universal morality—ideals nominally exported throughout Anatolia with the campaigns of the philosophically trained Alexander—in practice the successor states in Anatolia retained a more Persian style of autocratic governance and hierarchically organized bureaucracy than a Classical Athenian-style democracy (Lund 1992). Still, certain hallmarks of the Greek world's axial transition did make their way across the Hellespont. Notably, the practice of civic benefaction became both an important form of resource distribution and a symbol of the concern that elites had for the majority population. This form of prosocial behavior is often taken as a key indicator of the adoption, or internalization, of egalitarian, moral ideals (Mullins et al. 2018; Turchin 2014; Wilson 2015). As Lund (1992: 166) puts it, referring to royal benefactions, "though in crude terms this might be seen simply as a bribe, it also reflects the new ruler's concern to show himself truly royal, aware of his kingly obligations." At the same time, however, the practice of euergetism should be seen as rooted in the sharp socioeconomic inequalities that allowed elites to accumulate such masses of wealth, of which only a small fraction was "redistributed" through such benefaction (Cecchet 2014; Hoyer 2018).

The transition from Hellenistic to Roman rule in the Mediterranean Basin is discussed in several other chapters in this volume, so we will not say much on it here (see the Mediterranean Basin and Levant chapters in particular). It is worth noting, though, that Roman hegemony in the eastern Mediterranean, which began in earnest with the bequest of the Kingdom of Pergamon to Rome by King Attalus III upon his death in 133 BCE, brought no sharp changes to prevailing Hellenistic cultural, social, and institutional practices. This includes Anatolia, which piece by piece became incorporated into Rome's burgeoning empire. Rome, still a republic at this time, imposed its own layers of administration, concerned particularly with fiscal matters, but otherwise allowed Anatolian cities to retain their systems of civic rule, including councils, euergetism, and religious practices (Green 1990; Ma 2003). Particularly notable is that, even after Rome's transition from republic to principate, Roman emperors were venerated in the East as god-kings, resembling more the autocratic Hellenistic rulers than the "first among equals" image that emperors tended to favor in Italy and the Western provinces (Scheid 2011). Several centuries later, the ascension of Christianity as the dominant state religion in the early Byzantine period accompanied growing class and gender distinctions as well as an increasing centralization and institutionalization of bureaucratic hierarchies.[7] Put simply, the experience of Anatolia as well as the rest of the Roman Mediterranean took nearly the opposite course from that asserted by most proponents of the Axial Age, who tend to see Christianity as a secondary axial breakthrough that *should* have brought the Roman world closer to strong, institutionalized universalizing moral norms and egalitarian ideals, not further away.

Conclusions

Anatolia is a critical region not only for exploring the full implications of axiality, but for any global, cross-cultural historical study. The area has always been at the crossroads of history: supporting some of the earliest sedentary populations at the Neolithic transition and complex imperial formations in the early Bronze Age; acting as a conduit of social, economic, and cultural transfer between Europe and Asia throughout antiquity; sitting on the frontier of great empires as Rome and Parthian and then Sasanian Persia fought for hegemony; then taking on the mantle of Classical civilization from Rome during the long Byzantine period. Throughout, the societies of Anatolia have witnessed complex, often contradictory cultural and political influences, repeatedly documented in the preceding pages.

One element that comes across time and again in this sweeping overview of Anatolian history is the central role played by Anatolian societies in developments traditionally lauded as axial. The Bronze Age societies of the second millennium BCE, notably the vast Hittite Empire, had a clear and powerful impact on later developments in areas like Greece and the Levant—two of Jaspers' five core areas of axial transition. Hittite society, while "archaic" in some respects, nevertheless displayed many precedents of axial traits, much earlier than most scholars begin the Axial Age (Assmann 2012). Not only was Anatolia precocious in its axiality, but even during the mid-first millennium BCE, the period of axiality posited by most scholars, Anatolia formed a key node in a rich network of economic, political, and ideological exchange between societies around the Mediterranean Basin and in West Asia. Through this network, many of the ideals and institutional structures identified as axial were developed and transmitted between societies (Bryce 2002).

It is remarked on in other chapters (e.g. the Iran, Egypt, and Levant chapters) how traditional notions of the Axial Age that see each "axial awakening" as an independent, autochthonous development do a disservice to the complex interconnections between societies across Afro-Eurasia during the first millennium BCE. The experiences of Anatolian societies at this time and earlier further underscores this view. Indeed, the expansion of Anatolian civilizations from the Neolithic onwards had "an overwhelming impact on the formation of Bronze Age culture in Crete, as

---

7   See the Mediterranean Basin chapter in this volume for details.

well as the Mycenaean and Greek culture which grew out of it, later determining the cultural fate of Graeco-Roman antiquity" (Taracha 2009: 1) along with the axial modes of thought and practice arising in the Levant. This makes it all the more notable—indeed regrettable—that the region has been excluded from almost every account of the Axial Age.

Although an important and, at times, dominating presence through the Bronze and Iron Ages, once Anatolia was brought under Achaemenid rule in the sixth century BCE, the region experienced only periodic bursts of political independence. Even in these "independent" kingdoms, though, political administration, the authority of rulers, and the prevailing ideologies concerning moral norms and the distribution of rights and responsibilities tend to mirror those within the wider sociopolitical context of the time. From the mid-first millennium BCE to the Byzantine period, where this chapter comes to a close, Anatolian societies experienced the same complex developments in terms of the key markers of axiality as the other large, imperial societies in the region discussed in more detail in this volume's chapters on Iran, the Levant, and the Mediterranean Basin. This experience was, in essence, one of contrasts. On the one hand, we witness a clear rise in ideals espousing universal application of moral norms, of equitable treatment of various segments of a population, of more regularized, institutionalized forms of administering the law, and arguments against the unchecked power and divine prestige afforded to rulers. Yet at the same time, the practical experience of these societies belied many of these ideals, as strict divisions between class, status, and gender were enforced both in ideology and in law, and rulers maintained their autocratic authority and, for a remarkably long time, their claims to divinity (or at least divine authority).

The presence of nominally axial traditions such as Zoroastrianism, Judaism, Greek and Hellenistic philosophy, and later Christianity did little if anything to dissolve these strict divisions and inequalities in practice. Anatolia, typically neglected in cross-cultural studies on the Axial Age, adds much-needed richness to the concept of the Axial Age, showing how critical developments across West Asia and the Mediterranean were in fact quite interconnected. The region also provides further nuance, as the ideological and institutional developments within Anatolian societies display elements that fit within, but also some that contradict, traditional accounts of a mid-first millennium BCE axial transition. This chapter offers much evidence that agrees with many of the conclusions presented in other chapters in this volume and demonstrates, hopefully, why it is crucial to expand analysis of axiality beyond the typical Eurasian core of much previous work on the Axial Age.

CHAPTER 9

NORTH AFRICA | Egypt
Jenny Reddish & J.G. Manning

Period	Dynasty/Polity	Approx. dates
Bronze Age		
Predynastic	Dynasty 0	4400–3100 BCE
Early Dynastic	Dynasties 1–2	3100–2686
Old Kingdom	Dynasties 3–6	2686–2150
First Intermediate Period	Dynasties 7–10	2150–2016
Middle Kingdom	Dynasties 11–12	2016–1700
Second Intermediate Period	Dynasties 13–17	1700–1567
New Kingdom	Dynasties 18–20	1567–1070
Iron Age / Archaic		
Third Intermediate Period	Dynasties 21–25	1070–656
Saite Period	Dynasty 26	656–525
Persian Period	Dynasties 27–30	525–323
Greco-Roman	Ptolemaic	323–30
	Roman Empire	30 BCE–284 CE
	Eastern Roman Empire	284–395
Late Antique	Byzantine Empire	395–642
Early Medieval	Early Islamic Caliphate ("Rāshidūn")	642–661
	Umayyad Caliphate	661–750
	ʿAbbāsid Caliphate	750–850
	Ṭūlūnid and Ikhshīdid Dynasties	868–969
	Fāṭimid Caliphate	909–1171
	Ayyūbid Sultanate	1171–1250

Table 7. Periods of Egyptian history mentioned below. Dates for Predynastic to Greco-Roman periods based on the *Oxford History of Ancient Egypt* (Shaw 2000b: 480–89).

Introduction

Rivaled only by Mesopotamia in the antiquity of its civilization, the fertile strip of land flanking the Nile River in modern-day Egypt has been home to complex societies for over five millennia. During the late Neolithic, regional population centers grew up at sites like Abydos, Naqada and Hierakonpolis in Upper Egypt (the area between the First Cataract of the Nile and the Faiyum region) (Stevenson 2016). Cemeteries at these fourth-millennium sites have produced evidence for elite burials (433–37). At Abydos, hundreds of ivory and bone labels inscribed with an early form of writing were found in one tomb (Van De Mieroop 2011: 43). Lower Egypt (the northern Nile Valley, dominated by the Delta as the river fans out into the Mediterranean) also shows signs of an emerging elite, though somewhat later than in the south (Stevenson 2016: 446–48). In general, increasing social inequality, a greater commitment to sedentary settlement and cereal farming, and the invention of writing laid the foundations for the rise of a centralized state and a ruling dynasty around 3200–3100 BCE (Anđelković 2014). Though Egypt's monarchs liked to portray the foundation of the state as a unification of two independent kingdoms, Upper and Lower Egypt, through military conquest, archaeological research has revealed a much more complex process of cultural, economic and political coalescence (John Baines, pers. comm. 2019; Van De Mieroop 2011: 35–36).

With the exception of periods of instability and decentralization, Egypt was ruled by these powerful kings, in tandem with an elaborate secular and religious bureaucracy, until the last "native" rulers were unseated by Persian and Macedonian invasions in the mid-fourth century BCE (Perdu 2010; Ruzicka 2012: 3, 211). The Greco-Macedonian Ptolemies maintained much of the political structure of the older Dynastic state and effectively ruled as pharaohs. However, they were ousted by the Romans in 30 BCE, who held sway in Egypt—ruling first from Rome and then from Constantinople as Byzantine emperors—until it was absorbed into the Muslim world in the seventh century.

Despite the long duration of civilization in the Nile Valley, the region has been sidelined in discussions of the Axial Age. Pharaonic Egypt was excluded from Karl Jaspers' original five core axial areas of China, India, Iran, the Levant, and Greece. When it is mentioned in this connection, it is usually to serve as an example of an archaic, pre-axial culture. The work of Egyptologist Jan Assmann (1989, 2005, 2012), who argues that this scheme ignores the appearance of some key "axial" traits in Egyptian society well before the first millennium BCE, is a notable exception. The research of Egyptologists has shown that universalizing morality and some currents of egalitarian thought began to emerge in Egypt as early as the Old Kingdom, although these were counterbalanced by more hierarchical tendencies both in ideology and practice. As we note below, the perception of Akhenaten's religious reforms in the fourteenth century BCE as the sole dynamic moment against a background of timeless Pharaonic civilization is not justified. The Middle Kingdom in particular was a time when literature grappled with the problem of suffering, the nature of the gods, and the proper forms for human society.

The arrival of the Ptolemies brought Hellenic philosophical schools along with the more "traditional" worship of Greek deities (Morrison 2010: 758–61). According to dominant narratives of the Axial Age, the introduction of Greek culture into Egypt should have produced an increase in egalitarian ethics and universalizing morality, but the evidence for such a transformation is fairly weak. (Indeed, as we discuss below, the paramount indigenous concept of cosmic balance and ethical "rightness"—*maat*—exemplifies moralizing strands in Egyptian intellectual history that predate the Ptolemies by thousands of years.) By the Late Antique period, when Egypt formed part of the Eastern Roman Empire, religion and ethics in the province included strands of thought from Christian sects (some considered heresies), Judaism, Greco-Roman paganism, and the ancient beliefs of the Pharaonic age. Islam, like Christianity an egalitarian faith stressing a universalizing cosmology, clear moral prescriptions, and ethical imperatives for all people including ideals of equality and exhortations to prosocial behavior, was added to this complex mixture with the Arab invasion in 639–642 CE.

This chapter will first provide a very brief outline of Egyptian history from the beginning of the Old Kingdom c. 2650 BCE to the fall of the Fāṭimid Dynasty, then ruling from Cairo, in 1171 CE (Lev 2010: 210). It proceeds to explore a wealth of historical evidence concerning the key variables relevant to discussions of the Axial Age outlined above. What stance did Egyptian religious and philosophical thought take on the proper relations between rulers, elites, and commoners, and how did this change over the course of the Pharaonic, Greco-Roman and Islamic eras? In which periods can we speak of universalizing moral traditions in the Nile Valley? The chapter will also examine the evidence for connections between moral ideologies, institutions promoting social equality, and manifestations of "prosociality" in the region: for instance, charitable works and the production of public goods.

Historical and religious background

Pharaonic Egypt is customarily divided into the Old, Middle, and New Kingdoms—conceived of as periods of stability and centralized rule—separated by three Intermediate Periods characterized by political fragmentation (Van De Mieroop 2011: 19–20). The centuries between the Third Intermediate Period and the Macedonian invasion (more specifically, 664–332 BCE) are referred to as the Late Period (Lloyd 2000a). This scheme is largely an invention of nineteenth- and early twentieth-century Egyptologists (Morenz and Popko 2010: 102; Schneider 2003: 241–42), but continues to furnish a useful framework for Ancient Egyptian history. Further chronological divisions are provided by the concept of royal dynasties as set down by the Ptolemaic-period historian Manetho in the third century BCE (Malek 2000: 84).

Throughout the Pharaonic period, Egyptian religion centered around the worship of an extensive pantheon of gods and goddesses, some of whom assumed ascendancy at different periods of Dynastic history. Due to scarcity of evidence, the religious practices of the general population are less well understood than the "state religion" of the great temples, although altars, small statues of gods, and stelae inscribed with devotional texts and images have all been found in private households (Stevens 2009). We know that some deities could be approached by ordinary people through prayers and magic (for instance, the goddess Hathor heard petitions for fertility), while others communicated chiefly with the king or priests (Szpakowska 2010: 511). The gods varied in their precise relationships to the human social realm, but no aspect of life in Pharaonic Egypt was considered free from divine influence. As well as the gods, Egyptians could interact with the "justified" and "unjustified" dead (*akhu* and *mwt*) (509).

Certain remarkably consistent themes characterized Egyptian religion. In particular, the concept of *maat*—the correct moral order of the universe—structured Egyptian thought in a wide array of contexts. Usually translated as "order," "harmony," or "justice," *maat* served as a moral ideal for everyday social relations as well as a fundamental cosmic principle (Assmann 2006: 15–17). Its opposite was *isfet* (chaos), but it was also contrasted with evil and wrongdoing (176). Also central to the Egyptian worldview was an enduring concern with the afterlife (Szpakowska 2010: 507). Finally, it is impossible to understand the Pharaonic state without a consideration of the divine nature of Egyptian kingship (Baines 1995: 6, 10).

By the second half of the first millennium BCE, however, the political position of Egypt's divine kings had been weakened considerably by foreign invasions and internal conflict. When Alexander the Great entered the region in 332 BCE, he found a state torn apart by conflicts between the occupying Persians, native Egyptian dynasts and *machimoi* (militia), and mercenaries from across the eastern Mediterranean (Lloyd 2000a: 377–82; Manning 2010: 26–27). He had little difficulty in bringing an end to Persian rule and (though this is disputed) may even have been crowned pharaoh at Memphis, carrying out the required rituals and assuming the trappings of Egyptian divine kingship (Lloyd 2000a: 382; 2000b: 388–89).[1] After Alexander's death in Babylon in 323 BCE and two decades of civil war among his followers, his general Ptolemy emerged victorious as King of Egypt (Hölbl 2001: 12–14; Lloyd 2000b: 389). Later proclaimed Soter—"the savior"—by his son, he founded a Greco-Macedonian dynasty that was to rule Egypt for almost three centuries (Mikalson 2006; Thompson 2005: 113). This is known as the Hellenistic period, a term denoting the wider Greek world in ancient times. Alexander's successors—Greco-Macedonian generals—ruled over large tracts of territory in the eastern Mediterranean and western Asia.

In 30 BCE, the famous suicide of Cleopatra VII after the defeat of the Egyptian navy, commanded by her lover and Roman general Marc Antony, at the Battle of Actium marked the fall of the Ptolemaic Dynasty (Venning 2011: 334–35). For Rome, the battle was a decisive moment in the transition from Republic to Empire; the victor, Octavian, would soon become the first Roman emperor, adopting the name

---

1   Burstein (1991) has cast doubt on this, noting that the only ancient source for Alexander's coronation as pharaoh is the *Alexander Romance* of Pseudo-Callisthenes: a writer not renowned for his reliability.

Augustus (Venning 2011: 337–40). Egypt was now annexed to Rome as the province of Aegyptus (Pfeiffer 2012: 83; Vandorpe 2010: 173–75). Both native Egyptian and Greco-Mediterranean culture and religion, the influence of which had grown under the Ptolemies, continued to flourish under the Romans (Frankfurter 1998: 7), not to mention the beliefs and practices of Jewish, Arab, Syrian, and other communities well established in Egypt since Pharaonic times (Capponi 2010: 185). The economic importance of the fertile Nile floodplain also grew, as Egypt became a key source of grain for the empire's Mediterranean core (Van De Mieroop 2011: 321). The province remained a vital (if often troublesome) strategic possession for Rome until the Sasanian Persian invasions of the early seventh century CE (Power 2012: 86).

After the death of Theodosius I, the last Roman emperor to control both the western and eastern provinces, in 395 CE, the Roman Empire was to all intents and purposes split into two (Barnwell 1992: 1). Egypt formed a key part of the Eastern Roman (or Byzantine) Empire, governed from Constantinople (Istanbul in modern-day Turkey). With notable exceptions—such as the "turmoil" of the sixth century, when Egypt was racked by the Plague of Justinian, an earthquake, and sectarian religious conflict—the Nile Valley saw long periods of peace under Byzantine rule (Capponi 2010: 193–95). It was also during the Byzantine period that Christianity became dominant in Egypt. Christian symbols, beliefs and practices had in fact found a foothold among some Egyptians well before the legalization of the new faith by Constantine the Great in 313 CE (Capponi 2010: 193; Frankfurter 1998: 269). After this date, though, it received institutional backing and Alexandria in particular grew into an important seat of ecclesiastical power (Capponi 2010: 193).

By the mid-seventh century CE, the hegemony of Constantinople in North Africa was on the wane. As part of a general assault on Byzantine power, the armies of the Persian Sasanian Empire invaded Egypt, capturing Alexandria in 619 and Upper Egypt in around 621 CE (Power 2012: 86). The Sasanians could not hold onto their conquests for more than a decade, however, and in 629 Byzantium regained Egypt (86). These struggles between the latest incarnations of the Roman and Persian Empires for control of the country were brought to an end by the Arab military expansion after the death of the Prophet Muḥammad. First invading Egypt in 639, Arab armies encountered relatively little violent resistance, and over a three-year period the region was absorbed into the young Islamic Caliphate (Bowman 1986: 52–53). This brought a large new Arab Muslim population into the region and prompted the conversion of much of the Egyptian populace.

From this date onwards, Egypt formed part of successive Islamic sultanates and caliphates, sometimes as a province of larger empires stretching across North Africa and West Asia and sometimes functioning as a politically autonomous unit. Until the assassination of Caliph ʿAlī in 661 CE, Egypt formed part of a large imperial state, stretching from Iran to Tunisia and ruled by the *rāshidūn,* or "rightly guided," caliphs (Bosworth 1996: 1–2). After 'Alī's death, Mu'āwiya, the governor of Syria and member of the influential Umayyad family, founded what became known as the Umayyad Caliphate (Aghaie 2005; Hawting 2002). Under Mu'āwiya and his successors, the caliphate grew to encompass a vast territory that included Mesopotamia, Syria, Arabia and Egypt (Robinson 2010b: 209; Raymond 2000: 17).

The Umayyads' hold over Egypt lasted until 750 CE, when the dynasty was defeated by the 'Abbāsids (Bosworth 1996: 4). Though they moved the seat of power from Damascus to modern-day Iraq, the 'Abbāsids inherited the Umayyad territory and Egypt remained a province within an empire governed from western Asia (Bosworth 1996: 8). From 868 to 969 CE, the Ṭūlūnid and Ikhshīdid Dynasties were generally able to govern Egypt as if it were an autonomous state, though they continued to pay lip service to the 'Abbāsid caliphs (Raymond 2000: 26, 34; Sundelin 2013: 430–31).

In the mid-tenth century, Egypt was conquered by the Fāṭimids, who adhered to a form of Shī'a Islam known as Ismā'īlism and were in open rivalry with the 'Abbāsids (Bosworth 1996: 64). The Fāṭimid *imām*-caliphs retained control of Egypt—in the later phases via their increasingly powerful viziers—until they were succeeded by the Ayyūbid Dynasty (Lev 2010: 210–13). The first Ayyūbid ruler in Egypt was Saladin, famous from European sources as a formidable adversary during the Crusades; he was a member of the Kurdish Ayyūbid family and a Sunnī Muslim (Jubb 2005: 238). The period covered by this chapter ends with the military coup that unseated the Ayyūbids in Egypt, led by the Mamluks (high-ranking slave soldiers) in 1249 CE (Levanoni 1990: 137).

From pharaohs to caliphs: Religion and the position of the ruler in Egypt

One of the features of supposedly pre-axial states according to most Axial Age proponents is the elevation of rulers to the status of gods, concomitant with a lack of institutional constraints on their political power (Bellah 2011). Conversely, an increasingly skeptical attitude towards this "archaic" identification of kings with gods and towards rulers' claims to natural superiority over the general population is thought to characterize societies undergoing axial transformations (571).

This section will first examine the changing role of the divine pharaoh—both ideologically and in practice—over the course of the Old, Middle, and New Kingdoms and the first millennium BCE before 332. It proceeds to ask how the ruler's position changed after the arrival of Alexander the Great, ushering in a period in which Egypt was ruled by Greco-Macedonian kings and then by absentee Roman emperors. Ideologies of rule and political structures changed once again in the first millennium CE, first with the conversion of Roman emperor Constantine to Christianity and the later adoption of Christianity as the official religion of the Roman Empire in 380 CE, and secondly with the Arab invasion in the seventh century

CE. These events brought significant changes to the ways in which rulers in Egypt legitimated their authority, engaged with religion, and constrained their actions in accordance with their faith. The arrival of new forms of religion also had important consequences for the broader populations of the time, bringing different ideals of morality and concepts of equality, as will be discussed briefly at the end of this chapter. It is important to stress at the outset, though, that the full flourishing of Abrahamic religions (Christianity and then Islam) in Egypt began as late as the fourth century *CE*, a full millennium after the central time of the Axial Age proposed by Jaspers and his followers.

Egyptian kings had been considered mediators between gods and humans from as early as the Late Predynastic period (Baines 1995: 6, 10). In both pictorial and written sources, the monarch is portrayed as descending from the gods and as rejoining them after his death (Kemp 1983: 71–72; Malek 2000: 92; Szpakowska 2010: 511–12). In the Fourth Dynasty (c. 2613–2494 BCE), the king acquired the title of son of Re, the omnipresent sun-god (Szpakowska 2010: 508, 511). He was also associated with the falcon-god Horus, who triumphed over his brother Seth (508). Until the mid-second millennium BCE, iconographic conventions in Egyptian art meant that only the king could be depicted directly interacting with divine beings, reflecting his unique status and privileged relationship with the gods (Baines 1995: 10, 2007: 17).

The concept of divine kingship was reinvigorated during the reign of Akhenaten (c. 1352–1336 BCE) of the Eighteenth Dynasty, harking back to a model of rule last seen during the Old Kingdom. Sometimes described as history's first monotheist, Akhenaten promoted the sole worship of Aten (the sun-disc) and himself as Aten's living embodiment (Hornung 1999: 88–92; Van Dijk 2000: 268). He also founded a new capital, Akhetaten, now known as Amarna. Some have seen features of "proto-axiality" in Akhenaten's insistence that there was one true, universal god (Marshall 2016: 37). Others reject this, viewing the reaffirmation of the king's divinity during this period as a decidedly archaic trait (e.g. Bellah 2011: 277). It should also be noted that some elements of Amarna-period religious thought—a focus on one god above all others and, as discussed in greater detail below, a universalizing religious discourse—have precursors in earlier Egyptian history and would continue to be important after Akhenaten's revolution (Assmann 2012: 401, 2014: 1–2). Rather than a "great man" appearing *ex nihilo* to proclaim an entirely novel religious message, Akhenaten can thus be understood within the broader context of Egyptian theology and morality.

At other points in Pharaonic history, Egyptians made distinctions between the mortal human on the throne and the "everlasting" sacred nature of the office of kingship itself (Baines 1995: 6). This "desacralization" of Egyptian kingship became more marked over the course of Pharaonic history (Baines 1991: 198, 1995, 4–7). In the Late Period, the king was increasingly described as an "instrument" of the gods, a shift in terminology that reflected the pharaohs' decreasing political and religious influence in the last millennium BCE (O'Connor 1983: 190).

Moreover, even in the earliest periods, the king's divine status did not mean that he could do as he pleased. His role was to serve as the earthly guarantor of *maat*, providing a moral justification for his rule and—at least in theory—preventing the arbitrary exercise of power (Kemp 1983: 74–76; Silverman 1995). The gods had given him this responsibility and in all periods he remained subordinate to them (Baines 1995: 11). One of his most important duties was to ensure the Nile flooded at the right time and to the right extent to keep the people well fed and prosperous (an inundation too high or low could spell disaster for the year's harvest). In this respect, the ideology of *maat* was not confined to the ritual sphere, but was expressed in concrete form; the kings and their officials organized land reclamation projects and irrigation works as well as providing famine relief when the crops failed (Callender 2000: 152; Malek 2000: 94; Nicholson and Shaw 2000: 515).

There was no formal separation of executive, legislative, judiciary, and military powers in the Old, Middle, or New Kingdoms. The law, moreover, did not serve to constrain the pharaoh's activities, but rather cemented his authority and enhanced his ability to exert control over the population (Kemp 1983). The king also personally appointed the most senior officials, including the vizier, his seal-bearers, and, in the more administratively centralized periods, all major state-level and provincial officials (Morris 2010: 215). Both before and after the professionalization of the army in the Middle Kingdom, the top military officers generally answered to royal authority and in some periods the pharaoh himself led troops into battle (Morenz and Popko 2010: 111; Spalinger 2013: 422–24). In the Old Kingdom, the ruler could in theory seize any piece of land or natural resource for his own use (Malek 2000: 95). Together with the deeply sacred character of Egyptian kingship, these features of the Dynastic state have been held up by several Axial Age proponents (e.g. Bellah 2011: 276; Marshall 2016: 37) as proof of the "pre-axiality" of ancient Egyptian civilization.

It is true that the absence of *formal* institutions designed to guard against the arbitrary exercise of royal power sets Egypt apart from the "liberal" and constrained rule typified by later, post-axial states such as the later Roman Republic. In practice, however, Egyptian kings faced several significant informal constraints (Baines 1995: 8). Even during periods of centralization, royal control of the various *nomes* (provinces) was limited by local potentates and influential temple elites (García 2013; Seidlmayer 2000: 118). Perhaps most famously, the power of the Priesthood of Amun at Thebes grew to challenge that of the king and his officials at several points during the New Kingdom (Bryan 2000: 261; Morenz and Popko 2010: 119; Naunton 2010: 121). By the Third Intermediate Period, the High Priests of Amun—doubling as military generals—had gained effective control over Middle and Upper Egypt and formed a "theocratic state," leaving the Twenty-first Dynasty only nominally in power in this region (Morenz and Popko 2010: 119; O'Connor 1983: 232).

The king's lofty and ritualized position could place him at a remove from the everyday functioning of the state, and in some senses the effective head of government was the vizier (Haring 2010: 219–21). The scope of authority of this office became more well defined over the course of Dynastic history. For instance, towards the end of the Old Kingdom, during the Fifth Dynasty, viziers who were not members of the royal family began to be appointed (221). *Duties of the Vizier*, a text first attested in the New Kingdom but likely composed during the Middle Kingdom, resembles a "treatise of administration," setting out the responsibilities of this important role (Grajetzki 2013: 229). The *Duties* is concerned with defining appropriate, ethical conduct for officials of all ranks (who also served as judges); it stresses the importance of impartial judgment and the protection of the weaker party in court cases (Haring 2010: 222). The vizier could sanction his subordinates for laxity or abuse of their position (222). The Middle Kingdom also saw a comprehensive restructuring of state administration, with many new official titles appearing and old ones disappearing (Grajetzki 2013: 217). In short, while royal ideology and most monumental art throughout the Dynastic period continued to proclaim the awesome power of the king, a long-term trend towards more impersonal and routinized modes of governance can be discerned. A respect for impartial adherence to protocol has been identified in some Axial Age literature (e.g. Eisenstadt 1986b) as a feature of axial or post-axial societies, but the ancient Egyptian evidence suggests that its roots should be sought in earlier periods.

Egyptian literature, especially from the Middle Kingdom onwards, also distinguished between "good" and "bad" kings, providing a kind of indirect critique of royal behavior (Manning 2010: 43). Middle Kingdom narrative texts such as *The Tale of the Eloquent Peasant* and *The Tale of Sinuhe* use the voices of different characters to explore fundamental questions about how the state should work (Enmarch 2010: 670–72). They make clear that kings (as well as officials) were expected to concern themselves with the well-being of their subjects and to protect the weak from oppression. The *Teaching for King Merikare*, while it sets out a more militaristic image of the ideal ruler, stresses that not even kings will escape judgment after death for their actions while alive (673). That the ideas contained within this long textual tradition had an impact on royal self-presentation is shown by the *Edict of Horemheb* (c. 1320 BCE), a pharaoh of the Eighteenth Dynasty. The *Edict* sets out a series of measures designed to curb abuses of power by state officials, thereby portraying Horemheb as a benevolent protector (Kemp 2006: 305–06).

The *Demotic Chronicle* presents a particularly clear case of the critique of rulers' behavior. Probably first composed during the reign of Nectanebo II (360–42 BCE) but surviving only in a copy from the late third or second century BCE, it recounts and passes judgment on the deeds of the last native Egyptian rulers (Bresciani 1994; Quack 2015: 34–39). For instance, Amyrtaeus of the Twenty-eighth Dynasty is portrayed in a negative light: "As he ordered injustice to be done, one considered the things that were done to him. His son was not allowed to succeed him. Furthermore, he was deposed while he was still alive" (Quack 2015: 36). The chronicle contains more explicit and direct criticism of rulers than is found in texts from the New Kingdom and earlier periods. While some early scholars (e.g. Eduard Meyer, cited in Quack 2015: 39) have attributed this to Jewish influence, its moral worldview is clearly informed by ancient Egyptian ideals of kingship and the deities it invokes are Egyptian. Falling squarely within the Axial Age period, the *Demotic Chronicle* presents a problem for scholarly accounts that exclude Egypt from the proposed axial transformations of the eastern Mediterranean in the mid-first millennium BCE.

Alexander's conquest of Egypt in the fourth century did not betoken a complete break with Egyptian traditions of rulership; on the contrary, the Ptolemaic Dynasty adopted many of the same roles as their Pharaonic predecessors. As cultural inheritors of intellectual traditions identified as "axial" by Karl Jaspers and later Axial Age proponents—notably, the Platonic-Socratic, Aristotelian, Stoic, and Epicurean schools of philosophy (Beard et al. 1998; Larson 2016; Mikalson 2006)—it could reasonably be expected that these foreign rulers would preside over a shift in ideologies of rule, perhaps adopting a less exalted position. This was far from the case. According to tradition, Alexander the Great set the tone by being crowned pharaoh at Memphis and, in addition, declaring himself the son of Ammon-Zeus (a hybrid Egyptian-Greek god) (Vandorpe 2010: 161). Whether or not these events really took place, we known that the Ptolemies took on the attributes of the divine pharaohs and, in exchange for the support of the priestly establishment, they funded monumental temple-building projects: some of Egypt's best-preserved and most renowned sacred buildings date to this period (Frankfurter 2010: 530). Some of the old informal constraints on Egyptian rulership, such as the traditional role of the pharaoh in ensuring the well-being of the people and the fertility of the land, continued to find expression in the Ptolemaic period.

Within the Hellenistic world as a whole, there existed a tension between the conviction that the ideal and ethical society was governed democratically through an assembly of its citizens—and, as a corollary, that monarchy was a form of government suited only to "barbarians" such as the peoples of Egypt and Persia—and the uncomfortable reality of widespread sacral kingship across Egypt, western Asia, Macedonia, and Greece proper (Larson 2016; Murray 2007: 14;). Indeed, Philip II of Macedon (Alexander's father) had portrayed himself as semi-divine, descended from Herakles, son of Zeus (Gabriel 2010: 21). The strands of Greek thought critical of tyrants and god-kings who acted above the law, wielding power with impunity, were counterbalanced by texts and other cultural products that stressed the potential virtues of sovereign kingship when exercised wisely (Munn 2006: 16–20; Murray 2007: 14). The Ptolemaic kings and queens could therefore count on two separate sources of legitimacy for their rule, which, together with the environmental and economic factors that made the Nile Valley a particularly attractive possession, may have helped them to hold onto power longer than other Hellenistic dynasties in Persia or Asia Minor (modern Turkey) (Adams 2006: 38–43). Evidently, the arrival in Egypt of a ruling class heir to the "axial" political and philosophical traditions of Classical Greece did not lead to the emergence of effective institutional constraints on the ruler's power.

The role of Egypt's rulers continued to draw on multiple and sometimes conflicting sources of legitimacy after the country fell to Rome in 30 BCE. The Roman emperor was ostensibly the *princeps*, "first citizen," not a divine monarch. Roman law was more comprehensive than any that had hitherto been applied within Egypt and exerted a more effective constraint on the activity of the population, including that of officials and—significantly—rulers. The emperor's position was largely a secular one, backed by law and precedent and the combination of official positions he held (Noreña 2010). However, in the former Hellenistic states that became Roman provinces, including Egypt, Roman emperors sought to conform to existing practices. In essence, they portrayed themselves differently in the different provinces of the empire; in Egypt, temple decrees and artistic representations show that they were treated as pharaohs and honored as divine, just as the Ptolemies had been *(Frankfurter 1998: 10;* Martyndale-Howard 2015; Price 1986; Scheid 2011*)*.

This tension between the more "traditional" Egyptian practice of divinely sanctioned rule by autarchic god-kings and more secularized rule by human agents grounded in legal and political institutions (a more typically "post-axial" basis of authority) was only really resolved in the fourth century CE, once the Roman Empire adopted Christianity as the official state religion. Christian doctrine admits of no god-kings and it was therefore this period in which Pharaonic rule truly came to an end. Importantly, Christian emperors legitimated their authority through both their control of Rome's traditional institutions of power and their maintenance of Christian ritual and doctrine (McCormick 1997).

The Islamic conquest of Egypt brought many important changes to the region, but there were also many continuities. Like the Christian Roman emperors, Islamic caliphs and sultans were not deified in life or after death, although they similarly drew legitimacy largely from their roles as upholders of the state ideology (Yaran 2007). As successors to the Prophet Muḥammad, Islamic rulers were subject to few formal, institutionalized checks on their authority. Indeed, in the power they wielded and their claims to administer and arbitrate the rule of law—based as it was on Islamic ideology and their interpretation of it—caliphs and sultans ruled in a similar manner to the earlier pharaohs charged with maintaining *maat* on earth. In practice, however, advisors, administrators (for example *qāḍīs*, judicial officials), and religious scholars responsible for interpreting Islamic scripture offered powerful voices limiting or directing the actions of the ruler (Lindsay 2005; Rohe 2015; Weiss 1998; Yaran 2007). The ideological foundations of Islamic rule and concepts of justice cut both ways, though; the caliphs demanded obedience as upholders and protectors of Islam, but Muslims were obliged to intervene when rulers became tyrannical and started to act in contravention to Islam (Black 2011; Darling 2013).

Ideologies of rule and institutional constraints on rulers are far from the only features of Axial Age discussions, however. The emergence of an egalitarian ethic and universalizing morality within religious and philosophical thought is frequently considered the hallmark of axial transformation (see, for example, Baumard and Boyer 2013; Bellah 2011; Eisenstadt 2005). We now review the evidence for the presence or absence of these ideological currents in Egyptian history from the beginning of the Old Kingdom to the fall of the Ayyūbids.

Universalizing morality and egalitarian ethics

Turning now to the moral basis of religious thought more broadly during the region's long history, we can identify several interlinked trends with respect to universalizing morality and egalitarian ethics. In Pharaonic Egypt, there was a broadening of the notion of virtue from the First Intermediate Period onwards, as the maintenance of *maat* on earth was transformed from a royal prerogative into a personal imperative. Accompanying the widening concern with moral conduct at all levels of society was the expectation that good deeds would be rewarded and bad deeds punished in the afterlife, and an increasingly intimate relationship between gods and humanity. Egyptologists often write of a growth in "personal piety" during the New Kingdom, the Third Intermediate, and Late periods in particular (see below for a discussion). With respect to egalitarianism, expressions of basic human equality appear in sources from as early as the First Intermediate Period, and existed in complex tension with the social conservatism mandated by Egyptian ideals of order and harmony. We can also identify a greater role for universalizing thought in Egyptian religion from the New Kingdom onwards, as foreign lands began to feature in sacred texts as an important part of creation rather than threatening realms of chaos.

Even in the earliest phases of Egyptian state formation, the gods were not considered morally neutral, but took an active interest in human affairs and in the maintenance of *maat* in the social and political realms (Assmann 2006; Morris 2010: 216). As discussed above, ideologies of rule held that the gods had chosen and approved the king so that he could carry out this sacred duty. However, during the First Intermediate Period and the Middle Kingdom, the concept of *maat* began to be used in a more personal sense and in a broader range of contexts. Written evidence from tombs and funerary monuments makes it clear that living a virtuous, just, and ordered life—that is, a "maatian" life—was the responsibility of non-royal elites as well as the upwardly mobile middle classes and even the poorer members of society (Goelet, Jr. 2008: 140). In texts from the New Kingdom, the emphasis shifts slightly; individuals were to live according to *maat* not (or not only) because it would lead to success both before and after death, but because it was the will of the gods (Assmann 1989: 72–75; Ockinga 2005).

A stronger focus on personal virtue within Egyptian society went hand in hand with expectations of punishment for wrongdoing in the afterlife. Divine tribunals had been treated as a potential danger of the journey between this world and the next since the Old Kingdom (Assmann 2005: 136). However, the Coffin Texts, a body of spells and prayers found inscribed on coffins from the First Intermediate Period onwards, make it clear that in this period everyone could now expect to be judged in the next world and to account for their conduct on earth (Goelet, Jr. 2008: 140). The concept of an inevitable divine judgment after death was further elaborated and formalized in the New Kingdom through texts like the *Book of Going Forth by Day* (also known as the *Book of the Dead*) (Ockinga 2005; Quirke 2005). Assmann (2005: 136–39) has interpreted the idea of a universal judgment of the dead as one of the "antecedents of axiality" in Egypt, and it is noteworthy that these concepts began to gain currency as early as the First Intermediate Period, over a thousand years before the beginning of the Axial Age, c. 800 BCE.

One school of thought holds that there was a "democratization of the afterlife" between the late Old Kingdom and the Middle Kingdom (Wilkinson 2010b: 144). According to this theory, whereas in the Old Kingdom only the king could hope to achieve immortality as a divine being after death, by the Middle Kingdom non-royal elites and minor officials could aspire to the same fate (Callender 2000: 150, 168–69; Wilkinson 2010b: 144). Even those of relatively low status now took part in the rites of the god Osiris, once restricted to the king (Callender 2000: 168–69; Van De Mieroop 2011: 120). The idea that "all people" had a *ba*, an animating life force, also became prevalent during the Middle Kingdom (Callender 2000: 169); another early indication of universalizing religious currents in Egypt.[2]

The "democratization" theory has recently been criticized for resting on negative evidence for the restriction of a beatified afterlife to the pharaoh in the Old Kingdom: one scholar (Hays 2015: 201–02) points out that the absence of certain ritual texts from non-royal elite tombs may reflect iconographic conventions (known as "decorum") rather than the tomb owners' beliefs about what would become of them in the afterlife. Assumptions that the Egyptian peasant had no hope of achieving immortality after death until the First Intermediate Period also appear to be

---

2   Precisely who fell into the category of "all people" in the Middle Kingdom Egyptian worldview is discussed below, when we examine the status of foreigners in Egypt.

contradicted by the grave goods and evidence for ritual activity associated with a wide range of Predynastic graves as well as the Old Kingdom peasant burials at Nag‘ al-Dayr (Snape 2011: 7–11; Trigger 1993: 107–08). In short, even during the height of pharaonic power in the highly stratified Old Kingdom state, the royal family may not have had a monopoly on immortality in the company of the gods.

Some scholars believe that during the New Kingdom and especially after the Amarna experiment of Akhenaten was over, there was a flowering of "personal piety" among the general populace. This term refers to a more direct relationship with the gods, without the mediation of kings and priests; Bussmann (2017: 74) defines it as the expression of "an intimate relationship between a benign god and a human individual." It is true that prayers directed from individuals to the state gods became common in the New Kingdom, often addressing Amun "as one's personal savior and guide, a champion of personal justice, mercy, and benefaction" (Szpakowska 2010: 508). After Akhenaten, letters and prayers more often use expressions like "who places [a certain god] in his heart" (Bussmann 2017: 72). Abundant evidence also survives from the Third Intermediate Period and the Late Period for pious practice, for instance from mortuary inscriptions (Szpakowska 2010: 515).

However, debates on this topic are complex and long-standing. It is not clear whether the absence of written evidence for non-royal or non-elite "piety" in pre-New Kingdom contexts reflects a real lack of interest in such relationships with the divine, or merely shifting representational and textual conventions. With the relaxing of decorum over the course of the Dynastic period, a greater range of subjects became socially appropriate. It may be that religious texts from the New Kingdom onwards merely represent beliefs and practices that had hitherto been widespread but unexpressed in official contexts (Baines 2017: 24–25; Baines and Frood 2011). Indeed, Bussmann (2017) points to the wealth of material evidence for devotional practices among the general population, in the form of local shrines and votive offerings, from the third millennium BCE onwards. He believes that the personal piety phenomenon of the New Kingdom in fact reflects a *loss* of intimacy with the gods, produced by the exclusion of local communities from cult activities in official temples (86).

The question of whether Egyptian religious and philosophical traditions could properly be called "egalitarian" is a complex issue. Undercurrents of egalitarian thought and universality certainly appear in several sources, some of them very early indeed. For instance, one spell from the *Coffin Texts*, first appearing in the First Intermediate Period (late third millennium BCE), has a creator god declare:

I made the four winds, that every man might breathe, wherever he may be … I made the great inundation, that the bereft might share in it like the great … I made every man like his fellow; I did not command them to do evil, but it was their own hearts which overthrew what I devised ... I created the gods from my sweat, and men are the tears of my eye (Ray 2002: 30).

The text hints at a common origin for all of humankind and highlights the benevolence of this (unnamed) deity in providing for rich and poor alike through the annual Nile floods. Ray (2002: 31) believes that it is no coincidence that this spell was in circulation during the period of political upheaval after the collapse of the Old Kingdom, when old hierarchies broke down and the ability of rulers and elites to ensure order was in doubt. It is plausible that periods of political fragmentation caused Egyptians to question social hierarchy and encouraged the development of ideas of fundamental human equality. Even under the strong centralized state of the Old Kingdom, however, Egyptian "wisdom literature" stressed the importance of respecting men for their achievements and personal qualities rather than their social origins (Trigger 1993: 61–62). In one text in circulation during the Middle Kingdom, a king advises his son on selecting officials: "Do not prefer the wellborn to the commoner, / Choose a man on account of his skills" (Lichtheim 1975: 101). This principle had force through the Middle Kingdom and beyond (Enmarch 2010: 673).

As a general rule, elites and commoners were not believed to be fundamentally different in substance or origin (John Baines, pers. comm. 2017), and vertical social mobility was seen as desirable (Eyre 1987: 38). With the exception of the king's special status, disparities in economic and political power between social classes were not seen as divinely ordained (Assmann 1989: 61). Nonetheless, it is clear from the archaeological and written evidence that Egyptian society was structured by deep inequalities in wealth and power. How can we reconcile these strands of egalitarianism with the realities of Pharaonic society throughout its long history?

Tensions between the equality of humans expressed in Egyptian religious thought and the necessity of conserving the hierarchical order of society are perhaps best encapsulated by the concept of *maat*. *Maat* imposed a moral obligation to protect the weak from injustice and the oppression of the strong. However, the proposed solution to injustice and the suffering of the poor (certainly during the Old and Middle Kingdoms) was generally strong, centralized rule by the king and his officials as protectors of the people (Assmann 1989: 60–62). Paradoxically, hierarchy and political domination were justified precisely because they were believed to result in a fairer state of affairs than would develop in a society with no effective government. *Maat* thus encouraged conformity to unequal patterns of social and political life in the name of order and justice (O'Connor 1983: 189).

Before the beginning of the New Kingdom, Egyptian egalitarian thought also tended to exclude foreigners, who served as a foil to the concept of *maat* (Assmann 2012: 377; Poo 2005: 86). In iconography and in written documents, the inhabitants of the world beyond the Nile Valley and Delta—an island of civilized order in the midst of a sea of chaos—were usually portrayed as barbaric enemies to be defeated (Shaw 2000a: 320; Wilkinson 2010a: 58; Van Dijk 2000: 265). As peaceful relations with foreign polities increased and Egypt itself became more cosmopolitan (Shaw 2000a: 320), religious attitudes towards foreigners also became more favorable, culminating in the universalizing religion of Akhenaten in the fourteenth century BCE (Assmann 2012: 377; Poo 2005: 86).

It should be noted that even during the New Kingdom and after its disintegration (when Egypt was ruled by dynasties of Libyan and Kushite origin), xenophobia retained a place in the ideology and iconography of the state (Wilkinson 2010a: 58), and Egyptians often saw themselves as culturally and militarily superior to their neighbors (O'Connor 1983: 194). But the key difference from the Thutmosid period onwards was that the inhabitants of the world beyond the Nile Valley now stood in a relationship to the gods equivalent to that of the Egyptians themselves; the universalizing and egalitarian currents within Egyptian religion no longer ceased to apply at the borders of the Pharaonic state.

With the arrival of the Ptolemies and a new Greek-speaking elite, the influence of Hellenistic culture in Egypt grew. This included philosophical ideals, particularly those stemming from Classical Athens, that favored democratic rule, secular law, and an egalitarian ethic. Greek philosophy generally "taught a universalizing frame of reference," encouraging its adherents to view others as equals (Jennifer Larson, pers. comm. 2016; Baloglou 1998). This ideology was spread at the point of Alexander the Great's spear throughout the eastern Mediterranean and western Asia. There is some evidence that Greek political thought and practices found a foothold among the most important custodians of Pharaonic Egyptian tradition—the priesthood—in the form of the decrees issued by several synods of priests in the late third and second centuries BCE (Manning 2010: 99). The synods themselves were unprecedented, possibly taking their cue from the Greek practice of holding deliberative assemblies, and the decrees closely parallel those of contemporary Greek *poleis* beyond Egypt (Manning 2010: 99; van Minnen 2007).

Interestingly, the Greek concept of *dikē* (justice) overlaps with *maat*, but also differs from it in key ways. Both were concerned with ensuring proper conduct and maintaining social order and applied equally to rulers and ruled. However, the physical manifestation of *maat* in the Egyptian environment, for instance through the orderly flooding of the Nile, is an aspect lacking from the concept of *dikē*. Greek gods in general were also less concerned with human moral behavior than Egyptian deities, although they were believed to punish injustice, while legal and moral "rightness" were often intimately linked in the Greek world (Petrovic and Petrovic 2016). The extent to which these Greek ideologies impacted the daily lives of the rural Egyptian population is debatable. Certainly during the earlier phases of Ptolemaic rule, a "double society" developed in which Greek and Egyptian communities were subject to different judicial systems, and ethnic Greeks tended to dominate the civic life of the new cities (Lloyd 2000b: 409; Manning 2003: 53, 131). After 200 BCE, social boundaries and identities became more blurred (Vandorpe 2010: 171–73). Nevertheless, as we note above, there was an undeniable tension between Hellenistic and traditional Egyptian institutions and ideas, which persisted throughout the Hellenistic and much of the imperial Roman periods.

Typical treatments of the Axial Age suggest that egalitarian ideals gradually became more and more part of the cultural and institutional fabric of societies that embraced "axial" ideologies, including Greco-Roman philosophy and Christianity. The egalitarianism expressed in Greek and Roman philosophy, as we explain below, in fact did little to alter the actual levels of equality within Egyptian society that had developed over previous eras. It is noteworthy that early Christian doctrine in the region likewise reinforced many traditional distinctions along the lines of class, gender, and ethnicity (James 2008; McCormick 1997). Christianity is often hailed for its egalitarian and philanthropic ideals, at least in comparison with more "archaic" religious systems. Indeed, it expressed a clear universality and strong dedication to moral correctness, as discussed above. Nevertheless, the Byzantine emperors, sitting atop a religious hierarchy that also included priests, deacons, and bishops, had a clear set of privileges and authority, enforced by religious as well as legal mechanisms. This set them apart from the rest of the population.

Like Christianity, Islam was and is an explicitly egalitarian and universalizing religion, at least on a doctrinal level. It too developed in the wake of "axial" transformations and ideologies, notably Judaism and Greco-Roman philosophy along with early Christianity itself. Islamic doctrine from the earliest periods held that all men were equal before Allah, regardless of ethnicity, language, or place of origin (Yaran 2007: 12). Some scholars of early Islam argue also that women were offered more equitable treatment under the Islamic dynasties than in any prior period, though others disagree with this rosy assessment.[3] In practice, many stark inequalities were not only tolerated under Islamic rule, but sometimes religiously justified. High-ranking administrators were drawn from the Islamic elite, excluding women, foreigners, non-Muslim populations, and those of low social class (Cortese and Calderini 2006).

Egalitarianism, social mobility, and prosociality in practice
The evidence for universalizing religion, deities concerned with the morality of human behavior, egalitarian ethics, and other "axial" religious traits in Egypt thus predates the proposed Axial Age by many centuries. The rich written record demonstrates that they can be traced back to Pharaonic Egypt, which appears in many treatments of the Axial Age as a quintessentially archaic society. However, our

---

3   A useful overview of the debate is offered by Young and Göçek (2016).

discussion so far has been confined to ideological currents identifiable from written sources such as biographies, "wisdom literature," and administrative documents. Here, we examine the "fit" between these principles and more concrete manifestations of equality or hierarchy in Egypt from the Old Kingdom to the Islamic period.

Egalitarianism and structural inequalities

From the earliest beginnings of the state in the Nile Valley in the fourth millennium BCE, Egyptian society was structured by hereditary inequality. Though the precise shape of the social "pyramid" varied through time, in general it took the form of: a small elite, composed of the royal family and high-ranking officials; a middle class of lower-ranking bureaucrats, wealthy farmers and artisans; and the much more numerous lower classes, which included slaves and enserfed farmers (Frood 2010: 476; O'Connor 1983: 192–94). Both ancient and modern commentators have tended to emphasize positive valuations of women and female power in Pharaonic Egypt, but gender inequality also made itself felt at all levels of society (Frood 2010: 470). Men dominated the bureaucracy and public life, and representations of women in art and literature tended to define them primarily in relation to their male relatives: as wives, daughters, and mothers.

Moreover, universalizing and egalitarian currents within Egyptian philosophy and religion did not lead to calls for the abolition of slavery. This pattern may be familiar from the Classical Greek world, in which philosophers promoting a universalizing frame of reference had no qualms about personally owning slaves (Larson 2016). The forms of servitude referred to by the term "slavery" were of course different in Pharaonic Egypt and Classical Greece, and there is a great deal of debate among Egyptologists about the role and character of unfree labor (encompassing corvée labor, "serfdom," and chattel slavery) from the Old Kingdom onwards (Loprieno 1997: 185). Seen through the filter of the Hebrew Bible, Egypt was a "house of slavery" (*bet abadim* in Hebrew) (185); in many popular representations of Egypt today, the pyramids serve as the ultimate symbol of the pharaohs' despotic cruelty. However, it is likely that most of the workers who constructed the monumental tombs and temples of the Old and Middle Kingdoms were conscripted for certain periods of time (Caminos 1997: 21–22; Frood 2010: 485; Kemp 2006: 180–83). This corvée labor was arduous and compulsory, but the conscripts received rations and, unless they attempted to escape, were eventually allowed to return home (Caminos 1997: 21–22; Kemp 2006: 181).[4] Egyptian views on the social order did not make clear distinctions between "slaves" and "free" peasants. In the Old Kingdom at least, the majority of the population were theoretically in a state of subjection to (or dependence on)

---

4   The great monuments of Pharaonic Egypt have this much in common with the Suez Canal, constructed using corvée labor in the nineteenth century (Brown 1994: 116).

the king (Loprieno 1997: 189, 195). In practice, though, the forms of social control of the Egyptian population were more nuanced and complex. It is worth noting that for some ecologically informed scholarship, the real despotic power in the Nile Valley was not the pharaoh but the great river itself. Following the sociologist Michael Mann (1986: 108–15), Manning (2010: 44) has argued that the unpredictability of the Nile floods, along with the narrow area of land available for cultivation either side of the river, produced a "social caging" effect that enabled the effective exertion of centralized control over Egyptian communities. This control—regardless of the content of some Pharaonic royal ideology and iconography—was exercised not through capricious authoritarianism, but via a bureaucratic system that functioned relatively autonomously (44–45).

To return to our discussion of slavery, it is clear that although chattel slavery did not serve as the foundation of Egyptian economy (Malek 2000: 94), more permanent forms of bonded labor were certainly present and became more pronounced in the New Kingdom. From early on in the region's history, foreigners captured in war could be bought and sold by private households and were sometimes set to work on temple-building projects (Eyre 2010: 302; Loprieno 1997: 193). The numbers of these slaves were swelled in the New Kingdom by Egypt's increasingly frequent military campaigns abroad and by slave markets (Brier and Hobbs 2008: 80–81). In the same period, we hear of settlements of enslaved female workers, compared by one author to "prisoner-of-war labor camps" (Frood 2010: 486). Amid the political decentralization of the first millennium BCE, slave labor became less prevalent in Egyptian society, and documents of the Late Period do not treat slaves as a formal category of people with a precise legal definition (Lloyd 1983: 314; Loprieno 1997: 212–13). A constant theme throughout the period was that—like Greek and Roman traditional religion (Larson 2016)—Egyptian religion and philosophy did not view these various forms of unfree labor as morally problematic (John Baines, pers. comm. 2017).

Slavery, moreover, remained a feature of Egyptian society through the Christian and Islamic periods (Prinzig 2010; Soha 2016). This again demonstrates a contradiction between doctrine and reality, or at least complicates the relationship between the two. Islamic law viewed slavery in general as an intrusive practice; it forbade the enslavement of free members of Islamic society, including the *dhimmī* (non-Muslims residing in the Abode of Islam). Still, the existence of slavery was accepted and regulated by Islamic law, providing some rights and protections for the enslaved. Further, religious and ethnic distinctions structured the attitudes of Islamic law towards slavery, as only non-Muslims captured during a legitimate war, or the sons and daughters of slaves already in captivity, were regarded as legal slaves (Soha 2016).

Social mobility

Vertical social mobility, personified by the figure of the self-made man, was highly valued in Egyptian moral and political thought from the Old Kingdom onwards (Trigger 1993: 61–62). Higher status and perhaps even administrative roles could be attained through scribal education at fee-charging schools, but these opportunities were limited and only open to the wealthier members of the lower classes (Trigger 1993: 61). In comparison with other ancient societies, Egyptian categories of social status were "relatively fluid" (Baines 2007: 15), but it is likely that ideals of social mobility were not fully realized (Trigger 1993: 61–62).

Like its Pharaonic Egyptian counterpart, traditional Greek religion reinforced numerous social distinctions. The divisions structuring Egyptian society were transformed under the Hellenistic rulers, with many new institutions sprouting up to favor the newly arrived Greco-Macedonian elite. Administrative positions were not legally restricted to the Greek-speaking population, and the native Egyptian elite (now often fluent in Greek) played an active role in the economy and politics of Ptolemaic Egypt (Manning 2003: 131; Ritner 2008: 5). Nevertheless, they were largely displaced from the most important administrative roles and maintained their dominant position only within the temple system (Ritner 2008: 4).

Roman citizenship and upper-class status both conferred considerable economic benefits in Egypt during the Roman period. Roman citizens living in the province were exempt from the poll tax, and members of the upper classes had to pay less than those from lower social strata (Peacock 2000: 417). Rome imposed socially restrictive policies on the inhabitants, for example forbidding Egyptians to serve in the army legions (a prime route to citizenship) (Ritner 2008: 5–6). It has been suggested that this ethnic discrimination was due to the immense importance of the Nile floodplain as "granary" of the empire; it may have been an attempt to prevent upward social mobility that could potentially threaten grain production and supply (2–6).

Class and religious affiliation also remained important through the Christian and Islamic periods. Social mobility was, in general, low. The educated, propertied elites enjoyed great advantages in terms of access to prestigious (and often lucrative) administrative or religious offices, to economic power, and to certain legal privileges. Lower-class Egyptians and those practicing religions other than those supported by the state were not excluded from all aspects of social, economic, or political life. Indeed, Christians often held important official posts in successive Islamic empires (Robinson 2010b: 219). Still, the barrier to elite status was prohibitive for most. An important difference between the Christian and Islamic periods in Egypt is that the Christian Byzantine rulers sought rather actively to suppress the practice of other religions, notably traditional Roman paganism (Kazhdan and MacCormick 1997; Treadgold 1997). Judaism continued to be practiced in certain places, like

Alexandria, though in dwindling numbers compared to earlier times. The Islamic caliphates and sultanates, on the other hand, embraced religious pluralism within their societies, for the most part leaving non-Muslim subjects unfettered to pursue spiritual fulfillment through practicing their traditional religions (Robinson 2010a: 686; Raymond 2000).

Prosociality

In the preceding sections, we demonstrated how Pharaonic Egyptian morality and religious ideology incorporated some statements of egalitarianism and condemned injustice, which was understood to include the suffering and oppression of the poor. To some extent, these principles led to the promotion of "prosocial" behavior, designed to temper the worst excesses of inequality. The corpus of wisdom literature stresses the importance of hospitality to one's neighbors and to vulnerable members of the local community, such as widows (Frood 2010: 475). Texts from as early as the Old Kingdom also reveal a strong sense of duty among the elite towards those less fortunate than themselves. The concept of *imakhu*, meaning something close to "honored" or "provided for," encapsulates Egyptian ideals of the role of the elite as providers, whose relationship to other members of the community was akin to that of the head of a household to his dependents (Kemp 1983: 103). The biographies of officials recorded in funerary contexts enumerate their charitable activities as a matter of course, often using formulaic phrases (Lichtheim 1975: 17). On the façade of his tomb at Saqqara, the Sixth-Dynasty official Nefer-seshem-ptah proclaimed:

[I have gone from my town,
[I have descended from my nome,]
[having done] justice for its lord,
having contented him with what he loves.
I spoke the good, I repeated the good,
[I grasped the right manner,]
[for I wanted the good] for people.
I judged two parties so as to content them,
I saved the weak from one stronger than he as best I could,
[I spoke truly, I acted justly.]
[I gave bread to the hungry,] clothes to the naked,
I landed one who was stranded,
I buried him who lacked a son,
I made a boat [for the boatless,]
[and supported] the orphan.
I never spoke evil against anyone to a potentate (Lichtheim 1992: 13–14).

The tone here is typical of many official biographies throughout the Pharaonic period. What is less clear is whether these texts reflect real efforts to alleviate poverty on the part of officials, or merely pay lip service to the ideals of *maat* and *imakhu*. It appears that there were no formal mechanisms in place to compel elites to fulfill their charitable duties (John Baines, pers. comm. 2017). This contrasts, for example, with the Islamic period in Egypt, in which almsgiving (*zakāt*) was an obligation sometimes (though not always) enforced by the state (Kuran 2003). It is also evident that the philanthropic behavior expected of the elite was in no way incompatible with the maintenance of their superior status and wealth. Rather than demanding large-scale redistribution, *imakhu* was a fundamentally conservative and paternalistic notion: the elite bestowed "protection" on those below them in the hierarchy and received "love" in return (Assmann 1989: 73). In terms of cosmology, humans may have been created equal, but in practice the Egyptians accepted disparities in status and wealth as an inevitable part of life (John Baines, pers. comm. 2017).

In connection with prosociality, one important practice that arguably increased in importance in Egypt during the Hellenistic period was that of elite benefaction (Fischer-Bovet 2014: 330–32). Both temple priests and the Ptolemies, as pharaohs, continued to provide goods and services to the Egyptian population in the service of maintaining *maat*, as discussed above (John Baines, Oxford Workshop 2017)— maintaining irrigation channels or providing alimentary support to quarry workers, for instance. The Hellenistic and later Roman religious philosophies that arrived in Egypt from the late first millennium BCE onwards did not include precepts encouraging charity or almsgiving, as was prevalent in early Christian doctrine (Jennifer Larson, pers. comm. 2016). However, widespread in Greco-Roman culture was a strong tradition of elites engaging in prosocial acts based on a sense of "civic duty" (Hoyer 2013; Verboven 2002). In addition to this, the more well-off Greco-Macedonian population, for instance officials and veteran soldiers, also engaged in much prosocial activity, spurred on by similar motivations. Though not backed by the same religious and moral force as priests' activity, these civic benefactions still carried considerable ideological weight and led to the creation and maintenance of important infrastructure throughout Egypt, such as roads, bridges, and temples (Fischer-Bovet 2014; Monson 2010).

After the adoption of Christianity as the Roman Empire's official religion, elite, civic-minded prosociality gave way to religiously inspired notions of Christian charity and benefaction (Miller 2008). Similarly, charitable giving and prosociality enjoyed strong ideological support from Islam. Almsgiving is the "third pillar" of Islam and is considered obligatory for all Muslims, part of ensuring the social welfare of the Islamic community (Yaran 2007: 12). In Egypt, the principle of extending hospitality to strangers was institutionalized in *funduqs*, which served as hostels for travelers, places of trade for merchants, but also as "instruments of religious charity"

(Constable 2003: 42). *Funduqs* provided a range of charitable services such as housing for the needy, alimentary support, and even medical care (Raymond 2000). They were generally established through a *waqf*, an endowment of money set aside in perpetuity for a certain (usually "prosocial") purpose, for which the initial donation came from wealthy elites or rulers (Constable 2003: 42). By the Fāṭimid period, religious houses known as *ribāṭs* were established exclusively for the use of women, allowing widows and pious women to live in seclusion (Raymond 2000). Islamic state ministries in Egypt also continued the millennia-old tradition of using state resources to support necessary infrastructure, notably through building and maintaining irrigation works, public bathhouses, and marketplaces in nearly every city in the region (Lindsay 2005)—a remarkably similar set of "public goods" to that provided by the earliest pharaohs.

Conclusions

A dominant theme emerging from the preceding discussion is how remarkably consistent many of the ideological and institutional features of Egyptian life have been over the region's long history. There were of course significant changes over the course of the Pharaonic period, notably an increasing emphasis on personal piety and the "desacralization" of the pharaoh at certain points. From the mid-first millennium BCE on, moreover, the region was dominated by powers originating outside the Nile Valley; the Achaemenid Persians, Hellenistic Ptolemies, pagan Roman and later Christian Byzantine emperors, and various Islamic rulers took control of this productive and important region in succession. Each "foreign" ruling power and each era brought its own changes to ideological and institutional structures. The Hellenistic and Roman rulers were not only accompanied by large numbers of immigrants from the wider Mediterranean world, but also brought an expanded focus on urban growth and civic infrastructure, butting heads with, and eventually succeeding in undercutting the power of, the traditional Egyptian priesthood. Christian and Islamic rule, in turn, reimagined the role of the leader, stripping away the idea of the king as a god on earth and placing additional, institutionalized constraints on rulers' authority and legitimacy.

Such changes were undoubtedly significant, but it is equally clear that each era built on its predecessors, adopting many older traits and norms. Continuity is clear in a host of areas: in the importance of moral precepts concerning order and justice; in a tempered egalitarianism that sought to promote universality while still tolerating hierarchies and disparities in wealth, opportunity, and status; a well-developed legal system setting out the duties and responsibilities of diverse Egyptian populations; and in the promotion of prosocial activity, by the state and by individuals, seeking to ensure the welfare of all members of society.

Egypt, then, offers a confounding picture for traditional articulations of the Axial Age. On the one hand, the region experienced many of the key transformations often hailed as "axial," but over a millennium earlier than the period normally associated with the Axial Age, c. 800–200 BCE; this might suggest that Egypt belongs in the pantheon of axial regions, but with an amended timeline.[5] On the other hand, the early appearance of these transformations, at least relative to other regions, and their persistence through time and in various ideological and sociopolitical instantiations might suggest that Egypt was a somewhat precocious region and that the institutional and ideological developments we trace here gave some advantage to its societies. Taking stock of the region's dynamics over the very long term, as we do here, raises the possibility that Egypt was not merely one example among a group of regions that developed similar traits independently, as scholars assert for the typical "axial" regions of Greece, the Levant, Iran, India, and China. Rather, it may be that Egypt's precocious development inspired or even directly influenced the emergence of apparently similar traits in other areas, from the Italian Peninsula to the Aegean to Anatolia, the Levant, Iran, and beyond. However, these are issues for future work to address.

---

5   As repeatedly suggested by Assmann (2005, 2012, 2014).

SOUTHEAST ASIA | Lower Mekong Basin

Jill Levine & Miriam T. Stark

Period	Polity	Approx. dates
Neolithic		2500–1500 BCE
Bronze Age/Prehistoric		1500–500
Iron Age/Protohistoric/Early Historic		500 BCE–500 CE
Historic	Funan	225–640
Pre-Angkor	Chenla	640–802
Angkor	Early Angkor	802–1080
	Classic Angkor	1080–1220
	Late Angkor	1220–1431
Early modern	Khmer Kingdom	1431–1593
	Ayutthaya	1593–1767

Table 8. Periods and dates of polities mentioned in text that were based in or that occupied the Lower Mekong Basin

Introduction

Compared with other parts of Afro-Eurasia, discussed in several of the other chapters in this volume, the Lower Mekong Basin in what is today Cambodia saw the rise of complex social formations relatively late. The Neolithic (2500–1500 BCE) and Bronze Age/Prehistoric (1500–500 BCE) periods saw the development of agriculture and village settlements, but it was only in the period from 500 BCE to 500 CE that societies in the region began to produce iron tools and engage in long-distance maritime trade, and village clusters evolved into complex polities (Stark 2004: 91). The territory of modern Cambodia was occupied by groups of loosely confederated principalities (Jacques 1986: 84), collectively known as Funan, in the early third to early seventh centuries and Chenla in the seventh to eighth centuries CE, until the rise of the Khmer Empire in the ninth century. The Lower Mekong Basin—along with much of Mainland Southeast Asia—was dominated by Angkor from the eleventh to the fourteenth century; decline began in the fourteenth century, and power moved south to a series of capitals during the fifteenth and sixteenth centuries. The Kingdom of Ayutthaya, based to the west in modern-day Thailand, ascended to regional power following the decline of the Angkor state.

Following Jaspers (1953), most formulations of the Axial Age thesis assert that moralizing and universalizing ideologies and philosophies spread from the traditional "axial" regions—what is today Greece, Israel-Palestine, Iran, India, and China—to other parts of the globe, stimulating the development of constraints on executive power as well as institutions designed to curb inequality. We examine here the Lower Mekong Basin to determine whether the spread of Hinduism and Buddhism from South Asia supports this view, or whether the ideologies, institutions, and practices that emerged in the Lower Mekong Basin followed a different trajectory. Our analysis begins with the Early Funan "state" that Chinese emissaries reported by the third century CE and ends with the conquest of the area by the Ayutthaya Kingdom. Our conclusions are mixed. Many traditional Axial Age assumptions are not borne out by historical developments in the Mekong Basin. For example, rule by divinely sanctioned kings (if not living gods) operating with no effective limits—supposedly diagnostic features of "archaic" societies—giving way to constrained, institutionalized forms of power argued to follow axial transformations in other parts of the world (e.g. Bellah 2011; Eisenstadt 1986b) does not adequately describe the experience of Southeast Asia. Indeed, the idea of sacred, absolute kingship seems not to have been present in the region before the first millennium CE, developing only after exposure to South Asian political models and "axial" ideologies. Even then, rulers' behavior was always constrained by the elite "entourage" on whom kings depended for support. There appears, then, no typically "archaic" period in the Lower Mekong Basin, nor, thus, any sort of transition into a "post-axial" form of rule.

On the other hand, Hindu and Buddhist thought did contribute to several transformations of Mekong society that fit more comfortably with Axial Age theories, including an intensification of prosocial activity and the limitation of royal authority, albeit through mostly informal pressures rather than institutionalized regulation. In sum, this chapter demonstrates that the Mekong Basin's long and rich history offers an important example of the diverse paths that different societies took as ostensibly axial ideologies and practices spread throughout Eurasia.

Historical background

The traditional time frame for the Axial Age (800–200 BCE) straddles the Late Bronze Age/Prehistoric (1100–500 BCE) and the Iron Age/Protohistoric periods (500 BCE–500 CE) in Mainland Southeast Asia. The Bronze Age/Prehistoric saw significant technological changes, village-based craft specialization, and increased interaction between communities (Eyre 2011; White and Pigott 1996). Inhabitants of the Mekong Basin during this time used valuable items made of bronze to display status and wealth, having received the technology indirectly from Eurasian steppe cultures via China's Gansu corridor; bronze appeared in Southeast Asia (and the Mekong Basin) no later than 1200 BCE (White and Hamilton 2009).

The succeeding Iron Age/Protohistoric period (Protohistoric after c. 200 BCE) saw the rise of more complex settlements, intensified agriculture, and macroregional interactional networks (Bellina et al. 2014; Favereau and Bellina 2016; King et al. 2014; Rispoli et al. 2013). Most peoples in Mainland Southeast Asia's river valleys and deltas lived in settled rice-farming communities during this time. Iron Age/ Protohistoric political systems in Southeast Asia have been described as "mandalas," in which small polities were loosely integrated into larger kingdoms through dynamic processes of alliance and patronage (Stark 2004: 96). A few scholars have seen the rise in agglomerated village settlement along with scattered evidence for defensive fortifications and perhaps forged weapons as indications of increasing violence throughout the region (e.g. O'Reilly 2014). Most, however, note how rare evidence for warfare is during this period,[1] stressing rather the relatively harmonious intellectual and economic connections that characterized much of Southeast Asia. Notably, maritime trade in the Iron Age/Protohistoric period led to increased interaction with other societies throughout Asia as well as westward into the eastern Mediterranean (Bellina et al. 2014). Stone and glass beads from South Asian sources were prominent in local elite burials, signaling social status (Calo et al. 2015; Carter 2015), and social stratification was pronounced during this period as well (Stark 2004: 96). While state formation in the region generally lagged behind that of nearby contemporary societies in East and South Asia, we do note the development in this period of urban clusters, some connected to satellite settlements in the interior river valleys, while coastal areas exhibited smaller but agglomerated settlements.

The Funan Kingdom (225–640 CE) was one of the earliest large-scale, more or less centralized societies in the region, though similar other formations developed roughly contemporaneously in other parts of Southeast Asia.[2] Funan developed out of Protohistoric polities in the Mekong Delta (Stark 1998). Village communities in Southeast Asia had been interacting through trade since at least 2000 BCE (Hung et al. 2007). In the Funan period, however, many core settlements across the delta were connected by the Mekong, its tributaries, and some 200 km of canals; there may in fact have been multiple settlement centers in what is now southern Cambodia (Stark 2003: 92–93). Scholars agree that Angkor Borei is one of the most likely candidates as a Funan "capital." Linked directly to coastal settlements that engaged in maritime trade, like Óc Eo (located in modern Vietnam), the ancient city is located in an ideal region for rice cultivation (Ng 1979; Stark 2003). Stark (2006: 419) estimates that first-millennium CE Angkor Borei could have housed as many as 20,000 inhabitants.

Modern information on Funan comes from third- to sixth-century CE Chinese historical documents as well as epigraphic and archaeological work. Inscriptions from Funan were written in Sanskrit and Khmer using Brāhmī-derived scripts; the first Khmer inscription dates to 611 CE (Cœdès 1942: 21). While no written records from South Asia have been found that describe Funan, Chinese records and

---

1   Outside, perhaps, of northern Vietnam (e.g. Kim 2015).
2   The settlement of Co Loa in northern Vietnam, for instance (Kim et al. 2010).

Funan-period artifacts suggest a close relationship between South Asia, the Mekong Delta, and a South China Sea maritime network during this time (Bellina and Glover 2004). Chinese sources suggest that Funan was a center for maritime trade. Emperor Wu of the Chinese Han Dynasty sent two ambassadors to Funan in the third century CE. The ambassadors' report included descriptions of Funanese rice cultivation, defensive settlements, writing, legal processes, and taxation. Diplomacy and trade between China and Funan continued intermittently through the sixth century (Cœdès 1968: 10). Archaeological excavations in 1944 CE confirmed the presence of long-distance trade, occupational specialization, and writing in the Funanese port city of Óc Eo (Malleret 1962). Chinese sources record a multi-century dynastic history, though the political structure of Funan remains unclear. There is evidence that Funan might have been a mandala network, made up of smaller polities, or perhaps the most powerful polity within such a network (Jacques 1986). Funan was most likely governed by a system of hierarchical settlement chiefs, not quite "kings" in the traditional (Western) understanding (Vickery 1998: 19–20). Chinese accounts do note the presence of well-defined social stratification in Funanese society (Pelliot 1903: 261).

Some scholars use the term Chenla as a gloss for the post-Funan rise of multiple competing polities across the Lower Mekong basin during the seventh to early ninth centuries CE. While there are a number of theories on the reason for Funan's fall, historians have not reached any consensus (Manguin 2009). The transition between Funan and Chenla is difficult to detect archaeologically (Heng 2016) and may reflect hegemonic cycling among polities, rather than a sequential transition from one established regional power to another. Pre-Angkor period (sixth- to eighth-century CE) inscriptions indicate that there was a political hierarchy dominated by a deified ruler and local temples, controlled by settlement chiefs, that served as economic and ritual centers (Vickery 1998). Sambor Prei Kuk, for example, was a major pre-Angkorian center; the settlement includes a large moat and around 200 temples and other structures (Heng 2012).

The political landscape transformed in the early ninth century with the rise of the Angkor (or Khmer) Empire, which held sway over the region for the following six centuries. The Sdok Kak Thom inscription (dating to 1069 CE), found in a Thai temple, recounts the ascension of a ruler named Jayavarman II (r. 802–35 CE) and his followers, who moved to the Tonle Sap region from what is now eastern Cambodia to announce himself as a "universal ruler" (Cœdès 1928: 117–19). This campaign laid the basis for the Angkor state. Jayavarman II gave his own followers positions of power in the conquered regions, turning former Chenla polities into provinces of the Angkor Empire. Angkor government centered on a divine king. This sacred Angkor king is often seen as an absolute ruler, as there were generally little or no formal limits on his authority. In practice, however, the state apparatus contained nobles and royal priests who acted to constrain the king's power through informal means. The common people farmed, built temples, went to war, and otherwise supported the state. The Classic Angkor period is usually dated from 1082 CE with the rise of the Mahidharapura Dynasty (Briggs 1951: 178). The subsequent reign by Jayavarman VII (1181–1218 CE) marks the peak of the Angkor Empire's geographic extent and prestige. Jayavarman VII commanded the construction of state temples like Ta Prohm and Preah Khan; he created the great city of Angkor Thom; he consolidated road networks; and he built hospitals and resthouses along the routes radiating out from the capital to provincial centers (Hendrickson 2010).

The Late Angkor period (1220–1431 CE), marked by decline and warfare, began after the death of Jayavarman VII. Myriad factors contributed to Angkor's decline: social, climatic, and geopolitical. Ming China's maritime trade network drew Southeast Asian polities closer to coastal trading zones, while climatic instability (droughts and associated floods) challenged political organizational capacities through the thirteenth and fourteenth centuries (Buckley et al. 2010; Lieberman and Buckley 2012). The Angkor period came to an end with the rise of the Thai Kingdom of Ayutthaya (also known as Siam) to regional dominance in the fifteenth century.

Founded in 1351 CE, Ayutthaya was a large mercantile state with trade relationships with what are today China, India, Malaysia, and Arabia (Baker and Phongpaichit 2009: 10). In 1431 CE, an army from Ayutthaya attacked the Angkor complex, kidnapped a number of people, and installed an Ayutthayan royal as the ruler (Baker and Phongpaichit 2017: 66). Some of the Khmer royalty remained at Angkor with reduced power, while Khmer elites retained control of several sites to the south, including Phnom Penh (Hall 2018). By the seventeenth century, Ayutthaya had gained control of most of Mainland Southeast Asia, consolidated its hold over the Mekong Basin, and replaced Śrī Laṅkā as the preeminent regional center of Buddhism (Wyatt 1984: 130–31). The kingdom fell to the Burmese army in 1569 CE, but regained its independence in 1593 CE. Fighting and turmoil continued throughout the region until 1867 CE, when the territory of modern-day Cambodia sought protection from its predatory neighbors through French colonial control. However, Ayutthaya survived as an independent kingdom until the "Siamese Revolution" of 1932 CE, when the reigning king was deposed and the modern nation-state of Thailand established. Cambodia gained its independence in 1953 CE.

Ideological and religious background
Hinduism and Buddhism were introduced to Southeast Asia during the Iron Age/Protohistoric period through several mechanisms (Ray 2014; Skilling 2011). Traders, *brāhmaṇas* (those belonging to the South Asian priestly class), and missionaries traveled to the region along the "maritime Silk Road," namely via the Indian Ocean. Aśoka (r. 268–32 BCE), ruler of the vast South Asian Mauryan Empire and staunch

supporter of Buddhist practice, may have sent Buddhist missionaries to Southeast Asia in this period (Ray 2005), though the religion did not become widespread until a few centuries later (Bellina and Glover 2004). The region has seen many different schools of Hinduism and Buddhism through its history. Hinduism—albeit a version that incorporated local gods and indigenous beliefs—arrived during the Iron Age/Protohistoric period; Khmer people joined Śaivite and Vaiṣṇavite cults as early as the as the fifth century CE (Sanderson 2003). Brāhmaṇic religious practice in Funan, Chenla, and Angkor included a powerful priestly class and a hereditary social hierarchy; practitioners of all three Indic-derived ideologies believed in reincarnation and karma (Lockard 2009: 22). It is difficult to assess exactly when Mahāyāna Buddhism (which emerged in South Asia around 100 BCE) took root in Southeast Asia (Harris 2005: 4). All we do know is that the practice became the dominant form of Buddhism practiced in the Lower Mekong Basin for much of the first millennium CE. After the fall of Angkor, a long-standing Mahāyāna majority was eclipsed by the Theravāda community throughout Southeast Asia today (226).

Little information survives about everyday religious practice in Funan and Chenla, but inscriptions, architecture, and relics provide evidence for the syncretism of Hindu, Mahāyāna Buddhist, and indigenous iconography and beliefs (Cœdès 1968: 58). In Funan-era evidence, Hindu motifs proliferate in portable objects, from gold leaf and amulets to statuary representing Viṣṇu, Kṛṣṇa, and Rāma (Lavy 2003; Le Thi Lien 2008, 2015). Rulers participated in the cult of the *lingam*, a phallic representation of Śiva (Sanderson 2003: 403–09). Elites were required to make payments to fund the construction of local temples (Jacques and Lafond 2007: 43–63). The first known Buddhist statues in the Lower Mekong region date to the sixth and seventh centuries CE (Harris 2005: 4). Buddhism also seems to have played an important role in interactions between Funan and China. Chinese records show that Funanese monks visited China in 484 and 546 CE, while Chinese emissaries visited Funan at least three times between 460 and 524 CE (Cœdès 1968: 57–62). Buddhist missionaries were present in the Lower Mekong by the fifth century (Pelliot 1903), which helped to strengthen cultural links between the two regions.

During the pre-Angkor/post-Funan period, (sixth to eighth centuries CE), Hinduism had become the officially supported "state religion," though Buddhism was a substantial minority faith (Bhattacharya 1997). Hinduism remained the official religion of the Lower Mekong Basin for much of the Early and Classic Angkor periods. The patronage of Hindu gods is apparent in the material record: Angkor Wat, constructed by Suryavarman II (r. 1113–50 CE), was dedicated to Viṣṇu (Cœdès 1968: 162). However, Buddhist images were also common in Angkor temples at the same time (Roveda 2012). In the Classic Angkor period, Jayavarman VII (r. 1181–1218 CE) transformed the state and elevated Mahāyāna Buddhism to the status of official ideology. While in general the importance of Hinduism declined in the early second millennium, Jayavarman VIII (r. 1243–95 CE) promoted Hindu forms of worship after Jayavarman VII's death and destroyed many of the Buddhist images his predecessor had commissioned (Roveda 2004: 34). Hindu elements remain in Khmer ideology, as brāhmaṇa priests are still part of the Cambodian court today.

The Khmer people also continued to practice what is termed indigenous religion, especially in rural temples, performing rituals for spirits called *neak ta*. In many Southeast Asian cultures, ancestors provided the living with assistance and protection, but caused disaster if they were not appeased (Miksic and Goh 2017: 173). Ancestor worship remained important for both elites and the general population, and local customs and beliefs intermingled with Hindu and Buddhist practices (Ang 1988). In indigenous Khmer religious thought, mountains represented powerful spirits and ancestors could best be reached at their summit (Mabbet and Chandler 1995: 110). The association of certain mountains with Hindu gods like Śiva and Viṣṇu may, thus, represent a blending of imported religion and indigenous belief. By the seventh century, Hindu and Buddhist rituals had merged with local customs in Southeast Asia, but elites began to practice new rituals that excluded the common people (Miksic and Goh 2017: 9–10). In addition, despite some overlap in belief and ritual, state and local traditions operated in distinct spheres. Inscriptions show a society divided by language; Sanskrit was used in high temples and Khmer in local villages (Chandler 2009: 52–53; Mabbett and Chandler 1995: 112).

In the thirteenth century, after a long period in which Mahāyāna was the dominant form of Buddhism in the Angkor Empire, the pendulum began to swing towards Theravāda. Some Theravāda practices were present in the Lower Mekong Basin from the Funan period onwards, possibly influenced by the Mon culture to the west (Harris 2005: 4–5), but its political influence was negligible. During the Late Angkor period, however, the Khmer began to embrace this school of Buddhism (19–24). In the late thirteenth century the Chinese ambassador Zhou Daguan visited Angkor and saw monks dressed in characteristically Theravāda style, with shaved heads and yellow robes (Marston and Guthrie 2004: 9). The increasing popularity of Theravāda across Mainland Southeast Asia in this period may have undermined the Mahāyāna-supporting Angkor complex as a Buddhist religious center, contributing to its decline (Fletcher et al. 2017: 282). Theravāda was also the state religion of the Thai kingdom of Ayutthaya (Baker and Phongpaichit 2017: 210), which gained control over the Mekong region after the fall of Angkor.

Some argue that Theravāda is structured more hierarchically, which may explain, at least in part, its support by rulers and political elites fighting for power with Hindu and Mahāyāna elites throughout the region; across Southeast Asia, however, Theravāda monastic orders (the *saṅgha*, or community of Buddhist monks) have periodically posed a political challenge to colonial and postcolonial states (Harris 2007).

Universalizing morality and egalitarian ethics

As noted elsewhere in this volume, both Hinduism and Buddhism are generally regarded as moralizing and universalizing faiths, with the latter known also as equality-promoting, features that have contributed to their inclusion as core axial ideologies by Jaspers and most scholars following him. In general, Hinduism as practiced in Southeast Asia entailed a belief in karma, a concept that bestows all events and social circumstances with moral significance (Lockard 2009: 22). In South Asia, Hindus believed that punishment and rewards for their actions were realized through reincarnation rather than in a single lifetime (Shattuck 1999: 29). As we note above, practitioners in first-millennium CE Southeast Asia merged both Hinduism and Buddhism with popular indigenous traditions and beliefs. A seventh-century CE inscription from Talang Tuwo in modern-day Indonesia, for instance, shows clearly the localization of Mahāyāna Buddhist tradition in the region. The text urges moral behavior from followers, setting out a series of "moral prescriptions ... addressed to the faithful, who, if they follow them, may lay claim to the greatest joys of Buddhism" (Cœdès 1930: 50).

Ancestral spirits monitored behavior and enforced correct action throughout the premodern Mekong Basin. Inscriptions show that early Khmer kings recognized the power of local neak ta spirits, the "owners" of the land, and portrayed themselves as taking over some of their spiritual functions (Work 2017). Failure to fulfill one's duties to one's ancestors, for instance by neglecting to carry out the proper annual rituals, produced misfortune in the past and is still considered a cause by many today. This long-standing blend of indigenous and South Asian ideologies culminated in a complex and dynamic moral and ritual framework (Chandler 2009: 115; Miksic and Goh 2017: 9).

Any attempt to separate Hindu from Buddhist influences in Southeast Asian contexts is likewise fraught. Both Buddhist and Hindu ideologies emphasize reincarnation, for example, and bas-relief scenes depicting the 32 separate hells in Angkor Wat's southern gallery offer warning to those committing the worst transgressions. Suffering rebirth into these hells is a distinctly Buddhist representation in a monument dedicated to the Hindu deity Viṣṇu (Brown 2004: 359). The prevalence of such syncretic beliefs and practices complicates any simple understanding of causal influence in the development of moralizing ideology; the importance of good moral conduct, clearly, was emphasized in the Mekong Basin before the arrival of South Asian religions. Yet, the first-millennium CE embrace of Hindu and Buddhist practice also had a significant influence on local religious life.

Universalizing morality and egalitarianism in practice

Hindu thought generally does not promote egalitarianism and from its outset it was compatible with the South Asian division of society into four *varṇas* (priests and scholars, rulers and warriors, traders and farmers, and laborers) as well as the more fine-grained *jāti* ("caste") system (see the chapter on India in this volume for further discussion). Khmer states were organized into hereditary social classes, but this system was less strict than the *varṇa* and *jāti* system in contemporary South Asia (Mabbett 1977). The ruler and his (or her) entourage included *brāhmaṇas* and a large coterie of bureaucrats to whom the ruler had granted titles and who occupied the upper levels of Angkorian society. Parallel to this court population (and on a slightly lower rung) were mid-level elites and provincial rulers; temple personnel may also have been in this group. Most Angkorian Khmers, however, occupied the lowest stratum of the hierarchy. A shared belief in Hinduism did not entail equality between the ruling class and masses or any notion of universal morality. The general population was also further stratified into fairly rigid social categories, including temple personnel, peasants, and slaves (Sahai 1978). Miksic (2007: 86) argues that in Southeast Asian Hindu contexts, unlike in most of South Asia, "The same person could belong to several *varṇas* at one time. ... There is no reference to caste in relation to marriage or food restrictions." Nevertheless, social mobility within Khmer states was still limited. Chandler (2009: 55) writes that the concept of *varṇas* applied only to a small, relatively lofty segment of society: "These people included clerks, artisans, concubines, artists, high officials, and priests, as well as royal servants, relatives, and soldiers." The majority of the population farmed rice and were not included in these hierarchies.

Slavery, an extreme form of inequality and a useful proxy for the application of universalizing ideology, is accepted in traditional Hinduism. In the Mekong Basin, the term *knum* appears in inscriptions dating to the seventh to eighth centuries. *Knum* is often translated as "slave," though the term could also be interpreted as "dependent" or "servant" (Martin 1998: 290–95). In some cases, *knum* were purchased by elites and donated to temples. They mainly farmed land owned by the temple and took care of the temple's domestic animals. There were, however, many categories of unfree laborers in the pre-Angkor period, including those working in the fields and those who held administrative positions in temples (Chandler 2009: 56). In the Angkor period, there is also evidence for the practice of chattel slavery (Mabbett 1983).

This system remained in place after the decline of Angkor and the introduction of Theravāda Buddhism (Harris 2005: 71–72). Buddhism calls for the extension of compassion to all people and stresses that the ability to reach enlightenment is universal, yet these moral tenets did not lead to calls for the abolition of slavery. Harris (71–72) cites evidence for the persistence of slavery in the Mekong Basin into the twentieth century. Slavery was also present in the Kingdom of Ayutthaya (Baker and Phongpaichit 2009: 15). There is, thus, no evidence that the adoption of the "axial" ideology of Buddhism in the Mekong Basin, either in its Mahāyāna or Theravāda forms, led to any large-scale programs of reform aiming to flatten out social hierarchies. This is consistent with what we have found for other regions where "axial" religions emerged or were introduced (e.g. see the chapters on India, the Mediterranean Basin, and the Inland Niger Delta). In terms of slavery at least, one of the clearest and most extreme instantiations of human inequality, religions and ideologies generally adapted to suit the practice, rather than the other way around.

Gender equality

Likewise, unequal gender relations persisted in the Mekong Basin throughout the period under consideration here. Hindu thought has traditionally viewed women as subordinate to men (Whaling 2009: 81). Women in Southeast Asia, however, most likely had a better position in society than those in South Asia during contemporary periods. Records from the seventh- to eighth-century Mekong Basin point to the political influence of royal women (Jacobsen 2008: 22–28; Vickery 1998: 185–86) and rural populations in the region have traditionally practiced matrilineality: the tracing of descent and inheritance of wealth and status through female relatives (Vickery 1998). Queenship was not uncommon in the pre-Angkorian Mekong Basin and a series of queens from the eighth to ninth centuries (the queens of Śambhupura) appear in inscriptions from the north of the region (Jacobsen 2003). Queens largely disappear by the following Angkorian period, although elite women continued to enjoy high status and royal genealogies were frequently traced through the female line (Jacobsen 2008: 59–63).

Khmer women, like their compatriots across much of Southeast Asia, had relatively favorable social positions in the premodern Lower Mekong Basin. That this was embedded in indigenous culture (rather than adopted with the spread of "axial" religions deriving from South or East Asia) is suggested by the erosion of women's status in the Angkorian period. This trend is somewhat surprising as it coincides with the rise in popularity of Mahāyāna Buddhism, a tradition notable for its generally positive representation of women (Paul 1985: 303–11). As Jacobsen (2008) explains, the status of women in the region continued to fall in the post-Angkorian period (fifteenth to eighteenth centuries CE) with the introduction of didactic texts, known as *cpap*, that outlined fairly restrictive "appropriate behavior" for women. In the period of Ayutthaya rule, the legal system treated women as the property of men. Even queens were seen as the property of kings (Baker and Phongpaichit 2017: 110).

Mahāyāna and Theravāda Buddhism both emphasize the fundamental equality of all humans (Schmidt-Leukel 2006: 86). Theravāda practice in many ways replaced elite control over ideological authority, making religious practice more accessible to commoners through the *saṅgha* community (Chandler 2009). We discuss the position of monarchs in the region in more detail below, but here it is sufficient to note that there is no evidence of the decline of social hierarchies linked to the state support of Buddhist thought. Instead, the emergence of both Mahāyāna Buddhist and Hindu religious institutions in the first-millennium CE Lower Mekong Basin likely formalized and legitimized emerging social stratification. Mainland Southeast Asian Theravāda Buddhism, which flourished after the thirteenth century, valued "ordered relationships and harmony" between the sexes, between age groups, and between officials and laity (Mabbett and Chandler 1995: 112). It could thus serve ideologically to underpin social hierarchies and support the authority wielded by rulers, rather than undermine it (Harris 2005: 74). In fact, social hierarchies were further solidified in the period of Ayutthaya rule, as bureaucratic positions became restricted to the nobility (Baker and Phongpaichit 2009: 15). The introduction of neither Hindu nor Buddhist (Mahāyāna and later Theravāda) traditions, then, produced a concrete shift towards economic and social equality in the complex states of the Lower Mekong Basin.

Prosociality

Hinduism and Buddhism both promote "merit-making" through giving. In the early complex societies of the Lower Mekong region, there is evidence for the practice of donation by elites to Hindu as well as Buddhist temples (Chandler 2009: 34–35; Vickery 1986). After the shift to dominant Mahāyāna Buddhism in the Classic Angkor period, rulers began to undertake great acts of charity, providing for the care of the elderly and infirm as well as constructing public works such as canals and roads (Hendrickson 2010). Jayavarman VII left an inscription claiming that he "suffered from the maladies of his subjects more than from his own; for it is the public grief which makes the grief of kings, not their own grief" (Kulke 2014: 336). He built hospitals, resthouses, and improved the roads in the Angkor Empire (Briggs 1951: 209–36). Charity was also practiced by the rulers of Ayutthaya in the form of alms (Baker and Phongpaichit 2017: 110). The florescence of charity among the rulers and elites of Classic Angkor appears to be linked to state support for Mahāyāna Buddhism in particular, which features in the Axial Age literature as a "secondary breakthrough" after the initial emergence of Buddhism in the last millennium BCE (e.g. Wittrock 2005: 69). However, the aim of royal and elite benefaction was always to relieve suffering and produce merit for the donors themselves, never to do away with social hierarchies altogether.

The most notable works of prosociality in the period under review here were the enormous hydraulic projects undertaken by several rulers to bring water to people and crops in the Mekong Basin and beyond, especially in the Angkor period. Massive diversions of water and the creation of artificial lakes, like the famed Lolei Baray, not only provided for the material well-being of inhabitants, but also served ideological purposes and demonstrated the sheer power and resources commanded by Angkor rulers. Harris (2005: 19) summarizes well the interplay between all of these motivations:

The various hydraulic projects at Angkor may all be reduced to a simple form of a baray [artificial lake] surrounding a temple-mountain. In essence the mountain collects heavenly water and is fructified by the encounter. The water then runs down into a baray, from where it fertilizes the surrounding soils. We find this arrangement first at Kulen, but it may also be observed at Angkor Wat and the great Buddhist temple complexes of Jayavarman VII. From his cosmic center the king ruled; he both "consumed" his domains and, by the proper performance of the royal cult, radiated back quasi-divine power. In this way, order and prosperity were sustained.

Traditional Khmer moral norms, however, also emphasize the importance of mutual aid among kin (Delvert 1961: 218), making it difficult to disentangle indigenous from South Asian influences on practices of almsgiving and temple donation. In addition, temple donations in the Angkor Empire could be interpreted as a form of taxation rather than spontaneous prosocial giving. Temples served as a source of social welfare and security for their surrounding populations, providing education and supporting artisans. The inhabitants of the Khmer states did not amass large stores of personal wealth: goods were either used immediately or donated to temples (Harris 2005: 50).

Rulership and institutions of authority
There were close ties between religion and royal authority in the Lower Mekong Basin. In the early Southeast Asian polities that adopted Hinduism, rulers were often seen as representatives of Śiva. Hall (2011: 51–52) writes that "since Siva's authority over all that exists was absolute, in theory the rulers' own powers on earth had no limit." There is evidence of Śiva worship in the Lower Mekong Basin starting in the Late Funan period (Le 2008) and this cult was closely linked to royal power. As well as associating themselves directly with South Asian divine beings, local rulers across Southeast Asia drew legitimacy from their performance of Brāhmaṇic rituals and feats of asceticism (Hall 2011: 51–52).

The connection between rulers and gods evolved throughout the Chenla and Angkor periods. Most Chenla rulers were officially assigned divine status only after death and were seen as only semi-divine during their lifetime. As far as we know, Jayavarman I (r. c. 635–80 CE) was the first Chenla ruler to adopt the title of *vrah kamratan an* (holiest holy) while still living (Jacobsen 2008: xx). Because it was applied to both royals and Hindu gods, this title simultaneously conveyed a sense of these early rulers' earthly power and their relationship with the divine (Coe 2003: 68–69; Jacobsen 2008: xx).

Jayavarman II, considered the first king of the Angkor Empire, took sacred kingship in the Mekong Basin one step further in declaring himself *cakravartin* (universal ruler) or *devarāja* ("king of the gods" in Sanskrit) in a ceremony on Mount Mahendra in 802 CE (Wolters 2008: 165, 176). His successors continued the tradition, claiming to be incarnations of Śiva or Viṣṇu and building monuments dedicated to these gods (Kulke 1978). There were few formalized constitutional checks on Angkorian rulers' power beyond the power of moral authority, at least in terms of the sort of legal checks on authority and division of powers normally cited in models of axial transformations (e.g. Bellah 2011; Eisenstadt 2005). However, the activities of non-royal elites, including court notables and religious officials, likely provided powerful informal constraints on their authority, preventing the arbitrary exercise of power (Mabbett 1978). Further, written codes of conduct from South Asian sources, such as the Arthaśāstra, seem to have provided at least inspiration for statecraft and may perhaps have functioned like the institutionalized codes of conduct anticipated by axial theorists. Such limits, indeed, became more pronounced over time as Buddhist expectations of appropriate conduct by rulers gradually replaced (and to an extent merged with) syncretic Hindu and indigenous practices. Notions of divine kingship persisted during the periods of later Angkor history when Buddhism was dominant—Jayavarman VII, for instance, appears to have combined concepts of the king's divinity with the Mahāyāna Buddhist veneration of bodhisattvas in his monumental building projects (Hansen 2004: 106). However, the monarch's divine status became seen less as an expression of his inherent righteousness and benevolence and more as an ideal for him to live up to; with perhaps the threat of removal for failing to do so (Harris 2005: 80).

Benda (1962: 121) argues that the Theravāda Buddhism adopted in the region by the early thirteenth century "created a quasi-egalitarian religious community of which even the monarchs themselves became, albeit for short times and mainly symbolically, members." The kings of this period had many ritual duties and typically held daily audiences with their subjects (Harris 2005: 51). Harris (50) writes that while rulership was more or less hereditary, kings in the post-Classic period might have sometimes been chosen by committee for their spiritual merit. The saṅgha held considerable influence in the Theravāda state and may have been able to constrain royal power from the Late Angkor period onwards (Benda 1962: 121; Coe 2003: 195). At the same time, Theravāda Buddhist rulers were believed to possess supernatural abilities to control nature, a concept that ultimately reinforced royal authority (Harris 2005: 50).

The role of the ruler in the early Ayutthaya state provides more insight into Theravāda kingship. While the Ayutthaya state supported Theravāda Buddhism, its ideologies of kingship also drew from earlier Angkorian, Mahāyāna, and Brāhmaṇic traditions. In early Ayutthaya, the king was called a *mahasommutirat* (ruler by general consent), which is a more limited, perhaps "axial" concept than the idea of divinely sanctioned kingship seen in earlier periods (Baker and Phongpaichit 2017: 108). Baker and Phongpaichit (108–09) note that the ideal of the bodhisattva king also likely restricted the range of action available to the ruler by forcing him to act within Buddhist ideology, interpretable by powerful members of the saṅgha. However, another Ayutthayan belief held that the Buddhist king was created by 11 Hindu gods (108–09). The king was thus still seen as a divine figure, though was apparently subject to more constraints than his predecessors in earlier periods. Others, however er (e.g. Tambiah [1978] 2013: 505), note that the Buddhist king remained the node around which all other authority pivoted, serving "as wielder of dharma (the moral law), as the *cakravartin* (universal emperor) and bodhisattva (buddha-to-be)." While little reliable information on the structure of the Ayutthayan government is available (Wilson 1980: 31), the king's role in this period seems to have been more nuanced (at least in terms of ideologies of rulership) than that of the Angkor cakravartin.

Neither Hindu nor Buddhist ideals of universalism, then, prevented rulers in the Mekong Basin from claiming divine legitimation. On the contrary, adopting these South Asian ideologies—their rituals, traditions of literacy, and iconographic languages—allowed local rulers to make the first claims to kingship in the region in the early first millennium CE (Wolters 1979). This undercuts the idea that the importation to Southeast Asia of "axial" ideologies from South Asia led to the emergence of more critical attitudes to rulership and legitimate authority, as models of the Axial Age predict (e.g. Bellah 2011; Eisenstadt 1986b, 1986c). This should not, perhaps, be surprising, as Buddhist practice across Asia has coexisted quite comfortably with sacred monarchy from its inception to the present day (see the chapters on South and East Asia in this volume for more details). At the same time, we should not fall into the trap of portraying the power of the kings of Funan, Chenla, and Angkor as absolute. As we have seen, the political realities of rival elite factions—and, increasingly from the Late Angkor period onwards, the saṅgha of Theravāda monks and nuns—served to limit what was possible for rulers. Mahāyāna and Theravāda varieties of Buddhism also enshrined compassion for the suffering of one's people as the mark of a good, virtuous king, encouraging royal investment in public works.

Conclusion

Indigenous social structures, beliefs, and practices shaped the manner and form of the supposedly axial religions that Lower Mekong Basin residents adopted by the early first millennium CE. By then, long-term trends in Mainland Southeast Asia towards increased social complexity and greater connectivity with other societies of eastern Eurasia made its inhabitants receptive to South Asian models of rulership and authority, grounded in concepts and rituals that we now term "Hinduism." The introduction of this axial faith, then, produced the opposite effect from that predicted by Axial Age models; rather than bringing about a re-evaluation of sacred rulership, Hinduism allowed it to flourish.

State-sponsored Mahāyāna Buddhism espoused universalizing morality and forms of egalitarianism from the early second millennium CE, though also ultimately served the ideological needs of the rulers who patronized it. The economies of the Khmer states (like those of other Mainland Southeast Asian polities) depended on vast reserves of unfree labor; strict social hierarchy and limited social mobility persisted throughout the first and early first millennium CE. In terms of gender equality, while Buddhist ideals and indigenous traditions allowed women to attain certain prestige, at least relative to other traditions across Afro-Eurasia,[3] this did not translate into anything like gender equality. Further, the social opportunities available to women only narrowed over time, particularly in the post-Angkor phase, as discussed above.

Conversely, one "axial-type" transformation in the history of the Mekong Basin may be identified during the later Angkor period, as the adoption of Mahāyāna Buddhism as the most important state religion under Jayavarman VII promoted greater acts of prosocial spending. It is difficult, however, to pinpoint the precise impetus for this development and, as we noted above, indigenous moral norms also valued the provision of mutual aid among kin. Further, Mahāyāna did not remain the dominant form of Buddhist practice, as Theravāda became the favored religion by the Khmer period.[4] Nevertheless, while it is difficult to attribute any clear causal role to Buddhist ideals, it is notable that the royal support of both forms of Buddhism—a core "axial" ideology—did coincide with a period of fairly active creation of public goods by Angkorian rulers. The network of patronage that emerged under this system also acted as a funnel for resources, including time as well as material, to flow from elite patrons to their less well-off clients.

The issue is made more complex by the striking similarities in cultural pedigree between the societies of South and Southeast Asia, including modern-day India, southern China, and Mainland and Island Southeast Asia: a cultural region sometimes known as "monsoon Asia" (Mus 2011: 21–22). These South Asian developments themselves were heavily enmeshed in ideological interchange with the rest of western Eurasia, notably Roman and Persian societies (Bellina and Glover 2004). When the supposedly axial faiths of South Asia were introduced into Southeast Asia, then, the two regions already shared a deep cultural heritage supported by continual movement of peoples throughout the wider South Asian region; this shared heritage included beliefs in spirits of place and notions of appropriate ethical conduct, linking them also into a wider cultural sphere encompassing nearly all of Afro-Eurasia.[5] This underscores the importance of taking a long view of historical developments, as the chapters in this volume attempt to do.

---

3   See the other chapters in this volume for detailed discussions of this theme.
4   The precise details of this transition, though, are difficult to reconstruct.
5   These linkages are brought out throughout this volume; see the Introduction and Conclusion chapters especially for more thorough discussions.

The history of rulership in the Mekong River Basin is similarly complex. Even Jayavarman II and other Angkorian rulers who portrayed themselves as semi-divine *cakravartins* did not enjoy the near unlimited authority of the typical "archaic" king modeled by many Axial Age proponents. While there were still few clear formal checks on royal power, the power and authority of temple officials and elites provided powerful informal constraints. It could be argued that a more notable axial shift came in the thirteenth century CE with the rise of Theravāda Buddhism as the major, state-supported faith. The constraints imposed on the kings of Late Angkor and succeeding Southeast Asian polities by Theravāda monks—some institutionalized but still largely informal—limited the scope of royal authority more effectively than under previous regimes. Although the role of the king and prevailing concepts of kingship certainly became more complex in this period, it is unclear how this affected royal authority in practice. In the Ayutthaya Kingdom, kings were still shrouded in an aura of divinity despite the practice of Theravāda. It remains, thus, uncertain how the introduction of Theravāda to Southeast Asia affected the political position of the king and the structure of the state more generally.

We end this chapter, then, as we began; the Mekong Basin has a long and complex history, which neither unambiguously supports nor refutes traditional models of axial transitions. In many respects, early Mekong Basin polities like Funan and Chenla displayed typically "archaic" features, including limited social mobility, strong ideological support for hierarchy, and no clearly defined limits on the exercise of royal authority. On the other hand, many of these features changed little even after the establishment of Mahāyāna and later Theravāda Buddhism as official religions. Then again, the Buddhism practiced by the rulers of Angkor and Ayutthaya was not the same as the Buddhism of South or East Asia highlighted by Axial Age scholars. Rather, it was a blended tradition absorbing many local customs and beliefs. Complicating matters even further are the shared sociocultural traits between Southeast Asia and regions typically considered "core" axial regions, like South and East Asia. This realization begs important questions about early Bronze and Iron Age interactions throughout Eurasia, belying the oft-espoused notion that certain regions were isolated and fully autochthonous in their axial transformations (Jaspers 1953: 10).[6]

The only conclusion that can be safely drawn from this survey of the Mekong Basin's history, then, is that no conclusion can be drawn. This is not to say that this historical journey has been without merit, for the experience of rulers and ruled in the region over the long course of the period discussed here offers much-needed nuance to any story of the spread and development of axial traditions through eastern Eurasia.

---

6   The importance of interactions and cultural connections in the development of axial (and pre-axial) ideologies and ruling strategies are discussed throughout this volume; see especially the Egypt, Anatolia, and Iran chapters.

EAST ASIA | Japan

*Thomas Cressy**

Period	Polity	Approx. dates
Jōmon Period	Initial Jōmon	9200–5300 BCE
	Early Jōmon	5300–3500
	Middle Jōmon	3500–2500
	Late Jōmon	2500–1200
	Final Jōmon	1200–500
Bronze/Iron Age	Yayoi	500 BCE–250 CE
	Kofun	250–538
Classical	Asuka	538–710
	Nara	710–794
	Heian	794–1185
Early Medieval	Kamakura Shogunate	1185–1333

Table 9. Periods and dates of polities mentioned in text that were based in or that occupied Japan

Introduction

The introduction to this volume mentions Japan as a curious example of a region to which "axial" cultural traits and religious ideologies—namely, Buddhism along with Chinese Confucian-influenced practices—had spread, but which did not seem to generate "axial" reforms in the ways these ideologies had inspired, it is argued, in other parts of South and East Asia. It is also often argued that non-axial elements (such as the divinity of rulers and the reinforcement of social hierarchies) remained prominent in Japan throughout the first millennium CE, despite the presence of egalitarian and moralizing ethics in Shintō and Buddhist thought as well as the formation of formal legal and administrative structures around the middle of this millennium. Eisenstadt (1996) even remarked explicitly that Japan remained "pre-Axial" throughout most of its history. This chapter will deal with the precise circumstances and concepts of morality, egalitarian ethics and the relationship between the position of the ruler and religion in the Japanese context.

Japan, on the periphery of the "core" axial territories, poses many questions about the development of religious and philosophical thought as presented in prominent Axial Age theories. Over its long history, Japan has witnessed a complex interaction

---

* Gina Barnes and Eugene N. Anderson also contributed to this chapter by reading and providing feedback on previous drafts.

between supposedly pre- and post-axial characteristics, such as universalizing morality, egalitarianism, relations between rulers and ruled and the blending of local and "foreign" custom. Buddhism was brought to Japan from South Asia via China and Korea, along with Confucian ideas about rulership and political organization from the mainland as well. These novel ideologies merged with local beliefs and social structures in complex ways, which challenge traditional assumptions of a discrete, axial-type "turn." This chapter surveys how egalitarianism, universalizing morality and notions of rulership developed and changed over time in Japan, but also how these ideas were (or were not) adopted in practice. It focuses on ancient history from the Jōmon until around the end of the Heian period.

Historical and religious background

Based on current archaeological evidence, the defining aspect of Jōmon culture appears to be large and dense settlements of hunter-gatherers organized around key resources with subsistence strategies such as storage pits, but also the presence of sophisticated material culture, long-distance trade and much ceremonial and ritual activity—all of which have a very high degree of temporal and regional variation, over an almost 10,000-year period, that cannot be completely pinned down to a fixed set of cultural traits (Habu 2008: 572). The Jōmon culture is also an unusual example of a hunter-gatherer society with very early evidence of sedentism and the use of pottery. Population peaked in the Middle Jōmon and was particularly dense in north-eastern Japan, which was followed by a steady population decrease in the Late and Final Jōmon periods. This has been interpreted as a function of the limited population size sustainable in hunter-gatherer societies, although such theories cannot explain the population drop, which others have attributed to global cooling and thus harsher living conditions from the Middle Jōmon onward (572–73). The Jōmon people, then, offer an example of around 10,000 years of internal expansion and population booms of a hunter-gatherer society with sophisticated material culture, followed by 3,000 years of internal contraction and decline, possibly accompanied by decreasing complexity (though this is unclear) (583).

More recently, interpretations of the Jōmon people as "merely" a hunter-gatherer-fishing society have been called into question. Bleed and Matsui (2010: 364) suggest that the development of highly regularized bows is testament to Jōmon peoples' ability to carefully harvest plants nurtured for this specific use. Furthermore, Nasu and Momohara (2016: 504–10) suggest that they were likely long cultivating chestnuts and the lacquer trees that provided resources for their craft; rice agriculture was adopted on a small scale from the East Asian mainland during the first millennium BCE, particularly in Kyūshū, which indicates much earlier contact with the continent than is suggested by typical narratives, which place this during the later Yayoi period. This has led Kaner and Ishikawa (2007: 5) to suggest that Late and Final Jōmon society in Kyūshū could be considered "truly Neolithic," namely, agricultural but lacking metal technology. Even though there was contact with continental culture, reflected in the appearance of rice agriculture, metallurgy does not seem to have yet been adopted, despite often being lumped with rice agriculture as part of a complete "cultural package" taken from Korea or China. In this sense, it is unlikely that other aspects of continental thinking, such as the "axial" philosophies of Confucius or Laozi, were imported from Warring States China (770–221 BCE) even at the very end of the Jōmon period. On the other hand, there is evidence of metal tools following Chinese and Korean forms in use in Japan between 1200 and 800 BCE, as well as a lacquer container lid similar in style to that used in contemporary northern China. This suggests either that foreign invaders appeared at this time or, more likely given similarities in the ceramics and pottery that have been uncovered, that there was cultural contact, particularly through the Korean Peninsula (Bleed and Matsui 2010: 360). Despite this, it seems the most significant activities of the Jōmon people remained the same, with a focus on fishing, hunting and harvesting other available resources rather than adopting continental technologies and ideologies (with the exception of rice cultivation in isolated areas), and the later presence of certain objects and rice farming, suggestive of overseas cultural contact or immigration to Japan (367).

The famous clay figurines (*dogū*) of the Jōmon culture were clearly central to ritual practices and beliefs and there are no parallels or similar practices in other regions or contemporaneous cultures, showing them to be uniquely Jōmon (Maringer 1974: 128). These often loosely resembled the human form, but sometimes took on the forms and features of animals that were part of Jōmon life, such as boars, dogs, monkeys, bears, sea mammals, insects, shellfish, birds, snakes, frogs, fish and plants or mushrooms too—all of which suggests to Kaner (2009: 32) that this could be seen as a "pantheon of spirits," each with symbolic or ritual meaning. Furthermore, some of these clay figurines appear to be wearing the same clay masks that were likely used by the later Jōmon as ritual funerary ornaments: examples have been found in their grave pits and burial jars (34–35). By around 2000 BCE, the production of clay figurines had spread from a few mountainous centers to all over the main island, Honshū, and the figurines gained more female bodily features; in later Jōmon contexts, however, they have largely been found in domestic settings rather than burial grounds, suggesting a kind of cultic and domestic reverence (Maringer 1974: 132–34). Harada (2009: 58) suggests that rituals involving breaking and disposing of parts of the doll expressed ideas of the sacred and enacted communication with the many animal spirits of Jōmon ideology, and perhaps traces of such beliefs can be found in Japanese Shintō and myths in their prayers to the various enshrined animal *kami* (deities or spirits). However, it is difficult to know in detail what these religious practices and beliefs were, and there is no contemporary documentary evidence of how the Jōmon people perceived these spiritual and symbolic objects (Kaner 2009: 39). Nevertheless, recent research has now argued for a revaluation of the dating of the Yayoi period, pushing the Jōmon-Yayoi transition far into what is traditionally called the Final Jōmon period, and thus the beliefs thought to be distinctively Yayoi, such as the worship of *kami* that controlled the weather and crops, have become blurred with the animism of the Jōmon (Kaner 2011: 458). Kaner has, in fact, recently attempted to re-evaluate Jōmon ritual and religious practices in light of such archaeological discoveries, drawing especially on scholarship by Naumann (2000) and Kobayashi (2004).

The most recent studies of Jōmon ritual activity, however, reveal strong connections between spiritual beliefs and hunting, fishing, and burial cults—which are represented not only by clay figurines, but also by clay masks, phallic stones, zoomorphic ceramic figurines and stone pillars; it is especially interesting that many Jōmon sites themselves were constructed to align with the movements of the sun and moon, which, alongside distinctive mountain peaks, appear to have played a central role in Jōmon cosmology (Kaner 2011: 458–59). The animist aspect of these early Japanese religious practices is also difficult to pin down in detail, as the faces of the clay dolls appear to resemble smaller animals, including dogs (the only domestic animals in Jōmon culture), yet the animals hunted were not represented in these dolls. More importantly, Kaner argues for a focus on the transformation of the human form, whether through masks or the fashioning of humanoid figurines. This is reflected in the cultural elaboration of other practices of transformation, including the cooking of natural resources into edible foodstuffs (461–62).

The transition from Jōmon culture to that of the Yayoi era is characterized by the changes in ritual and religious practices brought about by the adoption of rice agriculture, thought to have entered Kyūshū from the Korean Peninsula. The most recent dates for this technological transfer place it at some point between 900 and 700 BCE (Miyamoto 2019: 110), and it was followed by the further consolidation and spread of technologies, artefact styles and burial practices from the Korean Peninsula to Kyūshū (Barnes 2015: 271). By the Yayoi period (500 BCE–250 CE), we see the emergence of the first agriculturally based society on the Japanese islands that was also characterized by the use of bronze and iron, defying "classification by Western archaeological standards" as neither Neolithic, Bronze Age, nor Iron Age; it is rather argued to be a unique creative mix of transformations of adopted traditions (Barnes 2014a: 833). The western island of Kyūshū appears to have been the first place where such cultural transformations began, while wet rice agriculture had been adopted as far as eastern Japan by 100 BCE (Barnes 2007: 78). By the end of the third century CE, rice was being cultivated in the very north of Honshū; significantly, though, skeletal remains indicate that at that time, a large number of the inhabitants of the westernmost regions were almost indistinguishable from contemporaneous populations in the Korean Peninsula and what is now China (Kidder 2007: 65–70). Nakahashi (2000: 12–13) has argued that 80–90% of their genome was identical to the populations in continental East Asia, although this is based on later evidence rather than genetic data from Yayoi. Bronze and cast-iron objects from the Bo-hai Bay region of China dating to 175–100 BCE have been found in burial sites in northern Kyūshū, and iron-forging techniques were also transferred from the south of the Korean Peninsula between 100 BCE and 200 CE (Barnes 2007: 35–36). As Kidder (1993: 107) states, physically larger immigrants brought with them wet-rice agriculture, iron and bronze, moated villages with watchtowers, and bronze mirrors; they joined or allied with or fought with other groups in the geographical area. These groups were eventually unified under a center of authority powerful enough to build large tombs from Queen Himiko's so-called Yamatai polity onward (Kidder 2007: 59). The Nara Basin was the likely center of this power according to Barnes (2014a: 841), beginning what is termed the Kofun period from around 250 CE, after the death of Himiko.

As no Chinese sources exist for the majority of the Kofun period, it is known as a historical "void" in Japan (Barnes 2007: 20), but archaeological evidence has provided some clues to what may have occurred in this period. As Kaner (2011: 464) explains, *kofun* means "old tombs" and this period is characterized by the construction of large tombs for elites. Another new development was the ritual authority given to the bronze mirrors and beadstone products (replaced by iron tools, weapons, armor, stoneware, gilt-bronze ornaments and gold jewelry around 400–475 CE) that were deposited in the mounted tombs—with the Miwa court as the political center of the Japanese isles (Barnes 2007: 9–10). This "elite Mounded Tomb Culture and cult system" had been incorporated by the regional chiefdoms in western Japan by the late third century; the system further progressed in the fifth century into one in which local chiefs were given court titles of the Yamato Kingdom and thereby absorbed into this state (Barnes 2014a: 846). Power over domains was, therefore, achieved through status rather than military conquest. A tributary system was then instituted, under the influence of Chinese and Korean state administrative practices, in which chiefdoms were divided into territorial units that performed prescribed manufacturing and service roles, especially making luxury goods for use in elite palaces. This activity was inclusive of and benefited greatly from the influx of refugees from the Korean Peninsula, many of whom were skilled in such crafts, replacing the earlier traditions focused on ritual objects such as bronze mirrors (846–48).

The Kofun period also witnessed one of the most impactful changes in ancient Japanese society: the arrival of religious, philosophical and political ideologies from mainland East Asia. In addition to the material and intellectual culture of Buddhism, Confucianism and Daoism, Chinese writing, artistic techniques, medical knowledge, and political and social configurations all flowed to the Yamato court, and thus to the many families and clan chiefs in competition for political power (Deal and Ruppert 2015: 5–6). Though the precise details are difficult to discern, the traditional narrative has immigrants, merchants and others bringing these traditions from the continent starting around 400 CE. However, it is argued that, as part of the diplomatic relations between Yamato and its allies, the gift of images of Buddha and scriptural scrolls to the sovereign Kinmei in 538 CE[1] represents the start of official discourse and debate on what the state was to do with such beliefs, marking the end of Kofun and the transition into the Asuka period.

A major source of these ideas, especially Buddhist thought, was the Korean Peninsula. The Korean Paekche Kingdom needed a military ally for its war against China and other Korean kingdoms; as part of this political context, gifts of Buddhist imagery and texts (as well as other resources) were given to the Yamato court in the sixth century CE to secure their military support. Experts in Buddhist thought also traveled from Korea and became central to the spread of Buddhism in Japan, mainly through the patronage of the Soga clan, whose origins may have been outside of Japan (Deal and Ruppert 2015: 22). According to the *Nihon Shoki* ("Chronicles of Japan"), by 624 CE, this clan, combined with other immigrant kinship groups, had overseen the construction of 46 Buddhist temples, home to 816 monks and 519 nuns (12–17). Despite some official recognition and reverence of Buddhist values by Queen Suiko and Prince Shōtoku, the Soga gained great power at court through their symbolic and ritual control of Buddhism. This power was considered such a threat that the leader of the Soga clan was assassinated in a plot in 645 CE, which was also the year King Kōtoku made the Taika ("Great Change") Reforms. These were modeled on the Chinese Tang Dynasty, which had established a permanent legal, military and political center of power in the government under an absolute monarch, as well as bringing Buddhist rituals and institutions under state control (33–34). A "Monastic Office" was also established, which included a system of ranks and training for monks and nuns; through this institution, in 679 CE, King Tenmu prescribed the attire and colors monks and nuns were to wear and measures were put in place to ensure further state control of temples built by powerful clans. For example, in 689 CE, an edict was issued that required all who wished to take Buddhist vows and join a monastic community to obtain the ruler's permission. Interestingly, the official state adoption of Buddhism seems to have been an attempt to control sources of symbolic and ritual power rather than being driven by a sort of "axial awakening," bringing new ideals of ethical responsibility, morality or principles of distributed authority.

---

1   This may have occurred slightly later, namely in 552 CE, according to the date given in the *Nihon Shoki*, a historical chronicle completed over a century later (Barnes 2014: 848).

Shortly after these reforms were instituted, Queen Jitō declared herself empress, or "divine sovereign") over all of Nippon (Japan)—a term echoing the Chinese "Mandate of Heaven," in which a divine ruler oversaw a centralized, hierarchical administration.[2] The new system that accompanied this change replaced the structure of the old Yamato court, in which various kings and clan leaders shared (and vied for) executive authority (Deal and Ruppert 2015: 41). In 701 CE, the state's Taihō Code further regulated monks and nuns along the same lines as the Tang Chinese laws, establishing "proper" relations between the ruler and the wider Buddhist community. As Barnes states (2014a: 848), during the Asuka period, Buddhism gave elites a new material culture to express status—elite resources were diverted from tomb building towards Buddhist temple building based on Chinese architectural precedents. Chinese cities also provided a model for Japanese urban planning, both for the short-lived capital of Fujiwara-kyō, built in 694 CE but abandoned due to an outbreak of a plague, and its successor city Heijō-kyō (modern-day Nara, based on the Chinese capital, Chang'an, and built in the Nara Basin in 710 CE). The foundation of Heijō-kyō marks the beginning of the Nara period.

A system of roads and regional districts, provinces, governmental offices and Buddhist monasteries and nunneries characterized Nara-era Japan (Barnes 2014a: 848; Deal and Ruppert 2015: 36–37). Capital cities had previously been moved after the death of a ruler to avoid the "pollution" death was believed to emit, but the foundation of the new capital as the center of ruling power along Tang Chinese models altered this pattern (Deal and Ruppert 2015: 41). During the early Nara period, when the capital was moved from Fujiwara-kyō, the four official state temples, rather than being abandoned as "polluted" old buildings, were each dismantled and then reconstructed at the new capital, showing their importance as ceremonial sites for the well-being of the state (37). Further, the ties between Buddhism and state power grew during the Nara period, especially through the *kokubunji* system, which established state temples in each province and provided an effective means of extending authority and bureaucratic hierarchy over land throughout the polity. The national temples were entrusted with the task of conducting rituals to gain protection for the state as a whole. However, temples were also able to amass great wealth in their own right, especially in land, building a potentially independent seat of political power (41–42).

Temple officials were also capable of enforcing law and collecting taxes, and were funded by the state to increase the production of Buddhist symbols. This was achieved especially by transcribing *sūtras* that would promote the well-being of the monarch and the welfare of the state; over 100,000 scrolls were transcribed with state sponsorship, suggesting such *sūtras* were genuinely believed to be effective (Deal and

---

2   See the North China chapter in this volume for further discussion of the "Mandate of Heaven."

Ruppert 2015: 45–46). However, non-Buddhist practices and cult groups still continued and were subject to suppressive measures, such as the ejection of male and female practitioners of magic from the capital in 781 CE (Kidder 2007: 130).

The year 794 CE marks the start of the Heian period. The capital was moved from Heijō-kyō to Heian-kyō (meaning "tranquil and peace capital"), modern-day Kyōto, for what the reigning emperor Kanmu stated were economic reasons: the location was accessible by both land and water. This move also coincided with the introduction of new Buddhist ideas from China to Japan by primarily Japanese pilgrims, significantly establishing the lineages of Shingon and Tendai in the capital (Deal and Ruppert 2015: 54). Deal and Ruppert (72) argue that, by 950 CE, the Heian royal court had consolidated many of the era's notable ritual practices, along with political and cultural features that allowed the influential Fujiwara clan to dominate the government and cultural life of the court. These features remained in place long after the end of the Heian period. There were also attempts to reconcile indigenous Japanese gods with Buddha; in 859 CE, the monk Eryō, for example, described such gods as "traces" of the Buddha (72). Our chapter closes with the end of the Heian period in the late twelfth century, as elaborate internal power dynamics, court intrigues and the imperial court's isolation from the realities of government eventually weakened the central government and allowed for the rise of a provincial warrior class and decentralized rule, resulting ultimately in the establishment of the Kamakura Shogunate (Henshall 2012: 29–30).

Religion and ideologies of rule

At present, no evidence suggests the presence of divinely legitimized rulership in Jōmon society. There is clear evidence of elites, and luxury items were used in their burial rituals, but it is still not discernible who the rulers of any specific group were and how their power related to contemporary religious practices. However, there was then a process of what Barnes terms "ritual replacement," in which the Chinese-imported Jōmon/Yayoi ritual practices of the first millennium BCE, featuring bronze bells (dōtaku), were replaced by the worship of the spirits of leaders. This reflects the emergence of ruling chiefs revered as gods after the adoption of rice agriculture (Kaner 2011: 463). Yayoi chiefs in Kyūshū were also markedout in their burials by the inclusion of conch-shell bracelets from the Ryūkyū Islands (Barnes 2007: 71). Furthermore, Mizoguchi (2002: 154) has identified a "shamanistic leader" from a grave in Fukuoka. This individual had been buried with bronze weapons, characteristic of the Sino-Korean influence on Japan during the Yayoi period and perhaps a means of making claims to political authority, but also with a mirror, which demonstrated his religious authority. Such mirrors had a ritual use in conjuring a spiritual "other" for the community in their reflective surfaces (Kaner 2011: 463). Although this example was male, from the earliest times for which good evidence is available, shamans, diviners and even later Buddhist exorcists (all prominent figures in Japanese life) appear to have been mostly women. Their importance rested on the need to read and interpret the signs and omens of the spirits to decide on future action for the whole group, and the Yayoi period was no exception (Barnes 2007: 127–28). In the case of rulers, such as Himiko, Chinese historical chronicles provide some clues to this relationship between divination and authority. Such texts touch on the magical and mystical nature of rulership in Japan—specifically citing the divination rituals using oracle bones (Kaner 2011: 464). Although the *Nihon Shoki* was compiled nearly half a millennium after Himiko's reign, it is the earliest surviving Japanese collection of myths and history, and its representation of female figures does not seem at odds with Chinese descriptions of Himiko. Barnes (2006: 42) argues that its characterization of women as able to foretell the future through divination, interpret dreams, cast curses and perform sacrifices can serve as a reliable marker of female ritual prowess.

After years of infighting and war with no clear leadership between c. 147 and 189 CE, the reign of the powerful Queen Himiko restored order and brought several key ideological developments. Himiko is described in the *Records of Wei* (*Weizhi*), an account of "the Kingdom of Wa" (namely Japan) compiled in the Chinese Kingdom of Wei in 297 CE, as an unmarried woman involved in "magic and sorcery," who ruled with strict laws and had a man to attend to her clothes and food and act as her mouthpiece.[3] According to the *Weizhi*, in previous times, there were over 100 chiefdoms on the Japanese Islands, 13 of which visited the imperial Han Chinese court, but, by the late third century, the number of Wa chiefdoms had diminished to 30, 14 of which sent envoys and interpreters back and forth to the Wei court. It is also recorded that a Chinese visitor found thousands or tens of thousands of households in different domains ruled by leaders with subordinates, but all were subjects of Queen Himiko's "domain" (Kidder 2007: 12–14).

It is difficult to know the precise role of spiritual and religious practices in Japanese rulership, but the *Weizhi* claims that Himiko was "skilled in the Way of Demons, keeping all under her spell" (Kidder 2007: 16). It notes that, for the seventy or eighty years before her rule, the polity was ruled by a man and there was constant chaos and fighting, but she brought about stability while also maintaining a mysterious persona; she was rarely seen and lived in a palace protected by armed guards, where she was attended to by 1,000 maids and one man who carried her messages and served her food and drink (16). The *Weizhi* entry for 247 CE records that, after

---

3   This account was, notably, written long after Himiko's lifetime and the stories it conveys of the Japanese ruler arrived on the mainland only through numerous intermediaries: merchants, sailors, diplomats and other travelers. While we should certainly not take every word at face value, it does encapsulate well the (perhaps semi-legendary) stories about Himiko's rule and the grandiose court life of her kingdom.

Himiko had passed away, a large mount was erected for her and over a hundred of her attendants were sacrificed. After her passing, there was reportedly a period of unrest under her male successor. Stability was restored when a 13-year-old female relative of Himiko was made the ruler (17).

The practice of constructing large burial mounds and performing human sacrifices for deceased rulers can be traced to similar funerary rites found in ancient China, according to Kidder; the Chinese examples predate parallel practices on the Korean Peninsula. It is possible that the practice was introduced to Japan over centuries of diplomatic and cultural exchange with China, traceable to 57 CE (Barnes 2007: 51–52; Kidder 2007: 95). Still, these tomb-building practices, along with a cult of worship based on ritual objects (such as the association of gods with mirrors from China), took a new direction under Himiko's rule. In the royal ideology of the time, she seems to have occupied an "exalted position" as mediator between gods and humans and as the ruler who brought strife and disorder to an end, which for Kidder (2007: 106–07) provided a blueprint for the emergence of the goddess Amaterasu centuries later. Although the long-standing Japanese association of supernatural communication with women may partly explain why female rulership was perceived as bringing stability and legitimacy, Barnes (2007: 181–85) has proposed further ways in which Himiko was able to use spiritual means to legitimize her ruling position. These include her possible associations with the Queen Mother of the West, a mythical figure popular in Chinese Daoism at the time.

Early Kofun elite graves often contained "deity-beast mirrors," bronze mirrors from China, decorated with images of gods and animals and connected especially with the cult of the Queen Mother of the West. The earliest deity-beast mirror has been dated to 167 CE, and examples began to be imported to Japan around 196 CE (Barnes 2007: 179). These mirrors may have been brought over earlier by people displaced by the Yellow Turban Daoist revolt. When the mirrors were bestowed by Himiko's court in the Miwa region, these ritual objects may have legitimated regional elites' positions: just as the Queen Mother conferred the right to rule on earth, Himiko distributed ritual goods to legitimize local authority. In the Chinese mythology, the Queen Mother guided the dead to the next world, which would explain the placement of the mirrors in tombs (Barnes 2014b: 12–14). The Queen Mother is said to have resided in a cave or stone apartment, carrying a staff. This is referenced by Early Kofun tombs, which are differentiated from Yayoi tombs by their stone chambers and the inclusion of beadstone staffs as grave goods. Although formal embassies to China are not recorded before those with the Wei Dynasty in 238 CE, the mirrors could have been brought to Japan before this date through population movements from China or by elites trading with the Gongsun polity in north-eastern China (15–18). In this regard, it is suggestive that the embassy from Himiko to Wei in 238 CE occurred in the same year that Gongsun's territory was brought under direct Wei rule: Himiko may have wished to ensure the flow of Chinese mirrors. Indeed, the sudden contact with Wei would make sense given the reliance of the Miwa court on prestige goods to distribute to local elites and ensure that they participated in extracting labor for the court, which would in turn be used to build impressive mound tombs, enhancing the status of elites (Kidder 2007: 105). Himiko, who appears to have used deity-beast mirrors, Queen Mother of the West iconography and burial mounds to build her ritual authority, can be interpreted as a female shaman founding her authority on her ability to communicate with or act as the analog of the Queen Mother. She was a "high ritual priestess" with authority over male local rulers who required her "goddess-granted ruler legitimacy" and safe passage to the next world (Barnes 2014b: 22–24). Barnes also argues that such an interpretation would explain the disaster and conflict created by a man attempting to rule after her, a situation only calmed when Himiko's 13-year-old female relative Iyo was placed on the throne. It could perhaps also explain the resemblance of the myths surrounding the later Japanese sun goddess (Amaterasu) to those of the Queen Mother of the West, on which they may have been based (19–22).

This new form of ritual activity and role of the ruler were characteristic of the Kofun period from the mid-third century CE onward. The monumental Hashihaka keyhole tomb constructed after Himiko's death elevated the region above all others and the spread of such tomb culture placed the chiefs into an elite network toward the end of the third century (Barnes 2007: 95–98). The erection of tombs was likely intended to establish the ruler's or chief's home in the next world, recalling burial practices in ancient northern China, where drainage systems were built underneath some tombs, and warehouses installed nearby, to provide drinking water and food in this afterlife "home" (Kidder 2007: 80). Brown (1993: 113) has noted that the construction of grand tombs for the burial of kings—a practice first found in China between 721 and 481 BCE—flourished in both the Nara Basin of Japan and on the Korean Peninsula during the fourth century CE, showing enough shared features to suggest a common period of cultural transition. Such practices can be seen as part of a formulation of new rituals and beliefs based on earlier Chinese precedents, including the provision of the great tombs of elites with terracotta guardians, or the aforementioned Chinese "Queen Mother of the West" myth and associated veneration of women with supernatural powers. All of these practices were adapted by the Miwa court in reverence of Himiko as well as the sacred mountain of Miwa in Nara. The selection of Mount Miwa was significant in linking political authority to the land under the concept of *shinken* ("godly authority") over the region, enforced by associated ritual activity. This turn to the land and food (in warehouses) as the focus of ritual activity can be seen in other spheres as well. Shows of military might, with newly developed bronze weaponry, also formed part of this ritual display of strength and access to the resources of the land—the uses of which were under the control of rulers due to their privileged relationship with the divine (Kaner 2011: 464–465).

In both western Kyūshū and southern Korea, there was a shared culture of burying objects with individuals according to a ranking system—jars, bells and weapons in the case of Kyūshū (Barnes 2014: 838). Such expressions of rank point to a political ideology that relied on differential access to the gods and high-value ritual materials. Some additional ruling strategies seem to have been adopted directly from Chinese practice, such as gridded capital cities laid out according to geomantic divinations and administrative ranks based on Confucian political ideology (Barnes 2014: 848). During the fourth and fifth centuries, the regional rulers of the Yamato state were referred to as *kimi* (literally "precious body") and the ruler of the state was an *ōkimi* ("ō" meaning "great"). A hierarchical succession from brother to brother appears to have been prevalent in the fifth century (marking a change from the female rule so revered in the third and fourth centuries), until the reign of Keitai (507–531 CE), who implemented the practice of keeping records of aristocratic family lineages and vertical succession to legitimize her ruling house and solidify succession (Barnes 2014: 845). During the Yayoi and Kofun periods, we see an increasing role for religion and ritual practices in the legitimacy of rulers, linked with the mystification of the land and control over material resources. There was likewise increasing stratification, achieved in part through the adoption of Confucian administrative practices adapted from Chinese contexts; this seems to bely the "axial" anticipation that Confucianism would foster the reverse.

The relationship between religion and the position of the ruler underwent further transformation in the following Asuka period, linked to the arrival of Buddhism on the islands from South Asia (by way of China and Korea). Two distinct stages of Buddhism's relation to the ruler can be identified: an early period spanning 538–645 CE, and the period in which Hakuhō Buddhism became prominent, from 645 to 710 CE. As mentioned, Buddhist materials were included in official diplomatic tributes: King Sŏng of Paekche made a gift of such materials to the Japanese court in either 538 or 552 CE. The *Nihon Shoki*, compiled under the Japanese emperor's orders in 720 CE and written in Chinese, provides an account of a court dilemma over what to do with the Dharma (Buddhist teachings) acquired from King Sŏng's visit. Although it is unwise to take the accounts of this later text at face value, the tale notes that the ruler, Kinmei (r. 540–71 CE), declared that he had never heard of such a fine teaching as the one King Sŏng presented to him, and asked his officials whether this Dharma (i.e. Buddhism) should be accepted in his country; one of his ministers, Soga no Iname, is then said to have declared that Japan should not be the only country to reject such teachings, whereas Mononobe no Okoshi represented the other viewpoint, namely that Japan had worshiped "180 deities" of "heaven and earth" since ancient times, and worshiping a foreign deity would make these gods angry. Deal and Ruppert (2015: 2) state that, after this event, Soga was granted permission to venerate the Buddha and prove the efficacy of the new religion, and so took the Korean Buddhist statue given by Sŏng to his own home and transformed it into a temple. This led to the outbreak of civil war between the Soga and Mononobe clans over which form of ritual practices was to be patronized by the Japanese rulership. By the close of the sixth century, the Soga had emerged victorious (11).

This was also a significant victory for Buddhism over the previous "*kami* cult" spiritual practices, but the royal court remained ambivalent and was slow to patronize Buddhism, leaving the Soga clan to build temples and craft Buddhist images—all powerful symbols of the political, ritual and cultural influence the Soga wielded in the late sixth and early seventh centuries (Deal and Ruppert 2015: 17–19). The Yamato court's move to establish a Chinese-style centralized bureaucracy also reflects the interest in Buddhism and Confucian-based political Chinese models at the highest levels. According to later historical texts, during the reign of the sovereign Suiko and her chief minister Prince Shōtoku, reverence for the Buddha, the Dharma and the Buddhist community was made an official requirement of government officials in the Seventeen-Article Constitution of 604 CE (11). Shōtoku was himself represented as the founder of Japanese Buddhism and a devout worshiper in the *Nihon Shoki*, but this is rather a later rewriting of history, which aimed to shift the achievement of championing Buddhism from the Soga clan (of which he was part of) to the imperial line that the chroniclers were trying to legitimize (12–23). As Deal and Ruppert (17) explain, the transmission of Buddhism throughout East Asia was marked by the construction and patronage of temples, spurred largely by the symbolic power and prestige Buddhism afforded. Yamato kings still held onto older Japanese ranking systems throughout the sixth and early seventh centuries as they appealed to the Chinese court for official recognition. However, this indigenous ranking system was gradually formalized and aligned with Chinese models, first in 603 with graded court ranks, then in 648 with the introduction of the *kabane* (eight surname titles) system, which privileged selected lineages in the ranks of the court nobility; further changes took place in the late seventh century and beyond (Kiley 1977: 365–76). Furthermore, the ritual construction of a new palace upon the death of the ruler (due to concerns about "spiritual pollution" from the dead) showed that pre-Buddhist ideas still had a considerable influence on royal ritual and symbolic power (Barnes 2014: 845–46). The rise of Hakuhō Buddhism (c. 645–710 CE) marks the period in which patronage of Buddhism began to move from aristocratic families like the Soga clan to the rulers themselves, starting with the assassination of Soga no Iruka and the Taika Reforms in 645 CE and continuing through the introduction of the *ritsuryō* system (based on Chinese Confucian bureaucratic statecraft) (Deal and Ruppert 2015: 33). Kōtoku, who became sovereign a few days after Soga no Iruka's assassination, is recorded as issuing imperial edicts to monks and nuns at the Asukadera temple, stating:

> We [the imperial government] now wish to reiterate our desire to revere the Buddha's true teaching and to shine widely the light of this great Dharma. Therefore, we appoint the following priests Dharma teachers: The Korean Dharma masters Fukuryō, Eun, Jōan, Ryōun, and Eshi, and the temple heads Sōmin, Dōtō, Erin, and Emyō. We separately appoint Dharma teacher Emyō the head priest of the temple Kudara-dera. These Dharma teachers will thoroughly instruct the monastic community and lead them in the practice of the Buddha's teaching so the Buddha's Dharma is properly followed. From the emperor to the managerial class, we will all assist in the building of temples. We will now appoint temple head priests and lay administrators. Temples will be visited to determine the actual situation pertaining to monks and nuns, their servants, and their rice fields. All findings will be presented to the emperor (Deal and Ruppert 2015: 34–35).

This quote illustrates the Taika Reforms' aim of centralizing power away from clans, who had previously held a monopoly on Buddhist ritual and any corresponding symbolic power, as well as the desire to choose and control those who held such ritual authority. Tenji (r. 661–72 CE) established many Buddhist temples, including the famous Kawaradera and, like many Tang Chinese rulers, dedicated several to deceased relatives or founded them in hopes of curing his relatives' or consorts' illnesses. Under Tenmu's reign (672–86 CE), the Buddhist practices of copying and reciting *sutras*, along with major temple-building projects, became a significant part of state administration and worked to further centralize rule over the Japanese territory. Tenmu even renamed the Kudara Ōdera temple the "Great Official Temple" (Daikan Daiji) to create a central place of worship for heads of state. It is also said that he was an ardent promoter of Buddhist values and hosted over 2,400 monks and nuns for a Buddhist vegetarian meal in his palace; he placed restrictions on hunting and which animals could be eaten; and he issued an edict that all provinces should conduct a ritual to free all animals in captivity, among other acts (Deal and Ruppert 2015: 35–38). His successor, Empress Jitō (r. 690–97 CE), continued this strong royal support for and control over Buddhism. Significantly, she was the first Japanese ruler to refer to herself as *tennō* ("heavenly sovereign," usually translated as "emperor" or "empress").

As Deal and Ruppert (2015: 34–35) explain, the Hakuhō period of Japanese Buddhism is distinctive for the establishment of state temples, with state-sponsored ritual practices and state control of the Buddhist community—all of which were used to promote the idea of a unified, centralized state headed by the royal family, whose patronage of the religion was codified in new laws and policies. Elite individuals and clans continued to build temples, but the state-built ones carried the symbolic weight of "official" Buddhist practice. Sources indicate that in 624 CE, there were 46 temples, most or all of which were controlled by clans; by 692 CE, there were 545 temples, mostly state-controlled (35–36). There had been earlier examples of royal attempts at controlling monastic positions and the conduct of monks, for example under Queen Suiko, the earliest being an edict of monastic codes and a three-person council to monitor the monastic community after a monk murdered his grandfather with an axe in 623 CE. However, overall, the Hakuhō period is characterized by the emergence of a "heavenly sovereign" as leader of a newly unified "Nippon" (Japan), drawing legitimacy from his or her role as upholder of the Dharma. State-sponsored Buddhism subverted the power that the competing clans of the Yamato Kingdom had previously held, bolstered by their monopoly on Buddhist rituals and material symbols. This drive towards centralized rule also led to the reworking of Japanese past. Under Empress Jitō, notably, earlier rulers were mythologized as belonging to a lineage of "emperors" that could be traced back to the sun goddess (Kidder 2007: 3). The reinterpretation of the past through the lens of the present led to a merging of local spiritual practices and Buddhism that remained unchallenged until Japan's nineteenth-century modernization efforts (Kaner 2011: 466). Such increases in the size and complexity of the centralized state bureaucracy from the Taika Reforms onward, however, faced a challenge: in the first decade of the eighth century, severe plagues caused the first Japanese state-planned permanent city, Fujiwara-kyō, to be abandoned and the capital to be moved to Nara—forcing a return to the previous practice of moving palaces, despite the aim of permanence (Kidder 2007: 142).

The Nara period saw a further entwining of Buddhist practice with political authority. Six "research groups" into Buddhist doctrine were established within temples, each receiving significant support from rulers (Deal and Ruppert 2015: 42). The first example of a ruler becoming a Buddhist monk also dates to this period; Emperor Shōmu (r. 724–49 CE) abdicated the throne after his ordination. His daughter, Empress Kōken, succeeded him until she too ordained as a nun and abdicated, before returning to reign as the only ordained sovereign in Japanese history, providing a great deal of support for the transcription of *sūtras*. Her mother (and Shōmu's consort) Kōmyō Kōgō was also a devout Buddhist; in 740 CE, she vowed to copy more than 7,000 Buddhist texts—a project that she continued for around twenty years. Shōmu's reign was characterized by the patronage of Buddhist rituals (copying and chanting *sūtras*), the sponsorship of temple building, the crafting of Buddhist imagery and the creation of the Chinese-inspired "national temple system" (*kokubunji*) in 741 CE as a way to secure peace, prosperity and the religiously legitimized succession of rulers. Shōmu also sent 10 copies of the *Lotus Sūtra* to each province for it to be taught, as the *sūtra* stated that the places where it is taught would have no enemies or diseases, only prosperity. This shows Shōmu's deep conviction that Buddhist rituals were vital for the protection, peace and prosperity of the state.

Likewise, in this period, a Buddhist monk named Dōkyō received official political authority after being appointed to increasingly powerful roles within the government by Empress Kōken. Following a failed revolt and Kōken's return to power under the name Shōtoku in 764 CE, Dōkyō was appointed the "Buddhist Prime Minister of State" (*daijōdaijin zenji*), blurring the line between Buddhist and state power. This entanglement was furthered in 766 CE when Dōkyō was named "Imperial Office of the Dharma King" (*hōō kyūshiki*). The growing political power of Buddhist monks caused much concern to elite clans, however. After his powerful patron, the Empress Shōtoku, passed away in 770 CE, Dōkyō was exiled from the capital to end his presence at court. In 772 CE, the succeeding Emperor Kōnin instituted official roles in imperial court ceremonies to restrict the official ordination ritual to 10 monks (and no nuns), which Deal and Ruppert (2015: 65) suggest may have been a way to legitimize himself as a male patron of Buddhism in contrast to previous female rulers. This is a significant development, as the restriction of roles for women that accompanied the widespread, state-sponsored adoption of Buddhism stands in contrast to the millennia-old tradition of female spiritual and ritual leadership in the Japanese archipelago. This trajectory differs from that predicted by Axial Age theories that envisage the spread of egalitarianism and universalizing ethics along with "axial" ideologies. The decline in female autonomy in Japan was likely reinforced from the mid-seventh century onward by the influence on the central court of Confucianism, which encouraged the subservience of women to men, holding that a woman should serve her father before marriage, her husband in marriage and her son after her husband's death (Barnes 2006: 2).

The association between royal power and religious practice was manifest in the Heian period as well. Heian rulers showed great respect for and interest in Buddhist innovations and sectarian distinctions in Buddhist practice. In 798 CE, during the reign of Emperor Kanmu, Usa Shrine in Kyūshū is mentioned in state records as housing a "great bodhisattva" as a *kami*. In Mahāyāna Buddhist thought, *bodhisattvas* are beings who have almost reached enlightenment but who delay their ultimate attainment of *nirvāṇa* in order to help others realize the truth; the Usa shrine thus demonstrates the blending of local forms of Buddhism with Japanese concepts of *kami* worship. In 816 CE, the state records claimed that "this great Bodhisattva is thus the august spirit of the retired sovereign," referring to "Emperor" Ōjin (a ruler erroneously recorded as ruling Japan in the third and fourth centuries CE in the *Nihon Shoki* and *Kojiki*, another chronicle) (Deal and Ruppert 2015: 81). Tenth-century Buddhist "praise portraits" (a kind of "preaching with pictures") portrayed Japanese royal figures like Prince Shōtoku as well as Buddhist masters from Japan, South Asia and China. From the late tenth century, retired sovereigns played a central role in elaborate performative liturgies, which now included music, dance and other performances, as well as hosting such performances and holding banquets in royal temples. This shows how the association of Japanese sovereigns with Buddhist cosmology developed during the Heian period (86). It is important for an understanding of the relations between ruler and religion in Japan to consider the new forms of Buddhism that developed in this period and the increasing role of the religion as a strategy for gaining and consolidating political authority.

Heian emperors from Kanmu onward continued to act as important patrons of Buddhist rituals and material culture, and did not seem to feel threatened by the increasing independence and influence Buddhist institutions received as they became more firmly established within wider Japanese society (Deal and Ruppert 2015: 54). Indeed, by this time, the courtly elite were probably more familiar with Buddhist practices than with the indigenous religious practices of the populace. This is apparent from the decision of Emperor Daigo in 905 CE to order the cataloging of local religious practices, shrines, gods, and their relationship with the myths of ancient times; this work came to fruition and such practices were given an official imprimatur by the state in the *Engishiki* (meaning the ceremonies of the Engi era, i.e. Daigo's reign), completed in 927 CE (131).

Over the course of the tenth century, rulers and noble clans took great pains to preserve knowledge of an increasingly diverse set of ritual practices, and also began to write diaries intended as instruction for participation in court rituals and duties (Deal and Ruppert 2015: 72–73). From the late eleventh century, retired sovereigns had the authority to appoint monks to administer monastic affairs (including shrine priests and mountain-dwelling hermits, who worshiped indigenous Japanese gods and combined esoteric and exoteric forms of Buddhism) (84). Indeed, at this time, the retired sovereign was typically the most powerful individual at court. The royal court of the time was animated by the need to gain "merit" (a Buddhist concept) through the performance and sponsorship of ritual activity and the production of copies of *sūtras*; all this took place against the backdrop of power struggles, within which Buddhism had much influence in swaying the ideas and actions of institutions. Despite the increasing independence of temples and the monastic elite from state oversight, the ruler was still an important figure and temples often served as temporary palaces for current and former sovereigns. Until the twelfth century, they hosted grand rituals to enhance the longevity of royals.

Even after the adoption of Buddhism as an "official" state ideology, rulers still drew much of their legitimacy from the lineages they descended from (as mythologized in the *Nihon Shoki*, for example) and retained a perceived divinity by tracing their ancestry back to the sun goddess. Indeed, the connection of sovereignty with the divine became progressively stronger as Buddhism was increasingly connected with ideologies of rule: from chieftains legitimized through divination, to the innovations of Himiko and the subsequent expansion of the cult activities of the royal court, to the fully fledged "divine rulers" of the Nara and Heian periods. In some senses, the influence of China's Confucian-based legal system and administrative organization helped foster the regularization and proto-bureaucratization of Japan: key aspects of "axiality" identified in the literature. On the other hand, ritual and symbolic power was still achieved through spiritual means, a trait generally considered a marker of "archaic" societies.

Universalizing morality and egalitarian ethics

It is difficult to ascertain whether there were clearly moralizing aspects or egalitarian beliefs within the cosmology of the Jōmon people. There may have been ritual specialists and, if so, they may have embodied stratified religious authority, but this remains uncertain. The extent to which ritualized burial practices and associated luxurious objects imply social hierarchy is hotly debated among scholars (see for instance Kaner 2011: 461). By the end of the Jōmon period, we are on firmer ground in inferring social stratification. Isotopic analysis of skeletal remains has shown clear dietary differences between those who were buried with opulent jewelry and other accessories and those who were not (Kaner 2011: 376; Kiriyama and Kusaka 2007). However, it has been argued that the increased prevalence of ceramic figurines in non-elite burials near the end of the period, coming at a time of profound change accompanying the growth of rice-farming, illustrates a resistance to this more stratified form of social organization (Kaner 2011: 462).

In Yayoi ritual activities, burned animal bones were used to communicate with the spirit world, much like the earlier divination rituals attested in China. On Kyūshū, prestige goods, such as shell bracelets from the Ryūkyū Islands, were used to show the status and wealth of individuals, but this was not the case everywhere. In the eastern Seto region, it is clear that bronze bells (cast by specialists using materials obtained in long-distance trade) were used in rituals to ensure agricultural fertility and community solidarity rather than for prestige (Barnes 2007: 67–68). However, in Yayoi culture as a whole, etched designs on pottery vessels and bronze bells, as well as the use of mirrors in ritual activity to communicate with spirits, point towards the presence of shamans and thus the importance of social status founded in ritual authority. Incipient stratification is also suggested by grave clusters, which demonstrate an increasing concern with ancestral rights to land and an awareness of lineage groupings (Kaner 2011: 462). According to Kidder (2007: 228), Yayoi rituals had a bonding societal effect, protecting the community as a whole against malignant spirits, which could be interpreted as an essentially egalitarian function for ritual. However, these evil spirits tended to manifest themselves in various ways, the identification of which was the task of elite shamans (Kaner 2011: 462–63). The aforementioned Chinese text the *Weizhi*, written and based on phenomena observed in the third century, records one such shaman on the mission boats that crossed the ocean from Japan to China, stating:

> When missions cross the ocean to visit China there is always one man who does not comb his hair, does not remove the lice, lets his clothes become dirty, does not eat meat, and does not get near women. He is like a mourner and works like a diviner or an ascetic/abstainer. If there is good luck, in view of this they all give him slaves and valuable things, but if disease or injuries occur, they dispatch him because as the diviner he had not been respectful [of his vows] (quoted in Kidder 2007: 15).

The privileged position of the diviner is shown here, but his privileges are dependent on producing good luck. Chieftains also had access to similar spiritual resources. During this period, land and nature began to be seen as things to be tamed and transformed for human use (Kaner 2011). Objects created from nature also appear to have been imbued with special powers. Swords and spears were seen as able to create water and each weapon was an individual that had to be treated with awe and respect so as not to bring about misfortune (Kidder 2007: 84). Chieftains and shamans acted as mediums for this spiritual energy, controlling its interpretation and using it as a show of power and legitimacy in an emerging hierarchical social structure. Barnes (2007: 114) suggests that the hierarchization of society can also be traced to a process of "ritual replacement," in which the worship of the spirits of rulers (practiced in northern Kyūshū) started to replace bell rituals dedicated to the spirit of rice throughout the Japanese Islands.

The *Nihon Shoki*, which was being compiled during the reign of Empress Jitō, provides an account of the arrival of Buddhist objects at court in 552 CE as a gift from King Sŏng of Paekche. Although Buddhism could arguably have arrived in earlier tributary exchanges between the continent and the Yamato court, this account emphasizes the Korean king's statement that the Dharma he presented was so profound that even Confucius or the Duke of Zhou could not comprehend it. According to Sŏng, it promised limitless and immeasurable "meritorious karmic consequence" and was "like a person who has a wish-fulfilling gem whose every desire is granted" (Deal and Ruppert 2015: 1). The In the *Nihon Shoki* it is also stated that Prince Shōtoku's Seventeen-Article Constitution of 604 CE called for obedience to the Buddhist Dharma and to imperial orders and for the chastisement of evil, suggesting that the moralizing aspects of Buddhist teachings were starting to gain official recognition (11).

In the decades before the 645 CE Taika Reforms, Buddhist practice remained largely centered on ritual activity and material expressions, such as images and temples, rather than scriptural study; there is little to no evidence of formal Buddhist doctrine in the Asuka period (Deal and Ruppert 2015: 18). State-sponsored rituals were performed in temples on a large scale in the Hakuhō (late Asuka) period, usually for the prosperity of the state and the health and well-being of ruling elites: these practices were founded on the Buddhist notion of karmic consequence, which held that following the Dharma, chanting the most revered *sūtras*, and praying to buddhas and *bodhisattvas* would produce beneficial results (37–38). Initially, such rituals were restricted to the temples at the capital, but after 670 CE, they were also being performed in provincial temples. Copying, chanting and lecturing on Buddhist texts had come to be viewed as an activity with great merit, especially in its increasing significance to the Japanese state; the two main *sūtras* in use for such Buddhist rituals were Chinese versions of the *Golden Light Sūtra* and the *Humane Kings Sūtra*, which state that the ruler who praises the *sūtras* and upholds the Dharma will have his country and personal well-being protected by the Four Heavenly Kings (fierce guardian deities), while countries whose rulers did not do so risked disaster. It was believed that chanting or copying such *sūtras* in rituals would actualize the sacred words.

Buddhist practices were further popularized in the reign of King Tenmu, who (as we noted above) also pursued explicitly moralizing reforms, including placing restrictions on when hunting could occur and which animals and fish could be eaten, and issued an edict requiring all provinces to observe a ritual that liberated all animals in captivity (Deal and Ruppert 2015: 38). Although horse sacrifice had continued after being officially banned in the Taika Reforms, it appears that Tenmu was the ruler who ended the long-standing tradition of sacrificing a horse to accompany its owner into the next world (although, as Kidder [2007: 147] explains, Tenmu did not include deer in his list of off-limit animals and he himself went on a hunting expedition in 683 CE). Tenmu also issued an edict in 684 CE requiring all hair to be tied up, much like in Tang China, with the curious exception of practitioners of magic, showing a recognition of non-Buddhist diviners too at this time.

Illness and death were also significant events that seemed to provide an incentive for rulers to act upon Buddhist notions of morality and egalitarian ideals. For example, when Tenmu's consort became ill, he commanded 100 people to become Buddhist priests in the hope of curing the illness, and the memorial service for his own death in 687 CE became the model for the rituals performed on the deaths of subsequent rulers (Deal and Ruppert 2015: 38). It is recorded that when Tenmu fell ill, a dizzying array of measures were taken in an attempt to cure him: among other things, *sūtras* were read to Yakushi (the Buddha of healing); the temple buildings were swept clean; prisoners were released; officials were promoted and ranks given to others; prayers were held and offerings were given to the gods; clergymen received imperial gifts; princes and temples were awarded more land; special ceremonies and vegetarian feasts were held at Kawara temple; provinces were ordered to hold proto-Shintō purification ceremonies; countrywide taxes were reduced by half and debts for the previous year were cancelled; and images of the *bodhisattva* of compassion, Kannon, were carved (Kidder 2007: 158–59). All these practices formed part of a demonstration of the ruler's power and generosity on a very large scale, incorporating ideas from Confucianism and indigenous Japanese religion as well as Buddhism (159). He did indeed live an extra four months, and thus, the introduction of the Buddhist Dharma, framed as a "wish-fulfilling gem," into Asuka Japan is significant in that it encouraged the state to perform "prosocial" activities make grand displays of generosity in order to gain merit, and thus tangible benefits in the health of the ruler.

Toward the end of the Asuka period, the increasing importance of scripture can be observed. The *Nihon Shoki* (still being compiled at this time) asserts that bad things happen to those who oppose Buddhism, suggesting that supporters of Buddhism or even priests may have written parts of this document (Deal and Ruppert 2015: 10). Kidder (2007: 6) also notes that some features of the *Nihon Shoki*'s style and content are clearly derived from Chinese philosophy and phraseology, such as references to "heaven-approved reigns," the connections between natural disasters and earthly events, and omens and official responses to them. Many of these phrases have been matched with earlier Chinese sources, suggesting that the editors were comfortable with borrowing from Chinese texts (6).

After the Taika Reforms and the further entrenching of the Tang-style *ritsuryō* bureaucracy, a "Bureau of Divination" was established, charged with viewing celestial events, calculating the calendar, announcing the time, and recording unusual natural phenomena. Further, the *Nihon Shoki* first references the idea of yin and yang in 671 CE and lists many Koreans as rank-holding members of the bureau that dealt with such practices (Kidder 2007: 156–57). Institutional developments at this time show the increasing importance in Japan of "moralistic punishment," a feature expected of axial civilizations. The state's developing cosmology framed acts such as rejecting Buddhism as punishable through both karmic retribution and judicial processes, and the application of formal legal codes in the *ritsuryō* system could be viewed in this light. However, it is still difficult to know whether this was carried out for "prosocial" purposes or rather to further consolidate state power through religion and laws, or perhaps both.

By the Nara period, several texts mythologizing earlier Japanese rulers and historical contexts as ancestral to the Yamato royal line had been compiled. The *Kojiki* (completed in 712 CE) records an imperial lineage and a cosmology involving three deities: the Sun Goddess (Amaterasu) and her brothers the Moon God and Sea God. These gods and the eight Japanese islands were created by two older deities, Izanagi and Izanami, with Izanami's death bringing about their birth. The *Kojiki* includes many examples of what Kidder (2007: 2–3) describes as "figments of the imagination," providing a lineage of divine emperors that can be traced back to Amaterasu, as well as many stories of how Japan and the Japanese people originated (which do not match the earlier Chinese records or the archaeological evidence). Similarly, the *Nihon Shoki* (completed in 720 CE) incorporates tales of rulers such as Empress Jingu, who supposedly ruled during Himiko's time and led an invasion of Korea as a divine leader under the aegis of the gods (Kidder 2007: 137). It is quite possible that this fictional ruler was based on Himiko or was a means to legitimate the resurgence of female rulership in the Nara and late Asuka periods.

Coexisting with this indigenous cosmology of Japanese rulers and deities was the deepening interest in Buddhism along "orthodox" Chinese lines. As mentioned in the preceding section, "research groups" were established for six lineages of Buddhism. Each lineage was entrusted with the keeping of specific texts, which could be accessed freely by monks and nuns from other lineages, showing a degree of institutional informality and fluidity. The ordination of Buddhist monks and nuns to the temples teaching these lineages of Buddhism was an unsystematic state ritual overseen by 10 monks, until the Chinese monk Ganjin arrived in 754 CE, bringing more orthodox rituals and rules. Ganjin's teachings changed the number of monks from 10 to the "doctrinally correct" 24, and followed wider East Asian Mahāyāna practice in requiring monks to observe 250 precepts and nuns to observe 348: far higher than the required 10 precepts for the ordination prior to this (Deal and Ruppert 2015: 50). The imposition of more precepts for nuns than monks formed part of a larger trend of women being placed in inferior positions to men in monastic regulations. Government reforms had codified monks and nuns as equals with equal responsibilities to protect the nation in rituals, yet along Tang Chinese lines, they were unequally valued. For example, monasteries built in the period were staffed by 20 monks, while the nunneries were made physically smaller and staffed by only 10 nuns (65).

Although compiled in the early Heian period, three volumes of Buddhist tales from the Nara period, *Nihonkoku genpō zen'aku ryōiki* ("Miraculous Tales from the Country of Japan Concerning Immediate Recompense for Good and Bad Actions"), were completed in 823 CE by the monk Kyōkai, giving a valuable account of his Buddhist world view while writing in the late Nara and early Heian periods. These supernatural stories focus on karma and the power of Buddhist rituals, with good actions yielding good results and immoral actions having negative consequences. The karmic repercussions occur in this life, the next or the one after in the cycle of birth, death and rebirth (with the possibility of being born into an unpleasant Buddhist hell in transition to another life) (Deal and Ruppert 2015: 52). The tales also show that it is possible for all humans to tap into the power of the universe for salvation, through belief in and rituals for the buddhas and *bodhisattvas*, as well as creating, revering and taking care of paintings and statues of them. Chanting and hearing *sūtras* or reading, writing, copying, and owning *sūtras* (particularly the

Lotus Sūtra) were also said to activate such power. Notably, there are several stories illustrating female devotion to Buddhist practices and arguing for the equality of men and women in the karmic order (65). Importantly, these clearly universalizing and equity-promoting norms, increasing in popularity along with the growth of Buddhist thought in Japan, support traditional narratives of axiality. It needs to be stressed, though, that many of these narratives promote Buddhist practice explicitly in conjunction with a mythology touting the relationship of rulers to the divine and relating good karma directly to the state of the country and the health of the sovereign; these ideas, supporting strong, divinely legitimated rulers, are more characteristically "archaic." Further, the privileged position women had long held in spiritual matters was lost following the implementation of Tang models in the late Nara period and the progressive exclusion of women from positions of religious authority from this time onward.

During the Heian period, Buddhism became increasingly divided into separate sects. In 803 CE, Emperor Kanmu declared that, of the 10 yearly ordinations that had been held since 696 CE, 5 each were to be given to the Sanron and Hossō lineages, providing state recognition of differences between the sects for the first time. The number of ordinations per year was increased to 12 in 806 CE: 3 each to the Sanron and Hossō and 2 each to Kegon and Ritsu, with another 2 being assigned to the monk Saichō's new Tendai lineage, giving it official recognition (Deal and Ruppert 2015: 47). Tendai, along with Shingon (founded by the monk Kūkai), was a new lineage that emerged through debates within the monastic community around the ideas brought to Japan by those who had studied in China. The founders of these lineages, Saichō and Kūkai, were independent from the state and traditional Buddhist temples, unlike most monks during the preceding Nara period, but they still relied on patronage from the court and were expected to support the state through rituals to protect to the country (54). These lineages introduced the division between exoteric and esoteric Buddhism into the Japanese context: simply put, exoteric strands of practice (more common in Tendai) emphasized clear statements of doctrine, while esoteric practices (a feature of Shingon) centered on initiation and knowledge transmitted secretly (71). Furthermore, unlike the Hossō lineage, which taught that evil people could not attain buddhahood, the Tendai view was that all sentient beings possessed "Buddha nature" and thus had the potential to attain enlightenment. Deal and Ruppert (59) argue that the version of Tendai that merged with esoteric Buddhism was a Japanese innovation, as contact with China became very limited in the ninth century; although the roots of Tendai were in Chinese Tiantai Buddhism, once in Japan the sect developed more or less independently. The main innovations of Shingon were brought about by a study of Chinese translations of Buddhist texts, which contributed to the formation of a ritual practice emphasizing the "Dharma body of the Buddha" and the "three mysteries" (referring to the speech, mind and body of the "cosmic Buddha," Mahāvairocana) (62). Central to these new traditions was the assertion that all humans, elite or commoner, and even other living beings, could attain enlightenment.

The messages of these universalizing doctrines led the courtier Minamoto Tamenori to write in his *The Three Jewels* of 984 CE that the poor, elderly and ill may all be manifestations of buddhas or "holy ones," or fathers and mothers from different eras, and deserve compassion; he saw giving as a "field of merit" to help the unfortunate or lower classes, and distinctions between people as empty and insubstantial (Deal and Ruppert 2015: 75). In the Heian capital, there was also a growing interest among elite families in achieving rebirth in the "Pure Land," a celestial realm presided over by the buddha Amida, through chanting and contemplation, particularly after the monk Genshin completed a guide to reaching this land in 985 CE. There was great anxiety that, at the time of one's death, distracted thought could lead a person away from the Pure Land to a bad rebirth, and thus many monks produced writings for deathbed rites to avoid such misfortune. Especially from the late tenth century onward, elite literary texts also took on Buddhist themes, such as Princess Senshi's *Collection of Waka of the Awakening Mind* (1012 CE) and several other collections of court poetry by various authors. Japanese monks continued to make pilgrimages to China, now under the Song Dynasty, collecting and sending back new Chinese translations of *sūtras*, which entered the Japanese Buddhist canon; there also began a practice of copying sacred works by Japanese masters as a ritual that laid the foundation for new lineages. This practice also characterized later Japanese Buddhism (95–96). Importantly, traditional Japanese deities were understood to be intimately related to Buddhas throughout the Heian period. Early forms of Shintō were codified in the *Engishiki* of 927 CE, which enumerated indigenous gods, folk practices and rituals and clarified their relationships with Buddhist shrines and their obligations to the imperial state, leading to mutual influences between Buddhist and *kami*-centered rituals (Kidder 2007: 131).

Overall, this section has explored the implications of religious and ritual activity from the Jōmon to the Heian period, stressing how the deliberate adoption of "axial" ideologies from East and South Asia—Chinese Confucian political philosophy and Buddhist practices—were used to bolster the central authority of the state and to underpin the legitimation of rulers. There are examples of how, from the end of the Asuka period onward, Buddhism in Japan increasingly took on "axial"-like qualities, such as providing a universal moral framework and insisting on the equal access of all living beings to spiritual reward. Yet social hierarchies remained, and in particular, women's attainment of high-status ritual roles in the early Japanese state was not permanent. Below, we discuss how such concepts manifested themselves in practice.

Universalizing morality, egalitarianism and constraints on rulers' authority in practice

Jōmon people have traditionally been regarded as egalitarian hunter-gatherers, in contrast to the following, more socially stratified Yayoi culture, which adopted continental East Asian rituals, metallurgy and rice agriculture. This view went largely unchallenged until Hiroshi Watanabe (1990) proposed that the Jōmon should be categorized with other North Pacific coastal stratified societies, in which social distinction derived from the roles and primary targets of hunters. Hunting big game, like bears, required particular technology and inspired specific ritual practices, which in turn needed sophisticated ornaments and valuables, and groups passed on this social status vertically. Pearson (2007: 364–65) summarizes his arguments:

> Since big game hunting did not provide food for basic subsistence, it could be said that its importance lay in the social reproduction of these groups [i.e. those who participate in hunting big game and those who do not]. In sum, the elite controlled superior technology, mobilized the community into collective rituals, and had access to refined exotic luxuries as social badges, thereby controlling the means of social reproduction.

Although the above statement essentializes all of Jōmon-period Japan as one culture without regional variation, it is important to note how thinking on this era has evolved. Some objects, such as lacquer and ceramic items, were used by all members of the social group, but in general burial data does seem to support this reading of Jōmon society as stratified. Individuals were buried with different qualities and types of objects: some were buried with no items, some with everyday items, and others with more extravagant and luxurious items such as jewelry made from jade and shells—a trend that begins around 6000 BCE and becomes progressively stronger, and is particularly salient on Hokkaidō and in the Tōhoku region of Honshū by the third millennium BCE (Pearson 2007: 376). A distinct class of elites, marked out by burial mounds and luxurious grave goods, only started to appear toward the end of the first millennium. For much of the Jōmon period, there is no strong evidence for inherited status; the impression given by archaeological remains is rather of hunter-gatherer societies with advanced lacquer and ceramic technology, though there is no clear indication of how this labor was organized and who benefited from it. As Barnes (2015: 282) explains, 10% of excavated Late and Final Jōmon burials have yielded personal ornaments and specialist prestige goods, and by the Final Jōmon there was a trend toward young people being buried with grave goods, perhaps indicating an emerging hereditary system of rank (282). Furthermore, by 600 BCE in north Kyūshū, Pacific conch-shell bracelets obtained from the Ryūkyū Islands were used as grave goods to signal elite status, and, in combination with other exotic goods like Chinese mirrors, delineated a three-tiered hierarchy of elites (327–28).

As discussed in previous sections, by the Yayoi period we witness a marked increase in the uniformity of ritual practices, displayed through the spread of bronze bells and mirrors and bones used for divination (Kaner 2011: 462). Barnes (2007: 78–79) has suggested, drawing an analogy with the Chinese Han Dynasty's control over the flow of prestige goods to "barbarians" as part of a "divide and rule" strategy, that Late Yayoi chiefs on Kyūshū controlled the distribution of valuable goods (iron weapons and tools by this time) to other chieftains outside of Kyūshū, and that military conflict may have been motivated by the desire for such valuables. Indeed, she argues elsewhere (2015: 329) that the hierarchical structure of these competitive and cooperative networks among northern Kyūshū chieftains was reliant on the supply of prestige goods from the Chinese Lelang Commandery. This is further supported by evidence that the structure largely fell apart when Wang Mang usurped the Han throne and the flow of prestige goods (bronze mirrors) was restricted, forcing the Yayoi people to resort to crafting their own versions after about 50 CE. In this sense, one important restriction on elites' power at this time seems to be the availability of ritual and prestige goods from China. Furthermore, Yayoi society was bonded together through a reverence for, and perhaps fear of, spirits, and the meanings of different rituals and the materials necessary for their performance was largely controlled by shamanic elites. As well as denoting increased conflict between different human groups, the rise of enclosed and moated settlements may be seen as a social expression of this fear. Such settlements were centered around central "shrine-like" buildings with raised platforms, which may have served as dwellings for Yayoi "spiritual-political leaders" (Kidder 2007: 77). These buildings are typical of Yayoi Japan, different from anything found on the Asian mainland (Kaner 2011: 463).

According to the *Weizhi*, throughout Wa (the Japanese Islands) during this period, taxes were collected and trade was conducted at central marketplaces in each district; elites were attended to and those of lower rank had to get off the road to let higher-ranking men pass, kneeling to show respect. Men of status had indigenous ranked titles (which did not correspond to the titles in use in China or Korea) and four or five wives (Kidder 1993: 97–98). The *Weizhi* also records details of the hierarchical ranks present in Japan, providing translations of the Japanese indigenous terms for rulers, nine different ranks of officials, and also the rank of a border guard, showing that some form of ranking system was already in place in this period (even if it was conceptualized in terms of, and translated into, Chinese hierarchical ranking systems). As Barnes (2007: 71, 2014a: 840, 2015: 329) notes, even before Himiko, there is some evidence that Yamato chieftains received audiences in China and voluntarily submitted to the Han court in exchange for valuable goods that would have symbolically solidified their authority and the legitimacy of their rule in Japan (such as iron from Korea).

Himiko herself courted favor with Chinese rulers, sending slaves to the Wei court in 238 CE as a form of tribute, for which she received the title "Ruler of Wa Friendly to Wei" along with a golden seal and purple ribbon (Kidder 2007: 16–17). Notably, this and similar gifts of slaves to Chinese rulers suggests the presence of unfree labor, a clear marker of social inequality, during the Yayoi period. Furthermore, strong social distinctions were made between fathers and sons and men and women (15). By this time, tattoo patterns on faces and bodies, which in previous times do not appear to have distinguished elites and commoners, may have marked which chiefdom one belonged to and displayed one's rank. Although there was a female ruler by the end of the Yayoi period, a gendered hierarchy was expressed through punishments handed down for crimes. It is noted by contemporary Chinese sources that, if a man committed a minor crime, his wife and children were enslaved and, for more serious offenses, his household and relatives were all "eradicated" (16). It also mentioned that lower social classes were subordinate to their "supervisors." In this sense, however stratified Jōmon societies may or may not have been, it is unmistakable that, by the end of the Yayoi period, there was a hierarchical ranking system as well as inequalities between men and women, adults and children, and free and enslaved (or enslavable) people.

By around 300 CE, ritual authority was generated largely through displays of significant objects, like weapons, as well as control over access to and the interpretation of spiritual power. This authority was largely monopolized by elite families, who used it to consolidate their social status. The focus of ritual activity was no longer local communities but rather the land, rice fields and ritual objects themselves (Kaner 2011: 464). At the level of the emerging state, Barnes (2014b: 23) has proposed that Himiko's legitimacy relied on her ability to act as a go-between between her subjects and the divine, or even to embody the Queen Mother of the West, enabling her to act as a supernatural granter of authority to local rulers. This role relied on her ability to obtain Daoist deity-beast mirrors from China, which featured iconography connected to the Queen Mother cult (Barnes 2014b: 23). "Axial" concepts of universal morality and equality seem a poor fit for such a stratified system. Interestingly, in the Yayoi period, there was a large influx of migrants to western Japan from Korea and China, who seem to have been welcomed and treated generously for their cultural and technological contributions. This shows that, from at least Himiko's reign onward, being an "outsider" was no barrier to participating in Japanese society, perhaps due to the ruling elite's reliance on Chinese ritual objects and Korean metallurgy to solidify their own authority as interpreters of omens and communicators with spirits.

The start of the Kofun period was marked by the construction of huge tombs in the Yamato area, which relied on access to a large labor pool from populations within the confederacy of chiefdoms (Kidder 2007: 106). As Barnes (2014a: 834–35) states, the appearance of such tombs for local rulers is evidence of the further stratification of society during this period. Although there was some regional variation in funerary monuments in this period (Kidder 2007: 99), in general mounded tombs—testifying to the large-scale mobilization of labor—and a standardized suite of luxury grave goods defined an elite class set apart from commoners, and have allowed graded regional political hierarchies to be reconstructed (Barnes 2007: 8–9, 2014a: 834–85). The mounds were built in separate locations from the cemeteries of commoners or settlements, eventually leading in later times to exclusive clan cemeteries in such locations (Barnes 2007: 168). The distribution of prestige goods, such as mirrors, in graves suggests that social mobility was possible through their acquisition and the subsequent recognition of membership in the elite culture granted by those of higher rank, who may have even gifted them in exchange for pledges of allegiance or alliance. Although such goods have been recovered only from graves, tales in the *Nihon Shoki* explicitly depict Kofun chieftains carrying them (Barnes 2007: 170). Overall, the prestige goods used to symbolize elites' elevated social status were less regionally variant than tomb-building itself, unified in a "peer polity" framework extending as far as the Korean peninsula (Barnes 2014a: 843).

By the fifth century CE, in this hierarchical system of hereditary regional rulers, the demand for valuable goods to display status led to the formal organization of craftspeople into groups with special status, hierarchically organized with managers (*muraji*) to oversee the work and delivery of goods to court. These managers eventually gathered kinship groups around them to form court clans (*uji*). This development also reflects the increasing importance of crafts (stoneware, gold jewelry, woven cloth, etc.) from the continent for display in the Yamato palace and as gifts to the aristocracy (Barnes 2014a: 847–48). This in turn afforded many opportunities for refugees from the continent skilled in such crafts, which replaced the now out-of-fashion bronze mirrors, staffs and stone bracelets of the Early Kofun period (847–48). Interestingly, these immigrants and others, as part of cross-continental contacts with Yamato, may have brought with them and disseminated Buddhism before the sixth-century date given in later official narratives of Buddhist transmission. Deal and Ruppert (2015: 6) suggest that this transmission may have fostered a political desire to try and control the dissemination of the Buddhist ideology currently spreading outside the realm of the ruling class. There were also direct requests from Yamato kings to the Chinese court for titles, five of which were successful in the fifth century alone (Barnes 2014: 845).

The start of the Asuka period was a time when Buddhist materials and scriptures were flowing officially to the Yamato court from their ally, Paekche, on the Korean Peninsula. However, the meanings of Buddhist doctrines and ceremonies required time to be learned and performed in the Japanese context (Deal and Ruppert 2015: 7). The ambivalence of the Yamato kings toward Buddhist doctrine and gifts in this period allowed noble clans, particularly the Soga, to take on the role of patronizing Buddhist practices until the Taika Reforms. The Soga, as well as other powerful families like the Hata, found that their adoption of Buddhism and construction of temples in the Nara Basin placed them in conflict with other powerful families who favored the older *kami* cult practices, the state not yet holding full symbolic or ritual power over either. Official exchange between courts was supplemented by the practical knowledge brought by migrants to Japan, who acted as bearers of Chinese culture; the Buddhist, Confucian and Daoist ideas they brought shaped technological developments, government, and administrative and economic systems in Yamato and Asuka Japan to a great extent (Deal and Ruppert 2015: 15). The intermarriage of many of these settlers from China and Korea into Japanese families, including important noble clans, gradually removed distinctions between immigrant groups and native Japanese. Even the *Nihon Shoki*, with its exaggerated depictions of Prince Shōtoku's piety and patronage of Buddhism, boasts of his studies with Korean Buddhist monks, underscoring the continued importance of mainland teachings during the Asuka period. There are many other accounts of monks from the Korean Peninsula bringing Buddhist material culture, ritual practices and thought; in 577 CE, for example, a "precept master," "meditation master," a nun, an incantations master, a Buddhist statue maker and a temple architect are all recorded as arriving at court (Deal and Ruppert 2015: 16).

The *Nihon Shoki* entry for 584 CE likewise records that Soga no Umako appointed a monk from the Korean kingdom of Koguryŏ, called Hyep'yŏn, as his Dharma teacher and built a temple for the first three Buddhist monastic initiates, all of them daughters of families with immigrant ancestry, setting the precedent for the later official state model for appointing "official nuns." This may seem surprising considering the somewhat less egalitarian treatment of women in other contemporary Buddhist contexts throughout Asia, but in Japan—as discussed above—women had long played an essential role as mediums between the divine and (especially royal) humans through important ritual practices, making them "natural" acolytes of the Buddha. Women were also the first to travel outside the Japanese archipelago to learn more about Buddhism, specifically to Paekche (Deal and Ruppert 2015: 64). The Soga and other pro-Buddhist families were primarily concerned with Buddhist practices and material culture rather than abstract thought, with Asuka-period rituals focusing on immediate and personal problems and concerns like illnesses, natural disasters, and defeating enemies—in other words, the "this-worldly benefits" (*genze riyaku*) that Buddhist images and temples were believed to help bring about (18–19). Practitioners of Buddhism, including many women, gained eminence at this time largely due to their ability to speak for the higher powers of the supernatural world and act as oracles guiding future action, as leaders sought to harness such power in grounding their own authority (Kidder 2007: 146–47). Women from aristocratic families were also strong patrons of Buddhism at the time and were heavily involved in *sutra* copying and the creation of images of the Buddha and *bodhisattvas* (Deal and Ruppert 2015: 64). In light of all this, one could argue there was more equality for women in ritual matters in Japan than in "axial" China at this point, yet doctrine and morality were not the focus of Buddhist practice in Japan.

As noted above, the authority and power that Buddhism offered came to be of great interest to the state and received royal patronage by the mid-seventh century CE; this was accompanied by many regulations and laws that reflected Buddhist values as well as the implementation of Tang-style administrative organization. However, the enforcement of Buddhist ideals in practice was inconsistent (Deal and Ruppert 2015: 40). For instance, the floods and famine of the early Asuka period led some to cannibalism; the practice of horse sacrifice continued despite being banned in the Taika Reforms; and there is evidence that "river sacrifice" (the sacrificing of female slaves to a "deity-dragon-king" in an attempt to lower dangerously rising water levels) took place near Fujiwara-kyō between 694 and 710 CE (Kidder 2007: 146–47). All of this occurred despite official proclamations that Buddha and his teaching's condemnation of such practices were to be revered. Similarly, regardless of the Soga's enthusiastic embrace of Buddhism, Nara remained a hotbed of indigenous occult activity, which reached its climax under the female sovereign Kōgyoku (642–45 CE). An example is the popular cosmology taught by Ōfube no Ō (and supported by numerous male and female sorcerers), which enticed people to worship a caterpillar-like insect said to be the god of the "Eternal World"; the people who joined this cult ignored their daily work duties, threw away their belongings, and spent their time dancing in the street. Such practices lasted until an elite friend of Prince Shōtoku put a permanent stop to it by intimidating the sorcerers. Kidder (2007: 130) argues that the subsequent Taika Reforms were a way to strengthen the government's ability to deal with subaltern organizations that threatened social order by establishing an official religion to legitimately combat "weird happenings" like the Ōfube cult. Leaders such as Kōgyoku and Kōmyō (the mother of Empress Kōken), who played a central role in establishing state Buddhism, exemplify the strong support Buddhism had from women of the ruling elite (Deal and Ruppert 2015: 64). The preceding discussion is crucial to any consideration of a possible "axial turn" in Japan, in that is shows how the introduction of axial thought faced localized practices and resistance to the doctrines and ideals of Buddhism and Confucianism.

In addition to the state sponsorship of Buddhist rituals, during the Nara period, many elite families converted parts of their homes into private monasteries and invited monastics to live with them in their home and engage in rituals to protect the well-being and health of their family. The Fujiwara clan, for instance, built the famous Kōfukuji temple for this reason (Deal and Ruppert 2015: 64). The application of Tang-influenced religious and administrative systems also brought social change, but unlike in Tang China, Japanese temples did not confiscate peasants' land (which was allocated to both females and males, another key difference from the Chinese context), but instead absorbed peasants as a labor force, leading eventually to a loss of revenue for the central government. Taxes themselves (especially in the form of grain) were held locally rather than channeled to the capital (Barnes 2015: 378). The transcription of *sūtras* from China was a state-sponsored ritual for the well-being of the monarch and the welfare of the state, but also gained prominence as an individual activity designed to achieve personal aims, such as curing disease or ensuring a good rebirth for deceased family members (Deal and Ruppert 2015: 45). State and elite sponsorship of Buddhist rituals and temples was widespread, and corvée labor was extracted from peasants to build great temples like Tōdaiji in Nara (Deal and Ruppert 2015: 64).

Funds were also raised from the general populace by monks. Some of these monks, operating outside of the official monastic system, were not recognized by the state; they faced punishment if caught (Deal and Ruppert 2015: 48). Despite such laws, the unofficial monk Gyōki managed to gain considerable influence in the capital and countryside as a wandering monastic, preaching the Dharma and engaging in public works projects such as building safe houses for travelers, temples for unofficial monks, bridges, and irrigation systems. Emperor Genshō issued an edict in 717 CE to combat such unofficial monks, requiring all monks to live in temples and specifically mentioning Gyōki as one who disrupted towns and villages. However, the state in fact called on his help later to build a very large bronze image of the Buddha. This was due to his ability to raise money from his thousands of followers, the labor and money being difficult to muster using state resources alone, and in 745 CE he was made the first ever *daisōjō*—the highest official monastic rank—in recognition of his contribution (Deal and Ruppert 2015: 49).

In the decade before Gyōki's recognition as *daisōjō*, Japanese monks were being sent to China to find Buddhist specialists to establish official ordinations, illustrating how Tang China was in many ways still regarded as the center of authentic Buddhist knowledge and practice at this time. As previously mentioned, after the Japanese adoption of Tang-style administration, including regulations regarding monastic life, social and legal distinctions between men and women became sharper compared to previous periods. This likewise led to severe restrictions on the ritual activities of nuns, decreasing their authority and causing the number of officially ordained nuns to drop rapidly. By the following Heian period, women were even more excluded from monastic positions of authority and ritual responsibility, though elite women remained active supporters of Buddhism throughout Japan, and there is archaeological evidence that there was still a considerable number of nunneries (Deal and Ruppert 2015: 65–66).

The separation of male from female authority in official Buddhist practice intensified over the course of the Heian period. Nunneries became managed by monks and women were no longer formally ordained; these shifts were reflected by restrictions on the behavior of elite laywomen, such as the promotion of chastity for widows (Deal and Ruppert 2015: 65). Alongside these developments, Heian elites began to ignore the previous Confucian-based legal system (*ritsuryō*), while new Buddhist lineages were developing outside of state control. The introduction of a regent system, requiring a regent for adult as well as child sovereigns, allowed the men of the Fujiwara family to gain power as regents. The clan further secured power by ensuring that Fujiwara women married into the royal line. Heian elites were also drawn to the new Buddhist lineages, which were able to secure increasing independence from government control (5). It was argued at the time that these new esoteric teachings could only be learned by direct transmission from master to disciple through imitation, and that reading texts alone would not allow one to perform the rituals correctly. The Fujiwaras' patronage of prominent monks allowed them to further consolidate de facto power, as ideological authority became increasingly concentrated in the teachings of individual monks rather in the *sūtras* themselves.

The Fujiwara rise to power coincided with the establishment of the Northern Song Dynasty (960–1127 CE) in China, reigniting religious interactions between Japan and the mainland, which was still viewed as the prime source of Buddhist knowledge and documents (Deal and Ruppert 2015: 94–95). In the context of power struggles between the royal house, particularly the retired emperors, and the high-ranking males of the Fujiwara clan, it was increasingly difficult for members of any "outsider" clan to forge successful political careers. Yet Buddhist institutions were becoming less and less reliant on either the state or wealthy patrons like the Fujiwaras for funds, as they were able to collect funds directly from the general populace for the creation of Buddhist images and architecture. The monk Chōgen exemplifies this trend: the retired emperor Go-Shirakawa enlisted him to repair the Great Buddha housed in Tōdaiji in the 1180s CE, which earned Chōgen an official position as the "great fundraiser" (91–97). Piggott's (1982: 52–53) analysis of the *shōen* (manor) system of the Tōdaiji temple revealed the "gigantic effort" of religious institutions to maintain income from land and private estates in the eleventh and twelfth centuries, when the dearth of state funding caused severe financial shortages.

Overall, Buddhism or spiritual practices were never a direct constraint on the power of the executive, but rather a tool that could be used by competing groups to gain authority and legitimacy. The fact that local spiritual practices, Chinese philosophy, Buddhist practices and texts, deities and divinized former rulers, buddhas and *bodhisattvas*, and ruling sovereigns were all brought under the umbrella of the ruling ideology exposes the importance of religious thought and practice in underpinning state authority throughout the periods explored here. Yet both the Soga and Fujiwara clans were able to challenge state authority with the aid of the same practices, and local rituals survived alongside these official ideologies (particularly in the Asuka period). Peasants were required to provide labor for Buddhist temple-building projects and were a source of income for monks, giving rise to a growing band of non-official monks who could muster considerable resources to assist the state when asked. The hierarchization that this entailed occurred despite universalizing doctrines proclaiming the equality of all, connected by karma. These ideas gained prominence at a time when women were being made more powerless than ever, at least in terms of ritual authority and positions of responsibility in religious institutions. However, they were key in easing the transition of migrants into Japanese society: the perceived value and power of Chinese thought provided a means of upward social mobility. Holders of Buddhist knowledge and influential interpreters of doctrine could also informally constrain the sovereign's power; this was exploited by those wealthy elite families who could muster the resources to become patrons of renowned Buddhist monks and centers.

Conclusion

From the evidence examined above, it is very difficult to come up with any firm conclusion about a Japanese "Axial Age," at least one that follows a trajectory similar to those described for other parts of Eurasia. Although doctrines characteristic of axial thought arrived in Japan, the ways these were assimilated were contextually specific and hybridized with local beliefs and practices, exemplified by the persistence of *kami* worship and other indigenous elements woven into Japanese Buddhism. Further, these ideas were adopted in Japan largely due to the perception of Chinese rituals and culture as effective and desirable as methods for gaining and legitimizing power by specific elites, and do not seem to have been driven by a wider ideological shift in moral or ethical precepts. There were clear moralizing aspects to these religions, but these seem to have found expression through the perception that rewards would accrue to elites and rulers who performed the proper rituals, rather than through a truly universalizing mindset. Furthermore, Japanese institutionalized religion shows some resistance to, or at least selectivity in the adoption and adaption of, the egalitarian strands of these religions. For instance, the increasing influence of state-sanctioned Buddhism actually resulted in the loss of women's privileged place in ritual and religious practices, rather than the reverse, which may have been expected from egalitarian doctrines. Similarly, rather than a transformation from an archaic model of divinely sanctioned rule to an axial mode of institutionally constrained rulership, sovereigns of Japan in fact became increasingly deified and reliant on religious legitimation following the adoption of Buddhism as a state religion. In this sense, Japan does not seem to fit a typical axial mode of dynamic transformation—rather, it serves as an example of the fascinating transformations, negotiations and shifting perceptions involved in adopting such forms of thought.

WEST AFRICA | Inland Niger Delta

Jenny Reddish*

Period	Polity	Approx. dates
Bronze Age	Jenné-jeno Phase I	250 BCE–50 CE
Iron Age	Jenné-jeno Phase II	50–400
	Jenné-jeno Phase III	400–900
Classical–medieval	Jenné-jeno Phase IV	900–1400
Early medieval	Wagadu / Ghana Empire	5th–12th c.
Medieval–early modern	Kingdom of Sosso	12th–13th c.
	Mali Empire	13th–15th c.
	Kingdom of Gao	8th c.–1469
	Songhay Empire	1469–1591

Table 10. Periods and polities mentioned in text that were based in or that occupied the Inland Niger Delta[1]

Introduction

As the Niger, the longest river of West Africa, descends in a north-easterly direction from its source in the mountains of Guinea, it forms a large interior floodplain in the modern nation-state of Mali (Gallais 1967; R. McIntosh 1998: 1). Over several millennia, this region (known variously as the Macina, Middle Niger, or Inner Niger Delta) played host to the emergence of urban life, economic specialization, and distinctive forms of social complexity (R. McIntosh 1998, 2005). These long-term developments began to accelerate from the early first millennium CE onwards, producing the earliest cities of sub-Saharan Africa yet to be identified (LaViolette and Fleisher 2005; R. McIntosh 1998: xv). The Inland Delta's landscape is dotted with hundreds of ancient (pre-Islamic) tell sites—mounds formed entirely from the debris of human occupation and often blanketed with sherds of pottery (MacDonald 1997; R. McIntosh 2005: 3). Nevertheless, for reasons we address below, the complex pre-Islamic civilization of the region was entirely overlooked by archaeologists and historians until the late twentieth century (R. McIntosh 2005: 6; S. McIntosh and R. McIntosh 1993).

---

*   Susan McIntosh also contributed to this chapter by reading and providing feedback on previous drafts.

1   The date ranges given here are approximate and still debated among scholars. Dates for the urban phases at Jenné-jeno come from R. McIntosh and S. McIntosh (1981: 15), while those for the medieval kingdoms and empires are based mostly on Conrad (2015).

In parallel with the local growth of urban clusters in the Middle Niger such as Jenné-jeno and Dia, kingdoms and empires that drew their power from superior military technology and control over long-distance trade began to spread across the Western Sahel[2] in the latter half of the first millennium CE (MacDonald 2013: 829). The first of these great "medieval" West African states, Ghana or Wagadu, was succeeded by the Mali Empire in the thirteenth century, which was in turn overshadowed by the growth of Songhai power during the fifteenth century. Middle Niger cities became strategically important for state-building dynasties during this period, though they were not always under direct rule.

To say that the Inner Niger Delta has been overlooked in theories of the Axial Age is something of an understatement. The entirety of the African continent, except for Egypt and the Mediterranean littoral, was excluded from consideration in Karl Jaspers' (1953) original formulation of the Axial Age concept. For him, northern Asia, Africa, and the Americas had all failed to produce anything "of importance to the history of the spirit" (22). This attitude towards African history, entirely congruent with Hegel's (1956: 91) description of the continent as "enveloped in the dark mantle of night," is perhaps one reason for the neglect of the Inner Niger Delta's pre-Islamic archaeological remains—not only in scholarship on the Axial Age, but really in works of global or comparative history generally. Another, more proximate reason, though, is the unusual character of the Niger's ancient urban sites. Ancient Middle Niger societies lacked a written record, public monuments, material expressions of hierarchy, and other traits that characterize primary urbanism elsewhere (West Asia, for example) (R. McIntosh 2005: 5; S. McIntosh and R. McIntosh 1993). As we discuss below, however, archaeological investigations over the last four decades have revealed a complex and differentiated political landscape, long predating the arrival of Islam and other influences from the "axial core" to the north. Founded on horizontal forms of authority and complementary socioeconomic specialization (R. McIntosh 1998), we may even say that the development of the Middle Niger civilization represents an alternate type of response to the same kinds of developments, conflicts, and complexities that stimulated "axial" thinking in mid-first-millennium BCE Eurasia: namely, what constitutes legitimate authority, what role do religious ideals have in secular life, and how should wealth and power be distributed?

This chapter reviews the evidence for universalizing morality and egalitarian ethics, both identified as characteristically "axial" ideological currents in the Axial Age literature, in the Inland Niger Delta between around 2000 BCE and 1400 CE.

---

2   The Sahel, meaning "shore" in Arabic, is the band of land flanking the southern edge of the Sahara: a zone of transition between the desert to the north and the tropical forests to the south (Foley et al. 2003). Another term used in discussions of West African history, "the Sudan" or "Sudanic belt," does not refer to the modern nation-state of Sudan but denotes roughly the same area as the Sahel.

Alongside this discussion, we also address attitudes to rulership and sources of political and legal authority in the region.

Historical background: c. 2000 BCE–1400 CE

At the dawn of the second millennium BCE, a period of warm, wet climatic conditions in West Africa, during which the Sahara had supported lakes, greenery, and much more animal life than it does today, was coming to an end (Connah 2013: 358–59; R. McIntosh 1998: 75–76). As the desert advanced and the climate fluctuated dramatically, human populations moved southwards and began to experiment with new modes of subsistence. In modern south-eastern Mauritania, for instance, an early complex tradition known as Tichitt-Walata (c. 1900–400 BCE) developed. The Tichitt-Walata people engaged in pearl millet farming and cattle pastoralism, built large stone-walled residential compounds, and interred their dead in grave tumuli (MacDonald 2013). To the south-east, the Middle Niger—including basins like the Méma, which has since dried out—became a valuable refuge. The inhabitants of this landscape of shifting channels and seasonal lakes by the later first millennium BCE included a mixture of mobile pastoralists, cultivators of grain crops such as millet, sorghum, and African rice, gatherer-hunters, and fishers (Connah 2013; S. McIntosh 2008: 356; R. McIntosh and S. McIntosh 1988: 144–45).

Over the course of the last millennium BCE, there was also a trend towards more settled lifestyles in the region, with the concomitant growth of permanent architecture and larger sites. Clusters of settlement mounds grew up at Akumbu in the Méma and around Dia on the Diaka River (R. McIntosh 1998: 166–76). Unlike the Late Stone Age Tichitt-Walata settlements, which were large but organizationally simple, several of these early Iron Age sites have provided evidence for specialist communities of artisans and food producers as well as sophisticated iron metallurgy (MacDonald 2013; Rashid 2006: 121). However, a true watershed in the urbanization of the Middle Niger was reached with the foundation of Jenné-jeno and its satellites around 250 BCE in the Upper Delta (MacDonald 2013; R. McIntosh 2005: xv). By the mid-first millennium CE, it was a mature city tied into long-distance exchange networks and by c. 900 CE the central mound covered 33 ha (S. McIntosh and R. McIntosh 1995: 18). A city wall, perhaps a flood defense rather than a protective bastion against attack, was also built (S. McIntosh and R. McIntosh 1993). Radiocarbon dates from the site have confounded prior assumptions of historians that West African urbanism was late and derivative of North African models (R. McIntosh and S. McIntosh 1981). In fact, this thriving city predated the establishment of regular long-distance trade with North Africa and the arrival of Islam in the region by several centuries (Sinclair et al. 1993: 27; Stahl 2004: 150). Moreover, hundreds of tell sites here are yet to be excavated, testifying to a complex pre-Islamic civilization only recently "discovered to the world" (R. McIntosh 2005: 6).

While the cities of the Inland Delta were growing and prospering, other important developments were taking place to the West. Wagadu (called Ghana in the Islamic sources and Awkar by Berber traders) is the earliest historically documented empire of West Africa (Davidson 1998: 26). Its earliest beginnings are hazy. Many scholars locate them among Soninke-speaking communities in the grasslands northwest of the Inland Niger Delta (MacDonald 2013; Munson 1980). However, others have recently suggested that earliest Wagadu was in fact centered on the Middle Niger itself (Dueppen 2016: 251; MacDonald 2013: 838). Whatever the precise location of the empire's heartland, a Soninke ruling dynasty emerged from around 400 CE, likely spurred by increasingly complex interregional exchange networks in copper, livestock, and grain, and managed to exert its authority over neighboring communities and lucrative trade routes (S. McIntosh 2008). Wagadu's influence spread rapidly over the course of the following centuries, benefiting especially from the advent of regular trans-Saharan trade in gold, salt, and slaves. "Ghana" appears in the writings of Muslim scholars from North Africa and Spain, who fantasized about this "land of gold," from the eighth century onwards. At its height in the mid-eleventh century, the polity covered a vast swath of the western Sahel and encroached on the Inland Niger Delta, though the forms of control it exerted varied widely within this territory (R. McIntosh 1998: 370–71; S. McIntosh 2008; Simonis 2010: 36). Further to the east, the polity known in Arabic texts as Kawkaw developed in the Gao region of the Niger Bend. The Arabic written sources and archaeological evidence of long-distance trade and probable elite residences permit the identification of another hierarchically organized kingdom here from the ninth century onwards (Cissé et al. 2013; Insoll 1996, 2000).

The power of Wagadu's rulers began to wane in the eleventh century CE. A variety of explanations have been advanced for this, from climatic upheavals to the activities of the Almoravids, a Muslim Berber dynasty to the north (R. McIntosh 1998: 258–60). The Almoravids wrested control of Awdaghust, an important Saharan trade entrepôt, from Wagadu in 1055 CE, but recent scholarly consensus allots them a comparatively minor role in the fall of the empire (Conrad and Fisher 1982, 1983). Conversion to Islam among its elite, contrary to earlier images of a clash of civilizations between the Berber Muslims and pagan West Africans, was most likely a gradual and complex process (El Fasi and Hrbek 1980: 100; R. McIntosh 1998: 259). Regardless, the slow decline of Wagadu led to a power vacuum in the region, which was filled with several smaller successor states, including the Sosso and Méma Kingdoms (R. McIntosh 1998: 247).

In the early thirteenth century, several Malinke chiefdoms from the Upper Niger region united against the Sosso and slowly aggregated into what would become the Mali Empire. This was the largest of the West African empires, covering the old Wagadu territory as well as extending westwards to the Atlantic coast, south to the tropical forest belt, and east to Gao and Timbuktu in the Niger Bend region (Lapidus 2012: 592; R. McIntosh 1998: 251). The apogee of the empire is considered to correspond to the reign of Musa I of the Keita Dynasty, the *mansa* (emperor) in the early fourteenth century (Bell 1972). One of the most well-known figures in precolonial West African history, Musa I, is also famed for his patronage of Islam in Mali and for his lavish distribution of gold on his pilgrimage to Mecca in 1324–25 CE (Schultz 2006). The empire flourished from the early thirteenth to the late fourteenth century, at which point it started to decline (MacDonald et al. 2011: 52). Though it likely survived in some form for several centuries, the Songhai Empire, founded by non-Mande speakers and centered on the Niger Bend north-east of the Inland Delta, increasingly came to dominate the Sahel after 1400 CE (Insoll 1994: 327; Jansen 1996b; Oliver and Atmore 2001: 67).

The precise relationship of these sprawling polities ruled by warrior dynasts to the well-established societies of the Inner Niger Delta—to the "elder world," to use a phrase applied by Roderick McIntosh (2008) to the ancient cityscape around Timbuktu—remains a subject of debate. Were cities like Jenné-jeno and Dia under the direct rule of Wagadu, Mali, and Songhai, and what form did external imperial power take in this region? Early Muslim visitors to the region and later Arabic chronicles (*ta'rīkhs*) are strangely silent on the matter (R. McIntosh 1998: 250). As Middle Niger settlements, including Timbuktu, Gao, and the new town of Jenné (founded close to Jenné-jeno) were reoriented towards long-distance trade, they became increasingly attractive to state-building ruling dynasties, who competed to reap the rewards control over these commercial hubs could bring (Rashid 2006: 122). However, clear evidence for the administrative status of the Inner Delta heartland within the new over-kingdoms is lacking, and R. McIntosh (1998: 264) has suggested that by the time of the Mali Empire, its towns may have "settled into a peaceful, semi-autonomous relationship" with the Mandinka rulers. Overall, it is likely that the degree of local political independence waxed and waned.

What we can say with more certainty, drawing on archaeological evidence, is that the period from the thirteenth century CE onwards brought significant depopulation and declining local prosperity on the Middle Niger (R. McIntosh 1998, 2005: 177–79, 2008; Togola 2000). Jenné-jeno's satellite sites Hambarketolo and Kaniana were abandoned some time before 1100 CE, and the main settlement was abandoned by 1400 CE (R. McIntosh and S. McIntosh 1995: 63; R. McIntosh 1998: 245–47). Climatic fluctuation, disruptions to agriculture and pastoralism, and perhaps also epidemics all played a role in this process. It is also possible that these same stresses allowed more vertical forms of political organization and hierarchy to emerge and gain ascendancy across West Africa—a shift we address in more detail below.

Egalitarianism, universalizing morality, and attitudes to legitimate authority in the Middle Niger region

In both recent and earlier scholarship on the Axial Age, the period from around 800 to 200 BCE in the five "core" axial regions of China, India, Iran, the Levant, and Greece is presented as one of extraordinary development in intellectual life and systems of morality. We are particularly interested here in the arguments for a shift towards egalitarianism and universalizing morality, reflexive critique of the existing political order, and the decoupling of divine and temporal power (for example, the desacralization of kingship) (e.g. Armstrong 2006; Bellah 2011; Eisenstadt 2005). What light can the history of the Middle Niger between roughly 2000 BCE and 1400 CE shed on such schemes? More often than not, the vast expanse of the African continent south of the Sahara simply does not feature in these discussions, as noted in the introduction to this chapter. Consequently, its potential contribution to scholars' understanding of the relationship between religion and ethical philosophy, inequality, and political structures goes unexplored. This is unfortunate, because the Inner Niger Delta in particular presents us with an alternative historical trajectory for the development of urbanism and social complexity, in tandem with indigenous religious systems that—at least before the mid-first millennium CE—did not necessarily serve to cement elite power or provide divine legitimacy to inequality and exploitation, as is often assumed to be the norm for pre- or non-"axial" society. In this section, we examine the evidence for egalitarian ethics, universalizing morality and local theories of political authority in the Middle Niger up to the end of the fourteenth century CE.

Before the rise of Wagadu (c. 2000 BCE—800 CE)

The implied baseline from which axial transformations are traced is a supposed prototypically "archaic" civilization, presided over by a god-king and equipped with a religion that justifies inequality within human society by presenting it as natural and divinely bestowed. The hierarchically organized states of ancient Mesopotamia, Pharaonic Egypt, and China during the Shang and Zhou Dynasties function as such exemplary pre-axial societies (Jaspers 1953; Marangudakis 2006),[3] though it is often implied that such archaic forms of rule are a universal, natural phase in societal development. However, despite abundant evidence of complex urban life, the material record from the Middle Niger suggests that no initial "despotic," archaic phase occurred here. Jenné-jeno and its sister cities are of deep historical significance not only because they testify to early, independently developed urbanism in

---

3   Though see the chapters on Egypt, Iran, and North China in this volume for a critical examination of these claims.

West Africa, but also due to their particular social structure as revealed by archaeo-logical investigation.

Over multiple excavation seasons at Jenné-jeno and surrounding sites, archae-ologists Susan and Roderick McIntosh—to their great surprise—failed to discover evidence of a ruling dynasty, a bureaucratic apparatus, or vertical social stratification before the rise of the Sahelian empires (MacDonald 2013; R. McIntosh 2005). The material manifestations of state power, including grand tombs and monuments re-quiring large-scale mobilization of labor; the use of writing for either bookkeeping, law codes, or royal propaganda; and specialized buildings for administration, are all absent (S. McIntosh and R. McIntosh 1993). This fact may go some way towards explaining why the Middle Niger's ancient civilization was only recognized as such in the mid-1970s. Archaeologists primed to associate primary urbanism with Meso-potamian-style temples and palaces walked over the region's thick carpets of broken pottery and mounds of melted mudbrick without ever recognizing their significance.

Jenné-jeno and its sister sites are nevertheless fully urban according to defini-tions that emphasize the role played by the city in the landscape and its relationship with nearby settlements. Like archaeologists working in other parts of Africa, Rod-erick McIntosh (2005: 17) favors such a functional approach, citing Bruce Trigger's (1972: 577) description of the city as a "unit of settlement which performs specialized functions in relation to a broader hinterland" (see also Norman 2012: 145–46). In the Inland Niger Delta, archaeological survey has revealed a differentiated urban landscape, with evidence for specialist activities such as ironworking and ceramic production concentrated in certain locations (MacDonald 2013: 836–37; R. McIn-tosh 2005). After 400 CE at Jenné-jeno, even different stages in the production of iron objects (smelting and smithing) became spatially separated (R. McIntosh 2005: 152–53).

Susan McIntosh and Roderick McIntosh have therefore argued consistently that both Jenné-jeno and the wider Middle Niger landscape was organized "heterarchi-cally"; that is, characterized by both economic and occupational specialization and the absence of centralized power (R. McIntosh 2005; S. McIntosh and R. McIntosh 1993; Stahl 2004: 150).[4] A still-developing school of thought within archaeology, anthropology, and related disciplines (see e.g. Ehrenreich et al. 1995; S. McIntosh 1999a) has explored heterarchy as an alternative "pathway to complexity" (S. McIn-tosh 1999b) in human history, one that nurtures resistance to hierarchy and thus also to the despotic state. One form this can take is the evolution of counterpoised sources of power: if the economic and political power of each specialized group is

---

4   One influential definition of heterarchy comes from the anthropologist Carole Crumley (1995: 3): "the relations of elements to one another when they are unranked or when they possess the potential of being ranked in different ways."

counterbalanced by that of other groups, no one group is allowed to grow dominant. Moreover, due to the complexity of social identities, any given individual will likely be a member of multiple such groups and so obliged to negotiate between competing loyalties, providing a further barrier to the concentration of decision-making authority in the hands of a few elites. In the McIntoshes' reconstruction of the social world of the ancient Inland Niger Delta, the constituent elements were "corporations," a term encompassing ethnic and kin groups, secret societies, and organizations of artisans and traders (R. McIntosh 1998: 9–10; R. McIntosh 2000; S. McIntosh 1999b: 15).

This view of the ancient Inland Niger Delta is of course not universally accepted. Stahl (2004: 151) appears skeptical of the leap made by the McIntoshes from archaeologically visible patterns to politics and ideology, and comments that their image of a heterarchical society at Jenné-jeno and elsewhere "requires further support." Some more general discussions of the concept of heterarchy (noted in Levy 2007: 191–92) criticize it as insufficiently defined or "too loosely applied" in archaeological contexts. Nevertheless, to the best of our knowledge, no comprehensive alternative theories of the political organization of the ancient Middle Niger societies have been proposed that could stand in opposition to the McIntoshes' heterarchy. Proceeding, then, from current scholarly opinion on the implications of the archaeological evidence and local oral tradition, what can we usefully say about the development of egalitarian ethics and universalizing ideology over time in the pre-Islamic Middle Niger?

Roderick McIntosh (1998: 5) has argued for a long-lived set of values corresponding to the distributed power relations of the Inland Niger Delta; what he calls a "symbolic reservoir of beliefs" (see also R. McIntosh and S. McIntosh 1988: 156). In cultural-historical terms, this floodplain was the crucible for the mixing of two great traditions that still structure West African societies today: the Soninke from the north of the Inland Delta, and the Malinke from its south (R. McIntosh 1998: 15). Both form part of the still larger Mande-speaking cultural sphere. In addition, there were the "autochthons" of the Inland Delta, such as the Bozo, who may have been present here for many centuries before the arrival of Soninke and Malinke speakers (Arazi 2005; MacDonald 1994; R. McIntosh 1998: 15). In McIntosh's view, certain Mande "core rules" of social life and action in the landscape are very old indeed, dating back millennia to the Late Stone Age (pre-Jenné-jeno) and to the era of urbanization and prosperity in the Inland Delta in the first millennium CE (R. McIntosh 2000: 159, 167–71).

Extrapolating backwards from historical Mande contexts, R. McIntosh (2000) argues that these rules demanded moral reciprocity both between human individuals and between human communities and the landscape (see also McNaughton 1988: 15–21). Mande concepts of landscape envision a grid underlain by currents of *nyama*, a vital force that is more concentrated in some localities than others (R. McIntosh 1998, 2000; Togola 2000). A particularly durable Mande trope is the *dalimasigi* (knowledge quest), in which a charismatic and skillful individual travels over the *nyama* grid and enters into relations with spirits of the land on behalf of the wider community (Conrad 2008; R. McIntosh 1998, 2005). By placating or subduing these beings, these heroes or heroines can transform potentially dangerous *nyama* and (for example) make certain locations habitable for humans or enable the extraction and working of iron (R. McIntosh 1998).[5] This worldview is laden with ethical expectations: knowledge quests are undertaken for the common good and not for personal gain, and places of concentrated *nyama* should never be "monopolized" by individuals or corporations (R. McIntosh 2005: 139–41). Parallels can be drawn between these values and the promotion of "prosociality," argued to characterize societies undergoing axial transformations (see Atran 2016; Turchin 2012). It is also on these foundations that Mande theories of legitimate authority rest. We discuss these in more detail below for the period in which ruling dynasties held sway over much of the Sahel, but here it is sufficient to note that—if McIntosh is correct—the moral values of the early Inland Niger Delta culture strongly proscribed the kind of self-serving despotism anticipated by Axial Age theorists for the initial, "archaic" phases of urbanization.

Despite the unusually rich trove of oral traditions preserved by Mande *jeliw* (a hereditary "caste" of historians, genealogists, and political mediators [Hoffman 2000; R. McIntosh 2000]) and the results of decades of modern archaeological research in the Inland Niger Delta, the reconstruction of trends in political and religious values in the region before the introduction of writing remains a fraught task. Our image of the shifting "symbolic reservoir" will probably always lack temporal resolution. In keeping with the distributed power relations of Middle Niger societies and the importance they ascribed to occult knowledge (McNaughton 1988: 13–14), it seems likely that the "ideology" of the delta had no canonical form promulgated from on high (for instance, no equivalent to the Christian orthodoxy reached after the First Council of Nicaea) and that its moral norms and core assumptions about the world often remained unspoken. This unspokenness was perhaps a strength rather than a weakness. And, as Sinopoli et al. (2015: 391) have argued, the maintenance of "distributed power relations" in complex societies requires ideological as well as material reinforcement.

To conclude this section, a case can certainly be made for ideological egalitarianism, in the sense of resistance to the concentration of wealth and power, in the pre-Islamic Inland Niger Delta. This extended, it seems, to the divine sphere as well, as there is no indication of any sort of omniscient "high god" who maintained moral or ethical norms and punished transgressions; what can be termed "divine power"

---

5   Note the interesting parallels with ideological traditions in other "non-axial" regions in the Americas and Polynesia, outlined in other chapters in this volume.

was a diffused, localized, "natural" force rather than one concentrated in the hands of one or several anthropomorphic beings as is common in the main axial religious traditions. Material support for this comes from the clustered "heterarchical" structure of the urban landscape, from the absence of signs of a wealthy ruling class, and also from the artwork recovered from ancient tells like Jenné-jeno. The terracotta sculpture of the Inland Delta, for instance, is remarkably diverse in both style and content, indicating a lack of aesthetic canonization or elite control over craft production (R. McIntosh and S. McIntosh 1988: 155–56). The presence or absence of universalizing currents of thought is a thornier question. Though Roderick McIntosh (1998) has argued for a common reservoir of beliefs and practices from which all inhabitants of the landscape could draw, there was evidently great diversity in identities and social roles in the region. The probable importance of occult knowledge as closely guarded property of corporations (R. McIntosh 2005: 101) also militates against any simplistic equation of the Middle Niger's "elder world" with the universalizing axial traditions of mid-first-millennium BCE Eurasia (see e.g. Baumard and Boyer 2013; Eisenstadt 2005). It may be more accurate to identify the pivotal ethical values of Middle Niger societies in this period as those of complementarity, reciprocity, and resistance to hierarchy.

The age of Islam and empire in the Middle Niger, c. 800–1400 CE

In this section, we ask how ideology and practice concerning status, gender, and the position of rulers changed during the rise and fall of West African kingdoms and empires before 1400 CE. Can we identify strands of egalitarianism and universalizing morality in this tumultuous period of the Middle Niger's history? How did Islam and local traditions of morality and ritual practice interact? We also examine more concrete manifestations of social stratification, such as the growth of bonded labor and economic inequality.

As we mentioned briefly above, the late first and early second millennia CE saw the emergence and consolidation of new forms of political organization in this region. For the first time, rulers and wealthy elites began to leave their mark on the sociopolitical landscape of the Middle Niger. This transformation, described by R. McIntosh (1998: 295) as heralding "three and a half centuries of warrior-state chaos," may be seen as a local expression of a broader shift across the Western Sahel from heterarchy to hierarchy and more coercive forms of rulership (Stahl 2004: 151). After 700 CE, a new system of religious belief and practice—Islam—was introduced south of the Sahara by Arab and Berber Muslim traders (Levtzion and Pouwels 2000; Webb 2006: 44). These merchants, and the clerics and scholars who followed on their heels, also brought writing, and state bureaucracies began to emerge in the region (Lapidus 2012: 590; Levtzion and Pouwels 2000: 3–4). In contrast to the early history of Jenné-jeno, Dia, and other Inland Delta sites, historians can therefore make use of roughly contemporary written records for this period.[6]

The dynasties that gained ascendancy in early second-millennium CE West Africa have often been portrayed as exploitative and predatory; utilizing superior military technology to dominate sedentary populations and siphon off wealth from the growing interregional and trans-Saharan trade (Goody 1971; R. McIntosh 2000; Stahl 2004: 151–52). Borrowing a phrase from Abdoulaye Bathily, a historian of the Upper Senegal region, R. McIntosh (2000: 170) goes so far as to describe them as "aristocracies of terror." With this language, we are back in more familiar territory for theories of the Axial Age. These dynasts, though the economic base of their power was very different, sound close to the archetypal despots thought to sit at the apex of pre-axial state hierarchies in West Asia and China. According to Axial Age theories, however, medieval Islamicate societies are decidedly "post-axial." The more oppressive aspects of rule by Islamic dynasties in medieval West Africa provide a degree of support for the position (e.g. see the chapters on Egypt and Iran in this volume) that the egalitarianism of axial transformations was only weakly institutionalized in later societies, and that the post-axial world (especially the first millennium CE in Afro-Eurasia) saw a resurgence of more "archaic" forms of governance. We explore these issues below.

Both archaeology and Arabic written sources point to the emergence of wealthy and powerful elites during the late first and early second millennium in West Africa. For instance, according to the eleventh-century Andalusian scholar al-Bakrī, who compiled reports of merchants and other travelers to the lands south of the Sahara, the funeral rites of the king of Ghana (Wagadu) involved the construction of a wooden hut to house his body (Collins and Burns 2013: 82). Before earth was piled over the building to create a mound, the king's retainers were placed inside, it seems while still living, so that they could serve him in death as in life (Law 1985: 61). Support for al-Bakrī's claims comes from the large grave tumuli that sprang up in the Middle Niger region towards the close of the first millennium CE, including two (El Ouladji and Koi Gourrey, also known as Killi) with evidence of human sacrifice (Connah 2001: 127; Desplagnes 1903, 1951; Dueppen 2016: 251). Law (1985) explicitly links the occurrence of funerary sacrifice in early second-millennium West Africa to the power held by rulers over the rest of the population, and indeed the practice has been viewed as an expression of extreme inequality (Turchin et al. 2015).

These rich tombs, equipped with grave goods and servants in the expectation of life after death, also raise the interesting question of the relationship of religious ideology to "royal" power in the region in the late first and early second millennium CE. In Axial Age theories, claims that the ruler's position is divinely willed (or

---

6   However, as we shall see, these sources bring their own interpretative problems.

even that he or she is a living god) often feature as a hallmark of pre-axial political orders (e.g. Bellah 2011). Was kingship sacred in West Africa during this period? In the preceding discussion of the early urban civilization of the Inland Niger (before around 800 CE), we saw how archaeologists have argued for an ethical outlook at this time that opposed hierarchy and sought to harness the dangerous yet sacred power of *nyama* for the benefit of multiple groups inhabiting the Inland Delta. In the later first millennium, however, old religious motifs appear to have been put to quite different uses. The McIntoshes (R. McIntosh 2000: 170; R. McIntosh and S. McIntosh 1988: 154) suggest that the rulers of Wagadu subverted older ideas about *nyama* and its proper use by co-opting a pre-existing "snake and rainmaker cult" to shore up their own power. According to Soninke oral tradition, Dinga, the founding ancestor of Wagadu, subdued "water genies" in various Sahelian locations, while his son Diabe placated the powerful snake Bida through the annual sacrifice of a beautiful virgin (Gomez 2018: 32; R. McIntosh 1998: 259–60). The precise details of the ideological charters adopted by emerging (especially pre-Mali Empire) Middle Niger elites at this time are difficult to ascertain, but one compelling possibility is that the potent symbols of the Mande hero and the *dalimasigi* quest served to legitimate their control over wealth, trade, and labor.

The religious landscape of the medieval Sahel, including the Middle Niger, was complicated by the intrusion of Muslim beliefs and practices, which trickled across the Sahara and became especially influential in the later empires (such as Mali and Songhai). In the mid–1320s CE, Mansa Musa of the Mali Empire made the pilgrimage to Mecca (Lapidus 2002: 402; Sapong 2016). His vast entourage of retainers and slaves and the masses of gold distributed on the journey ensured that he was remembered for many centuries in North Africa and Europe (Conrad 2001; Schultz 2006). Like other Sahelian kings and "chiefs" during this period, Musa also brought literate Muslim officials and clerics into the heart of Malian government. Islamic judicial institutions, centers of scholarship, and mosques sprang up across the region, and the development of formal bureaucracies gave Sahelian rulers a greater degree of administrative control over subject populations than had hitherto been possible (Lapidus 2002: 401–09; R. McIntosh 1998: 250).

With its insistence that "there is no god but God" and its critical attitude towards untrammeled royal authority (Denny 2016: 99; Sonn 1996), it could be reasonably expected that Islam would clash with the indigenous veneration of local spirits of water, earth, plants, and animals (Brooks 1993: 35) and the funerary rites of West African dynasts. However, in many ways the new religion functioned as an additional and non-exclusive wellspring of symbols that could be manipulated in the service of dynastic power. While in practical terms Arabic literacy was a powerful administrative tool, rulers could also benefit from the prestige associated with Islam by providing patronage for scholars, instituting daily Muslim prayers, and making the *ḥajj* (pilgrimage to Mecca). But not all kings (certainly not in Wagadu, and not even in the Mali Empire) converted, and even those who did adopted a syncretic approach (Dunn 2012: 294). Rather than abandoning ancient West African sources of legitimacy, they often retained a quasi-divine status and were venerated after death (Lapidus 2002: 401–02). In his account of his visit to Mali in the fourteenth century, the celebrated Moroccan scholar-explorer Ibn Baṭṭūṭa complained about the levels of ritual distance placed between him and high-ranking Malian hosts, representatives of the *mansa* (Dunn 2012: 299). His reaction can perhaps be traced to the differing ideologies of rule in fourteenth-century Morocco—where the Marinid rulers styled themselves as protectors of Sunnī Islam, but made no claims to personal divinity (Lapidus 2002: 327) and where the notional equality of all Muslim men was solidified through performance of hospitality rituals—and the Mali Empire.

Both the material and written record therefore furnishes evidence of the increasingly lofty ideological position of rulers across the medieval Sahel. Emerging royal and other elite roles were legitimated by a complex mélange of Islamic and indigenous West African religion and ritual. There are also some indications that the broader social organization of the region took on more hierarchical forms at this time, especially during the long dry phase from c. 1100 to 1500 CE (Brooks 1993: 97–99). According to the oral traditions of Wagadu, the clans known as *wago* constituted a class of hereditary nobles, descended from the four original soldier-commanders of the empire's provinces (Gomez 2018: 32). Likewise, Brooks (1993: 34) argues that in the early second millennium CE, a tripartite social division came to structure many of the communities inhabiting the western Sudanic belt, consisting of a stratum of the ruling elite together with free farming people; an intermediate class of hereditary occupational groups; and a class of slaves. In this view, such divisions originated among Mande-speaking people (especially the Malinke, who formed the elite of the Mali Empire) and spread along with their military conquests (Brooks 1993; Kea 2004: 735). The equestrian nobility accumulated wealth via tribute and taxation. They also developed relationships of simultaneous dominance over and dependence on emerging commercial diasporas and craft associations (*nyamakalaw*) of smiths, bards, and leatherworkers (Arazi 2005: 184–85; Brooks 1989). Though the *nyamakalaw* likely developed from earlier, first-millennium CE groupings of artisans, it has been argued that by 1300 CE they had become more rigid "castes," with endogamous marriage rules and prescribed social roles (Tamari 1991).

The third and lowest stratum in this social system, enslaved people, requires further comment. Though slaves may have been present in limited numbers in some regions of the Sahel from the fourth century CE (MacDonald 2013: 833), they became an important basis of state power—as exchange commodities or as producers of trade goods and grain—only in the late first millennium (Stahl 2004: 152). The emergence of a dense web of commercial connections between northern West Africa and the Mediterranean world at this time was accompanied by a rapid rise in the frequency of slave raiding (Rashid 2006; Webb 2006). Somewhat ironically, the spread of Islam, with its supposedly egalitarian moral precepts, did little to curb the growth of slaving south of the Sahara. Instead, Muslim traders facilitated and seem to have encouraged the transport of war captives both within the Sahel and across the vast desert to the north (Webb 2006). Some measure of protection from enslavement could be achieved by converting to Islam, but non-Muslims, and especially those dwelling outside the sphere of control of large states, were forced to fight or flee (Stahl 2004: 153). It should be noted, though, that the forms of bound labor practiced within Wagadu, Sosso, Mali, and other Sahelian states differed in crucial ways from the chattel slavery of the trans-Atlantic slave trade after 1500 CE. For instance, those who had been enslaved and set to work on agricultural land or in domestic contexts could "easily work themselves into freedom" according to Davidson (1998: 164). Arabic written sources hold that the Malian king Sakura was originally a slave of the royal family who was freed and usurped the throne (Levtzion 1963: 345).

Across the western Sahel, then, it seems that older, more heterarchical modes of social organization were replaced after around 800 CE by centralized state apparatuses, divinely sanctioned elites, ranked social strata, and an expanding slave trade—in these respects, an axial transformation in reverse. The role of Islamic doctrine and practice in this process is a complex issue. Equity-promoting and universalizing currents were certainly present in West African varieties of Islam. Many of the Berbers responsible for the introduction of the religion to West Africa in the late first millennium were Khārijites, believers in the "absolute equality of Muslims" and in the duty to oppose tyrannical hereditary rule (Iliffe 2017: 45–54; Marlow 1997: 14–15). Ideas of transcendence of ethnic identity undoubtedly also accompanied the religion across the Sahara to West Africa. Aḥmad Bābā, a scholar from Timbuktu, stated unequivocally in his *Miʻrāj al-ṣuʻūd* that there was "no difference between one race and another" (quoted in Bachir Diagne 2008: 26). As Malinke and Soninke living on the southern fringes of the Sahara, including the Middle Niger region, converted to Islam, then, they became members of a transcontinental "brotherhood of shared norms and trust" (Dunn 2012: 293). However, as we have seen, the core egalitarian tenets of this religion, which features in Axial Age schemas as a secondary axial "breakthrough" (e.g. Eisenstadt 1986c), did not prevent the association of Muslim clerics, officials, and traders with hereditary sacred rulers or their involvement in the slave trade.

It is important to recognize that the arrival of Islam, literacy, and associated forms of governance did not effect a complete break in culture or social structure. Dunn (2006: 293–94) stresses the continuities between pre-Islamic and Islamic-period West African societies, noting that the same general basis of political economy characterized the empires of Wagadu, Mali, and Songhai (spanning the period from the fifth to the sixteenth century CE). There were also key differences between Muslim societies south and north of the Sahara, notably in matters of gender. Women occupy a prominent role in Mande myths and the epic tradition, often appearing as heroines, and everyday gender relations seem to have been relatively equable and unconstrained. In the fourteenth century, the aforementioned Ibn Baṭṭūṭa was dismayed by what he saw as a failure to conform to proper Islamic standards of morality (Dunn 2012: 299–300). According to his account of his travels, after he admonished a Massūfa (Berber) scholar of the town of Walata for allowing his wife to converse with an unrelated man in the courtyard, the man replied: "the association of women with men is agreeable to us and a part of good conduct, to which no suspicion attaches. They are not like the women of your country" (Dunn 2012: 300). In this respect, medieval Mande social mores may have been more egalitarian in gender terms than many axial as well as post-axial societies in Eurasia. This is unsurprising: sexual equality is a notable blind spot of the first-millennium BCE axial "breakthroughs" (evidenced throughout the chapters in this volume).

It could be said that despite its militaristic and exploitative aspects, the Mande expansion brought its own forms of universalizing morality and constraints on power, and that increasing stratification in the late first and early second millennia was tempered by the retention of a high degree of social mobility. The diffusion of common ideals and certain norms of ethical conduct towards others took place as more and more communities were integrated into "Greater Mande" via the conquests of Malinke horse warriors and the movements of various Mande traders and artisans from the late first millennium onwards. For instance, Brooks (1993: 37–38) identifies "landlord-stranger reciprocities" as a pillar of social life in medieval and later West Africa. Remarked on by Ibn Baṭṭūṭa in the Mali Empire as well as later European explorers (Jansen 1996a: 122), these norms enabled the free movement of travelers and traders in safety. The voluminous literature on the historical fluidity of social identity in the Sahel shows, too, how easily migrants and even captives could be absorbed into host societies. The rigid hierarchies that developed in certain post-axial civilizations of the first millennium CE, for instance the Byzantine Empire, appear to have been absent in the West African context.

Another factor that complicates the overall picture of increasing stratification and hierarchy from the early first millennium to the early second millennium is the presence (or more likely persistence) of indigenous traditions of critique of untrammeled power. Even within the tripartite hierarchical structures of the early medieval states, authority was premised on one's ability to mediate effectively, to maintain equable distributions of resources, and to "command admiration and respect" (Brooks 1993: 34; R. McIntosh 2005: 139). The Sunjata Epic, the most important epic poem of the Malinke people, offers a window onto Mande political theory (Johnson 1999). It portrays Sunjata, semi-legendary founder of the Mali Empire, as a liberator of his people from the oppressive rule of Sumaworo, a blacksmith-king gone bad (Dunn 2012: 294). Sunjata is an exemplar of generous and wise leadership, and his victories eventually bring peace to the land (Kesteloot et al. 1991: 24). Though set in the thirteenth century, the oral nature of the epic causes problems of dating and authenticity. Nevertheless, several scholars (e.g. Conrad 2004; R. McIntosh 2015) are inclined to view Mande epic literature as representative of deep-time political values in the region. Such values perhaps served as an informal constraint on the ability of equestrian warrior elites to dominate subject populations. As R. McIntosh insists (1998: 144), "the long history of the Mande is the long evolution of heterarchy."

The Mande suspicion of despotic power raises a crucial, broader point. In recent years, there has been a reassessment of the coercive nature of political structures in the West African empires, and even of their "empire" status. Did Islamic and subsequently Western scholars fail to recognize the "radically different" forms of government present in the medieval Sahel, and therefore force them into categories more familiar to their readers (R. McIntosh 2005: 13, 2013: 165)? R. McIntosh points out that while Arab scholars spoke of kings and empires south of the Sahara, archaeologists have so far failed to find palaces or monumental state architecture, and—rather tellingly—disagree on the locations of the capitals of these states (MacDonald 2016; R. McIntosh 2005: 13). There is more evidence of centralized power in the Mali and Songhai Empires than in the earlier, more mysterious Wagadu (R. McIntosh 1998: 229). In general, though, this lack of evidence holds true throughout the period under review here.

One possibility is that the adoption of ostentatious modes of royal display in medieval West Africa was a sort of veneer overlaying societies that were still to a large extent characterized by relatively low levels of stratification (MacEachern 2005: 451; Stahl 2004: 152). Stahl (2004: 148) stresses the consequences of the population's ability to "vote with their feet"—to move away from excessively oppressive rulers—for the development of strategies of governance in the complex Iron Age societies (after c. 500 CE) of Africa's tropical belt, and similar arguments can be made for the drier region to the north (e.g. Jansen 1996a: 124). Because land was plentiful, "wealth in people" became more important than control over territory, and high levels of mobility meant that rulers had to strive to win the allegiance of followers (Stahl 2004: 148).

The common thread in the history of the Western Sahel in the late first and early second millennia CE is the complex interplay (both in theory and practice) of hierarchical and more egalitarian features: an interplay that was firmly rooted in the local environment and political context. R. McIntosh (1998) has written of the resilience of the Middle Niger's ancient "civil society" right up to the present day. Despite considerable destruction and depopulation, heterarchical modes of political organization have persisted alongside more centralized power structures and indigenous religion alongside Islam. Axial Age schemes seem to be of limited utility in explaining these historical trajectories.

Conclusions

This chapter has reviewed what archaeology, written records, and later oral tradition can tell us about universalizing morality, egalitarian ethics, and attitudes to legitimate authority in the Inland Niger Delta from c. 2000 BCE to 1400 CE. The absence of documentary evidence from West Africa before the arrival of Arabic literacy means that the religious ideologies of the pre-Islamic Middle Niger can only be tentatively reconstructed. However, archaeologists active in the region in recent decades, especially Roderick and Susan McIntosh, have argued consistently that the complex early civilization of the region was organized "heterarchically." The Inland Niger Delta, if we accept their claims, had its own distinctive traditions of egalitarianism and institutionalized mechanisms for checking the growth of inequality.

Although this chapter has been concerned chiefly with the urban phases of occupation in the delta (after c. 250 BCE)—along with their relationship to less sedentary warrior elites and tribute-takers—it was arguably during the early periods following the mid-Holocene warm, humid phase that the foundations for a politics of heterarchy were laid. This was likely linked to environmental factors: from the late millennia BCE onwards, the region was home to an unpredictable ecological mosaic of river channels, alluvium, and swampland, encouraging the emergence of an array of interdependent subsistence strategies and fluid political formations (R. McIntosh 1998, 2005; Stahl 2004). The first millennium CE brought the "golden age" of heterarchical urban complexity on the Middle Niger floodplain, with long-term trends towards increasing economic specialization and denser trade networks (MacDonald 2013; R. McIntosh 2005). After around 800 CE, the region witnessed a general shift towards more hierarchical and coercive forms of political organization (Stahl 2004). This process intensified in the 1100–1500 CE period of arid conditions, in which equestrian warrior elites drawing on both Mande and Islamic sources of legitimacy expanded their influence over much of the western Sahel.

The Middle Niger's historical trajectory is therefore hard to square with Axial Age schemas, which tend to posit an initial, despotic phase of civilization before an eruption of egalitarian thought and universalizing morality, keyed to the mid-first millennium BCE in China, India, Iran, the Levant, and Greece, then a gradual diffusion of these developments to other regions. The existence of an initial, archaic phase of domination by an oppressive ruling elite is not supported by the archaeological evidence from the Inland Niger Delta. Perhaps most problematic is the fact that the arrival of Islam, viewed by Axial Age theorists as a late-flowering product of the axial ideologies of the last millennium BCE—one of the "secondary breakthroughs" (Eisenstadt 1986c: xii)—in fact seems to have accompanied a *rise* in inequality and a growth in various forms of bonded labor across the Sahel. Overall, then, the changing political and ideological landscape of the Middle Niger between around 1000 BCE and 1400 CE provides meager support for Axial Age theories.

SOUTH AMERICA | Highland Peru

Dennis Spencer & R. Alan Covey*

Period	Approx. dates
Late Archaic Period	5000–2200 BCE
Formative Period	2200–450
Late Formative Period	450 BCE–200 CE
Early Intermediate Period	200–650
Middle Horizon	650–1000
Late Intermediate Period	1000–1400
Inca Empire	1400–1532
Spanish Empire, Habsburg Dynasty	1532–1700

Table 11. Periods and polities mentioned in text that were based in or that occupied Highland Peru

Introduction

The Cuzco region, located in what is today southern Peru, was the homeland of the Incas, who built the largest empire in the pre-Columbian Americas. At its peak, the Inca Empire (called Tawantinsuyu, "the four parts together," in Quechua) held somewhere between 6 and 14 million people, with an estimated 20,000 people living in the capital of Cuzco (N. D. Cook 2004). The Cuzco Valley lies in a mountainous region, with the snow-capped Ausangate peak visible from the Cuzco Basin, and the Verónica and Sahuasiray peaks found nearby. Nestled between these steep natural barriers lies the Cuzco Basin itself, an impression left by an ancient lake bed: an advantageous setting both in defensive terms and also as a hub for contacts between the surrounding mountains with neighboring settlements in nearly every direction. The Cuzco Valley floor was heavily cultivated from the Formative Period, and agricultural terraces further increased the area in which food could be grown (Bauer 2004: 66, 77). Maize in particular was an extremely important crop for the inhabitants of the region. The stone walls of terraces absorbed heat during the day and released it at night, protecting the maize from the frosts that occur at high altitudes (McEwan 2006: 123).

The earliest populations of the Cuzco region (8000–5000 BCE) were nomadic hunter-gatherers, but the transition to sedentary lifestyles began during what is known as the Late Archaic period (5000–2200 BCE) (Bauer 2004: 37). The

---

* Agathe Dupeyron also contributed to this chapter by reading and providing feedback on previous drafts.

domestication of key crops (e.g. maize, potato, quinoa) and animals (llama, alpaca, guinea pig) was mostly complete by around 2000 BCE, although it is likely that maize did not become an important staple food in the Cuzco Valley until about 2,000 years later (Kuznar 2001; Moseley and Heckenberger 2013: 648).As agriculture became more important in the Cuzco region, settlements became permanent and expanded. Several polities arose during the first millennium, most notably the Wari and the Tiwanaku states. Both extended their control over new populations around the seventh century CE, although we do not know exactly what motivated this expansion (Isbell 2008). The Wari were the more successful of the two, owing largely to their canal-fed terrace systems, which were easier to transplant to new colonies. By using terrace farming, the Wari were able to use water far more intensively than other polities in the Andean highlands, and this advantage increased when drought struck (Williams 2002). Both polities continued to control large areas until around the tenth century.

By the end of the seventh century CE, Wari influence extended over a wide swath of the modern Peruvian highlands and a few coastal areas, evidenced by material culture such as pottery styles and funerary remains. However, the form and extent of Wari control over the communities of the region is hotly debated. Wari has been characterized by some scholars (e.g. Isbell 1991; Isbell and Schreiber 1978; Schreiber 1992) as a large, centralized state or empire. Schreiber (1992) coined the term "mosaic of control" to refer to the variety of ruling strategies—from direct administration to indirect control via local elites—that she discerned in the archaeological record of the Middle Horizon. Others assert that it was a much smaller polity, centered on the great city of Wari in the Ayacucho Valley and exerting only loose control or cultural influence beyond its heartland (Covey et al. 2013: 549–50; Jennings 2010). They point out that there were large areas where Wari influence was negligible, even in some places over which the state might have claimed authority. Areas surrounding planned Wari architectural complexes, such as Pikillacta in the Cuzco region, might have been under direct Wari control, but other regions that traded occasionally for Wari pottery and textiles were home to independent polities whose rulers cooperated with Wari colonists and state representatives, or to sparsely scattered village communities that lacked political hierarchies. Beyond the Ayacucho Valley and their scattered enclaves throughout the Central Andes, the Wari appear to have built power through trade, forging ties with the elites of other societies through gifts, exchanges, and marriage alliances. It was likely a combination of drought and internal conflict that broke up the Wari state around the eleventh or twelfth century (Finucane et al. 2007). Population estimates for the city of Wari at its peak range from 20,000 (McEwan and Williams 2012: 67) all the way to 70,000 people (Isbell 1997: 186), but figures for the total population of the state are more difficult to produce due to scholarly disagreements about what constituted "Wari rule."

The collapse of Wari and Tiwanaku left a power vacuum in the Andean highlands. The unpredictable and more arid climate after 1000 CE meant that any polity able to grow food more efficiently had a major competitive advantage. One such group emerged in the central highlands, where the Incas were able to extend control over productive valley-bottom lands that they terraced and irrigated. What brought the Incas to power was not a sudden or dramatic technological transformation—rather, Inca agricultural intensification projects gradually drew new settlers to the Cuzco Basin, and rulers began to dominate their neighbors and improve lands in surrounding valleys. Over a century or so, the Incas built alliances and carried out conquests that brought most of the Cuzco region under their control. By 1400 CE, they were engaged in campaigns of imperial expansion beyond the Cuzco region and, in just over a century, they extended their dominion as far north as southern Colombia as well as south into what is today central Chile and north-west Argentina (Covey 2006).

By the early sixteenth century, the Inca Empire dominated the Central Andes, stretching from present-day southern Colombia to central Chile (D'Altroy 2014). But from the 1520s onwards, the European presence to the north, in Central America, triggered a series of devastating epidemics—of smallpox, measles, bubonic plague, and other diseases—in Inca lands (Alchon 2003: 75–76). Among the casualties was the emperor Huayna Capac, who died unexpectedly as he was campaigning on the northern frontier in 1528 (J. H. Rowe 2006: 2). Internal tensions among the Inca nobility then erupted in a civil war, from which Atahuallpa, one of Huayna Capac's sons, emerged victorious (2–3). However, in 1532, the conquistador Francisco Pizarro led a small force of Spaniards into the Andes, captured Atahuallpa, and later had him publicly executed (D'Altroy 2014: 107). The conquerors slowly consolidated their power in the Andes with the aid of Inca nobles willing to ally with the Spanish as client kings. While the Spanish certainly faced resistance, such as the rebellion led by Manco Inca in 1536–37 (Lamana 2008: 125), they eventually succeeded in laying claim to the territory of the Inca Empire.

Universalizing morality, egalitarian ethics, and social mobility

In this section, we examine the evidence for and against the development of universalizing religion, egalitarian ideologies, and social mobility—all facets of "axial" transformations identified in the literature on the Axial Age—in the Central Andes. The absence of written records means that the development of the religious beliefs and practices of pre-Columbian cultures here must be reconstructed through a combination of archaeological evidence, iconographic analysis, and knowledge of later, historic-period societies. Complementarity and reciprocity emerge as key themes in Andean ideology, though without the same universalizing and equity-promoting features that most Axial Age proponents assert accompanied transformations in

Eurasia. With the additional caveat in mind that scholars' understanding of ancient Andean worldviews is partial, there are few indications of strongly universalizing, moralizing religion or ideological support for equality in the region's history.

Tiwanaku and Wari material culture has some key iconographic motifs in common, in particular a figure known as the "Staff Deity." This motif, which depicts an individual seen frontally and grasping a staff in each hand, has deep roots in the Andes, appearing in the artwork of the Early Horizon Chavín culture (c. 900–200 BCE) as well as the still older Norte Chico civilization (c. 2600–2000 BCE) of the Late Archaic desert coast (Cook 2012; Haas and Creamer 2004: 46–49). During the Middle Horizon, c. 650–1000 CE, a cluster of images composed of the Staff Deity, a "Rayed Head," and attendants viewed in profile spread throughout both the Wari and Tiwanaku spheres, from the northern Peruvian coast to northern Argentina. Isbell (2008: 732–34) has suggested that together they "represent the ideological core of a new religion." This visual language crops up in varied contexts across the Middle Horizon Andes; interestingly, however, localized architectural styles and ritual practices were maintained beyond the Tiwanaku and Wari core areas. For instance, Véronique Bélisle (2011: 222; 2019) has identified local ceremonial architecture at Ak'awillay in the Cuzco region, as well as the use of hallucinogenic snuff in ways that differed from both Tiwanaku and Wari practices.

Does the proliferation of Staff Deity and Rayed Head imagery in the first millennium CE amount to evidence of a universalizing, moralizing religion in the pre-Columbian Andes? Certainly there was widespread participation, as shown by signs of large-scale feasting at Tiwanaku and the Wari sites of Pikillacta, Conchopata, and Wari itself (Berryman 2010; Cook and Glowacki 2002: 184–86; McEwan and Williams 2012: 71), as well as by the imitation of Wari and Tiwanaku material culture far beyond the heartlands of these two states. Delaere et al. (2019: 8234) have noted that the fierce, fanged Staff Deity, staring out frontally at the viewer, "could support the notion of a supernatural punisher." However, it is unclear whether this supernatural power was concerned with human behavior, or was revered—and perhaps feared—for holding power over vital aspects of the agricultural cycle, such as rainfall. Further, at least in the case of the Wari, who had a much stronger presence in the Cuzco region than the Tiwanaku state, the ethical system emphasized respect for the increasingly institutionalized social hierarchies of the period, not any universalizing precepts. Wari iconography features many scenes of political domination and ritualized violence, interpreted by Anita G. Cook (2004) as expressions of an elite seeking to legitimize its position. Ritual activities linked to human sacrifice and the taking of trophy heads also took place in D-shaped temples, which are found in the Ayacucho Valley and, more rarely, elsewhere in the Wari sphere of influence (McEwan and Williams 2012: 67). For instance, at Conchopata in the polity's heartland, 31 trophy heads prepared from recently deceased adults, many showing cranial injuries, were found inside a D-shaped structure along with finely decorated pottery and sacrificed camelids (Tung 2014: 246). Isotope analysis showed that the sacrificed individuals were not local to the region (246). One possible interpretation of these remains is that the ceremonies in D-shaped structures entailed the symbolic subjugation of defeated enemies. Monumental architecture in both the capital and the provinces also shows a concern with controlling and restricting access, perhaps indicating the presence of a priestly elite (Schreiber 2001: 92).

Overall, the florescence of art and ritual in the Middle Horizon appears to have served the ideological purposes of the elites of the Tiwanaku and Wari states, who may have positioned themselves as intermediaries between the general population and sources of supernatural power (e.g. Delaere et al. 2019; McEwan and Williams 2012). They were not always successful; in the Cuzco Valley, the abandonment of the Wari administrative complex of Pikillacta after c. 900 CE was accompanied by widespread burning, hinting at local resistance to Wari imperial ideology and attempts to extract labor and tribute from local populations (Bauer 2004: 68). The city of Wari itself may also have been sacked around 1100 CE (González-Carré et al. 1997: 90–99). It is possible that egalitarian or at least anti-hierarchical schools of thought found expression among the subject populations of the Middle Horizon Central Andes, but in the absence of written evidence this is hard to confirm.

After the collapse of the Wari state and its withdrawal from the Cuzco region, the Inca polity emerged slowly, consolidating fragmented small polities and ethnic groups into a larger political entity. Much more is known about Andean religion, morality, and political thought during the period of Inca dominance, thanks in large part to the chronicles compiled in the early years of the Spanish colonial period. Inca ritual practice, in common with other historic Andean societies, centered on sacred natural phenomena such as bodies of water and mountains, known as *wak'a* (Hispanicized as *huaca*) (D'Altroy 2014: 248; Jennings 2003). Other *wak'a* were associated with the resting places of their ancestors, the veneration of whom was the other major tenet of Andean religion. Some of these *wak'a*, known as *paqarina* (or *pacarina*), were believed to be the origin points of different groups. For example, Lake Titicaca features in many Andean myths as the site of the creation of humankind by the god Viracocha. Lakes, mountains, and springs elsewhere mark the places where humans emerged after Viracocha caused them to disperse (Bray 2013: 165). Andean societies associated with these sites would honor their ancestors through offerings. Further, if a group of people was relocated from one region to another, as happened occasionally, the relocated people would generate a new *paqarina* by taking something from the old *paqarina*, like a small amount of water, and pouring it into the new site. This helped to ensure the spiritual grounding for the new settlement (Sherbondy 1992: 56–57).

Wak'a and *paqarina* were the links that connected the entire Central Andean religious system, in which death and water created a cycle of creation and renewal

(Glowacki and Malpass 2003; Jennings 2003). In this cycle, vitality flowed throughout the earth and sky, mediated and controlled by a range of supernatural forces (Jennings 2003). For Central Andean people, the performance of rituals was a way of showing respect to such forces, with whom they were engaged in ongoing reciprocal relationships. Everyday reverence was met with the conditions (such as sunlight and favorable weather) needed to live in the Andes, while failure to make the obligatory reverence disrupted those cycles. Many rituals, mostly performed near wak'a, sought to feed the ancestors and other powerful beings through offerings including chicha (maize beer) and coca leaves (Jennings 2003). These offerings maintained the relationships between the living and the dead and legitimized a settlement's right to land and water (Bray 2013). Reciprocity was vital for everyday kin-based interactions. Poverty was defined not merely by a lack of material goods, but by a weak network of kin and allies who could share labor and food. When workers were called up for military duty and other forms of service, their relatives would tend to their fields and store their produce. Members of the same community would also assist people who could not support themselves, such as the sick or elderly without family. A household consisting of a large extended family could be far more productive than a smaller one, incentivizing dense webs of social relations among Andean populations (D'Altroy 2014). In terms of gender relations, too, Andean societies have historically tended to view men and women as complementary parts of a whole, rather than positing a strict hierarchy. Men and women existed in clearly defined but parallel spheres, and it was their joining that was necessary to bring about creative acts, such as house-building, farming, herding, and child-rearing. This concept is further illustrated by Inca concepts of parallel descent; men traced their descent through the male line, while women traced theirs back through their mothers (Powers 2000).

The relationship between the general population and local nobles also entailed mutual, reciprocal obligations and some prosocial activity on the part of the Inca state and elite. In return for agricultural labor and military service (a rotational corvée system called the mit'a in Quechua), the Andean nobility sponsored ceremonial feasts in which peasant communities participated. There was also an expectation that the Inca would provide the necessary tools and supplies, and would feed workers while they carried out these tasks. This meant that imperial labor service guaranteed a period of food security, eating state food rations from storehouses. Moreover, though the Inca state did not have explicitly defined, institutionalized responsibilities towards its subjects, it did provide public goods such as irrigation and stored food that could be distributed in times of scarcity (Bauer and Covey 2002: 851–52; D'Altroy and Hastorf 1984). In addition, charitable behavior was a key aspect of the self-representation of Inca royalty, who adopted the title waqchakuyaq, or "Lover and Benefactor of the Poor" (D'Altroy 2014: 179). On the other hand, we have very little evidence of egalitarian institutions or ideological support for equality in the Inca Empire. There were clear distinctions between commoners and the elite. While individual bravery and achievement were generously rewarded, the nature of the reward granted was very different based on the social status of the individual (D'Altroy 2014: 349). Additionally, the elite rarely faced consequences for crimes unless they had committed a particularly offensive act and even then, nobles would be disciplined far less severely than commoners.

Likewise, social mobility was largely absent in Inca society, although the elites of ethnic groups in the Cuzco region who showed loyalty to the Inca state were named Incas by privilege, thereby increasing their status (Malpass 2009: 34; Yaya 2008: 51). The only other clear case of social mobility was through the female *aqllawasi* system, in which provincial girls were selected to live in cloistered quarters and be trained for religious service. Elite status was hereditary and when an official died the most qualified adult male in the family was chosen to succeed him (D'Altroy 2014). Ethnicity was also a powerful organizing principle throughout the empire. Governors were usually ethnic Incas. For the most part, though, the emphasis on ethnic identity (Incas versus other Andean groups) restricted major status changes. The Incas required the various groups under their rule to dress in ways that signaled their specific ethnic identities, for example through different styles of headdress (Urton 2015: 130). Nor did they attempt to supplant local forms of ritual practice among the populations they ruled. Instead, they became patrons of the cult activities dedicated to powerful entities in local landscapes as well as at regional pilgrimage destinations, which people visited to consult oracles or celebrate the creation of the universe.

In this respect, Inca ruling strategies contrast sharply with those of the Spanish conquerors who arrived in the early sixteenth century. Whereas the Inca layered the state ideology over the beliefs and practices of subject populations without seeking to replace them, the Spanish viewed *wak'a* as diabolical and attempted to find and destroy them. As part of a concerted effort towards the "extirpation of idolatry" (de Arriaga [1621] 2015), they tried to prevent Andean people bringing *wak'a* into Christian ceremonies and were at pains in printed confessional manuals to delineate the difference between *wak'a* worship and veneration of saintly images. These new rulers, then—professing a faith descended from the "axial" ideologies of classical Judaic and Greek societies[1]—attempted to impose a kind of universalizing morality on Andean societies, one that was intolerant of pre-existing traditions.

One further aspect of pre-Columbian Andean ritual practice that remains to be addressed here—a subject of debate for Spanish, mestizo, and indigenous chroniclers—is human sacrifice. This has been viewed in some Axial Age discussions as a classically "archaic" or "pre-axial" trait, an expression of extreme social inequality (e.g. Bellah 2011: 213, 503–04). We know that ritual killing of various forms took place

---

1   See the chapters on the Levant and Mediterranean Basin in this volume for further details.

in Wari and in many other pre-Inca polities, such as the coastal Moche and Chimú, and continued—albeit only on rare occasions—under the Inca. Head-taking and the sacrifice of defeated enemies was practiced by the Wari elite class and does appear to have served as an expression of dominance (Tung and Knudson 2010; see discussion above). In the Inca Empire, boys and girls were chosen for their purity, killed and dedicated to the Sun, the emperor, or military victory. Prisoners of war were also sometimes offered up to honor the Sun and symbolize Inca power (D'Altroy 2014: 277). Events such as earthquakes, eclipses, and epidemics would call for sacrifices too, and momentous events such as the death of a ruler led to sacrifices that could number in the thousands (277). We do not know exactly why Inca ideology called for sacrifice, but Spanish chroniclers wrote that the intent was to ensure that the best of humanity would join the Creator, the Sun, deceased rulers, and other deities (277). Some forms of Inca sacrifice, such as the ceremonies referred to as *qhapaq ucha*, were viewed as a great honor. This is evident from the rich regalia in which child victims were dressed, the litters used to carry them, and the special status bestowed on their parents (Benson 2001: 18; D'Altroy 2014: 277–79). We should also bear in mind that Andean people seem to have conceived of death not as an abrupt end to life, but as a transition to another mode of being; in one case described by a Spanish "extirpator," Rodrigo Hernández Principe, a girl from the coast was ritually killed and became a revered "goddess" (Benson 2001: 18–19). It may be oversimplifying, then, to view all Inca human sacrifice as a demonstration of the absolute power of the elite over the social strata from which the sacrifices were drawn. Similarly, Bellah's and other Axial Age theorists' consignment of sacrificial rites and cannibalism to an archaic, pre-axial past appears to gloss over the central scene of sacrifice at the heart of Christianity, along with the ritual consumption of human flesh during the Eucharist—quite literally in the case of Christians who believe in transubstantiation.

The lack of written sources for the pre-Inca period means that the kind of analysis conducted by Axial Age proponents for ancient Afro-Eurasian societies, tracing the historical development of certain beliefs and attitudes, is not possible here. Some Andean specialists believe that the ethical system and the conceptions of the sacred documented in the Inca chronicles and later Andean ethnography originate much further back in time. For instance, Glowacki and Malpass (2003) suggest that the Wari (like the Incas) also venerated *wak'a*. Providing aid to others within one's *ayllu*—an expansive concept that can refer to a family occupying a single household at the smallest scale and to an entire ethnic group at the largest—is vital in today's highland Andean communities, and Albarracín-Jordán (1996) has argued that this type of social unit, with its accompanying ritual and moral obligations, was also present in prehistoric contexts such as the Tiwanaku Valley during the Middle Horizon. However, the presence of Wari *wak'a* or pre-Inca *ayllu* remains a matter of debate, and there is a risk of circular argument here: using Inca chronicles to inform our understanding of pre-Inca societies, and then, on that basis, positing ancient origins for many historically attested Inca practices. Ultimately, it is difficult to trace the long-term development of moral and political thought in the Central Andes with any temporal precision.

Historical records make possible more fine-grained accounts of the development of political and religious thought after the Spanish Conquest. For instance, MacCormack (1988) has argued that the events of the sixteenth century and the introduction of Christian ideas of the Last Judgment led Andeans to elaborate the indigenous concept of *pachacuti*, referring to a great upheaval in the "established order" and the dawn of a new era. Before Spanish contact, Inca historical myth was relatively shallow, not needing to delve back more than 200 years or so to claim greater ancestral authority than any of their potential rivals. But in contact with Spanish expressions of universal history along a biblical chronology that clearly predated the deepest reach of Andean oral histories, the Inca elite began to rework their founding myths. The semi-legendary "first Inca," Manco Capac, became enshrined in the writings of chroniclers like the Inca Garcilaso de la Vega as an Inca cultural hero—founder of Cuzco, lawmaker, and originator of a new way of organizing society. The later royal ancestor Pachacuti Inca Yupanqui played a similar role, becoming a figure credited with establishing new rituals and institutions of law and order (MacCormack 1988). The renewed focus in colonial Andean society on mythic ancestors, coupled with the anticipation of future upheavals effected by messiah-like figures, may be interpreted as a shift towards the morally charged view of history and the eschatological outlook of the Judeo-Christian tradition. In fact, many Inca nobles converted to Christianity very soon after Spanish contact, even before they began to share oral histories with Spaniards: the chronicles are far from "pristine" expressions of pre-Columbian thought. A concern with the workings of the divine through human history features in discussions of the Levant's axial transformation in the last millennium BCE (e.g. Assmann 1990; Uffenheimer 1986; see the chapters on the Levant and Anatolia in this volume). However, these currents of thought have indigenous Andean precedents too, in the form of the *pachacuti* concept, and we should be aware of the way Christianity and European views of history were transformed by Andean people in the light of their own experiences and worldviews.

In the economic sphere, labor obligations owed by Andean populations to their rulers also underwent a transformation in the wake of the conquest. Inca labor tribute was replaced by the colonial *encomienda* system, which took the form of royal grants permitting the Spanish recipient (the *encomendero*) to receive labor and goods from a specified group of indigenous people. This was justified through the conceit that the *encomendero* had a responsibility to transmit Christian doctrine to the population of his *encomienda*, in return for which they gave him food from their lands and labor in his house and fields. The *encomenderos* used Inca human capital to gain significant political and economic power, with much of that money going back to the Spanish Crown in taxes. While they had the rights to the output of their *encomiendas*, the indigenous people were not their slaves, at least in the sense of chattel ownership. In practice, though, these relationships were coercive and exploitative; the demographic decline triggered by Old World diseases exacerbated Spanish pressure for tribute from the surviving Andean peasants, many of whom went into debt to meet these demands (N. D. Cook 2004: 76; Davies 1984: 23–26). From the 1570s CE, men were conscripted from hundreds of Andean communities to work in the mercury mines of Huancavelica and the silver mines of Potosí, in dire conditions that killed or maimed countless workers (Dell 2010; Robins 2011: 177–95).

It is clear that the arrival of the Spanish, inheritors of a "post-axial" tradition who justified their presence in the New World largely as part of a civilizing mission, resulted in increasingly unequal social structures and exploitative labor relations; the opposite of the trajectory predicted by Axial Age theories.

Rulership, the law, and institutions of authority

In this section, we review the evidence for the development of rulership—in ideology and practice—and governing institutions in the Central Andes, focusing on the better-documented Inca period.

There is good archaeological evidence for the emergence of rulers in this region over a long time period. Already during the Initial Period (c. 1800–900 BCE) and Early Horizon (c. 900–200 BCE), large-scale monumental sacred architecture suggests the presence of authorities capable of directing labor, and iconography depicts a range of supernatural beings: "strange deity-like animals or human-animal combinations" (Kembel and Rick 2004: 57). Kembel and Rick (2004: 54) suggest that rulership in this period was "theocratic," perhaps consisting of priestly elite groups based at centers like Chavín de Huántar and Kuntur Wasi, both highland sites. Similarly, the elaborate craftwork and iconographies of the complex Andean polities of the first millennium CE, including Wari and Tiwanaku, are often seen as a product of elite attempts to justify their privileged positions and lend themselves supernaturally-derived legitimacy (A. G. Cook 2004; Nash 2018). From its earliest appearance, then, authority in the Central Andes appears to have had a sacred basis. Indications of "despotic" authority are few and far between, however. The control of pre-Inca Central Andean rulers over their territories was generally fragile and weakly institutionalized (Earle and Jennings 2012: 218). Soft-power strategies, such as diplomatic marriages and the distribution of finely crafted artworks to local elites in exchange for loyalty and political service, were important. Even during periods of greater regional integration, like the Early and Middle Horizons, areas and communities beyond the centers of power moved in and out of central state control.

We can be more specific about Inca political organization. At the top of the hierarchy stood the king, known as the *Sapa Inca*, and his wife, the *Qoya*. They were believed to be descendants of the Sun and the royal ancestors, and royal mummies continued to be revered as *wak'a* even after their deaths (D'Altroy 2014). In Inca cosmology, the *Sapa Inca* occupied the center of the universe, serving as the mediator between the human and supernatural worlds, the living and the dead. He arrogated to himself the authority to summon his subjects, transform them, and define their labor obligations (Acuto 2012; Covey 2012). In practice, though, the imperial government had little direct presence in the everyday lives of the inhabitants of Tawantinsuyu. Noble Incas and local chiefs served as intermediaries between their communities and the central government. Although there were few formal constraints on the *Sapa Inca's* power, Cuzco's royal kin groups, known as *panaqa*, still wielded major political influence, including—so they claimed—the ability to raise or depose an emperor. *Panaqa* were corporate descent groups formed by the lifelong union of a king and queen, who carried out the acts of ancestral creation that produced offspring and transformed resources into an estate that could be passed on to that group after the pair's death. Inheritance in Inca society followed a split model, meaning that while the powers of the ruling couple passed directly to their heirs, their possessions and lands were transferred collectively to their *panaqa* (Conrad 1981; D'Altroy 2014: 177). Members of the *panaqa* managed their dead ancestors' property and used that property to care for their mummies and maintain their cult. However, because the dead king and queen's lands were given to their *panaqa* in perpetuity, the land would be lost to future administrations.

The power of the *Sapa Inca* was also counterbalanced by that of his wife, the *Qoya*, and the hierarchy of religious officials that she headed. Women dominated the priesthood and oversaw the production of festive foods and drink that reciprocated labor service, as well as the production of cloth and footwear for royal gifts and for the use of the military. The *Qoya* also ruled when the *Sapa Inca* was away on military campaigns, and during their expansion the Incas incorporated several Andean polities that were ruled by women into their empire, giving them the same rights as male rulers (Powers 2000: 512–13). Here we see that the Andean complementary relationship between men and women was also expressed in the upper reaches of the political hierarchy. Men occupied the highest-status official positions, but their female relatives enjoyed considerable scope for political action and influence. Under Spanish colonial rule, there was an overall shift towards more unequal gender relations in the Andes as women were excluded from holding public office and subjected to restrictions intended to preserve their chastity (Graubart 2007: 99; Powers 2002). The change was particularly marked in the religious sphere with the replacement of Andean ritual offices with an exclusively male Catholic priesthood. Axial Age theories often overlook this form of inequality—unequal access to ritual participation, training, and knowledge on the basis of gender—and in this case it is clear that the arrival (by force) of an "axial tradition" in the Andes constricted the range of such opportunities open to women.

Another proposed feature of "axial" transformations is the emergence of impersonal, rule-based bureaucratic structures and institutions that ensure the accountability of rulers. For instance, Shmuel Eisenstadt (1986b: 8) claimed that during the Axial Age "there began to develop autonomous spheres of law and conceptions of rights" in the eastern Mediterranean, Iran, India, and China. While political power in the Inca Empire remained highly personalized throughout its history (D'Altroy 2014: 463), there is some evidence for moves towards procedural checks on the activities of those in official positions. According to the sixteenth-century chronicler Juan de Betanzos (1996), the emperor held a yearly assembly to review the moral behavior of the Incas in the capital. In the provinces, representatives of the emperor oversaw the punishment of serious crimes, while local leaders could address minor lapses of custom. Nevertheless, there was no formal body of laws or independent judiciary (D'Altroy 2014: 358). Inca law was largely restricted to managing Cuzco and maintaining Inca control and protecting the elite's interests in the empire's provinces. Local legal customs were usually maintained in provincial areas.

The Inca Empire thus does not fit neatly into historical schemes developed for application to Eurasian states. Eisenstadt's arguments, which represent impersonal bureaucracies as a kind of developmental milestone, can be traced back to Max Weber's theories about the state and even further to Aristotle's *Politics* (Covey 2015). They face difficulties when applied to the Inca Empire because political power here flowed primarily via kinship networks. The Incas used polygyny to build the power of the palace, generating hundreds of royal sons and daughters who would grow up to serve as state officials directly representing the ruling couple in encounters with local officials who represented their own polities or kin networks. The Weberian concept of a shift from kin-based social structures towards civic modes of political organization, thought to characterize state-level societies, does not account for the variability of states as they have emerged beyond the broad band of land stretching from western to eastern Eurasia.

As mentioned repeatedly above, Spanish presence in the region brought many social and ideological changes to Andean society, though rarely in the ways anticipated by Axial Age theories or other models developed in exclusively Eurasian contexts. Spanish colonial rule was at once sharply hierarchical and diffuse and decentralized (A. A. Alves, pers. comm. 2018). The Habsburg king sat atop a well-defined, institutionalized layer of military, economic, religious, and political administration, though his authority was constrained at least somewhat by both papal decree[2] and court councils. With its clear legal limits on executive power and diffused decision-making,

---

2   The actual power of the Church *vis-à-vis* the Crown was, however, complex. In large part, Spanish rulers were able to ensure their interests were supported, as with the appointment of chosen bishops, or the religious authority granted to Spanish colonial officials. See e.g. McAlister 1984.

Habsburg-ruled Spain exemplifies the political organization of post-axial systems, and this regularity was exported to their American holdings as well. In the Andes, this took place from the 1540s onwards, as the chaotic and violent rule of the conquistadors gave way to a more stable and bureaucratic government answerable to the Crown (D'Altroy 2014: 468). This strong, centralized but constrained power, however, was at least partly offset by the authority given to the colonial *audiencias* (royal courts) and especially the viceroys who ruled Spain's overseas holdings largely unfettered as the king's representative (Elliott 1987). There was also an inherent tension between the secular and religious authority of colonial officials, whose conflicting interests had to be managed by the viceroy and other state officials, frustrating any attempts at strong central oversight (Elliott 2006).

Despite arguments that axial transformations decreased rulers' reliance on supernatural or religious bases of authority (e.g. Bellah 2011; Eisenstadt 2005), Habsburg kings certainly deployed their connection to and upholding of Catholic ideals to legitimate their rule (Maltby 2009). Nor was this merely a cynical attempt to justify their positions: King Philip II (r. 1556–98) built El Escorial, a palatial complex close to Madrid, to reproduce the Temple of Jerusalem, and tried to collect relics of all the Catholic saints—he ended up with more than 7,000, which he laid on his body when he felt pain. In Europe, Charles V, Philip II, and Philip III were all associated with medieval Joachimite prophecies about the Last World Emperor, who would bring about the last millennium before the world's end. It was partly these fervent beliefs in the fulfillment of prophecy and the need to win souls for Christ that motivated Spanish colonization of the Central Andes. But whatever the Spaniards' intentions may have been for the souls of Andeans, their rule in the Americas was undeniably exploitative (for instance through the *encomiendas*), and led to drastic demographic collapse and the transformation or destruction of older social and religious practices. In the decades after the arrival of Pizarro and his men, in the course of institutionalizing colonial rule in the Andes, Incas and others were reduced to the racialized category of "Indian" and portrayed as uncivilized. This served to rationalize the distinct inequities both within the Viceroyalty of Peru and between the European imperial core and its possessions.

Conclusion

Central Andean societies are rarely discussed in terms of axiality, but they can serve as an interesting counterpoint to the patterns that emerged in Afro-Eurasia, exposing the limits of Eurasian-centric concepts of ideology and rulership for understanding developments in other parts of the world.[3] Overall, there is no sign of anything like

---

3   This is underscored by the complex pictures of "axiality" that emerge from other chapters in this volume—those on the Inland Niger Delta, Hawai'i, and the Mississippi Valley as well as the Late Complexity Survey.

an "axial" transition in Andean history. There were strict hierarchies, inegalitarian institutions, a lack of social mobility, and (as far as we are aware) no strongly moralizing, equality-promoting deities throughout the period examined in this chapter. Most of these traits, which feature in Axial Age discussions as key markers of "archaic" or pre-axial societies, in fact became more pronounced as the Incas expanded their empire. This is noteworthy, as it might be expected that a large, powerful, territorially expansive empire like that of the Incas would have produced something akin to an axial transition in the way that the imperial formations across Afro-Eurasia are said to (though see the rest of this volume for discussions that complicate this picture).

Evidence of truly egalitarian ideologies or institutions is virtually absent for this region, then, but the question of universalizing morality is less settled. Certainly, shared cultural norms can be identified across a broad geographical region. Late prehistoric and historic Andean social relations were structured by notions of balance and reciprocity that were ethical as much as they were cosmological, carrying with them responsibilities towards the land and one's living and deceased kin (McEwan and Williams 2012: 80; Silverman 2004: 5). Accounts of axiality based narrowly on the rise of explicitly moralizing Eurasian religions such as Judaism and Buddhism thus encounter problems in theorizing the pre-Columbian belief systems of Andean communities, whose morality was no less real for being entangled with cosmology and ecology. As the anthropologist Catherine Allen (2015: 27) has commented, "matter and morality are inseparable aspects of each other" for Andean societies.

The Spanish did not bring to the Peruvian highlands anything like an "axial awakening"—a universalizing moral order that included constraints on rulers and equitable social mores—as anticipated by the idea of an Axial Age of global extent. Yet their presence certainly deeply influenced Andean culture and society. The critical questions, namely *why* in most respects an axial turn failed to take place in Peru, and why the arrival of the Spanish and their Christian doctrines inspired new forms of historical mythologizing but not new calls for universalism or more egalitarian and limited forms of rule, must remain matters for future discussion. Another key issue raised by this chapter concerns how "post-axial" societies such as Habsburg Spain balanced an ethos of egalitarianism in limited parts of their faith communities with the promotion of gender inequality and slavery on an unprecedented scale for others: namely, non-believers and those defined as racial others.

NORTH AMERICA | Mississippi Valley

Jill Levine & Peter N. Peregrine

Period	Polity	Approx. dates
Woodland	Early Woodland	600–150 BCE
	Middle Woodland	150 BCE–300 CE
	Late Woodland, Rosewood	300–450
	Late Woodland, Mund	450–600
	Late Woodland, Patrick	600–750
Mississippian	Emergent Mississippian, Sponemann–Collinsville–Loyd	750–900
	Emergent Mississippian, Merrell–Edelhardt	900–1050
	Middle Mississippian, Lohmann–Stirling	1050–1200
	Mississippian, Moorehead	1200–1275
	Mississippian, Sand Prairie	1275–1400
Protohistoric	Oneota	1400–1640
Post-Contact	Illinois Confederation / Illiniwek Nation	1640–1778

Table 12. Periods and dates mentioned in text

Introduction

The region known as the American Bottom is located near the confluence of the Mississippi and Missouri Rivers, east of modern St. Louis, Illinois. Archaeologists have defined several distinct phases in its prehistory, and Karl Jaspers' Axial Age, c. 800–200 BCE, coincides with the Early Woodland (600–150 BCE) and Middle Woodland (150 BCE–300 CE) periods. The Woodland cultures had no known contact with any Eurasian "world religion" in this period. While Woodland settlements were generally egalitarian, the succeeding Emergent Mississippian period, characterized by intensified cultivation, has produced evidence of low-level social hierarchy. The ancient city of Cahokia dominated the region in the eleventh and twelfth centuries CE, during which time archaeological evidence shows a remarkable level of complexity and organization. After the decline of Cahokia, the people of the American Bottom lived in smaller settlements that do not appear to have been integrated into large-scale polities. In this chapter, we will trace the rise and fall of social complexity in the American Bottom, attempting to piece together the prevailing religious and ideological systems underpinning these complex social formations using archaeological and historical evidence and looking for signs of an "axial transition."

Historical and ideological background

The Early Woodland societies in North America emerged from Late Archaic culture. The Late Archaic peoples of the American Bottom were hunter-gatherers who settled on the Mississippi floodplain and began to cultivate food crops (McElrath et al. 2009: 364–66). Late Archaic settlements included domestic structures, pits, and possible food storage sites. Archaic and Woodland peoples both constructed large mounds for ceremonial and burial purposes.

The Early Woodland in the American Bottom has been divided into three phases: Carr Creek, Florence, and Ringering (Kelly 2002: 138). Woodland settlements featured "hearths, pits and refuse areas" (141). Burials, some in earthen mounds, were accompanied by rituals involving the use of red ocher (Hunter 2001: 84). Archaeologists have found evidence for the cultivation of little barley, maygrass, goosefoots and squash (Kelly 2002: 142). Hunting, fishing, and gathering were also important for subsistence in the Early Woodland period (Hunter 2001: 83).

The Middle Woodland period in the American Bottom was marked by "elaborate ritual and burial ceremonialism" and the gradual introduction of the Havana ceramic tradition (Kelly 2002: 144). Ritual seems to have been organized by formal leaders, perhaps shamans or "big men." These individuals were marked out in death through grave goods, including elaborate personal ornaments and ritual equipment such as large obsidian blades, copper and stone effigy figures, and engraved staffs of office. Effigy tobacco pipes were common, suggesting that tobacco ceremonialism was widespread. Materials for these objects traveled great distances: obsidian from the Yellowstone region, copper from the Lake Superior Basin, and shell from the Gulf Coast. Most of these exotic items have been found in ritual centers with large enclosures in geometric patterns and numerous burial mounds. The mounds themselves contain multiple interments and often have a central log-lined tomb, suggesting that there were some individuals of very high status in Middle Woodland societies (Johnson 2001: 323).

It was in this period that many sites began to be occupied year-round (Johnson 2001: 323). Kelly (2002: 147), however, notes that Middle Woodland sites are sometimes difficult to identify because of the "lack of diagnostic artifacts." While the Ohio Valley saw the introduction of maize consumption in the Middle Woodland period, evidence for this crop is lacking from the American Bottom (Kelly 2002: 144). Maize first appeared in the Woodlands archaeological record c. 100 CE, but it was not intensively cultivated until around 800 CE (Blitz and Porth 2013: 93). No evidence of its cultivation during this period in the American Bottom has been found (Simon 2017).

The Late Woodland period is divided into three phases: Rosewood (300–450 CE), Mund (450–600 CE), and Patrick (600–750 CE). These phases are distinguished by their ceramic and lithic deposits, as well as by the almost complete disappearance of long-distance trade and burial ceremonialism. In the 1970s and 1980s, archaeologist David Braun (in Kelly 2002: 151) concluded that the shift between the Middle and Late Woodland periods was partially characterized by the increased cultivation of starchy seed plants and alliances between local communities. However, the people of the American Bottom also utilized wild resources, including fruits, nuts, roots, seeds, and wild deer (Christiansen 2001: 250; Fritz 2019: 65). The Range site of the Patrick phase displays a settlement pattern of two clusters of households around a community square. One house, isolated from the main residential areas, may have been used for rituals and ceremonies (Kelly 2002: 154).

The Late Woodland people most likely lived in self-sufficient nuclear families (Christiansen 2001: 250). Community groups met for rituals that included feasts and marriages (Kelly 2002: 151). There is evidence for increased intergroup violence in most regions of North America beginning in the Rosewood phase (Blitz and Porth 2013: 90). The decline in regional ceremonialism and trade may also reflect increased conflict between local communities. This trend coincided with the rise of the bow and the decline of the atlatl. The bow also made hunting more accurate and efficient, which allowed Late Woodland groups to settle previously marginal ecological zones (Blitz and Porth 2013: 91–93).

The Emergent Mississippian period has been divided into multiple phases: Sponemann, Collinsville, Loyd (together spanning the period from 750 to 900 CE), Merrell, and Edelhardt (900–1050 CE). These phases have produced evidence for increasing social complexity. As noted, maize production intensified across the Woodlands region starting around 800 CE. It became the staple crop in most of the Midwest, perhaps paving the way for population growth (Blitz and Porth 2013: 92). However, the population of the largest Emergent Mississippian settlement was likely only around 500 people. Emergent Mississippian settlements featured houses clustered together into nucleated courtyard groups. Blitz and Porth (2013: 94) suggest that these settlement patterns were a defensive reaction to increased bow warfare. Settlements included ditches and in some cases palisades (Milner et al. 2013: 98). There is also evidence for increasingly differentiated social roles after 1000 CE, along with signs of growing centralization, including "community defense, organization of labor, and communal storage of maize in secure central places" (Blitz and Porth 2013: 94). Several of the new social roles are best explained as a direct response to the realities of increased intergroup conflict and bow warfare.

The site of the ancient city we now know as Cahokia, close to modern St. Louis, Illinois, was all but uninhabited until c. 1000 CE. During the Middle Mississippian period (1050–1275 CE), several groups settled here, leading to a massive population surge and the rise of the new city to the status of regional hegemon. Milner (in Peregrine et al. 2014: 15) estimated that at least 50,000 people lived within the boundaries of the Greater Cahokia area and 15,000 in the central administrative complex.

The previous settlement pattern of clusters of houses was replaced by "widely scattered single-family farmsteads" (Milner 2006: 100). Settlements included religious or political centers with multiple large mounds, towns with a single mound, villages, and hamlets (Peregrine 2001: 336).

Cahokia became a major ritual center beginning about 1050 CE. In the next century, more than 120 mounds were built, including the largest pre-Columbian structure in the Americas north of Mexico—Monks Mound. Monks Mound demonstrates the high level of social complexity and organization present at Cahokia: over a million cubic meters of earth were moved in the course of its construction (Milner 2006: 148). High levels of complexity are also suggested by the Great Plaza in front of Monks Mound, created by leveling a large area of floodplain, which may have required more labor than Monks Mound itself. There were perhaps a dozen such mound and plaza complexes in the Greater Cahokia region, all of which required complex organization and extensive mobilization of labor to build (Milner 2006: 101).

Mississippian religion shared many characteristics with Mesoamerican religions, such as a hybrid birdman deity, a cosmology in which the sky featured as "the realm of order and supernatural power," and a focus on the performance of rites of renewal and regeneration (Peregrine 2001: 337). It is likely that elites were deeply involved in religious ceremonies, including those connected with the care of ancestral remains as well as calendrical rituals and feasts. The timing of these ceremonies appears to have been worked out using large circles of posts, or "woodhenges," that allowed measurement of the sun's position throughout the year. Elites were identified by elaborate regalia, personal ornaments, and ritual paraphernalia that incorporated exotic materials obtained through extensive long-distance trade. It appears that some of these items were created by specialist craftspeople present at Cahokia itself. Shell beads and effigy pipes originating here were distributed throughout the midcontinent.

Archaeological evidence suggests that the political and ceremonial traditions serving as Cahokia's social glue began to weaken around 1150 CE. The evidence for political and social hierarchies is much weaker in the following Sand Prairie phase (1275–1400 CE), which was marked by decreasing social complexity (Emerson 1997: 6, 53). By 1350 CE, the great city of Cahokia had collapsed and its population dispersed. The overall population of the region reached its lowest point in centuries; Milner (1986: 227) estimated that the population density of an area of the Mississippi floodplain just south of Cahokia was between one and seven people per square kilometer.

Styles of material culture designated "Oneota" by archaeologists first appeared on the Mississippi floodplain in the thirteenth century, during the Sand Prairie phase, when new populations migrated into the region (Gibbon 2001: 392; Pauketat 1994: 47). They were most likely organized into tribes and clans (Gibbon 2001: 393). There is no archaeological evidence of durable social hierarchy (390–91) and population estimates are lacking (Hart 1990: 570–71). While the Oneota produced their own utensils for everyday use, there is evidence of trade with groups to the south (Gibbon 2001: 391–93). They subsisted on a combination of maize cultivation with hunting and gathering. Oneota archaeological history, however, is marked by warfare and violence—settlements show evidence of violence including decapitation, scalping, and mutilation. From the mid-fourteenth to the mid-fifteenth century, the Oneota lived in fortified villages on top of bluffs; by the mid-seventeenth century, they were living with the La Moine Mississippians in the fortified temple town of Crable, most likely driven there by violent conflict with other groups.

It is interesting to note the vacillation between more centralized and more decentralized polities in the American Bottom. In the Late Archaic and Early Woodland periods, groups lived more or less independently in small, mobile communities. During the Middle Woodland period, these communities gathered in ritual spaces for ceremonies led by formal leaders, and may have had some form of supra-community leadership between these ceremonies, as suggested by the presence of central log-lined tombs in some burial mounds. This centralization of ritual and perhaps political organization disappeared in the Late Woodland period, only to re-emerge in a highly complex form during the Mississippian period. However, by the Late Mississippian and Oneota periods, the complex ritual and political hierarchy of Mississippian societies had in turn broken down, with communities again largely independent of one another.

Archaeological evidence suggests that the populations encountered by French missionaries and traders in the central Mississippi Valley from the seventeenth century onwards were not descended from the Oneota (Hall 1997: 173). Rather, the most likely descendants of the Oneota groups are to be found among the historic residents of the Western Great Lakes, a region that was thrown into disarray by Iroquois raids after 1649 CE. The demographic history of the American Bottom itself in this period is also difficult to reconstruct. However, we know from French written sources that by 1700 CE it had been settled by groups belonging to the Illinois Confederation (or Illiniwek Nation), approximately a dozen indigenous tribes who spoke a common language and shared a similar culture (Illinois State Museum 2000; Temple 1966: 32–35). The Illinois might have migrated here from the Lake Michigan or Lake Erie Basin (Hall 1997: 173). They were mostly self-sufficient farmers and hunters, but also participated in a large trade network with tribes to the south and the west (Illinois State Museum 2000).

In 1640 CE, the first European reports were written on the Illinois, based on second-hand information from other indigenous groups (Illinois State Museum 2000). France claimed the "Illinois Country"—referring to a large region of the Midwest—as a colonial possession from the mid-1660s and 1670s CE. In the early years, French influence in the region was limited: only traders and missionaries interacted with the Illinois people (Walthall and Emerson 1992: 9–10). The Illinois maintained their autonomy for a time, but were considered (at least by the French authorities) under the "protection" of the French crown (Havard 2013: 117). In the late seventeenth century, they moved to large villages near French settlements (Morrissey 2015: 681–62). Historians traditionally view this shift in settlement pattern as an attempt to find refuge from violence and disease. However, Morrissey (681–82) has argued that the new villages were strategically positioned for "bison-hunting and slave raiding." The Illinois were officially incorporated into the French colony of Louisiane in 1717 CE (Walthall and Emerson 1992: 9–10). In 1719 CE, the large Illinois village of Kaskaskia had a French colonial government, which included a royal notary (Ekberg 2007: 31). French missionaries and other French settlers lived in Kaskaskia alongside the Illinois. Despite this coexistence and the sometimes peaceful relationships between French and Illinois in the early colonial period, the fact remains that the Illinois were devasted by European contact, enduring untold suffering and staggering depopulation, dropping from about 12,000 people in 1680 CE to just 1,900 in 1763 CE (Hauser 2015: 299). By the 1700s CE, only five Illinois tribes survived, and by the early nineteenth century only the Kaskaskia and Peoria tribes remained (Illinois State Museum 2000).

Scholars' understanding of Illinois religion is mainly based on observations by French colonists in the seventeenth century. According to these sources, the Illinois people worshiped Kitchesmanetoa as the creator of all things. French missionaries attempted to draw parallels between the Christian God and the Illinois' belief in a supreme deity (Illinois State Museum 2000). The Illinois believed that the earth rested on the back of an otter, and that the universe had three levels: the Upper World, inhabited by the sun and the thunder; the Middle World (earth); and the Lower World, home to monsters (Illinois State Museum 2000). Young Illinois went on vision quests in order to connect with personal spirits called *manitous* (Illinois State Museum 2000).

Universalizing morality and egalitarianism in the Mississippi Valley
Egalitarianism
In the Middle Woodland period, after c. 300 BCE, an increasing number of cone-shaped earthen mounds were built within the Hopewell culture, which extended across much of the Midwest (Iseminger 2010: 23–25). Often, they contained wealthy burials in log-lined tombs along with exotic and valuable grave goods; these individuals may have been kin group leaders or elders (23–25). The process of constructing these mounds likely served ideological purposes, perhaps reinforcing incipient social inequality in Woodland societies.

However, it appears that there were no durable hierarchies or social stratification at this time, and indeed the Late Woodland period saw a decrease in the number of high-status mound burials (Iseminger 2010: 23-25). There is no evidence of chiefdom-level political organization before the Mississippian period, and dwellings within settlements are relatively undifferentiated. For instance, the Range site from the Late Woodland Patrick phase (600-750 CE) featured different forms of houses clustered together. While to Kelly (2002: 155) this suggests some level of social division, Christiansen (2001: 260) maintains that "the typical archaeological indicators of ranking and stratification are not present at Patrick Phase sites." Iseminger's (2010: 26) description of Emergent Mississippian settlement patterns also suggests a relatively egalitarian society with no special dwellings for the elite: house clusters were organized around a central courtyard that probably played ceremonial and communal roles. Nor is there any evidence of slavery or serfdom, or any sign that human sacrifice—sometimes interpreted as a sign of social inequality—was performed.

On the whole, then, signs of institutionalized inequality are absent for the Late Woodland and Emergent Mississippian periods. These communities began to give way to more hierarchically organized social formations in the early phases of the Cahokia phenomenon. Archaeologists have uncovered structures at Cahokia that point to incipient social stratification. Milner (2006: 168) points to a florescence of mound-building activity after 1000 CE, suggesting the growth of an elite class. The palisade around Cahokia (built in the late 1100s) may also point to the presence of social stratification. According to Iseminger (2010: 138), the city continued for one mile outside the wall. The palisade may therefore have served to create a social distinction between the inhabitants of the central, walled area and those living outside it.

The presence of human sacrifice at Cahokia has also been interpreted as a marker of social hierarchy. Sacrificial rituals often mark certain groups as higher or lower status, and victims can include members of outgroups (like war prisoners and captives) or ingroups (such as elite retainers). The burials in Cahokia's Mound 72 provide an insight into human sacrifice as it was practiced in the ancient city. This ridge-topped mound contained at least 25 different burial groups and approximately 270 bodies in total (Thompson et al. 2015: 341). In excavations conducted in the late 1960s and early 1970s, archaeologists uncovered 15 individuals, including men, women and children, in the upper level of Feature 229 (Pauketat 2009: 158). Their remains had been treated with great ceremony, wrapped into bundles and lowered into the ground on stretchers. In the lower level of the feature were the bodies of 39 men and women who had been brutally executed (in some cases even decapitated) and thrown haphazardly into the pit (Pauketat 2009: 160). Analysis of dental metrics by Thompson et al. (2015: 349-50) found that these 39 sacrificial victims were biologically distinct from other individuals buried in Mound 72, suggesting "differing genetic and/or sociopolitical affiliations." They may have been war captives or belonged to marginalized groups living near Cahokia. However, this study also found that four groups of sacrificed individuals (mostly young women) in Mound 72, previously thought to represent a kind of human tribute from outlying communities dominated by Cahokia, had probably lived in or near Cahokia since birth. The variations in mortuary treatment between different burial groups in Mound 72 thus point to the presence of social divisions—though the precise form these divisions took remains unclear. Thompson et al. (2015: 354) conclude that more research must be done to better understand the ancient city's social stratification and its tribute relationships with other communities. Human sacrifice has only been studied in relation to Cahokia's Mound 72, and there is no evidence from preceding or succeeding periods.

Despite the evidence for inequality at Cahokia—including not only sacrificial victims but some spectacularly wealthy burials, including the well-known "birdman" (e.g. Pauketat 2004)—some aspects of egalitarianism seem to have been present in Cahokian culture. The ancient city hosted ritual feasts described as "collective experiences that defy pigeonholing into status categories" (Pauketat et al. 2002: 276). The feasts included both low- and high-status community members eating communally.

The Sand Prairie and Oneota periods saw decreasing social complexity in the region. Burial patterns in the cemeteries of the succeeding Sand Prairie period point to very few social or political divisions (Emerson 1997: 175). Oneota settlements were also more egalitarian than those at the height of the Cahokia phenomenon and there were no distinct social classes (Gibbon 2001: 391). This pattern of relative egalitarianism continued into the early Illinois period, but began to shift in the late seventeenth century as "chiefs" gained more formal power under French influence (Illinois State Museum 2000); a process we discuss in more detail below.

Moralizing and universalizing norms

Archaeologists still know very little about moralizing religion in the American Bottom before the arrival of Christianity. The Mississippian people probably practiced ritual purification (fasting and sweats), which may have included taking purgatives. However, based on current archaeological evidence, it is not possible to discern whether the connection between purification and morality that characterizes many Eurasian religions was also present in Mississippian cultures.

The Illinois story "How Wisakatchekwa Got into Some Trouble" illustrates the moral norms of this culture by distinguishing between correct and incorrect behavior. The story as we have it today is the version told in 1919 CE by George Washington Finley, one of the last speakers of the Peoria language. In the tale, Wisakatchekwa is tricked and punished by two old blind men after he moves their guide rope, causing them to fall into a river (Illinois State Museum 2000). While the story evokes the concepts of right and wrong, Wisakatchekwa was punished by the elders themselves, not by a spirit or any supernatural forces. In addition, while the Illinois believed in a Lower World populated by monsters, our sources do not mention whether in Illinois thought people were sent there as punishment after death for breaking moral taboos during life. Therefore, while Illinois culture no doubt encompassed moral norms and ideals of correct behavior, we cannot infer that their religion or cosmology was strongly moralizing.

Furthermore, the Illinois sold captives as slaves in the post-contact period. French observers wrote that the Illinois people either killed or captured all members of a village after an attack (Morrissey 2013: 678). The French concluded that they traditionally kidnapped outsiders to replace fallen warriors or kin (678). These captives would be strangers—not from allied tribes. By the late seventeenth century, however, the Illinois were also selling captives as commodities. In the 1720s CE, for example, the Illinois sold and traded Fox Nation captives to French colonists, who kept them as slaves (Rushforth 2012: 212). French colonists in Illinois Country kept indigenous and black people as slaves in the post-contact period. We do not know whether any aspect of Illinois religion or Illinois thought more broadly expressed any prohibitions on or censure of slavery, but what is clear is that contact with the French and competition over resources led to increased Illinois involvement in slaving.

Prosociality

There is not enough evidence to understand Mississippian attitudes towards prosocial activities. Late Woodland period settlements were relatively egalitarian, from which we can infer that there was likely some prosocial or charitable activity among kin or other groups. The communal structures in Emergent Mississippian settlements likewise seem to have been related to ceremonies which reinforced communal coordination and mutual support. At Cahokia, the communal feast ritual described above may have served to reinforce social bonds and group integration. However, we do not know whether prosociality was enforced by any specific religious ideology.

Overall, little is known about Illinois religion in the early historic period, but a story from the Winnebago oral tradition gives an example of Illinois prosociality. In the 1640s CE, 500 Illinois men carried food to a Winnebago village after the Winnebago suffered several disasters. In response, the Winnebago killed the entire Illinois party. Several years later, the Illinois attacked the Winnebago, killing and capturing most of the village (Illinois State Museum 2000). This story shows that the Illinois provided large-scale charity to members of other groups, but may have also served as a warning against extending this sort of prosocial behavior to those not belonging to allied tribes.

Rulership and institutions of authority

In the Middle Woodland period, the construction of large mounds may have been organized by kin group leaders or other informal leaders. As we noted above, evidence for high-status burials after 300 BCE, such as the log-lined tombs in Hopewell burial mounds, suggests that some form of leadership (though not necessarily hereditary) was present by this time (Iseminger 2010: 25). However, we can only speculate about the nature of leadership in the Early or Late Woodland periods. There were certainly no god-king figures, a feature often described in the Axial Age literature as characterizing the "archaic" (pre-axial) societies of Afro-Eurasia.

Some archaeologists believe that the institution of chiefship first appeared in the region in the Emergent Mississippian period, after 750 BCE (e.g. Iseminger 2010: 26). However, there is no evidence for a government or an administrative hierarchy in this period—it is more likely that emerging chiefs wielded only informal power, relying on the cooperation of kin group leaders and other elites.

The presence of formal political leaders is debated even for Cahokia at its height, during the Middle Mississippian period. Iseminger (2010: 27) believes fully-fledged chiefdoms were present in the Mississippian cultural sphere by around 1050 CE, but Peregrine et al. (2014: 31) point out that Cahokia has produced "no inscriptions, images, or even unambiguous houses or burials of political leaders." Leadership may thus have remained weakly institutionalized. One possibility is that the political and religious hierarchies of the Mississippian period were closely intertwined, with a ruler-priest or group of ruler-priests at the apex. The ruler (or rulers) would almost certainly have had to seek support from other groups of elites in order to govern effectively (Iseminger 2010: 27; Peregrine et al. 2014: 31). Further, "kings" were never present at Cahokia (Peregrine 2014: 31). Overall, the absence of written records or other record-keeping devices from Cahokia makes it difficult to understand the city's political and administrative structure, but it is clear that we are dealing here with a very different kind of society from the "archaic" Eurasian states that feature so prominently in Axial Age theories.

Interestingly, after the collapse of Cahokia there is very little evidence for centralized control over resources or for institutionalized rulership. Nothing from either the Sand Prairie or Oneota archaeological records leads us to speculate that chiefs were present. Archaeologists, in fact, have found no sign of elite activity of any kind at Sand Prairie phase sites (Emerson 1997: 148). The small communities occupying the American Bottom were relatively autonomous in this period (Milner 1983: 298). There may have been community or kin-group leaders, but there was likely no central administration or ruler with powers extending beyond the village. In Oneota society, villages were probably headed by "big men" (Gibbon 2001: 391), who had no hereditary claim to power.

Within the Illinois Confederation, "chiefs" rose to power based largely on their personal qualities, including their "ability to maintain social well-being" (Illinois State Museum 2000). Peace chiefs provided political leadership, led communal hunts, and supervised non-violent intertribal interactions, while separate war chiefs organized and led raids on other tribes (Illinois State Museum 2000). The Illinois did not have strongly institutionalized intertribal political institutions. Callender (1978: 675) notes that the Illinois political system was characterized by council meetings and collective decision-making. The peace chief may have cooperated closely with the general population of his tribe rather than exclusively with elders or elites. Nichols (1998: 2) writes that a chief made decisions only after a lengthy discussion had taken place and consensus had been reached among his people.

The role of the chief in Illinois culture differed from European settler-colonial modes of centralized leadership. French Jesuit missionary Father Gabriel Marest ([1712] 1959: 221) observed in 1712: "there are Chiefs among them [the Illinois], but the Chiefs have no authority; if they should use threats, far from making themselves feared, they would see themselves abandoned by the very men who had chosen them for Chiefs." Similarly, the missionary priest Louis Hennepin (quoted in Morrisey 2013: 55) wrote in 1680 CE that the Illinois had "no great Respect for their Chiefs."

French officials attempted to transform the traditional Illinois social structure into one they could more easily understand and control. In the late seventeenth century, the French began to give medals to Illinois chiefs to elevate their status. They also held such men responsible for the actions of others in their tribe (Illinois State Museum 2000). By the mid-eighteenth century, tribes had to gain approval from French officials when choosing a new leader (Illinois State Museum 2000). It is interesting to note here that proponents of the Axial Age theory argue that the appearance of a moralizing, axial ideology should result in chief executives becoming increasingly responsive to the needs of their people. However, French influence in the Mississippi Valley and the introduction of Christianity—a "second-order" axial religion—had the opposite effect on Illinois culture, creating an environment where leaders were as responsible to their colonial masters as they were to their own people.

Conclusion

The archaeological record suggests that settlements in the American Bottom were generally egalitarian until the rise of the ancient city of Cahokia around 1000 CE. At Cahokia, there is evidence of social hierarchies and increased inequality. In the wider region, too, increased social complexity most likely ushered in a more unequal age. After the decline of Cahokia, indigenous societies occupying the American Bottom were once again relatively egalitarian, though if any decisive ideological shift underpinned this shift in social structure, it is now inaccessible to us. We know little about the Mississippian concepts of morality and prosociality, but we have evidence for charity, communal feasting, and stories to encourage correct behavior before the arrival of the French.

Further, there may never have been a concept of absolute rule in the American Bottom and, if there was, it only existed briefly. Thus, the traditional path of axial transition—from god-king to institutionalized, responsive rule—has no relevance to the historical development of this region. Furthermore, it appears that most rulers were either directly responsible to their people or to elders, elites, and kin-group leaders. The spread of Christianity into the Mississippian region accompanied a political process in which chiefs became *less* responsive to the wider population and more responsible to the French colonial government, shrinking the scope of authority and the basis of legitimation rather than expanding it.

OCEANIA | Hawai'i

Dennis Spencer & Timothy Earle

Period	Polity	Approx. dates
Pre-unification period	Independent chiefdoms	1000–1778 CE
Unification period	'Umi-a-Liloa's Kingdom	1580–1778
	Kamehameha's Kingdom	1778–1819
European contact period	Kingdom of Hawai'i	1819–1854

Table 13. Periods and dates of polities mentioned in text that were based in or that occupied the Big Island of Hawai'i

Introduction and historical background

The Hawaiian archipelago sits isolated in the northern Pacific, more than 1,000 km of open ocean from the nearest inhabited island group. The Big Island (also known simply as Hawai'i) is the largest island, located at the south-eastern end of the archipelago over a volcanic hotspot. Four other major islands—Maui, Moloka'i, O'ahu, and Kaua'i—extend to the north-west. The first Polynesian settlers, numbering perhaps only 100, are thought to have reached the islands sometime between 1000 and 1100 CE (Athens et al. 2014). To establish a viable population, this purposeful colonizing effort would have required substantial seaworthy canoes, logistical planning, and repeated connections to island groups to the south. By 1650 CE, Hawaiian populations had grown quickly to an estimated 200,000 or more for the entire archipelago. The Hawaiian Islands had no semblance of urban centers. People lived in scattered settlements, originally along the coast, suggesting a maritime orientation, then moved inland and eventually settlement became focused on agriculturally rich zones of irrigated and dryland taro and sweet potato fields (Earle 1978; Kirch 2010). Of particular importance to Axial Age theories, the social and moral developments in the Hawaiian Islands were completely isolated from the Afro-Eurasian world system until the arrival of Europeans late in the eighteenth century.

Hawaiian societies lacked a writing system until European contact, so what we know about their political and religious life comes from archaeology and traditional histories. There is no archaeological evidence for complex social organization during the early period following colonization. The first settlers would have brought with them a Polynesian sense of social ranking, but early sites suggest a remarkably open and small-scale society. Nor are there any indications of political centralization, such as settlement hierarchies or religious monuments that required significant mobilization of labor. Regional chiefdoms and the subsequent island-wide "states" would emerge gradually over the centuries (Earle and Spriggs 2015; Kirch 2010).

As Hawaiian societies developed, agriculture began to be intensified through-out the archipelago. Geologically, the Hawaiian Islands are progressively younger from west to east, and the older western islands have excellent soil and permanent streams (Kirch 2007). On western islands such as Kaua'i and O'ahu, these favorable conditions allowed Hawaiians to develop extensive irrigation systems for the cultivation of taro. On the eastern islands such as Maui and especially the Big Island, irrigation was far less commonplace. Here, few streams, meager alluvial soils, and rocky conditions severely limited irrigation, and sweet potato, cultivated in dryland fields, became the crop of choice (Kirch 2007). This geological-agricultural difference ultimately had important political ramifications. Early in the Hawaiian cultural sequence, the landscapes of the older, fertile western islands were permanently altered through significant investments of labor to create irrigation systems. Once built, these terraces produced reliably high yields, enabling rapid population growth in the period from c. 700 to 1450 CE (Kirch 2007). The earliest Hawaiian irrigation was managed at the community level without the need for centralized planning, though as the chiefly elite developed, they exerted more control via land managers (konohiki) (Earle 1980). On the other hand, dryland agricultural systems required a smaller initial investment in construction but far more active maintenance and labor input than irrigated fields. Dryland farming was also riskier, as low rainfall could have disastrous consequences for the harvest (Kirch 2007). Furthermore, as population grew and soil nutrients were exhausted by intensification, it became more difficult to extract from dryland farming systems the food surpluses that fueled the political economy. Conquest warfare on the Big Island and subsequent state formation apparently arose here in part out of the need for reliable surplus extraction from dryland crops (Kirch 2007). Variability in harvests made food less secure, but conquest could obtain more extensive agricultural land and spread out the risks.

Over time, as documented best by the pattern of religious monuments, each island saw the emergence of multiple, independent chiefly polities (Kolb et al. 1994; Patrick Kirch, pers. comm. 2016). Separate polities, each with legitimizing religious ceremonies, continued to coexist on the Big Island until around 1580 CE, when 'Umi-a-Līloa is said to have been the first to consolidate the entire island into one polity. The oral traditions about 'Umi hold that he rebelled against his half-brother Hākau, combining military force and diplomatic marriage to unite the Big Island polities under his rule (Kirch 2010: 92–98). Archaeological work has confirmed at least the essence of this account by mapping the creation and spread of temples and farmland (Mulrooney and Ladefoged 2005). In particular, the Ahu-a-'Umi (Altar of 'Umi) is said to have been built for 'Umi. The ruins of this temple still stand, providing one of the only tangible links we have to the story of 'Umi (Kirch 2012).

After 'Umi's reign, the island fluctuated between being united under one ruler and being split into two or more smaller polities. While strong rulers such as 'Umi would be recognized by local chiefs, weaker or ineffective paramount authority was often ignored. Additionally, conflict within elite kin groups was commonplace, with brothers and half-brothers often either sharing the throne or outright opposing each other. The most famous instance took place in 1782 CE, when Kamehameha I rose against and killed his cousin Kīwalaʻō to become the sole ruler of the Big Island. Through the use of Western guns recently brought to the Pacific by European explorers at the end of the eighteenth century (Kirch 2010), Kamehameha managed to conquer and unite Hawaiʻi, Maui, and Oʻahu.

After ʻUmi, divine kings, reinforced by warrior might and a new system of land tenure, presided over what can be recognized as state-level polities (Kirch 2010). The study of precontact Hawaiian societies on the Big Island and Maui is of great comparative importance for historians and archaeologists, because the state emerged here independently from any other states (Hommon 2013; Kirch 2010). These island kingdoms were historically exceptional, arising outside of any world system, without markets or coinage, urbanization, metal, or writing. The case allows us to see that some of the most common features associated with "civilization" were not necessary for state formation.

The first European contact took place in 1778 CE, when the British explorer Captain James Cook arrived on Kauaʻi; in 1779 he reached the Big Island, landing at Kealakekua Bay. Soon afterwards, due to their central location in the Pacific and their excellent harbors, the Hawaiian Islands became an important supply base for fur traders, merchants, and whalers (Seaton 1974). They were also of major concern to the governments of the Western colonial powers (Britain, France, Russia, and eventually the United States), each looking to dominate Pacific trade and resource extraction. Kamehameha I (r. 1795–1819 CE) declared his allegiance to Britain, but the islands were not formally incorporated into the British Empire, an arrangement that continued under his successor Kamehameha II (r. 1819–1824 CE). The independence of the Kingdom of Hawaiʻi was internationally recognized in an 1843 CE treaty, but this did not prevent its annexation by the United States in 1898.

Religious and normative ideology

In this section, we give a brief overview of what is known about Hawaiian religion. Without a writing system, our understanding of the belief system of the early settlers of the Hawaiian Islands comes from a mixture of oral traditions (moʻolelo), comparisons with other Polynesian societies, and the archaeological record of religious monument construction. Kirch (2010: 87) has argued that the moʻolelo provide a "solid core of historical truth," and in addition to their vivid accounts of usurpations, conquests and chiefly rivalries, they can shed light on early Hawaiian beliefs and ritual practices and help to illuminate the archaeological data.

Archaeological surveys have found over 800 *heiau* (temples) throughout the islands. By using carbon dating and mapping the locations of these temples, we can gain valuable information about the development of Hawaiian religion and political organization (Kirch 2012; Mulrooney and Ladefoged 2005). The earliest examples date back to c. 1000–1200 CE and were very simple compared with the elaborately constructed later monuments. Most of the sites date from around 1650–1800 CE, by which time Hawaiian societies had already grown significantly in population and social complexity (Kolb et al. 1994).

Heiau were dedicated to the worship of various gods, but by around 1650 CE, the most important of these monuments were for Lono and Kū, the gods of agriculture/fertility and of war respectively (Kirch 1990; Kolb et al. 1994). Dedicated to the war god Kū, the largest temples on the islands were war temples, known as *luakini*, to be used by the king in preparation for battle. The temples built for Lono were also very important, as he was the god responsible for the fertility of the land and its people. During the annual *makahiki* ceremony, the king embodied the god Lono as he moved around the island in question from community to community, stopping at temples to receive designated tribute. Both kings and lesser chiefs could perform rituals at fertility *heiau*, and commoners continued to use smaller sacred sites, such as fishing shrines (Kirch 1990).

By analyzing which cultural traits are shared across various Polynesian societies and which are uniquely Hawaiian, it is possible to make inferences about which beliefs and cultural concepts the settlers of Hawaii brought with them and which they developed subsequently. It seems that the first settlers lacked the pantheon of four great gods that would later characterize Hawaiian religion. We know, however, that ancestral Polynesian religion included the veneration of ancestors, the *tupunga*,[1] who were believed to be the source of growth of the social unit and of *mana*, the vital power whose flow was necessary for life and fertility. Protecting and channeling *mana* was one of the primary roles of the *ariki*, the chief (Kirch 2012). If a chief were unable to perform adequately the rituals necessary to the well-being of his people, power would pass to a chief who could. This seems to have been used at times as justification of usurpation, but it makes clear that rule depended on religious sanctity, political stability, and economic sustainability. A notable proverb recorded in post-contact times held that "the land cannot live under an irreligious chief, a staff that breaks easily" (Handy and Pukui 1958), and this may convey something of the early Polynesian attitude towards rulers.

---

1   The asterisk before *tupunga* here indicates that the word belongs not to any living or historically recorded language but to "Proto-Polynesian": an ancestral language reconstructed based on triangulation between extant Polynesian languages.

For later Hawaiians, the gods—especially Kū, Lono, Kāne, and Kanaloa—became increasingly more important as sources of *mana*, alongside their ancestors (Kirch 2010: 56). Hawaiian kings were gods on earth, and were known as *ali'i akua*, or "god-kings." They were responsible for controlling the flow of *mana* from the gods and maintaining the order of the universe, and held the power of life and death over ordinary humans. The death of a king resulted in a kind of cosmic disorder; it would be followed by mass grieving, and his successor would be removed from the unholy scene before returning ten days later to reinstate order (Sahlins 1985). A Hawaiian king stood as "supreme mediator between men and gods" and at times received worship like a "true God" (*akua maoli*) (Valeri 1985: 141–43). Interestingly, however, and in contrast to the western Polynesian islands of Tonga, their burial sites were not monumentalized.

The belief that gods and ancestors were the source of *mana* was one of the key tenets underpinning social stratification in Polynesian societies, including Hawai'i. *Mana* was manifested in displays of accomplishment: power, strength, and skill. It was perceived as flowing from supernatural beings to humans, but did not flow equally to all people. Instead, it was transmitted through the paths of genealogical descent and rank that ordered Polynesian societies. Polynesian chiefs originally represented local ruling lineages bound by descent and *mana* to the group as a whole, but, in the more stratified examples, the distribution of *mana* between different social strata became more unequal. By the time of Cook's arrival, Hawaii was stratified into three broad social classes: the *ali'i* (elites), *maka'āinana* (commoners, literally translating to "people of the land"), and the less numerous *kauwā*, ("outcasts" or "slaves") (Kirch 2010: 34). High chiefs or kings became vehicles of *mana*, the point of contact between the divine and the rest of society (Kirch 2010). The Hawaiian proverb "The chief is a shark that travels on land" represents both the ferocity and otherness of the *ali'i* class from the perspective of the lower orders (Kirch 2012; Sahlins 1985).

Claims to power through ruling lineages were strengthened by the fact that Hawaiian commoners were forbidden to keep or recite their genealogies any further back than their grandparents (Kirch 2012: 219; Ralston 1984: 22). Kings, on the other hand, emphasized their genealogies as stretching back across 963 generations of ruling chiefs to the gods (Sahlins 1985: 51). Each new district chief or island king would also redistribute the lands among his immediate kinsmen, kinswomen, and followers, further preventing the growth of strong local lineages (Sahlins 1985: 45).

Another key tenet of pre-state Hawaiian ideology held in common across Polynesia was the idea of *kapu* (called *tapu* elsewhere in Polynesia). The *kapu* system was based on the belief that the world was created by two complementary elements: *Ao*, light, and *Po*, darkness. *Ao*, the male principle, represented the sacred, positive aspect of nature: the sky, light, and life. The female principle, *Po*, represented the unsacred, negative aspect of nature: earth, darkness, and death (Levin 1968). Beyond those major associations, many smaller features of the Hawaiian environment were seen as either sacred or unsacred, depending on whether they derived from *Ao* or *Po*. For example, summer was considered *kapu*, or sacred, while winter was *noa*, or common. This distinction even spread to foods, where pork and bananas were sacred while sweet potatoes were unsacred (Levin 1968).

By the late precontact period, the opposition between *kapu* and *noa* had come to structure all aspects of Hawaiian society, from the daily lives of the *maka'ainana* to courtly protocols. It undergirded an elaborate system of prohibitions, designed to ensure the correct flow of *mana* and protect the *ali'i* from contamination (Kirch 2010). Breaking some *kapu*, for instance by coughing or making noise during a religious service, was punishable by death (69). As the *ali'i nui* traveled through an area, his heralds went ahead of him to warn everyone but the highest-ranking chiefs to prostrate themselves on the ground on pain of death (Kirch 2012: 217). Different classes were also subject to different restrictions and punishments. For example, if a *maka'ainana* was caught wearing the loincloth of an *ali'i*, he would be sacrificed to the personal god of that chief, but if a lower-ranking chief did the same, he was rarely punished so harshly (Levin 1968). While we do not know whether Hawaiians believed that gods other than the divine chiefs would enforce morality, Hawaiian legends describe gods taking action against those who broke *kapu* (Patrick V. Kirch, pers. comm. 2016).

Kapu also created starkly different roles and opportunities for men and women. Women were seen as unsacred, particularly during menstruation. All shed blood was considered impure to various degrees, as it manifested a loss of integrity or life. Any lack of bodily integrity also implied a lack of social integrity, meaning that things such as menstrual blood and dead bodies brought disorder or weakness to the group. The notion of impurity also explains the close female connection with sorcery (Valeri 1985: 18–19. Among other restrictions and prohibitions, men and women therefore had to eat apart, and certain foods, such as pork, were prohibited to women. Men had to cultivate and prepare the sacred taro for eating. Additionally, it was forbidden for women to wear clothing that had been worn by a male and for relatives of the same sex but different generations to share clothing.

Limits on power

The first settlers of the Hawaiian Islands likely brought with them a social structure roughly corresponding to the "ancestral Polynesian" pattern that scholars have reconstructed through comparative linguistics. These early societies were headed by chiefs known as *ariki*, who had both secular and religious authority and performed sacred rituals on behalf of the group (Kirch 2012: 45). Under the ariki were the *fatu*, senior members of household groups probably responsible for economic coordination and rituals, as documented for early Hawai'i by a plethora of small shrines. By the time of European contact, however, Hawaiian society was extremely stratified. At the top sat the aforementioned *ali'i nui*, who ruled over an entire large island as well as neighboring smaller ones. Below him were the *kālaimoku* (a sort of "prime minister"), who advised the *ali'i nui* on secular affairs, and the *kahuna nui* (high priest), who officiated at important ceremonies (Kirch 2012: 204, 312–13). During times when the Big Island was more unified, the kingdom was divided into districts (*moku*), each headed by major chiefs known as *ali'i-'ai-moku*. Below them were the *ali'i-'ai-ahu-pua'a*, lower-ranking landowning chiefs of individual valleys or valley-sized island wedges. The lowest level of administration was made up of the *konohiki*, generally lower-ranking *ali'i* who served as "land managers" for the valley chiefs. Kinship ties were important in determining access to chiefly offices, and the highest positions in the hierarchy were awarded largely based on genealogical proximity to the king (Hommon 2013: 27–28). Loyal warriors of all ranks, including in some periods a very small number of *maka'āinana*, could also be rewarded with official positions (Kolb and Dixon 2002: 516–17).

While the position of king was ideally inherited by the eldest son of the previous ruler, many other principles and actions determined succession. The Hawaiians developed fine distinctions of chiefly rank based on the status and relatedness of one's parents, and full brother–sister marriage between two *ali'i* produced the highest-ranking offspring (Goldman 1970). Professional genealogists known as *kūauhau* were responsible for determining, or at least legitimizing, the heir to a throne. At times, half-brothers might rule together, with each brother controlling a separate region of the island, but such a balance was inherently unstable. Wars of succession were frequent, and those who lent military support to the contender to the throne who emerged victorious could expect to receive land and positions in the new political hierarchy (Earle 1978).

Armed conflict was probably present throughout Hawaiian history. For Polynesian chiefs, warfare was a way to preserve and display *mana* and status, while for their rivals it was a chance to increase *mana* and status for themselves (Kirch 1984). Warfare was a test of sanctity as much as military prowess; success in war was a sign of abundant *mana* and a justification of legitimacy. Kings' claims to power was strengthened by their association with the war god Kū (Kirch 2010). Prior to state formation, rivalry and conflict between high-ranking chiefs was common. Successful ruling chiefs would also amass large forces and war canoes to attack other islands in the hope of gaining power and territory (Kirch 1984). Early on, when warfare was between local chiefdoms, most combatants were commoner members of the polity, recruited and trained when conflict threatened (Hommon 2013). Later, however, a specialist class of highly trained warrior-chiefs emerged, who were vital in the wars of conquest, as when in the late eighteenth and early nineteenth centuries

Kamehameha I expanded his political domination. He maintained a large standing army that was scaled back during peacetime, though never in his lifetime fully disbanded.

In the late precontact period, the *ali'i nui* theoretically enjoyed absolute power (Seaton 1974: 198). However, their governments included a "council of chiefs," and the *ali'i nui* would often seek their advice before making important decisions. Keeping these influential *ali'i* on side also helped guard against the risk of their secession from the kingdom (Hommon 2013: 135). The councils of chiefs did not have a legal ability to impose sanctions on the *ali'i nui*, but they did provide legitimacy, especially critical during periods of succession. Nevertheless, the king stood above all other chiefs as the representative of the state as a whole. There are even examples of Hawaiians dating their lives relative to the actions of the king. One biography states, "I was born when Kamehameha conquered O'ahu ... I was old enough to carry stones when Kamehameha built the fish pond at Kiholo" (Sahlins 1985: 50).

No independent legislative body existed during the time of Kamehameha I, or, presumably, in earlier periods. *Kapu* effectively served as the system of laws, as it was a comprehensive list of dos and don'ts. As we noted in the previous section, the *kapu* system separated chiefs and commoners by giving special privileges to chiefs and designating them as sacred. Distinctive dress and certain ritual and behavioral restrictions also set them apart from commoners (Kirch 1984). By the time of Captain Cook's arrival, the *kapu* system strictly regulated contact between *ali'i* and commoners, and transgressions could be heavily punished (Kirch 2010).

Before unification, contact between different island kingdoms involved frequent diplomatic marriages between *ali'i*, some very limited trade, and military conflict with the aim of conquering more land. European arrival had a great impact on the entire archipelago. On the Big Island, Kamehameha was poised to take advantage of this because of his control of Kealakekua Bay, initially the most desirable port in the island chain for European ships (Levin 1968). He accumulated more Western guns than his rivals, and was able to conquer Maui, Moloka'i, and O'ahu (Kirch 2010). From his reign onwards, the Hawaiian Islands became a major center for Pacific supply and trade. In the early nineteenth century, *ali'i* diverted the labor under their control from subsistence farming to the now more profitable cultivation of sandalwood, which was exchanged for European goods (Levin 1968). Together with the population collapse caused by the introduction of diseases such as syphilis, cholera, and smallpox (Kirch 2010), this transformed local economies and drastically altered older systems of land tenure and agriculture.

The earliest Western visitors to Hawai'i largely assimilated into the *kapu* system, and Kamehameha was keen to host skilled craftsmen such as carpenters and blacksmiths (Levin 1968). Western sea captains were treated as chiefs and could decide whether or not to enforce traditional *kapus* on their ships, which effectively functioned as their floating chiefdoms. Many captains allowed women, who provided pleasures to their crew, to eat traditionally prohibited foods such as pork while on their ships (Seaton 1974). In 1819, following the death of Kamehameha I, his son and heir Liloliho himself publicly violated the strict *kapu* against men and women eating together by feasting with female *ali'i*. Apparently at the behest of Ka'ahumanu, Kamehameha I's favorite wife and co-ruler at his death (Seaton 1974), this dealt the symbolic death blow to the *kapu* system, and idols and sanctuaries were burned soon afterwards.

Scholars disagree on why the *kapu* system was abolished. Some believe that Liloliho and his allies acted as they did in order to retain power (Levin 1968). By overthrowing the *kapu* system, they could ensure that succession would only be based on heredity and not on access to *mana*, which was more open to interpretation (Levin 1968). Other historians emphasize causes such as the unsettling effect that Western contact had on Hawaiian society, or the disillusionment of its people. Many Hawaiians had violated *kapus* in secret for years, perhaps most notably Ka'ahumanu herself. According to Archibald Campbell, a Scottish sailor who visited the islands from 1809 to 1810, "generally observed, the women very seldom scruple to break [*kapu*], when it can be done in secret ... I once saw the queen [Ka'ahumanu] transgressing in this respect, and was strictly enjoined to secrecy as she said it was as much as her life was worth" (quoted in Seaton 1974). After breaking *kapu* in secret without any divine retribution, many Hawaiians may have begun to question the legitimacy of the entire system. This sea change in Hawaiian society appears to have prefigured the subsequent creation of a legal system modeled directly on British law.

Egalitarianism and social mobility

Marriage patterns across Polynesia suggest the probable flexibility of early Hawaiian practice. During the protohistoric period for which accounts are available, marriage was quite informal and fluid. Marriage among commoners was rarely accompanied by major ceremony, although the union of two *ali'i* was the occasion for ritual exchanges of gifts and land (Linnekin 1990: 121–23). Particularly for the chiefly class, monogamy was not expected by either party (Silverman 1983). Different classes rarely intermarried, although occasionally an elite male would take a commoner woman as a secondary wife. Class endogamy helped reinforce and perpetuate social stratification over the generations. For anyone of lower rank seeking advancement, however, it was always possible to suggest that one's mother had been impregnated by a high-ranking chief while he was touring his lands.

Initially, Hawaiian society most probably built on the common Polynesian concept of hereditary chieftainship. The islands were divided into numerous small chiefdoms, each ruled by a senior line, as *mana* was passed down from parent to child. However, the difference in rank between chiefs and commoners was certainly not as pronounced as it became in later Hawaiian history. The population was so small that nearly all its members must have been closely related, making it difficult to support claims of privilege based on heritage alone. After these initial years, however, social stratification began to increase. While it is unknown precisely how or when this occurred, oral histories suggest that Hawaiian society became increasingly stratified sometime between 1400 and 1600 CE (Kirch 2010; Hommon 2013). One possible cause is the rising population numbers, which made communities less interrelated and inherited differences in status more sustainable. During the centuries between initial settlement and European contact, landholding patterns shifted from a situation in which local lineage groups held communal rights to land to one in which the hierarchy of chiefs controlled territorial units, demanding tribute from the *maka'āinana* inhabitants (Kirch 2010: 24).

By the time of Cook's arrival in Hawai'i, then, hereditary elites had become the owners of all land, highly trained warriors, and embodiments of divine power on earth. Within this class, social mobility existed through a spoils system. Each new ruler would systematically reward his supporters, meaning that it was possible to increase one's status through loyalty to a victorious ruler. On the other hand, *ali'i* who were defeated in war could lose their noble status and their lineage would become a common one, though in practice loss of life was the more likely outcome. This mobility did not extend to the lower classes, who had no way to greatly increase their status. Their labor was directed by community *konohiki* towards farming the land, building irrigation systems, monuments, and other facilities, and generally supporting the ruling class.

Prosociality and well-being

In precontact Hawaii, charitable behavior within communities was important; it was heavily looked down on not to share with people in need (Matsuda 1988). On the level of the polity and relations between *ali'i* and *maka'āinana*, however, the picture is more complex. While the most important Hawaiian crops, taro and sweet potato, were not amenable to long-term storage (Kirch 2010: 51), Hawaiian chiefs did keep storehouses for food known as *hale papa'a*. Scholars agree that this food was intended for redistribution, but they disagree on the intended recipients. Much of it was given out to other *ali'i* and priests (*kahuna*) during great feasts (Kirch 2001), but *ali'i* were probably also expected to provide food to *maka'āinana* when disasters like floods or drought threatened famine (Kirch 1984: 260; Sahlins 1958: 18). Overall, not much is known about food shortages in precontact Hawai'i, although the nineteenth-century Hawaiian historian Samuel Kamakau (quoted in Schmitt 1970) referred to a famine on Maui after a drought, during which people were reportedly forced to subsist on weeds.

Chiefs did contribute to other public goods in a variety of ways that served both their political agendas and the needs and desires of the *maka'āinana*. For example, they sponsored the construction of irrigation systems. Although irrigation was not developed extensively on the Big Island, it dominated subsistence production elsewhere. Hawaiian irrigation systems were comparatively small-scale and technologically simple, such that they could easily have been built and maintained at the community level or even by a few neighboring farmers (Earle 1978, but see also Allen 1991: 122). Chiefs were evidently deeply involved, at least in later periods, in the construction, reconstruction, and maintenance of these systems. The *konohiki* oversaw all work on the irrigation infrastructure, which benefited local farmers, but at the same time obliged them to work for the chiefs to produce surplus food beyond their own needs. Our best guess is that chiefs expanded the irrigation systems that were started by commoners (Kirch 1985). In terms of the cultural lives of the people, chiefs were directly responsible for building and maintaining temples (using *maka'āinana* labor) and for supporting annual ceremonial cycles, which were broadly considered necessary for the fertility, peace, health, and well-being of the polities. At the same time, of course, these ceremonies legitimized chiefly rule.

Conclusion

Due to its remote location and the technical challenges of discovery, Hawai'i was one of the world's last places to be settled. During their comparatively short history, however, Hawaiian societies underwent a remarkable series of sociopolitical transformations. The archipelago developed what are widely acknowledged to be "archaic states," thus representing one of the only locations where states developed independently in human history (Hommon 2013; Kirch 2010). By elaborating on concepts inherited from their Polynesian ancestors, Hawaiians created the *kapu* system that would become so important, linking religious, political, and social themes of Hawaiian society.

While the development of uniquely Hawaiian religion and morality began over a millennium after the traditional Axial Age timeline proposed for societies across Eurasia, some aspects of Hawaiian political development parallel the institutional changes described as characterizing axial transitions. For instance, while no formal legal code existed in Hawaiian societies before European contact, the *kapu* system— consisting of a set of morally charged proscriptions and obligations backed up by the threat of force—could be seen as playing an equivalent social role to the ancient Eurasian concepts of law (such as the Greek *nomos* or the Judaic divine law) that feature prominently in Axial Age theories (e.g. Eisenstadt 2003: 36–38; Raaflaub 2005). It regulated acts seen as unethical and encouraged prosociality. However, it is clear from the discussion above that *kapu* restrictions did not result in greater accountability of rulers or more equality before the law, as has been argued for the "axial" societies across Eurasia. Instead, the Hawaiian *kapu* system effectively reinforced social stratification and gender divisions to a degree not seen in other Polynesian island groups.

The related concept of *mana* also served to differentiate between groups along status and gender lines. As gods on earth and ultimate vessels for *mana*, Hawaiian kings had a divine mandate to rule, meeting the expectations for "archaic" rulers in Axial Age theories (e.g. Bellah 2011: 212–13). On the other hand, *mana* could be expressed through action and skill as well as birth, creating some degree of social mobility within, if not between, classes. Hawaiian social structure was rigid in theory but allowed some flexibility in practice, as genealogies were open to interpretation and constant renegotiation (Sahlins 1985: 20).

With the arrival of Europeans from the late eighteenth century onwards, Christianity—inheritor of the Greek and Judaic axial traditions—was introduced to the archipelago. In the early nineteenth century, the *kapu* system was dramatically jettisoned and Calvinist Christianity adopted by the chiefly elite, notably by Kamehameha I's widow Ka'ahumanu (Fish Kashay 2008). Western legal structures were also instituted (Merry 2000). *Kapu* restrictions were lifted and men and women found themselves able to eat freely with one another and worship together. However, it is difficult to see the cultural colonization and eventual American annexation of the Hawaiian Islands as an "axial transition" at all comparable to the developments in mid-first-millennium BCE Eurasia. The insertion of Hawaii into the global economy caused food shortage problems by diverting *maka'āinana* away from agriculture into sandalwood collection for trade that further enriched the *ali'i* (Sahlins 1990: 35). Moreover, under Western influence, the time-honored response of the commoners to oppressive chiefs, namely to move into a new district, was made more difficult by punitive labor laws (Sumner and Roumasset 1984). Overall, then, the trajectories described by Axial Age theories for the five regions of China, India, the Iranian Plateau, the Levant, and the Aegean do not map convincingly onto Hawaiian history.

SURVEY OF LATE COMPLEXITY SOCIETIES
Eva Brandl*

Traditional name(s)	Alternative name(s)	Location
Umo-ke, Eva'embo, Periho	Orokaiva	Papua New Guinea
A'chik	Garo	Northern India
Dayak	Iban	Borneo
Shuar, Achuar	Jívaro	Peru and Ecuador
Haudenosaunee	Iroquois	North America
Sakha	Yakut	Siberia

Table 14. Names and locations of the peoples discussed in this chapter

Introduction

The history of worldviews and the institutions that underpin them has fascinated the fields of sociology, psychology and anthropology since their inception. Perusing a vast body of information on cultures past and present, collected for the most part by missionaries and colonial officials, Victorian thinkers built grand models charting what they viewed as the evolution of civilization out of savagery and barbarism. The latter were defined as more primitive stages in the development of human culture. "Magical" rituals practiced by "primitive" peoples were seen as precursors to the organized religions and scientific insights of more advanced cultures (Frazer [1890] 1975). Others proposed that all religion had evolved from animism, or the belief that souls and spirits inhabit the material world, through polytheism to the more sophisticated belief systems of monotheistic religions (Tylor 1871). Only the latter were thought to underpin ethics. Conversely, primitive religion was thought to be devoid of moral content, or prescriptions about the right and wrong conduct among humans. These theorists proposed that the "more elementary religions seek the supernatural for the purely mundane rewards of long life, abundant land and food, the avoidance of physical catastrophes, and the defeat of enemies" (Wilson 1975: 561). Today, Victorian theories seem dated not only due to the colonial presumption of their times, but also because they lack a plausible mechanism that drives the transitions between these cultural stages. In the twentieth century, most social anthropologists abandoned grand models and comparative work in favor of composing detailed accounts of particular cultures.

---

*   Harvey Whitehouse also contributed to this chapter by reading and providing feedback on previous drafts.

More recently, several prominent scholars—such as Karen Armstrong (2006), Robert Bellah (2011) and Pascal Boyer and colleagues (Boyer et al. 2015)—have re-engaged with Jaspers' (1953) and Eisenstadt's (1986) arguments for the existence of an Axial Age. Supporters of the concept argue that prosocial religions first emerged at a specific turning point in the history of civilization, namely the mid-first millennium BCE. In addition, axial cultures are credited with narrowing the gap between rulers and ruled, limiting the arbitrary power of sovereigns and implementing a more equitable distribution of rights and responsibilities in society. Finally, supporters argue that reflexive thought, philosophical criticism and reasoning about universal principles emerged during that same period of time. More specifically, proponents of the concept hold that axial thinkers detached myth from immediate experience and thus transformed the religious and political premises of society into an object of rational deliberation (Bellah 2011: 275). This enabled them to introduce a level of logical abstraction and analytic thought that axial theorists argue was absent from both archaic and "tribal" religion (Bellah 2005: 78–81). In the literature on the Axial Age, these achievements are attributed to the influence of a small number of pivotal figures, namely the philosophers, thinkers and religious leaders of second-generation civilizations that succeeded the first empires. The proposed centers of this development were located across Afro-Eurasia, with particular importance attributed to Greece, the Levant, Iran, India and China. After their initial formulation and implementation in these regions, axial ideas and institutions then spread to other civilizations.

Conversely, axial theorists argue that genuine axial traits were absent from the small-scale societies that preceded the emergence of archaic states, but also from "tribal" cultures extant today and in the recent past (see Bellah 2005). Wherever "tribal" beliefs and practices show similarities with axial trends, they are still held to be different in kind (Bellah 2005). However, macro-theorists do not always put their claims to the test by consulting the ethnographic record in the breadth and detail required to support them. While some discuss ethnographic examples to support their argument, these often receive limited attention and are confined to a small number of cases. For example, in his impressive volume on the history of religious thought, Bellah (2011) only discusses three "tribal" societies (the Kalapalo of Mato Grosso, Walbiri Aborigines of Australia and Navajo Indians of the American Southwest) and two Polynesian chiefdoms (Tikopia and Hawai'i) in some detail. Norenzayan (2013) mentions the Hadza of Tanzania and the Kalahari San and makes passing reference to Fiji. His argument, as far as it acknowledges ethnographic data, mainly rests on cross-cultural comparative studies that critics have found to be flawed (e.g. Atkinson et al. 2015). Given the great diversity of indigenous social structures and belief systems, this is problematic. Accordingly, critics of macrohistorical works have noted that over-confident generalizations about hunter-gatherers and other small-scale societies are far too common in the literature (Geertz 2014).

In this chapter, we aim to address this gap by consulting a number of relevant ethnographic case studies that, to the best of our knowledge, have not been discussed in detail in any account dealing with themes surrounding axiality. We focus on three key traits commonly ascribed to the Axial Age: limits on the arbitrary powers of leaders; equity and egalitarianism; and moralizing religions. To this end, we describe systems of cooperation, leadership and equity in six small-scale societies. We then investigate indigenous myths and rituals and evaluate their relationship with social norms. We use a list of criteria compiled by Mullins, Hoyer, et al. (2018), which summarized common themes and arguments expressed in prominent accounts of axial transformations. A few key markers of "axiality" stand out, which will be explored here. First, that leaders in axial societies were not treated as divine rulers; their ability to exercise power in an arbitrary manner was constrained by mechanisms that could overturn their decisions or refuse to comply with them; and they could be impeached. These constraints are thought to be supported by a formal legal code and a body of professional bureaucrats who are held accountable to administrative procedures. Second, that axial cultures began to equate commoners with elites and even with rulers. This development was supported by the emergence of universalistic moral ideologies. The general application of law to all social strata, including the ruling elite, may have played a role in this process. Finally, that religious leaders and texts in axial societies recognized omniscient supernatural beings that showed interest in the moral conduct of humans. Accordingly, supernatural agents and their ritual specialists judged and punished immoral behavior.

Ethnographic background

Seshat: Global History Databank has collected data on a number of small-scale societies in disparate regions of the world. These populations vary considerably in their ancestral lifeways. However, they also share commonalities of interest to the idea of Axial Age theories. None possessed states or bureaucratic institutions, and none were led by a single ruler or chief executive. Surplus production was limited, as was specialization of roles. None practiced intensive agriculture. All possessed subsistence economies, some with extensive barter trade. Urbanization was absent, as were writing systems. Accordingly, they differed considerably from the societies that brought forth the proposed axial transformation, which were generally states.

The way these small-scale societies organized cooperation and social structure also differed considerably from axial civilizations. For example, the states noted in most Axial Age literature tend to channel cooperation through formal institutions, such as state-run police forces and standing armies that enforce coordination with the power of law. On the other hand, acephalous societies, or those devoid of rulers, such as "stateless" hunter-gatherers, horticulturalists and pastoralists cooperate from the "bottom up." Many hunter-gatherers move freely between camps, hunt and forage together, and share food with those they reside with, many of whom are unrelated (Hill 2002; Hill et al. 2011). While some horticulturalists live in autonomous villages, other extensive farmers and many pastoralists form "clans" or corporate kin groups that regulate access to natural resources and social support. In daily life, much cooperation is flexible and occurs on an ad hoc basis. But it also involves more regulated forms of mutual aid, creating a web of obligations between distant relatives und unrelated friends. These obligations are reinforced through gift exchange, shared ceremonial activities and broader cultural norms and narratives. Marriage alliances between communities transform outsiders into in-laws. Fictive kinship, such as common descent from a semi-mythical ancestor, legitimates obligations between kin groups. Communal feasts and rituals provide opportunities to strengthen ties. In times of need, many small-scale societies extend coordination beyond the local community and cooperate at larger scales. For example, autonomous communities join forces in warfare when faced with an external threat. These alliances often remain temporary and disband once the threat is eliminated. In societies with more rigid corporate kin groups, different segments of a "tribe," "nation," or clan may coordinate warfare in a more routine way such that specific segments support each other against specific enemies (see Evans-Pritchard [1940] for an illustration of the concept among the Nuer, a Nilotic culture based in what is now South Sudan). Finally, influential individuals and their households gain prestige from generosity and hospitality, enhancing their status in the community. While kinship undoubtedly plays a prominent role in structuring cooperation in many small-scale societies, the ties that are cultivated through the above activities often reach beyond close biological kin.

Studying indigenous societies brings its own unique challenges. In the absence of written records, historical data on small-scale societies are often limited. Reconstructions of precolonial history rely on a combination of genetics, linguistics, archaeology and oral traditions. However, reconstructing worldviews of the past from these sources is likewise fraught with difficulty. While bones fossilize, ideas do not; scholars must infer them in an indirect, roundabout manner that is wide open to speculation and untested assumptions. Accordingly, we make no attempt to trace the historical depth of these traditions, and we do not treat them as pristine remnants of archaic cultures. Rather, we conceive of them as practices observed in a particular place at a specific point in time. To this end, we examine ethnographies, in particular early works which strove to provide holistic accounts of the societies studied. They provide a glimpse into ritual practices and belief systems as they were encountered by anthropologists in the nineteenth and early twentieth centuries. We supplement these sources with later works.

We now provide brief historical overviews of the peoples and periods under discussion in this chapter.

Orokaiva of Papua New Guinea

The *Orokaiva* are a Melanesian population located in Papua New Guinea. Their ethnonym is of colonial origin (Crocombe and Hogbin 1963: 1). Prior to the colonial period, the population now known as Orokaiva were divided into various autonomous "tribes" speaking distinct but mutually intelligible dialects of a shared Papuan language (Latham and Beierle 2004). While there were terms for various "tribes" or geographic subgroups (such as *Umo-ke*, *Eva'embo* and *Periho*), there was no overarching term designating them as a whole (Latham and Beierle 2004). They cultivated roots and tubers such as taro, which formed their primary means of subsistence. They supplemented swidden horticulture with foraging, fishing, hunting and animal husbandry. Pigs were the most important domestic animals and played a prominent role in symbolism and ritual. Dogs and chickens were also raised (Latham and Beierle 2004). The Orokaiva resided in compact villages made up of family huts built from bush poles, palm wood and fronds (Dakeyne 1969: 10). In addition, villagers constructed men's houses named *oro* or *arijo*, which housed unmarried boys and served ceremonial functions (Williams and Murray 1930: 70).

The population was divided into numerous patrilineal clans (Latham and Beierle 2004). In theory, wives were expected to live with their husband's relatives, but in practice, married couples had some choice over where to settle. Generally, multiple branches of a clan were present in a settlement, and these often came to form marriage alliances with each other. Individuals also retained ties to villages where other branches of their clans were located (Latham and Beierle 2004). Rights in land were held and transmitted within patrilineages, but individual families owned their own garden plots within the territory controlled by their clan (Williams 1928: 124–29). Neighbors and relatives cooperated in the most laborious tasks, such as fencing, sago-making and clearing fields (Williams and Murray 1930: 318). Men also went on joint hunting and fishing expeditions and cooperated in arduous construction tasks, such as house building (Latham and Beierle 2004).

On a day-to-day basis, much cooperation was thus confined to the village. But neighboring villages and occasionally whole kin groups worked together to establish new settlements and clear bushland (Morawetz 1967: 6; Williams 1928: 151). Villages and clan clusters also formed more far-reaching alliances for the purpose of warfare (although how precisely these were organized is disputed: see Rimoldi et al. 1966: 36). Allied communities affirmed their obligations towards one another by celebrating lavish feasts and pig-killing ceremonies. On the occasion of such festivities, hosts shared food with their guests, who were expected to return the favor by holding a feast of their own (Williams and Murray 1930: 30). In addition, men formed formal friendships both during initiations and later in life (Reay 1953–54: 117). These ties entailed mutual obligations of loyalty and support. Men cultivated such ties with many partners, both close to home and in more distant villages (117). A man's friends or *naname* were expected to show him hospitality and readily harbored him after he had run into trouble at his home village (118). Furthermore, "*naname* [...] had a binding obligation to fight for one another" (118).

Prior to the colonial period, New Guinea was intermittently visited by Malay and Chinese traders as well as the Spanish and British. In the early eighteenth century, the island nominally became part of the Dutch East Indies. Attempts at establishing colonial control remained superficial until the late nineteenth century, when much of it was forcibly brought under British control (see Waddell and Krinks 1968: 13–21 for an overview).

A'chik (Garo) of northern India

The *Garo* are a Sino-Tibetan population inhabiting the Garo Hills region of northern India and neighboring areas of Bangladesh. The term "Garo" is of colonial origin and refers to a set of groups with distinct dialects and cultural traditions (for a detailed discussion of the emergence of Garo ethnic identity see Bal 2007). Garos have traditionally referred to themselves as *a'chik* or *a'chik mande* ('hill men') (Roy 1999). At the time much of the ethnographic research we will be referring to was carried out, the hills population subsisted on slash-and-burn horticulture, cultivating grains such as dry rice and millet along with root crops and vegetables. They lived in hilltop villages built from bamboo, local wood and grass (Roy 1999). These villages were of substantial size and surrounded by bamboo palisades for the purpose of defense (Playfair 1909: 40). Each village also had a *nokpante* or men's house, where unmarried boys spent the night and elders congregated to debate matters of common concern, among other functions (Choudhury 1958: 12–13).

The population was divided into various matrilineages known as *mahari* (Roy 1999). Matrilineal clans or *machong* held rights in land (Roy 1999). These female-centered kin groups were a major source of support for individuals. Men, who generally resided with their wife's relatives, could expect ongoing help and hospitality from their own mother and sisters (Goswami and Majumdar 1964: 220). This is expressed in the proverb: "when a man goes to his mother's or sister's house, he takes with him his empty stomach to be filled in, and when he goes to his wife and children he takes a basket full of provisions to feed them" (220). Transferring men in marriage established lasting obligations between the lineages of husband and wife. When an individual was widowed, the relatives of the dead spouse were obliged to replace their kinsman or kinswoman with a new partner (Burling 1963: 144, 263). While families usually farmed their garden plots on their own, assistance within the village was common. During festivals, wealthier families shared food with less fortunate ones: "Feasts are frequent enough for poor people to eat significantly better than they would if they relied entirely on their own gardens" (Burling 1963: 204). The principle of reciprocity also played an important role in social relationships. Mutual visiting was common, and those who had benefited from the hospitality of others were expected to return the favor (Goswami and Majumdar 1964: 63).

Neighboring villages often considered themselves to be related to each other because larger settlements had produced nearby "daughter" villages within living memory (Burling 1963: 235). These village clusters "generally include a few lineages which belong to the same sib" (237). A sib is a subdivision of a matrilineal descent group, distinguished from other segments through a given name (22). Members of the same sib were considered relatives and forbidden from marrying each other, but the sibs of the largest descent groups were scattered across the Garo Hills and thus had little impact on cooperation (22, 238). While members of the same cluster were well acquainted and bound by ties of kinship, it had "little except sentimental importance" (237).

The A'chik have a long history of confronting incursions. *Zamindars*, landowners who controlled the neighboring lowland territories and paid tribute to the South Asian Mughal rulers, occasionally attempted to extend their dominion over the hill country (see Bal and Chambugong 2014: 97). In the nineteenth century, British authorities launched a series of punitive expeditions after the hill population refused to pay taxes, and eventually gained control over the area (97).

Dayak (Iban) of Borneo

The *Iban*, also known as *Dayak* or Sea Dayak, trace their origins to the Kapuas Basin of Borneo (Sutlive and Beierle 1995). While some use the term "Iban" to refer to themselves, this label may have originated with other Bornean groups such as the Kayan (Sutlive and Beierle 1995). Other groups use the term "Dayak" exclusively (Sutlive and Beierle 1995). During a series of migrations and aggressive expansions, the Iban or Dayak established themselves in other regions, including Sarawak on the northern coast of the island. They share a Malayo-Polynesian language and form part of the non-Muslim population of the island (Sutlive and Beierle 1995). In the pre- and early colonial periods, they subsisted on slash-and-burn horticulture, specifically the cultivation of dry rice, which they supplemented with vegetables, root crops and maize. Hunting, fishing, gathering and animal husbandry also contributed to their diet (Sutlive and Beierle 1995). The population was scattered across dispersed communities that settled in longhouses built from wooden materials (Sandin and Sather 1980: 10). One "longhouse consists of a series of family apartments [named *bilek*], joined laterally, and connected by a communicating passageway, gallery and open-air verandah" (Sandin and Sather 1980: xx). These settlements functioned as autonomous political units, with no formal authority above them (Freeman 1955a: 8).

There were no clans or "tribes," and the marriage and residence systems were very flexible. While the longhouse apartment occupied by a mother and father would pass to one of their children, neither age nor sex determined who would inherit it (Freeman 1955a: 8). Sons and daughters could choose between living with their own or their spouse's family (Davison and Sutlive 1991: 159). "Marriage, indeed, is a crucial determinant of *bilek* family membership" (Freeman 1958: 29), as in-marrying spouses became full members of their partner's longhouse community. Each family within the community held its own farmland and produced its own food (Freeman 1955a: 21). When in need, families formed *bedurok* or labor exchange groups in which members of one household lent their services to another, and the latter reciprocated by helping them in turn (Freeman 1955a: 82–85). Politically, each longhouse formed an autonomous unit, but nearby longhouses were often bound to each other through intermarriage and joined forces in warfare (Sutlive and Beierle 1995).

In the sixteenth and seventeenth centuries, the Sultanate of Brunei attempted to extract tribute from the Dayak, but its control over this population remained superficial at best. Brunei later ceded parts of Borneo to James Brooke, a soldier of fortune who went on to establish a short-lived dynasty known as the White Rajahs. Brooke launched a series of punitive expeditions and installed government chiefs. Other Dayak communities came under the authority of the Dutch colonial administration. A concise history of Dayak rebellions and Dutch and British attempts to curb them is provided in Wadley (2001). Despite the presence of the (post-) colonial state, many communities have retained some autonomy in the regulation of local matters.

Shuar and Achuar (Jívaro) of Peru and Ecuador

The people often referred to as *Jívaro* traditionally inhabit the Andean lowlands of Peru and Ecuador and share a Jebero-Jívaroan language. They are divided into multiple subgroups such as the *Shuar, Achuar, Aguaruna* and *Huambisa* (Beierle 2006). These groups generally reject the term Jívaro in favor of their own designations and it is considered offensive. They have historically subsisted on swidden horticulture, planting root crops such as manioc and sweet potatoes along with other vegetables (Beierle 2006). They supplemented farming with hunting, fishing, and gathering (Beierle 2006). The population was dispersed into compact hamlets built in relative isolation (Dyott 1926: 160). Each hamlet was made up of one communal house, a large elliptical structure built from wood, lianas and cane stalks and occupied by a group of related families (Rivet 1907: 583–84). Some hamlets "form, however, larger or smaller groups, separated from each other by forest and yet connected with each other by narrow footpaths" (Brüning 1928: 52). Due to frequent hostilities, home-steads were separated by large tracts of no man's land (Bennett Ross 1984: 93).

These hamlets were politically autonomous (Beierle 2006). While some sourc-es speak of "tribes," there were no resource-holding corporate kin groups. In fact, these "tribes" did not recognize formal ownership of land or other natural resources; instead, families simply took possession of unoccupied lands by cultivating them (Harner 1973: 179–80). Individuals formed part of a "personal" bilateral kindred. In this type of kinship structure, each person belongs to a different kindred "with rights and obligations coinciding only with those of siblings of the same sex" (Beier-le 2006). Accordingly, the residents of a hamlet enjoyed considerable freedom in handling their own affairs. In times of war, multiple groups rallied together under a common war-leader to combat an external enemy, but these alliances remained fleeting and often dissolved after the threat was neutralized (Karsten 1935: 183, 267, 282–83). Accordingly, the number of supporters attached to a particular leader could fluctuate considerably and change within a short period of time.

The Incas famously tried and failed to impose tribute on these groups. After the fall of the Inca Empire, Spanish *conquistadores* began to penetrate lowland ter-ritory and quickly moved to exploit the gold deposits in this region. Many Shuar and Achuar resisted these incursions and successfully expelled the Spanish from their territory in 1599. Further expeditions were by and large unsuccessful (for an overview of colonial conflicts in this area see Karsten 1935: 3–9). While the Spanish Crown and its successor states Peru and Ecuador retained nominal control over Shuar and Achuar territory, most communities remained de facto autonomous.

Haudenosaunee (Iroquois) of North America

The *Haudenosaunee*, more commonly known as the League of the *Iroquois*, inhabited the Great Lakes area of North America. A confederacy of five "tribes" or "nations" founded in the sixteenth century, they were made up of the Mohawk, Oneida, On-ondaga, Cayuga and Seneca (Reid 1996). The Tuscarora joined them in the early eighteenth century as a sixth nation. The Haudenosaunee spoke Iroquoian lan-guages and formed part of what is now known as the Eastern Woodlands culture area. The nations of the league were bound to each other through "fictive relations of kinship" (Foley 1994: 46). The "tribes" or "nations" were governed by a group of chiefs, who congregated in a hierarchical system of councils to debate matters of common concern. At the top level of this system, the member nations were represented in a common league council.

The Haudenosaunee subsisted on shifting horticulture, with corns, beans and squash as the most important crops (Reid 1996). Horticulture was supplemented with hunting, fishing and gathering (Reid 1996). Communities celebrated planting, harvesting, the ripening of fruits and the renewal of nature in an annual festival cycle (see Morgan and Lloyd 1901a: 180–99). During these festivals, they gave thanks to the earth and its fruits, and to the spirits thought to animate them (180–99). Extended families lived in longhouses made from logs and bark, divided into a number of compartments that housed nuclear families (Lyford 1945: 11; Noon 1949: 29). The various "nations" or "tribes" owned privileged access to the natural resources in their territory: "Use of hunting territory, fishing sites, berry grounds, and medicinal plant stations were deemed local privileges belonging to the inhabitants of that place. Ultimately, such ownership rested in the tribe or 'nation'" (Fenton 1951: 42). Accordingly, "[n]o individual could obtain the absolute title to land, as that was vested by the laws of the Iroquois in all the people" (Moran and Lloyd 1901a: 317). But individuals gained use rights in lands which they had opened for cultivation (317).

Haudenosaunee society was organized in matrilineages (Reid 1996). A lineage in turn was made up of 15 matrisibs, which among some nations were further divided into moieties (Reid 1996). Maternal relatives "cooperated in economic activities and were obliged to avenge the death or injury of any other member" (St. John 1994: 119). Marriages established lasting obligations between the kin groups of bride and groom, and allied matrilineages exchanged produce and services. For example, new husbands were expected to share their hunt with their wife's relatives (Foley 1994: 12–13). In turn, wives and children had obligations to their husband's and father's lineage. Sons had to support their father's matrilineage in warfare and blood vengeance (Foley 1994: 17–18). Finally, in-laws performed mortuary rituals for each other (17–18). On the village level, much cooperation was organized through mutual aid societies. For example, the men of a village cleared fields, built palisades and went on communal hunting expeditions, while women gardened and harvested together (Foley 1994: 11).

The Haudenosaunee figured prominently in indigenous and colonial trade networks. The Confederacy aggressively expanded its role in the fur trade, subduing various competing tribes and imposing tribute on them. Initially playing off French and British interests against each other, they allied with the British in the early eighteenth century. The Confederacy struggled to maintain its autonomy vis-à-vis colonial incursions until the American Revolution, after which the various "nations" were increasingly resettled on reservations, leading to a dramatic loss of self-determination and devastating suffering (for an overview of Haudenosaunee colonial history with a focus on the Seneca nation, see Abler and Tooker 1978: 506–514).

Sakha (Yakut) of Siberia

The *Sakha*, often known as *Yakut* in ethnographic records, are a Turkic people inhabiting the Lena river valley of Siberia. Their ancestors migrated there from the Lake Baikal region in the fourteenth century and may have shared cultural roots with Mongols and Chinese Uyghurs (Balzer and Skoggard 1997). They subsisted on pastoralism, specifically the breeding of horses and cattle for meat and dairy. Animal husbandry was supplemented with hunting and fishing; cereal agriculture was not introduced until the region came under Russian control (Balzer and Skoggard 1997). Sakha families were transhumant, or semi-nomadic. In the summers, they occupied *urossy*, tents made from birch bark (Wrangel and Sabine 1842: 38). In the winters, they built yurts or earth huts, small cottages covered in earth, mud, clay and cow dung for insulation (Jochelson 1933: 139; Wrangel and Sabine 1842: 38).

The population was divided into patrilineal kin groups. Individuals were members of *aqa-usa* or patrilineages that derived from a common ancestor nine generations past (Balzer and Skoggard 1997). These lineages formed part of larger units named *aimak* or *nasleg*, which included up to 30 lineages. In turn, multiple *aimak* combined to form an even larger group known as *dzhon* or *ulus* (Balzer and Skoggard 1997). Paternal relatives were expected to support each other in times of need. For example, "support of the *kutalani*, i.e., of the persons unable to provide a subsistence for themselves (aged cripples, orphans, having neither father nor mother, etc.) constitutes an obligation of the clan or the separate families which compose it" (Kharuzin 1898: 41). Collaborative labor was common. When faced with large workloads, families combined to pitch hay together (Sieroszewski 1993: 498–500). In daily life, much cooperation was informal and spontaneous: "Two fisherman who come together at the same fishing place will immediately organize a company. They will fish together and divide the catch equally" (Sieroszewski 1993: 680). Larger groups of people congregated during seasonal festivals. These were arranged by influential men and featured ceremonial offerings of *kumiss* or fermented mare's milk, but also music, games and contests (Jochelson 1906: 263): "Other people, and frequently whole clans, were invited; and during the festival, defensive and offensive leagues were concluded" (263).

In the early seventeenth century, Cossack expeditions invaded Sakha territory, imposed tribute on the population and established Russian control (Jochelson 1933: 220–25). Russian colonists entered the region and established agricultural settlements (Jochelson 1933: 179–85). Czarist authorities established an administrative infrastructure in the region, and in addition to Russian officials, Sakha nobles often doubled as administrators in their districts, a quasi-feudal system that continued until the Soviet period.

Limits on the arbitrary powers of leaders
"Big men"
How did these societies enforce cooperation? In general terms, standard thinking on this critical issue holds that norm enforcement may be "soft," operating through social pressure, or "hard," operating through violence or threats thereof. Either may be enacted by independent third-party institutions such as courts; in a mutualistic

manner in which the victims of a transgression pursue the perpetrator themselves; or collectively, when the whole community decides the matter. States codify norms in formal laws, which are enforced by institutions that aim to monopolize the right to enact violence. Once a group of people has claimed such a monopoly, failure to limit their powers may result in despotism. Where present, limits on the arbitrary power of rulers operate through formal mechanisms, such as legislative councils and independent courts. These aim to prevent autocracy by redistributing power between rulers and other institutions.

However, as some axial theorists (see Bellah 2011) themselves have noted, mechanisms that distribute power horizontally are by no means limited to axial civilizations. In fact, many small-scale societies rely on informal leaders who lack power to coerce. Informal leaders, such as elders and "big men," hear disputes and act as intermediaries in personal conflicts. In some cases, they also conduct informal trials with the help of oaths and ordeals, painful tests of innocence in which injury and death are taken as proof of guilt. Even so, they cannot enforce their decisions single-handedly and must obtain the support of their peers to do so. While leaders enjoy the respect of their communities, their peers are not obliged to obey, and may withdraw support if they are found to be ineffective. These conditions favor charismatic leaders who are adept at persuasion. Furthermore, when disputes arose within the community, friends and relatives of the disputants were expected to step up and contribute towards resolving the matter. Accordingly, "power" and social control are distributed across the community, rather than being invested in a single ruler.

For example, the Orokaiva recognized no formal leadership positions or "tribal" institutions. Instead, communities relied on informal leadership by "big men" or elders, who enjoyed respect due to their generosity, experience and decision-making skills (Latham and Beierle 2004). Many were renowned warriors or magicians. Big men were also skilled at establishing social relationships through shared ritual activities (Iteanu 1990: 40–41). To this end, they arranged communal feasts and relied on the labor of their wives and the support of younger men throughout their careers (Newton 1985: 204). Despite their considerable prestige, "big men" had no formal authority to coerce or punish, and their followers were not obliged to support their decisions. Accordingly, "[t]his status confers no sanctioning authority" (Latham and Beierle 2004). Headmen and lineage or village elders likewise had no formal authority to punish; they were restricted to simply expressing their approval or disapproval of actions taken by their peers (Reay 1953-54: 115). Power transfers were informal, hereditary succession was only practiced in the largest clans, and even there it remained limited (Williams 1928: 125). Respected elders and other informal leaders resolved disputes within the community. However, as there were no recognized "tribal" leaders, no one individual had enough authority to command the allegiance of larger social units or resolve disputes between them (Rimoldi et al. 1966: 30).

Among the A'chik or Garo, elders and village headmen typically exercised informal social control on the local level. The kinship system was matrilineal and matrilocal. Accordingly, the male headmen or *nokmas* who looked after village affairs were not patriarchs. Rather, they came into power through marrying women who hailed from senior households and stood to inherit family lands (the system is explained in some detail in Burling 1963: 223–25). The marital bond between a lineage heiress and the village headman often produced long-standing alliances between their respective families (223). Multiple *nokmas* were often present in a single village (223). They possessed no formal powers. In fact, "[a]ll the symbols of office [such as powerful ceremonial drums] go with the house and not with the man" (Burling 1963: 224). Instead of operating through formal authority, the influence of respected men showed itself in the "softer" way of steering public opinion:

People admire the rich men, but they do not defer to them in any formal manner, and an observer could not possibly tell from watching a group of men in ordinary daily pursuits which of them were rich and which poor. [...] Village life is so organized that few important village-wide decisions must be made, but when problems do arise people are usually willing to go along with the decisions of the elite. The *nokma* must formally designate the day for ceremonies, but before doing so he informally samples the opinions of other wealthy men. If disagreements arise about the distribution of plots for cultivation, the wealthy men can usually carry along public opinion toward some solution (Burling 1963: 207–8).

Headmen and prestigious elders presided over informal village councils, which acted as mediators in disputes within the community. It must be noted that the *nokma* was not the sole person responsible for negotiating such matters. In most disputes the *mahari* or lineages of accused and accuser also played a role in working out some solution. For example, in the case of adultery, an unfaithful woman's *chratang* or male blood relations, such as her brothers and uncles, were expected to punish her and contribute towards some material compensation paid to the injured party (Burling 1963: 169–70). Conversely, whenever a woman was mistreated or betrayed by her husband, her lineage mates were expected to defend her (169–70). Before British punitive campaigns suppressed internal warfare, offenses against life and limb were met with communally sanctioned acts of vengeance. While *nokmas* and other elders may attempt to negotiate a peaceful settlement between the affected clans, "they have no authority to declare peace or war [...]. If any man complains of an injury, such as one of his family having been murdered by a foreigner, the whole clan is ready to avenge his cause, or to fight until their companion is satisfied" (Burling 1963: 297).

Among the Iban or Dayak, autonomous longhouse communities were headed by informal leaders named *tuai rumah*. These headmen adjudicated disputes between members (Sandin and Sather 1980: xxiii–xxiv). In this, they often did not act alone, but relied on the support of elders and friends of the disputants, who acted as go-betweens and attempted to restrain them (xxiii–xxiv). This was done to prevent violent conflict among allied settlements (xxiii–xxiv). While headmen certainly received respect for their mediating abilities and leadership skills, "their formal powers were limited almost entirely to the context of warfare" (Sandin and Sather 1980: xiv). In daily life, a headman's influence was based on persuasion, not force, and "his position is dependent on the continued goodwill and approval of his *anembiak*, as the other members of the house are called" (Freeman 1955b: 48). While headmen fulfilled ritual duties, their status had no sacred character (48). Neither were they entitled to special treatment; their communities regarded them as peers, not superiors:

> When a man does become a *tuai rumah* there is no kind of initiation ceremony, nor is he given any kind of honorific title. His kindred continue to use the ordinary terms of classificatory kinship [...], while strangers address him as *wai* (friend), or with his personal name (e.g. Nyala). Towards him there are no special attitudes of deference or respect, other than he is able to command by virtue of his own personal prowess and prestige. He receives no tribute of any kind, and is entitled to no special privileges—except in his relations with Government officials (48).

Furthermore, authority was vested in particular individuals, not chiefly lineages, and there was no hereditary succession (Davison and Sutlive 1991: 159). And while elders were respected, age alone did not qualify a man for leadership. Rather, "the emphasis is not primarily on age, but on the personal qualities of the individual concerned" (Freeman 1955b: 46).

However, we must note that some authors have questioned this view (a summary of the debate is provided in King 2017: 91–95). While the powers of headmen were indeed constrained by customary law, many longhouse leaders sought to appropriate other forms of authority, such as ritual offices, to increase their standing in the community. For instance, Rousseau (1980: 55) notes that "the *tuai rumah* can also become the religious leader. The *tuai burong*, or augur, has a prestigious position and plays a major role in the organization of the agricultural cycle."

In principle, every man could become headman, regardless of descent or family wealth. However, "the reality is very different: in 25 out of 40 cases, the *tuai rumah* has been succeeded by a member of his own household and, in 14 out of the 15 remaining cases, by a relative" (Rousseau 1980: 56). The same contradiction between ideology and real life was found among war-leaders. The *tau serang* (or *tuai serang*) was a war-leader who organized expeditions, and he could recruit warriors from several communities. The position was taken by men largely through their personal skill and bravery, though the function was often in practice hereditary (Rousseau 1980: 57).

Nevertheless, we must stress again that in principle, community leadership or the position of *tuai rumah* was open to anyone who sought it, and whom his peers considered to be qualified for the role. Despite the above qualifications, longhouse leadership was a far cry from despotism and bears a strong resemblance to the soft power of *nokmas* and big men.

Checks and balances

As we have seen, the societies discussed above lacked "tribal" institutions. Conversely, cultures that regularly cooperate beyond the level of the local community often possess formal councils where leaders congregate to debate matters of common concern. For example, Sakha society was composed of patrilineal "tribes" or *dzhon*, which controlled access to livestock and natural resources (Balzer and Skoggard 1997). Lineage elders congregated in councils to negotiate disputes between families and plan blood vengeance (the standard response to homicide). Councils were composed of typically male elders termed nobles (*toyons*) by Russian authorities (Balzer and Skoggard 1997). Assemblies of elders also fulfilled judicial duties, but these trials were based on assessing prior agreements between the contending parties (Samokvasov 1876: 28). Whenever disputes needed to be solved, individuals would seek help from their lineage elders and the leaders of their *nasleg* or clan (Samokvasov 1876: 4–5). Should the outcome prove unsatisfactory, disputants could turn to the headman of their *ulus* or tribe (4–5). "Tribal" councils also met to organize warfare and form alliances (Balzer and Skoggard 1997). Accordingly, sanctions were not imposed by a central leader or authority. Instead, there was a community of leaders that negotiated common affairs in a designated body.

Some societies with more formal means of social control, such as hereditary chiefships and councils, also possessed formal mechanisms for nominating and deposing leaders. In addition, some North American cultures differentiated between diplomatic and military offices, ensuring a rudimentary separation of powers. Accordingly, societies with "tribal" institutions and more formalized leadership positions also possessed formal mechanisms for limiting the powers of leaders. For example, Haudenosaunee political organization distinguished between villages, nations and the common confederate level. In broad terms, the political system acknowledged *sachems* or chiefs. The right to nominate candidates for this position was held in specific matrilineages (Reid 1996). Sachems were "appointed by the oldest woman of the maternal family in which the title descended. Her descendants and those who were related clanwise were his constituents" (Fenton 1951: 50). Accordingly, this type of chiefship was a hereditary public office. The women of the matrilineal kin group not only nominated, but also "dehorned" or deposed chiefs "who failed to represent the interests of [their] people" (Reid 1996).

Chiefs congregated in a system of "tribal" and confederate councils in order to debate matters of shared concern. According to Noon (1949: 39):

> The method by which the chiefs arrived at a decision is known as counselling or "passing the matter through the fire" [...] Fire is a purifying agent and as the decisions pass through the fire, differences of opinion (impurities) are removed and the final decision of the Firekeepers represents the purified (unified) opinion of the chiefs. Counselling began with the Mohawk chiefs conferring together, and having reached a decision, their speaker announced it to the Seneca. If these tribes found they were in agreement, the speaker of the "Three Brothers," who was usually a Mohawk, announced the decision of the "Three Brothers" side to the chiefs of the opposite side. In like manner, the chiefs of the Oneida and Cayuga arrived at a decision, which was then announced by the speaker of the "Two Brothers" side to the Firekeepers. The decision of the Firekeepers was final unless they chose to resubmit the matter to the chiefs.

Lineage *sachems* were not the only chiefs or title holders. Another important position was the office of pine tree chief, a non-hereditary title held by distinguished war-leaders and orators who had been chosen in reward for their achievements (Noon 1949: 39). On top of chiefly associations, warriors congregated to consult in their own councils, as did women (Foley 1994: 24). The league was governed by a constitution of sorts that was transmitted orally from generation to generation (Lyford 1945: 9–10). This system of distributing authority across a range of individuals and deliberative bodies piqued the interest of early anthropologists: "Their whole civil policy was averse to the concentration of power in the hands of any single individual, but inclined to the opposite principle of division among a number of equals" (Morgan and Lloyd 1901a: 68).

Community regulation

We have seen how the powers of social control invested in formal and informal leaders were limited. In addition, small-scale societies rely on various control mechanisms that do not revolve around leaders at all, such as gossip, social exclusion and retaliation. Individuals maintain the unwritten social contract that underpins cooperation through "mutual policing" or reciprocal control. They may avenge slights and offenses committed against themselves, their kinsmen and friends through self-help justice. This could take the form of retaliatory raids, killings, kidnappings or sorcery attacks directed at the family of the perpetrator. Where possible, they may negotiate a settlement with the other party instead. Repeat offenders, notorious cheapskates and other known rule-breakers also face subtler pressures such as gossip, which can do serious harm to someone's reputation. This could prompt one's peers to withdraw cooperation, excluding individuals condemned in the court of public opinion from sharing and exchange networks. Severe cases, such as individuals suspected of harming others through unprovoked witchcraft attacks, are sometimes dealt with through mob violence. For example, while formal legal codes were absent among the Orokaiva, the community still shared a set of agreed-upon moral norms called *igege* or *yege*, such as prohibitions against theft, adultery and assault, and restrictions on domestic violence (Williams and Murray 1930: 323). Within the community, public opinion remained a potent tool of social control, as "[f]ailure in one's obligations means loss of status, leads to gossip, derogatory remarks to one's face, perhaps even a harangue at night by a man at the other end in the village" (Schwimmer 1969: 182). In the case of grave offenses such as deadly witchcraft, adultery, assault or murder, the relatives of the victim retaliated with beatings, homicide or counter-magic (Reay 1953–54: 115–16). From a young age, boys were trained to "take revenge for the death of a clan member. A clan victim represented the clan and failure to avenge his death badly weakened their prestige and status" (Newton 1983: 489). Alternatively, or in the case of less grievous offenses, the victim and their relatives publicly shamed the perpetrator or shunned them (489).

Among the Shuar and Achuar, social control was based on fear of retaliation, which could take the form of physical violence or sorcery. However, the right to retaliate was not vested in any higher authority or institution. Instead, the kinsmen of the victim took matters into their own hands, responding to witchcraft attacks and murder with blood vengeance in the manner of "an eye for an eye":

> When a murder committed by tribesman is to be avenged, the social morality of the Jibaros requires that the punishment shall be meted out with justice, in so far that for one life which has been taken only one life should be taken in retaliation. Thereupon the blood-guilt is atoned for (*tumáshi akérkama*) and the offended family is satisfied (Karsten 1935: 274).

Just as the kinsmen of the victim were responsible for carrying out retaliation, the relatives of the killer were considered legitimate targets for blood vengeance. If the murderer could not be killed in person, his father or brother was a sufficient substitute (Karsten 1935). The obligation to avenge murder could be averted through gift-giving. For example, the killer and his family may seek to placate the relatives of the victim by gifting them a weapon, such as a blowgun or rifle (Brüning 1928: 73; Harner 1973: 172–73). Should the aggrieved party accept the offer, they see to it that no blood vengeance is pursued against the murderer (Brüning 1928: 73; Harner 1973: 172–73). Self-help justice was also applied in cases of adultery and assault. Men and women whose spouses had strayed would slash the offender (or their lover) with a machete, with some assistance from relatives who held down the guilty party (Harner 1973: 174-75). By contrast, conflicts within families were often solved informally and through personal sanctions, such as avoidance and exclusion. For example, brothers refused to visit each other's households if inherited possessions were not shared to everyone's satisfaction (Harner 1973: 179).

Informal communal mechanisms also played a prominent role among the Haudenosaunee. For example, Morgan wrote that "[t]he lash of public indignation [was] the severest punishment known to the red man" (Morgan and Lloyd 1901a: 324-25). He claims that fear of social censure was sufficient to discourage theft (324-25). Families dealt with violent offenses such as homicide through blood vengeance (322-24). To this end, the family of the victim enlisted the help of kinsmen and in-laws. For example, men were expected to support the vendettas pursued by their father's matrilineage and their mother-in-law (Foley 1994: 17, 21). Alternatively, the family of the victim and the family of the perpetrator could negotiate a peaceful settlement (Morgan and Lloyd 1901a: 322-23). In this, they were not left to their own devices. The clans or "tribes" of victim and perpetrator congregated in councils to investigate the matter, delivered messages between the two parties, and, if the perpetrator made an offer of peace, attempted to persuade the aggrieved party to accept it (322-23). Anthropologists have claimed that most disputes were settled peacefully through the custom of family intervention, for instance Selden (1994: 72), who argues that "Certainly any quarrels that arose under such a kinship society were apt to be peacefully settled, since pressure on the quarreling factions was exerted by families of two clans."

Summary of limits on the arbitrary powers of leaders

The cultures we examine here all sought to limit the powers of leaders. Big men lacked formal powers; they depended on the continued support of their followers and could not enforce their decisions without it. Cultures that recognized more formal public offices also possessed institutional mechanisms for power-sharing. Rather than being invested in a single authority, social control was distributed across the community, as was the right to enact violence in culturally sanctioned ways. In the absence of centralized authority, self-help, informal sanctions and the mediating role of kin groups and friendship networks all have a part to play in maintaining cooperation. The societies we examined accomplished this through mutual monitoring in small-scale communities, without the help of written legal codes or bureaucratic institutions. Our observations illustrate that these cultures were not somehow inherently acephalous, but actively endeavored to limit the centralization of power within society, a feat that requires constant hard work and vigilance (see Bellah 2011: 177-78).

Equity and egalitarianism

Status and prestige

In addition to limiting the powers of leaders, many small-scale societies profess egalitarian ideologies and seek to distribute wealth equitably. This is evident among "simple" hunter-gatherers (mobile foragers who consume any resources they acquire immediately and do not produce a surplus), many of whom are fiercely egalitarian (Woodburn 1982). They achieve this by guaranteeing individuals direct access to resources, mobility and means of coercion, and by imposing sharing with peers (Woodburn 1982). Furthermore, in such societies "[p]eople are systematically disengaged from property and therefore from the potentiality in property for creating dependency" (431). This prevents the accumulation of returns from hunting and gathering. By enforcing continuous redistribution, "simple" hunter-gatherers suppress competition over resources (Hayden 1995). Accordingly, "upstarts" who strive to dominate the group are quickly silenced by their peers. Conversely, subtle status distinctions were present in many horticultural societies and among "complex" hunter-gatherers, who are more sedentary and store surplus food. Warriors in particular enjoyed considerable prestige. In many contexts, wealthy families gathered heirlooms and prestige items to display their status, but their communities limit the fixation of these differences with informal means. These include ridiculing pretense and pompousness. Distinct social classes or castes are often absent, and honorific titles only convey limited authority on their bearer. Accordingly, these societies have sometimes been called "transegalitarian" (Hayden 1995).

For example, among the Orokaiva, slayers were admired for their fierceness in battle, and men aspired to achieve this designation as it would bring them honor (Williams and Murray 1930: 311–12). When warriors returned home from a successful raid, their community celebrated with a feast (described in Williams and Murray 1930: 171–174). Killers attained the right to bear the names of their victims. They could also be bestowed with special insignia named *esa*, manufactured from materials such as hornbill beaks and marsupial furs (177–78). Other ornaments were earned through performance of ceremonial activities such as pig sacrifices (177–78). While warriors were welcome to showcase their achievements and admired for it, they were not treated with any particular deference. The treatment of respected warriors in ceremonies illustrates this point through a mixture of admiration and mockery: "The *aguma* [an old warrior] exhorts the *ehamei* [children participating in an initiation ceremony] to bravery, and the reason for telling of his own prowess is to give them something to emulate [...] While the distinguished warrior is shouting his exploits, a chorus of young men stand by beating their drums and making fun of the old man in their songs" (190).

Finally, "big men" gained much prestige by sponsoring lavish feasts that showcased their generosity (Williams and Murray 1930: 316). These feasts featured pig-killing ceremonies (61) and hosts liberally distributed pork and taro to their guests (30). However, as we have seen above, the status of big men was of a charismatic nature and conferred no formal authority over their peers.

Similar dynamics were in place among the A'chik. Prior to the suppression of raiding by the British, head-hunting was an important means of gaining prestige:

> In the records of the district, it is mentioned that from one village alone more than two hundred human skulls were recovered. It was the custom amongst the Garos to preserve the head of the man killed by them as a trophy. More the number of skulls gathered by an individual more honoured was his place in the society. It was considered as an act of valour and won respect and prestige from the members of the society. They not only carried on organised raids on the villages in the neighboring districts, i.e., the villages in the districts of Mymensingh, now in East Pakistan, and Goalpara in Assam to collect the human heads but also carried on such raids on enemy villages within the districts of Garo Hills (Sinha 1966: 22).

At the time, houses displayed the skulls of slain enemies on their roofs and head-taking functioned as an "act of chivalry" (Marak 1997: 44). Accomplished warriors received a great deal of respect: "The more the number of skulls the higher was their position and respectability" (Sinha 1966: 65). While A'chik communities were forced to discontinue head-hunting in the late nineteenth century (Playfair 1909: 78), other roads to renown remained open. For example, prosperous households could gain prestige through hospitality. During festivals, they could afford to entertain numerous neighbors with beer, rice and curry (Burling 1963: 203). Ownership of ceremonial gongs, which were beaten during village festivals, also conferred prestige on households (Burling 1963: 204-05). Poorer households could not entertain so lavishly and had to resort to borrowing gongs from wealthy neighbors (204–05).

Nevertheless, social stratification was moderate. Apart from the role of *nokma*, no formal status differences or privileges separated prestigious from less prestigious households, and their lifestyles were more similar than they were different. "Rich people spend most of their time working in the fields like everyone else" (Burling 1963: 203). While feasts provide hosts with an opportunity to display their greater wealth in produce, the ideal of generosity demands that this surplus food is shared with others. In social systems such as these, ambitious families do not gain prestige by hoarding wealth, but by "giving it away." This is sustainable because redistributing resources creates lasting obligations that the recipients of such favors will be expected to repay in some form, such as by supporting their benefactor's future endeavors (Hayden 1995). Finally, we have seen above that while *nokmas* were respected leaders, they could not impose their will on others, especially regarding the most vital matters of war and peace.

Like the A'chik and Orokaiva, the Shuar and Achuar showed great respect towards warriors. Renowned war-leaders wore "elaborate feather headdresses and ornaments when visiting other households or receiving guests" (Harner 1973: 112). They were admired for their fierceness. However, fierceness should not be confused with hot-headedness, and self-control was an important marker of valiant men (Descola 1996: 268). Those who had led numerous successful raids were even thought of as spiritually potent: "Such a man is known as *kakaram* ("powerful" or "powerful one") [...]. He is believed to possess an unusually large quantity of *arutam* soul power [...], which both protects him from death and is believed to drive him on to kill as often as possible" (Harner 1973: 112). Some were considered so powerful that they were "rarely attacked because his enemies feel that the protection provided him by his constantly replaced souls would make any assassination attempt against him fruitless" (Harner 1962: 263). Younger men admired and wished to emulate them (Harner 1973: 112).

The "power" of big men also manifested itself in the size and prosperity of their estate, with "powerful" men commanding the most impressive and productive households (Harner 1973: 45). These qualities made them desirable not only as leaders, but also as hosts. Entertaining guests and sponsoring feasts were important means of attaining prestige. Status with neighbors was "greatly affected by one's generosity with beer and food. No one can expect to have many friends unless he is a good host" (Harner 1973: 81). As much gardening and food preparation was done by women, men who could count on the labor of multiple wives were better equipped to become respected hosts (81). The realm of hospitality was not separate from that of warfare. Through the practice of *tsantsa* feasts, hospitality, feasting and warfare were all entangled in this sphere of prestigious male activities. *Tsantsas* are shrunken head trophies produced after head-hunting raids. Head-takers hosted a series of feasts after returning from a successful expedition; during these festivities, hundreds of guests would congregate for days on end to celebrate, dance and consume large quantities of food and beer (Harner 1973: 190–91). This festival cycle was so lavish that it may exhaust the host's supply of gardening produce and could take years to complete (190–91). Nevertheless, head-takers performed it "to acquire prestige, friendship, and obligations through being recognized as an accomplished warrior and, through the feasting, by being a generous host to as many neighbors as possible" (191–2).

While big men were admired for their fierceness in battle, they were also expected to display "an amiable, honest, and magnanimous nature when dealing with those who are not their enemies" (Harner 1973: 110). Sons of leaders were thought to inherit the outstanding abilities of their fathers (Karsten 1935: 267). However, this did not lead to a customary system of power transfer. Individual achievement was still paramount as even the sons of prominent leaders had to become accomplished warriors in their own right before becoming a big man. Accordingly, differences in prestige and charisma did not translate into a system of fixed status distinctions or classes.

Similar themes are evident among the Haudenosaunee. We have seen above that chiefly titles were transmitted within certain matrilineages (Fenton 1951: 50; Reid 1996), but status was not limited to ascribed or hereditary positions. Men could also achieve prestige through success in warfare. Young men celebrated bravery in elaborate war dances and chants, during which they boasted about their own warlike exploits and those of their ancestors (Fenton and Gertrude 1953: 106). Distinguished warriors signaled their status with special ornaments "through an elaborate set of symbols that included eagle feathers, down, non-eagle feathers, paint, and weasel skin [... A] full war bonnet meant an Indian had been successful in ten battles" (Eva-neshko 1975: 14). Finally, in contrast to the *sachems*, there were some chiefly positions that could not be inherited, and candidates were appointed on the basis of individual merit alone. "A warrior might become a war chief through demonstrating bravery and leadership ability. Men of wisdom, intellectual superiority, or oratory skill might obtain pine tree chief status. Finally, men by virtue of age and wisdom could become chiefs of the village council" (Evaneshko 1975: 45).

Furthermore, some differentiation of wealth was present. Some wealthy and pres-tigious families could command a group of servants to perform household chores for them (Beauchamp 1900: 83). Accordingly, some writers speak of a "nobility" made up of esteemed families who were admired for their descent and conduct (Beauchamp 1900: 85). However, this did not amount to a rigid class system. Prestige was always earned through achievements and by living up to "behavioral ideals of generosity, patience, willingness to help, self-control, etc.," but this was only as lasting as the good conduct was maintained (Evaneshko 1975: 157).

The scope of equality and universalizing ideals

Woodburn (1982) has written that some hunter-gatherers may extend their egalitar-ian ideologies to all humans, at least in principle. Conversely, many other small-scale societies did not necessarily extend equality to all mankind. Rather, group mem-bership is a common prerequisite for receiving equal treatment and the right to be treated according to shared moral norms. Accordingly, egalitarianism is not neces-sarily conceived of in a universal manner. This aspect can be seen in the Orokaiva's treatment of strangers and enemies. Communities that housed no friends or *naname* were fair game for warfare (Reay 1953–54: 117–18). Slayers took pride in having killed enemies of all ages and sexes (Williams and Murray 1930: 311–12). This attitude was reinforced during initiations where "youths [were] exhorted to bravery and blood thirstiness" (Newton 1983: 491). During these rituals, the young novices are first secluded in a ceremonial hut, where they observe various taboos. When they re-enter the dancing ground, they are "decked out in full dancing regalia. The novices enter the dancing ground in a dense phalanx, brandishing mock spears and stone clubs" (Whitehouse 1996: 704). Other stages of the ritual "involve [...] the presentation of 'homicidal emblems' (*otohu*), at which time aged warriors recite the names of men they have killed in battle, before *otohu* are fastened to the foreheads of the novices" (704). *Otohu* "were given to a successful slayer of an enemy" (Bloch 1992: 18). They "could also be obtained at rituals such as initiation in return for the gift of a slaughtered pig" (18). These emblems formed part of a complex ritual system in which

> pigs and humans are interchangeable in certain contexts. The final pig hunt of the ritual becomes a symbolic war on outsiders [...]. The way the *otohu* is given is even more revealing. It is offered by an elderly man who has been a famous killer in his time. Before indirectly giving the *otohu* he recites the names of his past victims to the children, who are thereby encouraged to become killers in their turn. The pig hunt is thus revealed to be the first stage in an ever-amplifying hunt against neighbours and enemies (17).

The "initiation concludes with an open-ended menace to outsiders which can in certain circumstances be the beginning of serious hostility" (17). When expedient, this hostility is expressed in raids and killing expeditions that target enemy groups (18).

Prior to the suppression of warfare, the bodies of slain enemies were consumed in cannibal feasts and their skulls displayed afterwards (described in Williams and Murray 1930: 171–74). An early ethnographer summed up this attitude trenchantly: "Towards all outsiders the correct attitude was one of suspicion if not always of hostility; a complete stranger wandering alone would be regarded both as potential enemy and good meat" (Williams and Murray 1930: 312). Accordingly, treachery against enemies was not seen as wrong, but as good strategy (312).

This point about the limits of equality is also illustrated by the treatment of captives taken in war, which some small-scale societies practiced. These individuals often occupied an ambiguous position. As slaves, they were considered inferior and treated as such, but could become full members of their host community through adoption. These behaviors have been documented, for instance, among the Iban or Dayak. Their drive to acquire heads and farmland, inspired by status-seeking (see above), brought about a need for territorial expansion against other groups (Rousseau 1980: 58). Exploitation and violence were thus deflected away from the community and directed at outsiders (Rousseau 1980: 60). During raids on other places and cultures, warriors sometimes took captives, who were subsequently enslaved. Many longhouses, thus, distinguished *ulun* ("slaves") from *mensi saribu* ("commoners") and *raja berani* (prestigious individuals) (Sutlive and Beierle 1995). Occasionally, slaves were sacrificed "as part of the rites of expiation which always follow serious cases of incest" (Freeman 1955b: 30). After this practice was suppressed during the colonial period, monetary fines and animal sacrifices were substituted for human victims (30).

However, with the consent of their owners, slaves could emancipate themselves and become full members of the community by performing a ceremony named *gawai betembang*. To perform this ceremony, slaves had to provide a few jars of wine, some calico cloth and a pig whose liver was to be used in auguries (see Sandin and Sather 1980: 81–83). These could take several months to acquire (81–83). Their master would then host a feast for them and, during an elaborate procession around the longhouse, the slave proclaimed their new status as an equal member of the community (81–83). The newly emancipated individual was gifted with a spear, to be used against anyone who henceforth called them a slave (Freeman 1981: 45). Their former master would then refer to them as their adopted son or brother (45). Some sources suggest that most slaves were enfranchised eventually (48). Accordingly, inferiority was not a permanent state, but one that could be overcome by becoming a full member of the community. Others write that captives "maintained a low and dependent status in the society, even when they were adopted by their owner" (Rousseau 1980: 59), never quite achieving full equality with other members of the community. This disagreement may be due to regional differences between different groups.

Similar traditions have been documented among the Haudenosaunee. Within the league, all member nations were considered to form part of a shared community or longhouse (Lyford 1945: 10a). Each nation played a distinct role within the Confederacy, and these roles were expressed in terms that referenced longhouse architecture. For example, the centermost nation, the Onondaga, guarded the central fire of the longhouse and hosted the meetings of the confederate council. Conversely, the Mohawk and Seneca acted as doorkeepers, which was due to their location at the western and eastern edges of league territory (10a). Finally, "[i]n between these were the Oneida who kept the second fire and the Cayuga who kept the fourth fire. They were regarded as the younger brothers whose duty it was to care for the captives" (10a). The number of seats on the confederate councils varied from nation to nation, but overall each "tribe" had one vote. When deliberating, "each tribe conferred among its representatives, then the Mohawk and Seneca conferred together before handing the issue over to their "younger brothers," the Oneida and Cayuga. They in turn sent the issue to the Onondaga, who in their capacity as hosts presided over the meeting and gave final voice to the unanimous decision (Evaneshko 1975: 52–53).

The imagery of the longhouse is thus one of solidarity and shared interests, but the league did not always extend this image of brotherhood to strangers. The Confederacy strove to win new members and allies by peaceful means. Those who refused diplomatic relations faced violent reprisals. If a nation capitulated, "it was at once spared and usually allowed to retain its territory and most of its property. The people were required to acknowledge the Iroquois as their superior, to pay a modest tribute in wampum [beads] and furs, and refrain from any further war activity"; failing this, "the Iroquois did not hesitate to totally annihilate whole tribes" (Evaneshko 1975: 52).

This contrast in treatment was especially true of slaves, obtained through capture in warfare. Captives were dehumanized, tortured and even killed in a routine fashion. Among the Illinois, another confederation that extended into the Western Great Lakes, captives were made to chant death songs when they were introduced to the victors' settlement. They were "treated as chattel, given as gifts, and, if rejected, killed. In torture they were cruelly shown their utter powerlessness, their lack of allies or friends of any kind, and were stripped of the very marks of their humanity: their thumbs and their face" (Peregrine 2008: 226).

While some captives were killed, families also adopted prisoners of war to fill the place of a deceased relative (Morgan and Lloyd 1901b: 277). These newcomers "were for a long time subject to suspicion and in danger of their lives; any untoward event, physical disability of the captive, or the mere caprice of their owners being enough to order them out to be burnt" (Morgan and Lloyd 1901b: 278). Some captives were allocated to wealthy households, where they performed women's labor such as household chores and worked in the fields (Beauchamp 1900: 81–83; Morgan and Lloyd 1901b: 279).

Others became full members of their adoptive lineage and could even acquire chiefly titles (Beauchamp 1900: 83). These adopted captives then "took on the statuses, roles, and even names of deceased persons" (Peregrine 2008: 226), replacing them and also "becoming" those persons. Ethnographers even tell of captured warriors who became so assimilated into their host society that they proceeded to raid their native communities (Morgan and Lloyd 1901b: 278–79). Sources on the Western Great Lakes suggest that women often played a crucial role in determining the fate of captives:

Some of them have lost a husband or sons in the war, and if seeing a handsome prisoner, or more often actuated merely by whim or caprice they ask for them to replace the dead, the council never refuses them. As soon as they are declared free, they are unbound and the women or girls who have saved them lead them to their cabins. They wash their wounds, oil them, and make them look as well as they can; and a few days later a feast is given in the cabin at which the strangers are adopted as children of the house, as brothers, sons-in-law, or other relatives (Peregrine 2008: 227).

Adoptions transformed strangers into kin and, thus, into individuals who could inhabit a shared social contract with their captors. Accordingly, captives did not form a caste, and the status of slave was not passed down through the generations. Rather, their "position, particularly if of Iroquoian stock, would gradually improve, and in the second generation no difference would remain between slaves and masters" (Morgan and Lloyd 1901b: 278). Again, we see how community membership entails rights to equal treatment by the group. Conversely, outsider status is hazardous, and strangers must overcome this barrier to gain an equal footing with their captors.

Distinctions between kin and strangers, with strong differences in treatment, were also present among the Shuar and Achuar. These differences are particularly striking in the domain of warfare and the treatment of slain enemies. It must be noted that not all Shuar and Achuar groups share the same history in this regard. While the Shuar are noted for their production of shrunken heads, there is no memory of head-hunting among the Achuar (although they may have raided in the distant past) (Descola 1996: 272). For head-hunting tribes, legitimate targets of head-taking raids were "stranger" groups who spoke different dialects and had no kin ties to one's tribe (Descola 1996: 275–77). In contrast, victims of blood vengeance (this practice was discussed above) were not turned into head trophies (275–77). This was because they maintained ties to the killer's group and were known to them (275–77). Blood vengeance and head-hunting thus followed different rationales and concerned different classes of people. Further, there were specific instruments for mediating conflicts without resorting to vengeance, or at least to prevent conflict from spreading. War between tribes, however, was not as easily mitigated, except through "*maniakmu*, 'a killing,' or *nanki jukimiau*, 'a raising of spears'" (277).

Again, we observe a marked distinction between ingroup and outgroup relationships, with dramatic consequences for the treatment of individuals and what kind of violence is legitimate in confrontations with them. Our examples illustrate that the ideologies of the societies reviewed here (at least as documented by anthropologists) did not posit ethical imperatives that applied to all people regardless of what group they were affiliated with. Indeed, members of other societies were not always viewed as "people" at all, a worldview that is clearly distinct from the universalizing moral schemes associated with axial thought.

Stratification

At this point, we must note that "stateless" societies are not inherently egalitarian. Archaeological remains, along with ethnographic analogy, suggest that foragers of Upper Paleolithic Europe may have switched between egalitarian and hierarchical systems depending on the season (Wengrow and Graeber 2015). These alternations are not limited to the distant past. Similar fluctuations in social structure have been documented among living societies, such as the Inuit, the Kwakiutl of the American

Northwest Coast, the Nambikwara of central Brazil and some Great Plains cultures (Wengrow and Graeber 2015).

A similar ambiguity was also present among the Iban or Dayak, although it was not based on seasonal fluctuations. In principle, this society expressed a "strongly egalitarian ethos" (Davison and Sutlive 1991: 159), at least among "insiders" or free people. However, Iban society also acknowledged status distinctions between those who sought prestige and those who did not: "Pioneering [opening up new lands for farming], continuously successful farming, participation in warfare and successful headhunting were the main avenues of prestige in Iban society" (Rousseau 1980: 58), along with feasting. In principle, status and prestige were open to anyone who sought them. However, Iban communities allowed for distinctions between status-seeking, more prestigious families and "commoners" who could not or would not compete for status. Further, while status was earned, "the impetus and the means for its acquisition were inherited [...] Any Iban was theoretically allowed to gain prestige, but only a minority of the population felt obligated to do so" (Rousseau 1980: 59). *Tusut* ("pedigrees" of status) were often used to establish descent from supernatural beings and culture heroes, while charms imbued with supernatural power were also inherited.

Some sources suggest that that group of status-seeking families reproduced itself by participating in prestigious activities. The gains from these activities—including raids in which war captives and prestige items like jars and gongs could be gained—enabled them to embark on further ventures, cementing their reputation as prestigious people (Rousseau 1980: 59). Rice surpluses grown on newly acquired fields could also be traded in exchange for more prestige goods, or to finance *gawai* festivals.

Nevertheless, we must note that the differences between prestige-seekers and ordinary people did not amount to formal distinctions between castes or feudal classes, and some mobility was possible. Drawing on the Iban case, Rousseau (1980) has proposed that hierarchical social strata emerge when the more subtle and fluid status distinctions of acephalous societies become "fixed" in a class system. Precisely how and why this occurs continues to be a matter of debate, and this literature is too vast to be covered here. Generally, it is assumed that economic organization plays a major role in this process (see Hayden 1995). Economies where resources can be monopolized by a minority often experience stark inequality, even without a state. Consider the case of early medieval Iceland, for example, where a class of property holders secured access to land by supporting chieftains or local warlords, who could count on a group of armed followers to enforce such claims (Durrenberger 1988). This arrangement enabled property holders to appropriate the labor of landless people (Durrenberger 1988). Similar trends can be found in some pastoralist cultures, where families with substantially larger herds are often the most powerful. This allows them to establish patronage relationships with poorer individuals, who come to depend on them in exchange for political and military support. These relationships can be exploitative, with steep hierarchies between leaders and followers.

As with other pastoralist societies, wealth inequality was present among the Sakha. *Toyons*, whom the sources describe as a military aristocracy, formed a ruling class of sorts. Descent played a major role in defining their status. "The elders and princelings are chosen, in hereditary order, from among the children and descendants of elders and princelings for an indefinite term, usually an older person in preference to a younger one" (Samokvasov 1876: 2). Only when there was no suitable heir available were the princelings chosen from among the general population (3). *Toyon* households were often wealthy with substantial herds and greater access to grazing lands (Tokarev and Gurvich 1964: 271–72). Some could also rely on the labor of slaves, often prisoners of war who were compelled to serve them (Balzer and Skoggard 1997). These slaves were occasionally transferred between prestigious households as part of dowry payments (Sieroszewski 1993: 867, 880). Wealthy men were also more likely to have multiple wives (Samokvasov 1876: 14).

Nobles' prestige was reflected in their semi-mythical genealogies, in which "the *toyons* often derived their names from the great and powerful deities" (Tokarev and Gurvich 1964: 281). By contrast, most "commoners" were comparatively poor and of lower status. Exploitation of lower social classes took various forms. For example, "nobles" employed their greater wealth and status to extract cheap labor from the less fortunate. As a result, poor households came to depend on the goodwill of *toyons*, sometimes for prolonged periods of time. *Toyons* legitimated their superior status by presenting themselves as patriarchal benefactors, and often manipulated kinship networks in their own interest:

> The toyons liked to style themselves the forefathers, heads and sponsors of their clans; they skillfully fomented various interclan quarrels [...], thereby sustaining the fiction of community of clan interests. A poor kinsman used to call a toyon who had robbed him of his possessions *aga* (father), and was expected to look upon him as his benefactor (Tokarev and Gurvich 1964: 275–76).

Such exploitation exercised by *toyons* continued until land reforms were implemented in the early Soviet period (Tokarev and Gurvich 1964: 29).

Gender

The above discussion has focused on aspects of social structure that are either specific to men or shared among both sexes. But what about the relationship and respective status of men and women? The case of gender equality surely is a complicated matter; small-scale societies vary considerably in their treatment of gender status, which ranges from gender egalitarianism in some hunter-gatherers to male dominance in many pastoralist societies, with many ambiguous cases in between. Intriguingly, even societies where gender relations are fairly egalitarian in daily life, often limit leadership roles to men. The same is true of some status symbols and other forms of overt prestige.

This is thought to be the case among the Orokaiva. While husbands were nominally in control, married life was characterized by mutual obligations between men and women. Husbands were entitled to their wives' fertility and gardening labor, but so were women to their husbands' gardening land and produce (Schwimmer 1973: 90). This reciprocity between the genders was not extended to specifically male systems of status and prestige, such as warfare. Granted, women sometimes accompanied war parties, carrying provisions along with a kind of quarterstaff called a *poreha* and acting as armor-bearers to their husbands (Williams and Murray 1930: 92). While women sometimes joined the fighting, they more commonly played supporting roles. We have found no evidence of women being awarded the status of slayer. Additionally, they could not take up leadership roles occupied by elders and "big men." "In public life, i.e. in the affairs of clan and village, the woman takes only a small part, but is well contented to have it so" (Williams and Murray 1930: 93). Women were also denied some posthumous honors (211).

In other contexts, women exercise influence and even form their own status systems with distinct rituals, prestige objects and leadership positions. Among some horticulturalists, men and women play complementary roles in ritual and community leadership, underpinned by ideas about the complementary nature of male and female cosmic forces. For example, Dayak women could not act as headmen (Freeman 1955b: 46), and distinctions between the sexes were present. Women did not participate in head-hunting and therefore could not acquire status from raiding expeditions (Davison and Sutlive 1991: 163). However, they had their own sphere of prestigious activities, made up of weaving, cloth dyeing and the ritual activities associated with them (164). Iban symbolism even equates skilled weavers with warriors: "those women who are experienced in the ritual preparation of mordants used in the dyeing of cloth (*indu' tau' nakar, tau' ngar*) are said to be the female equivalent of great war-leaders (*orang tau' serang*)" (205). In another obvious equivalent to head-hunting, the most spiritually powerful designs and techniques were viewed as dangerous and risky to produce, requiring considerable skill and experience (Gavin 1995: 258–290). While practiced in the female domain, weaving thus formed part of a more comprehensive "value system based on bravery" (Gavin 1995: 286).

On the ritual and spiritual level, women's activities complemented those of men. This is evident in the concepts and rituals used to underpin head-hunting. Head-taking was thought to promote the fertility of the women, for "in symbolic terms, Iban men go headhunting in order to procure children for their wives" (Davison and Sutlive 1991: 194). At the same time, head trophies delivered seeds to increase the fertility of the soils farmed by women. Longhouse communities re-enacted these narratives after the conclusion of successful head-hunting expeditions. When the male warriors returned, women received the trophies and danced with them around the longhouse (Davison and Sutlive 1991: 193–94). During these celebrations, women welcomed the head trophies by wrapping them in their woven cloths, "containing the ritually powerful and dangerous head trophy, transforming its threatening and disruptive influence into one of beneficence for the longhouse community" (210). Prestigious activities associated with male aggression and warfare were thought to guarantee the livelihood of the community, but they had to be transformed within the female domain to become productive. While other writers have criticized the notion that child-bearing and cultivation are directly equated with head-taking, they acknowledge that trophy heads "bring fertility and prosperity" (Gavin 1995: 288) to the community, while "cloths [sic] affords protection in times of crisis and provides a means of communication with gods and spirits" (288). Accordingly, the well-being and continuation of the community was thought to depend on a cycle of weaving, warfare, procreation and farming that required both sexes to cooperate.

It is, thus, not surprising that ethnographers report fairly egalitarian gender relations for this society. Husbands consulted their wives before taking decisions on household affairs (Gomes 1911: 129) and both sons and daughters could inherit wealth (Sutlive and Beierle 1995), resulting in an "even distribution of jural rights and obligations" (Davison and Sutlive 1991: 163). While rituals related to head-hunting play a more prominent role than rituals associated with weaving, women are not considered inferior or subordinate to men (Gavin 1995). In fact, women set the stage for and control many public celebrations performed to honor men's achievements. Men and women were equal to some extent but not equated with one another, nor were they considered identical or interchangeable. Instead, the specific capacities and tasks attributed to men and women were thought to constitute society together.

In other horticultural societies, these complementary roles translated into real political influence for women. We have seen above that Haudenosaunee women formed their own councils (Foley 1994: 24). We have also seen that female, not male, elders appointed chiefs (Fenton 1951: 50). The matrons of chiefly lineages also deposed chiefs (Reid 1996). And even though women did not usually speak at chiefly councils (Beauchamp 1900: 88), they could influence the *sachems'* deliberations. They achieved this by appointing a male speaker who communicated their views to the council and by refusing to cooperate with unpopular decisions (Randle 1951: 171–72). Some sources even state that in the late seventeenth century, a high-ranking woman accompanied a delegation of male ambassadors to Québec to make peace with the French (Beauchamp 1900: 86).

In yet other contexts, men's houses and associated rituals are found in some matrilocal societies, where male solidarity in ritual is counterbalanced by female strength in kinship. This duality has been observed among the A'chik. Husbands and fathers acted as heads of household and took decisions about arrangements concerning family property (Goswami and Majumdar 1965: 28; Pathak 1995: 71). Headmanship was restricted to males "because a village *nokma* has certain ceremonial functions, and such ceremonial rites cannot be performed by a woman" (Goswami and Majumdar 1965: 30). Women were also excluded from the *nokpante* or men's house. The men's house acted as a dormitory for unmarried boys; furthermore, *nokmas* held assemblies there and male visitors were welcome to spend the night there (George 1995: 188). Women were generally not allowed to enter the *nokpante* by the front door (Goswami and Majumdar 1965: 30). Only a few select women were allowed to enter via the back door, and this was restricted to the carrying out of festivities (Choudhury 1958: 13).

Some ethnographers claim that men generally considered themselves superior to women, who were regarded as close to children in political status (Goswami and Majumdar 1965: 30). However, lineage membership and lands were transmitted from mother to daughter (Roy 1999). Accordingly, household property was held by the wife, not the husband: "No Garo man may possess property apart from his wife unless he has acquired it by his own exertion before his marriage and it is independent of his connection with his wife" (Marak 1997: 85). Women lived with maternal kin, and husbands transferred to their wife's village after marriage (Roy 1999). Women thus had unrestricted access to a familiar support network of kinswomen. In such a context, husbands do not have free reign over their wives. Husbands who wished to add a second wife to their household needed their first wife's consent and were usually required to choose a woman from the wife's lineage (Marak 1997: 155–56). In accordance with this matrilocal principle, A'chik families kidnapped eligible bachelors to supply husbands for their daughters (see Burling 1963: 83–92)—the reverse of bride capture, which is more common in patriarchal societies.

The above cases illustrate an important aspect of the social dynamics that underpin gender relations. Societies where women form strong support networks are not usually "matriarchal" in the sense that women rule over men, but they can limit men's power over women. Conversely, where women are isolated from such networks, they lack bargaining power. Anthropologists have hypothesized that male dominance also depends on the ability to monopolize material wealth in the form of land, labor and livestock, an argument that was initially put forward by Engels (1884). Lerner (1986) later attributed the creation of patriarchy to archaic states in West Asia. Others have argued that male control over women has come about through a reduction in women's ability to form alliances with other women; a converse increase in the importance of alliances among men; increased male control over resources; and the formation of hierarchies among men (Smuts 1995). Male-dominated societies, thus, often experience stark gaps between the haves and the have-nots. Older, wealthier and more influential men exploit these gaps by monopolizing women, and families begin to concentrate wealth in the male line (these dynamics are explored in e.g. Goody 1976; Holden and Mace 2003; White and Burton 1988). Patriarchal cultures thus come to concentrate wealth, resources and political power in men. They also evaluate the female body and its physical functions in ways that depart from more egalitarian systems. Many African hunter-gatherers profess egalitarian gender norms and view menstruation as a source of "transformative potency" (Power 2017: 198) that forms the basis of women's ritual power. Conversely, many farming and herding societies with patriarchal values view menstruation and pregnancy as powerful, but also polluting, shameful and suspect (198)—and therefore as a threat to the ritual domains of men.

Some of these dynamics can be observed among the Sakha. Sakha families transmitted property and clan membership through the male line. Accordingly, the property rights of women were very limited, and they did not stand to inherit wealth from their father (Kharuzin 1898: 43–44). At marriage, women transferred from their natal lineage to their husband's clan and were thus often cut off from the support networks of their kinsmen, who henceforth "look upon her as a severed member" (Kharuzin 1898: 43). In line with the patrilineal principle, Sakha families preferred sons over daughters and "Yakuts who do not have sons are scorned by their neighbors: they call them *khatirik-uoma*, i.e. 'fire from bark'" (Kharuzin 1898: 53). Mothers had greater moral authority than fathers when it came to selecting future spouses for their children (51), but husbands and fathers acted as heads of household. Prevailing norms supported their higher status. Husbands were allowed to beat their wives for infidelity, but also for seemingly minor offenses such as neglecting their duties around the house (42). Husbands also had the right to hire out their wives to other households, and to claim her earnings for themselves. Men were not required to be faithful, but women had to obtain their husband's consent before pursuing extramarital relations. And a "widowed daughter, returning to the parental home, again falls under the authority of the father; she is as devoid of rights as her young unmarried sister" (53). Likewise, upon the death of their father, unmarried women came under the protection of their brothers (45). Finally, pregnancy and childbirth were considered polluting, and this was thought to bring misfortune: "Custom forbids women, particularly when they are pregnant, to eat certain dishes, and to touch certain objects. They are considered to be unclean. They may spoil a hunter's rifle for him or bring bad fortune to a fisherman" (Sieroszewski 1993: 904).

Summary of equity and egalitarianism

The cultures examined here have ways of bestowing respect on accomplished individuals and thus recognize subtle distinctions of status. However, these titles are usually honorifics that do not confer hard power over others. In fact, most of the societies under consideration limit hierarchy and have egalitarian ideologies. However, our sources indicate that this sense of togetherness was limited to members of the same cultural or ethnic group, who share a specific social contract. It did not extend to strangers, although the latter are typically seen as alien rather than low status. Outsiders could overcome this barrier if they are accepted as full members of the community, but this is conditional on the latter's approval. Accordingly, their egalitarianism functioned independently of universalistic ideologies. Other small-scale societies experienced stark differences in material possession and some "stateless" cultures recognized distinctions between "nobles" and "commoners," with the former monopolizing wealth and influence. Finally, the treatment of women varies considerably between cultures. While some were clearly male-dominated, other were more egalitarian, with complementary roles in ritual and community leadership. Accordingly, while there are few genuine matriarchies, claims that women are universally and across all cultures subordinate to men (see Ortner 1974) have been greatly exaggerated.

Moralizing religions and rituals

The worldviews of small-scale societies differ considerably from one another. Some feature deities that regularly intervene in human affairs; others focus on spirits, impersonal forces and the ghosts of the ancestors. Most incorporate numerous types of forces and beings, with a mixture of benevolent and malicious spirits. Ideas about the afterlife differ as much from one society to another as do other aspects of their cosmos. Nevertheless, many share commonalities of interest to our topic. Crucially, beings and forces that a Western audience may consider "supernatural" are not experienced as remote or detached from the material world of ordinary life. Instead, "supernature, nature, and society were all fused in a single cosmos" (Bellah 2011: 266). Animism, or the notion that animals, plants, natural phenomena and material objects possess distinct souls or spiritual essences, is widespread.[1] Bird-David (1999) has proposed that animism is at its heart a "relational epistemology" in which people come to understand the world around them through the relationships they form with non-humans. Rather than viewing themselves as standing apart from "nature," animists perceive these relationships as characterized by mutual responsiveness and responsibility. The spirits of primordial ancestors are sometimes assimilated to culture heroes and mythical figures, embodying group identity and shared values. Often, dreams establish connections to the spirit world and receive much attention, as do hallucinogenic substances. Ideas about contamination and pollution are also prominent. Bodily fluids, corpses, territories guarded by malevolent ghosts, and

---

1   See Peoples et al. 2016; for a discussion of the meaning of "souls" in animist worldviews and how they differ from souls as conceived in Abrahamic religions, see Willerslev 2011.

animals, plants and substances associated with certain spirits are often considered powerful and harmful and placed under a taboo. Humans perform sacrifices to curry favor with spirits and manipulate invisible forces with "magical" rituals. Active high gods (all-powerful beings that intervene in human affairs, sometimes with the intention to punish people for moral transgressions, or alternatively to reward them for good deeds) are present in only a small number of hunter-gatherers (Peoples et al. 2016). However, they are not altogether absent from small-scale societies.

Given the diversity of indigenous worldviews, it is difficult to generalize about the moralizing character of indigenous religions. This is further complicated by the fact that indigenous notions of morality may differ considerably from those of the Western social scientists that take an interest in them. Furthermore, the ways in which those norms relate to ritual, myth and spiritual entities may also differ considerably from axial systems endowed with divine judges that dwell in some remote heavenly realm. However, this does not imply that indigenous rituals and cosmologies do not moralize at all. Some axial theorists have recognized this. For example, Bellah (2011) writes that in "tribal" societies, ritual and myth support a shared moral order. In this section we expand on that idea.

Animism and shamanism

Some small-scale societies do not rigidly differentiate between ritual offenses and polluting activities such as taboo violations on the one hand, and immoral behaviors that harm humans on the other. Rather, both are violations of proper conduct that require redress, because they threaten a deeper harmony that underpins the proper functioning of the world. These notions were often informed by highly complex and sophisticated ideas about the cosmos, while in daily life, more concrete entities tended to predominate. For example, the Sakha cosmos was made up of myriad spirit beings, including gods thought to inhabit nine heavenly realms in the east, among them deities associated with the sun, the hearth and fertility (Gogolev 1992: 80). Their cosmos also featured numerous other spirits or *ichchi*, which were thought to inhabit rocks, trees, natural forces, living beings and artefacts (Balzer and Skoggard 1997). The souls of sacred trees were particularly important. So too was the spirit of the hearth, to whom people offered food and drink. Eagles likewise enjoyed a special status, "reflected in beliefs about serious supernatural punishments for the hunting of eagles, said to be children of the sky god *Khotoi-aiyy*" (Balzer 1996: 309).

The Sakha's cosmos was divided "into *aiyy*—the divine, light, clean, and good—and *abahy*—the diabolical, evil, and unclean. Humanity, livestock, and useful animals and plants comprised *aijy*. Everything harmful and foul—that is, everything that causes harm to humanity—was the invention of *abahy*" (Gogolev 1992: 71). Sakha notions of "sin" or "misdeed" were broad, and incorporated domains that a Western audience would consider both mundane and spiritual:

Very characteristic of the Yakut beliefs is the absence of conceptions of paradise and hell and the lack of any idea of retaliation as we understand it. The Yakut word [abahy] usually translated, sin, means more properly, harm, damage; for instance, [abahy] is used when milk is spoiled by a mouse falling into it, or, when a man's bed is contaminated by a frog (Jochelson 1933: 104).

Contamination was feared, and offenses against spirit beings could provoke misfortune. Spirits or souls claimed rights over the animals, plants and objects they inhabited. Those who encroached on their territory without paying their proper respects were "liable to be punished in some way: by illness, epizooty [epidemic among animals], or some other calamity" (Jochelson 1933: 104). Those who had been afflicted with some disease or other forms of misfortune consulted shamans. Shamans held seances for healing rituals; to this end, they traveled to other cosmic realms to retrieve lost souls or capture harmful spirits (Balzer 1996: 306). In this they received assistance from spirit helpers. Mediating spirits took the form of animals, such as "raven and eagle [or] such birds as the loon, hawk, crane, woodgrouse, swan, lark, cuckoo, and sandpiper, and included bears, wolves, foxes, bulls, and dogs" (308). Their role is reflected in shamanic dress: "Some of the iron ornaments of the Sakha, Even, Evenk, and Yukagir shaman's cloak symbolize bird feathers, certain bird bones (especially the humerus), and, often, full bird forms of various bird helper spirits" (306). Helper spirits lend their abilities to the shaman, and so a shaman whose familiar is the eagle acquires the keen eyesight and flight of this animal (312). Shamans also had "doubles" such as the mother-beast spirit or *iio-kyyl* (308). This concept is rooted in a complex notion of the soul. Sakha are thought to possess "three main souls: the *iio-kut* or 'mother soul,' *buor-kut* or 'earth-clay soul,' and *salgyn-kut* or 'air-breath soul'" (308). All three of these souls undergo transformations when a person trains to become a shaman.

While many shamans acted as healers, shamans were not universally benevolent and some could be harmful. Ethnohistorians speak of the "implicit menace of Sakha stories about still-avoided shamans' graves, about ravens as bad omens, and about shamanic curses [...] that are said to have affected some families for several generations" (Balzer 1996: 313). However, misfortune was not only brought on by offending the spirits or the shamans who served them. For example, those who lied under oath were also thought to court disaster (see Sauer 1802: 123).

Among the Dolgani, a Yakut-speaking population of reindeer herders of mixed origin, some transgressions were also thought to cause harm in the afterlife. For example, men and women who died childless were turned into frightening ghosts (Popov 1946: 22–23). Widowers who remarried lost favor with the gods because such actions were believed to go against fate. This was the case because "the [first] woman he selected was believed to have been born specially for him and had been fated to be his wife" (Popov 1946: 22).

Some ethnographers claim that the Sakha had little sense of punishment or reward in the afterlife, even after Christianization (Sieroszewski 1993: 958). However, their belief system had other ways of supporting shared values. For example, notorious evildoers became impure or "defiled" by their actions, just like people who came into contact with polluting substances. They were therefore excluded from some ritual activities, which is evident from early accounts of thanksgiving ceremonies (e.g. Sauer 1802: 117–18).

Similar themes are evident in the shamanic worldviews of Altai people, another Turkic group in Siberia. Among the Altai, animals are categorically divided into wild and domesticated species, representing two different but parallel dimensions of reality (Broz 2007: 292–95). The wilderness, in the form of water, land and mountains, is owned by spirit masters (296). Some have argued that, while the spirit masters show concern for their domain and the rituals directed at them, they are not interested in humans' interpersonal conduct (Purzycki 2011). However, this does not mean that they were disconnected entirely from the values endorsed in Siberian societies. This is evident from the ethics of hunting. When humans hunt, they enter the realm of these spirits and, like guests, must maintain a respectful relationship with them to ensure successful hunts. Hunters pay their respects by performing certain rituals and giving gifts to the spirits, for example. Should they fail to do so, the spirit masters will perceive them as mere thieves and robbers and won't allow the hunt to go forward. They express their displeasure by punishing improper conduct, sometimes with fatal results: "For example hunters who went to hunt in a forbidden territory accidentally shot one of their number who was turned, by the local *eezi* [the spirit master], into a deer at the moment of shooting" (Broz 2007: 297). Hunters' relationship with the spirit world is also defined by a notion of balance and moderation. It is believed that for each hunter, it is appropriate to kill a certain number of animals over a lifetime. Should they exceed their allocated share, both they and their descendants will face repercussions, for example in the form of curses (298). This concept forms part of a more comprehensive moral framework that disapproves of greed and obstinacy and values restraint in all interactions, be it with humans or non-humans. Adhering to appropriate moral norms ensures that the perspectives of human hunters and spirit masters can meet during hunting expeditions in a manner that is respected by both parties (299). Accordingly, we might conclude that the Altai notion of moral conduct transcends humanity. In fact, humans and spirit masters participate in a shared moral universe that all parties must acknowledge to ensure a productive relationship between humans and the environment that sustains them.

Our Siberian cases illustrate how indigenous worldviews can support important norms (such as truthfulness and moderation) and institutions (such as marriage and procreation) in ways that differ starkly from the axial vision of a remote enforcer.

Sorcery and revenge magic

In some settings, there are no higher powers to adjudicate human misdeeds in the manner of a divine judge. Instead, spiritual forces enable supernatural retaliation, mirroring blood vengeance and other forms of self-help justice. Ghosts of the dead return from the grave to haunt those who wronged them, ill will manifests itself in powerful curses, and humans employ sorcery to inflict harm on enemies and to avenge slights committed against them. Barriers between "realms" are often broken down during shamanistic rituals and under the influence of hallucinogenic drugs, granting access to this deeper reality. The Shuar and Achuar, for instance, communicate not only with other humans, but also with spirits, plants and animals, all of which are thought to possess *wakan* or "souls" (Descola 1996: 375–76). This is accomplished through incantations, dreams and visionary trances. Productive exchanges with the environment, such as successful hunts, depend on the observance of rules of etiquette. For example, humans were expected to desist from causing unnecessary suffering to game animals (114). The latter were thought to bear grudges against hunters who had done so. Furthermore, the dead were thought to sometimes inhabit red deer, which were therefore not hunted, as per "injunction of the ancients" (114).

Their cosmos was suffused with *tsarutama*, an impersonal supernatural force that animated everything (Beierle 2006). This force, neither good nor evil, was especially strong in powerful entities such as the rain god, the anaconda, the sun and moon, the earth and the *chonta* palm. Understanding these forces was crucial because "normal waking life [...] is simply 'a lie' or illusion, while the true forces that determine daily events are supernatural" (Harner 1973: 153). Various types of souls played a prominent role, most importantly the *arutam* soul, which boys and men acquired through a strenuous vision quest. During this quest, boys went on a pilgrimage to a sacred waterfall, where they proceeded to fast, expose themselves to the elements and ingest tobacco water along with other hallucinogenic substances (Harner 1973: 135). If the quest was successful, their *arutam*, the spirit of an unknown ancestor, would then appear to them in visions and dreams (138–39). Those who acquired an *arutam* soul were then filled with a strong spiritual force: "This power, called *kakarma*, is believed to increase one's intelligence as well as simple physical strength, and also to make it difficult for the soul possessor to lie or commit other dishonorable acts" (135). Possessors of strong *arutam* souls attained great powers. They were immune to sorcery and physical attacks, and some were thought to become immortal (Beierle 2006).

This cosmos was shaped by a logic of reciprocity and retaliation that also characterizes human relationships. This is evident in the concept of the *muisak* or avenging soul. This soul returns from the dead to avenge slights committed against its bearer: "both the Jibaros and the Canelos Indians believe that old men may, after death or even in their lifetime, appear in the shape of jaguars, anacondas, or other formidable or dangerous animals and in this disguise punish their relatives for neglect of duty" (Karsten 1935: 252–53). Avenging spirits, though acting out of anger and malice, may thus encourage individuals to fulfill their obligations. Curses and sorcery may play a similar role (Harner 1973: 111).

Illness and death were readily attributed to such invisible forces (Harner 1973: 152–53). However, these powers were fueled by anger at being slighted, not by some higher, prosocial authority. Kinsmen who had failed to live up to expectations were vulnerable to sorcery, but so were warriors to the wrath of their victim's vengeful spirit. The souls of slain enemies seek to exact vengeance on their killer by causing nightmares or accidents (Descola 1996: 115). After their return from a successful raid, warriors had to purify and protect themselves with hen's blood, a ritual bath and the application of *genipa* body paint (Karsten 1935: 305). But as we have seen above, the killing of enemies was not met with disapproval. To the contrary, it was encouraged and celebrated. Hauntings from vengeful victims were therefore treated as "very temporary inconveniences [that] amount to very little compared with the glorious feat of arms of which they are the consequence" (Descola 1996: 115–16) and do not deter further killings. Once cleansed, the head-taker attempted to use the powers of his enemy's muisak "for increasing the power of women who are members of [his] household" (Harner 1973: 192–93). Ordinary dead people are thought to bother the living to "bewail their solitude" (Descola 1996: 114). Humans placated them with gifts of food and beer. However, people treated these hauntings as a nuisance rather than a serious threat. It therefore appears that the power of ghosts to inflict real harm is limited to specific circumstances.

Supernatural punishment

Some theorists have argued that small-scale societies have little use for divine judges, hellfire, karma or other forms of supernatural punishment (Norenzayan 2013). They argue that people living in a face-to-face society where everyone knows everyone else can sufficiently monitor each other's behavior without the need for spiritual intervention. And in some settings, non-human forces really played a very limited role in the enforcement of social norms. The A'chiks' *songsarek* or "native" cosmos included numerous shapeless spirits beings or "*mites*" (Roy 1999). These beings were associated with such forces as the sun, fertility, strength, thunder and prosperity. Some of them possessed a god-like character: "To some of these *mite* the Garo attribute the creation of all the creatures of the world, the control of natural phenomena and the granting of health, wealth and happiness to mankind" (Khaleque 1988: 132). These higher beings coexisted with lesser spirits, who were often malevolent and a frequent cause of illness and misfortune. Spirits were thought to inhabit a wide range of locations including both the village and the jungle as well as trees, streams, road forks and mountain tops (Burling 1963: 55).

Both kinds of spirit demanded that humans observe certain taboos. For example, "[s]ome crops must not be eaten before a certain ceremony. One doesn't beat drums while the rice is ripening, for to do so might offend the spirits or gods and bring suffering to the transgressor" (Burling 1963: 62). When suffering some misfortune, humans performed animal sacrifices and other offerings in order to appease the angry spirits. During these rituals, knowledgeable men would "offer an egg, a chicken, a pig, or even a cow, depending upon the seriousness of the disease and the demands of the *mite*" over a makeshift altar of bamboo and leaves, along with some rice beer (55). Ritual specialists were known as *kamal* (Roy 1999). In addition, each village possessed a number of ritual stones or *kosi.* These were cleansed once a year with the blood of a sacrificial animal in a communal ceremony (Marak 1997: 112). A notable ritual still practiced among some communities is the *wangala* dance. During this ceremony, *songsarek* families make offerings to deities and interpret omens about the fertility and good fortune of their crops (de Maaker 2013: 231). The village shaman or priest then chants the local creation myth. "*Wangala* dancing connects people to the deities, reiterating their claim to the land they live on, and the forests and fields that belong to it" (231–32).

While humans sought to maintain an active exchange with the spirits, our sources indicate that this relationship was not a moralistic one. Misfortune usually resulted from angering the spirits due to some taboo violation, not from immoral behavior towards other humans (Burling 1963: 61). Supernatural punishment for the latter was limited to a particular kind of property offense:

> When the dried fields are burned at the beginning of planting, *Saljong* sees the smoke of the fire and comes to join the people as they worship him in their fields. He supervises them as they fix the boundaries, and he blinds the people if they later move the markers—the only example of supernatural punishment for immoral behavior that I ever heard of (Burling 1963: 58).

Other cultures are deeply concerned with maintaining harmony and coherence in the spiritual and material worlds. Immoral behaviors and taboo violations disrupt this harmony, with disastrous consequences. This worldview has been documented, for instance, among the Iban or Dayak. Their pantheon featured numerous types of spirits and higher beings, ranging from animistic beliefs and lesser spirits, often malicious, to benevolent creator gods who inhabit the divine realm of *panggau libau.*

Despite their remoteness, the latter were "unseen," yet "ubiquitous" (Sutlive and Beierle 1995). Men and women sought to maintain a good relationship with these spirit beings by performing sacrifices for them. Most commonly, these sacrifices were food offerings named *piring*, "composed of rice cooked in bamboos, cakes, eggs, sweet potatoes, plantains, or other fruit, and sometimes small live chickens" (Gomes 1911: 202). These offerings were presented on a brass plate or a makeshift altar made with sticks and small pieces of wood, and the spirits were thought to come and "eat the soul or spirit of the food" (202).

Families sought *lantang*, or the blessing of the spirits, before clearing farmland (Jensen 1974: 165–68). Other offerings were made whenever new residents joined the longhouse community (Howell 1908–10: 24–28). Bards or *lemambang* performed incantations during such ceremonies (Sutlive and Beierle 1995). Augurs or *tuai burong* interpreted omens in order to determine whether the spirit world approved of the community's undertakings (Sandin and Sather 1980: xxxviii). But the relationship between humans and spirits was not confined to seeking good luck or auspicious signs. Spirit forces also responded to moral conduct among humans. This is evident in the Iban notion of *adat*, a body of customary laws that defined the rights and duties of all residents in the longhouse, including matters related to marriage and inheritance (Komanyi 1973: 90). These norms, orally transmitted between the generations, also specified how breaches of *adat* should be punished (Sandin and Sather 1980: xiii). The headman of the longhouse was responsible for safeguarding *adat* (3). He also consulted with other members of the community who were knowledgeable about customary law, including ritual experts such as augurs (3).

Norm violations were not mundane matters. In fact, transgressions were thought to destabilize the world, which could have catastrophic consequences:

An offence against *adat* disturbs the universal order, producing disorder and the undesirable "heated" or "feverish" state, *angat*. The results of disorder range from minor sickness to epidemics and crop failure. Lesser transgressions may affect only the *bilek* concerned, although this is not necessarily so since an offence against *adat* disrupts the total order. The consequences are more the result of this disturbance than punishment inflicted on the guilty. Serious transgression of *adat* invariably touches the whole community. Particularly blatant offences result in *kudi*, the state of sterility where the natural order ceases to function. [...] Poor harvests, barren soil, sickness, and early death, since they have spirit origins, are attributed to disturbances causing an imbalance in the universal order of behaviour; they should not occur but for a breach of *adat* (Jensen 1974: 113).

Perpetrators of serious transgressions became *busong*, or cursed (Sandin and Sather 1980: xxviii). Conversely, transgressions that caused personal injury to one's peers or damaged their property were thought to harm the victim's soul (xiv). Grave offenses such as incest threatened to bring misfortune on the community as a whole. The Iban notion of incest precluded relatives from specific generations (such as the mother's sister) from being legitimate partners in marriage (Sandin 1976: 34–37). Marriages in defiance of this taboo were thought to cause earthquakes and tidal waves (34–37). Communities sought to prevent such disasters by performing pig sacrifices and ceremonial baths (34–37). These were considered necessary to repair relations with the spiritual world. Intriguingly, and of interest to ideas of supernatural punishment and monitoring:

> many of the acts thought to cause *busong* are covert, like theft, adultery or other sexual delicts, and so are often undetected, or if suspected, are difficult to prove. Thus even though a wrongful act may remain unpunished, a sense of moral disapproval is reinforced by a belief that the culprit will eventually be visited with misfortune as a consequence of his actions. The Iban believe that anyone who successfully cheats another, or escapes punishment for his crimes, even though he might appear to profit temporarily, ultimately suffers supernatural *retribution*. In addition, a person who refuses to accept a judicial settlement is similarly thought to suffer *busong* (Sandin and Sather 1980: xxviii).

Accordingly, large-scale societies are not the only cultures that benefit from supernatural retribution. Even in small communities, some misdeeds may go undetected or unpunished, and curses enforce what cannot be enforced otherwise.

Ancestors, ritual and myth

In other contexts, culture heroes, mythical figures and the protagonists of folk tales may illustrate ideals of honorable conduct (whether they live up to them or not). As Bellah (2011: 142) puts it, "myth is [simply] an account of the way things are, a reference frame for understanding the world." During collective rituals, people identify with these mythical forces and beings to the extent that they establish an embodied connection with mythical time itself. "[R]itual performance recapitulates the mythical relation of powerful beings and humans" (Bellah 2011: 144). The relationship between humans and other forces is above all participatory, experiential and immediate. This manner of engaging with myth and ritual differs starkly from the doctrinal systems of axial religions, which rely on codified bodies of rules that regulate liturgy, theology and human conduct, and establish binding interpretations thereof (Whitehouse 2000). But the absence of doctrinal religion does not preclude indigenous myths and rituals from making moralizing statements about human conduct. Among Australian Aborigines and other indigenous societies, linkages between humans, ancestral beings and mythical time are thought to be the foundation of society, but also of the moral order that underpins the proper functioning of the cosmos (Bellah 2011: 150–51, 172).

Similar trends can be identified in Orokaiva groups. Their world was populated by "demigods" or culture heroes, ancestor spirits and animistic beliefs. They conceived of the cosmos as divided into two realms: "the human world, comprising villages and gardens, and the wild world, *ariri*, the bush, where everything is dangerous and inimical to man, and where the ghosts (*sovai*) have their abode" (Schwimmer 1973: 140–41). These spirits did not resemble the omnipotent creator god familiar to Jews, Christians and Muslims. To the contrary, spirits were not superior to humans: "So-called supernatural beings, like persons and things, are part of society. As such, they are also subordinated to the values that order society and their identity is determined in terms of relations" (Iteanu 1990: 37). Instead, all entities are defined by their position in ritual exchanges, specifically their ability to butcher, eat and distribute meat in culturally sanctioned ways. This ritual order is thought to create society by defining relationships between those who participate and by imposing distinctions between humans, animals and spirits. It is thus not surprising that, once contacted by Christian missionaries, Orokaiva were reluctant to accept claims about god's omnipotence (Schwimmer 1969: 129).

Orokaivan demigods—the most powerful ancestor spirits—were sources of moral order:

> If the Orokaiva, by and large, order their lives by the same moral principles, they would explain this by their common belief in certain demigods whom they all regard as their ancestors and as sources of authority, and who created certain institutions embodying moral norms to which they all subscribe. Not only do they obey the precepts of these demi-gods, they also re-enact their feats in ritual and identify with them during ceremonies, and in many of their regular expressive activities (Schwimmer 1973: 51).

In the Orokaivan system, vital social institutions, such as warfare, feasting and gift exchange, had come into being through the actions of primordial ancestors and other mythical figures (some of these myths and their implications for Orokaiva social philosophy are explored in Schwimmer 1973: 51–56). On the most fundamental level, the clan system itself was defined through its relationship with ancestor spirits: "What they [i.e. the clans] are above all [...] is a relationship of certain living people to certain dead spirits which were associated with the village of the living" (Bloch 1992: 14).

Mythology also provided a template for (temporarily) overcoming strife: feasting. In mythical time, a fight broke out in a community preparing a feast (Schwimmer 1973: 52). This prompts their parents to desert them. When found by their sons, they exhort their children to return to the feast, but refuse to leave with them, saying "We are staying here. In bad times you will hear no speech from us but if times are good, and you intend to hold a feast, then listen to our speech" (reported in Schwimmer 1973: 53).

This tale establishes a set of customs related to feasting, such as the construction of ceremonial houses for the purpose of giving a feast. The parents, or feast-givers, remove this ritual house from the festival after fighting breaks out. Accordingly, a "feast could be permitted only if perfect peace reigned among the guests. If the guests quarreled the demigod's spirit would at once depart and the feast would be ritually void or even calamitous" (Schwimmer 1973: 54). Communal feasting is also validated in a cannibal tale. This story is based on the figure of Totoima, a hybrid being who combined human and pig-like features, and who ate his own children (55–56). He was killed through some act of trickery to avenge his misdeeds (55–56). His body was cut up, distributed and consumed among the ancestors of the Orokaiva (55–56). Due to Totoima's *ivo* or spiritual power, "[t]hose who ate the joints multiplied miraculously so that their descendants peopled practically the whole of the Northern District" (55). Feasting provides an opportunity to re-enact this communion, which temporarily suspends the state of permanent strife between enemy groups.

The power gained from consuming Totoima was then passed down the generations in the patrilineages whose ancestors had been present at the feast. Their *ivo* was "transmitted to a man by his father at the time of conception, and is augmented by the fact of success, and particularly by the killing of an animal or an enemy, the eating of meat, or the making of gifts" (Schwimmer 1973: 69). In line with these views, those who occupied clan lands strongly identified with the lineage spirits that resided there (109).

Maintaining good relations with the dead was believed to sustain life among the living. Conversely, when angered, ancestors became dangerous and punished taboo violations (Williams 1928: 58). Illness and misfortune were thought to befall those who dared enter a dead man's gardens, but also those who failed to observe the offerings and other rituals meant to honor the dead (58). When Mt Lamington erupted in 1951, many Orokaiva interpreted the event as punishment for breaches of taboo, such as the use of firearms near the volcano; others were convinced that the spirits of the mountain had punished the colonial powers for killing indigenous people (Schwimmer 1977). Some accounts suggest that ancestors were also displeased about strife among their descendants. For example, when an Orokaiva community experienced a catastrophic crop failure in the 1970s, villagers assumed that conflicts and infighting among the residents had caused some spiritual force to punish them (Newton 1985: 93). While some suspected the work of a sorcerer, many attributed their misfortune to the Christian god and their own ancestors (93).

We conclude that, on one level, Orokaiva society possessed a social order validated by ancestors and culture heroes who provided templates for normal behavior. But beneath the normal social order lurked archaic powers that were potent but also highly dangerous. These forces did not follow normal social rules and distinctions. They were activated in dramatic collective rituals. During the *jape* ceremony of the initiation ritual, boys and girls re-entered the settlement after a period of seclusion. Adults assumed specific characters or personas on the occasion, who committed numerous acts of violence and taboo violation (sleeping with married women, for example). The powerful but dangerous spiritual force at work in these ceremonies "temporarily extinguishes social relations and obliterates the distinction between subjects, objects and supernatural beings" (Iteanu 1990: 47). This ceremonial destruction of the normal social order was followed by another lengthy period of seclusion for the initiates (46–47). The community re-established ordinary social relations some years after these events by giving a big feast and exchange ceremony during which gifts were offered. We might say that these rituals create and recreate social order out of chaos.

Ancestors, ritual and myth were also close to the foundation of Haudenosaunee society. Their cosmos was composed of multiple deities, souls and lesser spirits. These included the Three Sisters or the spirits of the sacred crops maize, beans and squash, which were celebrated in the annual thanksgiving festivals (see Morgan and Lloyd 1901a). The most important entity was the Great Spirit, "who was responsible for the creation of men, the plants and animals, and the forces of good in nature" (Reid 1996). Early anthropologists theorized that this moralistic concept of the Great Spirit was a product of the colonial encounter, when Christian concepts introduced by Jesuit missionaries were incorporated into the indigenous cosmos (Morgan and Lloyd 1901b: 233). According to Morgan and Lloyd (234), these encounters transformed Haudenosaunee beliefs into an "ethical religion." In addition, the precontact Haudenosaunee are said to have worshiped the sun, or a Sun God, to whom "were paid prayer and sacrifice and thanks for such good gifts as food, sunshine, and victory over the enemy" (234).

Other sources, however, contradict these claims about the nature of indigenous worldviews. They emphasize that the spirit world legitimated key values, such as obligations to kinsmen, loyalty to one's nation and respect for elders:

The myths of disorder and order established a set of relations where consensus, equity and hospitality were stressed. At the village level all the myths of disorder and order validated the authority of the elders, matrons and chiefs; while at the confederate level the epic of the establishment of the league validated the authority status of the civil chief. Actions harmful to the interests of those in positions of authority could result in cultural disaster and thus supernatural sanctions against factionalism existed (Foley 1994: 46–47).

Furthermore, "[s]haring took on a ritualized form and received a supernatural sanction in the dream quest behaviour and feasts for the dead" (Foley 1994: 47). The welfare of humans relied on their ability to maintain harmonious relations with the spirit world. The spirits of humans, animals and the forces of nature were all connected and communicated with each other (St. John 1994: 50–51). Haudenosaunee treated dreams as messages from the spirit world (Hewitt 1895: 110–11). The spirits of animals, rivers, crops and trees, among many others, appeared in dreams to give advice and make demands; the dreamer and his community strove to meet these demands. The "denial of a request [...] might upset the harmony between human and non-human persons" (St. John 1994: 57). Whenever the harmony of the cosmos had become disturbed, the spiritual connections between all animate things were vital to restoring balance in the world (50–51).

The people's welfare also depended on maintaining harmonious relations with the dead. The living were obliged to remember their ancestors and to offer up food and presents to them (Shimony 1961: 231). Those who neglected these observances were met with illness and death (231). Both elements combined in communal feasts of the dead. These were held whenever a village was moved to a new site. The ancestors accompanied the living to their new dwellings, and thus "the bones of the dead were gathered and relocated in a mass grave near the new village site" (Foley 1994: 37). Just like burial rites, feasts of the dead connected the living with their allies. The resident matrilineages invited guests and held a feast in which the latter received gifts (15–16). Over time, different kin groups and villages exchanged gifts with each other in this manner, and sharing of gifts became a matter of prestige, not only for the living members of a lineage, but also their ancestors (15–16). Thus, the feast of the dead "in which the belongings of deceased individuals are given as gifts to relatives, friends, and allies of the deceased is seen as one mechanism through which social links severed by death were reestablished" (Peregrine 2008: 229).

Summary of moralizing religions and rituals

We have seen how ritual and myth can support social order and shared values, whether "supernatural" agents directly punish humans for moral transgressions or not. We have documented one culture—the Iban or Dayak—with an elaborate cosmic architecture that is highly sensitive not only to breaches of taboo, but also to moral offenses against other humans. In most other cases, the relationship between "supernatural" beliefs and moral norms is more subtle and need not rely on enforcement "from above." The misfortunes a person might suffer after offending or harming someone do not always come from a higher cosmic authority, but from those who feel slighted by those actions. Where divine punishment, as conceived in Abrahamic religions, mimics impartial judges and formal law, sorcery attacks implement the logic of blood vengeance and self-help with the means of magic.

Conclusion

We have seen how small-scale societies organize cooperation in a range of informal ways, including kin ties and friendship networks, reciprocal exchange, and prestige systems. Alliances, (fictive) kinship and marriage exchange extend cooperation beyond the local community. Conformity with prosocial norms is ensured through various informal mechanisms of social control, such as gossip and public indignation, retaliation and dispute resolution by community leaders. In addition, many acephalous societies that cooperate at larger scales have formal councils for debating "tribal" affairs.

Intriguingly, some of the traits identified by Mullins, Hoyer, et al. (2018) as core facets of axiality identified in many prominent works on the subject are present in these cultures as well, albeit ambiguously: many small-scale societies possess egalitarian values; leaders are often viewed as charismatic figures, and some status distinctions are present, though leaders possess no formal authority to coerce, and no monopoly over the use of force; hierarchies are kept in check through informal means, such as social censure and the bestowal (or withdrawal) of community support; societies that recognize formal leadership positions also implement mechanisms for appointing and deposing leaders. Accordingly, egalitarian ideologies and limits on the power of leaders were not suddenly discovered by certain "advanced" civilizations or exceptional individuals. Rather, these achievements are present in a wide range of social systems. They rely on broader societal efforts and require much cooperation, monitoring and vigilance to maintain. Its wide geographic spread and commonality among many hunter-gatherers suggest that egalitarianism has deep roots in human history and predates the more hierarchical primary states that emerged in the Neolithic. Some axial theorists have acknowledged that archaic states displaced earlier, more egalitarian societies (Bellah 2005: 69–70). By promoting egalitarian ethical ideas with universal claims, axial thinkers achieved a "reassertion of fundamental human equality" (Bellah 2011: 606) rather than inventing it from scratch.

Nevertheless, we must not fall for romantic fantasies about "noble savages." Where present, egalitarianism had its limits. It breaks down where resources can be monopolized by a few; and societies with stark wealth inequality appear to develop hierarchical distinctions of status. Furthermore, egalitarian ideologies are not necessarily universal in scope, with group membership a prerequisite for such treatment. Many societies possess mechanisms for transforming strangers into peers, but those who do not undergo this are beyond the scope of ordinary social norms. Contrary to assumptions made by many Westerners, the kind of egalitarianism we described here is compatible with fairly extreme forms of warfare and violence. Further, the treatment of women varies considerably between different small-scale societies, ranging from relative equality or complementarity to male dominance. Conversely, it is worth noting that many axial religions, too, have often drawn firm boundaries around the community of believers and restricted the rights of "unbelievers" and apostates (examples can be found in other chapters in this volume). At the same time, cultures dominated by these religions limited the rights of women. Accordingly, the less equitable characteristics of the societies we described are not unique to them and are present in numerous supposedly axial systems as well.

The case for moralizing religions is more difficult. On the one hand, our material shows that the worldviews of the cultures we examined are conceptually very different from axial religions, with their emphasis on doctrine and direct "supernatural" enforcement. On the other, small-scale societies vary considerably in their worldviews and ritual practices. We have documented both ends of the spectrum: worldviews that acknowledge broad enforcement and those where the spiritual realm is indifferent to human morality, with many ambiguous cases in between. We also note that rituals and mythology may support important norms and values with the aid of a divine judge. This cautions against drawing broad conclusions about the nature of religion in these societies and calls for a more detailed exploration of the topic than we can provide here.

Recent revivals of the Axial Age argument have inspired productive conversations on the history of human culture and religion. To this end, further enquiry into the ethnographic record is needed, and some assumptions may have to be abandoned. With this chapter, we hope to make a timely contribution to this endeavor.

CONCLUSION | Was There Ever an Axial Age?

Harvey Whitehouse, Pieter François, Enrico Cioni, Jill Levine, Daniel Hoyer, Jenny Reddish, Peter Turchin

Introduction

The idea that a great moral and intellectual revolution occurred in a few regions of Eurasia during the last millennium BCE—well after the rise of complex societies—is not new. It dates back at least as far as the scholarship of the French Indologist Anquetil-Duperron (1771) and the Scottish folklorist Stuart-Glennie (1873). However, it was Jaspers in mid-twentieth-century Switzerland who first coined the term "Axial Age" (*die Achsenzeit*, in his native German) to characterize, among other developments, the rise of moralizing religions and more egalitarian principles of governance, which in turn spawned many hallmark features of modernity. Jaspers (1948, 1953) along with several later Axial Age proponents (e.g. Bellah 2011; Eisenstadt 1986b) argue that this "axial turn" constituted a radical departure from the coercive political systems typical of so-called "archaic" states headed by deified rulers, in which extreme forms of inequality such as slavery and human sacrifice were sanctioned. According to this theory, axial modes of thought first appeared in what is now China, India, Israel-Palestine, Iran, and Greece, finding expression in the ethical systems respectively known as Confucianism, Buddhism, Judaism, Zoroastrianism, and Greek philosophy (the five "axial religions"). These traditions emerged over a relatively short time span, roughly 800–200 BCE. But does it really make sense to describe this period as an "Axial Age"?

In this concluding chapter, drawing on the evidence of the volume as a whole, we argue that the idea of a single "age" is misleading, but also that some traditional notions of "axiality," specifically the shift from coercive to more ethical forms of governance, is indeed a discernible phenomenon in global history. At the root of this process, though, was not the emergence of novel ways of looking at the world transcending inherited traditions and focussing instead on universal, moralizing principles (Bellah 2011; Eisenstadt 2011; Jaspers 1953)—which in any case would require further explanation in turn—but the demands of increasingly complex societies. In our view, axiality is a consequence of passing a certain threshold in the scale and structure of human societies, one that has been reached at different points in time in different parts of the world. Our central proposal is that once this threshold is passed, societies must adopt more prosocial and egalitarian moral principles if they are to survive the twin specters of external conquest and internal collapse (Turchin 2016).

Recognizing that ethical concerns can change over time—for instance that authoritarian regimes using the threat of violence to control subject populations can give way to ones that emphasize consensus-building and reciprocal rights and obligations—is not an endorsement of unconstrained moral relativism. In fact, what is judged morally good is somewhat invariable across human societies, apparently stemming from psychological predispositions that emerged deep in our species' evolutionary history. The evidence for a universal human morality is compelling. For example, in a recent analysis of ethnographic writings on 60 societies worldwide, researchers found that seven cooperative rules (help your family, help your group, return favors, be brave, defer to superiors, divide resources fairly, and respect others' property) were morally prescribed in all the cultural groups surveyed and, crucially, none of these was ever deemed morally bad (Curry et al. 2019). The fact that these seven rules for cooperation are predicted by game theory and found throughout the natural world (Curry 2016) may explain why those solutions are also considered morally good in all human societies. That is, moral intuitions appear to be biologically and culturally evolved adaptations to various collective action problems. But whereas in small-scale societies, innate moral predispositions might be sufficient to sustain many forms of cooperation, they became less effective in larger-scale and more complex societies where problems of surveillance and enforcement were increasingly acute and new forms of political domination and economic exploitation created unprecedented forms of suffering and social injustice (Mullins et al. 2013; Norenzayan et al. 2016).

In the next section, we consider how this set of panhuman moral intuitions, which evolved in the context of small group living, was insufficient to ensure cooperation at larger scales. As societies first reached new thresholds of complexity, many of our innate moral sensibilities were distorted or overridden as a result of the exercise of extreme forms of top-down coercion and violence. However, beyond a certain threshold of social complexity, such despotism generally proved to be unsustainable. This is the point at which the core features of "axiality" emerged, empowering equitable moral norms similar to those prevalent in earlier, smaller-scale societies via novel mechanisms of doctrinal religious organization and ideological teaching and proselytizing.

Changing moral landscapes in world history

Ancient foraging societies faced many kinds of problems related to collective action, ranging from the coordination of subsistence activities, to the defending of one's band against raiding parties and animal predators, to the resolution of internal conflict and the management of bullies (Boehm 2012). However, many of these problems could be quite effectively managed using a suite of evolved psychological adaptations encouraging prosocial behavior, reputation management, third-party punishment, and so on. Relevant adaptations include shame (Fessler 2004), empathy (Decety 2010), kin psychology (Whitehouse and Lanman 2014), coalitional psychology (Billig and Tajfel 1973; Gavrilets 2015), and a host of other mechanisms that regulate adherence to norms and the sanctioning of transgressions (Richerson and Henrich 2012; Kelly and Davis 2018; Wilson et al. 2013). In other words, humans naturally tend to be conditional cooperators (Fehr and Fischbacher 2004) with a strong aversion to fairness violations (Haidt 2012; Haidt and Joseph 2008) and an appetite for "prosocial punishment" (Fehr and Gächter 2002). In simple societies, these tools for prosocial living are easily deployed and regularly sharpened and maintained through such cultural practices as collective ritual and social synchrony (Wiltermuth and Heath 2009), commensality and music (Morley 2013), and potent forms of group bonding based on shared traumatic ordeals (Whitehouse 1996, 2018). Indeed, the chapter surveying "late complexity" societies in this volume highlights the way many of these tools have been used by cultures from Papua New Guinea, northern South Asia, Borneo, the Amazon Basin, Siberia, and the Finger Lakes region of North America.

With the rise of farming and increasingly large-scale human settlements, however, the evolved moral toolkit designed to enable cooperation in small groups was placed under increasing stress. Dependence on social interactions between strangers became more and more commonplace, weakening social cohesion in society at large and making it harder to detect and punish cheaters, defectors, and free riders. Human societies evolved several adaptations to break through the limit to group size imposed by face-to-face interactions. One adaptation was the capacity to signal group membership with symbolic markers (Richerson and Boyd 1998; Turchin 2011). Markers such as dialect and language, clothing, ornamentation, and religion allowed humans to determine whether someone personally unknown to them was a member of their cooperating group. Another evolutionary innovation was hierarchical social organization—"chains of command" (Turchin and Gavrilets 2009). There is no limit to the overall group size that can be unified and organized by a hierarchical network, as long as the sufficient number of organizational levels is added, which is why armies and bureaucracies in scores of different cultural contexts tend to be organized in such a way. A third adaptation, which worked together with identity markers and hierarchies, was to establish routinized forms of ritual practice associated with a more "doctrinal mode of religiosity" (Whitehouse 1995, 2000, 2004). This was a cultural adaption for large-group living that allowed identity markers to become standardized across expanding regions and time spans through high-frequency (i.e. daily or weekly) collective rituals and public oratory. Not only did this allow social cohesion to be maintained in much larger populations, based on shared beliefs and practices associated with a spreadable religious tradition, it also provided a system of policing via orthodoxy checks imposed by a priestly hierarchy (Whitehouse 2004). The emergence of the doctrinal mode has been linked to the earliest phases in the rise of social complexity (Whitehouse and Hodder 2010; Whitehouse et al. 2013; Gantley et al. 2018; Whitehouse et al. 2019).

The dark side to more hierarchical forms of social organization, however, was the establishment of increasingly oppressive systems of governance, commonly referred to as archaic states (Bellah 2011; Flannery and Marcus 2012; Trigger 2003; Turchin 2016). In his survey of seven early civilizations, Trigger (2003) found that all of them practiced slavery, were ruled by divine kings, and engaged in human sacrifice. Data systematically collected in the Seshat Databank confirms this pattern for a much larger sample of past societies. In particular, the incidence of human sacrifice increases from very low levels (<10 percent of cases in the sample) for small-scale societies to very high levels—over 80 percent—for mid-scale societies (complex chiefdoms and archaic states), and then declines to low levels for very large-scale societies (Turchin et al. 2019). The chapters in this volume attest to these practices as well. Both slavery and god-kings (or, at least, rulers claiming some close affinity with divine agents) are found in nearly all parts of the world surveyed here. While we have chosen not to focus on human sacrifice in this particular volume, clear examples of it are mentioned in the Late Complexity Survey and the chapters on Highland Peru and the Inland Niger Delta.

History shows that top-down coercion is effective up to a point. In small and even medium-sized states with highly cohesive elites, for example, the general population can be kept in check by fear of imprisonment, torture, or worse. But the larger the state, the more likely it is that factions will form and gather the collective strength to mount coups and revolutions. These problems become more acute as societies grow in complexity and scale, becoming more internally diverse, for example through the absorption of multiple ethnicities and religious traditions. As a result, early "mega-empires" were regularly wracked by palace coups and ruler assassinations, elite infighting, and regional rebellions. This constitutes a turning point in the evolution of social complexity, one that takes us back to our moral intuitions at the same moment that it thrusts us forward into novel forms of ideology and organized religion.

Axiality adds a new layer of moral norms

The idea that axiality constitutes a new dimension of equity-promoting, morality-enforcing normative practices via new forms of ideology and religion requires some careful unpacking. First, we need to be clear what exactly we mean by "axiality" and how its core features relate to our species-specific moral intuitions. Recent efforts to identify a set of specific diagnostic features for the Axial Age have focused on 12 principles[1] (Mullins et al. 2018):

1. **Moralistic punishment**: violations of natural morality will be punished by higher authorities, whether by means of secular or supernatural sanctions in this life or the next.
2. **Moralizing norms**: peers and other members of a relational network are obliged to monitor and deter deviance within the community.
3. **Promotion of prosociality**: cooperative behavior should be actively encouraged and rewarded.
4. **Moralizing omniscient supernatural beings**: an "eye in the sky" watching over everyone, punishing sins and rewarding virtuous behavior.
5. **Rulers are not gods**: worldly leaders are merely human, just like everyone else.
6. **Equating elites and commoners**: moral rules apply to both elites and commoners, regardless of birth and social status.
7. **Equating rulers and commoners**: moral rules apply to both rulers and commoners, regardless of birth and social status.
8. **Formal legal code**: the rule of law is explicitly formulated.
9. **General applicability of law**: the law applies to all citizens equally.
10. **Constraints on the executive**: the executive's decisions are constrained by formal rules—such as a veto—or informal (but powerful) ideological constraints, e.g. requiring the tacit approval of a priesthood.
11. **Bureaucratization**: administration of a system of governance requires specialist skills, training, and salary.
12. **Impeachment**: excessive and arbitrary exercise of power by rulers can lead to their removal.

Analysis of the emergence of these 12 principles across a sample of 13 world regions (the Mediterranean Basin, Egypt, the Inland Niger Delta, the Levant, Anatolia, the south-western Iranian Plateau, South Asia, North China, the Lower Mekong Basin, Japan, the Hawaiian Islands, the Mississippi Valley, and Highland Peru) plus a survey of Late Complexity areas prior to the spread of modernity shows that a coherent turn towards axiality (using all of the above principles) did not occur everywhere, and in the regions where it did emerge, the patterns and rates of emergence differ. For example, in what is today Japan, Cambodia, China, and Greece, only some and not all of the 12 principles coalesced. In the Lower Mekong Basin in modern-day Cambodia, specifically, there is stronger evidence for an axial transformation following our

---

1   This list, though, does not cover all arguments made by proponents of the Axial Age idea. See Mullins et al. (2018) for in-depth discussion of the range of arguments made by previous scholars on this popular topic.

definition in the early second millennium CE rather than in the period between 800 and 200 BCE. Furthermore, this axial transformation is not closely linked with one of the axial ideologies; Hindu beliefs and practices had reached the region several centuries before and only long after the traditional end date of the Axial Age did a Southeast Asian form of Buddhist thought bring clear moralizing and egalitarian principles to the region (Harris 2005; Higham 2014; Miksic 2007; Vickery 1986). Even then, these served to prop up powerful, arguably "archaic"-style rulers rather than subverting their authority (see the Lower Mekong Basin chapter for details). Moreover, although the pattern across all the regions sampled was a progression from relatively few to relatively many principles of axiality being attested, the path was not necessarily a linear one, with losses as well as gains along the way. In the Italian Peninsula, for example, the introduction of Christianity certainly resulted in a more pronounced moralizing dimension compared to older local religions, but, at the same time, it was paralleled by the flourishing of supposedly pre-axial traits such as an increase in social inequality and the emergence of autocracy legitimated on religious grounds (a process outlined in the Mediterranean Basin chapter).

Another key feature of Jaspers' Axial Age—one followed by many commentators since—is his argument that these novel ideologies emerged autochthonously, quite independently of the others. Indeed, much of Jasper's argument can be traced to his initial observation that "the spiritual foundation of mankind arose in three *mutually independent* places, in the West—polarized in Orient and Occident—in India, and in China" (Jaspers 1953: 23, italics added), places that had experienced only "isolated and interrupted contacts ... [until] only a few centuries ago and properly speaking not until our own day" (10–11).[2] One need only look at the chapters in this volume on Anatolia, the Levant, Egypt, the Mediterranean Basin, and Iran to see how extensively archaeological and historical research, in the decades since Jaspers was writing, has unearthed evidence for sustained, impactful connections between all of these regions. Axial faiths such as Zoroastrianism, Rabbinic Judaism, and Greek philosophy not only developed through the exchange of ideas, but also owed much to earlier Hittite, Mesopotamian, and Egyptian ideals and practices.

Equally important for any assessment of the Axial Age hypothesis as traditionally formulated is the observation that the greatest concentration of the 12 principles was not in the first millennium BCE, but in the 2,000 years that followed. According to Eisenstadt (1996), for example, Japan can be seen as an extreme case in point. Due to the emperors' strong association with the divine and what he saw as a lack of tension between the political order and the realm of the sacred, Eisenstadt viewed Japan as pre-axial until the modern era—this despite the much earlier introduction and adoption of Buddhist and Confucian ideas. As the Japan chapter in this volume

---

2   See Mullins et al. (2018) for further discussion.

clearly articulates, the intermixing of faiths and political forms in this archipelago belies the idea of any clearly delineated "age" marking a transition between distinct eras. The long and complex dynamics discussed in the chapters on Iran, Anatolia, and Egypt underscore this point as well. Moreover, many of the 12 principles emerged much earlier than the Jaspers' model allows and in regions that were not part of the classical articulation of axiality. In Egypt, for instance, we see that an ideology emphasizing both personal piety (intimate relationships with the gods) and a moral imperative that everyone (from the humblest farmers to the living-gods who ruled as pharaohs) should live a "virtuous, just, and ordered life" emerged well before 800 BCE (see Egypt chapter). The Hittite civilization of Bronze Age Anatolia likewise witnessed the somewhat precocious development of a principle often ascribed to axial societies, namely the formalized and universally applied (though not exactly egalitarian) rule of law (see Anatolia chapter). There are also cases like the first-millennium CE Inland Niger Delta in what is today Mali, where we see evidence for societies organized "heterarchically" in an attempt to keep equitable, cooperative structures in place even in the face of increased social complexity, defying traditional models of "archaic" rule. Indeed, here and elsewhere (e.g. the Lower Mekong Basin), the arrival of supposedly axial or post-axial faiths like Hinduism, Buddhism, and Islam actually led to an increase in the number of *archaic* traits expressed, rather than the reverse.

Lastly, this volume seeks to incorporate the histories of areas that have been often neglected, in order to challenge the implication of many Axial Age narratives that areas outside of the five key regions only experienced axial transitions out of exposure to, or through the adoption of, "post-axial" social and religious forms. Close scrutiny of societies typically left out of discussions of axiality or modernity serves only to complicate the picture further. The chapter on the Hawaiian Islands, for instance, notes that no formal legal code, institutionalized constraints on rulers, or bureaucratic administration developed in the archipelago before European contact, but also that many hallmarks of axiality—including strong moralizing norms with clear enforcement mechanisms and inducements to act prosocially—were present alongside these nominally "archaic" traits. In the Central Andes, conversely, there are no obvious signs of anything like an axial transition, as most of the hallmarks of axiality remained absent even as the Incas expanded into a very large, complex empire. Interestingly, the arrival of the Christian Spanish in the area did not produce an axial revolution either, but in many ways resulted in even more oppressive rule and the disintegration of local communities, a far cry from the "universal moral ideals" expected of a post-axial society. A similar story can be told regarding the encounters with supposedly "axial" societies during periods of colonial rule experienced by many regions covered in the Late Complexity Survey chapter.

Thus, axiality is a more complex, patchy, widely distributed, and temporally extensive phenomenon than the original advocates of the concept appreciated. Nevertheless, axiality involved an expansion of moral rules and novel enforcement mechanisms that had been systematically distorted in the archaic states that came before the axial transition(s). The prevalence of divine kings declined, and those that remained (as in Southeast Asia and throughout the states of the eastern Mediterranean and West Asia during the early first millennium CE) were increasingly constrained by formal and informal limits. Moreover, while their equity-promoting aspects were certainly limited in practice (see below), ideologies across the geographic sample surveyed here became more vocal about the universal applicability of salvation and made at least nods towards egalitarianism; and, throughout the globe, rules and procedures became increasingly formalized, administration came to be regulated, and prosocial activity continued to be performed. In short, while we cannot find support for a discrete "age," there are numerous moments of "axiality" that are identifiable in the global historical record.

If we abandon the idea that a particular period led to the flowering of these traits in a handful of regions, how then can we explain the observed patterns? According to the logic of game theory, the function of dominance–submission displays is to obviate fighting over resources to a point at which everyone loses (e.g. the resource is destroyed or both antagonists incur unnecessary fitness costs). In small-scale societies, ritual bonding, strong kin networks, ease of surveillance, and graduated sanctions (ranging from shaming and gossip to collective execution and ostracism) served to foster the requisite levels of cooperation within groups. As noted, these mechanisms become strained as societies become larger and more hierarchical, and power becomes concentrated in self-reproducing elites, a pattern we see throughout the historical record (Turchin et al. 2018; for an important possible alternative trajectory, though, see the Inland Niger Delta chapter). Nevertheless, excessive concentration of arbitrary power in the hands of god-kings—as was prevalent in many of these growing societies, whether they are termed archaic or something else—meant that the benefits for lower ranking sectors of society were disproportionately meager and the brutality of dominant individuals excessive. These tendencies ran contrary to natural moral preferences for more egalitarian principles of governance and resource distribution. Hittite legal practices during the Bronze Age, for instance, though formalized and regularized to a significant extent, lacked substantive constraints on the power of the ruler, who acted as chief military, judicial, political, and religious officer; indeed, simply challenging his judgment was punishable by death (see the Anatolia chapter). Similarly, in a number of cases, the principle of sharing privileges fairly was blatantly flouted by elites, who hoarded wealth while large portions of the population were enslaved or impoverished. For example, the rulers of the Western Zhou kingdom of northern China, who took up the mantle of preserving the "Mandate of Heaven" (that is, they legitimated their authority by presenting themselves as chosen by the gods to preserve the good fortune and prosperity of their kingdom), ruled autocratically, maintaining strict social and economic hierarchies and offering no obvious indications of supporting egalitarian or cooperative institutions.

As the chapters in this volume illustrate time and again, it is difficult to maintain social cohesion at the scales and levels of complexity reached by these "archaic" states while supporting starkly inequitable distributions of land, wealth, and power. The 12 principles of axiality seem, then, to have restored some of this cooperation, or at least to have mollified the harsher edges of archaic rule, by postulating supernatural agents who cared about social justice, family values, the rule of law, and by constraining the powers of earthly rulers. Throughout the imperial period in China, for instance, rulers maintained almost unconstrained authority, often claiming the same Mandate of Heaven that had legitimated the Bronze Age rulers of the Western Zhou kingdom. In practice, though, the moralizing (and occasionally egalitarian) ideals of Confucian, Legalist, Mohist, and later Buddhist thought led to significant changes for the majority of the populace: the promotion, at least at times, of a policy of land distribution known as the equal-field system, the opening of political power to a wider segment of the population through meritocratic reforms, the state sponsorship of healthcare, pensions, and other social welfare programs, among other beneficial policies. The North China chapter, along with many other chapters in this volume, clearly illustrates this point.

Although the exact manner in which moral rules were upheld by axial ideologies varied across world regions, the tendency towards the stepwise constraining of harsh, autocratic rule, along with increasing support for these values, is unmistakable when viewed comparatively on a global scale and over several millennia. This is what we mean (or *should* mean) by "axiality." Two questions remain, however: what exactly drove this added layer of moral norms and enforcement, and why did it take the religious and ideological forms that it did? We will consider both questions in a further section. First, it is necessary to name the limits in practice, or blind spots, of these supposedly moralizing, universalizing trends.

The limits of axiality

Another clear pattern that shows up repeatedly in the preceding pages is that these axial ideologies, no matter how forceful they may have been in asserting the moral necessity of inclusivity and equality or universal access to salvation, were difficult to put into practice. Indeed, a common theme of the regional chapters here is that the treatment of women almost universally lagged behind that of other potentially disadvantaged groups. Even societies that embraced Buddhism, Christianity, or Islam—undoubtedly strongly moralizing and universalizing faiths—continued to tolerate disparities in the rights and privileges of different classes, denying positions of authority or wealth to women, and widely accepting (often justifying) the practice of slavery.

The chapter on the Mediterranean Basin demonstrates how, once Christianity had been fully embraced as the official religion of the later Roman and Byzantine Empires, commentators preached the ability of all—rich and poor, man and woman—to attain salvation. Yet at the same time they also quoted Bible verses to argue for the inherent inferiority of women and slaves, justifying their low (and immutable) positions in the social hierarchy. States that adopted Islam supported similar contradictions, although, as the Egypt chapter highlights, women were sometimes offered more privileges than counterparts elsewhere. Nevertheless, non-Muslim populations in the early medieval caliphates were subject to special taxation and denied certain rights, despite Islamic doctrinal statements that all people were equal, regardless of their ethnic, cultural or religious background.

Similar tensions between doctrine and practice existed in societies that embraced Buddhism as well, despite the faith being often lauded as the prototypical extreme moralizing religion. As the Axial Religion Overview chapter notes, the role of women in Buddhism is particularly fraught, as there has been much debate and controversy over the opinion of the Buddha himself, Siddhārtha Gautama, on the importance of gender for one's quest to attain enlightenment. There is evidence that Siddhārtha opposed the inclusion of women in the order of Buddhist practitioners, though women played active roles in the faith's spread into East and Southeast Asia. In Japan, notably, women were often the most active sponsors of Buddhist institutions and the dissemination of Buddhist texts. Similarly, the ostensible adoption of Buddhist ideals did not prevent these same societies from maintaining many inegalitarian practices, such as slavery, strict social class systems, and gender inequality. Indeed, in spite of the long history of women holding positions of prominence as patrons of Buddhist learning in Japan, by the late first millennium CE women were being systematically relegated to inferior positions or even excluded from official Buddhist roles (see the Japan chapter for details).

This is not to deny the gains made by many people who lived in societies where axial ideologies were embraced; the articulation of egalitarian, universalizing ideals in itself may have laid the foundation for later improvements in the real rights and privileges enjoyed by marginalized groups, however gradual these may have been. Still, it is important not to lose sight of the extent to which these supposedly moralizing religions helped to promulgate rules that restricted the rights of women, foreigners, and the poor, that allowed for and at times justified slavery, and that often sanctioned the violent devastation of indigenous populations (as is abundantly illustrated in the chapters on Highland Peru and the Mississippi Valley and in the Late Complexity Survey).

Axiality and the megasociety threshold

A plausible explanation for the rise of axiality is that societies past a certain threshold of social scale and complexity become vulnerable to collapse, whether due to internal divisions or external attack (cf. Mullins et al. 2018). Some evidence to support this view comes from a recent study of one major feature of axiality, the rise of moralizing gods (Whitehouse et al. 2019). In this study, we analyzed data on social complexity and religion over 10,000 years in over 400 societies drawn from a stratified sample of 30 world regions. Our principal interest in this study was in just one of the 12 features of axiality: the presence of "moralizing gods." To capture this, we used two types of measures, one widely used in the literature on "high gods" (Murdoch 1967) and another relating to broad supernatural punishment conceived as "a supernatural agent or process that reliably monitors and punishes selfish actions" (Watts et al. 2016). To be coded as present, the belief in such a supernatural process had to be widely held, relevant to sanctioning a variety of uncooperative behaviors, and applicable to a broad range of people in the community. We focused in particular on three aspects of natural morality: the rules to act fairly, reciprocate favors, and to be loyal to the group. If any of these three rules were supernaturally enforced, we counted "broad supernatural punishment" as present.

We found that belief in moralizing gods usually *followed* the rise of social complexity and tended to appear after the emergence of "megasocieties," corresponding to populations greater than around one million people. For example, the Achaemenid rulers of the Persian Empire (which was the first mega-empire to govern a population numbering in the tens of millions) adopted Zoroastrianism, a deeply moralizing and universalizing religion, as its central ruling ideology (see discussion in the Iran chapter in this volume). Another example is the adoption of Buddhism, another profoundly moralizing religion, by Aśoka the Great and his family, ruler of the large South Asian Mauryan Empire, and the religion's popularity among similarly large or growing societies throughout East and Southeast Asia shortly after (see the corresponding chapters in this volume for details). In China, the first glimmerings of moralistic supernatural punishment appear during the Western Zhou period, centuries after the rise of megasocieties there (see the North China chapter).

It appears, therefore, that a belief in moralizing gods was not a prerequisite for the expansion in the social scale of complex human societies, but may have been a cultural adaptation that only became necessary to maintain cooperation in societies once they had exceeded a certain size. In particular, the megasociety threshold may represent a point at which societies become fragile due to internal divisions based on ethnicity or class, exacerbated by harsh, exploitative rule. One striking example of how complex societies tend to increase in stability with time, as they accumulate various institutions (including, but not limited to, moralizing gods) is China. Scholars such as Victoria Tin-bor Hui (2005) have noted that the periodic state collapses that characterized the imperial period of Chinese history gradually became less severe (as measured, for example, by the degree to which population declined) and periods between a collapse and subsequent reunification became shorter; this is mirrored by an increase in the number and importance of moralizing ideologies present in the area, along with the adoption of more and more rules and policies aimed at distributing wealth and power. A similar model would explain many of the other patterns observed in the preceding chapters, even accounting for the apparently precocious appearance of axial-type traits by Bronze Age societies in, for instance, Egypt and Anatolia, following on the heels of imperialistic expansions.

Admittedly, the above account represents only part of the story about the rise of axiality in world history. It focuses on the emergence of just one of the 12 features of interest and only 3 of the 7 rules that we have claimed to constitute natural morality. And it fails to account for the apparent lack of axiality in the Inca state, a large, centralized empire that certainly passed the megasociety threshold. Likewise, in many cases, even in societies where many of these 12 principles were adopted, their application was in practice restricted to certain groups (e.g. male citizens; see discussion above), or they were soon diluted following the re-emergence of more "archaic" ruling strategies. For instance, this dilution can be seen in the increasingly autocratic forms of authority exercised by Byzantine emperors (compared with their earlier Roman counterparts), or in the case of the Lower Mekong Basin, where the political ideology became more rather than less typically archaic over time, despite the widespread adoption of Buddhism as state-sponsored faith (see the Mediterranean Basin and Lower Mekong Basin chapters for details).

Nevertheless, the chapters in this volume support our general reading of the dynamics of axiality and the importance of the megasociety threshold, while also demonstrating how complex and nuanced the situation becomes when a detailed exploration of a global sample of societies is undertaken. On current evidence it would seem that axiality was a new way of restoring faith in old morals, using novel tools to scale up the cohesion needed to keep societies going, rather than an entirely novel moral system. The next step will be to flesh out the picture with more detailed analyses encompassing more variables.

Conclusion

So, was there an Axial Age? We suggest the answer is "sort of," but it was not so much an age as a *stage* in the evolution of social complexity—its distribution globally was wider and its origins historically deeper than anybody previously imagined. We have argued that the initial rise of archaic states led to the distortion and repression of at least some components of natural morality and that axiality provided a way of restoring those principles, and especially their cohesion-building effects, under the guise of a more benevolent regime of supernatural enforcement in ways that applied equally to rich and poor, the powerful and the meek. Such a restoration, we have argued, was necessary for political systems to evolve beyond the megasociety threshold.

This conclusion has many wider ramifications. For example, if the original function of the rise of axial faiths in world history was to hold together fragile, ethnically diverse coalitions, what might declining participation in organized religion mean for the future of societies today? Could secularization in Europe, for example, contribute to the unraveling of supranational forms of governance in the region? If beliefs in moralizing gods decline, what will that mean for cooperation across ethnic groups in the face of migration, warfare, or the spread of xenophobia? Have the exceptions that were allowed to persist in practice alongside these ostensibly universalizing axial faiths left lingering social divisions, which are now resurfacing in many parts of the world? Or are the functions of axial religious ideologies simply being replaced by more secular liberal ideologies? And if so, can they be made fully universal and egalitarian, if not reproduced through cohesion-inducing rituals? Or are we now at the point of a new threshold, an "ultra-megasociety" that will require a whole new toolkit of cultural and institutional reforms to engender global cooperation? To answer these questions, we need to integrate findings from the cognitive, behavioral, and biological sciences with ever more sophisticated analyses of world history. This volume points the way and we hope that many more will follow.

BIBLIOGRAPHY

Abdi, Kamyar. 2012. "The Iranian Plateau from Paleolithic Times to the Rise of the Achaemenid Empire." In *The Oxford Handbook of Iranian History*, edited by Touraj Daryaee, 13–36. Oxford: Oxford University Press.

Abler, Thomas S., and Elisabeth Tooker. 1978. "Seneca." *Handbook of North American Indians*, vol. 15: *Northeast*, edited by Bruce G. Trigger, 505–17. Washington, DC: Smithsonian Institution. Retrieved from http://ehrafworldcultures.yale.edu/document?id=nm09-049.

Abulafia, David. 1999. "Minorities in Islam: Reflections on a New Book by Xavier de Planhol." *European Review* 7 (1): 93–103. doi: 10.1017/S1062798700003768.

Acuto, Félix A. 2012. "Landscapes of Inequality, Spectacle and Control: Inka Social Order in Provincial Contexts." *Revista de Antropología* 25: 9–64. doi: 10.5354/0719-1472.2012.20256.

Adams, Ellen. 2004. "Power and Ritual in Neopalatial Crete: A Regional Comparison." *World Archaeology* 36 (1): 26–42. doi: 10.1080/0043824042000192678.

Adams, Winthrop Lindsay. 2006. "The Hellenistic Kingdoms." In *The Cambridge Companion to the Hellenistic World,* edited by Glenn Bugh, 28–51. Cambridge: Cambridge University Press.

Adkins, Lesley and Roy A. Adkins. 1998. *Handbook to Life in Ancient Rome.* New York: Oxford University Press.

AFTAU [American Friends of Tel Aviv University]. 2009. "Was a 'Mistress of the Lionesses' a King in Ancient Canaan?" *Tel Aviv University American Friends.* https://www.aftau.org/news-page-archaeology?&storyid4677=1850&ncs4677=3 (accessed September 24, 2019).

Aghaie, Kamran Scot. 2005. "The Origins of the Sunnite–Shi'ite Divide and the Emergence of the Ta'ziyeh Tradition." *The Drama Review* 49 (4): 42–47.

Ahmed, Leila. 1992. *Women and Gender in Islam.* New Haven, CT: Yale University Press.

Albarracín-Jordán, Juan. 1996. "Tiwanaku Settlement System: The Integration of Nested Hierarchies in the Lower Tiwanaku Valley." *Latin American Antiquity* 7 (3): 183–210. doi: 10.2307/971574.

Alchon, Suzanne Austin. 2003. *A Pest in the Land: New World Epidemics in a Global Perspective.* Albuquerque, NM: University of New Mexico Press.

Alcock, Susan E. and John F. Cherry. 2013. "The Mediterranean World." In *The Human Past: World Prehistory and the Development of Human Societies*, edited by Chris Scarre, 472–517. 3rd ed. London: Thames & Hudson.

Al-Husain Zarrinkub, Abd. 1975. "The Arab Conquest of Iran and Its Aftermath." In *The Cambridge History of Iran, vol. 4: The Period from the Arab Invasion to the Saljuqs*, edited by R. N. Frye, 1–56. Cambridge: Cambridge University Press.

Allam, Schafik. 1990. "Women as Holders of Rights in Ancient Egypt (during the Late Period)." *Journal of the Economic and Social History of the Orient* 33 (1): 1–34. doi: 10.2307/3632040.

Allen, Catherine J. 2015. "The Whole World Is Watching: New Perspectives on Andean Animism." In *The Archaeology of Wak'as: Explorations of the Sacred in the Pre-Columbian Andes*, edited by Tamara L. Bray, 23–46. Boulder, CO: University Press of Colorado.

Allen, Jane. 1991. "The Role of Agriculture in the Evolution of the Pre-Contact Hawaiian State." *Asian Perspectives* 30 (1): 117–32.

Altekar, A. S. 1958. *State and Government in Ancient India.* New Delhi, India: Shri Jainendra Press.

Alvar, Jaime. 2008. *Romanising Oriental Gods: Myth, Salvation and Ethics in the Cults of Cybele, Isis and Mithras.* Translated and edited by Richard Gordon. Leiden: Brill.

Álvarez-Mon, Javier. 2012. "Elam: Iran's First Empire." In *A Companion to the Archaeology of the Ancient Near East,* edited by D. T. Potts, 740–57. Chichester, England: Wiley-Blackwell.

Álvarez-Mon, Javier, Mark B. Garrison and David Stronach. 2011. "Introduction." In *Elam and Persia,* edited by Javier Álvarez-Mon and Mark B. Garrison, 1–32. Winona Lake: Eisenbrauns.

Amiet, Pierre, Nicole Chevalier, and Elizabeth Carter. 1992. "Susa in the Ancient Near East." In *The Royal City of Susa: Ancient Near Eastern Treasures in the Louvre,* edited by Prudence O. Harper, Joan Aruz, and Françoise Tallon, 1–24. New York: The Metropolitan Museum of Art.

Andelković, Branislav. 2014. "The Molding Power of Ideology: Political Transformations of Pre-dynastic Egypt." *Issues in Ethnology and Anthropology* n.s. 9 (3): 713–22. doi: 10.21301/eap.v9i3.9.

Ando, Clifford. 2011. "From Republic to Empire." In *The Oxford Handbook of Social Relations in the Roman World,* edited by Michael Peachin, 37–66. Oxford: Oxford University Press.

Ang, Choulean. 1988. "The Place of Animism within Popular Buddhism in Cambodia the Example of the Monastery." *Asian Folkore Studies* 47 (1): 35–41.

Anquetil-Duperron, Abraham-Hyacinthe. 1771. *Zend-Avesta: Ouvrage de Zoroastre; Contenant les idées théologiques, physiques et morales de ce législateur.* 2 vols. Paris: Tilliard.

Aperghis, G. G. 2011. "Jewish Subjects and Seleukid Kings: A Case Study of Economic Interaction." In *The Economies of Hellenistic Societies, Third to First Centuries BC,* edited by Zosia Archibald, John K. Davies, and Vincent Gabrielsen, 19–41. Oxford: Oxford University Press.

Aperghis, G. G. 2004. *The Seleukid Royal Economy: The Finances and Financial Administration of the Seleukid Empire.* Cambridge: Cambridge University Press.

Arazi, Noemie. 2005. "Tracing History in Dia, in the Inland Niger Delta of Mali: Archaeology, Oral Traditions and Written Sources." PhD Diss., University College London.

Arbuckle, Benjamin S. 2014. "Pace and Process in the Origins of Animal Husbandry in Neolithic Southwest Asia." *Bioarchaeology of the Near East* 8: 53–81.

Arbuckle, Benjamin S., Sara Whitcher Kansa, Eric Kansa, David Orton, Canan Çakırlar, Lionel Gourichon, Levent Atıcı, et al. 2014. "Data Sharing Reveals Complexity in the Westward Spread of Domestic Animals across Neolithic Turkey." *PLOS One* 9: e99845. doi: 10.1371/journal.pone.0099845.

Archi, Alfonso. 2003. "Middle Hittite–'Middle Kingdom.'" In *Hittite Studies in Honor of Harry A. Hoffner Jr. on the Occasion of His 65th Birthday,* edited by Gary Beckman, Richard Beal, and Gregory McMahon, 1–12. Winona Lake: Eisenbrauns.

Armstrong, Karen. 2002. *Islam: A Short History.* New York: Modern Library.

Armstrong, Karen. 2006. *The Great Transformation: The World in the Time of Buddha, Socrates, Confucius and Jeremiah.* London: Atlantic Books.

Arnason, Johann P. 2012. "Rehistoricizing the Axial Age." In *The Axial Age and Its Consequences*, edited by Robert N. Bellah and Hans Joas, 337–65. Cambridge: The Belknap Press of Harvard University Press.

Arnason, Johann P., Kurt A. Raaflaub, and Peter Wagner. 2013. "Introduction." In *The Greek Polis and the Invention of Democracy: A Politico-Cultural Transformation and Its Interpretations*, edited by Johann P. Arnason, Kurt A. Raaflaub, and Peter Wagner, 1–18. Chichester, England: Wiley-Blackwell.

Arriaga, Father Pablo José de. [1621] 2015. *The Extirpation of Idolatry in Peru*. Translated by L. Clark Keating. Lexington, KY: University of Kentucky Press.

Asad, Talal. 1993. *Genealogies of Religion: Discipline and Reasons of Power in Christianity and Islam*. Baltimore, London: Johns Hopkins University Press.

Asher, Catherine B., and Cynthia Talbot. 2006. *India before Europe*. Cambridge: Cambridge University Press.

Assmann, Jan. 1989. "State and Religion in the New Kingdom." In *Religion and Philosophy in Ancient Egypt*, edited by W. K. Simpson, 55–88. New Haven, CT: Yale Egyptological Seminar, Department of Near Eastern Languages and Civilizations, Yale University.

Assmann, Jan. 1990. "Guilt and Remembrance: On the Theologization of History in the Ancient Near East." *History and Memory* 2 (1): 5–33. doi: 10.11588/propylaeumdok.00001948.

Assmann, Jan. 1992. "Akhanyati's Theology of Light and Time." *Proceedings of the Israel Academy of Sciences and Humanities* 7 (4): 143–76. doi: 10.11588/propylaeumdok.00002140.

Assmann, Jan. 2004. "Confession in Ancient Egypt." In *Rituals and Ethics: Patterns of Repentance. Judaism, Christianity, Islam*, edited by Adriano Destro and Mauro Pesce, 1–12. Leuven: Peeters.

Assmann, Jan. 2005. "Axial 'Breakthroughs' and Semantic 'Relocations' in Ancient Egypt and Israel." In *Axial Civilizations and World History*, edited by Johann P. Arnason, S. N. Eisenstadt and Björn Wittrock, 133–56. Leiden: Brill.

Assmann, Jan. 2006. *Maʾat: Gerechtigkeit und Unsterblichkeit im Alten Ägypten*. 2nd ed. Munich: Verlag C. H. Beck.

Assmann, Jan. 2012. "Cultural Memory and the Myth of the Axial Age." In *The Axial Age and Its Consequences*, edited by Robert N. Bellah and Hans Joas, 366–408. Cambridge: The Belknap Press of Harvard University Press.

Assmann, Jan. 2014. *From Akhenaten to Moses: Ancient Egypt and Religious Change*. Cairo: The American University in Cairo Press.

Athens, J. Stephen, Timothy M. Rieth, and Thomas S. Dye. 2014. "A Paleoenvironmental and Archaeological Model-Based Age Estimate for the Colonization of Hawaiʻi." *American Antiquity* 79 (1): 144–55.

Atkinson, Quentin D., Andrew J. Latham, and Joseph Watts. 2015. "Book Symposium: *Big Gods* by Ara Norenzayan. Are Big Gods a Big Deal in the Emergence of Big Groups?" *Religion, Brain and Behavior* 5 (4): 266–74. doi: 10.1080/2153599X.2014.928351.

Atran, Scott. 2016. "Moralizing Religions: Prosocial or a Privilege of Wealth?" *Behavioral and Brain Sciences* 39: e2. doi: 10.1017/S0140525X15000321.

Auer, Blain H. 2012. *Symbols of Authority in Medieval Islam: History, Religion and Muslim Legitimacy in the Delhi Sultanate*. London: I. B. Tauris.

Austin, Michel M. and Pierre Vidal-Nacquet. 1977. *Economic and Social History of Ancient Greece: An Introduction*. Translated and revised by Michel M. Austin. Berkeley: University of California Press.

Bachir Diagne, Souleymane. 2008. "Toward an Intellectual History of West Africa: The Meaning of Timbuktu." In *The Meanings of Timbuktu*, edited by Shamil Jeppie and Souleymane Bachir Diagne, 19–27. Cape Town: HSRC Press.

Bagnall, Nigel. 2003. *The Punic Wars 264–146 BC*. London: Routledge.

Bailey, Harold Walter. 1987. "Arya." In *Encyclopædia Iranica*, II/7, 681–83. Updated version available online at http://www.iranicaonline.org/articles/arya-an-ethnic-epithet (accessed September 13, 2017).

Baines, John, and Elizabeth Frood. 2011. "Piety, Change and Display in the New Kingdom." In *Ramesside Studies in Honour of K. A. Kitchen*, edited by Mark Collier and Steven Snape, 1–17. Bolton: Rutherford Press.

Baines, John. 1991. "Society, Morality, and Religious Practice." In *Religion in Ancient Egypt: Gods, Myths, and Personal Practice*, edited by Byron E. Shafer, 133–200. Ithaca: Cornell University Press.

Baines, John. 1995. "Kingship, Definition of Culture, and Legitimation." In *Ancient Egyptian Kingship*, edited by David O'Connor and David P. Silverman, 3–48. Leiden: E. J. Brill.

Baines, John. 2007. *Visual and Written Culture in Ancient Egypt*. Oxford: Oxford University Press.

Baines, John. 2017. "How Can We Approach Egyptian Personal Religion of the Third Millennium?" In *L'individu dans la religion égyptienne: Actes de la journée d'études de l'équipe EPHE (EA 4519) "Égypte ancienne: Archéologie, Langue, Religion," Paris, 27 juin 2014*, edited by Christiane Zivie-Coche and Yannis Gourdon, 13–36. Montpellier: Université Paul-Valéry Montpellier 3.

Baker, Chris, and Pasuk Phongpaichit. 2009. *A History of Thailand*. Cambridge: Cambridge University Press.

Baker, Chris, and Pasuk Phongpaichit. 2017. *A History of Ayutthaya*. Cambridge: Cambridge University Press.

Baker, David C. 2011. "The Roman Dominate from the Perspective of Demographic-Structural Theory." *Cliodynamics* 2 (2): 217–51. doi: 10.21237/C7clio22216.

Bal, Ellen. 2007. *They Ask if We Eat Frogs: Garo Ethnicity in Bangladesh*. Singapore: ISEAS Publishing.

Bal, Ellen, and Timour Claquin Chambugong. 2014. "The Borders that Divide, the Borders that Unite: (Re)interpreting Garo Processes of Identification in India and Bangladesh." *Journal of Borderlands Studies* 29 (1): 95–109. doi: 10.1080/08865655.2014.892695.

Balali, Mohammed Reza, Josef Keulartz, and Michiel Korthals. 2009. "Reflexive Water Management in Arid Regions: The Case of Iran." *Environmental Values* 18 (1): 91–112. doi: 10.3197/096327109X404807.

Baldick, Julian. 1990. "Mazdaism ('Zoroastrianism')." In *The World's Religions: The Religions of Asia*, edited by Friedhelm Hardy, 20–36. London: Routledge.

Baloglou, Christos P. 1998. "Hellenistic Economic Thought." In *Ancient and Medieval Economic Ideas and Concepts of Social Justice*, edited by S. Todd Lowry and Barry Gordon, 105–46. Leiden: Brill.

Balot, Ryan K. 2013. "Democracy and Political Philosophy: Influences, Tensions, Rapprochement." In *The Greek Polis and the Invention of Democracy: A Politico-Cultural Transformation and Its Interpretations*, edited by Johann P. Arnason, Kurt A. Raaflaub, and Peter Wagner, 181–204. Chichester, England: Wiley-Blackwell.

Balzer, Marjorie Mandelstam. 1996. "Flights of the Sacred: Symbolism and Theory in Siberian Shamanism." *American Anthropologist* 98 (2): 305–18. doi: 10.1525/aa.1996.98.2.02a00070.

Balzer, Marjorie Mandelstam, and Ian A. Skoggard. 1997. "Culture Summary: Yakut." New Haven, CT: HRAF. Retrieved from http://ehrafworldcultures.yale.edu/document?id=rv02-000.

Barbieri-Low, Anthony J., and Robin D. S Yates. 2015. *Law, State and Society in Early Imperial China: A Study with Critical Edition and Translation of the Legal Texts from Zhangjiashan Tomb No. 247n2.* Leiden: Brill.

Barjamovic, Gojko Johansen, Thomas Klitgaard, and Mogens Trolle Larsen. 2012. *Ups and Downs at Kanesh: Chronology, History and Society in the Old Assyrian Period.* Leiden: Nederlands Instituut voor het Nabije Oosten.

Barnes, Gina L. 2006. *Women in the Nihon Shoki: Mates, Mothers, Mystics, Militarists, Maids, Manufacturers, Monarchs, Messengers and Managers.* Durham East Asian Papers 20. Durham: Durham University Department of East Asian Studies.

Barnes, Gina L. 2007. *State Formation in Japan: Emergence of a 4th-Century Ruling Elite.* London: Routledge.

Barnes, Gina L. 2015. *Archaeology of East Asia: The Rise of Civilization in China, Korea and Japan.* Oxford: Oxbow Books.

Barnes, Gina. 2014a. "Complex Society in Korea and Japan." In *The Cambridge World Prehistory, vol. 2, East Asia and the Americas*, edited by Colin Renfrew and Paul G. Bahn, 833–51. Cambridge: Cambridge University Press.

Barnes, Gina. 2014b. "A Hypothesis for Early Kofun Rulership." *Japan Review* 27: 3–29. doi: 10.15055/00007148.

Barnwell, P. S. 1992. *Emperors, Prefects & Kings: The Roman West, 395–565.* Chapel Hill: University of North Carolina Press.

Barrett, T. H. 1996. *Taoism under the Tang.* London: Wellsweep Press.

Basavaraja, K. R. 1984. *History and Culture of Karnataka: Early Times to Unification.* Dharwad: Chalukya Publications.

Basham, A. L. 1967. *The Wonder That Was India.* London: Sidgwick and Jackson.

Bates, Robert, Barbara Levi, Jean-Paul Rosenthal, and Barry Weingast. 1998. *Analytic Narratives.* Princeton, NJ: Princeton University Press.

Bauer, Brian S. 2004. *Ancient Cuzco: Heartland of the Inca.* Austin, TX: University of Texas Press.

Bauer, Brian S., and Alan R. Covey. 2002. "Processes of State Formation in the Inca Heartland (Cuzco, Peru)." *American Anthropologist* 104 (3): 846–64. doi: 10.1525/aa.2002.104.3.846.

Bauer, S. W. 2010. *The History of the Medieval World: From the Conversion of Constantine to the First Crusade*. New York: W. W. Norton & Company.

Baumard, Nicolas and Pascal Boyer. 2013. "Explaining Moral Religions." *Trends in Cognitive Science* 17 (6): 272–80. doi: 10.1016/j.tics.2013.04.003.

Baumard, Nicolas, Alexandre Hyafil, and Pascal Boyer. 2015a. "What Changed during the Axial Age: Cognitive Styles or Reward Systems?" *Communicative and Integrative Biology* 8 (5): e1046657. doi: 10.1080/19420889.2015.1046657.

Baumard, Nicolas, Alexandre Hyafil, Ian Morris, and Pascal Boyer. 2015b. "Increased Affluence Explains the Emergence of Ascetic Wisdoms and Moralizing Religions." *Current Biology* 25 (1): 10–15. doi: 10.1016/j.cub.2014.10.063.

Bazzana, Giovanni Battista. 2010. "The Bar Kokhba Revolt and Hadrian's Religious Policy." In *Hadrian and the Christians*, edited by Marco Rizzi, 85–110. New York: De Gruyter

Beard, Mary, John North, and Simon Price. 1998. *Religions of Rome, vol. 1: A History*. Cambridge: Cambridge University Press.

Beauchamp, William M. 1900. "Iroquois Women." *Journal of American Folklore* 13 (49): 81–91. doi: 10.2307/533798. Retrieved from http://ehrafworldcultures.yale.edu/document?id=nm09-012.

Beavis, Mary Ann. 2007. "Christian Origins, Egalitarianism, and Utopia." *Journal of Feminist Studies in Religion* 23 (2): 27–49.

Bechert, Heinz and Richard Gombrich. 1984. *The World of Buddhism*. London: Thames & Hudson.

Beck, Hans, Antonio Duplá, Martin Jehne, and Francisco Pina Polo. 2011. "The Republic and Its Highest Office: Some Introductory Remarks on the Roman Consulate." In *Consuls and Res Publica: Holding High Office in the Roman Republic*, edited by Hans Beck, Antonio Duplá, Martin Jehne, and Francisco Pina Polo, 1–16. Cambridge: Cambridge University Press.

Beckman, Gary. 1995. "Royal Ideology and State Administration in Hittite Anatolia." In *Civilizations of the Ancient Near East*, vol. I, edited by Jack M. Sasson, John Baines, Gary Beckman, and Karen S. Rubinson, 529–43. New York: Charles Scribner's Sons.

Beckman, Gary. 2000. "Goddess Worship–Ancient and Modern." In *"A Wise and Discerning Mind": Essays in Honor of Burke O. Long*, edited by Saul M. Olyan and Robert C. Culley, 11–23. Providence: Brown Judaic Studies.

Beckman, Gary. 2002. "'My Sun-God': Reflections of Mesopotamian Conceptions of Kingship among the Hittites." In *Ideologies as Intercultural Phenomena: Proceedings of the Third Annual Symposium of the Assyrian and Babylonian Intellectual Heritage Project, Held in Chicago, USA, October 27–31, 2000*, edited by Antonio Panaino and Giovanni Pettinato, 37–43. Milan: University of Bologna.

Beckman, Gary. 2013. "Under the Spell of Babylon: Mesopotamian Influence on the Hittites." In *Cultures in Contact: From Mesopotamia to the Mediterranean in the Second Millennium B.C.*, edited by Joan Aruz, Sarah B. Graff, and Yelena Rakic, 284–97. New York: Metropolitan Museum of Art.

Beckwith, Christopher I. 2009. *Empires of the Silk Road: A History of Central Eurasia from the Bronze Age to the Present.* Princeton, NJ: Princeton University Press.

Beheim, Bret, Quentin Atkinson, Joseph Bulbulia, Will Gervais, Russell D. Gray, Joseph Henrich, Martin Lang, et al. 2019. "Corrected Analyses Show that Moralizing Gods Precede Complex Societies but Serious Data Concerns Remain." Preprint: https://psyarxiv.com/jwa2n/.

Beierle, John. 2006. "Culture Summary: Jivaro." New Haven, CT: HRAF. Retrieved from http://ehrafworldcultures.yale.edu/document?id=sd09-000.

Bélisle, Véronique. 2011. "Ak'awillay: Wari State Expansion and Household Change in Cusco, Peru (AD 600–1000)." PhD diss., University of Michigan.

Bélisle, Véronique. 2019. "Hallucinogens and Altered States of Consciousness in Cusco, Peru: A Path to Local Power during Wari State Expansion." *Cambridge Archaeological Journal* 29 (3): 375–91. doi: 10.1017/S0959774319000015.

Bell, Nawal Morcos. 1972. "The Age of Mansa Musa of Mali: Problems in Succession and Chronology." *The International Journal of African Historical Studies* 5 (2): 221–34. doi: 10.2307/217515.

Bellah, Robert N. 2005. "What Is Axial about the Axial Age?" *European Journal of Sociology / Archives Européennes de Sociologie / Europäisches Archiv für Soziologie* 46 (1): 69–89. doi: 10.1017/S0003975605000032.

Bellah, Robert N. 2011. *Religion in Human Evolution: From the Paleolithic to the Axial Age.* Cambridge: The Belknap Press of Harvard University Press.

Bellah, Robert N. 2012. "The Heritage of the Axial Age: Resource or Burden?" In *The Axial Age and Its Consequences*, edited by Robert N. Bellah and Hans Joas, 447–68. Cambridge: The Belknap Press of Harvard University Press.

Bellah, Robert. Forthcoming. "Challenges to Social Development in Modernity."

Bellah, Robert N., and Hans Joas, eds. 2012. *The Axial Age and Its Consequences.* Cambridge: The Belknap Press of Harvard University Press.

Bellina, Bérénice, and Ian Glover. 2004. "The Archaeology of Early Contact with India and the Mediterranean World, from the Fourth Century BC to the Fourth Century AD." In *Southeast Asia: From Prehistory to History*, edited by Ian Glover and Peter Bellwood, 68–88. New York: RoutledgeCurzon.

Bellina, Bérénice, Praon Silapanth, Boonyarit Chaisuwan, Cholawit Thongcharoenchaikit, S. Jane Allen, Vincent Bernard, Brigitte Borell, et al. 2014. "The Development of Coastal Polities in the Upper Thai-Malay Peninsula." In *Before Siam: Essays in Art and Archaeology*, edited by Nicolas Revire and Stephen A. Murphy, 69–89. Bangkok: River Books.

Benda, Harry J. 1962. "The Structure of Southeast Asian History: Some Preliminary Observations." *Journal of Southeast Asian History* 3 (1): 106–38. doi: 10.1017/S0217781100000582.

Benn, Charles. 2002. *Daily Life in Traditional China: The Tang Dynasty.* Westport, CT: The Greenwood Press.

Benn, Charles. 2004. *China's Golden Age: Everyday Life in the Tang Dynasty.* Oxford: Oxford University Press.

Bennett Ross, Jane. 1984. "Effects of Contact on Revenge Hostilities among the Achuará Jívaro." In *Warfare, Culture, and Environment*, edited by R. Brian Ferguson, 83–109. Orlando, FL: Academic Press. Retrieved from http://ehrafworldcultures.yale.edu/document?id=sd09-038.

Benson, Elizabeth P. 2001. "Why Sacrifice?" In *Ritual Sacrifice in Ancient Peru*, edited by Elizabeth P. Benson and Anita G. Cook, 1–20. Austin, TX: University of Texas Press.

Benveniste, Emile. 1929. *The Persian Religion According to the Chief Greek Texts*. Paris: Librairie Paul Geuthner.

Berquist, Jon L. 1995. "The Shifting Frontier: The Achaemenid Empire's Treatment of Western Colonies." *Journal of World-Systems Research* 1 (17): 71–90. doi: 10.5195/jwsr.1995.48.

Berryman, Carrie Anne. 2010. "Food, Feasts, and the Construction of Identity and Power in Ancient Tiwanaku: A Bioarchaeological Perspective." PhD Diss., Vanderbilt University.

Betanzos, Juan de. 1996. *Narrative of the Incas*. Translated and edited by Roland Hamilton and Dana Buchanan from the Palma de Mallorca manuscript. Austin: University of Texas Press.

Betlyon, John W. 2005. "A People Transformed: Palestine in the Persian Period." *Near Eastern Archaeology* 68 (1/2): 4–58.

Bhattacharya, Kamaleswar. 1997. "The Religions of Ancient Cambodia." In *Sculpture of Angkor and Ancient Cambodia: Millennium of Glory*, edited by Helen Jessup and Thierry Zephir, 34–52. Washington, DC: National Gallery of Art.

Bickerman, Elias J. 1983. "The Seleucid Period." In *The Cambridge History of Iran, vol. 3 (I): The Seleucid, Parthian and Sasanian Periods*, edited by Ehsan Yarshater, 3–20. Cambridge: Cambridge University Press.

Billig, Michael, and Henri Tajfel. 1973. "Social Categorization and Similarity in Intergroup Behaviour." *European Journal of Social Psychology* 3: 27–52. doi: 10.1002/ejsp.2420030103.

Bird-David, Nurit. 1999. "'Animism' Revisited: Personhood, Environment, and Relational Epistemology." *Current Anthropology* 40: 67–91. doi: 10.1086/200061.

Black, Anthony. 2008. "The 'Axial Period': What Was It and What Does It Signify?" *The Review of Politics* 70 (1): 22–39. doi: 10.1017/S0034670508000168.

Black, Antony. 2011. *The History of Islamic Political Thought: From the Prophet to the Present*. Edinburgh: Edinburgh University Press.

Bleed, Peter, and Akira Matsui. 2010. "Why Didn't Agriculture Develop in Japan? A Consideration of Jomon Ecological Style, Niche Construction, and the Origins of Domestication." *Journal of Archaeological Method and Theory* 17 (4): 356–70. doi: 10.1007/s10816-010-9094-8.

Blenkinsopp, Joseph. 1995. *Sage, Priest, Prophet: Religious and Intellectual Leadership in Ancient Israel*. Louisville: Westminster John Knox Press.

Blitz, John H., and Erik S. Porth. 2013. "Social Complexity and the Bow in the Eastern Woodlands." *Evolutionary Anthropology Issues News and Reviews* 22 (3): 89–95. doi: 10.1002/evan.21349.

Bloch, Maurice 1992. *Prey into Hunter: The Politics of Religious Experience*. Cambridge: Cambridge University Press.

Blois, Lukas de. 2002. "Monetary Policies, the Soldiers' Pay and the Onset of Crisis in the First Half of the Third Century A.D." In *The Roman Army and the Economy*, edited by Paul Erdkamp, 90–107. Leiden: Brill.

Boehm, Christopher. 2012. *Moral Origins: The Evolution of Virtue, Altruism, and Shame.* New York: Basic Books.

Boesche, Roger. 2002. *The First Great Political Realist: Kautilya and His Arthashastra.* Lanham, MD: Lexington Books.

Bosworth, Clifford Edmund. 1996. *The New Islamic Dynasties: A Chronological and Genealogical Manual.* Edinburgh: Edinburgh University Press.

Bottéro, Jean, and André Finet. 2001. *Ancient Mesopotamia: Everyday Life in the First Civilisation.* Edinburgh: Edinburgh University Press.

Bowman, Alan K. 1986. *Egypt after the Pharaohs, 332 BC–AD 642: From Alexander to the Arab Conquest.* Berkeley: University of California Press.

Boy, John D., and John Torpey. 2013. "Inventing the Axial Age: The Origins and Uses of a Historical Concept." *Theory and Society* 42 (3): 241–59. doi: 10.1007/s11186-013-9193-0.

Boyce, Mary M. 1987. "Avestan People." In *Encyclopædia Iranica*, III/1, 62–66. Updated version available online at http://www.iranicaonline.org/articles/avestan-people (accessed August 28, 2017).

Boyce, Mary. 1968. "The Pious Foundations of the Zoroastrians." *Bulletin of the School of Oriental and African Studies* 31: 270–89. doi: 10.1017/S0041977X00146518.

Boyce, Mary. 1975. *A History of Zoroastrianism, vol. I: The Early Period.* Leiden: E. J. Brill.

Boyce, Mary. 1979. *Zoroastrians: Their Religious Beliefs and Practices.* London: Routledge & Kegan Paul.

Boyce, Mary. 1982. *A History of Zoroastrianism, vol. II: Under the Achaemenians.* Brill: Leiden.

Boyce, Mary. 1983a. "Achaemenid Religion." In *Encyclopædia Iranica*, I/4, 426–29. Updated version available online at http://www.iranicaonline.org/articles/achaemenid-religion (accessed September 14, 2017).

Boyce, Mary. 1983b. "Iranian Festivals." In *The Cambridge History of Iran, vol. 3 (I): The Seleucid, Parthian and Sasanian Periods,* edited by Ehsan Yarshater, 792–812. Cambridge: Cambridge University Press.

Braund, David. 2003. "After Alexander: The Emergence of the Hellenistic World, 323–281." In *A Companion to the Hellenistic World*, edited by Andrew Erskine, 19–34. Malden: Blackwell Publishing.

Bray, Tamara L. 2013. "Water, Ritual, and Power in the Inca Empire." *Latin American Antiquity* 24 (2): 164–90. doi: 10.7183/1045-6635.24.2.164.

Bresciani, Edda. 1994. "Demotic Chronicle." In *Encyclopædia Iranica*, VIII/3, 276–77. Updated version available online at http://www.iranicaonline.org/articles/demotic-chronicle (accessed September 26, 2019).

Briant, Pierre. 1992. "Class System ii: In the Median and Achaemenid Periods." In *Encyclopædia Iranica*, V/6, 651–52. Updated version available online at http://www.iranicaonline.org/articles/class-system-ii (accessed September 25, 2019).

Briant, Pierre. 2002. *From Cyrus to Alexander: A History of the Persian Empire*. Translated by Peter T. Daniels. Winona Lake: Eisenbrauns.

Brier, Bob and Hoyt Hobbs. 2008. *Daily Life of the Ancient Egyptians*. 2nd ed. Westport: Greenwood Publishing Group.

Briggs, Lawrence Palmer. 1951. *The Ancient Khmer Empire*. Philadelphia: American Philosophical Society.

Brockington, J. L. 1981. *The Sacred Thread: Hinduism in its Continuity and Diversity*. Edinburgh: Edinburgh University Press.

Bronkhorst, Johannes. 2011. *Karma*. Honolulu: University of Hawaii Press.

Brooks, George E. 1989. "Ecological Perspectives on Mande Population Movements, Commercial Networks, and Settlement Patterns from the Atlantic Wet Phase (ca. 5500–2500 B.C.) to the Present." *History in Africa* 16: 23–40. doi: 10.2307/3171777.

Brooks, George E. 1993. *Landlords and Strangers: Ecology, Society, and Trade in Western Africa, 1000–1630*. Boulder, CO: Westview Press.

Brosius, Maria. 2010. "Women i: In Pre-Islamic Persia." Encyclopædia Iranica. Online edition. http://www.iranicaonline.org/articles/women-i (accessed August 25, 2017).

Brosius, Maria. 2016. "No Reason to Hide: Women in the Neo-Elamite and Persian Periods." In *Women in Antiquity: Real Women across the Ancient World*, edited by Stephanie Lynn Budin and Jean Macintosh Turfa, 156–74. London: Routledge.

Brosnan, Sarah. 2013. "Justice- and Fairness-Related Behaviors in Nonhuman Primates." *Proceedings of the National Academy of Sciences* 110, Supplement 2: 10,416–23. doi: 10.1073/pnas.1301194110.

Brosnan, Sarah, and Frans de Waal. 2014. "Evolution of Responses to (Un)Fairness." *Science* 346 (6207): 1251776. doi: 10.1126/science.1251776.

Brown, Delmer M. 1993. "The Yamato Kingdom." In *The Cambridge History of Japan, vol. 1: Ancient Japan*, edited by Delmer M. Brown, 108–62. Cambridge: Cambridge University Press.

Brown, Eric. 2009. "False Idles: The Politics of the 'Quiet Life.'" In *A Companion to Greek and Roman Political Thought*, edited by Ryan K. Balot, 485–500. Chichester, England: Wiley-Blackwell.

Brown, Nathan J. 1994. "Who Abolished Corvée Labour in Egypt and Why?" *Past & Present* 144: 116–37.

Brown, Peter. 1996. *The Rise of Western Christendom: Triumph and Diversity AD 200–1000*. Oxford: Blackwell.

Brown, Peter. 2012. *Through the Eye of a Needle: Wealth, the Fall of Rome, and the Making of Christianity in the West, 350–550 CE*. Princeton, NJ: Princeton University Press.

Brown, Robert L. 2004. "Ritual and Image at Angkor Wat." In *Images in Asian Religions: Texts and Contexts*, edited by Phyllis Granoff and Koichi Shinohara, 350–68. Vancouver: University of British Columbia Press.

Broz, Ludek. 2007. "Pastoral Perspectivism: A View from Altai." *Inner Asia* 9 (2): 291–310. doi: 10.1 163/146481707793646566.

Brubaker, Robert. 2000–2001. "Aspects of Mortuary Variability in the South Indian Iron Age." *Bulletin of the Deccan College Post-Graduate & Research Institute* 60–61: 253–302.

Brüning, Hans H. 1928. "Travelling in the Aguaruna Region." *Baessler-Archiv* 12: 46–85. Retrieved from http://ehrafworldcultures.yale.edu/document?id=sd09-026.

Bryan, Betsy M. 2000. "The Eighteenth Dynasty before the Amarna Period (c 1550–1352 BC)." In *The Oxford History of Ancient Egypt*, edited by Ian Shaw, 364–87. Oxford: Oxford University Press.

Bryant, Edwin. 2001. *The Quest for the Origins of Vedic Culture: The Indo-Aryan Migration Debate.* Oxford: Oxford University Press.

Bryce, Trevor. 2002. *Life and Society in the Hittite World.* Oxford: Oxford University Press.

Bryce, Trevor. 2003. *Letters of the Great Kings of the Ancient Near East: The Royal Correspondence of the Late Bronze Age.* London: Routledge.

Bryce, Trevor. 2011. "The Late Bronze Age in the West and the Aegean." In *The Oxford Handbook of Ancient Anatolia, 10,000–323 B.C.E.*, edited by Sharon R. Steadman and Gregory McMahon, 363–75. Oxford: Oxford University Press.

Bryce, Trevor. 2012. *The World of the Neo-Hittite Kingdoms: A Political and Military History.* Oxford: Oxford University Press.

Buckley, Brendan M., Kevin J. Anchukaitis, Daniel Penny, Roland Fletcher, Edward R. Cook, Masaki Sano, Le Canh Nam, et al. 2010. "Climate as a Contributing Factor in the Demise of Angkor, Cambodia." *PNAS* 107 (15): 6748–52. doi: 10.1073/pnas.0910827107.

Budin, Stephanie Lynn. 2004. *The Ancient Greeks: New Perspectives.* Santa Barbara: ABC-CLIO.

Buell, Denise Kimber. 2002. "Race and Universalism in Early Christianity." *Journal of Early Christian Studies* 10 (4): 429–68. doi: 10.1353/earl.2002.0061.

Burkert, Walter. 1992. *The Orientalizing Revolution: Near Eastern Influence on Greek Culture in the Early Archaic Age.* Translated by Margaret E. Pinder and Walter Burkert. Cambridge: Harvard University Press.

Burkes, Shannon. 2003. *God, Self, and Death: The Shape of Religious Transformation in the Second Temple Period.* Leiden: Brill.

Burstein, Stanley M. 1991. "Pharaoh Alexander: A Scholarly Myth." *Ancient Society* 22: 139–45.

Bussmann, Richard. 2017. "Personal Piety: An Archaeological Response." In *Company of Images: Modelling the Imaginary World of Middle Kingdom Egypt (2000–1500 BC). Proceedings of the International Conference of the EPOCHS Project, Held 18th–20th September 2014 at UCL, London,* edited by Gianluca Miniaci, Marilina Betrò, and Stephen Quirke, 71–92. Leuven: Peeters.

Callender, C. 1978. "Illinois." In *Handbook of North American Indians, vol. 15: Northeast,* edited by Bruce G. Trigger, 673–80. Washington, DC: Smithsonian Institution.

Callender, Gae. 2000. "The Middle Kingdom Renaissance (c.2055–1650 BC)." In *The Oxford History of Ancient Egypt,* edited by Ian Shaw, 364–87. Oxford: Oxford University Press.

Calo, Ambra, Bagyo Prasetyo, Peter Bellwood, James W. Lankton, Bernard Gratuze, Thomas Oliver Pryce, Andreas Reinecke, et al. 2015. "Sembiran and Pacung on the North Coast of Bali: A Strategic Crossroads for Early Trans-Asiatic Exchange." *Antiquity 89: 378–96.* doi: 10.15184/aqy.2014.45.

Caminos, Ricardo A. 1997. "Peasants." In *The Egyptians,* translated by Robert Bianchi, Anna Lisa Crone, Charles Lambert, and Thomas Ritter and edited by Sergio Donadoni, 1–30. Chicago: University of Chicago Press.

Canepa, Matthew P. 2009. *The Two Eyes of the Earth: Art and Ritual of Kingship between Rome and Sasanian Iran.* Berkeley: University of California Press.

Cantera, Alberto. 2015. "Ethics." In *The Wiley-Blackwell Companion to Zoroastrianism,* edited by Michael Stausberg and Yuhan Sohrab-Dinshaw Vevaina, 315–32. Chichester, England: Wiley Blackwell.

Capponi, Livia. 2010. "The Roman Period." In *A Companion to Ancient Egypt, vol. 1,* edited by Alan B. Lloyd, 180–98. Chichester, England: Wiley-Blackwell.

Carter, Alison K. 2015. "Beads, Exchange Networks and Emerging Complexity: A Case Study from Cambodia and Thailand (500 BCE–CE 500)." *Cambridge Archaeological Journal* 25 (4): 733–57. doi: 10.1017/S0959774315000207.

Carter, Elizabeth. 2011. "Landscapes of Death in Susiana during the Last Half of the 2nd Millennium B.C." In *Elam and Persia,* edited by Javier Álvarez-Mon and Mark B. Garrison, 45–58. Winona Lake: Eisenbrauns.

Carter, Elizabeth and Matthew W. Stolper. 1984. *Elam: Surveys of Political History and Archaeology.* Berkeley: University of California Press.

Carter, Elizabeth, Oscar White Muscarella, Matthew W. Stolper, Suzanne Heim and Joan Aruz. 1992. "The Neo-Elamite Period." In *The Royal City of Susa: Ancient Near Eastern Treasures in the Louvre,* edited by Prudence O. Harper, Joan Aruz, and Françoise Tallon, 197–214. New York: Metropolitan Museum of Art.

Cartledge, Paul. 1975. "Toward the Spartan Revolution." *Arethusa* 8 (1): 59–84.

Cartledge, Paul. 1993. *The Greeks: A Portrait of Self and Others.* Oxford: Oxford University Press.

Casanova, José. 2012. "Religion, the Axial Age, and Secular Modernity in Bellah's Theory of Religious Evolution." In *The Axial Age and Its Consequences,* edited by Robert N. Bellah and Hans Joas, 191–221. Cambridge: The Belknap Press of Harvard University Press.

Castleden, Rodney. 1990. *Minoans: Life in Bronze Age Crete.* London: Routledge.

Catling, Hector W. 1989. *Some Problems in Aegean Prehistory, c. 1450–1380 BC.* Oxford: Leonard's Head Press.

Cavanagh, William. 2008. "Death and the Mycenaeans." In *The Cambridge Companion to the Aegean Bronze Age,* edited by Cynthia W. Shelmerdine, 327–41. Cambridge: Cambridge University Press.

Cecchet, Lucia. 2014. "Giving to the Poor in Ancient Greece: A Form of Social Aid?" In *Gift Giving and the "Embedded" Economy in the Ancient World,* edited by Filippo Carlà and Maja Gori, 157–80. Heidelberg: Universitätsverlag Winter.

Chadwick, Henry. 1986. "Envoi: On Taking Leave of Antiquity." In *The Oxford History of the Roman World*, edited by John Boardman, Jasper Griffin, and Oswyn Murray, 449-78. Oxford: Oxford University Press.

Chakrabarti, Dilip. K. 2000. "Mahajanapada States of Early Historic India." In *A Comparative Study of Thirty City-State Cultures: An Investigation*, vol. 21, edited by Mogens Herman Hansen, 375-91. Copenhagen: Kongelige Danske Videnskabernes Selskab.

Chan, Joseph. 2014. *Confucian Perfectionism: A Political Philosophy for Modern Times*. Princeton, NJ: Princeton University Press.

Chandler, David P. 2009. *A History of Cambodia*. 4th ed. Boulder, CO: Westview Press.

Chen Shuguo. 2010. "State Religious Ceremonies." In *Early Chinese Religion: The Period of Division (220-589 AD)*, edited by John Lagerway and Pengzhi Lu, 53-143. Boston, MA: Brill.

Choksy, Jamsheed K. 2002. *Evil, Good, and Gender: Facets of the Feminine in Zoroastrian Religious History*. New York: Peter Lang.

Choudhury, Bhupendranath. 1958. *Some Cultural and Linguistic Aspects of the Garos*. Guahati, Assam: B. N. Dutta Barooah, B. L., Lawyer's Bookstall. Retrieved from http://ehrafworldcultures. yale.edu/document?id=ar05-005.

Christiansen, George. 2001. "Late Eastern Woodland." In *Encyclopedia of Prehistory, vol. 6: North America*, edited by Peter N. Peregrine and Melvin Ember, 248-68. New York: Springer Science+Business Media.

Cissé, Mamadou, Susan Keech McIntosh, Laure Dussubieux, Thomas Fenn, Daphne Gallagher, and Abigail Chipps Smith. 2013. "Excavations at Gao Saney: New Evidence for Settlement Growth, Trade, and Interaction on the Niger Bend in the First Millennium CE." *Journal of African Archaeology* 11 (1): 9-37. doi: 10.3213/2191-5784-10233.

Cizek, Alexandru. 1975. "From the Historical Truth to the Literary Convention: The Life of Cyrus the Great Viewed by Herodotus, Ctesias and Xenophon." *L'Antiquité Classique* 44 (2): 531-52. doi: 10.3406/antiq.1975.1787.

Cline, Eric H. 2004. *Jerusalem Besieged: From Ancient Canaan to Modern Israel*. Ann Arbor, MI: University of Michigan Press.

Coe, Michael D. 2003. *Angkor and the Khmer Civilization*. London: Thames and Hudson.

Cœdès, George. 1928. "XX. Les capitales de Jayavarman II." *Bulletin de l'Ecole française d'Extrême-Orient* 28: 113-123.

Cœdès, George. 1930. "Les inscriptions malaises de Çrivijaya." *Bulletin de l'Ecole française d'Extrême-Orient* 30: 29-80. Translated and published in 1992. *Sriwijaya: History, Religion and Language of an Early Malay Polity*. Collected Studies by George Cœdès and Louis-Charles Damais. Kuala Lumpur: Malaysian Branch of the Royal Asiatic Society.

Cœdès, George. 1942. *Inscriptions de Cambodge*, vol. 2. Paris: École Française d'Extrême Orient.

Cœdès, George. 1968. *The Indianized States of Southeast Asia*, edited by W. F. Vella and translated by S. B. Cowing. Honolulu: University of Hawai'i Press.

Cogan, Mordechai and Hayim Tadmor. 1977. "Gyges and Ashurbanipal: A Study in Literary Transmission." *Orientalia* 46 (1): 65-85.

Cohen, Shaye. 2014. *From the Maccabees to the Mishnah*. Louisville, KY: Westminster John Knox Press.

Colebrooke, H. T. 1805. "On the Védas or Sacred Writings of the Hindus." *Asiatick Researches* 8: 369–476.

Colish, Marcia L. 1990. *The Stoic Tradition from Antiquity to the Early Middle Ages, I: Stoicism in Classical Latin Literature*. Leiden: E. J. Brill.

Collins, Billie Jean. 2007. *The Hittites and Their World*. Atlanta, GA: Society of Biblical Literature.

Collins, Billie Jean. 2013. "Anatolia." In *The Cambridge Companion to Ancient Mediterranean Religions*, edited by Barbette Stanley Spaeth, 95–115. Cambridge: Cambridge University Press.

Collins, Robert O., and James M. Burns. 2014. *A History of Sub-Saharan Africa*. 2nd ed. Cambridge: Cambridge University Press.

Colpe, Carsten. 1983. "Development of Religious Thought." In *The Cambridge History of Iran, vol. 3 (I): The Seleucid, Parthian and Sasanian Periods*, edited by Ehsan Yarshater, 819–65. Cambridge: Cambridge University Press.

Connah, Graham. 2001. *African Civilizations: An Archaeological Perspective*. 2nd ed. Cambridge: Cambridge University Press.

Connah, Graham. 2013. "Holocene Africa." In *The Human Past: World Prehistory and the Development of Human Societies*, edited by Chris Scarre, 350–91. 3rd ed. London: Thames & Hudson.

Connolly, Joy. 2007. *The State of Speech Rhetoric and Political Thought in Ancient Rome*. Princeton, NJ: Princeton University Press.

Connolly, Joy. 2010. "Political Theory." In *The Oxford Handbook of Roman Studies,* edited by Alessandro Barchiesi and Walter Scheidel, 713–27. Oxford: Oxford University Press.

Conrad, David C. 2001. "Pilgrim Fajigi and Basiw from Mecca: Islam and Traditional Religion in the Former French Sudan." In *Bamana: The Art of Existence in Mali*, edited by Jean-Paul Colleyn, 25–33. New York: Museum for African Art.

Conrad, David C. 2004. "Introduction." In *Sunjata: A West African Epic of the Mande Peoples*, recorded, edited, and translated by David C. Conrad, narrated by Djanka Tassey Condé, xiv-xxxi. Indianapolis: Hackett Publishing Company.

Conrad, David C. 2008. "From the 'Banan' Tree of Kouroussa: Mapping the Landscape in Mande Traditional History." *Canadian Journal of African Studies / Revue Canadienne des Études Africaines* 42 (2/3): 384–408. doi: 10.1080/00083968.2008.10751389.

Conrad, David C. 2015. "Early Polities of the Western Sudan." In *The Cambridge World History, vol. 5: Expanding Webs of Exchange and Conflict, 500 CE–1500 CE*, edited by Benjamin K. Zedar and Merry E. Wiesner-Hanks, 586–609. Cambridge: Cambridge University Press.

Conrad, David C., and Humphrey J. Fisher. 1982. "The Conquest that Never Was: Ghana and the Almoravids, 1076. I. The External Arabic Sources." *History in Africa* 9: 21–59. doi: 10.2307/3171598.

Conrad, David C., and Humphrey J. Fisher. 1983. "The Conquest that Never Was: Ghana and the Almoravids, 1076. II. The Local Oral Sources." *History in Africa* 10: 53–78. doi: 10.2307/3171690.

Conrad, Geoffrey W. 1981. "Cultural Materialism, Split Inheritance, and the Expansion of Ancient Peruvian Empires." *American Antiquity* 46 (1): 3–26. doi: 10.2307/279981.

Constable, Olivia Remie. 2003. *Housing the Stranger in the Mediterranean World: Lodging, Trade and Travel in Late Antiquity and the Middle Ages*. Cambridge: Cambridge University Press.

Cook, Anita G. 2004. "Wari Art and Society." In *Andean Archaeology*, edited by Helaine Silverman, 146–66. Oxford: Blackwell.

Cook, Anita G. 2012. "The Coming of the Staff Deity." In *Wari: Lords of the Ancient Andes*, edited by Susan E. Bergh, 103–21. New York: Thames & Hudson.

Cook, Anita G. and Mary Glowacki. 2002. "Pots, Politics, and Power: Huari Ceramic Assemblages and Imperial Administration." In *The Archaeology and Politics of Food and Feasting in Early States and Empires*, edited by Tamara L. Bray, 172–202. New York: Kluwer Academic Publishers.

Cook, Noble David. 2004. *Demographic Collapse: Indian Peru, 1520–1620*. Cambridge: Cambridge University Press.

Corcoran, Simon. 2000. *The Empire of the Tetrarchs: Imperial Pronouncements and Government, AD 284–324*. Revised ed. Oxford: Clarendon Press.

Cornell, T. J. 1993. "The End of Roman Imperial Expansion." In *War and Society in the Roman World*, edited by John Rich and Graham Shipley, 139–70. London: Routledge.

Cornell, T. J. 1995. *The Beginnings of Rome: Italy and Rome from the Bronze Age to the Punic Wars (c. 1000–264 BC)*. London: Routledge.

Cortese, Delia, and Simonetta Calderini. 2006. *Women and the Fatimids in the World of Islam*. Edinburgh: Edinburgh University Press.

Covey, R. Alan. 2006. How the Incas Built Their Heartland: State Formation and the Innovation of Imperial Strategies in the Sacred Valley, Peru. Ann Arbor, MI: University of Michigan Press University Press.

Covey, R. Alan. 2012. Comments on Félix A. Acuto, "Landscapes of Inequality, Spectacle and Control: Inka Social Order in Provincial Contexts." *Revista de Antropología* 25: 9–64. doi: 10.5354/0719-1472.2012.20256.

Covey, R. Alan. 2015. "Kinship and the Inca Imperial Core: Multiscalar Archaeological Patterns in the Sacred Valley (Cuzco, Peru)." *Journal of Anthropological Archaeology* 40: 183–95. doi: 10.1016/j.jaa.2015.08.004.

Covey, R. Alan, Brian S. Bauer, Véronique Bélisle, and Lia Tsesmeli. 2013. "Regional Perspectives on Wari State Influence in Cusco, Peru (c. AD 600–1000)." *Journal of Anthropological Archaeology* 32 (4): 538–52. doi: 10.1016/j.jaa.2013.09.001.

Cranz, Isabel. 2017. *Atonement and Purification: Priestly and Assyro-Babylonian Perspectives on Sin and Its Consequences*. Tübingen: Mohr Siebeck.

Crawford, Dorothy. 1971. *Kerkeosiris: An Egyptian Village in the Ptolemaic Period*. Cambridge: Cambridge University Press.

Crawford, Michael. 1986. "Early Rome and Italy." In *The Oxford History of the Roman World*, edited by John Boardman, Jasper Griffin, and Oswald Murray, 13–49. Oxford: Oxford University Press.

Crocombe, R. G., and G. R. Hogbin. 1963. *Land, Work, and Productivity at Inonda.* New Guinea Research Bulletin. Canberra: New Guinea Research Unit, Australian National University. Retrieved from http://ehrafworldcultures.yale.edu/document?id=oj23-014.

Crumley, Carole. 1995. "Heterarchy and the Analysis of Complex Societies." *Archeological Papers of the American Anthropological Association* 6 (1): 1–5. doi: 10.1525/ap3a.1995.6.1.1.

Curry, Oliver S. 2016. "Morality as Cooperation: A Problem-Centred Approach." In *The Evolution of Morality*, edited by Todd K. Shackelford and Ranald D. Hansen, 27–51. Cham: Springer.

Curry, Oliver Scott, Matthew Jones Chesters, and Caspar J. Van Lissa. 2019. "Mapping Morality with a Compass: Testing the Theory of 'Morality-as-Cooperation' with a New Questionnaire." *Journal of Research in Personality* 78: 106–124. doi: 10.1016/j.jrp.2018.10.008.

Curry, Oliver S., Daniel A. Mullins, and Harvey Whitehouse. 2019. "Is It Good to Cooperate? Testing the Theory of Morality-as-Cooperation in 60 Societies." *Current Anthropology* 60 (1): 47–69. doi: 10.1086/701478.

Dakeyne, R. B. 1969. *Village and Town in New Guinea.* Case Studies in Australasian Geography. Croydon, Victoria: Longmans. Retrieved from http://ehrafworldcultures.yale.edu/document?id=oj23-018.

d'Alfonso, Lorenzo. 2014. "The Kingdom of Tarhuntassa: A Reassessment of Its Timeline and Political Significance." In *Proceedings of the Eighth International Congress of Hittitology, Warsaw, 5-9 September 2011*, edited by Piotr Taracha with the assistance of Magdalena Kapełuś, 221–39. Warsaw: Agade Publishing.

D'Altroy, Terence N. 2014. *The Incas.* 2nd ed. Chichester, England: Wiley Blackwell.

D'Altroy, Terence N., and Christine A. Hastorf. 1984. "The Distribution and Contents of Inca State Storehouses in the Xauxa Region of Peru." *American Antiquity* 49 (2): 334–49. doi: 10.2307/280022.

Dąbrowa, Edward. 2012. "The Arsacid Empire." In *The Oxford Handbook of Iranian History*, edited by Touraj Daryaee, 164–86. Oxford: Oxford University Press.

Dalby, Michael T. 1979. "Court Politics in Late T'ang Times." In *The Cambridge History of China, vol. 3: Sui and T'ang China, 589-906 AD, part 1*, edited by D. C. Twitchett, 561–681. Cambridge: Cambridge University Press.

Dales, George F. 1964. "The Mythical Massacre at Mohenjo-Daro." *Expedition Magazine* 6 (3): 37–44.

Dandamaev, Muhammad A. and Vladimir G. Lukonin. 1989. *The Culture and Social Institutions of Ancient Iran.* Cambridge: Cambridge University Press.

Dandamayev, Muhammad A. 1988. "Barda and Barda-Dari i: Achaemenid Period." In *Encyclopædia Iranica*, III/7, 762–63. Updated version available online at http://www.iranicaonline.org/articles/barda-i (accessed October 31, 2017).

Dandamayev, Muhammad A. 2006. "Neo-Babylonian and Achaemenid State Administration in Mesopotamia." In *Judah and the Judeans in the Persian Period*, edited by Oded Lipschits and Manfred Oeming, 373–98. Winona Lake: Eisenbrauns.

Darling, Linda T. 2013. *A History of Social Justice and Political Power in the Middle East: The Circle of Justice from Mesopotamia to Globalization.* London: Routledge.

Daryaee, Touraj. 2009. *Sasanian Persia: The Rise and Fall of an Empire*. London: I.B. Tauris.

Daryaee, Touraj. 2010. "The Fall of the Sasanian Empire to the Arab Muslims: From Two Centuries of Silence to Decline and Fall of the Sasanian Empire: The Partho-Sasanian Confederacy and the Arab Conquest of Iran." *Journal of Persianate Studies* 3: 239–54. doi: 10.1163/187471610X537280.

Daryaee, Touraj. 2012a. "Introduction." In *The Oxford Handbook of Iranian History*, edited by Touraj Daryaee, 3–12. Oxford: Oxford University Press.

Daryaee, Touraj. 2012b. "The Sasanian Empire (224–651 CE)." In *The Oxford Handbook of Iranian History*, edited by Touraj Daryaee, 187–207. Oxford: Oxford University Press.

Davidson, Basil. 1998. *West Africa before the Colonial Era: A History to 1850*. London: Routledge.

Davies, John K. 2006. "Hellenistic Economies." In *The Cambridge Companion to the Hellenistic World*, edited by Glenn R. Bugh, 73–92. Cambridge: Cambridge University Press.

Davies, Keith A. 1984. *Landowners in Colonial Peru*. Austin: University of Texas Press.

Davison, Julian and Vinson H. Sutlive Jr. 1991. "Children of Nising: Images of Headhunting and Male Sexuality in Iban Ritual and Oral Literature." In *Female and Male in Borneo: Contributions and Challenges to Gender Studies*, edited by Vinson H. Sutlive Jr. Williamsburg, VA: The Borneo Research Council; Department of Anthropology, College of William and Mary. Retrieved from http://ehrafworldcultures.yale.edu/document?id=0c06-035.

Dawson, Raymond, trans. 1993. *Confucius: The Analects*. Harmondsworth, UK: Penguin.

De Angelis, Franco. 2016. *Archaic and Classical Greek Sicily: A Social and Economic History*. Oxford: Oxford University Press.

de Bary, Theodore, and Irene Bloom, eds. 1999. *Sources of Chinese Tradition* I. 2nd ed. New York: Columbia University Press.

de Jong, Albert. 1995. "Jeh the Primal Whore? Observations on Zoroastrian Misogyny." In *Female Stereotypes in Religious Traditions*, edited by Rai Kloppenborg and Wouter J. Hanegraaff, 15–41. Leiden: Brill.

de Jong, Albert. 2015. "Religion and Politics in Pre-Islamic Iran." In *The Wiley-Blackwell Companion to Zoroastrianism*, edited by Michael Stausberg and Yuhan Sohrab-Dinshaw Vevaina with Anna Tessmann, 85–102. Chichester, England: Wiley-Blackwell.

De Maaker, Erik. 2013. "Performing the Garo Nation? Garo Wangala Dancing between Faith and Folklore." *Asian Ethnology* 72 (2): 221–39.

Deal, William E., and Brian Ruppert. 2015. *A Cultural History of Japanese Buddhism*. Chichester, England: John Wiley & Sons.

Decety, Jean. 2010. "The Neurodevelopment of Empathy in Humans." *Developmental Neuroscience* 32 (4): 257–67. doi: 10.1159/000317771.

Delaere, Christophe, José M. Capriles, and Charles Stanish. 2019. "Underwater Ritual Offerings in the Island of the Sun and the Formation of the Tiwanaku State." *PNAS* 116 (17): 8233–38. doi: 10.1073/pnas.1820749116.

Dell, Melissa. 2010. "The Persistent Effects of Peru's Mining Mita." *Econometrica* 78 (6): 1863–1903. doi: 10.3982/ECTA8121.

Delvert, Jean. 1961. *Le Paysan Cambodgien*. Paris: Mouton & Co.

Dench, Emma. 2003. "Beyond Greeks and Barbarians: Italy and Sicily in the Hellenistic Age." In *A Companion to the Hellenistic World*, edited by Andrew Erskine, 294–310. Malden: Blackwell Publishing.

Denny, Frederick. 2016. *An Introduction to Islam*. 4th ed. Abingdon: Routledge.

Descola, Philippe. 1996. *The Spears of Twilight: Life and Death in the Amazon Jungle*. New York: The New Press/Harper Collins.

Despeux, C., and L. Kohn. 2003. *Women in Daoism*. Cambridge, MA: Three Pine Press.

Desplagnes, Louis. 1903. *Etude sur les tumuli du Killi dans la région de Gaundam*. Paris: Masson et Cie.

Desplagnes, Louis. 1951. "Fouilles du tumulus d'El Oualedji (Soudan)." *Bulletin de l'Institut français d'Afrique noire* 13 (4): 1159–73.

Diakonoff, Igor M. 1985. "Elam." In *The Cambridge History of Iran, vol. 2: The Median and Achaemenian Periods*, edited by I. Gershevitch, 1–24. Cambridge: Cambridge University Press.

Dickinson, Oliver. 1994. *The Aegean Bronze Age*. Cambridge: Cambridge University Press.

Dikshit, Durga Prasad. 1980. *Political History of the Chalukyas of Badami*. New Delhi: Abhinav Publications.

Dimitrov, K. 2011. "Economic, Social and Political Structures on the Territory of the Odrysian Kingdom in Thrace (5th–First Half of the 3rd Century BC)." *ORPHEUS. Journal of Indo-European and Thracian Studies* 18: 4–24.

Dixon, Helen M. 2013. "Phoenician Mortuary Practice in the Iron Age I–III (c. 1200–c. 300 BCE) Levantine 'Homeland.'" PhD Diss., University of Michigan.

Docherty, Paddy. 2008. *The Khyber Pass: A History of Empire and Invasion*. New York: Union Square Press.

Doniger O'Flaherty, Wendy. 1980. "Introduction." In *Karma and Rebirth in Classical Indian Traditions*, edited by Wendy Doniger O'Flaherty, ix–xxv. Berkeley: University of California Press.

Donlan, Walter. 1973. "The Tradition of Anti-Aristocratic Thought in Early Greek Poetry." *Historia: Zeitschrift für Alte Geschichte* 22 (2): 145–54.

Donlan, Walter. 1993. "Duelling with Gifts in the Iliad: As the Audience Saw It." *Colby Quarterly* 29 (3): Article 3.

Donner, Fred M. 2010. *Muhammad and the Believers, at the Origins of Islam*. Cambridge, MA: Harvard University Press.

Donohue, John J. 2003. *The Buwayhid Dynasty in Iraq 334H./945 to 403H./1012: Shaping Institutions for the Future*. Leiden: Brill.

Dothan, Moshe. 1989. "Archaeological Evidence for Movements of the Early 'Sea Peoples' in Canaan." In *Recent Excavations in Israel: Studies in Iron Age Archaeology*, edited by Seymour Gitin and William G. Dever, 59–70. Winona Lake: Eisenbrauns.

Drews, Robert. 1993. "Myths of Midas and the Phrygian Migration from Europe." *Klio* 75: 9–26. doi: 10.1524/klio.1993.75.75.9.

Driessen, Jan. 2002. "'The King Must Die': Some Observations on the Use of Minoan Court Compounds." In *Monuments of Minos: Rethinking the Minoan Palaces*, edited by Jan Driessen, Ilse Schoep, and Robert Laffineur, 1–15. Liège: Université de Liège.

Duchesne-Guillemin, Jacques. 1953. *Ormazd et Ahriman. L'Aventure dualiste dans l'Antiquité.* Paris: Presses Universitaires de France.

Dueppen, Stephen A. 2016. "The Archaeology of West Africa, ca. 800 BCE to 1500 CE." *History Compass* 14 (6): 247–63. doi: 10.1111/hic3.12316.

Dumont, Louis. 1980. *Homo Hierarchicus.* Chicago: University of Chicago Press.

Dundas, Paul. 2002. *The Jains.* 2nd ed. London: Routledge.

Dunn, Ross E. 2012. *The Adventures of Ibn Battuta: A Muslim Traveller of the 14th Century.* Berkeley: University of California Press.

Dunstan, William E. 2011. *Ancient Rome.* Lanham: Rowman & Littlefield Publishers.

Durrenberger, E. Paul. 1988. "Stratification without a State: The Collapse of the Icelandic Commonwealth." *Ethnos* 3–4: 239–65. Retrieved from http://ehrafworldcultures.yale.edu/document?id=eq02-003.

Dusinberre, Elspeth R. M. 2003. *Aspects of Empire in Achaemenid Sardis.* Cambridge: Cambridge University Press.

Dusinberre, Elspeth R. M. 2013. *Empire, Authority, and Autonomy in Achaemenid Anatolia.* Cambridge: Cambridge University Press.

Dutcher-Walls, Patricia. 2002. "The Circumscription of the King: Deuteronomy 17:16–17 in Its Ancient Social Context." *Journal of Biblical Literature* 121 (4): 601–16. doi: 10.2307/3268573.

Dyott, George Miller. 1926. *On the Trail of the Unknown in the Wilds of Ecuador and the Amazon.* London: T. Butterworth. Retrieved from http://ehrafworldcultures.yale.edu/document?id=sd09-020.

Earle, Timothy. 1978. *Economic and Social Organization of a Complex Chiefdom: The Halele'a District, Kaua'i, Hawai'i.* Anthropological Paper No. 63. Ann Arbor, MI: University of Michigan Museum of Anthropology.

Earle, Timothy. 1980. "Prehistoric Irrigation in the Hawaiian Islands: An Evaluation of Evolutionary Significance." *Archaeology & Physical Anthropology in Oceania* 15 (1): 1–28. doi: 10.1002/j.1834-4453.1980.tb00316.x.

Earle, Timothy, and Justin Jennings. 2012. "Remodeling the Political Economy of the Wari Empire." *Boletín de Arqueología PUCP* 16: 209–26.

Earle, Timothy, and Matthew Spriggs. 2015. "Political Economy in Prehistory: A Marxist Approach to Pacific Sequences." *Current Anthropology* 56 (4): 515–44. doi: 10.1086/682284.

Ebrey, Patricia Buckley. 1993. *Chinese Civilization: A Sourcebook.* Pennsylvania: Free Press.

Ebrey, Patricia Buckley. 1996. *The Cambridge Illustrated History of China.* Cambridge: Cambridge University Press.

Eckstein, Arthur M. 2008. *Rome Enters the Greek East: From Anarchy to Hierarchy in the Hellenistic Mediterranean, 230–170 BC.* Malden, MA: Blackwell.

Eckstein, Arthur M. 2009. "Hellenistic Monarchy in Theory and Practice." In *A Companion to Greek and Roman Political Thought*, edited by Ryan K. Balot, 247–65. Chichester, England: Wiley-Blackwell.

Ehrenreich, Robert M., Carole L. Crumley, and Janet E. Levy, eds. 1995. *Heterarchy and the Analysis of Complex Societies*. Arlington: American Anthropological Association.

Eich, Peter. 2015. "The Common Denominator: Late Roman Imperial Bureaucracy from a Comparative Perspective." In *State Power in Ancient China and Rome*, edited by Walter Scheidel, 90–149. Oxford: Oxford University Press.

Eisenstadt, S. N. 1982. "The Axial Age: The Emergence of Transcendental Visions and the Rise of Clerics." *European Journal of Sociology / Archives Européennes de Sociologie* 23 (2): 294–314. doi: 10.1017/S0003975600003908.

Eisenstadt, S. N. 1986a. "Introduction: The Axial Age Breakthrough in Ancient Greece." In *The Origins and Diversity of Axial Age Civilizations*, edited by Shmuel N. Eisenstadt, 29–39. Albany: State University of New York Press.

Eisenstadt, S. N. 1986b. "Introduction: The Axial Age Breakthroughs—Their Characteristics and Origins." In *The Origins and Diversity of Axial Age Civilizations*, edited by S. N. Eisenstadt, 1–28. Albany: State University of New York Press.

Eisenstadt, S. N. 1986c. "Preface." In *The Origins and Diversity of Axial Age Civilizations*, edited by Shmuel N. Eisenstadt, xi–xiii. Albany: State University of New York Press.

Eisenstadt, S. N., ed. 1986d. *The Origins and Diversity of Axial Age Civilizations*. Albany, NY: State University of New York Press.

Eisenstadt, S. N. 1996. *Japanese Civilization: A Comparative View*. Chicago: The University of Chicago Press.

Eisenstadt, S. N. 2003. *Comparative Civilizations and Multiple Modernities*, part I. Leiden: Brill.

Eisenstadt, S. N. 2005. "Axial Civilizations and the Axial Age Reconsidered." In *Axial Civilizations and World History*, edited by J. P. Arnason, S. N. Eisenstadt, and B. R. Wittrock, 531–64. Leiden: Brill.

Eisenstadt, S. N. 2011. "The Axial Conundrum: Between Transcendental Visions and Vicissitudes of Their Institutionalizations: Constructive and Destructive Possibilities." *Análise Social* 46 (199): 201–17.

Ekberg, Carl. 2007. *Stealing Indian Women: Native Slavery in Illinois Country*. Chicago, IL: University of Chicago Press.

El Fasi, Mohammed and Ivan Hrbek. 1980. "Étapes du développement de l'Islam et de sa diffusion en Afrique." In *Histoire Générale de l'Afrique, vol. 3: L'Afrique du VIIe au XIe siècle*, edited by Mohammed El Fasi, 81–116. Paris: UNESCO.

Elkana, Yehuda. 1986. "The Emergence of Second-Order Thinking in Classical Greece." In *The Origins and Diversity of Axial Age Civilizations*, edited by Shmuel N. Eisenstadt, 40–64. Albany: State University of New York Press.

Eller, Cynthia. 2012. "Two Knights and a Goddess: Sir Arthur Evans, Sir James George Frazer, and the Invention of Minoan Religion." *Journal of Mediterranean Archaeology* 25 (1): 75–98. doi: 10.1558/jmea.v25i1.75.

Elliott, J. H. 1987. "Spain and America before 1700." In *Colonial Spanish America*, edited by Leslie Bethell, 59–111. Cambridge: Cambridge University Press.

Elliott, J. H. 2006. *Empires of the Atlantic World: Britain and Spain in America 1492–1830*. New Haven, CT: Yale University Press.

Elman, B. 2000. *A Cultural History of Civil Examinations in Late Imperial China*. Berkeley: University of California Press.

Emerson, Thomas E. 1997. *Cahokia and the Archaeology of Power*. Tuscaloosa, AL: University of Alabama Press.

Emmerick, R. E., trans. 2004. *The Sūtra of Golden Light (Suvarṇaprabhāsottamasūtra)*. Oxford: Pali Text Society.

Emmerick, Roland. 1970. *The Sūtra of Golden Light: Being a Translation of the Suvarṇabhāsottamasūtra*. London: Luzac.

Emon, Anver M. 2012. *Religious Pluralism: Dhimmīs and Others in the Empire of Law*. Oxford: Oxford University Press.

Engel, David M. 2003. "Women's Role in the Home and the State: Stoic Theory Reconsidered." *Harvard Studies in Classical Philology* 101: 267–88. doi: 10.2307/3658531.

Engels, Friedrich. [1884] 1985. *The Origin of the Family, Private Property and the State*. London: Penguin Books.

English, Paul Ward. 2009. "Qanats and Lifeworlds in Iranian Plateau Villages." Yale F&ES Bulletin 103, available online at http://environment.yale.edu/publication-series/documents/downloads/0-9/103english.pdf.

Enmarch, Roland. 2010. "Middle Kingdom Literature." In *A Companion to Ancient Egypt, vol. 2*, edited by Alan B. Lloyd, 663–84. Chichester, England: Wiley-Blackwell.

Eno, Robert. 2009. "Shang State Religion." In *Early Chinese Religion. Part One: Shang through Han*. Leiden: Brill.

Erickson, L. 1999. "The Problem of Zoroastrian Influence on Judaism and Christianity." Paper presented at the World Congress on Mullā Sadrā, Tehran, May 25–27, 1999.

Erskine, Andrew. 1991. "Hellenistic Monarchy and Roman Political Invective." *Classical Quarterly* 41 (1): 106–20. doi: 10.1017/S000983880000358X.

Eshel, Hanan. 2006. "The Bar Kochba Revolt, 132–135." In *The Cambridge History of Judaism*, edited by Steven T. Katz, 105–27. Cambridge: Cambridge University Press.

Esposito, John L. 1984. *Islam and Politics*. 4th ed. New York: Syracuse University Press.

Evaneshko, Veronica. 1975. *Tonawanda Seneca Ethnic Identity: Functional and Processual Analysis*. Ann Arbor, MI: University Microfilms International. Retrieved from http://ehrafworldcultures.yale.edu/document?id=nm09-059.

Evans, G. R. 2007. *The Church in the Early Middle Ages*. London: I. B. Tauris & Co.

Evans, Gillian R. 2007. *The Church in the Early Middle Ages*. London: I. B. Tauris.

Evans-Pritchard, E. E. 1940. *The Nuer: A Description of the Modes of the Livelihood and Political Institutions of a Nilotic People.* Oxford: Clarendon Press.

Eyre, Christopher J. 1987. "Work and the Organisation of Work in the Old Kingdom." In *Labor in the Ancient Near East*, edited by Marvin A. Powell, 5–47. New Haven, CT: American Oriental Society.

Eyre, Christopher J. 2010. "The Economy: Pharaonic." In *A Companion to Ancient Egypt, vol. 1*, edited by Alan B. Lloyd, 291–308. Chichester, England: Wiley-Blackwell.

Eyre, Chureekamol Onsuwan. 2011. "Social Variation and Dynamics in Metal Age and Protohistoric Central Thailand: A Regional Perspective." *Asian Perspectives* 49 (1): 43–84. doi: 10.1353/asi.2010.0005.

Favereau, Aude, and Bérénice Bellina. 2016. "Thai-Malay Peninsula and South China Sea Networks (500 BC–AD 200), Based on a Reappraisal of 'Sa Huynh-Kalanay'-Related Ceramics." *Quaternary International* 416: 219–27. doi: 10.1016/j.quaint.2015.09.100.

Fear, A. T. 1996. "Cybele and Christ." In *Cybele, Attis and Related Cults: Essays in Memory of M. J. Vermaseren*, edited by Eugene N. Lane, 37–50. Leiden: E. J. Brill.

Feder, Yitzhaq. 2011. *Blood Expiation in Hittite and Biblical Ritual: Origins, Context, and Meaning.* Atlanta, GA: Society of Biblical Literature.

Fehr, Ernst, and Simon Gächter. 2002. "Altruistic Punishment in Humans." *Nature* 415: 137–40. doi: 10.1038/415137a.

Fehr, Ernst, and Urs Fischbacher. 2004. "Social Norms and Human Cooperation." *Trends in Cognitive Sciences* 8: 185–90. doi: 10.1016/j.tics.2004.02.007.

Fenton, William N. 1951. "Locality as a Basic Factor in the Development of Iroquois Social Structure." In *Symposium on Local Diversity in Iroquois Culture*, edited by William N. Fenton, 35–54. Washington, DC: Smithsonian Institution. Retrieved from http://ehrafworldcultures.yale.edu/document?id=nm09-032.

Fenton, William N., and Prokosch Kurath Gertrude. 1953. "The Iroquois Eagle Dance, an Offshoot of the Calumet Dance." *Bureau of American Ethnology Bulletin* 156: 1–324. Retrieved from http://ehrafworldcultures.yale.edu/document?id=nm09-029.

Fessler, Daniel. 2004. "Shame in Two Cultures: Implications for Evolutionary Approaches." *Journal of Cognition and Culture* 4 (2): 207–62. doi: 10.1163/1568537041725097.

Figes, Orlando. 1996. *A People's Tragedy: A History of the Russian Revolution.* London: Jonathan Cape.

Finer, Samuel. 1999. *The History of Government, vol. I: Ancient Monarchies and Empires.* Oxford: Oxford University Press.

Finkelstein, Israel. 2013. *The Forgotten Kingdom: The Archaeology and History of Northern Israel.* Atlanta, GA: Society of Biblical Literature.

Finley, Moses I. 2002a. "The Silent Women of Rome." In *Sexuality and Gender in the Classical World: Readings and Sources*, edited by Laura K. McClure, 147–60. Oxford: Blackwell.

Finley, Moses I. 2002b. *The World of Odysseus.* Revised ed. New York: New York Review of Books.

Finucane, Brian Clifton, J. Ernesto Valdez, Ismael Perez Calderon, Cirilo Vivanco Pomacanchari, Lidio M. Valdez, and Tamsin O'Connell. 2007. "The End of Empire: New Radiocarbon Dates from the Ayacucho Valley, Peru, and Their Implications for the Collapse of the Wari State." *Radiocarbon* 49 (2): 579–92. doi: 10.1017/s003382220004248x.

Fischer-Bovet, Christelle. 2014. *Army and Society in Ptolemaic Egypt*. Cambridge: Cambridge University Press.

Fish Kashay, Jennifer. 2008. "From Kapus to Christianity: The Disestablishment of the Hawaiian Religion and Chiefly Appropriation of Calvinist Christianity." *Western Historical Quarterly* 39 (1): 17–39. doi: 10.2307/25443647.

Fitzjohn, Matthew. 2007. "Equality in the Colonies: Concepts of Equality in Sicily during the Eighth to Sixth Centuries BC." *World Archaeology* 39 (2): 215–28. doi: 10.1080/00438240701257655.

Flannery, Kent, and Joyce Marcus. 2012. *The Creation of Inequality: How Our Prehistoric Ancestors Set the Stage for Monarchy, Slavery, and Empire*. Cambridge, MA: Harvard University Press.

Fletcher, Roland, Brendan M. Buckley, Christophe Pottier, and Shi-Yu Simon Wang. 2017. "Fourteenth to Sixteenth Centuries AD: The Case of Angkor and Monsoon Extremes in Southeast Asia." In *Megadrought and Collapse: From Early Agriculture to Angkor*, edited by Harvey Weiss, 275–307. Oxford: Oxford University Press.

Floor, Willem. 2009. "Judicial and Legal Systems iv: Judicial System from the Advent of Islam through the 19th Century." In *Encyclopædia Iranica. Online edition.* http://www.iranicaonline.org/articles/judicial-and-legal-systems-iv-judicial-system-from-the-advent-of-islam-through-the-19th-century (accessed November 28, 2017).

Fogel, Robert, and Geoffrey Elton. 1983. *Which Path to the Past?* New Haven, CT: Yale University Press.

Foley, Denis. 1994. *An Ethnohistoric and Ethnographic Analysis of the Iroquois from the Aboriginal Era to the Present Suburban Era*. Ann Arbor, MI: University Microfilms International. Retrieved from http://ehrafworldcultures.yale.edu/document?id=nm09-060.

Foley, Jonathan A. Michael T. Coe, Marten Scheffer, and Guiling Wang. 2003. "Regime Shifts in the Sahara and Sahel: Interactions between Ecological and Climatic Systems in Northern Africa." *Ecosystems* 6 (6): 524–32. doi: 10.1007/s10021-002-0227-0.

Fowden, Garth. 1999. "Religious Communities." In *Late Antiquity: A Guide to the Postclassical World*, edited by G. W. Bowersock, Peter Brown, and Oleg Grabar, 82–106. Cambridge: The Belknap Press of Harvard University Press.

Fox, Robin Lane. 1986. *Pagans and Christians in the Mediterranean World from the Second Century AD to the Conversion of Constantine*. London: Viking.

Foxhall, Lin. 2002. "Access to Resources in Classical Greece: The Egalitarianism of the Polis in Practice." In *Money, Labour and Land: Approaches to the Economics of Ancient Greece*, edited by Paul Cartledge, Edward E. Cohen and Lin Foxhall, 209–20. London: Routledge.

François, Pieter, J. G. Manning, Harvey Whitehouse, Rob Brennan, T. E. Currie, Kevin Feeney, and Peter Turchin. 2016. "A Macroscope for Global History. Seshat Global History Databank: A Methodological Overview." *Digital Humanities Quarterly* 10 (4).

Frankfurter, David. 1998. *Religion in Roman Egypt: Assimilation and Resistance*. Princeton, NJ: Princeton University Press.

Frankfurter, David. 2010. "Religion in Society: Graeco-Roman." In *A Companion to Ancient Egypt, vol. 1*, edited by Alan B. Lloyd, 526–46. Chichester, England: Wiley-Blackwell.

Frankopan, Peter. 2015. *The Silk Roads: A New History of the World*. London: Bloomsbury.

Fraser, Chris. 2016. *The Philosophy of Mozi: The First Consequentialists*. New York: Columbia University Press.

Frazer, James George. [1890] 1975. *The Golden Bough: A Study in Magic and Religion*. Abridged ed. London: Macmillan.

Frederickson, H. George. 2002. "Confucius and the Moral Basis of Bureaucracy." *Administration and Society* 33 (4): 610–628. doi: 10.1177/0095399702336002.

Freeman, Derek. 1955a. *Iban Agriculture: A Report on the Shifting Cultivation of Hill Rice by the Iban of Sarawak*. Colonial Research Studies. London: Her Majesty's Stationery Office. Retrieved from http://ehrafworldcultures.yale.edu/document?id=oc06-001.

Freeman, Derek. 1955b. *Report on the Iban of Sarawak*, vol. 1: *Iban Social Organization*. Kuching, Sarawak: Government Printing Office. Retrieved from http://ehrafworldcultures.yale.edu/document?id=oc06-015.

Freeman, Derek. 1958. "The Family System of the Iban of Borneo." In *The Developmental Cycle in Domestic Groups*, edited by Jack Goody, 15–52. Cambridge: Cambridge University Press. Retrieved from http://ehrafworldcultures.yale.edu/document?id=oc06-006.

Freeman, Derek. 1981. *Some Reflections on the Nature of Iban Society*. Occasional Paper of the Department of Anthropology, Research School of Pacific Studies, Australian National University. Canberra: Dept. of Anthropology, Research School of Pacific Studies, Australian National University. Retrieved from http://ehrafworldcultures.yale.edu/document?id=oc06-019.

Fried, Lisbeth S. 2002. "Cyrus the Messiah? The Historical Background to Isaiah 45:1." *Harvard Theological Review* 95 (4): 373–93. doi: 10.1017/S0017816002000251.

Fried, Lisbeth S. 2004. *The Priest and the Great King: Temple-Palace Relations in the Persian Empire*. Winona Lake: Eisenbrauns.

Fritz, Gayle J. 2019. *Feeding Cahokia: Early Agriculture in the North American Heartland*. Tuscaloosa, AL: University of Alabama Press.

Frood, Elizabeth. 2010. "Social Structure and Daily Life: Pharaonic." In *A Companion to Ancient Egypt*, vol. 1, edited by Alan B. Lloyd, 469–90. Chichester, England: Wiley-Blackwell.

Frye, Richard N. 1984. *The History of Ancient Iran*. Munich: C. H. Beck'sche Verlagsbuchhandlung.

Frye, Richard N. 2002. "Ethnic Identity in Iran." *Jerusalem Studies in Arabic and Islam* 26: 78–83.

Frykenberg, Robert. 1989. "The Emergence of Modern 'Hinduism' as a Concept and as an Institution: A Reappraisal with Special Reference to South India." In *Hinduism Reconsidered*, edited by Gunther D. Sontheimer and Hermann Kulke, 24–49. New Delhi: Manohar.

Gabriel, Richard A. 2010. *Philip II of Macedonia: Greater than Alexander*. Washington, DC: Potomac Books.

Gafni, Isaiah. 1984. "The Historical Background." In *The Literature of the Jewish People in the Period of the Second Temple and the Talmud, vol. 2: Jewish Writings of the Second Temple Period: Apocrypha, Pseudepigrapha, Qumran, Sectarian Writings, Philo, Josephus*, edited by Michael Stone, 1–31. Philadelphia: Fortress Press.

Gagarin, Michael, and Paula Perlman. 2016. *The Laws of Ancient Crete c.650–400 BCE.* Oxford: Oxford University Press.

Gait, E. A. 1913. "Human Sacrifice (Indian)." In *Encyclopedia of Religion and Ethics*, vol. 6, edited by James Hastings, 849–53. Edinburgh: Clark.

Galinsky, Karl. 2007. "Continuity and Change: Religion in the Augustan Semi-Century." In *A Companion to Roman Religion*, edited by Jörg Rüpke, 71–82. Malden: Blackwell Publishing.

Gallais, Jean. 1967. *Le delta intérieur du Niger, étude de géographie régionale.* Dakar: IFAN.

Gantley, Michael, Amy Bogaard, and Harvey Whitehouse 2018. "Material Correlates Analysis (MCA): An Innovative Way of Examining Questions in Archaeology Using Ethnographic Data." *Advances in Archaeological Practice* 6 (4): 328–341. doi: 10.1017/aap.2018.9.

García, Juan Carlos Moreno. 2013. "The 'Other' Administration: Patronage, Factions, and Informal Networks of Power in Ancient Egypt." In *Ancient Egyptian Administration*, edited by Juan Carlos Moreno García, 1029–65. Leiden: Brill.

Gardner, Daniel K. 2014. *Confucianism: A Very Short Introduction.* Oxford: Oxford University Press.

Garnsey, Peter. 1996. *Ideas of Slavery from Aristotle to Augustine.* Cambridge: Cambridge University Press.

Gavin, Traude. 1995. "Iban Ritual Fabrics: Their Patterns and Names." PhD Diss., University of Hull.Gavrilets, Sergey. 2015. "Collective Action and the Collaborative Brain." *Interface* 12: 20141067. doi: 10.1098/rsif.2014.1067.

Geertz, Armin W. 2014. "Do Big Gods Cause Anything?" *Religion* 44 (4): 609–613. doi: 10.1080/00 48721X.2014.937052.

Genz, Hermann, and Dirk Paul Mielke. 2011. "Research on the Hittites: A Short Overview." In *Insights into Hittite History and Archaeology*, edited by Hermann Genz and Dirk Paul Mielke, 1–30. Leuven: Peeters.

George, Mathew. 1995. "Development of Education in Garo Hills: Continuity and Change." In *Hill Societies, Their Modernisation: A Study of North East with Special Reference to Garo Hills*, edited by Milton S. Sangma, 187–96. New Delhi: Omsons Publications. Retrieved from http://ehrafworldcultures.yale.edu/document?id=ar05-038.

Gershevitch, Ilya. 1959. *The Avestan Hymn to Mithra.* Cambridge: Cambridge University Press.

Gethin, Rupert. 1998. *The Foundations of Buddhism.* Oxford: Oxford University Press.

Gibbon, Guy E. 2001. "Oneota." In *Encyclopedia of Prehistory, vol. 6: North America*, edited by Peter N. Peregrine and Melvin Ember, 389–407. New York: Springer Science+Business Media.

Glassman, Ronald. 2017. *The Origins of Democracy in Tribes, City-States and Nation-States.* Cham: Springer.

Glatz, Claudia and Roger Matthews. 2005. "Anthropology of a Frontier Zone: Hittite-Kaska Relations in Late Bronze Age North-Central Anatolia." *Bulletin of the American Schools of Oriental Research* 339: 47–65. doi: 10.1086/BASOR25066902.

Glowacki, Mary, and Michael Malpass. 2003. "Water, Huacas, and Ancestor Worship: Traces of a Sacred Wari Landscape." *Latin American Antiquity* 14 (4): 431–48. doi: 10.2307/3557577.

Gnoli, Gherardo. 1993. "Conversion i: Of Iranians to the Zoroastrian Faith." In *Encyclopædia Iranica*, VI/3, 227–29. Updated version available online at http://www.iranicaonline.org/articles/arsacids-ii (accessed September 14, 2017).

Gnoli, Gherardo. 1999. "Farr(ah)." In *Encyclopædia Iranica. Online edition.* http://www.iranicaonline.org/articles/farrah (accessed November 28, 2017).

Goelet, Jr., Ogden. 2008. "Commentary." In *The Egyptian Book of the Dead: The Book of Going Forth by Day,* translated by Raymond O. Faulkner and edited by Ogden Goelet, Jr., Carol A. R. Andrews, and Eva von Dassow, 137–70. San Francisco, CA: Chronicle Books.

Gogolev, A. I. 1992. "Dualism in the Traditional Beliefs of the Yakuts." *Anthropology and Archeology of Eurasia* 31 (2): 70–84. doi: 10.2753/AAE1061-1959310270.

Goldin, Paul R. 2014. *Confucianism.* Abingdon: Routledge.

Goldin, Paul. 2001. "The Thirteen Classics." In *The Columbia History of Chinese Literature,* edited by Victor Mair, 86–96. New York: Columbia University Press.

Goldin, Paul. 2011. "Persistent Misconceptions about Chinese 'Legalism.'" *Journal of Chinese Philosophy* 38 (1): 88–104. doi: 10.1111/j.1540-6253.2010.01629.x.

Goldman, Irving. 1970. *Ancient Polynesian Society.* Chicago: University of Chicago Press.

Goldman, Leon. 2012. "Women ii: In the Avesta." In *Encyclopædia Iranica.* Online edition. http://www.iranicaonline.org/articles/women-ii-avesta (accessed September 6, 2017).

Goldstein, Jonathan A. 1990. "The Hasmonean Revolt and the Hasmonean Dynasty." In *The Cambridge History of Judaism, vol. 2: The Hellenistic Age,* edited by William D. Davies and Louis Finkelstein, 292–351. Cambridge: Cambridge University Press.

Gombrich, Richard. 1988. *Theravada Buddhism: A Social History from Ancient Benares to Modern Colombo.* London: Routledge.

Gomes, Edwin H. 1911. *Seventeen Years among the Sea Dyaks of Borneo: A Record of Intimate Association with the Natives of the Bornean Jungles.* London: Seeley and Co. Retrieved from http://ehrafworldcultures.yale.edu/document?id=oc06-007.

Gomez, Michael A. 2018. *African Dominion: A New History of Empire in Early and Medieval West Africa.* Princeton, NJ: Princeton University Press.

González-Carré, Enrique, Jaime Urrutía Ceruti, and Jorge Lévano Peña. 1997. *Ayacucho: San Juan de la Frontera de Huamanga.* Lima: Banco de Crédito del Perú.

Goodman, Martin. 1987. *The Ruling Class of Judaea: The Origins of the Jewish Revolt against Rome, A.D. 66–70.* Cambridge: Cambridge University Press.

Goody, Jack. 1971. *Technology, Tradition and the State in Africa.* Cambridge: Cambridge University Press.

Goody, Jack. 1976. *Production and Reproduction: A Comparative Study of the Domestic Domain* Cambridge Studies in Social Anthropology, no. 17. Cambridge: Cambridge University Press.

Goswami, M. C., and Dhirendra Narayan Majumdar. 1964. "Mahari among the Garo." *Journal of the University of Guahati* 15 (2): 214–22. Retrieved from http://ehrafworldcultures.yale.edu/document?id=aro5-020.

Goswami, M. C., and Dhirendra Narayan Majumdar. 1965. "A Study of Women's Position among the Garo." *Man in India* 45 (1): 27–36. Retrieved from https://ehrafworldcultures.yale.edu/document?id=aro5-021.

Gould, Ketayun H. 1994. "Outside the Discipline, Inside the Experience: Women in Zoroastrianism." In *Religion and Women*, edited by Arvind Sharma, 139–82. Albany: State University of New York Press.

Graeber, David. 2011. *Debt: The First 5,000 Years.* Brooklyn, NY: Melville House Publishing.

Graham, Alexander J. 1995. "The Odyssey, History, and Women." In *The Distaff Side: Representing the Female in Homer's Odyssey*, edited by Beth Cohen, 3–16. Oxford: Oxford University Press.

Grajetzki, Wolfram. 2013. "Setting a State Anew: The Central Administration from the End of the Old Kingdom to the End of the Middle Kingdom." In *Ancient Egyptian Administration*, edited by Juan Carlos Moreno García, 215–58. Leiden: Brill.

Graubart, Karen B. 2007. *With Our Labor and Sweat: Indigenous Women and the Formation of Colonial Society in Peru, 1550–1700.* Stanford: Stanford University Press.

Green, Adam S., and Cameron A. Petrie. 2018. "Landscapes of Urbanization and De-Urbanization: A Large-Scale Approach to Investigating the Indus Civilization's Settlement Distributions in Northwest India." *Journal of Field Archaeology* 43 (4): 284–99. doi: 10.1080/00934690.2018.1464332.

Green, Peter. 1990. *Alexander to Actium: The Historical Evolution of the Hellenistic Age.* Berkeley: University of California Press.

Green, Peter. 2013. *Alexander of Macedon, 356–323 B.C.: A Historical Biography.* Berkeley: University of California Press.

Greenewalt Jr., Crawford H. 1995. "Sardis in the Age of Xenophon." *Pallas* 43: 125–45. doi: 10.3406/palla.1995.1367.

Greenewalt Jr., Crawford H. 2011. "Sardis: A First Millennium B.C.E. Capital in Western Anatolia." In *The Oxford Handbook of Ancient Anatolia, 10,000–323 B.C.E.*, edited by Sharon R. Steadman and Gregory McMahon, 1112–30. Oxford: Oxford University Press.

Gregory, Peter and Patricia Buckley Ebrey. 1993. "The Religious and Historical Landscape." In *Religion and Society in T'ang and Sung China*, edited by Patricia Buckley Ebrey and Peter Gregory, 1–45. Honolulu: University of Hawaii Press.

Grenet, Frantz. 2015. "Zarathustra's Time and Homeland: Geographical Perspectives." In *The Wiley-Blackwell Companion to Zoroastrianism*, edited by Michael Stausberg and Yuhan Sohrab-Dinshaw Vevaina with Anna Tessmann, 21–30. Chichester, England: Wiley-Blackwell.

Grimm, Veronika E. 2006. "On Food and the Body." In *A Companion to the Roman Empire*, edited by David S. Potter, 354–68. Chichester, England: Wiley-Blackwell.

Gropp, Gerd. 2005. "Susa v: The Sasanian Period." In *Encyclopædia Iranica*. Online edition. http://www.iranicaonline.org/articles/susa-v (accessed August 11, 2017).

Gruen, Erich S. 1998. *Heritage and Hellenism: The Reinvention of Jewish Tradition*. Berkeley: University of California Press.

Gruen, Erich S. 2010. "Romans and Others." In *A Companion to the Roman Republic*, edited by Nathan Rosenstein and Robert Morstein-Marx, 459–77. Chichester, England: Wiley-Blackwell.

Gürkan, S. Leyla. 2008. *The Jews as a Chosen People: Tradition and Transformation*. New York: Routledge.

Haas, Jonathan, and Winifred Creamer. 2004. "Cultural Transformations in the Central Andean Late Archaic." In *Andean Archaeology*, edited by Helaine Silverman, 35–50. Malden, MA: Blackwell.

Habermas, Jürgen. 2010. *An Awareness of What Is Missing: Faith and Reason in a Post-Secular Age*. Cambridge: Polity.

Habib, I. 2005. "The Delhi Sultanate." In *The State and Society in Medieval India*, edited by J. S. Grewal, 37–44. Oxford: Oxford University Press.

Habu, Junko. 2008. "Growth and Decline in Complex Hunter-Gatherer Societies: A Case Study from the Jomon Period Sannai Maruyama Site, Japan." *Antiquity* 82 (317): 571–84. doi: 10.1017/S0003598X00097234.

Haerinck, Ernie. 1997. "Babylonia under Achaemenid Rule." In *Mesopotamia and Iran in the Persian Period: Conquest and Imperialism 539-351 BC. Proceedings of a Seminar in Memory of Vladimir G. Lukonin*, edited by John Curtis, 26–34. London: British Museum Press.

Hägg, Robin, ed. 1983. *The Greek Renaissance of the Eighth Century BC: Tradition and Innovation*. Stockholm: Svenska Institutet i Athen.

Hahm, David E. 2009. "The Mixed Constitution in Greek Thought." In *A Companion to Greek and Roman Political Thought*, edited by Ryan K. Balot, 178–98. Chichester, England: Wiley-Blackwell.

Haidt, Jonathan, and Craig Joseph. 2008. "The Moral Mind: How Five Sets of Innate Intuitions Guide the Development of Many Culture-Specific Virtues, and Perhaps Even Modules." In *The Innate Mind, vol. 3: Foundations and the Future*, edited by Peter Carruthers, Stephen Lawrence, and Stephen Stich, chap. 19. Online edition. Oxford: Oxford University Press. doi: 10.1093/acprof:oso/9780195332834.001.0001.

Haidt, Jonathan. 2007. "The New Synthesis in Moral Psychology." *Science* 316: 98–1002. doi: 10.1126/science.1137651.

Haidt, Jonathan. 2012. *The Righteous Mind: Why Good People Are Divided by Politics and Religion*. New York: Pantheon Books.

Haldon, John F. and Hugh Kennedy. 1980. "The Arab-Byzantine Frontier in the Eighth and Ninth Centuries: Military Organization and Society in the Borderlands." *Zbornik Radova Vizantološkog Instituta* 19: 79–116.

Hall, Kenneth R. 1993. "Economic History of Early Southeast Asia." In *The Cambridge History of Southeast Asia, vol. 1: From Early Times to c. 1800*, edited by Nicholas Tarling, 183–275. Cambridge: Cambridge University Press.

Hall, Kenneth R. 2011. *A History of Early Southeast Asia: Maritime Trade and Societal Development, 100–1500*. Lanham, MD: Rowman & Littlefield.

Hall, Kenneth R. 2018. "The Coming of the West: European Cambodian Marketplace Connectivity, 1500–1800." In *Cambodia and the West, 1500–2000*, edited by T. O. Smith, 7–36. London: Palgrave Macmillan.

Hall, Robert L. 1997. *An Archaeology of the Soul: North American Indian Belief and Ritual*. Urbana, IL: University of Illinois Press.

Halpern, Baruch and Kenneth S. Sacks, eds. 2017. *Cultural Contact and Appropriation in the Axial-Age Mediterranean World: A Periplos*. Leiden: Brill.

Halton, Eugene. 2014. "Islands of Light." In *From the Axial Age to the Moral Revolution: John Stuart-Glennie, Karl Jaspers, and a New Understanding of the Idea*, edited by Eugene Halton, 61–71. New York: Palgrave Macmillan.

Halton, Eugene. 2019. "John Stuart-Glennie's Lost Legacy." In *Forgotten Founders and Other Neglected Social Theorists*, edited by Christopher T. Conner, Nicholas M. Baxter, and David R. Dickens, 11–26. Lanham, MD: Lexington Books.

Hamblin, William J. 2006. *Warfare in the Ancient Near East to 1600 BC: Holy Warriors at the Dawn of History*. London: Routledge.

Hamilakis, Yannis. 2006. "The Colonial, the National, and the Local: Legacies of the 'Minoan' Past." In *Archaeology and European Modernity: Producing and Consuming the "Minoans,"* edited by Yannis Hamilakis and Nicoletta Momigliano, 145–62. Padua: Bottega d'Erasmo.

Hamilton, Sue. 2013. *Indian Philosophy: A Very Short Introduction*. Oxford: Oxford University Press.

Handy, E. S. Craighill, and Mary Kawena Pukui. 1958. *The Polynesian Family System in Ka'u, Hawai'i*. Wellington: Polynesian Society.

Hansen, Anne. 2004. "Cambodia." In *Encyclopedia of Buddhism*, vol. 1: A–L, edited by Robert E. Buswell, Jr., 105–10. New York: Macmillan Reference.

Hansen, Mogens, and Thomas Nielsen, eds. 2004. *An Inventory of Archaic and Classical Poleis*. Oxford: Oxford University Press.

Hansen, Valerie. 2012. *The Silk Road: A New History*. Oxford: Oxford University Press.

Hansman, John. 1985. "Anshan in the Median and Achaemenian Periods." In *The Cambridge History of Iran, vol. 2: The Median and Achaemenian Periods*, edited by I. Gershevitch, 25–35. Cambridge: Cambridge University Press.

Harada, Masayuki. 2009. "Dogu Broken and Enshrined: Traces of a Jomon World View." In *The Power of Dogu: Ceramic Figures From Ancient Japan*, edited by Simon Kaner, 50–59. London: British Museum Press.

Haring, Ben. 2010. "Administration and Law: Pharaonic." In *A Companion to Ancient Egypt, vol. 1*, edited by Alan B. Lloyd, 218–36. Chichester, England: Wiley-Blackwell.

Harl, Kenneth W. 2011. "The Greeks in Anatolia: From the Migrations to Alexander the Great." In *The Oxford Handbook of Ancient Anatolia, 10,000–323 B.C.E.*, edited by Sharon R. Steadman and Gregory McMahon, 752–74. Oxford: Oxford University Press.

Harner, Michael J. 1962. Jivaro Souls. *American Anthropologist* 64 (2): 258–72. Retrieved from http://ehrafworldcultures.yale.edu/document?id=sd09-032.

Harner, Michael J. 1973. *Jívaro: People of the Sacred Waterfalls*. Garden City, NY: Anchor Press/ Doubleday. Retrieved from http://ehrafworldcultures.yale.edu/document?id=sd09-034.

Harper, Prudence O., Joan Aruz, and Françoise Tallon. 1992a. "Chronology." In *The Royal City of Susa: Ancient Near Eastern Treasures in the Louvre*, edited by Prudence O. Harper, Joan Aruz, and Françoise Tallon, xviii–xix. New York: The Metropolitan Museum of Art.

Harper, Prudence O., Joan Aruz, and Françoise Tallon. 1992b. "Maps." In *The Royal City of Susa: Ancient Near Eastern Treasures in the Louvre*, edited by Prudence O. Harper, Joan Aruz, and Françoise Tallon, xiv–xvii. New York: The Metropolitan Museum of Art.

Harris, Edward M. 2002. "Did Solon Abolish Debt-Bondage?" *The Classical Quarterly* 52 (2): 415–30. doi: 10.1017/CBO9780511497858.013.

Harris, Ian Charles. 2005. *Cambodian Buddhism: History and Practice*. Honolulu: University of Hawai'i Press.

Harris, Ian Charles. 2007. *Buddhism, Power and Political Order*. London: Routledge.

Harris, William V. 2010. "Power." In *The Oxford Handbook of Roman Studies*, edited by Alessandro Barchiesi and Walter Scheidel, 564–78. Oxford: Oxford University Press.

Hart, John P. 1990. "Modeling Oneota Agricultural Production: A Cross-Cultural Evaluation." *Current Anthropology* 31 (5): 569–77. doi: 10.1086/203903.

Hartman, Charles. 2015. "Sung Government and Politics." In *The Cambridge History of China*, vol. 5: *The Five Dynasties and Sung China, 960–1279 AD, Part 2*, edited by J. W. Chaffee and D. Twitchett, 21–138. Cambridge: Cambridge University Press.

Hauser, Raymond E. 2015. "Illinois." In *Colonial Wars of North America, 1512–1763: An Encyclopedia*, edited by Alan Gallay, 299–300. Abingdon: Routledge.

Havard, Gilles. 2013. "'Protection' and 'Unequal Alliance': The French Conception of Sovereignty over Indians in New France." In *French and Indians in the Heart of North America, 1630–1815*, edited by Robert Englebert and Guillaume Teasdale, 113–37. East Lansing, MI: Michigan State University Press.

Hawkins, David. 1986. "Writing in Anatolia: Imported and Indigenous Systems." *World Archaeology* 17 (3): 363–76. doi: 10.1080/00438243.1986.9979976.

Hawkins, David. 2009. "Cilicia, the Amuq, and Aleppo: New Light in a Dark Age." *Near Eastern Archaeology* 72 (4): 164–73. doi: 10.1086/NEA25754025.

Hawting, Gerald R. 2000. *The First Dynasty of Islam: The Umayyad Caliphate AD 661–750*. 2nd ed. London: Routledge.

Hayden, Brian. 1995. "Pathways to Power: Principles for Creating Socioeconomic Inequalities." In *Foundations of Social Inequality*, edited by T. Douglas Price and Gary M. Feinman, 15–86. New York: Plenum Press.

Hays, Harold M. 2015. "The Contextualization of the Pyramid Texts and the Religious History of the Old Kingdom." In *Towards a New History for the Egyptian Old Kingdom*, edited by Peter Der Manuelian and Thomas Schneider, 200–26. Leiden: Brill.

Heath, Malcolm. 2008. "Aristotle on Natural Slavery." *Phronesis* 53 (3): 243–70. doi: 10.1163/156852808X307070.

Hegel, Georg W. F. 1956. *The Philosophy of History*. Translated by John Sibree. New York: Dover.

Heid, Stefan. 2007. "The Romanness of Roman Christianity." In *A Companion to Roman Religion*, edited by Jörg Rüpke, 406–26. Malden: Blackwell.

Hendrickson, Mitch. 2010. "Historic Routes to Angkor: Development of the Khmer Road System (Ninth to Thirteenth Centuries AD) in Mainland Southeast Asia." *Antiquity* 84: 480–96. doi: 10.1017/S0003598X00066722.

Heng, Piphal. 2012. "Speculation on Land Use in and around Sambor Prei Kuk." In *Old Myths and New Approaches: Interpreting Ancient Religious Sites in Southeast Asia*, edited by Alexandra Haendel, 180–98. Monash: Monash University Press.

Heng, Piphal. 2016. "Transition to the Pre-Angkorian Period (300–500 CE): Thala Borivat and a Regional Perspective." *Journal of Southeast Asian Studies* 47: 484–505. doi: 10.1017/S0022463416000369.

Hengel, Martin. 1990. "The Political and Social History of Palestine from Alexander to Antiochus III (333–187 B.C.E.)." In *The Cambridge History of Judaism, vol. 2: The Hellenistic Age*, edited by William D. Davies and Louis Finkelstein, 35–78. Cambridge: Cambridge University Press.

Henkelman, Wouter F. M. 2008. *The Other Gods Who Are: Studies in Elamite-Iranian Acculturation Based on the Persepolis Fortification Texts*. Leiden: Nederlands Instituut voor het Nabije Oosten.

Henkelman, Wouter F. M. 2011. "Parnakka's Feast: Šip in Parsa and Elam." In *Elam and Persia*, edited by J. Alvarez and M. B. Garrison, 89–166. Winona Lake: Eisenbrauns.

Henshall, Kenneth. 2012. *A History of Japan: From Stone Age to Superpower*. 3rd ed. New York: Palgrave Macmillan.

Herzfeld, Ernst. 1936. "The Iranian Religion at the Time of Darius and Xerxes." *Religions* 15: 20–8.

Hewitt, J. N. B. 1895. "The Iroquoian Concept of the Soul." *Journal of American Folklore* 8 (28): 107–16. Retrieved from http://ehrafworldcultures.yale.edu/document?id=nm09-013.

Hezser, Catherine. 2004. "Classical Rabbinic Literature." In *The Oxford Handbook of Jewish Studies*, edited by Martin Goodman. Oxford: Oxford University Press.

Higham, Charles. 2014. *Early Mainland Southeast Asia: From First Humans to Angkor*. Bangkok: River Books.

Hill, Kim. 2002. "Altruistic Cooperation during Foraging by the Ache, and the Evolved Human Predisposition to Cooperate." *Human Nature* 13 (1): 105–28. doi: 10.1007/s12110-002-1016-3.

Hill, Kim R., Robert S. Walker, Miran Božičević, James Eder, Thomas Headland, Barry Hewlett, B., A. Magdalena Hurtado, et al. 2011. "Co-Residence Patterns in Hunter-Gatherer Societies Show Unique Human Social Structure." *Science* 331 (6022): 1286–89. doi: 10.1126/science.1199071.

Hinz, Walther. 1972. *The Lost World of Elam: Re-Creation of a Vanished Civilization. Translated by Jennifer Barnes*. London: Sidgwick and Jackson.

Hirschman, Albert O. 1970. *Exit, Voice, and Loyalty: Responses to Decline in Firms, Organizations, and States*. Cambridge, MA: Harvard University Press.

Hjerrild, Bodil. 1990. "The Survival and Modification of Zoroastrianism in Seleucid Times." In *Religion and Religious Practice in the Seleucid Kingdom*, edited by Per Bilde, Troels Engberg-Pedersen, Lise Hannestad, and Jan Zahle, 140–50. Aarhus: Aarhus University Press.

Hodgson, Marshall G. S. 1974. *The Venture of Islam: Conscience and History in a World Civilization.* Chicago: University of Chicago Press.

Hoffman, Barbara G. 2000. *Griots at War: Conflict, Conciliation and Caste in Mande.* Bloomington: Indiana University Press.

Hoffner, Harry A. 2006. "The Royal Cult in Hatti." In *Text, Artifact, and Image: Revealing Ancient Israelite Religion*, edited by Gary M. Beckman and Theodore J. Lewis, 132–51. Providence: Brown Judaic Studies.

Hölbl, Günther. 2001. *A History of the Ptolemaic Empire.* London: Routledge.

Holcombe, Charles. 2001. *The Genesis of East Asia: 221 B.C.–A.D. 907.* Honolulu, HI: University of Hawaii Press.

Holcombe, Charles. 2011. *A History of East Asia: From the Origins of Civilization to the Twenty-First Century.* Cambridge: Cambridge University Press.

Holden, Clare Janaki, and Ruth Mace. 2003. "Spread of Cattle Led to the Loss of Matrilineal Descent in Africa: A Coevolutionary Analysis." *Proceedings of the Royal Society of London, Series B: Biological Sciences* 270 (1532): 2425–33. doi: 10.1098/rspb.2003.2535.

Hole, Frank. 1987. *The Archaeology of Western Iran: Settlement and Society from Prehistory to the Islamic Conquest.* Washington, DC: Smithsonian Institution Press.

Hommon, Robert J. 2013. *The Ancient Hawaiian State: Origins of a Political Society.* Oxford: Oxford University Press.

Horky, Phillip Sidney. 2009. "Persian Cosmos and Greek Philosophy: Plato's Associates and the Zoroastrian Magoi." *Oxford Studies in Ancient Philosophy* 37: 47–103.

Hornung, Erik. 1999. *Akhenaten and the Religion of Light.* Translated by David Lorton. Ithaca: Cornell University Press.

Horowitz, Wayne, Takayoshi Oshima, and Filip Vukosavović. 2012. "Hazor 18: Fragments of a Cuneiform Law Collection from Hazor." *Israel Exploration Journal* 62 (2): 158–176.

Horsley, Richard A. 1999. *Bandits, Prophets, and Messiahs: Popular Movements at the Time of Jesus.* Harrisburg, PA: Trinity Press International.

Houben, Jan E. M. 1999. "To Kill or Not to Kill the Sacrificial Animal (*Yajñapaśu*)? Arguments and Perspectives in Brahmanical Ethical Philosophy." In *Violence Denied: Violence, Non-Violence and the Rationalization of Violence in South Asian Cultural History*, edited by Jan E. M. Houben and Karel R. van Kooij, 105–83. Leiden: Brill.

Howell, William. 1908–1910. "Sea Dyak." *Sarawak Gazette* 38–40 [HRAF pagination: 1–118]. Retrieved from http://ehrafworldcultures.yale.edu/document?id=oc06-002.

Hoyer, Daniel. 2013. "Public Feasting, Elite Competition, and the Market Economy of Roman North Africa." *The Journal of North African Studies* 18 (4): 574–91. doi: 10.1080/13629387.2013.822304.

Hoyer, Daniel. 2018. *Money, Culture, and Well-Being in Rome's Economic Development, 0–275 CE*. Leiden: Brill.

Hsu C-y. 1999. "The Spring and Autumn Period." In *The Cambridge History of Ancient China From the Origins of Civilization to 221 BC*, edited by Michael Loewe and Edward L. Shaughnessy, 545–86. Cambridge: Cambridge University Press. http://www.iranicaonline.org/articles/jerusalem-and-iran.

Hui, Victoria Tin-bor. 2005. *War and State Formation in Ancient China and Early Modern Europe*. Cambridge: Cambridge University Press.

Hulsewé, A. F. P. 1955. *Remnants of Han Law*. Leiden: Brill.

Humphries, Mark. 2009. "The Shapes and Shaping of the Late Antique World: Global and Local Perspectives." In *A Companion to Late Antiquity*, edited by Philip Rousseau with the assistance of Jutta Raithel, 97–109. Chichester, England: Wiley-Blackwell.

Hung, Hsiao-Chun, Yohiyuki Iizuka, Peter Bellwood, Kim Dung Nguyen, Bérénice Bellina, Praon Silapanth, Eusebio Dizaon, et al. 2007. "Ancient Jades Map 3,000 Years of Prehistoric Exchange in Southeast Asia." *PNAS* 104 (50): 19745–50. doi: 10.1073/pnas.0707304104.

Hunt, Hannah. 2007. "Byzantine Christianity." In *The Blackwell Companion to Eastern Christianity*, edited by Ken Parry, 73–93. Oxford: Blackwell.

Hunter, Andrew. 2001. "Early Eastern Woodland." In *Encyclopedia of Prehistory, vol. 6: North America*, edited by Peter N. Peregrine and Melvin Ember, 81–97. New York: Springer.

Hussain, Ali J. 2005. "The Mourning of History and the History of Mourning: The Evolution of Ritual Commemoration of the Battle of Karbala." *Comparative Studies of South Asia, Africa and the Middle East* 25 (1): 78–88. doi: 10.1215/1089201X-25-1-78.

Hutter, Manfred. 2003. "Aspects of Luwian Religion." In *The Luwians*, edited by H. Craig Melchert, 211–80. Leiden: Brill.

Iliffe, John. 2017. *Africans: The History of a Continent*. 3rd ed. Cambridge: Cambridge University Press.

Illinois State Museum. 2000. "The Illinois." MuseumLink Illinois. Accessed February 19, 2019. http://www.museum.state.il.us/muslink/nat_amer/post/htmls/il.html.

Inglehart, Ronald. 2018. *Cultural Evolution: People's Motivations are Changing, and Reshaping the World*. Cambridge: Cambridge University Press.

Inglehart, Ronald, and Christian Welzel. 2005. *Modernization, Cultural Change, and Democracy: The Human Development Sequence*. Cambridge: Cambridge University Press.

Insoll, Timothy. 1994. "A Cache of Hippopotamus Ivory at Gao, Mali; and a Hypothesis of Its Use." *Antiquity* 69 (263): 327–36. doi: 10.1017/S0003598X00064723.

Insoll, Timothy. 1996. *Islam, Archaeology and History, Gao Region (Mali) ca. AD 900–1250*. Oxford: Archaeopress.

Insoll, Timothy. 2000. *Urbanism, Archaeology and Trade: Further Observations on the Gao Region (Mali): The 1996 Field Season Results*. Oxford: Archaeopress.

Isbell, William H. 1991. "Huari Administration and the Orthogonal Cellular Architecture Horizon." In *Huari Administrative Structures*, edited by William Isbell and Gordon McEwan, 293–316. Washington, DC: Dumbarton Oaks.

Isbell, William H. 1997. "Reconstructing Huari: A Cultural Chronology for the Capital City." In *Emergence and Change in Early Urban Societies*, edited by Linda R. Manzanilla, 181–227. New York: Plenum Press.

Isbell, William H. 2008. "Wari and Tiwanaku: International Identities in the Central Andean Middle Horizon." In *Handbook of South American Archaeology*, edited by Helaine Silverman and William H. Isbell, 731–60. New York: Springer.

Isbell, William H., and Katharina J. Schreiber. 1978. "Was Huari a State?" *American Antiquity* 43 (3): 372–89. doi: 10.2307/279393.

Iseminger, William. 2010. *Cahokia Mounds: America's First City*. Charleston, SC: The History Press.

Iteanu, Andre. 1990. "The Concept of the Person and the Ritual System: An Orokaiva View." *Man* 25 (1): 35. doi: 10.2307/2804108.

Jacobs, Bruno. 2006. "Achaemenid Satrapies." In *Encyclopædia Iranica*. Online edition. http://www.iranicaonline.org/articles/achaemenid-satrapies (accessed 17 February 2018).

Jacobsen, Trudy. 2003. "Autonomous Queenship in Cambodia, 1st–9th Centuries AD." *Journal of the Royal Asiatic Society* 3 (13): 357–75. doi: 10.1017/S1356186303003420.

Jacobsen, Trudy. 2008. *Lost Goddesses: The Denial of Female Power in Cambodian History*. Copenhagen: Nordic Institute of Asian Studies Press.

Jacques, Claude. 1986. "Le pays Khmer avant Angkor." *Journal des savants* 1–3: 59–95. doi: 10.3406/jds.1986.1494.

Jacques, Claude, and Philippe Lafond. 2007. *The Khmer Empire: Cities and Sanctuaries, Fifth to Thirteenth Centuries*. Bangkok: River Books.

James, Liz. 2008. "The Role of Women." In *The Oxford Handbook of Byzantine Studies*, edited by Elizabeth Jeffreys, John Haldon, and Robin Cormack, 643–51. Oxford: Oxford University Press.

Jansen, Jan. 1996a. "Polities and Political Discourse: Was Mande Already a Segmentary Society in the Middle Ages?" *History in Africa* 23: 121–28. doi: 10.2307/3171937.

Jansen, Jan. 1996b. "The Representation of Status in Mande: Did the Mali Empire Still Exist in the Nineteenth Century?" *History in Africa* 23: 87–109. doi: 10.2307/3171935.

Jaspers, Karl. 1948. "The Axial Age of Human History: A Base for the Unity of Mankind." Translated by Ralph Manheim. *Commentary* 6: 430.

Jaspers, Karl. 1953. *The Origin and Goal of History*. Translated by Michael Bullock. New Haven, CT: Yale University Press.

Jennings, Justin. 2003. "Inca Imperialism, Ritual Change, and Cosmological Continuity in the Cotahuasi Valley of Peru." *Journal of Anthropological Research* 59 (4): 433–62.

Jennings, Justin. 2010. "Becoming Wari: Globalization and the Role of the Wari State in the Cotahuasi Valley of Southern Peru." In *Beyond Wari Walls: Regional Perspectives on Middle Horizon Peru*, edited by Justin Jennings, 37–56. Albuquerque, NM: University of New Mexico Press.

Jensen, Erik. 1974. *The Iban and Their Religion*. Oxford Monographs on Social Anthropology. Oxford: Oxford University Press. Retrieved from http://ehrafworldcultures.yale.edu/document?id=oc06-021.

Jochelson, Waldemar. 1906. "Kumiss Festivals of the Yakut and the Decoration of Kumiss Vessels." In In *Boas Anniversary Volume*, edited by Berthold Laufer, 257–71. New York: G. E. Stechert and Co. Retrieved from http://ehrafworldcultures.yale.edu/document?id=rv02-039.

Jochelson, Waldemar. 1933. *The Yakut*. Anthropological Papers of the American Museum of Natural History, vol. 33, pt. 2. New York: The American Museum of Natural History. Retrieved from http://ehrafworldcultures.yale.edu/document?id=rv02-002.

Johansen, Peter G. 2014. "The Politics of Spatial Renovation: Reconfiguring Ritual Places and Practice in Iron Age and Early Historic South India." *Journal of Social Archaeology* 14 (1): 59–86. doi: 10.1177/1469605313515976.

Johnson, Jay K. 2001. "Middle Eastern Woodland." In *The Woodland Southeast*, edited by David G. Anderson and Robert C. Mainfort, 322–34. Tuscaloosa, AL: University of Alabama Press.

Johnson, John William. 1999. "The Dichotomy of Power and Authority in Mande Society and in the Epic of Sunjata." In In *Search of Sunjata: The Mande Oral Epic as History, Literature and Performance*, edited by Ralph A. Austen, 9–23. Bloomington: Indiana University Press.

Johnston, Philip S. 2002. *Shades of Sheol: Death and Afterlife in the Old Testament*. Downers Grove: InterVarsity Press.

Joukowsky, Martha Sharp. 1996. *Early Turkey: An Introduction to the Archaeology of Anatolia from Prehistory through the Lydian Period*. Iowa: Kendall/Hunt Publishing Company.

Jubb, Margaret. 2005. "The Crusaders' Perceptions of Their Opponents." In *Palgrave Advances in the Crusades,* edited by Helen J. Nicholson, 225–44. Basingstoke: Palgrave Macmillan.

Kaizer, Ted. 2009. "The Parthian and Early Sasanian Empires, c. 247 BC–AD 300." In *The Great Empires of the Ancient World,* edited by Thomas Harrison, 174–95. London: Thames & Hudson.

Kamath, Suryanath. 1980. *A Concise History of Karnataka: From Pre-historic Times to the Present.* Bangalore, India: Archana Prakashana.

Kaner, Simon. 2009. "Encountering Dogu." In *The Power of Dogu: Ceramic Figures From Ancient Japan*, edited by Simon Kaner, 24–39. London: British Museum Press.

Kaner, Simon. 2011. "The Archaeology of Religion and Ritual in the Prehistoric Japanese Archipelago." In *The Oxford Handbook of the Archaeology of Ritual and Religion*, edited by Timothy Insoll, 457–69. Oxford: Oxford University Press.

Kaner, Simon, and Takeshi Ishikawa. 2007. "Reassessing the Concept of the 'Neolithic' in the Jomon of Western Japan." *Documenta Praehistorica* 34: 1–7. doi: 10.4312/dp.34.1.

Kaniewski, David, Elise van Campo, Joël Guiot, Sabine Le Burel, Thierry Otto, and Cecile Baeteman. 2013. "Environmental Roots of the Late Bronze Age Crisis." *PLoS ONE* 8 (8): e71004. doi: 10.1371/journal.pone.0071004

Kaplan, Philip. 2006. "Dedications to Greek Sanctuaries by Foreign Kings in the Eighth through Sixth Centuries BCE." *Historia: Zeitschrift für Alte Geschichte* 55 (2): 129–52.

Karasu, Cem. 2003. "Why Did the Hittites Have a Thousand Deities?" In *Hittite Studies in Honor of Harry A. Hoffner Jr. on the Occasion of His 65th Birthday*, edited by Gary Beckman, Richard Beal, and Gregory McMahon, 221–36. Winona Lake: Eisenbrauns.

Karsten, Rafael. 1935. *Head-Hunters of Western Amazonas: The Life and Culture of the Jibaro Indians of Eastern Ecuador and Peru*. Commentationes Humanarum Litterarum. Helsingfors: Finska vetenskaps-societeten. Retrieved from http://ehrafworldcultures.yale.edu/document?id=sd09-001.

Katouzian, Homa. 2009. *The Persians: Ancient, Mediaeval and Modern Iran*. New Haven, CT: Yale University Press.

Kazhdan, Alexander P., and Michael MacCormick. 1997. *The Social World of the Byzantine Court*. Cambridge: Dumbarton Oaks Research Library and Collection.

Kea, Ray A. 2004. "Expansions and Contractions: World-Historical Change and the Western Sudan World-System (1200/1000 B.C.–1200/1250 A.D.)." *Journal of World-Systems Research* 10 (3): 723–816. doi: 10.5195/jwsr.2004.286.

Keay, John. 2013. *India: A History, from the Earliest Civilisations to the Boom of the Twenty-first Century*. London: HarperCollins.

Keightley, David N. 1978. *Sources of Shang History: The Oracle-Bone Inscriptions of Bronze Age China*. Los Angeles, CA: University of California Press.

Keightley, David N. 1999. "The Shang: China's First Historical Dynasty." In *The Cambridge History of Ancient China From the Origins of Civilization to 221 BC*, edited by Michael Loewe and Edward L. Shaughnessy, 232–291. Cambridge: Cambridge University Press.

Keith, Arthur Berriedale, trans. 1914. *The Veda of the Black Yajus School: Entitled Taittirīya Sanhitā*. Cambridge, MA: Harvard University Press.

Kelly, John E. 2002. "Woodland Period Archaeology in the American Bottom." In *The Woodland Southeast*, edited by David G. Anderson and Robert C. Mainfort, 134–62. Tuscaloosa, AL: University of Alabama Press.

Kelly, Daniel, and Taylor Davis. 2018. "Social Norms and Human Normative Psychology." *Social Philosophy and Policy* 35 (1): 54–76. doi: 10.1017/S0265052518000122.

Kembel, Silvia Rodriguez, and John W. Rick. 2004. "Building Authority at Chavín de Huántar: Models of Social Organization and Development in the Initial Period and Early Horizon." In *Andean Archaeology*, edited by Helaine Silverman, 51–76. Oxford: Blackwell.

Kemp, Barry J. 1983. "Old Kingdom, Middle Kingdom and Second Intermediate Period c. 2686–1552 BC." In *Ancient Egypt: A Social History*, edited by Bruce G. Trigger, Barry J. Kemp, David O'Connor, and Alan B. Lloyd, 71–182. Cambridge: Cambridge University Press.

Kemp, Barry J. 2006. *Ancient Egypt: Anatomy of a Civilization*. 2nd ed. London: Routledge.

Kennedy, Titus. 2013. "A Demographic Analysis of Late Bronze Age Canaan: Ancient Population Estimates and Insights through Archaeology." PhD Diss., University of South Africa.

Kenoyer, Jonathan M. 1989. "Socio-Economic Structures in the Indus Civilization as Reflected in Specialized Crafts and the Question of Ritual Segregation." In *Old Problems and New*

Perspectives in the Archaeology of South Asia, edited by Jonathan M. Kenoyer, 183–92. Madison: University of Wisconsin Press.

Keown, Damien. 2013. *Buddhism: A Very Short Introduction.* Oxford: Oxford University Press.

Kesteloot, Lilyan, Thomas A. Hale, and Richard Bjornson. 1991. "Power and Its Portrayals in Royal Mandé Narratives." *Research in African Literatures* 22 (1): 17–26.

Khaleque, Kibriaul. 1988. "Garo of Bangladesh: Religion, Ritual and World View." *Contributions to Southeast Asian Ethnography* 7: 129–156. Retrieved from http://ehrafworldcultures.yale.edu/document?id=ar05-014.

Khanbaghi, Aptin. 2006. *The Fire, the Star and the Cross: Minority Religions in Medieval and Early Modern Iran.* London: I. B. Tauris.

Kharuzin, Aleksai Nikolaevich. 1898. "Juridicial Customs of the Yakut." *Etnograficheskoe Obozrenie* 10 (37): 37–64. Retrieved from http://ehrafworldcultures.yale.edu/document?id=rv02-019.

Kidder, J. Edward, Jr. 1993. "The Earliest Societies in Japan." In *The Cambridge History of Japan, vol. 1: Ancient Japan*, edited by Delmer M. Brown, 48–107. Cambridge: Cambridge University Press.

Kidder, J. Edward, Jr. 2007. *Himiko and Japan's Elusive Chiefdom of Yamatai.* Honolulu: Hawaii University Press.

Kiley, Cornelius J. 1977. "Uji and Kabane in Ancient Japan." In *Monumenta Nipponica* 32: 365–76.

Kim, Nam C. 2015. *The Origins of Ancient Vietnam.* Oxford: Oxford University Press.

Kim, Nam C., Lai Van Toi, and Trinh Hoang Hiep. 2010. "Co Loa: An investigation of Vietnam's ancient capital." *Antiquity* 84: 1011–27. doi: 10.1017/S0003598X00067041.

King, Charlotte L., R. Alexander Bentley, Charles Higham, Nancy Tayles, Una Strand Viðarsdóttir, Robert Layton, Colin G. Macpherson, and Geoff Nowell. 2014. "Economic Change after the Agricultural Revolution in Southeast Asia?" *Antiquity* 88: 112–25. doi: 10.1017/S0003598X00050250.

King, Victor T. 2017. "Claiming Authority: Derek Freeman, His Legacy and Interpretations of the Iban of Borneo." *Bijdragen tot de taal-, land- en volkenkunde* 173 (1): 83–113. doi: 10.1163/22134379-17301005.

Kirch, Patrick V. 1984. *The Evolution of the Polynesian Chiefdoms.* Cambridge: Cambridge University Press.

Kirch, Patrick V. 1985. *Feathered Gods and Fishhooks: An Introduction to Hawaiian Archaeology and Prehistory.* Honolulu: University of Hawai'i Press.

Kirch, Patrick V. 1990. "Monumental Architecture and Power in Polynesian Chiefdoms: A Comparison of Tonga and Hawaii." *World Archaeology* 22 (2): 206–22. doi: 10.1080/00438243.1990.9980141.

Kirch, Patrick V. 2001. "Polynesian Feasting in Ethnohistoric, Ethnographic, and Archaeological Contexts: A Comparison of Three Societies." In *Feasts: Archaeological and Ethnographic Perspectives on Food, Politics, and Power*, edited by Michael Dietler and Brian Hayden, 168–84. Tuscaloosa, AL: University of Alabama Press.

Kirch, Patrick V. 2007. "Hawaii as a Model System for Human Ecodynamics." *American Anthropologist* n.s. 109 (1): 8–26. doi: 10.1525/aa.2007.109.1.8.

Kirch, Patrick V. 2010. *How Chiefs Became Kings: Divine Kingship and the Rise of Archaic States in Ancient Hawaii.* Oxford: Oxford University Press.

Kirch, Patrick V. 2012. *A Shark Going Inland Is My Chief: The Island Civilization of Ancient Hawaii.* Berkeley: University of California Press

Kiriyama, Kyoko, and Soichiro Kusaka. 2007. "Prehistoric Diet and Mortuary Practices in the Jomon Period: Isotopic Evidence from Human Skeletal Remains from the Yoshigo Shell Mound." *Journal of Archaeological Science: Reports* 11: 200–210. doi: 10.1016/j.jasrep.2016.11.048.

Kirkland, Russell. 2002. "The History of Taoism: A New Outline." *Journal of Chinese Religions* 30 (1): 177–193. doi: 10.1179/073776902804760257.

Kirkland, Russell. 2004. *Taoism: The Enduring Tradition.* New York: Routledge.

Kleeman, Terry F. 1998. *Great Perfection: Religion and Ethnicity in a Chinese Millennial Kingdom.* Honolulu, HI: University of Hawaii Press.

Klengel, Horst. 2011. "History of the Hittites." In *Insights into Hittite History and Archaeology*, edited by Hermann Genz and Dirk Paul Mielke, 31–46. Leuven: Peeters.

Knechtges, David R. 2010. "From the Eastern Han through the Western Jin (AD 25–317)." In *The Cambridge History of Chinese Literature, vol. 1: To 1375*, edited by Stephen Owen, 116–98. Cambridge: Cambridge University Press.

Knott, Kim. 2000. *Hinduism: A Very Short Introduction.* Oxford: Oxford University Press.

Kobayashi, Tatsuo. 2004. *Jomon Reflections: Forager Life and Culture in the Prehistoric Japanese Archipelago.* Oxford: Oxbow Books.

Kohn, Livia. 2000. *Daoism Handbook.* Leiden: Brill.

Kolb, Michael J., Ross Cordy, Timothy Earle, Gary Feinman, Michael W. Graves, Christine A. Hastorf, Ian Hodder, et al. 1994. "Monumentality and the Rise of Religious Authority in Precontact Hawai'i [and Comments and Reply]." *Current Anthropology* 35 (5): 521–47. doi: 10.1086/204315.

Kolb, Michael J., and Boyd Dixon. 2002. "Landscapes of War: Rules and Conventions of Conflict in Ancient Hawai'i (and Elsewhere)." *American Antiquity* 67 (3): 514–34. doi: 10.2307/1593824.

Kolbaba, Tia. 2008. "Latin and Greek Christians." In *The Cambridge History of Christianity*, edited by Thomas F. X. Noble and Julia M. H. Smith, 213–29. Cambridge: Cambridge University Press.

Komanyi, Margit Ilona. 1973. *Real and Ideal Participation in Decision-Making of Iban Women: A Study of a Longhouse Community in Sarawak, East Malaysia.* Ann Arbor, MI: University Microfilms. Retrieved from http://ehrafworldcultures.yale.edu/document?id=oc06-028.

Koshelenko, Gennadij A., and Victor N. Pilipko. 1994. "The Parthian Empire." In *History of Civilizations of Central Asia, vol. II: The Development of Sedentary and Nomadic Civilizations, 700 B.C. to A.D. 250*, edited by János Harmatta, B. N. Puri, and G. F. Etemadi, 127–45. Paris: UNESCO.

Kravitz, Kathryn F. 2003. "A Last-Minute Revision to Sargon's Letter to the God." *Journal of Near Eastern Studies* 62 (2): 81–95. doi: 10.1086/376363.

Kreyenbroek, Philip G. 2006. "Iran ix: Religions in Iran (1) Pre-Islamic." In *Encyclopædia Iranica*, XIII/4, 432–39. Updated version available online at http://www.iranicaonline.org/articles/iran-ix1-religions-in-iran-pre-islamic (accessed September 21, 2017).

Kuhrt, Amélie. 1983. "The Cyrus Cylinder and Achaemenid Imperial Policy." *Journal for the Study of the Old Testament* 25: 83–97. doi: 10.1177030908928300802507.

Kuhrt, Amélie. 2001 "The Achaemenid Persian Empire (c. 550–c. 330 BCE): Continuities, Adaptations, Transformations." In *Empires: Perspectives from Archaeology and History*, edited by Susan E. Alcock, Terence N. D'Altroy, Kathleen D. Morrison, and Carla M. Sinopoli, 93–123. Cambridge: Cambridge University Press.

Kuhrt, Amélie. 2007. *The Persian Empire: A Corpus of Sources from the Achaemenid Period*. London: Routledge.

Kulke, Hermann. 1978. *Devarāja Cult*. Translated by I. W. Mabbett. Ithaca, NY: Southeast Asia Program, Department of Asian Studies, Cornell University.

Kulke, Hermann. 2014. "From Aśoka to Jayavarman VII: Some Reflections on the Relationship between Buddhism and the State in India and Southeast Asia." In *Buddhism across Asia: Networks of Material, Intellectual and Cultural Exchange, vol. 1*, edited by Tansen Sen, 327–46. Singapore: Institute of Southeast Asian Studies.

Kulke, Hermann, and Dietmar Rothermund. 1990. *A History of India*. London: Routledge.

Kumaraswamy, P. R. 2007. "Islam and Minorities: Need for a Liberal Framework." *Mediterranean Quarterly* 18 (3): 94–109. doi: 10.1215/10474552-2007-019.

Kuran, Timur. 2003. "Islamic Redistribution through Zakat: Historical Record and Modern Realities." In *Poverty and Charity in Middle Eastern Contexts*, edited by Michael Bonner, Mine Ener, and Amy Singer, 275–94. Albany: State University of New York Press.

Kuznar, Lawrence. 2001. "Late Highland Andean Archaic." In *The Encyclopedia of Prehistory, vol. 7: South America*, edited by Peter N. Peregrine and Melvin Ember, 235–52. New York: Springer Science+Business Media.

Lachowski, J. 2003. "Sin (in the Bible)." In *The New Catholic Encyclopedia*, vol. 13, edited by Catholic University of America. Detroit: Thomson/Gale.

Laine, James W. 2014. *Meta-Religion: Religion and Power in World History*. Oakland: University of California Press.

Laliberté, André, David A. Palmer, and Wu Keping. 2011. "Religious Philanthropy and Chinese Civil Society." In *Chinese Religious Life*, edited by David A. Palmer, Glenn Shive, and Philip Wickeri, 139–154. New York: Oxford University Press.

Lamana, Gonzalo. 2008. *Domination without Dominance: Inca-Spanish Encounters in Colonial Peru*. Durham, NC: Duke University Press.

Laneri, Nicola and Mark Schwartz. 2011. "Southeastern and Eastern Anatolia in the Middle Bronze Age." In *The Oxford Handbook of Ancient Anatolia, 10,000–323 B.C.E.*, edited by Sharon R. Steadman and Gregory McMahon, 337–60. Oxford: Oxford University Press.

Langgut, Dafna, Israel Finkelstein, and Thomas Litt. 2013. "Climate and the Late Bronze Collapse: New Evidence from the Southern Levant." *Tel Aviv* 40 (2): 149–75. doi: 10.1179/033443513X137 53505864205.

Lapidus, Ira M. 2002. *A History of Islamic Societies.* 2nd ed. Cambridge: Cambridge University Press.

Lapidus, Ira M. 2012. *Islamic Societies to the Nineteenth Century: A Global History.* Cambridge: Cambridge University Press.

Larsen, Mogens Trolle. 2015. *Ancient Kanesh: A Merchant Colony in Bronze Age Anatolia.* Cambridge: Cambridge University Press.

Larson, Jennifer. 2016. *Understanding Greek Religion: A Cognitive Approach.* Abingdon: Routledge.

Latham, Christopher S., and John Beierle. 2004. "Culture Summary: Orokaiva." New Haven, CT: HRAF. Retrieved from http://ehrafworldcultures.yale.edu/document?id=oj23-000.

Lau, Ulrich and Thies Staack. 2016. *Legal Practices in the Formative Stages of the Chinese Empire: An Annotated Translation of the Exemplary Qin Criminal Cases from the Yuelu Academy Collection.* Leiden: Brill.

LaViolette, Adria and Jeffrey Fleisher. 2005. "The Archaeology of Sub-Saharan Urbanism: Cities and Their Countrysides." In *African Archaeology: A Critical Introduction*, edited by Ann Brower Stahl, 327–52. Malden: Blackwell.

Lavy, Paul. 2003. "As in Heaven, So on Earth: The Politics of Viṣṇu, Śiva and Harihara Images in Preangkorian Khmer Civilisation." *Journal of Southeast Asian Studies* 34 (1): 21–39. doi: 10.1017/S002246340300002X.

Law, Robin. 1985. "Human Sacrifice in Pre-Colonial West Africa." *African Affairs* 84 (334): 53–87. doi: 10.1093/oxfordjournals.afraf.a097676.

Le Roy Ladurie, Emmanuel. 1978. *Montaillou: The Promised Land of Error.* New York: Braziller.

Le Thi Lien. 2008. "Hindu Iconography in Early History of Southern Vietnam." *Taida Journal of Art History* 25: 69–96.

Le Thi Lien. 2015. "Hindu Beliefs and the Maritime Network in Southern Vietnam during the Early Common Era." *Journal of Indo-Pacific Archaeology* 39: 1–17. doi: 10.7152/jipa.v39i0.14748.

Leeming, Frank. 1980. "Official Landscapes in Traditional China." *Journal of the Economic and Social History of the Orient* 23: 153–204. doi: 10.1163/156852080X00078.

Legendre De Koninck, Héléne. 2004. "Angkor," translated by Jane Macauley. In *Southeast Asia: A Historical Encyclopedia*, edited by Keat Gin Ooi, 148–51. Santa Barbara: ABC-CLIO.

Lemos, Irene S. 2010. "The 'Dark Age' of Greece." In *The Edinburgh Companion to Ancient Greece and Rome*, edited by Edward Bispham, Thomas Harrison, and Brian A. Sparkes, 87–91. Edinburgh: Edinburgh University Press.

Leppin, Hartmut. 2007. "Old Religions Transformed: Religions and Religious Policy from Decius to Constantine." In *A Companion to Roman Religion*, edited by Jörg Rüpke, 96–108. Chichester, England: Wiley-Blackwell.

Lerner, Gerda. 1986. *The Creation of Patriarchy.* New York: Oxford University Press.

Lerner, Jeffrey D. 1999. *The Impact of Seleucid Decline on the Eastern Iranian Plateau: The Foundations of Arsacid Parthia and Graeco-Bactria.* Stuttgart: Franz Steiner Verlag.

Lev, Yaacov. 2010. "The Fāṭimid Caliphate (358–567/969–1171) and the Ayyūbids in Egypt (567–648/1171–1250)." In *The New Cambridge History of Islam, vol. 2: The Western Islamic World, Eleventh to Eighteenth Centuries,* edited by Maribel Fierro, 201–36. Cambridge: Cambridge University Press.

Levanoni, Amalia. 1990. "The Mamluks' Ascent to Power in Egypt." *Studia Islamica* 72: 121–44. doi: 10.2307/1595777.

Levin, Stephenie Seto. 1968. "The Overthrow of the Kapu System in Hawaii." *The Journal of the Polynesian Society* 77 (4): 402–30.

Levtzion, Nehemia. 1963. "The Thirteenth- and Fourteenth-Century Kings of Mali." *Journal of African History* 4 (3): 341–53. doi: 10.1017/S002185370000428X.

Levtzion, Nehemia, and Randall L. Pouwels. 2000. "Introduction: Patterns of Islamization and Varieties of Religious Experience among Muslims of Africa." In *The History of Islam in Africa,* edited by Nehemia Levtzion and Randall L. Pouwels, 1–18. Ohio: Ohio University Press.

Levy, Janet E. 2007. "Gender, Heterarchy, and Hierarchy." In *Women in Antiquity: Theoretical Approaches to Gender and Archaeology,* edited by Sarah Milledge Nelson, 189–216. Lanham: AltaMira Press.

Lewis, Bernard. 1993. *Arabs in History.* 6th ed. Oxford: Oxford University Press.

Lewis, David. 2011. "Near Eastern Slaves in Classical Attica and the Slave Trade with Persian Territories." *The Classical Quarterly* 61 (1): 91–113. doi: 10.1017/S0009838810000480.

Lewis, Mark Edward. 1999a. "Warring States Political History." In *The Cambridge History of Ancient China From the Origins of Civilization to 221 BC,* edited by M. Loewe and E. L. Shaughnessy, 587–650. Cambridge: Cambridge University Press.

Lewis, Mark Edward. 1999b. *Writing and Authority in Early China.* Albany, NY: State University of New York Press.

Lewis, Mark Edward. 2006. *The Construction of Space in Early China.* Albany, NY: State University of New York Press.

Lewis, Mark Edward. 2007. *The Early Chinese Empires: Qin and Han.* Cambridge, MA: Harvard University Press.

Lewis, Mark Edward. 2009. *China's Cosmopolitan Empire: The Tang Dynasty.* Cambridge, MA: Harvard University Press.

Lichtheim, Miriam. 1975. *Ancient Egyptian Literature,* vol. 1: *The Old and Middle Kingdoms.* Berkeley: University of California Press.

Lichtheim, Miriam. 1976. *Ancient Egyptian Literature,* vol. 2: *The New Kingdom.* Berkeley: University of California Press.

Lichtheim, Miriam. 1992. *Maat in Egyptian Autobiographies and Related Studies.* Freiburg-Göttingen: Vandenhoeck & Ruprecht.

Lieberman, Victor and Brendan Buckley. 2012. "The Impact of Climate on Southeast Asia, circa 950–1820: New Findings." *Modern Asian Studies* 46 (5): 1049–96. doi: 10.1017/S0026749X12000091.

Liebeschuetz, Wolf. 2007. "Was There a Crisis of the Third Century?" In *Crises and the Roman Empire: Proceedings of the Seventh Workshop of the International Network Impact of Empire (Nijmegen, June 20-24, 2006)*, edited by Olivier Hekster, Gerda de Kleijn, and Daniëlle Slootjes, 11–20. Leiden: Brill.

Lim, Richard. 2010. "Late Antiquity." In *The Edinburgh Companion to Greece and Rome*, edited by Edward Bispham, Thomas Harrison, and Brian A. Sparkes, 114–20. Edinburgh: Edinburgh University Press.

Lincoln, Bruce. 2007. *Religion, Empire and Torture: The Case of Achaemenian Persia, with a Postscript on Abu Ghraib*. Chicago: University of Chicago Press.

Lindsay, James E. 2005. *Daily Life in the Medieval Islamic World*. Indianapolis: Hackett Publishing Company.

Lindsay Adams, Winthrop. 2006. "The Hellenistic Kingdoms." In *The Cambridge Companion to the Hellenistic World*, edited by Glenn R. Bugh, 28–51. Cambridge: Cambridge University Press.

Linnekin, Jocelyn. 1990. *Sacred Queens and Women of Consequence: Rank, Gender, and Colonialism in the Hawaiian Islands*. Ann Arbor, MI: University of Michigan Press.

Lipiński, Edward. 1995. "The Phoenicians." In *Civilizations of the Ancient Near East*, vol. 2, edited by Jack M. Sasson, 1321–33. New York: Scribner.

Lipschits, Oded. 2005. *The Fall and Rise of Jerusalem: Judah under Babylonian Rule*. Winona Lake: Eisenbrauns.

Lipschits, Oded. 2006. "Achaemenid Imperial Policy, Settlement Processes in Palestine, and the Status of Jerusalem in the Middle of the Fifth Century B.C." In *Judah and the Judeans in the Persian Period*, edited by Oded Lipschits and Manfred Oeming, 19–52. Winona Lake: Eisenbrauns.

Liverani, Mario. 2005. *Israel's History and the History of Israel*. Translated by Chiara Peri and Philip R. Davies. London: Equinox.

Liverani, Mario. 2014. *The Ancient Near East: History, Society and Economy*. Translated by Soraia Tabatabai. London: Routledge.

Liverani, Mario. 2016. "Conservative versus Innovative Cultural Areas in the Near East ca. 800-400 BC." In *Eurasia at the Dawn of History: Urbanization and Social Change*, edited by Manuel Fernández-Götz and Dirk Krausse, 198–210. Cambridge: Cambridge University Press.

Llewellyn-Jones, Lloyd. 2013. *King and Court in Ancient Persia 559 to 331 BCE*. Edinburgh: Edinburgh University Press.

Lloyd, Alan B. 1983. "The Late Period, 664–323 BC." In *Ancient Egypt: A Social History*, edited by Bruce G. Trigger, Barry J. Kemp, David O'Connor, and Alan B. Lloyd, 279–348. Cambridge: Cambridge University Press.

Lloyd, Alan B. 2000a. "The Late Period (664–332 BC)." In *The Oxford History of Ancient Egypt*, edited by Ian Shaw, 364–87. Oxford: Oxford University Press.

Lloyd, Alan B. 2000b. "The Ptolemaic Period (332–30 BC)." In *The Oxford History of Ancient Egypt*, edited by Ian Shaw, 388–413. Oxford: Oxford University Press.

Lloyd, Alan B. 2007. "Darius I in Egypt: Suez and Hibis." In *Persian Responses: Political and Cultural Interaction with(in) the Achaemenid Empire*, edited by Christopher Tuplin, 99–116. Swansea: The Classical Press of Wales.

Lockard, Craig A. 2009. *Southeast Asia in World History*. Oxford: Oxford University Press.

Loewe, Michael. 1986. "The Concept of Sovereignty." In *The Cambridge History of China*, vol. 1, edited by Denis Twitchett and Michael Loewe, 726–746. Cambridge: Cambridge University Press.

Loewe, Michael. 1999. "The Heritage Left to the Empires." In *The Cambridge History of Ancient China From the Origins of Civilization to 221 BC*, edited by M. Loewe and E. L. Shaughnessy, 967–1032. Cambridge: Cambridge University Press.

Loewenstein, Karl. 1973. *The Governance of Rome*. The Hague: Martin Nijhoff.

Logue, Wendy. 2004. "Set in Stone: The Role of Relief-Carved Stone Vessels in Neopalatial Minoan Elite Propaganda." *Annual of the British School at Athens* 99: 149–72. doi: 10.1017/S0068245400017056.

Lomas, Kathryn, and T. J. Cornell. 2003. "Introduction: Patronage and Benefaction in Ancient Italy." In *'Bread and Circuses': Euergetism and Municipal Patronage in Roman Italy*, edited by Tim Cornell and Kathryn Lomas, 1–11. New York: Routledge.

Loprieno, Antonio. 1997. "Slaves." In *The Egyptians*, translated by Robert Bianchi, Anna Lisa Crone, Charles Lambert, and Thomas Ritter and edited by Sergio Donadoni, 185–219. Chicago: University of Chicago Press.

Lowe, Candice Marie. 2004. "All the Harappan Men Are Naked, but the Women Are Wearing Jewelry." In *Ungendering Civilization*, edited by K. Anne Pyburn, 193–209. New York: Routledge.

Lund, Helen S. 1992. *Lysimachus: A Study in Early Hellenistic Kingship*. London: Routledge.

Lupack, Susan. 2011. "A View from Outside the Palace: The Sanctuary and the *Damos* in Mycenaean Economy and Society." *American Journal of Archaeology* 115: 207–17.

Lyford, Carrie A. 1945. *Iroquois Crafts*, edited by Willard W. Beatty. Washington, DC: United States Department of the Interior, Bureau of Indian Affairs. Retrieved from http://ehrafworldcultures.yale.edu/document?id=nm09-011.

Ma, John. 2003. "Kings." In *A Companion to the Hellenistic World*, edited by Andrew Erskine, 177–95. Oxford: Blackwell Publishing

Mabbett, Ian W. 1977. "Varnas in Angkor and the Indian Caste System." *The Journal of Asian Studies* 36 (3): 429–42. doi: 10.2307/2054092.

Mabbett, Ian W. 1978. "Kingship in Angkor." *Journal of the Siam Society* 66 (2): 1–58.

Mabbett, Ian W. 1983. "Some Remarks on the Present State of Knowledge about Slavery in Angkor." In *Slavery, Bondage and Dependency in Southeast Asia*, edited by Anthony Reid, 44–63. New York: St. Martin's Press.

Mabbett, Ian W., and David Chandler. 1995. *The Khmers*. Oxford: Blackwell.

MacCormack, Sabine. 1988. "Pachacuti: Miracles, Punishments, and Last Judgment: Visionary Past and Prophetic Future in Early Colonial Peru." *The American Historical Review* 93 (4): 960–1006. doi: 10.1086/ahr/93.4.960.

MacDonald, Kevin, Seydou Camara, Sirio Canós Donnay, Nikolas Gestrich, and Daouda Keita. 2011. "Sorotomo: A Forgotten Malian Capital?" *Archaeology International* 13: 52–64. doi: 10.5334/ai.1315.

MacDonald, Kevin. 1994. "Socio-Economic Diversity and the Origins of Cultural Complexity along the Middle Niger (2000 B.C. to A.D. 300)." PhD Diss., University of Cambridge.

MacDonald, Kevin. 1997. "More Forgotten Tells of Mali: An Archaeologist's Journey from Here to Timbuktu." *Archaeology International* 1: 40–42. doi: 10.5334/ai.0112.

MacDonald, Kevin. 2013. "Complex Societies, Urbanism, and Trade in the Western Sahel." In *The Oxford Handbook of African Archaeology*, edited by Peter Mitchell and Paul J. Lane, 829–44. Oxford: Oxford University Press.

MacDonald, Kevin. 2016. "Ghana, Empire of." In *The Encyclopedia of Empire*, edited by John M. MacKenzie. Online edition. Malden: Wiley-Blackwell.

MacEachern, Scott. 2005. "Two Thousand Years of West African History." In *African Archaeology: A Critical Introduction*, edited by Ann Brower Stahl, 441–66. Oxford: Blackwell.

Mack, Alexandra. 2002. *Spiritual Journey, Imperial City: Pilgrimage to the Temples of Vijayanagara.* New Delhi, India: Vedams.

MacMullen, Ramsay. 1981. *Paganism in the Roman Empire.* New Haven, CT: Yale University Press.

MacSweeney, Naoíse. 2008. "The Meaning of 'Mycenaean.'" In *SOMA 2005: Proceedings of the IX Symposium on Mediterranean Archaeology, Chieti (Italy), 24–26 February 2005*, edited by Oliva Menozzi, Marialuigia Di Marzio, and Domenico Fossataro, 105–10. Oxford: British Archaeological Reports.

Macuch, Maria. 1981. *Das sasanidische Rechtsbuch "Matakadan I Hazar Datistan" (Teil II).* Wiesbaden: Harrassowitz.

Macuch, Maria. 2009. "Judicial and Legal Systems iii: Sasanian Legal System." *Encyclopædia Iranica* XV (2): 181–96. http://www.iranicaonline.org/articles/judicial-and-legal-systems-iii-sasanian-legal-system (accessed 28 November 2017).

Macuch, Maria. 2015. "Law in Pre-Modern Zoroastrianism." In *The Wiley-Blackwell Companion to Zoroastrianism*, edited by Michael Stausberg and Yuhan Sohrab-Dinshaw Vevaina, 289–98. Chichester, England: Wiley Blackwell.

Madan, A. P. 1990. *The History of the Rashtrakutas.* New Delhi: Harman.

Madigan, Kevin. 2015. *Medieval Christianity: A New History.* New Haven, CT: Yale University Press.

Magdalene, Rachel. 2009. "Judicial and Legal Systems i: Achaemenid Judicial and Legal Systems." In *Encyclopædia Iranica*, XV/2, 174–77. Updated version available online at http://www.iranicaonline.org/articles/judicial-and-legal-systems-i-achaemenid-judicial-and-legal-systems (accessed September 18, 2017).

Mahmoudian, Seyed Ali, and Seyed Navid Mahmoudian. 2012. "Water and Water Supply Technologies in Ancient Iran." In *Evolution of Water Supply through the Millennia*, edited by Andreas N. Angelakis, Larry W. Mays, Demetris Koutsoyiannis, and Nikos Mamassis, 93–99. London: IWA Publishing.

Mairs, Rachel. 2015. "Bactria and India." In *The Oxford Handbook to Ancient Greek Religion*, edited by Esther Eidinow and Julia Kindt, 637–649. Oxford: Oxford University Press.

Maisels, Charles K. 1999. *Early Civilizations of the Old World: The Formative Histories of Egypt, the Levant, Mesopotamia, India, and China*. London: Routledge.

Malandra, William W. 2005. "Zoroastrianism i: Historical Review up to the Arab Conquest." In *Encyclopædia Iranica*. Online edition. http://www.iranicaonline.org/articles/zoroastrianism-i-historical-review (accessed August 27, 2017).

Malek, Jaromir. 2000. "The Old Kingdom (c. 2686–2160 BC)." In *The Oxford History of Ancient Egypt*, edited by Ian Shaw, 83–107. Oxford: Oxford University Press.

Malleret, L. 1962. *L'Archéologie du delta du Mekong, vol. 3: La culture du FouNan, texte et planches*. Paris: Publication d l'École Française d'ExtrêmeOrient.

Malpass, Michael A. 2009. *Daily Life in the Inca Empire*. 2nd ed. Westport, CT: Greenwood Press.

Maltby, William S. 2009. *The Rise and Fall of the Spanish Empire*. New York: Palgrave Macmillan.

Manguin, Pierre-Yves. 2009. "The Archaeology of Funan in the Mekong River Delta: The 'Oc Eo Culture' of Vietnam." In *Arts of Ancient Viet Nam: From River Plain to Open Sea*, edited by Nancy Tingley, Andreas Reinecke, and Pierre-Yves Manguin, 100–18. Houston; New York: The Museum of Fine Arts, Houston; Asia Society.

Mann, Michael. 1986. *The Sources of Social Power, vol. 1: A History of Power from the Beginning to A.D. 1760*. Cambridge: Cambridge University Press.

Manning, J. G. 2003. *Land and Power in Ptolemaic Egypt: The Structure of Land Tenure*. Cambridge: Cambridge University Press.

Manning, J. G. 2010. *The Last Pharaohs: Egypt under the Ptolemies, 305–30 BC*. Princeton, NJ: Princeton University Press.

Manning, Patrick, Pieter Francois, Daniel Hoyer, and Vladimir Zadorozhny. 2017. "Collaborative Historical Information Analysis." In *Comprehensive Geographic Information Systems, vol. 3: GIS Applications for Socio-Economics and Humanity*, edited by Bo Huang, 119–44. Amsterdam: Elsevier.

Manning, Sturt W. 1986. "The Military Function in Late Minoan I Crete: A Note." *World Archaeology* 18 (2): 284–88. doi: 10.1080/00438243.1986.9980004.

Marak, Kumie R. 1997. *Traditions and Modernity in Matrilineal Tribal Society*. Tribal Studies of India Series. New Delhi: Inter-India Publications. Retrieved from http://ehrafworldcultures.yale.edu/document?id=ar05-011.

Marangudakis, Manussos. 2006. "The Social Sources and Environmental Consequences of Axial Thinking: Mesopotamia, China, and Greece in Comparative Perspective." *European Journal of Sociology / Archives Européennes de Sociologie* 47 (1): 59–91. doi: 10.1017/S0003975606000038.

Marest, Gabriel. [1712] 1959. "Letter from Father Gabriel Marest, Missionary of the Society of Jesus, to Father Germon, of the Same Society." In *The Jesuit Relations and Allied Documents*, vol. 66, edited by Reuben Gold Thwaites, 218–95. New York: Pageant.

Marfoe, Leon. 1979. "The Integrative Transformation: Patterns of Sociopolitical Organization in Southern Syria." *Bulletin of the American Schools of Oriental Research* 234: 1–42. doi: 10.2307/1356463.

Marinatos, Nanno. 2004. "Minoan and Mycenaean Civilizations." In *Religions of the Ancient World: A Guide*, edited by Sarah Iles Johnston, 206–09. Cambridge: The Belknap Press of Harvard University Press.

Maringer, Johannes. 1974. "Clay Figurines of the Jōmon Period: A Contribution to the History of Ancient Religion in Japan." *History of Religions* 14 (2): 128–39. doi: 10.1086/462719.

Markoe, Glenn E. 2005. *The Phoenicians*. Revised ed. London: Folio Society.

Marlow, Louise. 1997. *Hierarchy and Egalitarianism in Islamic Thought*. Cambridge: Cambridge University Press.

Marshall, Paul. 2016. *A Complex Integral Realist Perspective: Towards a New Axial Vision*. London: Routledge.

Marston, John Amos, and Elizabeth Guthrie. "Introduction." In *History, Buddhism, and New Religious Movements in Cambodia*, edited by John Amos Marston and Elizabeth Guthrie, 1–12. Honolulu: University of Hawai'i Press.

Martin, Luther H. 2018. *Studies in Hellenistic Religions*. Edited by Panayotis Pachis. Eugene: Cascade Books.

Martin, Marie Alexandrine. 1998. "L'esclavage au Cambodge aux temps anciens d'après les sources *épigraphiques* et bibliographiques." In *Formes extrêmes de dépendance*, edited by G. Condominas, 285–314. Paris: Éditions de l'EHESS.

Martyndale-Howard, Jodie. 2015. "Augustus: Caesar and God. Varying Images of the First Roman Emperor." In *Fresh Perspectives on Graeco-Roman Visual Culture: Proceedings of an International Conference at the Humboldt-Universität*, edited by Christoph Klose, Lukas C. Bossert, and William Leveritt, 77–86. Berlin: Humboldt-Universität zu Berlin.

Marx, Karl, and Friedrich Engels. [1848] 1977. "The Communist Manifesto." In *Karl Marx: Selected Writings*, edited by David McLellan, 221–47. Oxford: Oxford University Press.

Mathisen, Ralph W. 2006. "Peregrini, Barbari, and Cives Romani: Concepts of Citizenship and the Legal Identity of Barbarians in the Later Roman Empire." *The American Historical Review* 111 (4): 1011–40. doi: 10.1086/ahr.111.4.1011.

Mathur, Aparna. 2007. *The Arthasastra Tradition and Ancient Indian Value-System*. New Delhi: Anamika Publishers & Distributors.

Matsuda, Mari J. 1988. "Law and Culture in the District Court of Honolulu, 1844–1845: A Case Study of the Rise of Legal Consciousness." *The American Journal of Legal History* 32 (1): 16–41. doi: 10.2307/845993.

Matthee, Rudi. 2010. "Was Safavid Iran an Empire?" *Journal of the Economic and Social History of the Orient* 53 (1/2): 233–265. doi: 10.1163/002249910X12573963244449.

Matthews, Roger. 2013. "Peoples and Complex Societies of Ancient Southwest Asia." In *The Human Past: World Prehistory and the Development of Human Societies*, edited by Chris Scarre, 432–71. 3rd ed. London: Thames & Hudson.

Mazar, Amihai. 2010. "Archaeology and the Biblical Narrative: The Case of the United Monarchy." In *One God—One Cult—One Nation: Archaeological and Biblical Perspectives*, edited by Reinhard G. Kratz and Hermann Spieckermann, 29–58. Berlin: Walter de Gruyter.

McAlister, Lyle N. 1984. *Spain and Portugal in the New World, 1492–1700*. Minneapolis, MN: University of Minnesota Press.

McAuliffe, Katherine, and Laurie Santos. 2018. "Do Animals Have a Sense of Fairness?" In *Atlas of Moral Psychology*, edited by Kurt Gray and Jesse Graham, 393–401. New York: Guilford Press.

McCormick, Michael. 1990. *Eternal Victory: Triumphal Rulership in Late Antiquity, Byzantium and the Early Medieval West*. Cambridge: Cambridge University Press.

McCormick, Michael. 1991. "Imperial Cult." In *The Oxford Dictionary of Byzantium*, edited by Alexander Kazhdan, 989–90. Oxford: Oxford University Press.

McCormick, Michael. 1997. "Emperors." In *The Byzantines*, edited by Guglielmo Cavallo, 231–54. Chicago: University of Chicago Press.

McElrath, Dale L., Andrew C. Fortier, Brad Koldehoff, and Thomas E. Emerson. 2009. "The American Bottom: An Archaic Cultural Crossroads." In *Archaic Societies: Diversity and Complexity across the Midcontinent*, edited by Thomas E. Emerson, Dale L. McElrath, and Andrew C. Fortier, 317–76. Albany, NY: SUNY Press.

McEwan, Gordon F. 2006. *The Incas: New Perspectives*. Santa Barbara, CA: ABC-CLIO.

McEwan, Gordon F., and Patrick Ryan Williams. 2012. "The Wari Built Environment: Landscape and Architecture of Empire." In *Wari: Lords of the Ancient Andes*, edited by Susan E. Bergh, 66–83. London: Thames & Hudson.

McIntosh, Jane. 2008. *The Ancient Indus Valley*. Santa Barbara: ABC-CLIO.

McIntosh, Roderick J. 1998. *The Peoples of the Middle Niger*. Oxford: Blackwell.

McIntosh, Roderick J. 2000. "Social Memory in Mande." In *The Way the Wind Blows: Climate, History, and Human Action*, edited by Roderick J. McIntosh, Joseph A. Tainter, and Susan Keech McIntosh, 141–80. New York: Columbia University Press.

McIntosh, Roderick J. 2005. *Ancient Middle Niger: Urbanism and the Self-Organizing Landscape*. Cambridge: Cambridge University Press.

McIntosh, Roderick J. 2008. "Before Timbuktu: Cities of the Elder World." In *The Meanings of Timbuktu*, edited by Shamil Jeppie and Souleymane Bachir Diagne, 31–44. Cape Town: HSRC Press.

McIntosh, Roderick J. 2013. "Captain of 'We Band of Brothers': An Archaeologist's Homage to Nehemia Levtzion." In *Engaging with a Legacy: Nehemia Levtzion (1935–2003)*, edited by E. Ann McDougall, 162–71. London: Routledge.

McIntosh, Roderick J. 2015. "Climate Shock and Awe: Can There Be an 'Ethno-Science' of Deep-Time Mande Palaeoclimatic Memory?" In *Climate Cultures: Anthropological Perspectives on Climate Change*, edited by Jessica Barnes and Michael R. Dove, 273–88. New Haven, CT: Yale University Press.

McIntosh, Roderick J. and Susan K. McIntosh. 1981. "The Inland Niger Delta before the Empire of Mali: Evidence from Jenne-Jeno." *The Journal of African History* 22 (1): 1–22. doi: 10.1017/S0021853700018983.

McIntosh, Roderick J. and Susan K. McIntosh. 1988. "From Siècles Obscurs to Revolutionary Centuries on the Middle Niger." *Archaeology in Africa* 20 (1): 141–65. doi: 10.1080/00438243.1988.9980062.

McIntosh, Roderick J. and Susan K. McIntosh. 1995. "Stratigraphy, Features and Chronology." In *Excavations at Jenné-Jeno, Hambarketolo, and Kaniana (Inland Niger Delta, Mali), the 1981 Season*, edited by Susan K. McIntosh, 27–129. Berkeley: University of California Press.

McIntosh, Susan K., ed. 1999a. *Beyond Chiefdoms: Pathways to Complexity in Africa*. Cambridge: Cambridge University Press.

McIntosh, Susan K. 1999b. "Pathways to Complexity: An African Perspective." In *Beyond Chiefdoms: Pathways to Complexity in Africa*, edited by Susan K. McIntosh, 1–30. Cambridge: Cambridge University Press.

McIntosh, Susan K. 2008. "Reconceptualizing Early Ghana." *Canadian Journal of African Studies / Revue Canadienne des Études Africaines* 42 (2/3): 347–73. doi: 10.1080/00083968.2008.10751387.

McIntosh, Susan K. and Roderick J. McIntosh. 1993. "Cities without Citadels: Understanding Urban Origins along the Middle Niger." In *The Archaeology of Africa: Food, Metals and Towns*, edited by Thurstan Shaw, 622–42. London: Routledge.

McIntosh, Susan K. and Roderick J. McIntosh. 1995. "Background to the 1981 Research." In *Excavations at Jenné-Jeno, Hambarketolo, and Kaniana (Inland Niger Delta, Mali), the 1981 Season*, edited by Susan K. McIntosh, 1–26. Berkeley: University of California Press.

McKnight, J. Michael Jr. 1977. "Kingship and Religion in India's Gupta Age: An Analysis of the Role of Vaisnavism in the Lives and Ideology of the Gupta Kings." *Journal of the American Academy of Religion* 45 (2): 727–51. doi: 10.1093/jaarel/XLV.2.227.

McMahon, Gregory, and Sharon R. Steadman. 2011. "Introduction: The Oxford Handbook of Ancient Anatolia." In *The Oxford Handbook of Ancient Anatolia, 10,000–323 B.C.E.*, edited by Sharon R. Steadman and Gregory McMahon, 3–11. Oxford: Oxford University Press.

McNaughton, Patrick R. 1988. *The Mande Blacksmiths: Knowledge, Power, and Art in West Africa*. Bloomington: Indiana University Press.

McNeill, John T., and Helena M. Gamer. 1990. *Medieval Handbooks of Penance: A Translation of the Principal "Libri Poenitentiales" and Selections from Related Documents*. New York: Columbia University Press.

McNeill, William H. 1993. "The Age of Gunpowder Empires, 1450–1800." In *Islamic & European Expansion: The Forging of a Global Order*, edited by Michael Adas, 103–39. Philadelphia: Temple University Press.

Mellink, Machteld J. 1992. "The Native Kingdoms of Anatolia." In *The Cambridge Ancient History, vol. III, part 2: The Assyrian and Babylonian Empires and Other States of the Near East, From the Eighth to the Sixth Centuries B.C.*, edited by John Boardman, I. E. S. Edwards, N. G. L. Hammond, E. Sollberger, and C. B. F. Walker, 619–65. Cambridge: Cambridge University Press.

Merry, Sally Engle. 2000. *Colonizing Hawai'i: The Cultural Power of Law.* Princeton, NJ: Princeton University Press.

Michalowski, Piotr. 2005. "Mesopotamian Vistas on Axial Transformations." In *Axial Civilizations and World History,* edited by Johann P. Arnason, S. N. Eisenstadt, and Bjørn Wittrock, 157–82. Leiden: Brill.

Michel, Cécile. 2011. "The Kārum Period on the Plateau." In *The Oxford Handbook of Ancient Anatolia, 10,000–323 B.C.E.,* edited by Sharon R. Steadman and Gregory McMahon, 313–36. Oxford: Oxford University Press.

Mikalson, Jon D. 2006. "Greek Religion: Continuity and Change in the Hellenistic Period." In *The Cambridge Companion to the Hellenistic World,* edited by Glenn R. Bugh, 208–22. Cambridge: Cambridge University Press.

Miksic, John N. 2007. *Historical Dictionary of Ancient Southeast Asia.* Lanham, MD: Scarecrow Press.

Miksic, John N., and Geok Yian Goh. 2017. *Ancient Southeast Asia.* London: Routledge.

Miller II, Robert D. 2014. "The Judges and the Early Iron Age." In *Ancient Israel's History: An Introduction to Issues and Sources,* edited by Bill T. Arnold and Richard S. Hess, 165–89. Grand Rapids: Baker Academic.

Miller, Margaret C. 2002. "Greece ii: Greco-Persian Cultural Relations." In *Encyclopædia Iranica,* XI/3, 301–19. Updated version available online at http://www.iranicaonline.org/articles/greece-ii (accessed October 22, 2017).

Miller, Timothy S. 2003. *The Orphans of Byzantium: Child Welfare in the Christian Empire.* Washington, DC: The Catholic University of America Press.

Miller, Timothy. 2008. "Charitable Institutions." In *The Oxford Handbook of Byzantine Studies,* edited by Robin Cormack, John F. Haldon, and Elizabeth Jeffreys, 621–29. Oxford: Oxford University Press.

Milner, George R. 1983. "Mississippian Sand Prairie Phase Mortuary Complex." In *The Florence Street Site,* by Thomas E. Emerson, George R. Milner, and Douglas K. Jackson, 220–302. Urbana, IL: University of Illinois Press.

Milner, George R. 1986. "Mississippian Period Population Density in a Segment of the Central Mississippi River Valley." *American Antiquity* 51 (2): 227–38. doi: 10.2307/279938.

Milner, George R. 2006. *The Cahokia Chiefdom: The Archaeology of a Mississippian Society.* Gainesville, FL: University Press of Florida.

Milner, George R., George Chaplin, and Emily Zavodny. 2013. "Conflict and Societal Change in Late Prehistoric Eastern North America." *Evolutionary Anthropology* 22: 96–102. doi: 10.1002/evan.21351.

Mishra, Jayashri. 1992. *Social and Economic Conditions under the Imperial Rashtrakutas.* New Delhi: Commonwealth.

Mitchell, Stephen. 1993. *Anatolia: Land, Men, and Gods in Asia Minor, vol. I: The Celts and the Impact of Roman Rule.* Oxford: Clarendon Press.

Mitchell, Stephen. 2003. "The Galatians: Representation and Reality." In *A Companion to the Hellenistic World*, edited by Andrew Erskine, 280–93. Malden: Blackwell Publishing.

Miyamoto, Kazuo. 2019. "The Spread of Rice Agriculture during the Yayoi Period: From the Shandong Peninsula to the Japanese Archipelago via the Korean Peninsula." *Japanese Journal of Archaeology* 6 (2): 109–24.

Mizoguchi, Koji. 2002. *An Archaeological History of Japan, 30,000 B.C. to A.D. 700.* Philadelphia: University of Pennsylvania Press.

Momigliano, Arnaldo. 1975. *Alien Wisdom: The Limits of Hellenization.* Cambridge: Cambridge University Press.

Monson, Andrew. 2012. *From the Ptolemies to the Romans: Political and Economic Change in Egypt.* Cambridge: Cambridge University Press.

Monson, Andrew. 2015. "Hellenistic Empires." In *Fiscal Regimes and the Political Economy of Premodern States*, edited by Andrew Monson and Walter Scheidel, 169–207. Cambridge: Cambridge University Press.

Morawetz, David. 1967. *Land Tenure Conversion in the Northern District of Papua.* New Guinea Research Bulletin. Canberra: New Guinea Research Unit, Australian National University. Retrieved from http://ehrafworldcultures.yale.edu/document?id=oj23-017.

Morenz, Ludwig D., and Lutz Popko. 2010. "The Second Intermediate Period and the New Kingdom." In *A Companion to Ancient Egypt*, vol. 1, edited by Alan B. Lloyd, 101–19. Chichester, England: Wiley-Blackwell.

Morgan, Lewis Henry, and Herbert M. Lloyd. 1901a. *League of the Ho-De'-No-Sau-Nee or Iroquois*, vol. 1. New York: Dodd, Mead and Company. Retrieved from http://ehrafworldcultures.yale.edu/document?id=nm09-001.

Morgan, Lewis Henry, and Herbert M. Lloyd. 1901b. *League of the Ho-De'-No-Sau-Nee or Iroquois*, vol. 2. New York: Dodd, Mead and Company. Retrieved from http://ehrafworldcultures.yale.edu/document?id=nm09-002.

Morley, Iain. 2013. *The Prehistory of Music: Human Evolution, Archaeology, and the Origins of Musicality.* Oxford: Oxford University Press.

Morony, Michael G. 2012. "Iran in the Early Islamic Period." In *The Oxford Handbook of Iranian History*, edited by Touraj Daryaee, 208–26. Oxford: Oxford University Press.

Morris, Ellen F. 2010. "The Pharaoh and Pharaonic Office." In *A Companion to Ancient Egypt*, vol. 1, edited by Alan B. Lloyd, 201–17. Chichester, England: Wiley-Blackwell.

Morris, Ian. 1986. "Gift and Commodity in Archaic Greece." *Man* n.s. 21 (1): 1–17. doi: 10.2307/2802643.

Morris, Ian. 1988. "Tomb Cult and the 'Greek Renaissance': The Past in the Present in the 8th Century BC." *Antiquity* 62 (237): 750–61. doi: 10.1017/S0003598X00075207.

Morris, Ian. 1996. "The Strong Principle of Equality and the Archaic Origins of Greek Democracy." In *Dēmokratia: A Conversation on Democracies, Ancient and Modern*, edited by Josiah Ober and Charles Hedrick, 19–48. Princeton, NJ: Princeton University Press.

Morris, Ian. 2010. *Why the West Rules—For Now.* New York: Farrar, Straus & Giroux.

Morris, Ian. 2013. *The Measure of Civilization: How Social Development Decides the Fate of Nations.* Princeton, NJ: Princeton University Press.

Morris, Ian. 2015. *Foragers, Farmers, and Fossil Fuels: How Human Values Evolve.* Princeton, NJ: Princeton University Press.

Morrison, A. D. 2010. "Greek Literature in Egypt." In *A Companion to Ancient Egypt,* vol. 2, edited by Alan B. Lloyd, 755-78. Chichester, England: Wiley-Blackwell.

Morrissey, Robert Michael. 2013. "The Terms of Encounter: Language and Contested Visions of French Colonization in the Illinois Country, 1673-1702." In *French and Indians in the Heart of North America,* 1630-1815, edited by Robert Englebert and Guillaume Teasdale, 43-75. East Lansing, MI: Michigan State University.

Morrissey, Robert Michael. 2015. "The Power of the Ecotone: Bison, Slavery, and the Rise and Fall of the Grand Village of the Kaskaskia." *Journal of American History* 102 (3): 667-92. doi: 10.1093/jahist/jav514.

Moseley, Michael E., and Michael J. Heckenberger. 2013. "From Village to Empire in South America." In *The Human Past: World Prehistory and the Development of Human Societies,* edited by Chris Scarre, 640-77. 3rd ed. London: Thames & Hudson.

Mouritsen, Henrik. 2004. *Plebs and Politics in the Late Roman Republic.* Cambridge: Cambridge University Press.

Mouton, Alice, and Ian Rutherford. 2013. "Luwian Religion, a Research Project: The Case of 'Hittite' Augury." In *Luwian Identities: Culture, Language and Religion between Anatolia and the Aegean,* edited by Alice Mouton, Ian Rutherford, and Ilya Yakubovich, 329-44. Leiden: Brill.

Mouton, Alice, Ian Rutherford and Ilya Yakubovich, eds. 2013. *Luwian Identities: Culture, Language and Religion between Anatolia and the Aegean.* Leiden: Brill.

Müller, Friedrich Max. 1867. *Essays on Mythology, Traditions, and Customs.* London: Longmans, Green, and Co.

Mullins, Daniel Austin, Daniel Hoyer, Christina Collins, Thomas Currie, Kevin Feeney, Pieter François, Patrick E. Savage et al. 2018. "A Systematic Assessment of 'Axial Age' Proposals Using Global Comparative Historical Evidence." *American Sociological Review* 83 (3): 596-626. doi: 10.1177/0003122418772567.

Mullins, Daniel A., Harvey Whitehouse, and Quentin D. Atkinson. 2013. "The Role of Writing and Recordkeeping in the Cultural Evolution of Human Cooperation." *Journal of Economic Behavior and Organization* 90: 141-151. doi: 10.1016/j.jebo.2012.12.017.

Mulrooney, Mara A., and Thegn N. Ladefoged. 2005. "Hawaiian Heiau and Agricultural Production in the Kohala Dryland Field System." *The Journal of the Polynesian Society* 114: 45-67.

Munn, Mark H. 2006. *The Mother of the Gods, Athens, and the Tyranny of Asia: A Study of Sovereignty in Ancient Religion.* Berkeley: University of California Press.

Munson, Patrick J. 1980. "Archaeology and the Prehistoric Origins of the Ghana Empire." *The Journal of African History* 21 (4): 457-66. doi: 10.1017/S0021853700018685.

Murdock, George P. 1967. "Ethnographic Atlas: A Summary." *Ethnology* 6: 109-236.

Murdock, George P., and Douglas R. White. 1969. "Standard Cross-Cultural Sample." *Ethnology* 8 (4): 329–69. doi: 10.2307/3772907.

Murray, Oswyn. 1986. "Life and Society in Classical Greece." In *The Oxford History of Greece and the Hellenistic World*, edited by John Boardman, Jasper Griffin, and Oswyn Murray, 240–76. Oxford: Oxford University Press.

Murray, Oswyn. 2007. "Philosophy and Monarchy in the Hellenistic World." In *Jewish Perspectives on Hellenistic Rulers*, edited by Tessa Rajak, Sarah Pearce, James Aitken, and Jennifer Dines, 13–28. Berkeley: University of California Press.

Murthy, H. V. Sreenivasa and R. Ramakrishnan. 1978. *A History of Karnataka*. New Delhi: S. Chand.

Mus, Paul. 2011. *India Seen from the East: Indian and Indigenous Cults in Champa*. Translated by I. W. Mabbett and edited by I. W. Mabbett and D. P. Chandler. Caulfield: Monash University Press.

Muscarella, Oscar White. 1995. "The Iron Age Background to the Formation of the Phrygian State." *Bulletin of the American Schools of Oriental Research* 299/300: 91–101. doi: 10.1163/9789004236691_019.

Nafplioti, Argyro. 2008. "'Mycenaean' Political Domination of Knossos Following the Late Minoan IB Destructions on Crete: Negative Evidence from Strontium Isotope Ratio Analysis (87Sr/86Sr)." *Journal of Archaeological Science* 35 (8): 2307–17. doi: 10.1016/j.jas.2008.03.006.

Nakahashi, Takahiro. 2000. "Population Movements in the Yayoi Period." In Newsletter Special Issue *Nihon-jin to Nihon Bunka*, edited by K. Ōmoto, 12–13. Kyoto: Nichibunken.

Nakassis, Dimitri. 2013. *Individuals and Society in Mycenaean Pylos*. Leiden: Brill.

Nakhai, Beth Alpert. 2003. "Canaanite Religion." In *Near Eastern Archaeology: A Reader*, edited by Suzanne Richard, 343–48. Winona Lake: Eisenbrauns.

Naqvi, Syed. 1993. "The Indus Valley Civilization—Cradle of Democracy? (Reflections)." *UNESCO Courier* February: 48.

Nash, Donna J. 2018. "Art and Elite Political Machinations in the Middle Horizon Andes." In *Images in Action: The Southern Andean Iconographic Series*, edited by William H. Isbell, Mauricio I. Uribe, Anne Tiballi, and Edward P. Zegarra, 479–500. Berkeley: UCLA Cotsen Institute of Archaeology Press.

Nashat, Guity. 2003. "Women in Pre-Islamic and Early Islamic Iran." In *Women in Iran: From the Rise of Islam to 1800*, edited by Guity Nashat and Lois Beck, 11–47. Urbana: University of Illinois Press.

Nasr, Seyyed Hossain. 1975. "Philosophy and Cosmology." In *The Cambridge History of Iran, vol. 4: The Period from the Arab Invasion to the Saljuqs*, edited by R. N. Frye, 419–41. Cambridge: Cambridge University Press.

Nasu, Hiroo, and Arata Momohara. 2016. "The Beginnings of Rice and Millet Agriculture in Prehistoric Japan." In *Quaternary International* 397: 504–512. doi: 10.1016/j.quaint.2015.06.043.

Naumann, Nelly. 2000. *Japanese Prehistory: The Material and Spiritual Culture of the Jomon Period*. Berlin: Harrassowitz Verlag.

Naunton, Christopher. 2010. "Libyans and Nubians." In *A Companion to Ancient Egypt*, vol. 1, edited by Alan B. Lloyd, 120–39. Chichester, England: Wiley-Blackwell.

Newton, Janice. 1983. "Orokaiva Warfare and Production." *Journal of the Polynesian Society* 92 (4): 487–507. Retrieved from http://ehrafworldcultures.yale.edu/document?id=oj23-030.

Newton, Janice. 1985. "Orokaiva Production and Change." Pacific Research Monograph. Canberra: Development Studies Centre, Australian National University. Retrieved from http://ehrafworldcultures.yale.edu/document?id=oj23-029.

Ng, R. C. Y. 1979. "The Geographical Habitat of Historic Settlement in Mainland Southeast Asia." In *Early South East Asia: Essays in Archaeology, History and Historical Geography*, edited by R. B. Smith and W. Watson, 263–72. New York: Oxford University Press.

Nichols, Roger L. 1998. *Indians in the United States and Canada: A Comparative History*. Lincoln, NE: University of Nebraska Press.

Nicholson, Paul T. and Ian Shaw. 2000. *Ancient Egyptian Materials and Technology*. Cambridge: Cambridge University Press.

Niemeyer, Hans Georg. 2006. "The Phoenicians in the Mediterranean between Expansion and Colonisation: A Non-Greek Model of Overseas Settlement and Presence." In *Greek Colonisation: An Account of Greek Colonies and Other Settlements Overseas*, vol. 1, edited by Gocha R. Tsetskhladze, 143–68. Leiden: Brill.

Nigosian. 1993. *The Zoroastrian Faith*. Montreal: McGill-Queen's University Press.

Noll, K. L. 2007. "Canaanite Religion." *Religion Compass* 1 (1): 61–92.

Noon, John A. 1949. *Law and Government of the Grand River Iroquois*. Publications in Anthropology. New York: Viking Fund. Retrieved from http://ehrafworldcultures.yale.edu/document?id=nm09-009.

Noreña, Carlos. 2010. "The Early Imperial Monarchy." In *The Oxford Handbook of Roman Studies*, edited by Alessandro Barchiesi and Walter Scheidel, 533–46. Oxford: Oxford University Press.

Norenzayan, Ara. 2013. *Big Gods: How Religion Transformed Cooperation and Conflict*. Princeton, NJ: Princeton University Press.

Norenzayan, Ara, Azim F. Shariff, Aiyana K. Willard, Edward Slingerland, Will M. Gervais, Rita A. Mcnamara, and Joseph Henrich. 2016. "The Cultural Evolution of Prosocial Religions." *Behavioral & Brain Sciences* 39: 1–65. doi: 10.1017/S0140525X14001356.

Norman, Neil L. 2012. "From the Shadow of an Atlantic Citadel: An Archaeology of the Huedan Countryside." In *Power and Landscape in Atlantic West Africa: Archaeological Perspectives*, edited by J. Cameron Monroe and Akinwumi Ogundiran, 142–66. Cambridge: Cambridge University Press.

Nylan, Michael. 2001. *The Five "Confucian" Classics*. New Haven, CT: Yale University Press.

O'Connor, David. 1983. "New Kingdom and Third Intermediate Period, 1552–664 BC." In *Ancient Egypt: A Social History*, edited by Bruce G. Trigger, Barry J. Kemp, David O'Connor, and Alan B. Lloyd, 183–278. Cambridge: Cambridge University Press.

O'Reilly, Dougald J. W. 2014. "Increasing Complexity and the Political Economy Model: A Consideration of Iron Age Moated Sites in Thailand." *Journal of Anthropological Archaeology* 35: 297–309. doi: 10.1016/j.jaa.2014.06.007.

Ober, Josiah. 2008. *Democracy and Knowledge: Innovation and Learning in Classical Athens.* Princeton, NJ: Princeton University Press.

Ober, Josiah. 2015. *The Rise and Fall of Classical Greece.* Princeton, NJ: Princeton University Press.

Obeyesekere, Gananath. 1980. "The Rebirth Eschatology and Its Transformations: A Contribution to the Sociology of Early Buddhism." In *Karma and Rebirth in Classical Indian Traditions,* edited by Wendy Doniger O'Flaherty, 137–64. Berkeley: University of California Press.

Ockinga, Boyo. 2005. "Ethics and Morality." In *The Oxford Encyclopedia of Ancient Egypt,* edited by Stephen G. J. Quirke. Online edition. Oxford: Oxford University Press.

Oded, Bustanay. 1974. "The Phoenician Cities and the Assyrian Empire in the Time of Tiglath-Pileser III." *Zeitschrift des Deutschen Palästina-Vereins* 90 (1): 38–49.

Olivelle, Patrick. 2013. *King, Governance, and Law in Ancient India: Kautilya's Arthashastra.* Oxford: Oxford University Press.

Oliver, Roland, and Anthony Atmore. 2001. *Medieval Africa, 1250–1800.* Cambridge: Cambridge University Press.

Olsen, Barbara A. 1998. "Women, Children and the Family in the Late Aegean Bronze Age: Differences in Minoan and Mycenaean Constructions of Gender." *World Archaeology* 29 (3): 380–92. doi: 10.1080/00438243.1998.9980386.

Ortner, Sherry B. 1974. "Is Female to Male as Nature Is to Culture?" In *Woman, Culture, and Society,* edited by Michelle Zimbalist Rosaldo and Louise Lamphere, 68–87. Stanford, CA: Stanford University Press.

Osborne, Robin. 1997. "Law, the Democratic Citizen and the Representation of Women in Classical Athens." *Past & Present* 155: 3–33. doi: 10.1093/past/155.1.3.

Osborne, Robin. 2013. "Democracy and Religion in Classical Greece." In *The Greek Polis and the Invention of Democracy: A Politico-Cultural Transformation and Its Interpretations,* edited by Johann P. Arnason, Kurt A. Raaflaub, and Peter Wagner, 274–97. Chichester, England: Wiley-Blackwell.

Ostwald, Martin. 1986. *From Popular Sovereignty to the Sovereignty of Law: Law, Society, and Politics in Fifth-Century Athens.* Berkeley: University of California Press.

Ownby, David. 1999. "Chinese Millenarian Traditions: The Formative Age." *The American Historical Review* 104 (5): 1513–30. doi: 10.1086/ahr/104.5.1513.

Palaima, Thomas G. 1995. "The Nature of the Mycenaean Wanax: Non-Indo-European Origins and Priestly Functions." In *The Role of the Ruler in the Prehistoric Aegean: Proceedings of a Panel Discussion Presented at the Annual Meeting of the Archaeological Institute of America, New Orleans, Louisiana, 28 December 1992, with Additions,* edited by Paul Rehak, 119–39. Liège: Histoire de l'art et archéologie de la Grèce antique, Université de Liège; Austin: Program in Aegean Script and Prehistory, University of Texas at Austin.

Palumbi, Giulio. 2011. "The Chalcolithic of Eastern Anatolia." In *The Oxford Handbook of Ancient Anatolia, 10,000–323 B.C.E.*, edited by Sharon R. Steadman and Gregory McMahon, 205–28. Oxford: Oxford University Press.

Papadakis, A. 1991. "Epithimion." In *The Oxford Dictionary of Byzantium*, vol. 1, edited by A. Kazhdan, 112–13. Oxford: Oxford University Press.

Papadopoulos, John K. 1996. "Dark Age Greece." In *The Oxford Companion to Archaeology*, edited by Brian M. Fagan, Charlotte Beck, George Michaels, Chris Scarre, and Neil Asher Silberman, 253–55. Oxford: Oxford University Press.

Papaioannou, Stratis. 2009. "The Byzantine Late Antiquity." *A Companion to Late Antiquity*, edited by Philip Rousseau with the assistance of Jutta Raithel, 17–28. Chichester, England: Wiley-Blackwell.

Papio, Michael C. 2004. "Slavery." In *Medieval Italy: An Encyclopedia*, vol. 2, edited by Christopher Kleinhenz, 1049–52. London: Routledge.

Parpola, Asko. 1999. "The Formation of the Aryan Branch of Indo-European." In *Archaeology and Language III: Artefacts, Languages and Texts*, edited by Roger Blench and Matthew Spriggs, 180–207. London: Routledge.

Pathak, Manjushree. 1995. "Concept of Maintenance in Garo Customary Law." In *Hill Societies, Their Modernisation: A Study of North East with Special Reference to Garo Hills*. New Delhi: Omsons Publications. Retrieved from http://ehrafworldcultures.yale.edu/document?id=ar05-025.

Pauketat, Timothy R. 1994. *The Ascent of Chiefs: Cahokia and Mississippian Politics in Native North America*. Tuscaloosa, AL: University of Alabama Press.

Pauketat, Timothy R. 2004. *Ancient Cahokia and the Mississippians*. Cambridge: Cambridge University Press.

Pauketat, Timothy R. 2009. *Cahokia: Ancient America's Great City on the Mississippi*. New York: Viking.

Pauketat, Timothy R., Lucretia S. Kelly, Gayle F. Fritz, Neal H. Lopinot, Scott Elias, and Eve Hargrave. 2002. "The Residues of Feasting and Public Ritual at Early Cahokia." *American Antiquity* 67: 257–279. doi: 10.2307/2694566.

Paul, Diane Y. 1985. *Women in Buddhism: Images of the Feminine in Mahāyāna Tradition*. Berkeley, CA: University of California Press.

Peacock, David. 2000. "The Roman Period (30 BC–AD 395)." In *The Oxford History of Ancient Egypt*, edited by Ian Shaw, 414–36. Oxford: Oxford University Press.

Pearson, Richard. 2007. "Debating Jomon Social Complexity." *Asian Perspectives* 46 (2): 361–88.

Peatfield, Alan A. D. 2016. "A Metaphysical History of Minoan Religion." In *Metaphysis: Ritual, Myth and Symbolism in the Aegean Bronze Age*, edited by Eva Alram-Stern, Fritz Blakolmer, Sigrid Deger-Jalkotzy, Robert Laffineur, and Jörg Weilhartner, 485–95. Leuven: Peeters.

Pelliot, Paul. 1903. "Le Fou-nan." *Bulletin de l'École française d'Extrême-Orient* 3: 248–303. doi: 10.3406/befeo.1903.1216.

Peoples, Hervey C., Pavel Duda, and Frank W. Marlowe. 2016. "Hunter-Gatherers and the Origins of Religion." *Human Nature* 27 (3): 261–282. doi: 10.1007/s12110-016-9260-0.

Perdu, Olivier. 2010. "Saites and Persians (664–332)." In *A Companion to Ancient Egypt*, vol. 1, edited by Alan B. Lloyd, 140–58. Chichester, England: Wiley-Blackwell.

Perdue, Leo G. 2008. *The Sword and the Stylus: An Introduction to Wisdom in the Age of Empires.* Grand Rapids: William B. Eerdmans Publishing Company.

Peregrine, Peter N. 2001. "Mississippian." In *Encyclopedia of Prehistory, vol. 6: North America*, edited by Peter N. Peregrine and Melvin Ember, 335–38. New York: Springer.

Peregrine, Peter N. 2003. "Atlas of Cultural Evolution." *World Cultures* 14.

Peregrine, Peter N. 2008. "Social Death and Resurrection in the Western Great Lakes." In *Invisible Citizens: Captives and Their Consequences*, edited by Catherine M. Cameron, 223–32. Salt Lake City: University of Utah Press.

Peregrine, Peter N., Scott Ortman, and Eric Rupley. 2014. "Social Complexity at Cahokia." *SFI Working Paper*. Santa Fe, NM: Santa Fe Institute.

Perlman, Paula J. 2004. "Writing on the Walls: The Architectural Context of Archaic Cretan Laws." In *Crete beyond the Palaces: Proceedings of the Crete 2000 Conference*, edited by Leslie Preston Day, Margaret S. Mook, and James D. Muhly, 181–98. Philadelphia: INSTAP Academic Press.

Perono Cacciafoco, Francesco. 2017. "Linear A and Minoan: Some New Old Questions." *Lingvistică* 1/2: 154–70.

Petrie, Cameron. 2005. "Exploring Routes and Plains in Southwest Iran: Settlement on the Susiana Plain." *ArchAtlas*, Version 4.1. Accessed August 11, 2017. http://www.archatlas.org/Petrie/SusianaPlain.php.

Petrie, C. A., R. N. Singh, C. A. I. French, J. Bates, C. Lancelotti, S. Neogi, A. K. Pandey, et al. 2017. "Land, Water and Settlement in Northwest India 2008–2012: A Review of Progress." In *South Asian Archaeology 2012. Man and Environment in Prehistoric and Protohistoric South Asia: New Perspectives*, edited by V Lefèvre, A. Didier, and B. Mutin, 243–55. Turnhout: Brepols.

Petrovic, Andrej and Ivana Petrovic. 2016. *Inner Purity and Pollution in Greek Religion*, vol. 1: *Early Greek Religion*. Oxford: Oxford University Press.

Pfeiffer, Stefan. 2012. "The Imperial Cult in Egypt." In *The Oxford Handbook of Roman Egypt*, edited by Christina Riggs, 83–100. Oxford: Oxford University Press.

Pfoh, Emanuel. 2016. *The Emergence of Israel in Ancient Palestine: Historical and Anthropological Perspectives*. London: Routledge. doi: 10.4324/9781315539140.

Piggott, Joan R. 1982. "Hierarchy and Economics in Early Medieval Tōdaiji." In *Court and Bakufu in Japan*, edited by Jeffrey Mass, 45–91. New Haven, CT: Yale University Press.

Pines, Yuri. 2002. *Foundations of Confucian Thought: Intellectual Life in the Chunqiu Period*. Honolulu, HI: University of Hawaii Press.

Pines, Yuri. 2009. *Envisioning Eternal Empire: Chinese Political Thought in the Warring States Period*. Honolulu, HI: University of Hawaii Press.

Playfair, Alan. 1909. *The Garos*. London: David Nutt. Retrieved from http://ehrafworldcultures.yale.edu/document?id=ar05-002.

Pomeroy, Sarah B., Stanley M. Burstein, Walter Donlan, and Jennifer Tolbert Roberts. 2004. *A Brief History of Ancient Greece: Politics, Society, and Culture*. Oxford: Oxford University Press.

Poo, Mu-chou. 2005. *Enemies of Civilization: Attitudes towards Foreigners in Ancient Mesopotamia, Egypt, and China*. Albany: State University of New York Press.

Popov, A. A. 1946. "Family Life of the Dolgani People." *Sovetskaya Etnografiya* (4): 50–74. Retrieved from http://ehrafworldcultures.yale.edu/document?id=rv02-057.

Possehl, Gregory. 2002. *The Indus Civilization: A Contemporary Perspective*. Oxford: AltaMira.

Potts, Daniel T. 2004. *The Archaeology of Elam: Formation and Transformation of an Ancient Iranian State*. Cambridge: Cambridge University Press.

Potts, Daniel T. 2012. "The Elamites." In *The Oxford Handbook of Iranian History*, edited by Touraj Daryaee, 37–56. Oxford: Oxford University Press.

Pourshariati, Parvaneh. 2009. *Decline and Fall of the Sasanian Empire: The Sasanian-Parthian Confederacy and the Arab Conquest of Iran*. London: I. B. Tauris.

Power, Camilla. 2017. "Reconstructing a Source Cosmology for African Hunter-Gatherers." In *Human Origins: Contributions from Social Anthropology*, edited by Camilla Power, Morna Finnegan, and Hillary Callahan, 180–203. New York: Berghahn.

Power, Timothy. 2012. *The Red Sea from Byzantium to the Caliphate: AD 500-1000*. Cairo: The American University in Cairo Press.

Powers, Karen Vieira. 2000. "Andeans and Spaniards in the Contact Zone: A Gendered Collision." *American Indian Quarterly* 24 (4): 511–36. doi: 10.1353/aiq.2000.0025.

Powers, Karen Vieira. 2002. "Conquering Discourses of 'Sexual Conquest': Of Women, Language, and Mestizaje." *Colonial Latin American Review* 11 (1): 7–32. doi: 10.1080/10609160220133655.

Prasad, P. 1998. *Famines & Droughts: Survival Strategies*. Jaipur, India: Rawat Publications.

Price, Simon R. F. 1986. *Rituals and Power: The Roman Imperial Cult in Asia Minor*. Cambridge: Cambridge University Press.

Prinzig, Günter. 2010. "On Slaves and Slavery." In *The Byzantine World*, edited by Paul Stephenson, 92–102. New York: Routledge.

Puett, Michael. 2002. *To Become a God: Cosmology, Sacrifice, and Self-Divination in Early China*. Cambridge, MA: Harvard University Press.

Puett, Michael. 2014. "Ghosts, Gods, and the Coming Apocalypse: Empire and Religion in Early China and Ancient Rome." In *State Power in Ancient China and Rome*, edited by Walter Scheidel, 230–95. Oxford: Oxford University Press.

Purzycki, Benjamin Grant 2011. "Tyvan *Cher Eezi* and the Socioecological Constraints of Supernatural Agents' Minds." *Religion, Brain & Behavior* 1(1): 31–45. doi: 10.1080/2153599X.2010.550723.

Purzycki, Benjamin Grant, Cody T. Ross, Coren Apicella, Quentin D. Atkinson, Emma Cohen, Rita Anne McNamara, Aiyana K. Willard et al. 2018. "Material Security, Life History, and Moralistic Religions: A Cross-Cultural Examination." *PLOS ONE* 13 (3): e0193856. doi: 10.1371/journal.pone.0193856.

Quack, Joachim Friedrich. 2015. "'As He Disregarded the Law, He Was Replaced during His Own Lifetime': On Criticism of Egyptian Rulers in the So-Called Demotic Chronicle." In *Antimonarchic Discourse in Antiquity*, edited by Henning Börm, 25–43. Stuttgart: Franz Steiner Verlag.

Quigley, Declan. 2003. "On the Relationship Between Caste and Hinduism." In *The Blackwell Companion to Hinduism*, edited by Gavin Flood, 495–508. Oxford: Blackwell.

Quinn, Josephine. 2018. In *Search of the Phoenicians*. Princeton, NJ: Princeton University Press.

Quirke, Stephen G. J. 2005. "Judgment of the Dead." In *The Oxford Encyclopedia of Ancient Egypt*, edited by Stephen G. J. Quirke. Online edition. Oxford: Oxford University Press.

Raaflaub, Kurt A. 1996. "Equalities and Inequalities in Athenian Democracy." In *Dēmokratia: A Conversation on Democracies, Ancient and Modern*, edited by Josiah Ober and Charles Hedrick, 139–74. Princeton, NJ: Princeton University Press.

Raaflaub, Kurt A. 2005. "Polis, 'The Political,' and Political Thought: New Departures in Ancient Greece, c. 800–500 BCE." In *Axial Civilizations and World History*, edited by Johann P. Arnason, S. N. Eisenstadt, and Björn Wittrock, 253–86. Leiden: Brill.

Raaflaub, Kurt A. 2013. "Perfecting the 'Political Creature': Equality and 'the Political' in the Evolution of Greek Democracy." In *The Greek Polis and the Invention of Democracy: A Politico-Cultural Transformation and Its Interpretations*, edited by Johann P. Arnason, Kurt A. Raaflaub, and Peter Wagner, 323–50. Chichester, England: Wiley-Blackwell.

Raaflaub, Kurt A. and Robert W. Wallace. 2007. "'People's Power' and Egalitarian Trends in Archaic Greece." In *Origins of Democracy in Ancient Greece*, edited by Kurt A. Raaflaub, Josiah Ober, and Robert W. Wallace with chapters by Paul Cartledge and Cynthia Farrar, 22–48. Berkeley: University of California Press.

Radcliffe-Brown, A. R. 1952. *Structure and Function in Primitive Society*. London: Routledge & Kegan Paul.

Ragab, Ahmed. 2015. *The Medieval Islamic Hospital: Medicine, Religion, and Charity*. Cambridge: Cambridge University Press.

Rainey, Anson F. Z"L. 2015. *The El-Amarna Correspondence: A New Edition of the Cuneiform Letters from the Site of El-Amarna Based on Collations of All Extant Tablets*. Collated, transcribed and translated by Anson F. Z"L Rainey and edited by William Schniedewind and Zipora Cochavi-Rainey. 2 vols. Leiden: Brill.

Rainey, Anson. 2008. "Who Were the Early Israelites?" *Biblical Archaeological Review* 34 (6): 51–55.

Rainey, Lee Dian. 2010. *Confucius and Confucianism: The Essentials*. Oxford: Wiley-Blackwell.

Ralston, Caroline. 1984. "Hawaii 1778–1854: Some Aspects of *Maka'ainana* Response to Rapid Cultural Change." *The Journal of Pacific History* 19 (1): 21–40. doi: 10.1080/00223348408572478.

Randle, Martha Champion. 1951. "Iroquois Women, Then and Now." In *Symposium on Local Diversity in Iroquois Culture*, edited by William N. Fenton, 167–87. Washington, DC: Smithsonian Institution. Retrieved from http://ehrafworldcultures.yale.edu/document?id=nm09-037.

Raschke, Manfred G. 1976. "New Studies in Roman Commerce with the East." In *Politische Geschichte (Provinzen und Randvölker: Mesopotamien, Armenien, Iran, Südarabien, Rom und der Ferne Osten)*, edited by Wolfgang Haase, 604–1362. Berlin: Walter de Gruyter.

Rashid, Ismail. 2006. "Class, Caste & Social Inequality in West African History." In *Themes in West Africa's History*, edited by Emmanuel Kwaku Akyeampong, 118–40. Athens: Ohio University Press.

Rawlings III, Hunter R. 2008. "Thucydides on the Purpose of the Delian League." In *The Athenian Empire*, edited by Polly Low, 49–57. Edinburgh: Edinburgh University Press.

Rawson, Elizabeth. 1986. "The Expansion of Rome." In *The Oxford History of the Roman World*, edited by John Boardman, Jasper Griffin, and Oswyn Murray, 50–73. Oxford: Oxford University Press.

Ray, Himanshu Prabha. 2005. "The Axial Age in South Asia: The Archaeology of Buddhism (500 B.C.–A.D. 500)." In *Archaeology of Asia*, edited by Miriam T. Stark, 303–23. Malden, MA: Blackwell.

Ray, Himanshu Prabha. 2014. "Multi-Religious Maritime Linkages across the Bay of Bengal during the First Millennium CE." In *Before Siam: Essays in Art and Archaeology*, edited by Nicolas Revire and Stephen A. Murphy, 135–51. Bangkok: River Books.

Ray, John. 2002. *Reflections of Osiris: Lives from Ancient Egypt*. Oxford: Oxford University Press.

Raymond, André. 2000. *Cairo*. Cambridge: Harvard University Press.

Raz, Gil. 2012. *The Emergence of Daoism: Creation of Tradition*. New York: Routledge.

Reay, Marie. 1953–1954. "Social Control amongst the Orokaiva." *Oceania* 24: 110–18. Retrieved from http://ehrafworldcultures.yale.edu/document?id=oj23-003.

Rees, Roger. 2004. *Diocletian and the Tetrarchy*. Edinburgh: Edinburgh University Press.

Regev, Eyal. 2013. *The Hasmoneans: Ideology, Archaeology, Identity*. Göttingen: Vandenhoeck & Ruprecht.

Rehak, Paul and John G. Younger. 1998. "Review of Aegean Prehistory VII: Neopalatial, Final Palatial, and Postpalatial Crete." *American Journal of Archaeology* 102 (1): 91–173.

Reid, Gerald. 1996. "Culture Summary: Iroquois." New Haven, CT: HRAF. Retrieved from http://ehrafworldcultures.yale.edu/document?id=nm09-000.

Rezakhani, Khodadad. 2013. "Arsacid, Elymaean and Persid Coinage." In *The Oxford Handbook of Ancient Iran*, edited by Daniel T. Potts, 766–77. Oxford: Oxford University Press.

Richerson, Peter J., and Robert Boyd. 1998. "The Evolution of Human Ultrasociality." In *Ethnic Conflict and Indoctrination*, edited by I. Eibl-Eibesfeldt and F. K. Salter, 71–95. Oxford: Berghahn Books.

Richerson, Peter, and Joseph Henrich. 2012. "Tribal Social Instincts and the Cultural Evolution of Institutions to Solve Collective Action Problems." *Cliodynamics* 3: 38–80. doi: 10.2139/ssrn.1368756.

Rimoldi, Max, Cromwell Burau, and Robert Ferraris. 1966. *Land Tenure and Land Use among the Mount Lamington Orokaiva*. New Guinea Research Unit Bulletin. Canberra: New Guinea Research Unit, Australian National University. Retrieved from http://ehrafworldcultures.yale.edu/document?id=oj23-007.

Rinpoche, Samdhong. 1972. "The Social and Political Strata in Buddhist Thought." In *The Social Philosophy of Buddhism*, edited by Samdhong Rinpoche. Varanasi: The Central Institute of Higher Tibetan Studies.

Rispoli, Fiorella, Roberto Ciarla, and Vincent C. Pigott. 2013. "Establishing the Prehistoric Cultural Sequence for the Lopburi Region, Central Thailand." *Journal of World Prehistory* 26: 101–71. doi: 10.1007/s10963-013-9064-7.

Ritner, Robert K. 2008. "Egypt under Roman Rule: The Legacy of Ancient Egypt." In *The Cambridge History of Egypt, vol. 1: Islamic Egypt, 640–1517*, edited by Carl F. Petry, 1–33. Cambridge: Cambridge University Press.

Rivet, Paul. 1907. "Jivaro Indians: Geographic, Historical and Ethnographic Research." *L'Anthropologie* 18: 333–68, 583–618. Retrieved from http://ehrafworldcultures.yale.edu/document?id=sd09-012.

Robins, Nicholas A. 2011. *Mercury, Mining, and Empire: The Human and Ecological Cost of Colonial Silver Mining in the Andes*. Bloomington, IN: Indiana University Press.

Robinson, Chase F. 2010a. "Conclusion: From Formative Islam to Classical Islam." In *The New Cambridge History of Islam, vol. 1: The Formation of the Islamic World, Sixth to Eleventh Centuries*, edited by Chase F. Robinson, 173–225. Cambridge: Cambridge University Press.

Robinson, Chase F. 2010b. "The Rise of Islam, 600–705." In *The New Cambridge History of Islam, vol. 1: The Formation of the Islamic World, Sixth to Eleventh Centuries*, edited by Chase F. Robinson, 683–95. Cambridge: Cambridge University Press.

Rohe, Mathias. 2015. *Islamic Law in Past and Present*. Leiden: Brill.

Roller, Lynn E. 1999. In *Search of God the Mother: The Cult of Anatolian Cybele*. Berkeley: University of California Press.

Roller, Lynn E. 2011. "Phrygia and the Phrygians." In *The Oxford Handbook of Ancient Anatolia, 10,000–323 B.C.E.*, edited by Sharon R. Steadman and Gregory McMahon, 560–78. Oxford: Oxford University Press.

Roosevelt, Christopher H. 2009. *The Archaeology of Lydia: From Gyges to Alexander*. Cambridge: Cambridge University Press.

Roosevelt, Christopher H. 2012. "Iron Age Western Anatolia: The Lydian Empire and Dynastic Lycia." In *A Companion to the Archaeology of the Ancient Near East*, edited by Daniel T. Potts, 897–913. Malden: Wiley-Blackwell.

Rose, Jenny. 2014. *Zoroastrianism: An Introduction*. London: I. B.Tauris.

Rose, Jenny. 2015. "Gender." In *The Wiley-Blackwell Companion to Zoroastrianism*, edited by Michael Stausberg and Yuhan Sohrab-Dinshaw Vevaina, 273–88. Chichester, England: Wiley Blackwell.

Roth, Rudolf. 1850. "Die Sage von Çunaḥçepa." *Indische Studien* 1: 457–64.

Rousseau, Jérôme. 1980. "Iban Inequality." *Bijdragen tot de taal-, land- en Volkenkunde / Journal of the Humanities and Social Sciences of Southeast Asia* 136 (1): 52–63. doi: 10.1163/22134379-90003537.

Roveda, Vittorio. 2004. "The Archaeology of Khmer Images." *Aséanie* 13: 11–46. doi: 10.3406/asean.2004.1809.

Roveda, Vittorio. 2012. "Buddhist Iconography in Brahmanical Temples of Angkor." In *Materializing Southeast Asia's Past: Selected Papers from the 12th International Conference of the European Association of Southeast Asian Archaeologists*, edited by Marijke J. Klokke and Veronique Degroot, 56–81. Singapore: NUS Press.

Rowe, Greg. 2006. "The Emergence of Monarchy: 44 BCE–96 CE." In *A Companion to the Roman Empire*, edited by David S. Potter, 115–25. Chichester, England: Wiley-Blackwell.

Rowe, John H. 2006. "The Inca Civil War and the Establishment of Spanish Power in Peru." *Ñawpa Pacha* 28 (1): 1–9. doi: 10.1179/naw.2006.28.1.002.

Roy, Kumkum. 1994. *The Emergence of Monarchy in North India*. Oxford: Oxford University Press.

Roy, Sankar Kumar. 1999. "Culture Summary: Garo." New Haven, CT: HRAF. Retrieved from http://ehrafworldcultures.yale.edu/document?id=ar05-000.

Rubin, Benjamin B. 2008. "(Re)presenting Empire: The Roman Imperial Cult in Asia Minor, 31 BC–AD 68." PhD Diss., University of Michigan.

Runciman, W. G. 2012. "Righteous Rebels: When, Where, and Why?" In *The Axial Age and Its Consequences*, edited by Robert N. Bellah and Hans Joas, 317–34. Cambridge: The Belknap Press of Harvard University Press.

Rushforth, Brett. 2012. *Bonds of Alliance: Indigenous and Atlantic Slaveries in New France*. Chapel Hill, NC: University of North Carolina Press.

Ruzicka, Stephen. 2012. *Trouble in the West: Egypt and the Persian Empire, 525–332 BCE*. Oxford: Oxford University Press.

Saddhatissa, H., trans. 1994. *The Sutta-Nipāta*. London: RoutledgeCurzon.

Sage, Paula Winsor. 1995. "Dying in Style: Xenophon's Ideal Leader and the End of the *Cyropaedia*." *The Classical Journal* 90 (2): 161–74.

Sahai, Sachchidanand. 1978. "Central Administration in Ancient Cambodia." *The South East Asian Review* 3 (1): 17–40.

Sahlins, Marshall. 1958. *Social Stratification in Polynesia*. Seattle: University of Washington Press.

Sahlins, Marshall. 1985. *Islands of History*. Chicago: University of Chicago Press.

Sahlins, Marshall. 1990. "The Political Economy of Grandeur in Hawaii from 1810 to 1830." In *Culture through Time: Anthropological Approaches*, edited by Emiko Ohnuki-Tierney, 26–56. Stanford, CA: Stanford University Press.

Samokvasov, D. I. A. 1876. *A Collection of Customary Law of the Siberian Natives*. Warsaw: Ivan Noskovskii. Retrieved from http://ehrafworldcultures.yale.edu/document?id=rv02-035.

Sams, G. Kenneth. 2005. "Gordion: Exploration over a Century." In *The Archaeology of Midas and the Phrygians: Recent Work at Gordion*, edited by Lisa Kealhofer, 10–21. Philadelphia: University of Pennsylvania Museum of Archaeology and Anthropology.

Sams, G. Kenneth. 2011. "Anatolia: The First Millennium B.C.E. in Historical Context." In *The Oxford Handbook of Ancient Anatolia, 10,000–323 B.C.E.*, edited by Sharon R. Steadman and Gregory McMahon, 604–22. Oxford: Oxford University Press.

San Tan Koon. 2014. *Dynastic China: An Elementary History*. Malaysia: The Other Press

Sancisi-Weerdenburg, Heleen. 2013. "Exit Atossa: Images of Women in Greek Historiography on Persia." In *Herodotus: Volume 2: Herodotus and the World*, edited by Rosaria Vignolo Munson, 135–47. Oxford: Oxford University Press.

Sanderson, Alexis. 2003. "The Śaiva Religion among the Khmers, Part I." *Bulletin de l'École Française d'Extrême-Orient* 90/91: 349–462. doi: 10.3406/befeo.2003.3617.

Sanderson, Alexis. 2009. "The Saiva Age — The Rise and Dominance of Saivism during the Early Medieval Period." In *Genesis and Development of Tantrism*, edited by Shingo Einoo, 41–350. Tokyo: Institute of Oriental Culture, University of Tokyo.

Sandin, Benedict. 1976. *Iban Way of Life: A Translation from Tusun Pandiau*. Kuching: Borneo Literature Bureau. Retrieved from http://ehrafworldcultures.yale.edu/document?id=oc06-032.

Sandin, Benedict, and Clifford Sather. 1980. *Iban Adat and Augury*. George Town, Penang: Penerbit Universiti Sains Malaysia for School of Comparative Social Sciences. Retrieved from http://ehrafworldcultures.yale.edu/document?id=oc06-029.

Sapong, Nana Yaw B. 2016. "Mali Empire." In *The Encyclopedia of Empire*, edited by John M. MacKenzie. Online edition. Malden: Wiley-Blackwell.

Sauer, Martin. 1802. *Account of a Geographical and Astronomical Expedition to the Northern Parts of Russia by Commodore Joseph Billings, in the Years 1785–1794*. London: T. Cadell. Retrieved from http://ehrafworldcultures.yale.edu/document?id=rv02-006.

Savage, Patrick E., Harvey Whitehouse, Pieter François, Thomas E. Currie, Kevin C. Feeney, Enrico Cioni, Rosalind Purcell, et al. Forthcoming. "Reply to Beheim et al.: Reanalyses Confirm Robustness of Original Analysis." *SocArXiv* preprint: https://osf.io/preprints/socarxiv/xjryt.

Schäfer, Peter. 2003. *The History of the Jews in the Greco-Roman World*. Revised ed. London: Routledge.

Scheid, John. 2011. "Graeco-Roman Cultic Societies." In *The Oxford Handbook of Social Relations in the Roman World*, edited by Michael Peachin, 535–47. 1st ed. Oxford: Oxford University Press.

Scheidel, Walter. 2005. "Human Mobility in Roman Italy, II: The Slave Population." *Journal of Roman Studies* 95: 64–79.

Schick, Robert. 1998. "Archaeological Sources for the History of Palestine: Palestine in the Early Islamic Period: Luxuriant Legacy." *Near Eastern Archaeology* 61 (2): 74–108. doi: 10.2307/3210639.

Schippmann, Klaus. 1987. "Arsacids ii: The Arsacid Dynasty." In *Encyclopædia Iranica*, II/5, 525–36. Updated version available online at http://www.iranicaonline.org/articles/arsacids-ii (accessed August 17, 2017).

Schmidt, Karl J. 2015. *An Atlas and Survey of South Asian History*. Armonk: M. E. Sharpe.

Schmidt-Leukel, Perry. 2006. *Understanding Buddhism*. Edinburgh: Dunedin Academic Press.

Schmitt, Robert C. 1970. "Famine Mortality in Hawaii." *The Journal of Pacific History* 5: 109–15. doi: 10.1080/00223347008572167.

Schmitt, Rüdiger. 1983. "Achaemenid Dynasty." *Encyclopædia Iranica* I: 414–426. http://www.iranicaonline.org/articles/achaemenid-dynasty (accessed 28 November 2017).

Schmitt, Rüdiger. 1987. "Aryans." *Encyclopædia Iranica*, II/7, 684–87. Updated version available online at http://www.iranicaonline.org/articles/aryans (accessed September 13, 2017).

Schneider, Thomas. 2003. "Die Periodisierung der Ägyptischen Geschichte: Problem und Perspektive für Ägyptologische Historiographie." In *Menschenbilder—Bildermenschen: Kunst und Kultur im Alten Ägypten*, edited by Tobias Hofmann and Alexandra Sturm, 241–56. Norderstedt: Books on Demand GmbH.

Schoep, Ilse. 2002. "The State of the Minoan Palaces or the Minoan Palace-State?" In *Monuments of Minos: Rethinking the Minoan Palaces*, edited by Jan Driessen, Ilse Schoep, and Robert Laffineur, 15–33. Liège: Université de Liège.

Schoep, Ilse. 2006. "Looking Beyond the First Palaces: Elites and the Agency of Power in EM III–MM II Crete." *American Journal of Archaeology* 110 (1): 37–64.

Schouten, Jan Peters. 1995. *Revolution of the Mystics: On the Social Aspects of Vīraśaivism*. Kampen: Kok Pharos.

Schrecker, John E. 2004. *The Chinese Revolution in Historical Perspective*. Westport, CT: Praeger.

Schreiber, Katharina J. 1992. *Wari Imperialism in Middle Horizon Peru*. Ann Arbor, MI: Museum of Anthropology, University of Michigan.

Schreiber, Katharina J. 2001. "The Wari Empire of Middle Horizon Peru: The Epistemological Challenge of Documenting an Empire without Documentary Evidence." In *Empires: Perspectives from Archaeology and History*, edited by Susan E. Alcock, Terence N. D'Altroy, Kathleen D. Morrison, and Carla M. Sinopoli, 70–92. Cambridge: Cambridge University Press.

Schultz, Warren. 2006. "Mansa Musa's Gold in Mamluk Cairo: A Reappraisal of a World Civilizations Anecdote." In *History and Historiography of Post-Mongol Central Asia and the Middle East: Studies in Honor of John E. Woods*, edited by Judith Pfeiffer and Sholeh A. Quinn in collaboration with Ernest Tucker, 428–49. Wiesbaden: Harrassowitz Verlag.

Schwartz, Benjamin, ed. 1975. "Wisdom, Revelation, and Doubt: Perspectives on the First Millennium BC." *Themed issue of Daedalus* 104 (2).

Schwartz, Martin. 1985. "The Religion of Achaemenian Iran." In *The Cambridge History of Iran, vol. 2: The Median and Achaemenian Periods*, edited by I. Gershevitch, 664–97. Cambridge: Cambridge University Press.

Schwartz, Seth. 2004. "Historiography on the Jews in the 'Talmudic Period' (70–640 ce)." In *The Oxford Handbook of Jewish Studies*, edited by Martin Goodman. Oxford: Oxford University Press.

Schwartz, Seth. 2011. "Ancient Jewish Social Relations." In *The Oxford Handbook of Social Relations in the Roman World*, edited by Michael Peachin, 551–66. Oxford: Oxford University Press.

Schwimmer, Eric G. 1969. *Cultural Consequences of a Volcanic Eruption Experienced by the Mount Lamington Orokaiva*. Eugene, OR: Dept. of Anthropology, University of Oregon. Retrieved from http://ehrafworldcultures.yale.edu/document?id=oj23-022.

Schwimmer, Eric G. 1973. *Exchange in the Social Structure of the Orokaiva: Traditional and Emergent Ideologies in the Northern District of Papua*. London: C. Hurst. Retrieved from http://ehrafworldcultures.yale.edu/document?id=oj23-005.

Schwimmer, Eric G. 1977. "What Did the Eruption Mean?" In *Exiles and Migrants in Oceania*, edited by Michael D. Lieber, 296–341, 401–14. Honolulu: University Press of Hawaii. Retrieved from http://ehrafworldcultures.yale.edu/document?id=oj23-024.

Scullard, Howard H. 1989. "Carthage and Rome." In *The Cambridge Ancient History, vol. VII, pt. 2: The Rise of Rome to 220 B.C.*, edited by F. W. Walbank, A. E. Astin, M. W. Frederiksen, and R. M. Ogilvie, assisted by A. Drummond, 486–569. Cambridge: Cambridge University Press.

Seaton, S. Lee. 1974. "The Hawaiian *Kapu* Abolition of 1819." *American Ethnologist* 1 (1): 193–206. doi: 10.1525/ae.1974.1.1.02a00100.

Seeher, Jürgen. 1995. "Forty Years in the Capital of the Hittites: Peter Neve Retires from His Position as Director of the Ḫattuša-Boğazköy Excavations." *The Biblical Archaeologist* 58 (2): 63–67. doi: 10.2307/3210476.

Seeher, Jürgen. 2011. "The Plateau: The Hittites." In *The Oxford Handbook of Ancient Anatolia, 10,000–323 B.C.E.*, edited by Sharon R. Steadman and Gregory McMahon, 376–92. Oxford: Oxford University Press.

Seidel, Anna. [1978] 2008. "The Emperor and His Councillor: Laozi and Han Dynasty Taoism." *Studies in Chinese Art History* 17: 125–165. doi: 10.3406/asie.2008.1274.

Seidlmayer, Stephan. 2000. "The First Intermediate Period (c. 2160–2055 BC)." In *The Oxford History of Ancient Egypt*, edited by Ian Shaw, 108–36. Oxford: Oxford University Press.

Sekunda, Nicholas Victor. 1985. "Achaemenid Colonization in Lydia." *Revue des Études Anciennes* 87 (1–2): 7–30. doi: 10.3406/rea.1985.5544.

Selden, Sherman Ward. 1994. *Legend, Myth and Code of Deganawidah and Their Significance to Iroquois Cultural History*. Ann Arbor, MI: University Microfilms International. Retrieved from http://ehrafworldcultures.yale.edu/document?id=nm09-061.

Shahbazi, Alireza Shapour. 2012. "The Achaemenid Persian Empire (550–330 BCE)." In *The Oxford Handbook of Iranian History*, edited by Touraj Daryaee, 120–41. Oxford: Oxford University Press.

Shai, Itzhaq and Joe Uziel. 2010. "The Whys and Why Nots of Writing: Literacy and Illiteracy in the Southern Levant during the Bronze Ages." *Kaskal* 7: 67–83. doi: 10.1400/172116.

Shaki, Mansour. 1994. "Den." *Encyclopædia Iranica*, VII/3, 279–81. Updated version available online at http://www.iranicaonline.org/articles/den (accessed September 5, 2017).

Shaki, Mansour. 2009. "Judicial and Legal Systems ii. Parthian and Sasanian Judicial Systems." *Encyclopædia Iranica*, XV/2, 177–80. http://www.iranicaonline.org/articles/judicial-and-legal-systems-ii-parthian-and-sasanian-judicial-systems (accessed 20 September 2019).

Sharma, R. S. 2007. *India's Ancient Past*. Oxford: Oxford University Press.

Shattuck, Cybelle. 1999. *Hinduism*. London: Routledge.

Shattuck, Cybelle. 2002. *Hinduism*. London: Routledge.

Shaw, Ian. 2000a. "Egypt and the Outside World." In *The Oxford History of Ancient Egypt*, edited by Ian Shaw, 308–23. Oxford: Oxford University Press.

Shaw, Ian, ed. 2000b. *The Oxford History of Ancient Egypt*. Oxford: Oxford University Press.

Shayegan, M. Rahim. 2013. "Sasanian Political Ideology." In *The Oxford Handbook of Ancient Iran*, edited by Daniel T. Potts, 805–13. Oxford: Oxford University Press.

Shelmerdine, Cynthia W. 2008. "Background, Sources, and Methods." In *The Cambridge Companion to the Aegean Bronze Age*, edited by Cynthia W. Shelmerdine, 1–18. Cambridge: Cambridge University Press.

Shelmerdine, Cynthia W., and John Bennet. 2008. "Economy and Administration." In *The Cambridge Companion to the Aegean Bronze Age*, edited by Cynthia W. Shelmerdine, 289–309. Cambridge: Cambridge University Press.

Sherbondy, Jeanette E. 1992. "Water Ideology in Inca Ethnogenesis." In *Andean Cosmologies through Time: Persistence and Emergence*, edited by Robert V. H. Dover, Katharine E. Seibold, and John H. MacDowell, 46–66. Bloomington, IN: Indiana University Press.

Sherwin-White, A. N. 1977. "Roman Involvement in Anatolia, 167–88 B.C." *The Journal of Roman Studies* 67: 62–75. doi: 10.2307/299919.

Sherwin-White, Susan, and Amélie Kuhrt. 1993. *From Samarkhand to Sardis: A New Approach to the Seleucid Empire*. London: Duckworth.

Shi, Veronica. 2016. "The Function of the 'Axial Age' in Karl Jaspers' Philosophy of History: A Critical Response to *The Origin and Goal of History*." Unpublished paper.

Shimony, Annemarie. 1961. *Conservatism among the Iroquois at the Six Nations Reserve*. Yale University Publications in Anthropology. New Haven, CT: Department of Anthropology, Yale University. Retrieved from http://ehrafworldcultures.yale.edu/document?id=nm09-065.

Shults, F. LeRon, Wesley J. Wildman, Justin E. Lane, Christopher J. Lynch, and Saikou Diallo. 2018. "Multiple Axialities: A Computational Model of the Axial Age." *Journal of Cognition and Culture* 18 (5): 537–64. doi: 10.1163/15685373-12340043.

Siddiqui, Iqtidar Husain. 1986. "Water Works and Irrigation System in India during Pre-Mughal Times." *Journal of the Economic and Social History of the Orient* 29 (1): 52–77. doi: 10.2307/3632072.

Siddiqui, Iqtidar Husain. 2012. "Science of Medicine and Hospitals in India during the Delhi Sultanate Period." *Indian Historical Review* 39 (1): 11–18. doi: 10.1177/0376983612449526.

Sieroszewski, Wacław. 1993. *The Yakut: An Experiment in Ethnographic Research*. Moscow: Assotsiatsiia "Rossiiskaia polit. entsiklopediia." Retrieved from http://ehrafworldcultures.yale.edu/document?id=rv02-001.

Silverman, David P. 1995. "The Nature of Egyptian Kingship." In *Ancient Egyptian Kingship*, edited by David O'Connor and David P. Silverman, 49–92. Leiden: E. J. Brill.

Silverman, Helaine. 2004. "Introduction: Space and Time in the Central Andes." In *Andean Archaeology*, edited by Helaine Silverman, 1–15. Oxford: Blackwell.

Silverman, Jane. 1983. "To Marry Again." *The Hawaiian Journal of History* 17: 64–75.

Silverstein, Adam J. 2010. *Islamic History: A Very Short Introduction*. Oxford: Oxford University Press.

Simon, Kara. 2013. *Civil Society in China: The Legal Framework from Ancient Times to the "New Reform Era."* Oxford: Oxford University Press.

Simon, Mary L. 2017. "Reevaluating the Evidence for Middle Woodland Maize from the Holding Site." *American Antiquity* 82 (1): 140–50. doi: 10.1017/aaq.2016.2.

Simonis, Francis. 2010. *L'Afrique soudanaise au Moyen Age: Le temps des grands empires (Ghana, Mali, Songhai)*. Aix-Marseille: CRDP de l'Académie d'Aix-Marseille.

Sinclair, Paul J. J., Thurstan Shaw, and Bassey Andah. 1993. "Introduction." In *The Archaeology of Africa: Food, Metals and Towns*, edited by Thurstan Shaw, Paul Sinclair, Bassey Andah, and Alex Okpoko, 1–32. London: Routledge.

Singer, Itamar. 2002. *Hittite Prayers*, edited by Harry A. Hoffner, Jr. Leiden: Brill.

Singer, Itamar. 2006. "The Failed Reforms of Akhenaten and Muwatalli." *British Museum Studies in Ancient Egypt and Sudan* 6: 37–58.

Sinha, Tarunchandra. 1966. *The Psyche of the Garos*. Calcutta: Anthropological Survey of India, Govt. of India. Retrieved from http://ehrafworldcultures.yale.edu/document?id=ar05-018.

Sinopoli, Carla. 2001. "On the Edge of Empire: Form and Substance in the Satavahana Dynasty." In *Empires: Perspectives from Archaeology and History*, edited by Susan Alcock, Terence D'Altroy, Kathleen D. Morrison and Carla Sinopoli, 155–78. Cambridge: Cambridge University Press.

Sinopoli, Carla M., Roderick J. McIntosh, Ian Morris, and Alex R. Knodell. 2015. "The Distribution of Power: Hierarchy and Its Discontents." In *The Cambridge World History, vol. 4: Early Cities in Comparative Perspective, 4000 BCE–1200 CE*, edited by Norman Yoffee, 381–94. Cambridge: Cambridge University Press.

Sivan, Hagith. 2008. "Jerusalem and Iran." In *Encyclopædia Iranica*, XIV (6): 632–34. New York: Columbia University Press. Updated version available online at

Skilling, Peter. 2011. "Buddhism and Circulation Ritual in Early Peninsular Southeast Asia." In *Early Interactions Between South and Southeast Asia: Reflections on Cross-Cultural Exchange*, edited by Pierre-Yves Manguin, A. Mani, and Geoff Wade, 371–84. Singapore: Institute of Southeast Asian Studies.

Skjærvø, Prods Oktor. 2012. "Avestan Society." In *The Oxford Handbook of Iranian History*, edited by Touraj Daryaee, 57–119. Oxford: Oxford University Press.

Skjærvø, Prods Oktor. 2014. "Achaemenid Religion." *Religion Compass* 8 (6): 175–87. doi: 10.1111/rec3.12110.

Slingerland, Edward, et al. 2019. "Historians Respond to Whitehouse et al. (2019), 'Complex Societies Precede Moralizing Gods Throughout World History.'" *PsyArXiv* preprint: https://psyarxiv.com/2amjz/.

Smith, Adam T. 2000. "Rendering the Political Aesthetic: Political Legitimacy in Urartian Representations of the Built Environment." *Journal of Anthropological Archaeology* 19 (2): 131–63. doi: 10.1006/jaar.1999.0348.

Smith, Brian. 1994. *Classifying the Universe: The Ancient Indian Varna System and the Origins of Caste*. Oxford: Oxford University Press.

Smith, Kidder. 2003. "Sima Tan and the Invention of Daoism, 'Legalism,' et cetera." *The Journal of Asian Studies* 62 (1): 129–156. doi: 10.2307/3096138.

Smith, Robert Houston. 1990. "The Southern Levant in the Hellenistic Period." *Levant* 22 (1): 123–30. doi: 10.1179/lev.1990.22.1.123.

Smuts, Barbara. 1995. "The Evolutionary Origins of Patriarchy." *Human Nature* 6 (1): 1–32. doi: 10.1007/BF02734133.

Snape, Steven. 2011. *Ancient Egyptian Tombs: The Culture of Life and Death.* Chichester, England: Wiley-Blackwell.

Snodgrass, Anthony M. [1971] 2000. *The Dark Age of Greece: An Archaeological Survey of the Eleventh to the Eighth Centuries BC.* Reprinted with a new introduction. New York: Routledge.

Soar, Kathryn. 2009. "Old Bulls, New Tricks: The Reinvention of a Minoan Tradition." In *The Past in the Past: The Significance of Memory and Tradition in the Transmission of Culture*, edited by Mercourios Georgiadis and Chrysanthi Gallou, 16–27. Oxford: Archaeopress.

Soggin, J. Alberto. 1999. *An Introduction to the History of Israel and Judah.* Translated by John Bowden, 3rd ed. London: SCM Press.

Soha, El Achi. 2016. "Slavery." In *The Oxford Encyclopedia of Islam and Law*, edited by John L. Esposito. Online edition. Oxford: Oxford University Press.

Sohrab-Dinshaw Vevaina, Yuhan. 2015. "Theologies and Hermeneutics." In *The Wiley-Blackwell Companion to Zoroastrianism*, edited by Michael Stausberg and Yuhan Sohrab-Dinshaw Vevaina with Anna Tessmann, 211–34. Chichester, England: Wiley-Blackwell.

Sonn, Tamara. 1996. "Political Authority in Classical Islamic Thought." *American Journal of Islamic Social Sciences* 13 (3): 366–81.

Sonn, Tamara. 2010. *A Brief History of Islam.* Chichester, England: Wiley-Blackwell.

Sowerwine, James E. 2011. *Caliph and Caliphate: Oxford Bibliographies Online Research Guide.* Oxford: Oxford University Press.

Spalinger, Anthony. 2013. "The Organisation of the Pharaonic Army (Old to New Kingdom)." In *Ancient Egyptian Administration*, edited by Juan Carlos Moreno García, 393–478. Leiden: Brill.

St. John, Donald Patrick. 1994. *Dream-Vision Experience of the Iroquois: Its Religious Meaning.* Ann Arbor, MI: University Microfilms International. Retrieved from http://ehrafworldcultures.yale.edu/document?id=nm09-062.

Stahl, Ann Brower. 2004. "Political Economic Mosaics: Archaeology of the Last Two Millennia in Tropical Sub-Saharan Africa." *Annual Review of Anthropology* 33: 145–72. doi: 10.1146/annurev.anthro.33.070203.143841.

Stark, Miriam T. 1998. "The Transition to History in the Mekong Delta: A View from Cambodia." *International Journal of Historical Archaeology* 2 (3): 175–203. doi: 10.1023/A:1027368225043.

Stark, Miriam T. 2003. "Angkor Borei and the Archaeology of Cambodia's Mekong Delta." In *Art and Archaeology of Fu Nan*, edited by James C. M. Khoo, 87–106. Bangkok: The Southeast Asian Ceramic Society.

Stark, Miriam T. 2004. "Pre-Angkorian and Angkorian Cambodia." In *Southeast Asia: From Prehistory to History*, edited by Ian Glover and Peter Bellwood, 89–119. London: RoutledgeCurzon.

Stark, Miriam T. 2006. "Early Mainland Southeast Asian Landscapes in the First Millennium A.D." *Annual Review of Anthropology* 35: 407–32. doi: 10.1146/annurev.anthro.35.081705.123157.

Starnes, Casey. 2009. "Ancient Visions: The Roots of Judeo-Christian Apocalypse." In *End of Days: Essays on the Apocalypse from Antiquity to Modernity*, edited by Karolyn Kinane and Michael A. Ryan, 27–46. Jefferson: McFarland & Company.

Starr, Chester G. 1984. "Minoan Flower Lovers." In *The Minoan Thalassocracy: Myth and Reality*, edited by Robin Hägg and Nanno Marinatos, 9–12. Stockholm: Svenska institutet i Athen.

Stausberg, Michael. 2000. "Hell in Zoroastrian History." *Numen* 56: 217–253. doi: 10.1163/156852709X404991.

Stausberg, Michael and Yuhan Sohrab-Dinshaw Vevaina. 2015. "Introduction: Scholarship on Zoroastrianism." In *The Wiley-Blackwell Companion to Zoroastrianism*, edited by Michael Stausberg and Yuhan Sohrab-Dinshaw Vevaina with Anna Tessmann, 1–18. Chichester, England: Wiley-Blackwell.

Stein, Burton. 1998. *A History of India*. Oxford: Blackwell.

Steinmetz, Sebald. 1898/99. "Classification des types sociaux." *L'Année Sociologique* 3: 43–147.

Stepaniants, M. T. 2002. "The Encounter of Zoroastrianism with Islam." *Philosophy East and West* 52 (2): 159–172. doi: 10.1353/pew.2002.0030.

Stevens, Anna. 2009. "Domestic Religious Practices." In *UCLA Encyclopedia of Egyptology*, edited by Willeke Wendrich and Jacco Dieleman. Accessible online at http://digital2.library.ucla.edu/

Stevenson, Alice. 2016. "The Egyptian Predynastic and State Formation." *Journal of Archaeological Research* 24: 421–68. doi: 10.1007/s10814-016-9094-7.

Stiner, Mary C., Hijlke Buitenhuis, Güneş Duru, Steven L. Kuhn, Susan M. Mentzer, Natalie D. Munro, Nadja Pöllath, et al. 2014. "A Forager-Herder Trade-Off, from Broad-Spectrum Hunting to Sheep Management at Aşıklı Höyük, Turkey." *Proceedings of the National Academy of Sciences* 111: 8404–09. doi: 10.1073/pnas.1322723111.

Stockwell, Stephen. 2010. "Before Athens: Early Popular Government in Phoenician and Greek City States." *Geopolitics, History, and International Relations* 2 (2): 123–35.

Stockwell, Stephen. 2012. "Israel and Phoenicia." In *The Edinburgh Companion to the History of Democracy*, edited by Benjamin Isakhan and Stephen Stockwell, 71–81. Edinburgh: Edinburgh University Press.

Stolper, Matthew W. and Béatrice André-Salvini. 1992. "The Written Record." In *The Royal City of Susa: Ancient Near Eastern Treasures in the Louvre*, edited by Prudence O. Harper, Joan Aruz, and Françoise Tallon, 253–78. New York: The Metropolitan Museum of Art.

Stone, Lawson G. 2014. "Early Israel and Its Appearance in Canaan." In *Ancient Israel's History: An Introduction to Issues and Sources*, edited by Bill T. Arnold and Richard S. Hess, 127–64. Grand Rapids: Baker Academic.

Strootman, Rolf. 2015. "Seleucid Empire." In *Encyclopædia Iranica*. Online edition. http://www.iranicaonline.org/articles/seleucid-empire (accessed November 27, 2017).

Stuart-Glennie, John S. 1873. In *The Morningland: Or, the Law of the Origin and Transformation of Christianity, vol. 1: The New Philosophy of History*. London: Longmans, Green, and Company.

Sullivan, C. S. 2003. "Merit." In *The New Catholic Encyclopedia*, vol. 9, edited by Catholic University of America. Detroit: Thomson/Gale.

Sumner, J. La Croix, and James Roumasset. 1984. "An Economic Theory of Political Change in Premissionary Hawaii." *Explorations in Economic History* 21 (2): 151–68. doi: 10.1016/0014-4983(84)90022-6.

Sun, Anna Xiao. 2017. *Confucianism as a World Religion: Contested Histories and Contemporary Realities.* Princeton, NJ: Princeton University Press.

Sundelin, Lennart. 2013. "Egypt: Tulunids and Ikhshidids, 850–969." In *Encyclopedia of African History*, vol. 1, edited by K. Shillington, 430–31. London: Routledge.

Sundermann, Werner. 2009. "Manicheism i: General Survey." In *Encyclopædia Iranica.* Online edition. http://www.iranicaonline.org/articles/manicheism-1-general-survey (accessed December 4, 2017).

Sutlive Jr., Vinson H., and John Beierle. 1995. "Culture Summary: Iban." New Haven, CT: HRAF. Retrieved from http://ehrafworldcultures.yale.edu/document?id=oc06-000.

Szpakowska, Kasia. 2010. "Religion in Society: Pharaonic." In *A Companion to Ancient Egypt*, vol. 1, edited by Alan B. Lloyd, 507–26. Chichester, England: Wiley-Blackwell.

Taffet, Avia and Jak Yakar. 1998. "Politics and Religion in Urartu." In *Essays on Ancient Anatolia in the Second Millennium B.C.*, edited by H. I. H. Prince Takahito Mikasa, 133–52. Wiesbaden: Harrassowitz Verlag.

Tamari, Tal. 1991. "The Development of Caste Systems in West Africa." *The Journal of African History* 32 (2): 221–50. doi: 10.1017/S0021853700025718.

Tambiah, Stanley J. 2013 [1978]. "The Galactic Polity in Southeast Asia. Reprint." *HAU: Journal of Ethnographic Theory* 3(3): 503–534. doi: 10.14318/hau3.3.033.

Taracha, Piotr. 2009. *Religions of Second Millennium Anatolia.* Wiesbaden: Harrassowitz Verlag.

Tartaron, Thomas F. 2007. "Aegean Prehistory as World Archaeology: Recent Trends in the Archaeology of Bronze Age Greece." *Journal of Archaeological Research* 16: 83–161. doi: 10.1007/s10814-007-9018-7.

Tatišvili, Irene. 2010. "Some Remarks on a Passage of the Apology of Ḫattusili III." In *Pax Hethitica: Studies on the Hittites and Their Neighbours in Honour of Itamar Singer*, edited by Yoram Cohen, Amir Gilan, and Jared L. Miller, 356–61. Wiesbaden: Harrassowitz Verlag.

Tavernier, Jan. 2013. "Elamite and Old Iranian Afterlife Concepts." In *Susa and Elam: Archaeological, Philological, Historical and Geographical Perspectives*, edited by Katrien De Graef and Jan Tavernier, 471–89. Leiden: Brill.

Temple, Wayne. 1966. *Indian Villages of the Illinois Country: Historic Tribes.* 2nd ed. Springfield, IL: Illinois State Museum.

Thapar, Romila. 1971. "The Image of the Barbarian in Early India." *Comparative Studies in Society and History* 13 (4): 408–36. doi: 10.1017/S0010417500006393.

Thapar, Romila. 1997. *Ashoka and the Decline of the Mauryas.* Oxford: Oxford University Press.

Thomas, Carol G. 1976. "The Nature of Mycenaean Kingship." *SMEA* 17: 109–11.

Thomas, Zachary. 2016. "Debating the United Monarchy: Let's See How Far We've Come." *Biblical Theology Bulletin: Journal of Bible and Culture* 46 (2): 59–69. doi: 10.1177/0146107916639208.

Thompson, Andrew R., Kristin M. Hedman, and Philip A. Slater. 2015. "New Dental and Isotope Evidence of Biological Distance and Place of Origin for Mass Burial Groups at Cahokia's Mound 72." *American Journal of Physical Anthropology* 158: 341-357. doi: 10.1002/ajpa.22791.

Thompson, Dorothy J. 2005. "The Ptolemies and Egypt." In *A Companion to the Hellenistic World*, edited by Andrew Erskine, 105-20. Malden: Blackwell Publishing.

Thompson, Laurence. 1989. "On the Prehistory of Hell in China." *Journal of Chinese Religions* 17 (1): 27-41. doi: 10.1179/073776989805896107.

Thonemann, Peter. 2013. "Phrygia: An Anarchist History, 950 BC-AD 100." In *Roman Phrygia: Culture and Society*, edited by Peter Thonemann, 1-40. Cambridge: Cambridge University Press.

Thonemann, Peter. 2016. *The Hellenistic Age*. Oxford: Oxford University Press.

Thuesen, Ingolf. 2002. "The Neo-Hittite City-States." In *A Comparative Study of Six City-State Cultures: An Investigation Conducted by the Copenhagen Polis Centre*, edited by Mogens Herman Hansen, 43-56. Copenhagen: Den Kongelige Danske Videnskabernes Selskab.

Tilly, Charles. 1992. *Coercion, Capital, and European States, AD 990-1992*. Cambridge, MA: Blackwell.

Togola, Téréba. 2000. "Memories, Abstractions, and Conceptualization of Ecological Crisis in the Mande World." In *The Way the Wind Blows: Climate, History, and Human Action*, edited by Roderick J. McIntosh, Joseph A. Tainter, and Susan Keech McIntosh, 181-92. New York: Columbia University Press.

Tokarev, S. A., and S. I. Gurvich. 1964. "The Yakuts." In *The Peoples of Siberia*, edited by M. G. Levin and L. P. Potapov, 243-304, 904-05. Chicago: University of Chicago Press. Retrieved from http://ehrafworldcultures.yale.edu/document?id=rv02-053.

Torpey, John. 2017. *The Three Axial Ages: Moral, Material, Mental*. New Brunswick, NJ: Rutgers University Press.

Treadgold, Warren T. 1997. *A History of the Byzantine State and Society*. Stanford: Stanford University Press.

Trigger, Bruce G. 1972. "Determinations of Growth in Pre-Industrial Societies." In *Man, Settlement, and Urbanism*, edited by Peter J. Ucko, Ruth Tringham, and G. W. Dimbleby, 575-99. London: Duckworth.

Trigger, Bruce G. 1993. *Early Civilizations: Ancient Egypt in Context*. Cairo: The American University in Cairo Press.

Trigger, Bruce G. 2003. *Understanding Early Civilizations*. Cambridge: Cambridge University Press.

Tripolitis, Antonía. 2002. *Religions of the Hellenistic-Roman Age*. Grand Rapids: William B. Eerdmans Publishing Company.

Tsetskhladze, Gocha R. 2006. "Revisiting Ancient Greek Colonisation." In *Greek Colonisation: An Account of Greek Colonies and Other Settlements Overseas*, vol. 1, edited by Gocha R. Tsetskhladze, xxiii-lxxxiii. Leiden: Brill.

Tung, Tiffiny A. 2014. "Making Warriors, Making War: Violence and Militarism in the Wari Empire." In *Embattled Bodies, Embattled Places: War in Pre-Columbian America*, edited by Andrew K. Scherer and John W. Verano, 227-56. Washington, DC: Dumbarton Oaks.

Tung, Tiffiny A., and Kelly J. Knudson. 2010. "Childhood Lost: Abductions, Sacrifice, and Trophy Heads of Children in the Wari Empire of the Ancient Andes." *Latin American Antiquity* 21 (1): 44–66. doi: 10.7183/1045-6635.21.1.44.

Tuplin, Christopher. 2008. "The Seleucids and Their Achaemenid Predecessors: A Persian Inheritance?" In *Ancient Greece and Ancient Iran: Cross-Cultural Encounters*, edited by Seyed Mohammad Reza Darbandi and Antigoni Zournatzi, 109–36. Athens: National Hellenic Research Foundation.

Turchin, Peter. 2011. "Warfare and the Evolution of Social Complexity: A Multilevel Selection Approach." *Structure and Dynamics* 4 (3, Article 2): 1–37.

Turchin, Peter. 2012. "Religion and Empire in the Axial Age." *Religion, Brain & Behavior* 2 (3): 256–60. doi: 10.1080/2153599X.2012.721220.

Turchin, Peter. 2014. "Cultural Evolution and Cliodynamics." *Cliodynamics: The Journal of Quantitative History and Cultural Evolution* 5 (1): 1–3. doi: 10.21237/C7clio5125308.

Turchin, Peter. 2016. *Ultrasociety: How 10,000 Years of War Made Humans the Greatest Cooperators on Earth.* Chaplin, CT: Beresta Books.

Turchin, Peter. 2018. "Fitting Dynamic Regression Models to Seshat Data." *Cliodynamics* 9 (1): 25–58. doi: 10.21237/C7clio9137696.

Turchin, Peter, Rob Brennan, Thomas E. Currie, Kevin C. Feeney, Pieter François, Daniel Hoyer, J. G. Manning et al. 2015. "Seshat: The Global History Databank." *Cliodynamics* 6: 77–107. doi: 10.21237/C7clio6127917.

Turchin, Peter, Agathe Dupeyron, Thomas E. Currie, Harvey Whitehouse, Pieter François, Kevin C. Feeney, Daniel Hoyer, et al. In Prep. "The Rise and Fall of Human Sacrifice in the Evolution of Sociopolitical Complexity."

Turchin, Peter, and Sergey Gavrilets. 2009. "Evolution of Complex Hierarchical Societies." *Social History and Evolution* 8 (2):167–198.

Tylor, Edward B. 1871. *Primitive Culture: Researches into the Development of Mythology, Philosophy, Religion, Art, and Custom.* London: John Murray.

Uffenheimer, Benjamin. 1986. "Myth and Reality in Ancient Israel." In *The Origins and Diversity of Axial Age Civilizations*, edited by Shmuel N. Eisenstadt, 135–68. Albany: State University of New York Press.

Uhalde, Kevin. 2012. "Justice and Equality." In *The Oxford Handbook of Late Antiquity*, edited by Scott Fitzgerald Johnson, 764–79. Oxford: Oxford University Press.

Urton, Gary. 2015. "Ethnicity." In *Encyclopedia of the Incas*, edited by Gary Urton and Adriana von Hagen, 130–31. Lanham, MD: Rowman & Littlefield.

Valeri, Valerio. 1985. *Kingship and Sacrifice: Ritual and Society in Ancient Hawaii.* Translated by Paula Wissing. Chicago: University of Chicago Press.

Vallat, François. 1998. "Elam vi: Elamite Religion." In *Encyclopædia Iranica*, VIII/3, 335–36 and VIII/4, 342. Updated version available online at http://www.iranicaonline.org/articles/elam-vi (accessed August 22, 2017).

Van de Mieroop, Marc. 2007. *A History of the Ancient Near East ca. 3000–323 BC.* 2nd ed. Malden, MA: Blackwell.

Van De Mieroop, Marc. 2011. *A History of Ancient Egypt.* Chichester, England: Wiley-Blackwell.

van den Hout, Theo P. J. 2011. "The Written Legacy of the Hittites." In *Insights into Hittite History and Archaeology*, edited by Hermann Genz and Dirk Paul Mielke, 47–84. Leuven: Peeters.

van der Spek, Robartus Johannes. 2014. "Cyrus the Great, Exiles, and Foreign Gods: A Comparison of Assyrian and Persian Policies on Subject Nations." In *Extraction & Control: Studies in Honor of Matthew W. Stolper*, edited by Michael Kozuh, Wouter F. M. Henkelman, Charles E. Jones, and Christopher Woods, 233–64. Chicago: The Oriental Institute of the University of Chicago.

Van Dijk, Jacobus. 2000. "The Amarna Period and the Later New Kingdom (c. 1352–1069 BC)." In *The Oxford History of Ancient Egypt*, edited by Ian Shaw, 265–307. Oxford: Oxford University Press.

van Dommelen, Peter. 2005. "Colonial Interactions and Hybrid Practices: Phoenician and Carthaginian Settlement in the Mediterranean." In *The Archaeology of Colonial Encounters: Comparative Perspectives*, edited by Gil J. Stein, 109–41. Sante Fe: School of American Research Press.

van Minnen, Peter. 2007. "Review of Das Dekret von Kanopos (238 v. Chr.). Kommentar und historische Auswertung eines dreisprachigen Synodaldekretes der ägyptischen Priester zu ehren Ptolemaios' III. und seiner Familie by Stefan Pfeiffer." *Gnomon* 79 (8): 709–13.

Van Norden, Bryan. 2007. *Virtue Ethics and Consequentialism in Early Chinese Philosophy.* Cambridge: Cambridge University Press.

Van Norden, Bryan. 2011. *Introduction to Classical Chinese Philosophy.* Indianapolis: Hackett Publishing.

van Seters, John. 1972. "The Terms 'Amorite' and 'Hittite' in the Old Testament." *Vetus Testamentum* 22 (1): 64–81. doi: 10.1163/156853372X00488.

Vanderhooft, David. 2006. "Cyrus II, Liberator or Conqueror? Ancient Historiography Concerning Cyrus in Babylon." In *Judah and the Judeans in the Persian Period*, edited by Oded Lipschits and Manfred Oeming, 351–72. Winona Lake: Eisenbrauns.

Vandorpe, Katelijn. 2010. "The Ptolemaic Period." In *A Companion to Ancient Egypt, vol. 1*, edited by Alan B. Lloyd, 159–79. Chichester, England: Wiley-Blackwell.

Vanschoonwinkel, Jacques. 2006. "Greek Migrations to Aegean Anatolia in the Early Dark Age." In *Greek Colonisation: An Account of Greek Colonies and Other Settlements Overseas*, vol. 1, edited by Gocha R. Tsetskhladze, 115–42. Leiden: Brill.

Venetis, Evangelos. 2012. "Iran at the Time of Alexander the Great and the Seleucids." In *The Oxford Handbook of Iranian History*, edited by Touraj Daryaee, 142–63. Oxford: Oxford University Press.

Venning, Timothy. 2011. *A Chronology of the Roman Empire.* London: Continuum.

Verboven, Koenraad. 2002. *The Economy of Friends: Economic Aspects of Amicitia and Patronage in the Late Republic.* Brussels: Editions Latomus.

Vickery, Michael, 1986. "Some Remarks on Early State Formation in Cambodia." In *Southeast Asia in the 9th to 14th Centuries*, edited by David G. Marr and A. C. Milner, 95–115. Singapore: Institute of Southeast Asian Studies.

Vickery, Michael. 1998. *Society, Economics, and Politics in pre-Angkor Cambodia: The 7th-8th Centuries*. Tokyo: Centre for East Asian Cultural Studies for UNESCO.

Voegelin, Eric. 1974. *Order and History, vol. 4: The Ecumenic Age*. Baton Rouge: Louisiana State University Press.

Voigt, Mary M. and Robert C. Henrickson. 2000. "Formation of the Phrygian State: The Early Iron Age at Gordion." *Anatolian Studies* 50: 37–54. doi: 10.2307/3643013.

von Falkenhausen, Lothar. 2006. *Chinese Society in the Age of Confucius (1000–250 BC): The Archaeological Evidence*. Los Angeles, CA: Cotsen Institute of Archaeology, University of California, Los Angeles.

von Glahn, Richard. 2016. *An Economic History of China: From Antiquity to the Nineteenth Century*. Cambridge: Cambridge University Press.

Waddell, Eric, and P. A. Krinks. 1968. *Organisation of Production and Distribution among the Orokaiva: An Analysis of Work and Exchange in Two Communities Participating in Both the Subsistence and Monetary Sectors of the Economy*. New Guinea Research Bulletin. Canberra: New Guinea Research Unit, Australian National University. Retrieved from http://ehrafworldcultures.yale.edu/document?id=oj23-008.

Wadley, Reed L. 2001. "Trouble on the Frontier: Dutch-Brooke Relations and Iban Rebellion in the West Borneo Borderlands (1841–86)." *Modern Asian Studies* 35 (3): 623–44. doi: 10.1017/S0026749X01003055.

Wallace, Robert W. 2016. "Equality, the *Dêmos*, and Law in Archaic Greece." In *Symposion 2015: Conferências sobre a História do Direito grego e helenístico (Coimbra, 1–4 Setembro 2015) / Vorträge zur griechischen und hellenistischen Rechtsgeschichte (Coimbra, 1.–4. September 2015)*, edited by Delfim F. Leão and Gerhard Thür, 1–14. Vienna: Verlag der Österreichischen Akademie der Wissenschaften.

Wallace, Saro. 2018. *Travellers in Time: Imagining Movement in the Ancient Aegean World*. Abingdon: Routledge.

Wallace, Shane. 2014. "Defending the Freedom of the Greeks: Antigonos, Telesphoros, and the Olympic Games of 312 B.C." *Phoenix* 68 (3/4): 235–46. doi: 10.7834/phoenix.68.3-4.0235.

Wallace, Vesna. 2015. *Buddhism in Mongolian History, Culture, and Society*. New York: Oxford University Press.

Walthall, John A., and Thomas E. Emerson. 1992. "Indians and French in the Midcontinent." In *Calumet and Fleur-De-Lys: French and Indian Interaction in the Midcontinent*, edited by John A. Walthall and Thomas E. Emerson, 1–13. Washington, DC: Smithsonian Institution Press.

Walzer, Michael, Menachem Lorberbaum, Noam Zohar, and Yair Lorberbaum. 2000. *The Jewish Political Tradition, vol. 1: Authority*. New Haven, CT: Yale University Press.

Watanabe, Hitoshi. 1990. *Jomonshiki Kaisoka Shakai* [Jomon-type stratified society]. Tokyo: Rokko Shuppan.

Waters, Matthew W. 2000. *A Survey of Neo-Elamite History*. Helsinki: The Neo-Assyrian Text Corpus Project.

Waters, Matthew W. 2014. *Ancient Persia: A Concise History of the Achaemenid Empire, 550–330 BCE*. Cambridge: Cambridge University Press.

Watts, Joseph, Oliver Sheehan, Quentin D. Atkinson, Joseph Bulbulia, and Russell D. Gray. 2016. "Ritual Human Sacrifice Promoted and Sustained the Evolution of Stratified Societies." *Nature* 532: 228–31. doi: 10.1038/nature17159.

Webb Jr., James L. A. 2006. "Ecology & Culture in West Africa." In *Themes in West Africa's History*, edited by Emmanuel Kwaku Akyeampong, 33–51. Athens: Ohio University Press.

Weber, Alfred. 1935. *Kulturgeschichte als Kultursoziologie*. Leiden: A. W. Sijthoff.

Weber, Max. 1949. *The Theory of Economic and Social Organization*. Translated by A. M. Henderson and Talcott Parsons. Glencoe, IL: The Free Press.

Weber, Max. 2013. *Economy and Society: An Outline of Interpretive Sociology*, edited by Guenther Roth and Claus Wittich. 2 vols. Berkeley, CA: University of California Press.

Weinfeld, Moshe. 1986. "The Protest against Imperialism in Ancient Israelite Prophecy." In *The Origins and Diversity of Axial Age Civilizations*, edited by Shmuel N. Eisenstadt, 169–82. Albany: State University of New York Press.

Weiss, Bernard G. 1998. *The Spirit of Islamic Law*. Athens: University of Georgia Press.

Weller, Robert P., Julia Huang, Wu Keping, and Fan Lizhu. 2018. *Religion and Charity: The Social Life of Goodness in Chinese Societies*. Cambridge: Cambridge University Press.

Wells, Bruce. 2005. "Law and Practice." In *A Companion to the Ancient Near East*, edited by Daniel C. Snell, 183–95. Malden: Blackwell Publishing.

Wengrow, David, and David Graeber. 2015. "Farewell to the 'Childhood of Man': Ritual, Seasonality, and the Origins of Inequality." *Journal of the Royal Anthropological Institute* 21 (3): 597–619. doi: 10.1111/1467-9655.12247.

Wenke, Robert J. 1981. "Elymeans, Parthians, and the Evolution of Empires in Southwestern Iran." *Journal of the American Oriental Society* 101 (3): 303–15. doi: 10.2307/602592.

Whaling, Frank. 2009. *Understanding Hinduism*. Edinburgh: Dunedin Academic Press.

Wheeler, Mortimer. [1947] 1979. "Harappan Chronology and the *Rig Veda*." In *Ancient Cities of the Indus*, edited by G. Possehl, 289–92. New Delhi, India: Vikas.

White, Douglas R., and Michael L. Burton. 1988. "Causes of Polygyny: Ecology, Economy, Kinship, and Warfare." *American Anthropologist* 90 (4): 871–87. doi: 10.1525/aa.1988.90.4.02a00060.

White, Joyce C., and Elizabeth G. Hamilton. 2009. "The Transmission of Early Bronze Technology to Thailand: New Perspectives." *Journal of World Prehistory* 22 (4): 357–97. doi: 10.1007/s10963-009-9029-z.

White, J. C., and V. C. Pigott. 1996. "From Community Craft to Regional Specialization: Intensification of Copper Production in Prestate Thailand." In *Craft Specialization and Social Evolution: In Memory of V. Gordon Childe*, edited by B. Wailes, 151–75. Philadelphia: University of Pennsylvania Museum of Archaeology and Anthropology.

Whitehouse, Harvey. 1995. *Inside the Cult: Religious Innovation and Transmission in Papua New Guinea*. Oxford: Oxford University Press.

Whitehouse, Harvey. 1996. "Rites of Terror: Emotion, Metaphor, and Memory in Melanesian Initiation Cults." *Journal of the Royal Anthropological Institute* 4: 703–715. doi: 10.2307/3034304.

Whitehouse, Harvey. 2000. *Arguments and Icons: Divergent Modes of Religiosity*. Oxford: Oxford University Press.

Whitehouse, Harvey. 2004. *Modes of Religiosity: A Cognitive Theory of Religious Transmission*. Walnut Creek, CA: AltaMira Press.

Whitehouse, Harvey. 2018. "Dying for the Group: Towards a General Theory of Extreme Self-Sacrifice." *Behavioral and Brain Sciences* 41: e192. doi: 10.1017/S0140525X18000249.

Whitehouse, Harvey, Pieter François, Patrick E. Savage, Thomas E. Currie, Kevin C. Feeney, Enrico Cioni, Rosalind Purcell, et al. 2019. "Complex Societies Precede Moralizing Gods throughout World History." *Nature* 56: 226–29. doi: 10.1038/s41586-019-1043-4.

Whitehouse, Harvey, and Ian Hodder. 2010. "Modes of Religiosity at Çatalhöyük." In *Religion in the Emergence of Civilization: Çatalhöyük as a Case Study*, edited by Ian Hodder, 122–45. Cambridge: Cambridge University Press.

Whitehouse, Harvey, and Jonathan A. Lanman. 2014. "The Ties that Bind Us: Ritual, Fusion, and Identification." Current Anthropology 55 (6): 674–95. doi: 10.1086/678698.

Whitehouse, Harvey, Camilla Mazzucato, Ian Hodder, and Quentin D. Atkinson. 2013. "Modes of Religiosity and the Evolution of Social Complexity at Çatalhöyük." In *Religion at Work in a Neolithic Society: Vital Matters*, edited by Ian Hodder, 134–55. Cambridge: Cambridge University Press.

Whiten, Andrew. 2011. "The Scope of Culture in Chimpanzees, Humans and Ancestral Apes." *Philosophical Transactions of the Royal Society* B 366: 997–1007. doi: 10.1098/rstb.2010.0334.

Wiesehöfer, Josef. 1986. "Ardašīr I i: History." In *Encyclopædia Iranica*, II/4, 371–76. Updated version available online at http://www.iranicaonline.org/articles/ardasir-i (accessed August 18, 2017).

Wiesehöfer, Josef. 2009. "The Achaemenid Empire." In *The Dynamics of Ancient Empires: State Power from Assyria to Byzantium*, edited by Ian Morris and Walter Scheidel, 66–98. Oxford: Oxford University Press.

Wiesehöfer, Josef. 2013. "Law and Religion in Achaemenid Iran." In *Law and Religion in the Eastern Mediterranean: From Antiquity to Early Islam*, edited by Anselm C. Hagedorn and Reinhard G. Kratz, 41–58. Oxford: Oxford University Press.

Wilkinson, Toby. 2010a. "The Early Dynastic Period." In *A Companion to Ancient* Egypt, vol. 1, edited by Alan B. Lloyd, 48–62. Chichester, England: Wiley-Blackwell.

Wilkinson, Toby. 2010b. *The Rise and Fall of Ancient Egypt: The History of a Civilisation from 3000 BC to Cleopatra*. London: Bloomsbury.

Willerslev, Rane. 2011. "Frazer Strikes Back from the Armchair: A New Search for the Animist soul." *Journal of the Royal Anthropological Institute* 17 (3): 504–26. doi: 10.1111/j.1467-9655.2011.01704.x.

Williams, F. E. 1928. *Orokaiva Magic*. London: Oxford University Press; H. Milford. Retrieved from http://ehrafworldcultures.yale.edu/document?id=oj23-002.

Williams, F. E., and Hubert Murray. 1930. *Orokaiva Society*. London: Oxford University Press. Retrieved from http://ehrafworldcultures.yale.edu/document?id=oj23-001.

Williams, Patrick Ryan. 2002. "Rethinking Disaster-Induced Collapse in the Demise of the Andean Highland States: Wari and Tiwanaku." *World Archaeology* 33 (3): 361-74. doi: 10.1080/00438240120107422.

Wilson, Andrew I. 2008. "Hydraulic Engineering and Water Supply." In *The Oxford Handbook of Engineering and Technology in the Classical World*, edited by John Peter Oleson, 285-318. Oxford: Oxford University Press.

Wilson, Constance M. 1980. "Nineteenth-Century Thai Administration: Are Our Models Adequate?" In *Royalty and Commoners: Essays in Thai Administrative, Economic, and Social History*, edited by Constance M. Wilson, Chrystal Stillings Smith, and George Vinal Smith, 29-40. Leiden: Brill.

Wilson, David Sloan. 2015. *Does Altruism Exist? Culture, Genes, and the Welfare of Others*. New Haven, CT: Yale University Press.

Wilson, David Sloan, Elinor Ostrom, and Michael E. Cox. 2013. "Generalizing the Core Design Principles for the Efficacy of Groups." *Journal of Economic Behavior & Organization*, Supplement 90: S21–S32. doi: 10.1016/j.jebo.2012.12.010.

Wilson, E. O. 1975. *Sociobiology: The New Synthesis*. Cambridge, MA: Harvard University Press.

Wiltermuth, Scott S., and Chip Heath. 2009. "Synchrony and Cooperation." *Psychological Science* 20: 1–5. doi: 10.1111/j.1467-9280.2008.02253.x.

Winternitz, Rudolf. 1887. "Einige Bemerkungen über das Bauopfer bei den Inder." *Mittheilungen der anthropologischen Gesellschaft in Wien* 17: 37–40.

Wittrock, Björn. 2005. "The Meaning of the Axial Age." In *Axial Civilizations and World History*, edited by Johann P. Arnason, S. N. Eisenstadt, and Björn Wittrock, 51-86. Leiden: Brill.

Wittrock, Björn. 2012. "The Axial Age in Global History: Cultural Crystallizations and Societal Transformations." In *The Axial Age and Its Consequences*, edited by Robert N. Bellah and Hans Joas, 102–25. Cambridge: The Belknap Press of Harvard University Press.

Wolpert, S. A. 1997. *A New History of India*. Oxford: Oxford University Press.

Wolters, Oliver W. 1979. "Khmer 'Hinduism' in the Seventh Century." In *Early South East Asia: Essays in Archaeology, History, and Historical Geography*, edited by R. B. Smith and W. Watson, 427-42. New York and Kuala Lumpur: Oxford University Press.

Wolters, Oliver W. 2008. *Early Southeast Asia: Selected Essays*, edited by Craig J. Reynolds. Ithaca, NY: Cornell Southeast Asia Program Publications.

Woodburn, James. 1982. "Egalitarian Societies." *Man* 17 (3): 431–51.

Woodhead, Linda. 2004. *Christianity: A Short Introduction*. Oxford: Oxford University Press.

Work, Courtney. 2017. "The Persistent Presence of Cambodian Spirits: Contemporary Knowledge Production in Cambodia." In *The Handbook of Contemporary Cambodia*, edited by Katherine Brickell and Simon Springer, 389-98. Abingdon: Routledge.

Wrangel, Ferdinand Petrovich, and Edward Sabine. 1842. *Narrative of an Expedition to the Polar Sea, in the Years 1820, 1821, 1822, and 1823*. New York: Harper and Brothers. Retrieved from http://ehrafworldcultures.yale.edu/document?id=rv02-024.

Wyatt, David K. 1984. *Thailand: A Short History*. New Haven, CT: Yale University Press.

Xiong, Victor Cunrui. 2009. *Historical Dictionary of Medieval China*. Plymouth: Scarecrow Press.

Yakubovich, Ilya. 2005. "Were Hittite Kings Divinely Anointed? A Palaic Invocation to the Sun-God and Its Significance for Hittite Religion." *Journal of Ancient Near Eastern Religions* 5 (1): 107–37. doi: 10.1163/156921205776137972.

Yakubovich, Ilya. 2011. "Luwian and the Luwians." In *The Oxford Handbook of Ancient Anatolia, 10,000–323 B.C.E.*, edited by Sharon R. Steadman and Gregory McMahon, 534–47. Oxford: Oxford University Press.

Yao Xinzhong. 2000. *An Introduction to Confucianism*. Cambridge: Cambridge University.

Yaran, Cafer S. 2007. *Understanding Islam*. Edinburgh: Dunedin Academic Press.

Yarshater, Ehsan. 1983. "Introduction." In *The Cambridge History of Iran, vol. 3 (I): The Seleucid, Parthian and Sasanian Periods*, edited by Ehsan Yarshater, xvii–lxxv. Cambridge: Cambridge University Press.

Yasur-Landau, Assaf, Eric H. Cline, Andrew J. Koh, David Ben-Shlomo, Nimrod Marom, Alexandra Ratzlaff, and Inbal Samet. 2015. "Rethinking Canaanite Palaces? The Palatial Economy of Tel Kabri during the Middle Bronze Age." *Journal of Field Archaeology* 40 (6): 607–625. doi: 10.1080/00934690.2015.1103628.

Yavari, Neguin. 2012. "Medieval Iran." In *The Oxford Handbook of Iranian History*, edited by Touraj Daryaee, 227–42. Oxford: Oxford University Press.

Yaya, Isabel. 2008. "The Importance of Initiatory Ordeals: Kinship and Politics in an Inca Narrative." *Ethnohistory* 55 (1): 51–85. doi: 10.1215/00141801-2007-046.

Young, Elizabeth L. and Fatma Müge Göçek. 2016. "Gender Equality." In *The Oxford Encyclopedia of Islam and Women*, edited by John L. Esposito, online edition. Oxford: Oxford University Press.

Young, Frances. 2006. "Prelude: Jesus Christ, Foundation of Christianity." In *The Cambridge History of Christianity Volume 1: Origins to Constantine*, edited by Margaret Mitchell and Frances Young, 1–34. Cambridge: Cambridge University Press.

Younger, John G. and Paul Rehak. 2008. "Minoan Culture: Religion, Burial Customs, and Administration." In *The Cambridge Companion to the Aegean Bronze Age*, edited by Cynthia W. Shelmerdine, 165–85. Cambridge: Cambridge University Press.

Zeder, Melinda A. 2011. "The Origins of Agriculture in the Near East." *Current Anthropology* 52 (4): S221–235. doi: 10.1086/659307.

Zhao, Dingxin. 2015. *The Confucian-Legalist State: A New Theory of Chinese History*. Oxford: Oxford University Press.

Zimansky, Paul E. 1995. "The Kingdom of Urartu in Eastern Anatolia." In *Civilizations of the Ancient Near East*, edited by Jack M. Sasson, 1135–46. New York: Scribner.

INDEX

A

Abahy, 380

Abū Bakr, 61

'Abbāsid Caliphate, 120–121, 135–136, 222

   'Abbāsid Dynasty, 139

   'Abbāsid period, 135–136

Acephalous societies, 349

Aceramic Neolithic, 176

Achaemenid Empire, 25, 42–43, 45, 97, 101, 115, 118, 122, 123, 127, 132, 136, 138–140, 145, 197–198, 201, 208, 215

   Achaemenid Iran, 129

   era of benevolent and humane rule, 137

   ethnoreligious hierarchy, 138–139

   fall of, 132

   gender equality in, 140–141

   imperial rule of Anatolia, 208–210

   legal practice, 141–142

   Levantine territories of, 97

   "oriental despotism" image, 137

   popular representations of, 136–137

   prosociality under, 141–142

   religious and cultural diversity of, 137

   religious ideology under, 128–131

   slavery and, 138

   society, division of, 139

   structural inequalities, 139

   tolerance of non-Zoroastrian practice, 138

   Zoroastrian faith, 41–42, 137–138

Achaemenid period, 129, 131, 136, 141–142, 208

Achaemenid Persians, 201

A'chik mande, 352

A'chik of northern India, 352–353

Achuar, 354

Ācārāṅga Sūtra, 171

Across the River (Achaemenid satrapy), 97

Act of chivalry, 366

Ādipurāṇa, 162–163

Aegean, societies of

   cultural integration and exchange across, 69

   "Late Bronze Age Crisis," 69

   migrations within, 69

   social and economic hierarchy, 72–73

   universalizing and egalitarian ideologies among, 73

African rice, 293

Afro-Eurasia, 332, 348

   relevance of Axial Age idea to, 19–20

Afterlife, 99

   Canaanite beliefs, 98

   concern with, 220

   democratization of, 229

   punishment for wrongdoing in, 229

Aguaruna, 354

Ahab, King, 108, 113

Ahu-a-'Umi, 336

Ahura Mazda, 42–45, 123, 128, 130–131, 137–138

Ai Khanoum, 153

Airlangga, 160

Aitareya Brāhmaṇa, 159

Akhenaten, 218, 223, 232

   Amarna experiment of, 230

   religious reforms of, 205

Akkadian Empire, 115, 117, 121, 125

Akumbu, 293

Alexander III of Macedon, 42, 70, 97, 132, 153, 220

   crowned pharaoh at Memphis, 226

   death of, 119

   "Lord of Asia" title, 119

Andean populations, 314

Andean religion, 313

Angkor Borei, 243

Angra Mainyu, 129

Anquetil-Duperron, Abraham-Hyacinthe, 14, 395

Antigonid Dynasty, 201

Anti-imperialist tradition, 101, 112

Antiochus III, 97

Antony, Marc, 220

Aśoka, King, 52

'Apiru, uprisings of, 94

Aqllawasi system, 315

Arabian Peninsula, 60

Arabic chronicles, 295

Arabic literacy, 302

Arab Muslims and non-Arab Muslim converts, 139

Archaic civilization, 296

Archaic period (Greece), 70

"Archaic" societies, 242

Archaic-style rulers, 400

Ardashir, 119–120

Arda Viraz Namag, 44

Aristocratic warrior ethos, 82

Aristotle's *Politics*, 320

Armstrong, Karen, 348

Arsaces, 119

Arsacid Empire, 119

Arthaśāstra, 39–40, 153, 161–162

Āryan culture, 150

Āryan invasions, 151

Āryan people, 150

Aśoka, 152–153

Aśoka's pillars, 152

Assmann, Jan, 25, 218

Aššurbanipal, 118, 208

Assyria, 92, 96–97, 109–111, 138, 199, 200, 203

Asuka period, 262–263, 268, 276–277, 280, 284–285, 286, 289

Atahuallpa, 311

Athenian democracy, 68

Athens, 11, 20, 68–70, 74, 79, 83, 335

Atlantic coast, 294

Augustus, 71, 80–81, 84–85, 202, 209, 221

Autochthons, 298

Autochthony, 110

Autonomous political action, 82

Avesta, 43, 129, 138–139

Avestan social divisions, 139

Awdaghust, 294

Axial Age, 292, 348, 349, 395–407
    arbitrary powers of leaders, 349
    arguments about, 33
    in Central Andes, 311
    definition, 13
    lingering impacts of, 15–16
    mid-first millennium BCE, 13
    second, 14
    theories, 13, 16, 92, 301, 320

Axial Age idea
    core elements of
        critical transformations, 17
        geographical boundaries, 16
        temporal boundaries, 16
    developments of, 14–16
        Bellah's works, 15
        Eisenstadt's works, 15
        Jaspers' analysis, 14–15
        lingering effects, 15–16
        Stuart-Glennie's analysis, 14
    disagreement between scholars on, 17–18
    exploring limits of, 18–19
    popularity of, 17
    relevance of, 19–20

Axial cultures, 17, 348–349

Axiality, 3–4, 7, 11–12, 14, 18–20, 24–25, 35–36, 38, 143–144, 214–215, 321–322, 349, 395–396
    limits of, 403–404
    megasociety threshold, 405–406
    moral norms, 398–403

Axial tradition, 319

Axial transformations, 15, 18, 21, 24, 27, 68, 73, 116, 198, 226, 228, 299, 301, 320–321, 349, 399–400

Axial transition, 323

Ayacucho Valley, 312

Azerbaijan, 41

B

Bābā, Ahmad, 304

Babylon, 96–97, 102, 104, 119, 137–138, 148, 220

Babylonian Empire, 97

Babylonian Talmud, 104

Baghdad, 62

Bahram II, 134

Bar Kochba revolt of 132–135 CE, 97

Basava, 158

Bathily, Abdoulaye, 301

Battle of Actium of 31 BCE, 71

Bedurok, 354

Bellah, Robert, 348

Berber Muslims, 294, 300

Bhagavad-gītā, 37

Biblical exegesis, 102

Biblical law, dating of, 99

Biblical literature, patriarchal streak in, 100–101

Big Island, Hawai'i, 335, 336

    Kealakekua Bay, 337

Big men, 324, 332

Bijjala II Kalacuri, 157

Black Death epidemic, 62

Bodhisattva, 51–52, 186

Bohai Bay region of China, 261

Book of Going Forth by Day, 229

Book of Isaiah, 97

Boyer, Pascal, 348

Brāhmanic tradition, 25, 50–51, 55, 167–169, 172, 246, 253

Brāhmanism, 50–51, 167–168, 179

Breakthrough, 304

Brhadratha, 153

Brāhmanic caste system, 50, 152

Broad supernatural punishment, 405

Bronze Age societies in northern China, 181

Brother–sister marriage, 341

Buddha, 11, 15, 50–51, 53–54, 163, 173–175, 262, 264, 269–270, 276, 278, 280, 285–288

Buddhism, 13, 25–26, 33, 35–37, 45–47, 50–54, 152, 155–157, 169–174, 179, 186–187, 190, 192, 194–195, 245–249, 253–258, 257, 261–263, 268–273, 277–280, 285–288, 395, 403–404

    adoption of, 273, 285, 289, 405–406

    egalitarian ideology, 53–54, 192, 274–289

    first schism of, 51

    five precepts of, 53, 190–191

    founder of, 50

    gender equality in, 54

    gods in, 53

    good deeds and bad deeds in, 53

    and ideologies of rule in Japan, 264–274

    influence in India, 152, 155, 156, 157

    lay followers, 53

    in Lower Mekong Basin, 246–247

    moral transgressions and, 54

    origin of, 50–51

    prosociality in, 194

    relation to ruler, 268

    social (in)equality in, 172–174

    spread of, 51–52, 152

    state religion of Northern Wei rule, 187

    state support for, 187

    universal moral code, 190–191

    in Western Jin period, 186

Buddhist ethical principles, 152

Buddhist monastics, 164

Bureaucratization, 399

Buwayhids, 121

Būyid Dynasty, 121, 135

Byzantine emperors, 202, 218, 233, 406

Byzantine Empire, 58–59, 71, 202, 210, 217, 305, 404

Byzantium, 57, 60, 64, 71, 76, 104, 202, 208, 221

C

Cahokia, 6, 24, 27, 323, 325, 326
  burials, 329
  Mound 72, 329, 330
  political and ceremonial traditions, 326
  sacrificial rituals, 329
Cakkavattisīhanāda Sutta, 163
Cālukya Dynasty, 146, 155–158, 161
Cambodia, 241. *See also* Lower Mekong Basin
Canaan, city-states of
  cultic temples, 98
  military threat to, 94
Canaanite, 91
  afterlife beliefs, 98
  civilization
    calamities faced by, 94
    collapse of, 94–95
  economy of, 93
  Egyptian overlordship, 93
  ideology, 99
  law codes, 107
  polities
    during Middle Bronze Age, 93
    rulership and institutions of authority,
      106–110
  religion, descriptions of, 98
  social structure
    hupsu farmers, 104
    slaves, 104
    social mobility, 105
    women, 104–105
  society, 92
    four classes of, 98
    migrations and political disintegration, 95
  uprisings against Egyptian officials, 93–94
Canaanite rulers, 107
  egalitarian, 108–109, 112, 113
  role in society, 106

Cantera, Alberto, 141
Cappadocian Kingdom, 197–198
Carr Creek, 324
Carthage, 71, 97
Caste
  ordered hierarchically, 39
  scriptural basis for, 38–39
  system, 39–40, 51, 54, 56, 159, 161, 167, 172–173,
    179, 248–249
Catholic and Protestant branches, 58
Catholic saints, 321
Cattle-herding cultures, 151
Cattle-herding migrants, 177
Censorate (China), 189
Central Andes, 310
Central Asian empires, 150
Charitable giving, 142
Charity, 22, 60, 111, 193–194, 238, 251
Chiefdom-level political organization, 329
China
  Axial Age, 189
  Shang and Zhou Dynasties, 296
  spread of Buddhism in, 52
  unified under imperial dynasties, 181
Chinese culture
  and Confucianism, 45
  key virtues in contemporary, 48
Chinese religion
  early, 182–183
  indigenous, 183, 189
Choksy, Jamsheed, 140
Christian and Jewish Romans, relations be-
  tween, 103–104
Christian God, 58, 62, 328
Christianity, 35–36, 42–43, 45, 56–58, 60, 62–63,
  85–86, 92, 111, 134, 142–143, 210, 213–215, 219,
  221–223, 233, 316–317, 400, 403
  adoption in Egypt, 221, 222, 223
  in Anatolia, 210
  gender egalitarianism, 58–59

institutions of authority and social organization, 59–60

origins of, 54–56

spiritual egalitarianism, 56, 58

spread of, 56–58, 76

    Constantine's conversion, 57

    early converts, 56

    to east, 57

    official state support, 57

    persecutions, 57

    in Persia, 134

virtuous and sinful acts, 58

Christianization, 382

Christian rulers, attributes of, 59

Christian teachings, 56, 59

Christian women, 59

Chunqiu, 183

Churches, 86

    Christian rulers supporting, 59

    Eastern and Western, 57–58

    Roman emperor's power over, 59

Cimmerians, 201

City kings, 106–107

Civic benefaction, 85

Civil society, 306

Classical Athens, 10, 74, 87, 211, 232

Cleopatra VII, suicide of, 220

Climatic fluctuation, 295

Coca leaves, 314

Code of Hammurabi, 107

Coffin Texts, 229–231

Collective governance, 74

Colonial *audiencias* (Spanish Empire), 321

Colonial *encomienda* system (Spanish Empire), 317

Communal feasting, 389

Communal storage of maize, 325

Community defense, 325

Conchopata, 312

Confucian *Analects*, 46, 185

Confucian charity, 194

Confucian classics, 47, 184, 186, 188, 193

Confucianism, 13, 33, 35–36, 52, 182, 184–185, 187–188, 190, 192–193, 195, 268, 395

    Chinese culture and, 45

    classification as "world religion," 45

    during Han Dynasty, 47

    "inclusive care," doctrine of, 193

    institutions of authority and social organization, 49

    key tenets of, 47–48, 185

    morality in, 190, 195

    origin of, 46

    path to social betterment, 48–49

    prosociality in, 193–194

    spread of, 46–47

Confucian scriptures, 52

Confucius, 11, 15, 21, 25, 45–46, 48, 54, 182–185, 184, 187, 190, 192

    bias against women, 192

    disciples and early followers, 46

Constantine, Emperor, 57, 71, 81, 202, 210, 222

Constantinople. *See* Byzantium

Copper, from Lake Superior Basin, 324

Cosmic order, 167

Cosmos, 50

Council of Elders (Phoenician), 109

Cretan religion

    beliefs and practices, 72

    in Middle and Late Minoan periods, 72

    social and economic hierarchy, 72–73

Crete, 69

Cross-cultural influence

    in Iran, 143

    in Levant, 110–112

    in South India, 176–178

Crumley, Carole, 297

Crusades, 62

Cultic temples, Canaanite, 98

Cuzco Basin, 309, 311

as site of intellectual transformations, 68

Greek cities, 70

Greek philosophy, 13, 42, 213, 232, 395, 400

Greek "renaissance," 69

"Greek-style" civic architecture, 106

Grenet, Frantz, 130

Guinea, mountains, 291

"Gunpowder empires," 62

Gupta Empire, 37, 154–155

H

Habiru, uprisings of, 94

Habsburg Dynasty, 309

Hadza of Tanzania, 348

Hajj (pilgrimage to Mecca), 302

Hakuhō Buddhism, 268–271

Hambarketolo, 295

Han Dynasty, 47, 184–186, 191

Han Feizi, 190

Harappan archaeological record, 167

Harappan Civilization. *See* Indus Valley
Civilization

Harappans
egalitarianism among, 166–167
rulership among, 159
structural gender inequality among, 167

Harṣa's empire, 156

Harṣavardhana, 156

Hashihaka keyhole tomb, 267

Hasmonean Dynasty, 97, 106

Ḥattuša, 199–200

Haudenosaunee (Iroquois), of North America,
355–356, 368

Hauntings, 384

Havana ceramic tradition, 324

Hawai'i, 27, 335, 336
civilization, 337
environment, 340
egalitarianism/social mobility in, 343
food shortages, 344

historical background of, 335–337

irrigation systems, 336, 345

Kū, Lono, Kāne, and Kanaloa, 339

landholding patterns, 344

limits on power, 340–343

morality, 335

population, 335

prosociality in, 344–345

religious and normative ideology, 337–340

Hazor, 107

Hebrew Bible, 55, 98, 137, 234
dating of, 99
on divine reward, 100
Isaiah 45, 137

Hebrew prophets of mid-first millennium BCE,
11, 15, 24

Heian emperors, 272, 273, 288

Heian period, 258, 264, 272–274, 279–280, 287

Hellenistic kingdoms, 26, 70–71, 75, 80, 110, 112,
139, 209

Hellenistic moral philosophy, 102

Hellenistic period, 75, 83, 91, 97, 100, 102–103,
110–111, 132, 208, 220, 238

Hellenistic sculpture, 154

Hellenization of Parthians, 123

Henkelman, Wouter, 126

Hennepin, Louis, 333

Henotheism, 131

Hephthalites, 155

Highland Peru, 28
Inca Empire, 309
rulership/institutions of authority, 318–321
universalizing morality/egalitarian ethics/so-
cial mobility, 311–318
Wari, 310–311

Himiko, Queen, 265–267

Hindu concepts of *cakravartin*, 26

Hindu deities, 37

Hinduism, 13, 35–39, 42, 44, 155, 177, 179, 242,
248–249, 251, 254

interaction and cross-cultural influence in, 143

old Achaemenid heartland, 119

Rāshidūn Caliphate and, 120

Seljuq Empire and, 121

social mobility in, 125–127

Umayyad Caliphate and, 120

universalizing morality in, 125–127

Iron Age Anatolia, 207

Iroquois, of North America, 355

Iseminger, 332

Islam, 16, 35–36, 42–43, 45, 58–64, 111, 120–121,
135–136, 139–140, 142, 178, 228, 233, 238,
294–295, 300, 304, 403

arrival in northern South Asia, 39

gender equality within, 63–64

institutions of authority, 64

morality, 62–63

origin of, 60

replacement of Zoroastrianism, 42–43

social organization, 64

spread of, 61–62

Islamic caliphates, 104, 110, 134, 139, 144, 221, 227,
237

'Abbāsid Caliphate, 222

Egypt absorbed into, 227–228

Fāṭimid imām-caliphs, 222

Persian religious ideology under, 134–136

"rightly guided" caliphs, 221–222

Umayyad Caliphate, 222

Islamic dynasties, in medieval West Africa, 301

Islamic God, 62–63

Islamic judicial institutions, 302

Islamic law, 64

Islamic period in Persia, 135

Islamic rule

cultural and religious pluralism under, 136

religious ideology under, 134–136

Islamic world, 61

golden age of, 62

political fragmentation of, 62

Israel, 205

as an Assyrian province, 96

economy of, 96

imposing tribute on other kingdoms, 95

and Judah, interrelations between, 95

military force of, 96

and Phoenicians, 92

population, 95

rebellion against Assyria, 96

trade links, 95–96

Israelite God, 205

Israelite kings, formal institutional powers of,
107–110

Israelite people

pre-monarchic ideology of, 99–100

vassals of Jewish God, 99

J

Jainism, 25, 37, 52, 147, 152, 158, 162–163, 165, 169,
172, 174–175, 175–176, 179

Jains, migration of, 155

Japan, 26, 257

Asuka period, 268, 277, 285

Buddhism's relation to ruler, 268

capital cities, 263

deity-beast mirror, 266

egalitarian ethics in, 274–289

grave goods, 268

Heian emperors, 272, 273, 288

Heian period, 258, 264, 272–274, 279–280, 287

human sacrifices for deceased rulers in, 266

Jōmon culture. See Jōmon culture

Kamakura Shogunate, 257, 264

Kofun period, 261, 267–268, 283

kokubunji system, 263

magical and mystical nature of rulership in,
265

morality in, 274–289

Nara period, 261, 263, 267, 285

reign of Keitai, 268

reign of Queen Himiko, 265–267

religion and ideologies of rule in, 264–274

Soga clan, 268–269

spread of Buddhism in, 262, 263

spread of Confucianism in, 47

state adoption of Buddhism, 262

Taihō Code, 263

tomb-building practices, 266

Wei Dynasty, 266–267

Yamato state, 268

Yayoi period. *See* Yayoi period

Japanese Buddhism, 269

Japanese Islands, chiefdoms on, 265

Japanese urban planning, 263

Jaspers, Karl, 46, 64, 110, 184, 292, 400

    analysis of Axial Age

        sages and ancient philosophers, 14–15

        sociopolitical transformations, 14, 15

    inclusion of Iran, 116

    insistence on autonomous nature, 111

    nominating the Jews as an "axial people," 111

Jayavarman II, 160, 244

Jayavarman VII, 245

Jehoram, Omrid king, 96

Jenné-jeno, 292, 293, 295–298, 300, 301

Jerusalem, 96

    Persian occupation, 97

    revival, 106

Jewish communities

    "problems of integration" faced by, 112

    in West Asia, 104

Jewish devastation, apocalyptic view of, 111

Jewish elites

    as administrators, 106

    as nodes of cross-cultural influence, 106

Jewish experience and ideology, 104

Jewish God. *See* YHWH (god), 99

Jewish monotheism, 110

Jewish thought, 102

    "axial" features of, 111

conflicting attitudes, 101

development of, 102, 111

egalitarian ideologies, 105–106, 112, 113

and practice, 102

universalizing claims of, 102, 112

Jewish tradition, 112

Jews

    migrating west, 104

    prophetic religion of, 111

Jezebel, 108

Jitō, Empress, 270

Jívaro of Peru and Ecuador, 354–355

Jizya, 139

Jōmon culture, 258–260, 274, 281

    clay figurines of, 259

    cosmology, 260

    hunter-gatherer society, 258

    ideology, 259

    Late and Final, 258–259

    metal tools, 259

    population size, 258

    ritual and religious practices, 259–260

    "truly Neolithic," 259

Jōmon Period, 257, 259, 274, 281

Jones, William, 150

Judah, Kingdom of, 96–97

Judaic elite, 102

Judaic ideology, 102

Judaic prophetic tradition, 111

Judaic thought

    alternate view of kingship, 110

    narratives of "exile and return," 102

Judaism, 13, 76, 92, 99, 102, 395

Judas Maccabeus, 106

Judean highlands, 95

Judeo-Christian, 53

K

Ka'ahumanu, 343

Kalahari San, 348

Qing Dynasty, 184

religious Daoist movements, 186

reunification of, 187

"six houses of thought," 185

Spring and Autumn period, 183

Sui Dynasty, 187

Tang Dynasty, 187, 188, 192

Three Kingdoms period, 186

universalizing morality in, 189–191

Warring States period, 183

Western Han, 184–186

    central government ruling, 184

    concept of ideological schools in, 185–186

    fajia thought, 192

    imperial academy in, 186

    popular religion, 186

    Wang Mang's coup, 184–185

Western Jin rule, 187

Western Zhou Dynasty, 182–183

    moral behavior during, 189

    traditional ideology, 188

Northern Black Polished Ware, 151

Northern China, 194–195

Northern Hinduism, 39

Northern India, polities of, 151

Northern Kingdom of Israel, 95, 108

Northern Levant, 92

Northern Song Dynasty, 182

Northern Song society, 187

Northern Wei Dynasty, 187, 191–192

Nyama, 299, 302

Nyamakalaw, 303

O

O'ahu, 335

Obsidian, from Yellowstone region, 324

Oceania. *See* Hawai'i

Ohio Valley, 324

Old Assyrian trade network, 199

Old Elamite period, 117

Old Kingdom, Egypt, 218–219, 223–225, 228–231, 234, 236–237

Old World diseases, 318

Oneota period, 326, 327, 330

Onondaga, 370

Ordinances of Government, The, 64

Organization of labor, 325

"Oriental despotism," 137

Orokaiva, 351, 365

    clans, 351

    demigods, 388

    of Papua New Guinea, 351–352

    pigs, 351

    society, 390

Otohu, 369

Ottoman Empire, 58, 62

P

Pabag, 119

Pachacuti, 317

Pagan rituals, Roman Empire, 57

Palatial system

    disintegration of, 69

    Late Bronze Age collapse of, 77

Palestine, 110

Pallavas, 156

"Pan-Aegean elite identity," 73

Panhuman moral intuitions, 396

Papua New Guinea, 351

Paqarina/pacarina, 313

Parni, 119

Parthian Empire, 119

    political and legal practices, 124

    religious aspects of, 123, 133

    social stratification, 139

    Zoroastrian practice, 42

Patriarchy, 100–101

Patrimony, 109

Patronage, 109

Penitentials, 60

Pre-unification period, Hawai'i, 335

Prosociality, 141–142, 299

   in Lower Mekong Basin, 251–252

   in North China, 193–194

   in Pharaonic Egypt, 237–239

   promotion of, 399

Prosocial punishment, 397

Protohistoric period, Hawai'i, 343

Protopalatial period, Crete, 82

Psychological adaptations, 396

Ptolemaic Dynasty, 119, 218, 220–221, 226–227

Ptolemaic Empire, 97

Public works, 184

Pulakeśin II, 156

Purāṇas, 37, 155

Puṣyamitra, 153

Puzur-Inshushinak, 117

Pylos polity, 82

Q

Qanat system, 142

Qhapaq ucha, 316

Qin Empire, 181

Qing Dynasty, 184

Qin Great Wall, 184

Qin Shi Huangdi, 181, 184

Qoya, 318

Quasipolities, 30

Quinoa, in Cuzco region, 310

R

Rabbinic Judaism, 35

Radiocarbon dates, 293

Raja berani (prestigious individuals), 369

Rāṣṭrakūṭa Empire, 156–157

Rayed Head, 312

Records of Wei (Weizhi), 265

Religion, 33, 76. *See also* Specific types

   Buddhism. *See* Buddhism

   Christianity. *See* Christianity

Confucianism. *See* Confucianism

Hinduism. *See* Hinduism

in history of Susiana, 121–125

Islam. *See* Islam

in post-Classical Mediterranean, 74–75

and rulership, 159–166

   among Harappans, 159

   Buddhist political theory, 163–164, 166

   divinely sanctioned, 159–161

   Islamic notions of, 165

   Jain approach to, 162–163, 166

   king's duty, 162, 163

   king's power, 161

   Vākāṭaka-Gupta period, 155

   Zoroastrianism. *See* Zoroastrianism

Religious Daoist movements, 186

Religious ideology

   under Achaemenid rule, 128–131

   in Elam, 125–126

   in later Iranian history, 132–136

Religious practices, collective, 33

Religious societies, Hellenistic and Roman, 74–75

Reputation management, 396

Ṛg Veda, 159

Rib-Adda, 94

Ricci, Matteo, 45

"Rightly guided" caliphs, 221–222

Ringering phase, 324

Rites of Zhou, 191

Ritual purification of Mississippian people, 330

Roman citizenship, 85

Roman Dominate, 91

Roman Empire, 72, 75. *See also* Eastern Roman Empire; Western Roman Empire

   Diocletian's accession, 71

   encroaching on Hellenistic kingdoms, 71

   internal revolt against monarchy, 70

   legal and economic structures of, 84–85

   new political institutions, 70–71

Made in the USA
Columbia, SC
16 December 2019

85046392R00285